Dear Mrs Burton

M000087943

Loved your cooking lessons. Hears just a little thank you and a help to make all those future buns and biscuit lessons Sucess full for the next classes.

I will miss you

Love Ashley

BIG BOOK OF
SWEET TREATS

BIG BOOK OF SWEET TREATS

130 sumptious recipes for indulging
in all things sweet

NEW HOLLAND

Reprinted in 2011
First published in 2010 by
New Holland Publishers (UK) Ltd
London • Cape Town • Sydney • Auckland

Garfield House
86–88 Edgware Road
London W2 2EA
www.newhollandpublishers.com

80 McKenzie Street
Cape Town 8001
South Africa

Unit 1, 66 Gibbes Street
Chatswood
NSW 2067
Australia

218 Lake Road
Northcote
Auckland
New Zealand

10 9 8 7 6 5 4 3 2

ISBN 978 1 84773 550 8

Editor: Amy Corstorphine
Design: Peter Gwyer
Production: Laurence Poos
Editorial Direction: Rosemary Wilkinson

Reproduction by Pica Digital Pte Ltd, Singapore
Printed and bound in India by Replika Press Pvt. Ltd.

Contents

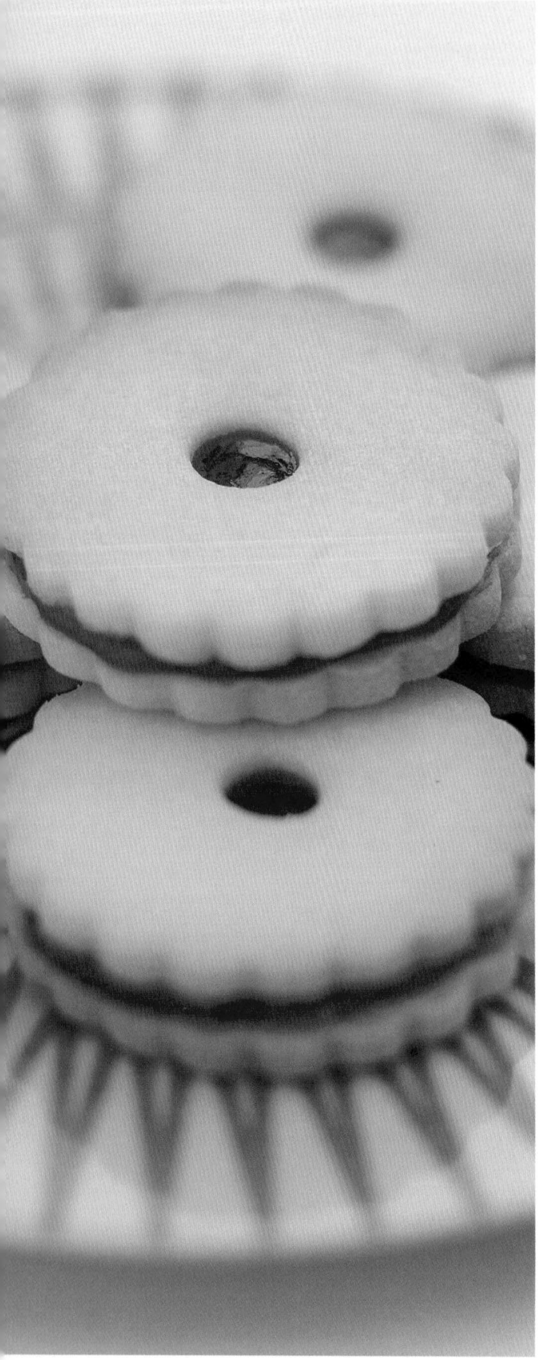

Introduction

Are you the type of person who sits down at a dinner party table and immediately checks for a spoon placed above your plate? Does your Christmas begin in early October, when you start scanning magazines and cookbooks for delicious new desserts and cakes to add to your already long list of Christmas musts? Have you ever popped into your local supermarket just to buy milk and suddenly found yourself, as if by magic, in the bakery section? If so, this is the book for you. You love to eat cake and, frankly, you deserve it! After all, life would be so boring without sweet treats and people like you.

Most supermarkets these days have seemingly endless rows of cakes, cookies and ready-made desserts, all delicious and mouthwateringly tempting. Which may make you wonder why you should bother making your own. Yet a quick scan of the ingredients label may give you the first reason – you probably won't recognize half of them and will set you thinking whether that is really what you want to be feeding your family and friends. Secondly, taking the time to buy all the ingredients and then making the dessert or cake

yourself simply shows you care. Time is a precious commodity these days – most of us spend life in a constant rush and actually spending some time preparing something for a family member or a friend is a great way to give something back. But above all else, the most important reason to make your own sweet treats is, of course, because it's just great fun!

In our experience, there's no better way to lure the kids from the computer or TV than to tempt them into the kitchen. Sweet treats are just that and shouldn't be eaten every day, but helping out in the kitchen with simple recipes for cakes and cookies is a great way to get children interested in cooking early on in life. Capitalize on this interest and their curiosity for all types of cooking will grow – bear in mind that what they taste now, they'll remember for the rest of their lives. Which is also why spending time in the kitchen should also be fun. It should be messy, sticky and tasty and everybody should be able to join in – kids will find something to stir or a spoon to lick, and granny can contribute with old family recipes. Some families even have a collection of recipes that have been passed down generation after generation and special occasions just wouldn't be the same without them. Maybe it's a special recipe for cookies that are only made for Christmas, or perhaps it's a special topping for your pancakes on Pancake Day that only you and your family know about. It's these little traditions and recipes that make baking so important in family life and really makes us who we are.

Another great thing about making sweet treats is that you don't really need any special or expensive equipment or use any complicated methods. In fact, you'll probably already have a few ingredients in your cupboard before you even start. Sometimes all you need is just some butter, flour, eggs and sugar – sometimes you don't even need an oven! Making sweet desserts and baking cakes are deceptively easy while simultaneously impressive. With a bit of care and some fancy decorations you'll add instant 'wow factor' to the end of any meal, a special occasion or even just afternoon tea. Even a rainy afternoon seems so much brighter after a batch of cookies. Make your own waffles and celebrate the season with local fruit and berries as a topping. Or why not treat someone special with breakfast in bed, surprising them with your own mix of luxury muesli – a very healthy sweet treat and a great start to the day.

Like every other type of cooking, desserts and cakes also reflect the times we live in. The more ingredients that become available to us, the more adventurous we become with trying out new flavours and flavour combinations. Our parent's generation had never heard of tiramisu or pannacotta, yet these are now common desserts at most restaurants as the more traditional hearty pies and steamed puddings are making way for lighter, more refreshing desserts such as sorbets and ice creams. Ice cream is no longer a treat for children on hot summer days but can now be found in all sorts of sophisticated flavours aimed at choosy adults. The best news of all is that it's really easy to make ice cream yourself. Ice cream is, in fact, one of the shop-bought desserts that contain the most additives and chemical substitutes instead of genuine flavouring. We're probably so used to the taste of chemically enhanced vanilla that most of us wouldn't recognize, or even appreciate, the subtle taste of real vanilla any more. Try making your own ice cream and you'll discover a new – old –world.

This book offers an exciting and varied range of sweet treats for every occasion. Cookies are great for kids but there are all sorts of flavours to experiment with – here you'll find all the classics as well as new versions to tempt your taste buds. Why not make a big batch and store in your cupboard for a quick pick-me-up! Cakes, cakes, cakes – you are sure to find a new favourite in this book because it's packed with every kind of cake you could think of – sponges, cupcakes, drizzle cakes, birthday cakes, cheesecakes... Or if you need a posh ending to your fancy dinner party or new inspiration for a family pudding, look no further. There's also pancakes and waffles, which are simple to make, the whole family will love them and you can vary the toppings endlessly to suit the chocoholics to the fruit lovers and anyone in-between. But if, after all this indulgence your conscience gets the better of you, you'll also find a great range of healthier option desserts with delicious fresh fruit. So go on, don't leave this book on the shelf with the rest of your cook books. It wants to get sticky and stained and most of all, it wants you to have fun because everyone deserves a sweet treat once in a while!

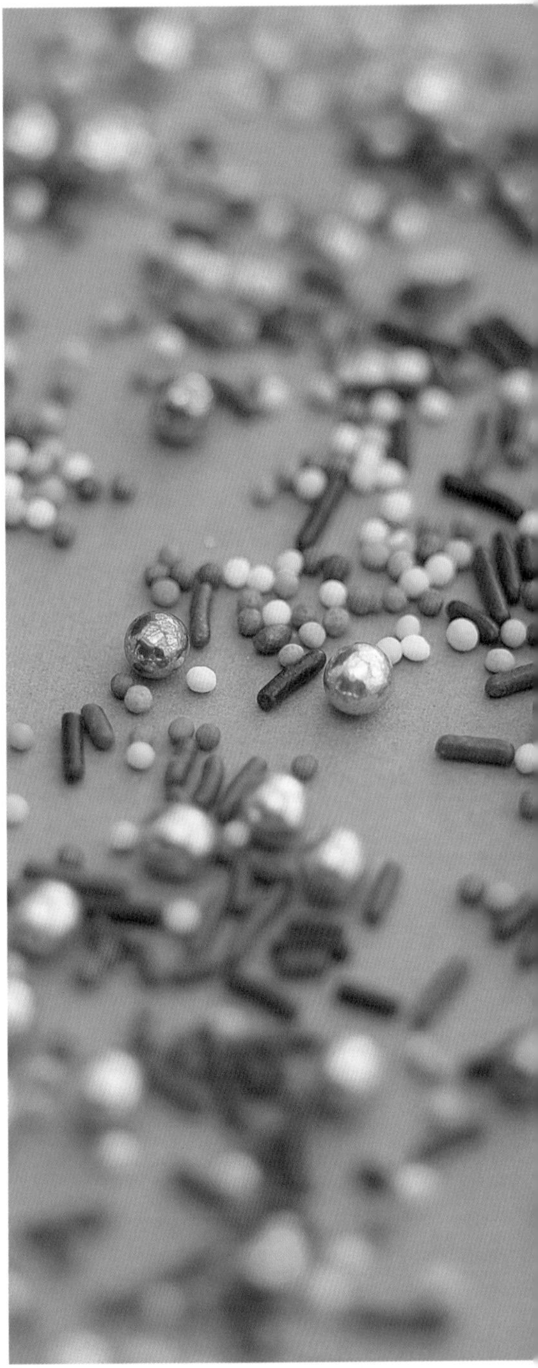

Recipe accompaniments

Basic pancake batter

125 g/4 oz plain flour
1 pinch of salt
1 egg
300 ml/10 fl oz milk
Vegetable oil

Makes 8 pancakes

Combine the flour and salt in a bowl, make a well in the centre and break in the egg. Add half the milk and gradually work into the flour using a whisk. Beat lightly until well combined and smooth – too much whisking causes the gluten in the flour to develop and will make the finished batter chewy. Add the remaining milk gradually, whisking gently until the batter has the consistency of pouring cream.

Transfer to a jug, cover loosely and leave in a cool place for 30 minutes. Pancakes made straightaway, without standing, will be lighter in texture and have a bubbly surface. On standing, the batter may begin to separate, so stir gently before using. If you leave it for a longer time, the batter may start to thicken and you will need to water it down again to achieve the correct consistency. Never leave the batter longer than 1 hour, unless covered and refrigerated, otherwise it will start to ferment.

Lightly brush a medium frying pan – 20 cm/8 in diameter base – with vegetable oil and heat until hot.

Pour away any excess oil – the pan should be practically dry. The cooking temperature is important in order to achieve a good finished texture. To gauge the correct temperature for cooking, drop a tiny amount of water on to the surface of the pan. If the drops stay in place, the pan isn't hot enough; if they disappear immediately it is too hot; but when they sizzle and spit across the surface, the pan is ready.

Holding the pan, pour in about 4 Tbsp batter into the middle then tilt the pan from side to side so the batter runs into a thin, even layer across the bottom of the pan.

Place the pan over moderate heat and cook for about 1½ minutes, or until the pancake browns around the edges and begins to curl away from the pan. Slide a palette knife under the pancake and flip it over. Brown the underside of the pancake for a further minute.

Turn the pancake out on to a wire rack lined with a clean tea towel and baking parchment. Fold the paper and towel over the pancake to keep it moist. Continue to make a further 7 pancakes, re-oiling the pan as necessary, and stacking the cooked pancakes between the sheets of parchment, until you are ready to serve. Pancakes will keep warm like this while you cook the remaining batter, but if you want to keep them warm for longer, transfer them still layered up, to a heatproof plate, cover with foil and place over a pan of gently simmering water or in the oven at a low (keep warm) setting.

Basic waffle batter

250 g/8 oz plain flour
½ tsp bicarbonate of soda
½ tsp salt
30 g/1 oz caster sugar (optional)
1 egg, separated
300 ml/10 fl oz milk
30 g/1 oz unsalted butter, melted

Makes 12 waffles

Prepare and preheat the waffle irons or waffle machine as directed. Combine the flour with the bicarbonate of soda, salt and sugar, if using, in a bowl and make a well in the centre. Add the egg yolk and milk, and gradually work into the flour using a whisk. Beat gently until smooth. Carefully stir in the melted butter.

In a grease-free bowl, whisk the egg white until stiff and carefully fold into the batter using a large metal spoon.

Pour over enough batter to ensure that the moulded surface of the lower plates are covered sufficiently (for an electric plate you will need about 3 Tbsp for each plate). Close the irons or lid and cook until the waffles are just brown on the outside, about 3 minutes. When the waffles are ready, remove them with a two-pronged fork or a wooden skewer, taking care not to scratch the non-stick coating. Place on a wire rack lined with a clean tea towel and baking parchment. Fold the paper and towel over the waffle to keep it moist. Continue to make waffles, about 12 in total, stacking the cooked waffles between sheets of parchment, until you are ready to serve.

Basic crêpe batter

125 g/4 oz plain flour
30 g/1 oz caster sugar (optional)
1 pinch salt
2 whole eggs
2 egg yolks
300 ml/10 fl oz milk
75 g/2½ oz unsalted butter, melted

Makes 12 crêpes

Combine the flour, sugar, if using, and salt in a bowl. Make a well in the centre and break in the eggs then add the extra yolks. Add half the milk and gradually work into the flour using a whisk. Beat lightly until smooth, taking care not to over-mix.

Add the remaining milk gradually, whisking gently until well combined. Transfer to a jug, cover loosely and leave in a cool place for 30 minutes. Stir 60 g/2 oz melted butter into the batter before using.

Lightly brush a small frying pan – 15 cm/6 in diameter base – with a little of the remaining butter and heat until hot. Holding the pan, pour in about 50 ml/2 fl oz batter and tilt the pan from side to side so that it runs into a thin, even layer across the bottom of the pan.

Place the pan over moderate heat and cook for about 1 minute, or until the crêpe browns around the edges and begins to curl away from the pan. Slide a palette knife under the crêpe and flip it over. Brown the underside for a further minute.

Turn out on to a wire rack lined with a clean tea towel and baking parchment. Fold the paper and towel over the crêpe to keep it moist. Continue to make a further 11 crêpes, brushing the pan with melted butter as necessary, gently stirring the batter each time it is used, and stacking the cooked crêpes between sheets of parchment, until you are ready to serve.

Basic lemon cupcakes

125 g/4½ oz butter, softened

125 g/4½ oz caster sugar

2 medium eggs

Finely grated rind and juice of 1 lemon

125 g/4½ oz self-raising flour

12- or 24-hole bun tray lined with paper cases

Makes 12 standard-size cupcakes or use half the quantities to make 18 to 24 mini cupcakes

Preheat the oven to 190° C/375° F (gas 5). Beat the butter and sugar together in a bowl until the mixture is light and fluffy. Add the eggs, lemon rind and juice and the flour to the bowl and beat the mixture until smooth. Divide the mixture between the paper cases and bake in the centre of the oven until the cakes have risen and are just firm to the touch in the centre.
The standard-size cakes will take about 12 to 15 minutes and the mini cakes will take 10 to 12 minutes.

Remove the cakes from the oven and transfer them to a wire rack to cool.

Basic plain cupcakes

125 g/4½ oz butter, softened

125 g/4½ oz caster sugar

2 medium eggs

125 g/4½ oz self-raising flour

2 Tbsp milk

12 or 24-hole bun tray lined with paper cases

Makes 12 standard-size cupcakes or use half the quantities to make 18 to 24 mini cupcakes

Preheat the oven to 190° C/375° F (gas 5). Beat together the butter and sugar in a bowl until light and fluffy. Add the eggs, flour and milk to the bowl and beat until the mixture is smooth. Divide the mixture between the paper cases and bake in the centre of the oven until the cakes have risen and are just firm to the touch in the centre. The standard-size cakes will take about 12 to 15 minutes and the mini cakes will take 10 to 12 minutes.

Remove the cakes from the oven and transfer them to a wire rack to cool.

Basic chocolate cupcakes

125 g/4½ oz butter, softened
125 g/4½ oz caster sugar
2 medium eggs
2 Tbsp milk
100 g/3½ oz self-raising flour
3 level Tbsp cocoa

12- or 24-hole bun tray lined with paper cases

Makes 12 standard-size cupcakes or use half the quantities to make 18 to 24 mini cupcakes.

Preheat the oven to 190° C/375° F (gas 5). Beat together the butter and sugar in a bowl until light and fluffy. Add the eggs and milk, and sift over the flour and cocoa, then beat until the mixture is smooth. Divide the mixture between the paper cases and bake in the centre of the oven until the cakes have risen and are just firm to the touch in the centre. The standard-size cakes will take about 12 to 15 minutes and the mini cakes will take 10 to 12 minutes.

Remove the cakes from the oven and transfer them to a wire rack to cool.

Candied citrus peel

4–6 mixed citrus fruits (grapefruit, oranges, lemons, limes)
300 g/10 oz caster sugar
200 ml/ 7 fl oz water

Using a wide, horizontal vegetable peeler, peel the skin from the fruit, making sure not to peel away the bitter white pith. Finely slice the peel into matchsticks. Set aside.

Combine 200 g/7 oz of the sugar with the water in a heavy-bottomed saucepan and bring to the boil. Boil the mixture gently until the sugar dissolves. Add the chopped peel, reduce the heat and simmer gently for 30 minutes. Remove the peel with a slotted spoon and place, separated, onto a plate. Place the remaining sugar in a bowl. Toss the cooled peel in the sugar, then leave to dry on a clean towel. Store in an airtight container.

Chocolate pastry

125 g/4 oz plain flour
1 Tbsp cocoa powder
Pinch of salt
60 g/2 oz caster sugar
60 g/2 oz unsalted butter
1 egg yolk
Few drops of vanilla extract
Approx. 1 Tbsp whole milk

Makes 23 cm/9 in pastry case or 12 x patty pan tins

Preheat the oven to 200° C/400° F (gas 6). Sieve the flour, cocoa, salt and sugar into a bowl, and rub in the butter to form a mixture that resembles fresh breadcrumbs. Mix in the egg yolk and vanilla extract and bring the mixture together adding milk if necessary, then knead gently to form a firm dough. Wrap and chill for 30 minutes.

Roll out the pastry thinly on a lightly-floured surface to fit a 23 cm/9 in fluted loose-bottomed flan tin. The pastry is very short so you may find it easier to mould the pastry into the tin. Prick the base all over with a fork and bake in the oven for 15–20 minutes until set and firm to the touch.

Sweet pastry

175 g/6 oz plain flour
100 g/4 oz butter
Pinch of salt
50 g/2 oz icing sugar, sifted
Rind of ¼ lemon, grated
½ large egg, beaten

Sift the flour onto a work surface, make a well in the centre and into it place the butter, salt, sugar, lemon rind and egg. Draw the fingers of one hand together and lightly and quickly combine the ingredients in the well with your fingertips until the misxture is soft and blended. Gradually draw in the flour from around the edges and, using the same fingertip movement, combine the ingredients to form a crumb-like mixture. Gather together and lightly press the moist crumbs into a soft ball. Gently knead the dough on a lightly-floured surface until smooth, ensuring you do not overwork the dough. Wrap in a plastc bag and chill for 2 hours before using.

Brisée pastry

225 g/8 oz plain flour
½ tsp salt
1 tsp caster sugar
115 g/4 oz butter
2 large egg yolks
3½ tbsps cold water

Sift the flour and salt onto a work surface and make a well in the centre. Into it place the sugar, butter, egg yolks and water. Using your fingertips, lightly and quickly work the ingredients in the well with a bird-like pecking motion until the mixture resembles scrambled eggs. Draw in the flour to form a crumb-like mixture then bring the mixture together with your hands to form a soft moist dough. Wrap in a plastic bag and chill for 2 hours.

Vanilla cream

284 ml/9½ fl oz double cream
2 tsp caster sugar
1 tsp pure vanilla extract, or pure vanilla bean paste

Add all the ingredients to a mixing bowl and beat into just firm peaks (the cream will thicken a little more as you pipe it). This classic cream filling, sometimes called Chantilly cream, works well for a multitude of cakes, roulades and éclairs.

Cream cheese frosting

300 g/10½ oz cream cheese
Finely grated rind and juice of 1 lemon
3-4 Tbsp icing sugar

Makes enough for 12 standard-size cupcakes or 24 mini cupcakes.

Beat the cream cheese to soften it, then beat in the lemon rind and juice. Finally, beat in icing sugar to taste.

Use full fat cream cheese as lower fat cheeses are usually softer and if used for making frostings the result may be too runny.

Chocolate trifle sponge

2 large eggs
60 g/2 oz caster sugar
30 g/1 oz plain flour
15 g/½ oz cocoa powder
2 tsp cornflour
30 g/1 oz butter, melted

Makes sufficient sponge for a large trifle

Preheat the oven to 180° C/350° F (gas 4). Grease and line with baking parchment a 20 cm/8 in square cake tin. Put the eggs and sugar in a large clean bowl and stand over a large bowl of hot water. Whisk until thick, pale and creamy – about 5 minutes. Remove from the bowl of water and continue to whisk for a further 3 minutes. You should be able to leave a trail from a spoon in the mixture when it is whisked sufficiently.

Sieve in the flour, cocoa and cornflour. Pour the melted butter around the edge of the mixture and carefully fold the mixture together using a large metal spoon. Pour into the prepared tin and bake in the oven for 20–25 minutes until well risen and just firm to the touch. Remove from the tin and cool on a wire rack.

Chocolate buttercream

175 g/6 oz butter, softened
4 level Tbsp cocoa
3 Tbsp boiling water
350 g/12½ oz icing sugar
Few drops of vanilla extract

Makes enough for 12 standard-size cupcakes or 24 mini cupcakes

Beat the butter in a bowl to soften it. Tip the cocoa into a seperate bowl, add the boiling waterto it and mix it to a paste, then add it to the butter and add the icing sugar and vanilla extract and beat until the icing is very smooth.

Swiss meringue buttercream

4 medium egg whites
250 g/9 oz caster sugar
Pinch of salt
250 g/9 oz unsalted butter, softened
Few drops of vanilla extract

Makes enough for 12 standard-size cupcakes or 24 mini cupcakes

Place the egg whites, sugar and salt in a bowl over a pan of simmering water and mix together well. Stir frequently while heating to prevent the egg whites from cooking.

After about 5 to 10 minutes, when the mixture is warm and the sugar crystals have dissolved, remove the bowl from the heat. Whisk the meringue to full volume and until the mixture is cool.

Add the butter and vanilla extract to the meringue – the mixture will reduce in volume and will appear curdled. Continue to whisk until the butter emulsifies completely into the meringue and forms a smooth, light and fluffy texture.

This buttercream is stable for 1 to 2 days at room temperature (no higher than 15° C/59° F), otherwise it may be refrigerated for up to two weeks.

Egg glaze

1 egg yolk
Pinch of salt
1–2 Tbsp milk

Beat all the ingredients together with a fork until well amalgamated. Use to brush over pastry before baking to ensure a rich, golden colour.

Chocolate-coated honeycomb

150 g/5 oz granulated sugar

2 Tbsp golden syrup

2 Tbsp set honey

2 tsp bicarbonate of soda

400 g/14 oz milk chocolate

Makes approx. 36 pieces (depending on size)

Grease and line an 18 cm/7 in square cake tin with baking parchment. Put the sugar in a large saucepan with the syrup and honey. Heat gently, stirring, until the sugar dissolves. Bring to the boil and cook, without stirring, for about 3 minutes until the mixture foams and turns a deep, golden caramel. Remove from the heat and quickly stir in the bicarbonate of soda. The mixture will immediately foam and bubble up in the saucepan, so quickly pour into the prepared tin while still foaming. Set aside to cool.

When the honeycomb has set, carefully remove from the tin and peel away the paper. Cut into pieces using a large sharp knife. Arrange the pieces on a board lined with baking parchment and set aside.

Break the chocolate into small pieces and place in a large heatproof bowl and stand over a pan of barely simmering water. Allow to melt then remove from the water and cool for 20 minutes.

Using small tongs, carefully dip the honeycomb pieces into the chocolate to cover them and place back on the parchment. Stand in a cool place to set. Any small smashed pieces can be tossed into the remaining melted chocolate and set to make honeycomb clusters.

Peel the sweets off the parchment and store in an airtight container between layers of greaseproof paper.

Dipping chocolate

To melt chocolate in the microwave: place the chocolate in a microwave-safe bowl. Microwave on medium power for 1 minute then stir. Repeat the process, stirring after every 30 seconds until the chocolate has melted.

To melt the chocolate on top of the hob: place the chocolate in a heatproof bowl that fits snugly on top of a saucepan. Bring a small quantity of water to a simmer in the saucepan and place the bowl on top. Reduce the heat and stir the chocolate until smooth and melted. Carefully remove from the heat and set aside.

To melt the chocolate in the oven: place the chocolate in a heatproof bowl in an oven preheated to the lowest temperature or Gas mark. Stir occasionally until the chocolate has melted. This usually takes about 5-10 minutes.

Custard sauce

4 level Tbsp cornflour
3 Tbsp caster sugar
600 ml/1 pt whole milk
2 egg yolks
Few drops vanilla extract
Few drops yellow food colouring (optional)

Makes approx. 600 ml/1 pt

In a saucepan, blend the cornflour with a little of the milk to make a smooth paste. Stir in the sugar and remaining milk. Heat, stirring over the heat until boiling and thick – you may find it easier to use a whisk to help keep the mixture smooth. Cook for 2 minutes.

Remove from the heat and cool for 10 minutes. Stir in the egg yolks and return to the heat. Cook through for 3 minutes, stirring but without boiling. Add vanilla extract to taste, and colour with food colouring if liked. To use cold, pour into a heatproof bowl and cover the surface with greaseproof paper to prevent a skin forming.

Marshmallow sauce

90 ml/3 fl oz golden syrup
60 g/2 oz caster sugar
1 large egg white

Makes 250 ml/8 fl oz

Combine the syrup and sugar with 1 tablespoon of water in a small saucepan. Bring to the boil, brushing the sides of the pan with a wet pastry brush to stop it crystallizing.

In a medium bowl, beat the egg white until stiff. When the syrup reaches 120° C/250° F, after about 7 minutes, slowly pour the syrup down the side of bowl, beating well until the mixture is shiny and fluffy. Use immediately, or store in an airtight container in the refrigerator for up to 1 week (it may need a stir before serving).

This sauce remains gooey when chilled or frozen.

Chocolate fudge sauce

75 g/2½ oz soft brown sugar
45 g/1½ oz butter
125 ml/4 fl oz golden syrup
1 Tbsp cocoa powder
150 ml/5 fl oz double cream
60 g/2 oz plain chocolate
½ tsp vanilla extract

Makes 350 ml/12 fl oz

Combine the sugar, butter, golden syrup and cocoa powder in a saucepan over a very low heat until the sugar has dissolved. Bring to a gentle boil and cook, uncovered, for 5 minutes. Remove the pan from the heat and stir in the cream, chocolate and vanilla extract. Stir well until the chocolate has melted. Return to the heat and cook for a further 1 minute or until smooth.

Serve the sauce hot over ice cream or allow to cool and swirl through ice cream.

This sauce will keep for up to 2 weeks in an airtight container in the refrigerator.

Chocolate sauce

180 g/6 oz continental plain chocolate, broken into pieces

15 g/½ oz unsalted butter

6 Tbsp double cream

3 Tbsp golden syrup

Few drops vanilla extract (optional)

Makes approx. 300 ml/10 fl oz

Put all the ingredients except the vanilla extract in a small heatproof bowl. Stand the bowl over a pan of gently simmering water and heat gently, stirring occasionally, until all the ingredients have melted together and the sauce is warm. Add a few drops of vanilla extract before serving. Serve warm – the sauce will harden on cooling.

Caramel sauce

400 g/14 oz caster sugar

125 ml/4 fl oz water

350 ml/12 fl oz double cream

2 Tbsp unsalted butter

1 tsp vanilla extract

1 tsp lemon juice

Makes 600 ml/1 pt

Combine the sugar and water in a heavy-bottomed saucepan over a medium heat. Stir until the sugar dissolves, then stop stirring and bring the syrup to the boil. Brush the sides of the pan with a wet pastry brush to keep the sugar from crystallising on the side of the pan. Swirl the pan as the syrup begins to brown. When the syrup is a dark amber colour (approximately 180° C/350° F on a sugar thermometer, watch carefully, the syrup can easily burn), reduce the heat to low and add the cream. Stir as the syrup bubbles and splatters until smooth. Add the butter and vanilla and stir until it melts. Finish the sauce with a squirt of lemon juice.

Allow the sauce to cool before using it in an ice cream recipe, or storing it in the refrigerator. It will keep for 2 weeks in an airtight container in the refrigerator.

Butterscotch sauce

150 g/5 oz golden syrup
60 g/2 oz unsalted butter
150 g/5 oz demerara or light brown sugar
150 ml/5 fl oz double cream
Few drops vanilla extract

Makes approx. 450 ml/15 fl oz

Put the syrup, butter and sugar in a saucepan and heat gently, stirring, until dissolved. Bring to a simmer and cook gently for a further 5 minutes. Remove from the heat and gradually stir in the cream and vanilla extract. Serve hot or cold.

Sugar syrup

350 g/12 oz caster sugar
600 ml/20 fl oz cold water

Makes approx. 600 ml/20 fl oz

Place the sugar in a saucepan and pour over the water. Heat, stirring, until the sugar dissolves. Increase the heat and bring to the boil. Simmer, without stirring, for 10 minutes. Remove from the heat and allow to cool.

Chocolate sugar syrup

350 g/12 oz caster sugar
600 ml/20 fl oz cold water
1 Tbsp cocoa powder

Makes approx. 600 ml/20 fl oz

Place the sugar in a saucepan and pour in the water. Heat, stirring, until the sugar dissolves. Raise the heat and bring to the boil. Simmer, without stirring, for 10 minutes. Remove from the heat. Sieve in the cocoa powder and whisk well. Set aside to cool.

Berry coulis

½ quantity Sugar syrup (*see page 24*)

250 g/8 oz of any of the following: raspberries, blackberries, blueberries or strawberries, washed and prepared

1–2 Tbsp freshly squeezed lemon juice (optional)

Each coulis makes approx. 550 ml/18 fl oz

Make the syrup as described on page 24 and, once the syrup has cooked, add your chosen fruit to it before it cools.

Once cold, transfer to a blender or food processor and blend for a few seconds until smooth. Strain through a nylon sieve to make a smooth sauce. If the sauce is too sweet, add lemon juice to sharpen. Cover and chill until required.

You can try adding extra flavourings to your chosen coulis, such as finely grated citrus rind, vanilla extract or rosewater.

Tropical fruit coulis

1 small ripe mango

½ small ripe papaya

1 ripe kiwi fruit, peeled and roughly chopped

6 Tbsp unsweetened pineapple juice

1–2 tsp runny honey

Makes approx. 450 ml/15 fl oz

Peel the mango and slice down either side of the smooth flat central stone. Discard the stone, chop the flesh and put in a blender or food processor. Scoop out the seeds from the papaya and peel away the skin. Chop the flesh and add to the mango along with the kiwi fruit and pineapple juice. Blend for a few seconds until smooth. Add honey to taste, cover and chill until required.

Sweet spiced butter

90 g/3 oz unsalted butter, softened

1 Tbsp caster sugar

1 tsp ground cinnamon

Makes approx. 100 g/3½ oz

Combine all three ingredients together in a small bowl until well mixed. Pile onto a double thick layer of clingfilm and roll up the butter into a thick roll about 2.5 cm/1 in thick. Wrap tightly and chill for at least 30 minutes until you are ready to use it.

Lemon curd

100 g/3½ oz unsalted butter

150 g/5 oz caster sugar

Finely grated zest and juice of 3 lemons

3 large eggs, beaten

Makes 400 ml/14 fl oz

Put the butter, sugar, lemon zest and juice in a heatproof bowl. Place over a pan of simmering water and stir over a low heat until the sugar has dissolved and the mixture is warm. Whisk the warm lemon mixture into the beaten eggs and strain through a non-metallic sieve. Return the mixture to the heatproof bowl and place over the still simmering water. Stir occasionally until the mixture thickens and coats the back of a wooden spoon. Do not allow the mixture to boil or it will curdle.

Pour the hot mixture into hot, sterilized jars and seal well. The lemon curd will keep for up to 1 month if stored in a cool place.

Fresh marzipan

225 g/8 oz almonds, finely ground
110 g/4 oz icing sugar, sifted
110 g/4 oz caster sugar
Few drops vanilla extract
2 tsps rum or brandy
2 large egg whites, whisked until foamy

Place the almonds, two types of sugar, vanilla and rum or brandy in a mixing bowl. Add enough whisked egg white to make a moist ball of paste. Knead until perfectly smooth and free of cracks. Keep covered in plastic wrap in the fridge until required. Well wrapped, it will keep for several months.

You can mould marzipan into pretty shapes and use them to decorate the tops of cakes. Gently knead the paste on a work surface lightly dusted with icing sugar until smooth and free of cracks. Divide it into small portions and press each one into your chosen decorative mould, level the top and scrape away any excess marzipan with a sharp knife. If using a soft, rubber mould, demould the shapes immediately. If the mould is made of rigid clear plastic, freeze the marzipan until it is hard then press the tip of a knife between the marzipan and the mould to prise it out. Marzipan bought from a good cake supplier is usually of good enough quality and slightly better for moulding than home-made marzipan.

Citrus zest icing

225 g/8 oz icing sugar, double sifted
3 tbsps lemon juice
Zest of 1 lime, grated
Zest of 1 lemon, grated
Zest of 1 orange, grated

Makes approx. 450 ml/15 fl oz

Add the icing sugar to a large mixing bowl and vigorously stir in the lemon juice until the consistency is smooth and shiny. Finally, add the grated fruit zest and mix thoroughly. Try lime, orange or lemon, or all three together to add a fresh zestiness to a variety of bakes. Drizzle over your favourite bakes and allow to set.

Raspberry vinegar

650 g/1 lb 5 oz fresh raspberries or blackberries, washed and hulled

600 ml/20 fl oz white wine vinegar or cider vinegar

Makes 500 ml/16 fl oz

Place 250 g/8 oz of the berries in a non-reactive bowl and pour over the vinegar. Cover and leave for 24 hours in a cool place. The next day, strain the liquid and discard the fruit. Place another 250 g/8 oz fruit in a non-reactive bowl and pour over the fruit-flavoured vinegar. Cover and leave as before. The next day, strain the liquid through muslin and discard the fruit. Put the remaining berries in a large sterilized bottle or jar and pour over the fruited vinegar. Seal well and leave to stand in a cool, dark place for at least 1 month before using.

White vanilla frosting

400 g/14 oz caster sugar

2 egg whites

Pinch cream of tartar

Pinch salt

1 tsp vanilla extract

Makes sufficient to fill and cover 20 cm/8 in round, deep cake

Put all the ingredients except the vanilla extract in a heatproof bowl and whisk to make a thick paste. Place the bowl over a pan of gently simmering water and whisk for 6–7 minutes until thick and peaking.

Remove from the heat and whisk in the vanilla extract. Use this frosting immediately, before it begins to set.

Royal icing

2 large egg whites
350–500 g/12½ oz–
1 lb 2 oz icing sugar

Makes enough for 12 standard-size cupcakes or 24 mini cupcakes

In a bowl, lightly beat the egg whites to break them down, then gradually beat in the icing sugar, using the paddle beater rather than a whisk. Add enough icing sugar until the mixture starts to thicken, then beat using the slowest speed of an electric mixer for about 10 minutes, until the icing is light and fluffy. Adjust the consistency if necessary by either adding more icing sugar if the mixture is too runny, or a few drops of water if it's too stiff – but beat for at least 2 to 3 minutes after each addition of icing sugar.

Still freezing method

If you do not own an ice cream maker you can still make every ice cream in this book by using the still freezing method. To freeze your ice cream mixture successfully, it is important to ensure you set your freezer temperature to -18° C/0° F or, alternatively, use the fast-freeze option if you have it. When your ice cream mixture is made, transfer it to a suitable freezer container, cover it and place it in the coldest part of the freezer. Leave for about 1–1½ hours, or until the sides and base are just frozen and the middle is a soft slush. Remove from the freezer and beat, using an electric whisk or food processor, until the ice crystals are uniform. It is important to work quickly to prevent the ice crystals from melting. Cover the mixture and quickly return to the freezer. Repeat this process two more times, at 1–1½-hour intervals. If you are adding large chunks, such as chocolate, biscuits or sweets, add them after the third or fourth beating. After the final beating allow the ice cream to freeze for at least 2 hours, or preferably overnight before serving.

It is not necessary to beat a semifreddo while still freezing – just cover the surface and freeze for at least 6 hours.

Biscuits & Pastries

Lemon and white chocolate biscuits

125 g/4½ oz butter, softened
125 g/4½ oz caster sugar
1 tsp pure lemon oil
1 egg
450 g/1 lb plain flour
1 tsp baking powder
2 Tbsp milk
300 g/10½ oz white chocolate

Makes 24–30

1. Preheat the oven to 170° C/325° F (gas 3). Line one or two baking sheets with baking parchment.

2. Beat the butter and sugar in a large bowl until pale and creamy. Add the lemon oil and beat for a further 30 seconds. Beat in the egg until just combined. In a separate bowl combine the flour and baking powder. Mix into the butter mixture, adding enough of the milk to make a dough. Chill if the weather is warm.

3. Roll out the dough on a lightly floured surface, about 4 mm/¼ in thick. Using a 6 cm/2½ in round cutter, cut the dough into rounds then transfer on to the prepared trays.

4. Bake for 15–18 minutes, or until lightly golden. Allow to cool slightly then transfer to a wire rack and allow to cool completely. When cool, melt the chocolate in the microwave or over a double boiler. Half dip the biscuits into the chocolate then leave to set on baking parchment in a cool place (see page 21).

Chocolate truffle cookies

250 g/9 oz continental plain chocolate (70% cocoa solids), broken

60 g/2½ oz cocoa powder, sifted

110 g/4 oz butter

3 eggs

200 g/7 oz caster sugar

1½ tsp vanilla extract

75 g/2¾ oz plain flour

¼ tsp baking powder

¼ tsp salt

150 g/5½ oz continental plain chocolate (70% cocoa solids), chopped into small chunks

Makes 40–42

1. Preheat the oven to 180° C/350° F (gas 4).

2. Combine the broken chocolate pieces, the cocoa powder and butter in a metal bowl and place over a pan of simmering water. Stir occasionally until the chocolate and butter have melted. Remove from the heat, stir to combine and set aside to cool.

3. Beat the eggs and sugar, using an electric mixer, until light and fluffy. Beat in the vanilla extract and chocolate mixture. Sift together the flour, baking powder and salt. Add to the butter mixture together with the chopped chocolate and stir until just combined.

4. Cover the dough and chill for at least 3 hours. Even after chilling, the dough will be quite soft. Quickly roll the dough into heaped teaspoon-sized balls (roughly 3 cm/1 in wide) and place 5 cm/2 in apart on ungreased or parchment-lined baking sheets. Bake for 10 minutes, or until the tops are crispy and the centres just set.

5. Allow to cool for 5 minutes on the baking sheets then transfer to a wire rack and allow to cool completely. Dust with cocoa powder to serve.

Ginger crunch

For the base:

225 g/8 oz plain flour

100 g/3½ oz caster sugar

1 tsp baking powder

2 tsp ground ginger

150 g/5½ oz butter, cut into cubes

For the icing:

150 g/5½ oz butter

60 ml/2 fl oz golden syrup

300 g/10½ oz icing sugar, sifted

2 Tbsp ground ginger

Makes 16–24

1. Preheat the oven to 180° C/350° F (gas 4). Line a deep-sided 18 x 27 cm/7 x 10¾ in shallow baking tin with baking parchment.

2. To make the base, put the flour, sugar, baking powder and ginger in a food processor. Pulse several times to combine then add the butter. Process for about 30 seconds, or until the mixture resembles fine breadcrumbs. This can also be done by hand. Press the mixture evenly into the tin and level off, using the back of a spoon.

3. Bake for 20–25 minutes, or until lightly golden. Remove from the oven and allow to cool completely.

4. To make the icing, put the butter and golden syrup in a medium saucepan and heat until just melted. Add the sifted icing sugar and ginger and cook for a further 1–2 minutes, stirring constantly until smooth. Remove from the heat and poor over the base. Leave to set. Remove from the tin and cut into squares or triangles to serve.

Hazelnut and chocolate flower cookies

100 g/3½ oz roasted hazelnuts
200 g/7 oz self-raising flour
100 g/3½ oz sugar
100 g/3½ oz unsalted butter
2 eggs
1–2 drops hazelnut essence (optional)
1 Tbsp cocoa

Makes 20 large cookies or 40 small biscuits

1. Finely grind the hazelnuts in a food processor. Mix the flour, sugar and butter together in a bowl until it forms a crumbly texture. Add the eggs, hazelnut essence, if using, and the ground hazelnuts. Mix into a soft sticky dough.

2. Divide the dough in half. Add 1 tablespoon of cocoa to one half of the dough and work in until even in colour. Form each portion into a roll, wrap in cling film, then refrigerate for 30 minutes.

3. To make the biscuits, remove the cling film, cut into 5 mm/¼ in thick slices and shape into 'flowers', alternating the petals and centres with hazelnut and chocolate dough. Place on a baking tray lined with non-stick baking paper and bake in an oven preheated to 180° C/350° F (gas 4) for 12 minutes. Allow the biscuits to cool for 1–2 minutes before removing from the baking tray.

White chocolate and macadamia cookies

125 g/4½ oz butter, softened
225 g/8 oz soft brown sugar
1 egg, lightly beaten
1 tsp vanilla extract
225 g/8 oz plain flour
½ tsp baking powder
1 pinch salt
200 g/7 oz white chocolate chunks or chips
150 g/5½ oz macadamia nuts, roughly chopped

Makes 20

1. Preheat the oven to 180° C/350° F (gas 4). Line a baking sheet with baking parchment.

2. Beat the butter and sugar together in a large bowl until pale and creamy. Add the egg and vanilla extract and stir to combine. Combine the flour, baking powder and salt together in a separate bowl and stir into the butter mixture until just combined. Fold through the chocolate chunks and macadamia nuts.

3. Place heaped tablespoonfuls of the mixture on to the prepared baking sheet, leaving a little space between them to allow for spreading.

4. Bake for 15–20 minutes, or until lightly golden. Allow to cool on the sheets for 5 minutes then transfer to a wire rack and allow to cool completely.

Popcorn balls

70 g/2½ oz popped popcorn
250 ml/9 fl oz molasses
150 g/5½ oz caster sugar
2 Tbsp white vinegar
2 Tbsp butter
125 ml/4½ fl oz water
½ tsp bicarbonate of soda
200 g/7 oz pecans or walnuts, chopped (or a combination of both)

Makes 10–14

1. Put the popped popcorn into two large, separate bowls (this will make combining with the molasses syrup a much easier task). Set aside.

2. Combine the molasses, sugar, white vinegar, butter and water in a saucepan over medium heat. Boil gently, without stirring, until the mixture begins to bubble and a sugar thermometer inserted reads 116° C/240° F (or until a small amount dropped into cold water forms a soft ball when pressed between finger and thumb). Stir in the bicarbonate of soda. Working quickly, pour the syrup over the two bowls of popcorn. Add the chopped nuts and stir to combine.

3. When the popcorn is cool enough to handle, butter your hands, scoop up the popcorn by the fistful and roll into balls. Wrap each ball individually in clingfilm.

4. Try to seek out molasses rather than using treacle in this recipe. Treacle will work, but molasses lends more of a caramel flavour.

Berry chocolate florentines

75 g/2¾ oz butter

75 g/2¾ oz light brown sugar

50 g/1¾ oz plain flour

50 g/1¾ oz flaked almonds, toasted

100 g/3½ oz mixed dried berries, e.g. cranberries, blueberries, cherries, strawberries

150 g/5½ oz plain chocolate, chopped

¼–½ tsp ground mixed spice

Makes 20–24

1. Preheat the oven to 180° C/350° F (gas 4). Line a large baking sheet with baking parchment.

2. Heat the butter and sugar together in a saucepan until the sugar dissolves and they bind together. Remove from the heat and mix in the flour, then add the nuts and berries.

3. Put tablespoonfuls full of the mixture, quite widely spaced, on the baking sheet and flatten slightly using the back of the spoon. You may need to bake them in two batches.

4. Bake the florentines for 10–12 minutes, or until spread flat and golden. While still hot, neaten up the edges using a knife and allow to cool completely on the baking sheet. Melt the chocolate over a saucepan of simmering water or in the microwave. Stir in the mixed spice and mix well. Using a palette knife, spread the chocolate over the flat side of the florentines and allow to cool before serving.

Ginger kisses

250 g/9 oz butter, softened

115 g/4¼ oz icing sugar, sieved

1 egg, lightly beaten

3 tsp ground ginger

225 g/8 oz plain flour

150 g/5½ oz cornflour

For the filling:

250 g/9 oz mascarpone

50 g/1¾ oz stem ginger, finely chopped

1 Tbsp stem ginger syrup

50 g/1¾ oz demerara sugar

½ tsp vanilla extract

Makes 20–24

1. Preheat the oven to 170° C/325° F (gas 3). Line two baking sheets with baking parchment.

2. In a large bowl beat the butter until pale and creamy. Gradually add the icing sugar, beating well after each addition until the mixture is light and fluffy. Beat in the egg until well combined. If the mixture starts to curdle, add a tablespoon of the flour.

3. In a separate bowl combine the ginger, flour and cornflour. Sift the dry ingredients into the butter mixture and mix thoroughly. Roll teaspoon-sized amounts into balls and press down with a fork.

4. Bake for 20–22 minutes, or until firm and lightly golden in colour. Transfer to a wire rack and allow to cool completely.

5. While the biscuits are cooling prepare the filling. Combine all the ingredients in a bowl and set aside. When the biscuits are cool enough spread the filling on half the biscuits then place the remaining biscuits on top.

Chocolate peanut butter pinwheels

125 g/4½ oz butter

220 g/7¾ oz caster sugar

125 g/4½ oz smooth peanut butter

1 egg, lightly beaten

2 Tbsp milk

275 g/9¾ oz plain flour

½ tsp salt

½ tsp bicarbonate of soda

175 g/6 oz plain chocolate, broken

1 tsp butter

Makes 48

1. Combine the butter, sugar and peanut butter in a large mixing bowl and beat with an electric whisk until smooth and creamy. Add the egg and milk and beat until smooth. In a separate bowl sift the flour, salt and bicarbonate of soda together. Add to the butter mixture and, using a wooden spoon, stir until just combined. Cover and refrigerate for 1 hour.

2. Combine the chocolate and 1 tsp butter in a saucepan over low heat and stir until melted. Set aside. Divide the dough into two equal parts and shape into balls. Flour a work surface and roll one ball into a 24 x 30 cm/ 9½ x 12 in rectangle, 5 mm/¼ in thick. Spread half of the chocolate mixture over the rectangle. Starting at a narrow end, carefully roll up the dough to the other end. Continue with the other roll. Place both rolls, seam-side down, on a parchment-lined baking sheet and chill for 20 minutes.

3. Preheat the oven to 200° C/400° F (gas 6). Transfer the rolls to a floured surface and slice into 1 cm/½ in wide cookies. Place on parchment-lined baking sheets and bake for 8–10 minutes, until set and slightly golden. Allow to cool for 5 minutes on the baking sheets then transfer to wire racks and allow to cool completely.

Smart cookies

50 g/2 oz polyunsaturated margarine

125 g/4 oz caster sugar

1 egg yolk

125 ml/4 fl oz unsweetened apple sauce

175 g/6 oz plain flour

½ tsp bicarbonate of soda

75 g/2¾ oz porridge oats

Makes 16

1. Preheat the oven to 190 °C/375 °F (gas 5). Line two baking sheets with baking parchment. In a bowl, beat together the margarine and sugar until blended, then beat in the egg yolk and apple sauce. Sift the flour and bicarbonate of soda over the mixture and stir in with the rolled oats to make a soft dough.

2. With lightly floured hands, roll the mixture into walnut-sized balls and place on the baking sheets, spacing slightly apart. Use the palm of your hand to flatten the cookies a little. Bake for 15 minutes, until firm. Allow to cool on the baking sheets for a few minutes, then transfer to a wire rack. When completely cold, store the cookies for up to a week in an airtight container.

Date and hazelnut crumble slice

For the filling:

400 g/14 oz dried stoned dates, roughly chopped

Grated rind of 2 lemons

250 ml/9 fl oz water

75 g/2¾ oz sugar

For the base:

225 g/8 oz plain flour

100 g/3½ oz caster sugar

1 tsp baking powder

125 g/4½ oz firm butter, cut into chunks

For the crumble topping:

100 g/3½ oz plain flour

50 g/1¾ oz light brown sugar

75 g/2¾ oz hazelnuts, roughly chopped

75 g/2¾ oz firm butter

Makes 8–16

1. Preheat the oven to 200° C/400° F (gas 6) and line an 18 x 27 cm/7 x 10 ¾ in baking tin with baking parchment.

2. Put the filling ingredients in a saucepan and bring to the boil. Reduce the heat and simmer for 10–15 minutes, or until thick. Allow to cool.

3. Mix together the flour, caster sugar and baking powder for the base. Using your hands or a food processor, rub in the butter to resemble fine breadcrumbs. Press the mixture firmly into the tin and bake for 15–18 minutes, or until brown around the edges. Remove from the oven.

4. Combine the crumble ingredients together in another bowl until the mixture is crumbly. Spread the date mixture over the cooked base then sprinkle over the crumble mixture, pressing it down firmly but gently. Return to the oven and cook for a further 15–20 minutes, or until the crumble topping is golden. Allow to cool completely in the tin before serving or serve warm with a spoonful of vanilla ice cream.

Chocolate chip oatmeal cookies

60 ml/2 fl oz vegetable oil
75 g/2¾ oz butter, softened
100 g/3½ oz caster sugar
110 g/4 oz light brown sugar
½ tsp vanilla extract
1 egg
100 g/3½ oz porridge oats
150 g/5½ oz plain flour
½ tsp bicarbonate of soda
½ tsp baking powder
pinch salt
150 g/5½ oz plain chocolate chips or plain chocolate, chopped

Makes approx. 24

1. Preheat the oven to 180° C/350° F (gas 4).

2. Combine the oil, butter and sugars in a large mixing bowl and cream until smooth. Beat in the vanilla and eggs, one at a time, then stir in the oats. In a separate bowl, sift the flour with the bicarbonate of soda, baking powder and salt. Using a wooden spoon, stir the flour mixture into the buttery oat mixture together with the chocolate chips. Stir until just combined.

3. Drop rounded tablespoonfuls of the dough, 5 cm/2 in apart, on to ungreased baking sheets. Bake for 10 minutes, until the surface is set and the centres slightly soft. Allow to cool on the baking sheets for 5 minutes then transfer to wire racks and allow to cool completely. The cookies will firm up slightly while cooling, so don't over-cook.

Mini macaroons

175 g/6 oz sweetened desiccated coconut

150 g/5½ oz caster sugar

2 egg whites, lightly beaten

4 sheets edible rice paper

Makes 24–36

1. Preheat the oven to 170° C/325° F (gas 3).

2. In a large bowl combine the coconut and caster sugar. Add the egg whites and stir in to form a fairly firm mixture.

3. Lay out the rice paper on one or two baking sheets. Shape the mixture into heaped teaspoon-sized balls and place on the rice paper, pressing down gently to flatten.

4. Bake for 10–12 minutes, or until lightly golden. Remove from the oven and allow to cool on the baking sheets. Tear away any excess rice paper to serve.

Gingerbread men

150 g/5½ oz butter

130 g/4½ oz caster sugar

1 egg

200 ml/7 fl oz treacle or molasses

450 g/1 lb plain flour

½ tsp baking powder

1 tsp bicarbonate of soda

1 tsp salt

1 tsp ground ginger

½ tsp ground cloves

½ tsp ground cinnamon

Suggested decorations:

Royal icing ***(see page 29)***

Silver balls

Chocolate drops

Hundreds and thousands

The yield depends on the size of cutter used. If you use 9 cm/3½ in cutters you will have 7 gingerbread men.

1. Combine the butter and sugar in a large bowl and beat, using an electric mixer, until light and fluffy. Add the egg and treacle and beat until smooth. In a separate bowl, sift the flour with the baking powder, soda, salt, cinnamon and cloves. Slowly add the flour mixture to the treacle mixture in three separate stages, stirring with a wooden spoon until combined.

2. Divide the dough into four balls, flatten and wrap in clingfilm then refrigerate for at least 1 hour before use.

3. Preheat the oven to 190° C/375° F (gas 5).

4. Roll the balls, one at a time, between two sheets of greaseproof paper to a 3 mm/⅛ in thickness. Peel off the top layer and cut into patterns. Carefully transfer cut-outs to ungreased baking trays. Bake for 10–15 minutes, until just cooked. Do not over-cook. Allow the gingerbread men to cool on trays, for 5 minutes, then transfer to racks and allow to cool completely. Decorate as you wish.

Bark

220 g/7¾ oz butter

120 g/4½ oz brown sugar

180 g/6 oz cream crackers

200 g/7 oz plain chocolate chips or plain chocolate, roughly chopped

100 g/3½ oz sliced almonds, lightly toasted

Makes approx. 42 pieces

1. Preheat the oven to 200° C/400° F (gas 6).

2. Line a baking tray with foil, shiny-side up. Cover the foil with the crackers. Do not overlap.

3. Melt the butter and sugar in a saucepan over medium heat. Bring the mixture to the boil, stirring well to ensure the butter and sugar are well blended. Pour the mixture over the crackers and bake for 2–4 minutes, until the butter mixture begins to bubble. Watch carefully. Remove from the oven and sprinkle with chocolate. Bake for a further 1 minute, until the chocolate is soft. Remove from the oven and spread the chocolate evenly to form an icing layer. Sprinkle with almonds. Place the tray in the fridge for about 1 hour, until cool. Remove the bark from the foil and break roughly into 5 cm square pieces.

4. Store the bark in an airtight container for up to 5 days, or freeze for up to 2 months.

Mini pain au chocolat

275 g/9 oz plain flour

1 Tbsp caster sugar

$1/2$ tsp salt

30 g/1 oz lard or white vegetable fat

1 tsp fast-acting dried yeast

150 ml/5 fl oz whole milk, slightly warm

90 g/3 oz piece unsalted butter

1 egg, beaten

12 small pieces (approx. 60 g/2 oz) plain chocolate

30 g/1 oz icing sugar

Makes 12

1. Sift the flour into a mixing bowl and stir in the sugar and salt. Rub in the fat to form fine breadcrumbs. Stir in the yeast. Make a well in the centre and pour in most of the milk. Mix with your fingers, then tip on to a lightly-floured work surface. Bring together and knead lightly until you have a dough slightly softer than a pastry mixture. Lightly flour the bowl and place the dough back in it. Cover loosely and stand in a warm place for about an hour until doubled in size.

2. Gently reknead the dough to form a smooth ball. Roll the dough out to form an oblong 38 x 15 cm/15 x 6 in and place the piece of butter in the centre. Fold the dough over the butter, top and bottom, to cover it and press the edges to seal. Roll the dough out gently to form an oblong the same size as before. Fold the top third down and the bottom third up, and turn 90 degrees. Cover and rest for 10 minutes. Repeat the rolling, folding and turning twice more. Transfer to a floured plate, cover and chill for 30 minutes.

3. Roll out to 30 x 20 cm/12 x 8 in. Cut in two lengthways and then cut each piece into six oblongs to give 12 pieces. Brush each with beaten egg and then place a piece of chocolate in the centre. On each piece fold the bottom third up and the top third down. Turn over and press down to seal the edges to enclose the chocolate. Transfer to a large baking sheet and cover loosely with greased clear food wrap. Stand in a warm place for about 30 minutes until slightly risen. Preheat the oven to 220° C/425° F (gas 7).

4. Brush with beaten egg and bake for about 15 minutes until puffed up and golden. Transfer to a wire rack to cool. Best served warm, dusted with icing sugar.

Peanut butter cookies

175 g/6 oz crunchy peanut butter (with no added sugar)

50 g/2 oz unsalted butter, at room temperature

50 g/2 oz golden caster sugar

40 g/3 Tbsp light brown sugar

1 egg, lightly beaten

125 g/4 oz self-raising flour

50 g/2 oz cornflakes, lightly crushed

Makes 20

1. Preheat the oven to 180° C/375° F (gas 5).

2. Line two baking sheets with baking parchment. Put the peanut butter and butter in a large bowl and beat together until well-mixed and creamy. Add the sugars and beat again. Gradually add the egg, a little at a time, beating well after each addition. Sift over the flour and mix to a stiff dough.

3. Put the crushed cornflakes on a plate. Roll the cookie dough into walnut-sized balls, then roll in the cornflakes to coat. Place on the prepared baking sheets, spacing them slightly apart, then flatten them a little with the palm of your hand (this will stop them rolling off the sheet)!

4. Bake for 10–12 minutes until firm, then remove from the oven and transfer to a wire rack to cool. Store in an airtight container for up to a week. Serve two or three cookies with a glass of milk, a smoothie or a small bowl of yoghurt and fresh fruit.

Chocolate chip slab cookies

220 g/7 3/4 oz butter, softened

200 g/7 oz brown sugar

1 tsp vanilla extract

300 g/10 1/2 oz plain flour

200 g/7 oz plain or milk chocolate chips or plain or milk chocolate, chopped into chunks

Makes 12–18 large squares

1. Preheat the oven to 180° C/350° F (gas 4). Lightly grease a 38 x 25 cm/15 x 10 in baking tin.

2. Beat the butter and sugar using an electric mixer until light and fluffy, about 5 minutes (the secret!). Beat in the vanilla extract. Stir in the flour and chocolate chips. Pat the dough into the prepared baking tray. Bake for 25–28 minutes, until the edges are slightly crispy. Allow to cool before slicing into squares.

Lemon and blueberry shortcake slice

For the base:

225 g/8 oz plain flour

100 g/3½ oz caster sugar

175 g/6 oz firm butter, cut into cubes

For the topping:

3 eggs

225 g/8 oz caster sugar

Juice (about 100 ml/3½ fl oz) and grated rind of 3 lemons

40 g/1½ oz flour

75 g/2¾ oz dried blueberries (optional)

Icing sugar, to serve (optional)

Makes 16–20

1. Preheat the oven to 180° C/350° F (gas 4). Line the base and sides of an 18 x 27 cm/ 7 x 10¾ in tin with baking parchment.

2. Put the flour and the first measure of sugar in a large bowl or food processor and mix to combine. Add the butter and rub together or process until the mixture resembles fine breadcrumbs. Press the crumbs evenly into the prepared tin and bake for 20–25 minutes, or until golden. Remove and reduce the temperature to 140° C/275° F (gas 1).

3. While the base is cooking, whisk together the eggs and the second measure of sugar, using an electric mixer, until very thick and pale, about 8–10 minutes. Stir in the lemon juice and rind then fold in the flour. Sprinkle the blueberries evenly over the base, if using. Pour over the egg mixture and bake for 35–40 minutes, or until set. Allow to cool in the tin before cutting into bars. Serve dusted with icing sugar, if liked.

Amaretti biscuits

Amaretti with fresh almonds:

200 g/7 oz almonds

20 bitter almonds (apricot kernels)

3 egg whites

200 g/7 oz sugar

1 tsp arrowroot

grated zest of 1 lemon

brown sugar for sprinkling

Amaretti with ground almonds:

15 bitter almonds (apricot kernels)

1 tsp brown sugar

3 egg whites

3 Tbsp caster sugar

150 g/5 oz ground almonds

brown sugar for sprinkling

Makes 25–30 biscuits

1. To make Amaretti with fresh almonds, blanch the almonds and bitter almonds in boiling water for a few seconds, then remove the skins. Finely grind in a food processor. Beat the egg whites, sugar and arrowroot into very stiff peaks, then fold in the ground almonds and lemon zest. Spoon onto a baking tray lined with non-stick baking paper to make approximately 30 biscuits. Sprinkle with brown sugar and bake in an oven preheated to 100° C/225° F (gas ¼) for 45 minutes to 1 hour, or until they easily detach from the paper but before they become brown. Allow them to cool in the oven.

2. To make Amaretti with ground almonds, blanch the bitter almonds in boiling water for a few seconds, then remove the skins. Finely grind in a food processor with the brown sugar. Beat the egg whites and caster sugar together, then fold in the ground almonds and bitter almonds. Spoon onto a baking tray lined with non-stick baking paper to make approximately 25 biscuits.

3. Sprinkle with brown sugar and bake in an oven preheated to 100° C/225° F (gas ¼) for 45 minutes to 1 hour, or until they easily detach from the paper but before they become brown. Allow them to cool in the oven. If the amaretti are too soft or chewy once cooked, reheat the oven to 180° C/350° F (gas 4), turn it off, and place the amaretti back in to harden.

Coconut marshmallows

300 g/10½ oz sweetened desiccated coconut

4 sachets unflavoured gelatine (about 4 Tbsp)

300 ml/10 fl oz water

600 g/1 lb 5 oz caster sugar

280 ml/10 fl oz golden syrup

¼ tsp salt

1 tsp coconut extract

Makes approx. 40 squares

1. Preheat the oven to 160° C/325° F (gas 3).

2. Spread the coconut evenly over a baking sheet and toast in the middle of the oven for about 10 minutes or until golden, stirring halfway through. Allow to cool.

3. Lightly oil the base and sides of a 28 x 43 x 5 cm/11 x 17 x 2 in baking dish. Line the dish with foil and then oil the foil. Cover the base of the dish with one third of the toasted coconut. Set aside the remaining coconut in an airtight container.

4. Combine the gelatine and 150 ml/5 fl oz of the water in the bowl of an electric mixer. Combine the sugar, syrup, remaining water and salt in a heavy saucepan. Bring to the boil and cook over high heat until a sugar thermometer inserted reads 116° C/ 240° F (or until a small amount dropped into cold water forms a soft ball when pressed between finger and thumb).

5. Using the whisk attachment of the electric mixer, whisk the hot syrup very slowly into the gelatine mixture, until the whole mixture is very stiff, about 15 minutes. Beat in the coconut extract. Pour the mixture over the foil-lined, coconut-covered baking dish. Hold the dish with two hands and tap on a worktop to level the surface. Cover with ⅓ of the toasted coconut. Cover with clingfilm and leave to rest at room temperature for 12 hours.

6. Place the remaining coconut in a large mixing bowl. Turn the marshmallow out on to a clean work surface. Using a large knife (dipped in water if it gets sticky) cut the marshmallow into 5 cm/ 2 in squares. Working in batches, toss the marshmallow squares in the bowl with the remaining coconut, pressing lightly to adhere. Store in an airtight container at room temperature for 1 week.

Blondies

350 g/12 oz white chocolate, broken into small pieces

90 g/3 oz butter

4 eggs, beaten

150 g/5 oz unbleached caster sugar

30 g/1 oz vanilla sugar

180 g/6 oz self-raising flour

180 g/6 oz ground almonds

60 g/2 oz milk chocolate

Serves 12

1. Preheat the oven to 180° C/350° F (gas 4). Grease and line with baking parchment an 18 x 28 cm/7 x 11 in rectangular cake tin.

2. Place 125 g/4 oz white chocolate pieces in a heatproof bowl with the butter. Place the bowl over a saucepan of gently simmering water. Allow to melt then remove from the water and cool for 10 minutes. Beat in the eggs and sugars. Sieve in the flour and add the ground almonds, and carefully fold into the mixture along with 180 g/6 oz chocolate pieces until well combined.

3. Transfer to the prepared tin and smooth over the top. Bake in the oven for about 40 minutes until risen, firm and golden. Allow to cool in the tin, then cut into 16 pieces. Carefully remove from the tin and transfer to a wire rack.

4. Melt the remaining white chocolate and the milk chocolate separately. Spoon a little of the two chocolates on to each slice and gently mix together, using a skewer, to give a marbled effect. Allow to set before serving.

Soft-bake blueberry and white chocolate cookies

180 g/6 oz unsalted butter, softened

150 g/5 oz light brown sugar

1 egg yolk

250 g/8 oz plain flour

1 pinch salt

½ tsp baking powder

1 tsp vanilla extract

125 g/4 oz white chocolate, cut into small chunks

150 g/5 oz fresh blueberries

Makes 30

1. Preheat the oven to 190° C/375° F (gas 5). Line two large baking trays with baking parchment.

2. In a mixing bowl, beat together the butter and sugar until light and creamy. Beat in the egg yolk and carefully stir in the flour, salt, baking powder, vanilla extract, chocolate chunks and blueberries to make a firm dough.

3. Form into walnut-sized balls and place, a little apart, on the prepared baking trays, then press down gently to flatten the tops. Bake in the oven for about 12 minutes until just firm and lightly browned. Cool for 10 minutes on the baking trays, then transfer to wire racks to cool further. Even more delicious served slightly warm with ice cream!

Pecan and caramel bars

For the base:

300 g/10½ oz plain flour

150 g/5½ oz soft brown sugar

150 g/5½ oz butter, cut into cubes

200 g/7 oz pecan nuts

For the topping:

175 g/6 oz butter

80 g/3 oz soft brown sugar

Makes 20

1. Preheat the oven to 180° C/350° F (gas 4).

2. To make the base, combine the flour, brown sugar and butter in a large bowl and blend with a fork until crumbly. Pat the mixture into a 23 x 33 cm/9 x 13 in baking tin. Sprinkle the pecan nuts on top and set aside.

3. Make the topping. In a saucepan combine the butter and brown sugar over medium heat. Bring to the boil and stir constantly for 1 minute. Pour the caramel mixture over the pecan-covered base.

4. Bake for 18–20 minutes, until the caramel bubbles and the crust is golden. Allow the tin to cool on wire racks before cutting into roughly 4 x 8 cm/1½ x 3¼ in bars. Store the bars in an airtight container for 3–5 days.

Raspberry Shrewsburys

250 g/9 oz flour
175 g/6 oz butter
125 g/4½ oz caster sugar
1 large egg yolk
200 g/7 oz raspberry jam
Juice of 1 lemon

Makes 20

1. Put the flour and butter in a food processor and process until the mixture resembles breadcrumbs. Add the sugar and egg yolk and process until the mixture starts to form a dough. Alternatively, cut the butter into small cubes and add to the flour. Using your fingers, rub the butter into the flour until it makes fine breadcrumbs. Add the sugar and egg yolks and mix to a smooth dough. On a lightly floured surface knead the dough until it comes together. Shape into a ball and wrap in baking parchment and chill for at least 30 minutes.

2. Preheat the oven to 170° C/325° F (gas 3). Line a baking sheet with baking parchment. Roll out the dough on a lightly floured surface to about 3 mm/⅛ in thick and cut out rounds using a 5–6 cm/2–2½ in crimped cutter. Re-roll the trimmings and cut out more rounds until you have 40. Use a 1 cm/½ in piping nozzle to remove the centre from 20 of the rounds.

3. Bake for 10–12 minutes, or until lightly golden in colour. Remove from the oven and allow to cool for a few minutes on the baking sheet then transfer to a wire rack and allow to cool completely.

4. While the biscuits are cooling, put the jam and lemon juice in a saucepan and heat to a simmer. Spoon or brush the jam over the base of a whole round and sandwich with a round with its centre removed on top. Continue until all are done.

Biscotti

250 g/9 oz plain flour

150 g/5½ oz caster sugar

1 tsp baking powder

100 g/3½ oz crystallized ginger, cut into chunks

125 g/4½ oz Brazil nuts, chopped into chunks

3 eggs

Variation: Omit the crystallized ginger and Brazil nuts and add:

200 g/7 oz whole almonds, blanched

150 g/5½ oz plain chocolate, cut into chunks

Or:

150 g/5½ oz pistachio nuts

150 g/5½ oz plain chocolate, cut into chunks

Makes approx. 30

1. Preheat the oven to 180° C/350° F (gas 4). Line two large baking sheets with baking parchment and set aside. Put all the dry ingredients in a large bowl and mix to combine. Add the eggs and stir until the mixture comes together in a ball, adding a little extra flour if it is too wet.

2. Halve the mixture and place each half on the baking parchment. Shape into long, flat log shapes about 25 cm/10 in long, 10 cm/4 in wide and 2.5 cm/1 in high. Bake for about 20 minutes, or until the logs are cooked through and only very lightly golden.

3. Remove from the oven and, when they are cool enough to handle, lift the logs on to a board, and slice thinly (about 7 mm/⅜ in thick) on the diagonal, then place the separate biscuits back flat on the baking sheets. Bake for 10 minutes then turn and bake for a further 5 minutes on the other side or until lightly golden and crispy. Transfer to a wire rack and allow to cool completely. These will keep in an airtight container for about 7–10 days.

Drop scones

- **3 heaped Tbsp self-raising flour**
- **1 lightly rounded Tbsp caster sugar**
- **¼ tsp cream of tartar**
- **1 egg, lightly beaten**
- **4 Tbsps milk**
- **Butter, for frying**
- **Butter, jam and thick cream, to serve**

Makes 10

1. Sift together the flour, sugar and cream of tartar. Make a well in the centre and drop in the egg with the milk and beat together to make a fairly thick batter with a dropping consistency.

2. Heat a griddle or frying pan and grease it lightly with butter, which should be hot and sizzling before you add the batter. Pour a dessertspoon onto the griddle or pan and when small bubbles start to rise to the surface, turn the scone over with a palette knife and cook it on the other side. Fit as many scones as you can onto the frying pan but make sure you leave enough space between them. When both sides are cooked and golden transfer the scones to a wire cooling rack and serve warm or cold thickly spread with butter, jam and a dollop of thick cream.

Apple scones

225 g/8 oz self-raising flour

Pinch of salt

55 g/2 oz butter, roughly chopped

55 g/2 oz sugar

225 g/8 oz Bramley (tart) cooking apple, peeled and grated

70 ml/2 $\frac{1}{2}$ fl oz milk

Egg glaze (*see page 19*)

Makes 15

1. Preheat the oven to 200° C/400° F (gas 6).

2. Put the flour, salt and butter into a large mixing bowl and rub in the butter using your fingertips until it resembles fine breadcrumbs. Mix in the sugar and the grated apple and combine with enough of the milk to make a soft dough.

3. Turn onto a floured board and knead lightly. Roll out the dough to a 1–2 cm/$\frac{1}{2}$–$\frac{3}{4}$ in thickness. Then cut into circles with a 5 cm/2 in floured biscuit cutter. Place the circles onto an ungreased baking sheet, brush over with a little egg glaze and bake for about 10 to 15 minutes. Check the scones after 10 minutes to see how they are progressing. If they look well risen with golden tops they are ready.

Cakes

Orchard fruit and berry sponge

750 g/1 lb 10 oz apple and pears, peeled, cored and chopped

4 Tbsp honey

1 tsp mixed spice

120 g/3¾ oz butter

120 g/3¾ oz light soft brown sugar

2 medium eggs, beaten

285 g/10 oz self-raising flour, sieved

150 g/5½ oz blackberries

1 eating apple, cored and finely sliced

Makes 8 slices

1. Preheat the oven to 180° C/350° F (gas 4). Butter and base line a 20 cm/8 in round loosed-bottomed cake tin.

2. Gently simmer the apples and pears with a little water for 10–12 minutes, until just soft. Add 3 Tbsp of the honey and the mixed spice and heat through for 1–2 minutes then leave to cool.

3. Cream together the butter and sugar until pale and fluffy then gradually beat in the eggs. Fold in the flour then stir in the apples and pears and half the blackberries.

4. Spoon the mixture into the prepared tin. Decorate the top with the thinly sliced apple and remaining blackberries. Bake for 45–50 minutes, until golden and cooked through – test by sticking a knife in the centre, the knife should come out clean.

5. Drizzle with the remaining honey and leave to cool for a few minutes in the tin before turning out and cooling completely on a wire cooling rack. Dust with sifted icing sugar to serve.

Banana pudding cake

225 g/7 1/2 oz unsalted butter
275 g/9 oz dark brown sugar
3 large ripe bananas
4 eggs, beaten
1 tsp vanilla extract
100 g/3 1/2 oz self-raising flour
1/2 tsp ground allspice
1 pinch salt
90 g/3 oz ground almonds

Serves 8

1. Preheat the oven to 180° C/350° F (gas 4).

2. Melt 100 g/3 1/2 oz butter in a saucepan and, when bubbling, add 150 g/5 oz of the sugar. Simmer gently for about 3 minutes, stirring occasionally, until syrupy. Pour into the base of a 23 cm/9 in round cake tin.

3. Peel the bananas, cut two in half, and then slice through lengthways. Fan the banana slices in a round over the base of the tin. Set aside. Mash the remaining banana.

4. In a mixing bowl, cream together the remaining butter and sugar together until pale, and fluffy in texture. Gradually whisk in the eggs with the vanilla and half the flour. Sieve in the remaining flour, ground allspice and salt and add the ground almonds. Fold in together with the mashed banana until well mixed and then pile on top of the fanned-out bananas.

5. Smooth over the top and bake in the oven for 40–45 minutes until lightly golden and firm to the touch. Cool in the tin for 10 minutes to serve hot, or allow to cool for longer before turning out to serve warm.

Old-fashioned marbled loaf cake

45 g/1½ oz plain chocolate
2 tsp hot, boiled water
½ tsp vanilla extract
180 g/6 oz unsalted butter, softened
180 g/6 oz caster sugar
3 large eggs, beaten
250 g/8 oz plain flour
1½ tsp baking powder
45 g/1½ oz ground almonds
1½ Tbsp milk

Serves 8

1. Preheat the oven to 180° C/350° F (gas 4). Grease and line a 1 kg/2 lb loaf tin with baking parchment. Break the chocolate into pieces and place in a small heatproof bowl over a pan of gently simmering water. Allow to melt, then remove from the water and set aside to cool for 15 minutes. Stir in the water and the vanilla extract.

2. Put the butter and sugar in a separate bowl and beat together until pale and fluffy. Beat in the eggs one at a time. Sieve in the flour and baking powder and add the ground almonds and milk. Gently fold the dry ingredients into the creamed mixture. Spoon half the mixture into another bowl and mix in the melted chocolate.

3. Drop alternate spoonfuls of the two mixtures into the prepared tin, gently swirling the two together to give a marbled effect. The mixture should be of dropping consistency, so thin with a little more milk if the mixture is too thick. Smooth the top and bake in the oven for about 45 minutes until risen, firm to the touch and a skewer inserted into the centre comes out clean. Cool in the tin for 15 minutes, then turn on to a wire rack to cool completely. Wrap the cooled cake well and stored for 24 hours before slicing thickly to serve.

Torta Bella

300 g/10½ oz white chocolate
150 g/5½ oz unsalted butter
5 eggs, separated
100 g/3½ oz sugar
2 Tbsp plain flour
icing sugar for dusting

For the chocolate strawberries:
20 strawberries, with stems
200 g/7 oz white chocolate
edible gold paper to decorate (optional)

Serves 12

1. Melt the white chocolate together with the butter and set aside to cool. In a large mixing bowl whisk the egg yolks and sugar together until pale yellow and foamy (it is better to do this by hand). While still whisking, add the cooled chocolate mixture, then the flour. In a separate bowl beat the egg whites into stiff peaks and gently fold into the mixture. Line the base and sides of a 23 cm/9 in round cake tin with non-stick baking paper. Pour in the mixture and bake in an oven preheated to 180° C/350° F for approximately 35 minutes or until a toothpick inserted into the cake comes out clean.

2. Remove the cake from the oven, dust with icing sugar, and allow it to cool in the tin for 2–3 hours. It will flatten while cooling, just like a soufflé.

3. To prepare the chocolate strawberries, lightly rinse and dry the strawberries. Melt the chocolate and, holding each strawberry by the stem, dip it halfway into the chocolate. Place the strawberries, chocolate end up, on a cooling tray to set, attaching a small piece of edible gold paper, if desired. Lift the cake from its tin by the baking paper and remove the paper. Place the cake on a serving plate and arrange the strawberries on top.

Tropical fruit chocolate box gateau

300 g/10 oz plain chocolate

Chocolate trifle sponge
(see page 18)

4 Tbsp coconut liqueur or syrup

180 g/6 oz white chocolate

150 ml/5 fl oz double cream

150 ml/5 fl oz coconut milk

Assorted prepared tropical fruit such as kiwi fruit, mango, pineapple, banana, star fruit, to decorate

Grated chocolate, to decorate

Serves 8

1. For the chocolate box, turn an 18 cm/7 in square cake tin upside down. Mould a double layer of foil around the tin, pressing it around the corners. Carefully remove the foil and turn the tin right side up. Carefully press the foil 'box' into the tin, making the foil as smooth as possible. Place a small piece of sticky tape at the top of the middle of each side to secure in place. It should be placed right at the very edge of the foil and fold it down to the edge of the tin. Place in the freezer for 20 minutes.

2. Break the plain chocolate into pieces and place in a heatproof bowl over a pan of barely simmering water until melted. Remove from the water.

3. Pour the hot chocolate into the foil-lined tin. Working quickly, tilt the tin to coat the bottom and the sides – you might want to wear gloves to do this as the tin will be very cold. Using a small spatula, spread the chocolate evenly right to the edges of the foil (do not cover the sticky tape), smoothing it into the corners. Chill in the fridge until set.

4. When the chocolate case is completely set, remove the sticky tape, carefully pull out the foil lining and peel it away from the chocolate. Put the chocolate box on a board. Trim the sponge to fit inside the chocolate box and carefully lower it into the bottom. Spoon the liqueur or syrup over the sponge. Chill until required.

5. Melt the white chocolate as above and set aside. Whip the cream until just peaking and then whisk in the coconut milk. Fold in the melted white chocolate and then spoon on top of the sponge. Smooth off the top and chill for at least 2 hours until firm. To serve, decorate the top with a selection of tropical fruit and sprinkle with grated chocolate.

Sweet cherry marzipan bread

250 ml/8 fl oz whole milk

1 pinch saffron

500 g/1 lb strong white bread flour

1 1/2 tsp salt

1 1/2 tsp instant or fast-acting yeast

250 g/8 oz ready-made marzipan, finely chopped

2 eggs, beaten

250 g/8 oz fresh cherries, stoned and halved

1 Tbsp icing sugar (optional)

Serves 12

1. Preheat the oven to 200° C/400° F (gas 6). Pour the milk into a saucepan and add the saffron. Heat gently until warm but not hot. Set aside to cool for 10 minutes.

2. Sift the flour and salt into a bowl and stir in the yeast and half the marzipan. Make a well in the centre and stir in half of the egg along with the saffron milk. Bring together to form a dough. Turn the dough out onto a lightly floured surface and knead until smooth. Lightly dust the mixing bowl with flour and replace the dough inside. Cover loosely and leave in a warm place for about 1 hour until doubled in size.

3. Re-knead the dough and place it on a large baking sheet lined with baking parchment. Press the dough into a round about 25 cm/10 in diameter. Brush all over with beaten egg then sprinkle the cherries evenly over the top and gently press into the dough. Cover loosely and set aside for about 40 minutes or until well risen.

4. Sprinkle with the remaining marzipan and bake in the oven for about 30 minutes until the marzipan is golden and the cherries are tender. Leave to cool on the baking tray. Best served warm and dusted with icing sugar, if liked.

Hot chocolate sandwich

2 slices Pane al cioccolato ***(see page 163)*****, brioche or other sweet bread, approx. 1 cm/½ in thick**

30 g/1 oz unsalted butter, softened

2 Tbsp chocolate spread

1 large banana, mashed

1 small milk chocolate flake bar, crumbled

Serves 1

1. Thickly butter the bread and place buttered side down on a board lined with baking parchment. Spread the unbuttered sides with chocolate spread.

2. On one slice, carefully spread the mashed banana and sprinkle with chocolate flakes. Peel the other slice of bread off the parchment and gently press, chocolate side down, on top to make a sandwich.

3. Heat a nonstick ridged griddle or frying pan until hot, and press the sandwich on to the pan for about 2 minutes. Turn over and cook for a further 2 minutes until golden and lightly charred. Drain and serve immediately.

Mini orange brioche surprises

- 250 g/8 oz strong white bread flour
- ½ tsp salt
- 1 Tbsp caster sugar
- 1¼ tsp instant or fast-acting dried yeast
- ½ tsp finely grated orange zest
- 30 g/1 oz candied orange peel, finely chopped
- 3 Tbsp whole milk, slightly warm
- 2 eggs, beaten
- 60 g/2 oz unsalted butter, melted
- 4 pieces (approx. 30 g/1 oz) plain chocolate
- Egg glaze (*see page 19*)

Makes 4

1. Sieve the flour, salt and caster sugar into a bowl and stir in the dried yeast, orange zest and orange peel. Make a well in the centre. Mix together the milk and beaten egg with the melted butter and pour into the centre of the well. Mix the ingredients together with your fingers, then tip on to a lightly-floured work surface, bring together and knead lightly for about 5 minutes until you have a dough slightly softer than a pastry mixture. Lightly flour the bowl and place the dough back in it. Cover loosely and stand in a warm place for about an hour until doubled in size.

2. Gently reknead the dough to form a smooth ball. Cut into four equal portions, flatten and place a piece of chocolate in the centre of each. Bring the dough up around the chocolate and form into a ball. If you have four 10 cm/4 in individual brioche tins, grease them and place a dough ball in each, otherwise greased muffin tins will work just as well. Cover loosely with lightly-oiled clear food wrap and leave in a warm place for about 45 minutes until doubled in size. Preheat the oven to 200° C/400° F (gas 6).

3. Glaze the brioche with the egg and bake in the oven for 20–25 minutes until risen and richly golden. Transfer to a wire rack to cool slightly. Serve warm.

Jumble slice

150 g/5 oz unsalted butter

500 g/1 lb milk chocolate, broken into small pieces

180 g/6 oz chocolate chip cookies, crushed into small pieces

60 g/2 oz glacé cherries, chopped

60 g/2 oz seedless raisins

60 g/2 oz mini marshmallows

125 g/4 oz honeycomb *(see page 20)*, lightly crushed

Serves 12

1. Line a 500 g/1 lb loaf tin with clear food wrap. Place the butter and chocolate in a saucepan over a very low heat, stirring occasionally, until melted. Set aside for 10 minutes.

2. Meanwhile put the remaining ingredients together in a mixing bowl and stir until well combined.

3. Pour the melted chocolate over the dry mixture and stir well, making sure that all the pieces are thoroughly coated. Transfer to the prepared tin, press down well, cover loosely and chill for at least 2 hours until firm and set.

4. Remove from the tin and discard the food wrap. Using a large sharp knife, cut into 12 slices to serve. Keep refrigerated.

Clementine and cranberry muffin cake

For the fruit:
2 clementines
85 g/3 oz kumquats, halved
140 g/5 oz fresh cranberries
2 Tbsp redcurrant jelly
70 g/2½ oz caster sugar
25 g/1 oz butter

For the cake mix:
225 g/8 oz plain flour
2 rounded tsps baking powder
Pinch salt
140 g/5 oz caster sugar
85 g/3 oz melted butter
1 large egg
284 ml/10 fl oz buttermilk
Icing sugar, to dust
Lightly sweetened crème fraîche, to serve

Serves 8 to 10

1. Add the whole clementines, unpeeled, to a medium-size saucepan and cover with boiling water. Cover with a lid and simmer for 2 hours over a low to moderate heat, checking the water levels every now and again. Remove the clementines from the heat and when they have cooled, split them open and remove the pips. Liquidize them to a smooth, orange-coloured purée and set aside.

2. Preheat the oven to 180°C/375°F (gas 4). In a flat, oven-proof container, mix the halved kumquats, cranberries, redcurrant jelly and sugar and dot over with the butter. Bake for 8 minutes, until the juices start to run and the fruit looks glossy. Baste a couple of times to amalgamate the fruit, then remove from the oven and leave the fruit to cool in the syrup.

3. To make the cake mix, sift the dry ingredients into a large mixing bowl. In a smaller bowl, mix in the cooled melted butter with the egg, buttermilk and puréed clementine. Make a well and pour in the clementine and buttermilk mixture and fold it in gently until nearly blended. Fold in half the braised fruit making sure not to over mix the mixture. Lightly butter a 23 cm/9 in round loose-bottomed tin 4 cm/1½ in deep. Spoon the mixture into the tin and sprinkle the remaining braised fruit on top. Bake for 30 minutes. When slightly cooled, turn out onto a wire cooling rack. Serve cut into wedges with a thick dusting of icing sugar and a spoonful of lightly sweetened crème fraîche.

Ginger cake with ginger polka dots

175 g/6 oz butter, softened

175 g/6 oz golden caster sugar

3 large eggs

1½ Tbsp black treacle

2½ Tbsp ginger syrup from a stem (preserved) ginger jar

225 g/8 oz self-raising flour

2 tsps ground ginger

1–1½ level Tbsp ground almonds

2 Tbsp single cream

One quantity of citrus zest icing (*see p.27*)

4–5 pieces of stem ginger, to decorate

Serves 12

1. Preheat the oven to 170°C/325°F (gas 3).

2. Cream the butter and sugar together until light and creamy. Gradually beat in the eggs, one by one, beating well between each addition. Fold in the treacle and the ginger syrup. Gradually fold in the flour sifted with the ground ginger. Then fold in the ground almonds, followed by the cream, until well combined.

3. Spoon the cake mix into a buttered 20 cm/8 in square tin lined at the base with baking parchment and smooth it level. Bake for 40 to 50 minutes, or until the centre of the cake is firm and slightly springy to the touch. Leave to cool slightly in the tin, then turn it out onto a wire cooling rack.

4. When the cake has sufficiently cooled, spread the citrus zest icing over the top, coaxing it towards the edges of the cake with a palette knife. Leave to set.

5. For the polka dot decoration, simply dot the icing with thinly-shaved ginger slices spaced a little apart. Serve cut into squares.

Dried cranberry marzipan cake

Half quantity of fresh marzipan *(see page 27)*

1 tsp vanilla extract

1 Tbsp rum

115 g/4 oz butter, softened

115 g/4 oz caster sugar

3 large eggs, beaten

140 g/5 oz dried cranberries, roughly chopped

115 g/4 oz ground almonds

2 tsp orange marmalade

115 g/4 oz plain flour, sifted

2 lightly rounded tsps baking powder, sifted

For the glaze:

2 Tbsp orange marmalade

2 Tbsp caster sugar

2 Tbsp water

Serves 10

1. Preheat the oven to 180° C/350° F (gas 4).

2. Cream the marzipan, vanilla extract, rum, butter and caster sugar together into a smooth paste. Add the eggs, gradually beating them well into the mixture until well combined, then fold in the remaining ingredients.

3. Spoon the mixture into a 900g/1 lb French-style loaf tin lined at the base with baking parchment and bake for about 1 hour. Cover with a double-folded sheet of baking parchment about 10 minutes before the end of baking to ensure the top of the cake does not over-brown. Leave to cool a little before turning out onto a wire cooling rack.

4. To make the glaze, add all the ingredients to a small saucepan and boil together until the syrup thickens. Brush the hot syrup over the surface of the cake.

Chocolate and marshmallow wedges

350 g/12 oz dark chocolate

250 g/9 oz butter

1½ Tbsp water

1½ Tbsp caster sugar

1½ tsp vanilla extract

1½ Tbsp orange juice

3 medium egg yolks, whisked lightly and strained

125 g/4½ oz digestive biscuits

175 g/6 oz pink and white marshmallows

1 Tbsp cocoa powder mixed with chocolate powder in equal amounts, to dust

Makes 8 slices

1. Melt the chocolate with the butter, water and sugar in a mixing bowl set over a pan of hot water taken off the heat. Stir until smooth, then remove the bowl from the heat and leave the mixture to cool a little.

2. Lightly whisk in the vanilla and orange juice followed by the egg yolks. Finely crush half of the biscuits and mix them into the chocolate mixture, followed by the remaining digestive biscuits roughly chopped. Finally add the marshmallows cut into halves and quarters. While the chocolate marshmallow mixture is still fairly fluid, pour it into a lightly buttered 20 cm/8 in round tin lined at the base with baking parchment. If the mixture has begun to set, press it into the tin and then smooth the top level with a palette knife. Cover the tin with plastic wrap and refrigerate for 6 hours, or preferably overnight until hard.

3. Turn out onto a plate and dust over the top of the cake with cocoa powder evenly mixed with chocolate powder. Cut the chocolate marshmallow biscuit cake into thick wedges while it is still chilled. Wrap in cellophane and tie each one with ribbon. Keep refrigerated until required.

Mini French loaf cake

55 g/2 oz caster sugar

55 g/2 oz self-raising flour, sifted

Small pinch of salt

55 g/2 oz butter

2 small eggs

25 g/1 oz almonds, finely ground

½ vanilla pod, split

2 Tbsp quince jelly or sieved apricot jam, to glaze

Icing sugar, to dust

Makes 1

1. Mix the sugar, sifted flour and salt together in a bowl. Melt but do not brown the butter and set aside to cool.

2. Lightly beat the eggs and mix them into the sugar and flour mixture and gradually add the cooled butter, ground almonds and the vanilla pod seeds (reserving the empty pod). Mix well but not too vigorously. Cover and refrigerate for 30 minutes to 1 hour.

3. Preheat the oven to 190° C/375° F (gas 5). Spoon the mixture into a lightly buttered 225 g/½ lb French loaf tin lined at the base with baking parchment and level the top with the back of a spoon. Lay the reserved split vanilla pod on top of the mixture and bake for 25 minutes until the cake looks lightly golden and domed with the pod peeping through the cooked cake mixture.

4. If you wish to glaze the cake, gently melt 2 Tbsp of quince jelly or sieved apricot jam until syrupy and brush it warm over the top. Leave to set and serve, cut in thin delicate slices arranged on a tea plate, lightly dusted with icing sugar.

Chocolate angel cake

100 g/3½ oz plain flour

2 Tbsp cocoa powder

180 g/6 oz caster sugar

Pinch of salt

7 large egg whites

1 level tsp cream of tartar

1 tsp vanilla extract

1 quantity of White vanilla frosting ***(see page 28)***

Edible silver dragées, to decorate

Serves 8–10

1. Preheat the oven to 180° C/350° F (gas 4). Grease and line a deep 20 cm/8 in diameter round cake tin with baking parchment. Sift the flour and cocoa powder with 7 Tbsp of the caster sugar and the salt in a bowl. Set aside.

2. Place the egg whites in a large grease-free bowl and whisk until foamy but not stiff. Add the cream of tartar and 2 Tbsp of the remaining caster sugar. Whisk until the egg whites form soft peaks. Add the vanilla extract and remaining sugar, and fold in using a large metal spoon. Gently sieve in the flour, cocoa and sugar mixture, folding it in as you go.

3. Transfer the mixture to the prepared tin and smooth the top. Bake in the centre of the oven for 30–35 minutes until firm to the touch and a skewer inserted into the centre comes out clean. Leave to cool in the tin for 15 minutes, then remove from the tin and transfer to a wire rack to cool completely.

4. Peel away the parchment and slice the cake horizontally in half. Spread half of the White vanilla frosting over one cake half and sandwich the other half on top. Transfer to a serving plate, cover the top with the remaining frosting and leave for 30 minutes to set before serving decorated with silver dragées.

Double chocolate muffins

50 g/2 oz creamed coconut
300 ml/10 fl oz boiling water
5 Tbsp sunflower oil
225 g/8 oz self-raising flour
25 g/1 oz unsweetened cocoa powder
1 tsp baking powder
100 g/3½ oz light brown sugar
75 g/2½ oz dairy-free chocolate or carob chips

9-hole bun tray lined with paper cases

Makes 9

1. Preheat the oven to 200 °C/400 °F (gas 6).

2. Grease a 9-hole muffin tray or line with paper muffin cases. Roughly chop the creamed coconut. Add to the boiling water in a jug and stir until dissolved. Add the oil, then leave the mixture until tepid.

3. Sift the flour, cocoa and baking powders into a mixing bowl. Stir in the sugar and chocolate or carob chips. Add the coconut mixture and briefly mix until just combined, but still a little lumpy.

4. Divide the mixture between the prepared muffin tray or cases and place in the oven. Immediately turn down the oven temperature to 180° C/350° F (gas 4) and bake for 16–18 minutes, until well risen and firm. Leave the muffins in the tin for a few minutes, then carefully transfer to a wire rack. Serve warm or cold.

Strawberry and cream cupcakes

For the cupcakes:

12 standard-size Plain cupcakes (*see page 14*)

6 Tbsp strawberry jam

For the topping:

284 ml/10 fl oz double cream

2 Tbsp icing sugar

6 medium strawberries, halved

12-hole bun tray lined with paper cases

Makes 12

1. Cut the tops off the cupcakes and spread the cut surface with jam, then replace the tops.

2. For the topping, pour the cream into a bowl and add the icing sugar. Lightly whip the cream until it forms soft peaks, then spoon onto the top of each cupcake. Finish by pressing half a strawberry on top. Keep the cakes chilled until ready for serving.

Chocolate chunk and raspberry muffins

250 g/8 oz self-raising flour

125 g/4 oz unbleached caster sugar

125 g/4 oz milk chocolate chunks

2 eggs, beaten

150 ml/5 fl oz whole milk

125 g/4 oz butter, melted

200 g/7 oz fresh raspberries

10-hole bun tray lined with paper cases

Makes 10

1. Preheat the oven to 190° C/375° F (gas 5).

2. Put 10 paper muffin cases into a tray of deep muffin tins.

3. Sift the flour into a bowl and gently stir in the sugar and chocolate chunks and make a well in the centre. Mix the eggs, milk and melted butter together and pour into the well, stirring to form a stiff batter, but taking care not to overmix. Carefully fold in the raspberries.

4. Divide the batter equally between the muffin cases. Smooth the tops slightly and bake in the oven for 35–40 minutes, until risen and lightly golden. Transfer to a wire rack to cool. Best served warm on day of baking.

Bakewell cupcakes

For the cupcakes:
125 g/4½ oz butter, softened
125 g/4½ oz caster sugar
Few drops of almond extract
2 medium eggs
2 Tbsp milk
100 g/3½ oz self-raising flour
30 g/1 oz ground almonds
2–3 Tbsp flaked almonds

For the topping:
5–6 Tbsp raspberry jam
Icing sugar, for dusting

12-hole bun tray lined with paper cases

Makes 12

1. Preheat the oven to 190°C/375° F (gas 5).

2. To make the cupcakes, beat the butter, sugar and almond extract together in a bowl until the mixture is light and fluffy. Add the eggs, milk, flour and ground almonds and beat until the mixture is smooth. Divide the mixture between the paper cases. Scatter the flaked almonds for the topping over the top of each and press them down slightly in to the mixture.

3. Bake in the centre of the oven for 12–15 minutes until the cakes have risen and are just firm to the touch in the centre and the almonds are a light golden colour. Remove the cakes from the oven and transfer them to a wire rack to cool.

4. Slice the tops off the cakes, spread with the jam, then replace the tops. Dust with icing sugar before serving.

Pistachio cupcakes

For the cupcakes:
60 g/2 oz pistachio nuts
125 g/4 1/2 oz self-raising flour
125 g/4 1/2 oz butter, softened
125 g/4 1/2 oz caster sugar
2 medium eggs
2 Tbsp milk

For the topping:
1 quantity of Cream cheese frosting ***(see page 17)***
100 g/3 1/2 oz pistachio nuts, chopped

12-hole bun tray lined with paper cases

Makes 12

1. Preheat the oven to 190° C/375° F (gas 5).

2. To make the cupcakes, place the pistachio nuts and flour into the bowl of a food processor, and whiz until the nuts are finely ground. Alternatively, finely chop the nuts and mix them into the flour. Beat the butter and sugar together in a bowl until light and fluffy, then add the flour mixture, eggs and milk to the bowl, and beat until smooth. Divide the mixture between the paper cases and bake in the centre of the oven for 12–15 minutes until the cakes have risen and are just firm to the touch in the centre. Remove the cakes from the oven and transfer them to a wire rack to cool.

3. For the topping, cover the cakes with the cream cheese frosting and scatter the chopped pistachio nuts over them.

Black Forest cupcakes

For the syrup:

150 ml/5 fl oz water

60 g/2 oz caster sugar

3 Tbsp Kirsch

For the cupcakes:

12 Chocolate cupcakes, *(see page 15)*

6 level Tbsp black cherry conserve

For the topping:

284 ml/10 fl oz double cream

12 fresh cherries with stalks

1–2 Tbsp grated plain chocolate

12-hole bun tray lined with paper cases

Piping bag fitted with a large star piping tube

Makes 12

1. To make the syrup, pour the water into a saucepan and add the sugar. Place the pan over a low heat and stir until the sugar has dissolved. Increase the heat and boil rapidly until the mixture has reduced by about half. Remove the pan from the heat and allow the syrup to cool for about 5 minutes, then stir in the Kirsch.

2. Cut the top off each cupcake and reserve the tops for 'lids'. Scoop out a small amount of the cake to create a small hollow in each. Brush the warm syrup into the hollows and spoon a little of the black cherry conserve into each hollow, then replace the lids on the cake.

3. For the topping, whisk the cream until it forms soft peaks, then spoon it into the piping bag. Pipe a swirl of cream on top of each cupcake. Place a cherry on top of each and sprinkle a little grated chocolate.

Lemon crunch cupcakes

For the cupcakes:
125 g/4½ oz butter, softened
125 g/4½ oz caster sugar
125 g/4½ oz self-raising flour
2 medium eggs
2 Tbsp milk
Finely grated rind of 1 lemon

For the topping:
3–4 level Tbsp granulated sugar
Juice of 1 lemon

12-hole bun tray lined with paper cases

Makes 12

1. Preheat the oven to 190°C/375° F (gas 5).

2. To make the cupcakes, beat the butter and sugar together in a bowl until the mixture is light and fluffy. Add the flour, eggs, milk and lemon rind to the bowl, and beat the mixture until smooth.

3. Divide the mixture between the paper cases and bake in the centre of the oven for 12–15 minutes until the cakes have risen and are just firm to the touch in the centre. Remove the cakes from the oven and transfer them to a wire rack.

4. Immediately sprinkle the sugar for the topping over the hot cakes. Spoon over the lemon juice and leave the cakes to cool.

Apple and cinnamon cupcakes

For the cupcakes:

125 g/4½ oz butter, softened

125 g/4½ oz light soft brown sugar

2 medium eggs

125 g/4½ oz self-raising flour

2 level tsp ground cinnamon

1 dessert apple, cored and grated

1 dessert apple, cored and sliced

For the topping:

4–6 Tbsp apricot glaze or sieved apricot jam

2 Tbsp water

12-hole bun tray lined with paper cases

Makes 12

1. Preheat the oven to 190° C/375° F (gas 5).

2. To make the cakes, beat together the butter and sugar in a bowl until the mixture is light and fluffy. Add the eggs and then sift the flour and cinnamon together into the bowl. Beat the mixture until smooth, then stir in the grated apple. Divide the mixture between the paper cases and arrange apple slices on the top of the cakes. Bake in the centre of the oven for 12–15 minutes until the cakes have risen and are just firm to the touch in the centre. Remove the cakes from the oven and transfer them to a wire rack.

3. For the topping, warm the apricot glaze or jam with the water, either in a saucepan or in a microwave oven, and brush it over the top of the hot cupcakes. Serve warm or cool.

Raspberry and white chocolate cupcakes

For the cupcakes:

50 g/2 oz butter, softened

50 g/2 oz caster sugar

1 medium egg

50 g/2 oz self-raising flour

1 Tbsp milk

50 g/2 oz white chocolate, chopped

For the topping:

100 ml/3½ fl oz crème fraîche

200 g/7 oz white chocolate, melted

24 raspberries

24-hole mini muffin tray lined with paper cases

Piping bag fitted with a large, plain piping tube, optional

Makes 24

1. Preheat the oven to 190° C/375° F (gas 5).

2. To make the cupcakes, beat the butter and sugar in a bowl until the mixture is light and fluffy. Add the egg, flour and milk to the bowl and beat until smooth. Fold in the chocolate. Divide the mixture between the paper cases and bake in the centre of the oven for 12–15 minutes until the cakes have risen and are just firm to the touch in the centre. Remove the cakes from the oven and transfer them to a wire rack to cool.

3. For the topping, stir the crème fraîche into the melted chocolate, and leave to cool and thicken slightly, if necessary. Spoon or pipe onto the cupcakes. Place a raspberry onto each cake before the chocolate topping sets.

Mini sticky jammy cakes

For the cupcakes:

60 g/2 oz butter, softened

90 g/3 oz smooth fruit jam

60 g/2 oz self-raising flour

1 medium egg

1 Tbsp milk

For the topping:

8–10 level Tbsp smooth fruit jam

24-hole mini muffin tray lined with paper cases

Makes 24

1. Preheat the oven to 190° C/ 375° F (gas 5).

2. Beat together the butter and jam in a bowl until the mixture is smooth. Add the flour, egg and milk to the bowl and beat the mixture well. Divide the mixture between the paper cases and bake in the centre of the oven for 12-15 minutes until the cakes have risen and are just firm to the touch in the centre. Remove the cakes from the oven and transfer them to a wire rack to cool.

3. For the topping, warm the jam and brush it thickly over the top of the hot cupcakes, then leave the cakes to cool completely before serving.

Butterfly cakes

For the cupcakes:

12 Plain cupcakes, (*see page 14)*

For the topping:

1 quantity of Chocolate buttercream (*see page 18*)

Icing sugar and cocoa, for dusting

12 chocolate buttons

Piping bag fitted with a star piping tube

Makes 12

1. Slice the tops off the cakes and cut the tops in half.

2. Fill the piping bag with the buttercream and pipe a swirl on top of each cake. Stick the top halves in place on top like wings. Pipe a little extra buttercream between the wings. Dust the cakes with a little icing sugar and cocoa, then press a chocolate button onto the top of each.

Coffee and walnut cupcakes

For the cupcakes:

150 g/5½ oz self-raising flour

60 g/2 oz walnuts

150 g/5½ oz butter, softened

150 g/5½ oz light soft brown sugar

3 medium eggs

2 Tbsp coffee granules

1 Tbsp boiling water

For the topping:

1 Tbsp coffee granules

1 Tbsp boiling water

90 g/3 oz butter, softened

175 g/6 oz icing sugar

12 walnut halves

Icing sugar, for dusting

12-hole bun tray lined with paper cases

Makes 12

1. Preheat the oven to 190° C/375° F (gas 5).

2. To make the cupcakes, tip the flour and walnuts into the bowl of a food processor and whiz until the nuts are finely ground.

3. Beat the butter and sugar in a bowl until the mixture is light and fluffy, then add the eggs, and the flour and walnut mixture. Tip the coffee granules into a small bowl, add the water and stir until the coffee has dissolved, then add to the cake ingredients in the bowl. Beat the mixture until smooth. Divide the mixture between the paper cases and bake in the centre of the oven for 15–20 minutes until the cakes have risen and are just firm to the touch in the centre. Remove the cakes from the oven and transfer them to a wire rack to cool.

4. To make the topping, tip the coffee granules into a mixing bowl, add the boiling water and stir until the coffee has dissolved. Add the butter to the bowl and beat until smooth, then gradually beat in the icing sugar to give a fluffy icing. Spread the icing over the top of the cupcakes and place a walnut half on the top of each. Dust with icing sugar before serving.

Raspberry swirls

For the biscuit cupcakes:

175 g/6 oz unsalted butter, softened

60 g/2 oz caster sugar

150 g/5½ oz plain flour

30 g/1 oz cornflour

For the topping:

4–5 Tbsp raspberry jam

Icing sugar, for dusting

12-hole bun tray lined with paper cases

Piping bag fitted with a large star piping tube

Makes 12

1. Preheat the oven to 180° C/350° F (gas 4).

2. To make the cupcakes, cream the butter and caster sugar until light and fluffy. Sift together the plain flour and cornflour, then gradually beat into the creamed mixture. Fill the piping bag with the creamed mixture and pipe into each paper case, leaving a small hole in the centre. Bake in the centre of the oven for 15–20 minutes, until lightly golden in colour. Remove the cakes from the oven and transfer to a wire rack to cool.

3. To finish the cakes, fill the holes in the centre with the jam. Dust with icing sugar.

Blueberry and cream cheese cupcakes

For the cupcakes:

12 Lemon cupcakes, *(see page 14)*

For the topping:

1 quantity of Cream cheese frosting *(see page 17)*

150–175 g/5½–6 oz blueberries

4 Tbsp blueberry jam, sieved

2 Tbsp water

12 sprigs mint

Makes 12

1. Spread the cream cheese frosting over the cupcakes. Arrange the blueberries on top of the cakes, pressing them into the frosting slightly to ensure they are secure.

2. Warm the jam with the water, either in a microwave oven or in a saucepan, then brush the glaze over the blueberries. Decorate with a sprig of mint on each cake.

Pretty and pink

For the cupcakes:

24 Plain mini cupcakes (*see page 14*)

For the topping:

4 Tbsp smooth strawberry jam

1 quantity of Swiss meringue buttercream (*see page 19*)

Pink food colouring

Pink nonpareils (sprinkles)

Large piping bag fitted with a star piping tube

Makes 24

1. For the topping, beat the raspberry jam into the buttercream. Add a little pink food colouring to give the buttercream a deeper pink colour. Fill the piping bag with the mixture and pipe a swirl onto each cupcake. Scatter over the nonpareils.

Flapjacks

For the flapjacks:

150 g/5 1/2 oz butter

150 g/5 1/2 oz light soft brown sugar

3 Tbsp golden syrup

275 g/9 1/2 oz porridge oats

For the topping:

60 g/2 oz plain chocolate-flavour cake covering, melted

12-hole bun tray lined with paper cases

Small disposable piping bag

Makes 12

1. Preheat the oven to 160° C/325° F (gas 3).

2. To make the flapjacks, melt the butter, sugar and golden syrup in a small saucepan. Stir the oats into the melted mixture and mix well. Spoon the mixture into the paper cases and press it down firmly. Bake the cupcakes in the centre of the oven for 15–20 minutes, or until the mixture is bubbling and is a pale golden colour. Remove the cakes from the oven and transfer them to a wire rack to cool.

3. For the topping, spoon the melted chocolate into the piping bag and cut off the tip to give a small hole. Pipe random lines of chocolate over the cupcakes. Leave in a cool place for the chocolate to set before serving.

Date and banana

For the cupcakes:

125 g/4½ oz gluten-free flour

30 g/1 oz light soft brown sugar

125 g/4½ oz dates, stoned and chopped

1 level tsp gluten-free baking powder

2 medium eggs

4 Tbsp sunflower oil

1 ripe banana, peeled and mashed

For the topping:

Cream cheese frosting (*see page 17*)

12-hole bun tray lined with paper cases

Makes 12 standard-size cupcakes

1. Preheat the oven to 200° C/400° F (gas 6).

2. To make the cupcakes, tip the flour and sugar into a bowl and stir in the dates and baking powder. In a separate bowl, lightly whisk the eggs and oil together and stir in the mashed banana. Stir this into the dry mixture.

3. Divide the mixture between the paper cases and bake in the centre of the oven for 15 to 20 minutes until the cakes have risen and are just firm to the touch in the centre. Remove the cakes from the oven and transfer them to a wire rack to cool.

4. For the topping, spread the cream cheese frosting over the cupcakes and texture the surface with a fork.

Lemon and yoghurt muffins

225 g/8 oz plain flour

2 rounded tsp baking powder

Pinch salt

140 g/5 oz caster sugar, or 5 Tbsp runny honey

1 large egg, beaten

284 ml/9 ½ fl oz natural yoghurt

1 Tbsp freshly grated unwaxed lemon rind

85 g/3 oz butter, melted

8 cardamom seeds, crushed to a powder

8 very thin slices of lemon, halved, to decorate

Lemon curd (*see page 26*) and crème fraîche, to serve

8–12 hole bun tray lined with paper cases

Makes 8 to 9

1. Preheat the oven to 180° C/350° F (gas 4).

2. Sift the flour, baking powder and salt into a large mixing bowl. If you are using honey instead of sugar, mix it in along with the egg, yoghurt and lemon rind. Stir the melted butter into the mixture, add the cardamom powder and fold lightly together until just mixed.

3. Spoon the mixture into the muffin paper cases set inside holes of the tin so that they are two-thirds full. Lightly press a few lemon segments over the top of each muffin and bake them for 25 minutes until springy to the touch. When the muffins have cooled slightly, remove them from the tin to a wire cooling rack. Serve with a little dollop of lemon curd and crème fraîche on the side.

Sunshine muffins with an orange glaze

For the muffin mix:

225 g/8 oz plain flour

2 rounded tsp baking powder

Pinch of salt

140 g/5 oz golden caster sugar

85 g/3 oz butter

1 large egg, lightly beaten

175 ml/6 fl oz cultured buttermilk

Juice of 1½ oranges

Zest of 2 oranges, grated

1 Tbsp orange marmalade

For the orange glaze:

Juice and finely grated zest of ½ orange

5–6 Tbsp icing sugar, double sifted

1 tsp of marmalade

8–12 hole bun tray lined with paper cases

Makes 9 to 10

1. Preheat the oven to 180° C/350° F (gas 4).

2. To make the muffin mix, sift the dry ingredients into a large mixing bowl and set aside. Melt the butter in a small saucepan over a low heat, then leave it to cool slightly. In another mixing bowl mix together the egg, buttermilk, orange juice and zest, and when cooled, the melted butter.

3. Pour in the buttermilk mixture over the dry ingredients and fold it in gently with the marmalade until just blended, making sure not to over mix.

4. Spoon the mixture into muffin paper cases set inside the holes of the tin, almost to the top. Bake for 25 minutes until the muffins look golden and puffed up and the centres bounce back when lightly touched. Remove from the oven and turn them out onto a wire cooling rack.

5. To make the orange glaze, add the orange juice to a small mixing bowl and slowly beat in the zest, icing sugar and marmalade. The icing should cover the back of the spoon, but still be thin and fluid. Drizzle the icing in a loose zigzag pattern over the tops of the muffins about 10 minutes before serving so that the glaze looks fresh and shiny.

Nut butter muffins with peanut butter icing

For the muffin mix:

225 g/8 oz plain flour

2 rounded tsps baking powder

70 g/2½ oz golden caster sugar

85 g/3 oz butter

175 g/6 oz crunchy peanut butter

200 ml/7 fl oz plain yoghurt

100 ml/3½ fl oz Canadian maple syrup

1 large egg, lightly beaten

55 g/2 oz cashew nuts, halved

For the peanut butter icing:

3 Tbsp crunchy peanut butter

6 Tbsp icing sugar, double sifted

5–6 Tbsp hot water

12-hole bun tray lined with paper cases

Makes 10 muffins

1. Preheat the oven to 180° C/350° F (gas 4).

2. Sift the flour, baking powder and sugar into a large mixing bowl and set aside. Melt the butter, remove it from the heat and mix in the peanut butter. Mash it lightly with a fork until just softened, then mix in the yoghurt, maple syrup and beaten egg.

3. Pour the yoghurt mix over the dry ingredients. Fold lightly together until just blended, being careful not to over mix. Divide the mixture equally between the muffin paper cases set inside the holes of the tin. Sprinkle some of the cashew nut halves over the centre of each muffin.

4. Bake for about 20–25 minutes, but check after 20 minutes. If the cakes feel springy to the touch and look nicely risen and golden they are ready. Transfer them to a wire cooling rack.

5. To make the icing, warm the peanut butter in a small saucepan and remove it from the heat. Mix with the icing sugar and hot water until smooth. Coat the tops of the muffins with the warm icing and leave them to set.

Desserts

Pane al cioccolato

400 g/14 oz strong white bread flour

30 g/1 oz cocoa powder

½ tsp salt

2 Tbsp dark brown sugar

30 g/1 oz unsalted butter

1 tsp instant or fast-acting dried yeast

60 g/2 oz plain chocolate chips

250 ml/8 fl oz whole milk, slightly warm

1 egg white, beaten

1 Tbsp caster sugar

Serves 12

1. Sieve the flour, cocoa and salt into a bowl and stir in the brown sugar. Rub in the butter and stir in the yeast and chocolate chips. Make a well in the centre.

2. Pour the milk into the centre of the well. Mix with your fingers, then tip on to a lightly-floured work surface, bring together and knead lightly for about 5 minutes until you have a firm, pliable dough. Lightly flour the bowl and place the dough back in it. Cover loosely and stand in a warm place for about an hour until doubled in size.

3. Gently reknead the dough to form a smooth ball. Place in the centre of a lightly-greased baking sheet. Cover loosely with oiled, clear food wrap and leave in a warm place for about 45 minutes or until doubled in size. Preheat the oven to 200° C/400° F (gas 6).

4. Brush the dough ball all over with egg white and sprinkle with sugar. Bake in the oven for about 30 minutes until risen and firm – it should sound hollow when tapped. Cool for 15 minutes then transfer to a wire rack to cool completely. Serve warm or cold.

Creamy lemon meringue pie

- **300 g/10 oz ready-made shortcrust pastry**
- **4 Tbsp cornflour**
- **275 g/9 oz caster sugar**
- **Juice and finely grated rind of 2 small lemons**
- **300 ml/10 fl oz double cream**
- **2 large eggs, separated**
- **1 large egg white**
- **Shredded lemon rind, to decorate**
- **Pouring cream, to serve**

Serves 6–8

1. Preheat the oven to 200° C/400° F (gas 6). Roll out the pastry to fit a 2.5 cm/1 in deep, 20 cm/8 in round pie dish and lightly prick the base. Bake in the oven for 15 minutes until lightly golden. Set aside to cool.

2. Mix the cornflour, 125 g/4 oz caster sugar, lemon juice and rind together in a saucepan and add a little cream to form a paste. Stir in the remaining cream and cook over medium heat, stirring, until just boiling and thick. Cook for 1 minute longer then set aside to cool for 10 minutes. Stir in the egg yolks. Pour into the pastry case and cool completely.

3. In a large heatproof bowl, whisk the egg whites until stiff. Place the remaining sugar in a saucepan with 50 ml/2 fl oz water and heat, stirring until the sugar has dissolved. Bring to the boil and cook until the temperature reads 121° C/240° F on a sugar thermometer. Pour the hot syrup in a steady stream into the egg whites, and continue to whisk for a further 5 minutes. Spoon over the lemon filling to cover completely.

4. Preheat the grill to medium. Cook the topping for 2–3 minutes until golden all over. Serve immediately, sprinkled with lemon rind, with pouring cream to accompany.

Berry pavlova

4 large egg whites

1 pinch salt

½ tsp cream of tartar

400 g/14 oz caster sugar

1 tsp Raspberry vinegar ***(see page 28)***

Few drops vanilla extract

Juice and finely grated rind of 2 lemons

300 ml/10 fl oz whipping cream

300 g/10 oz assorted prepared fresh berries: blueberries, strawberries, blackberries and raspberries

Serves 8

1. Preheat the oven to 140° C/275° F (gas 1). Line a large baking sheet with baking parchment and draw a 24 cm/10 in circle on the paper.

2. In a large, grease-free bowl, whisk the egg whites with the salt and cream of tartar, until stiff and dry. Gradually whisk in 150 g/5 oz of the sugar, and then carefully fold in a further 150 g/5 oz sugar, together with the vinegar and vanilla extract, to form a thick, glossy meringue.

3. Pile the meringue on to the baking sheet, keeping within the marked circle, smoothing and scooping the meringue from the sides back on top to make a thick "cake". Bake in the oven, on the bottom shelf, for about 1½ hours, until pale cream in colour, crisp on the outside, yet marshmallowy inside. Turn off the oven and leave to cool – it will probably sink in the middle.

4. Meanwhile, place the lemon juice and rind in a small saucepan with the remaining sugar and stir over a low heat until dissolved. Bring to the boil and simmer gently for 2–3 minutes until syrupy. Set aside to cool.

5. When ready to serve, whip the cream until just peaking, and pile on top of the meringue. Sprinkle with the berries and drizzle with lemon syrup. Serve immediately.

Blue cheese cheesecake

180 g/6 oz digestive biscuits, crushed

90 g/3 oz unsalted butter, melted

250 g/8 oz strong-flavoured blue cheese, e.g. mature Stilton, Roquefort or Danish Blue

150 ml/5 fl oz soured cream

3 eggs

200 g/7 oz black grapes

Celery leaves, to garnish

Serves 8

1. Preheat the oven to 180° C/350° F (gas 4). Grease and line the base and sides of a 20 cm/8 in round spring-release cake tin.

2. Place the crushed biscuits in a bowl and mix in the melted butter. Press on to the base of the tin using the back of a spoon and chill until required.

3. Crumble the blue cheese into a blender or food processor and add the soured cream and eggs. Blend for a few seconds until smooth. Pour over the biscuit base. Bake in the centre of the oven for about 40 minutes until just set. Leave to cool in the tin. When cool, release from the tin and place on a serving plate. Cover and chill for 2 hours.

4. To serve, wash the grapes, halve and remove the pips. Arrange on top of the cheesecake and garnish with celery leaves. Cut into 8 slices to serve.

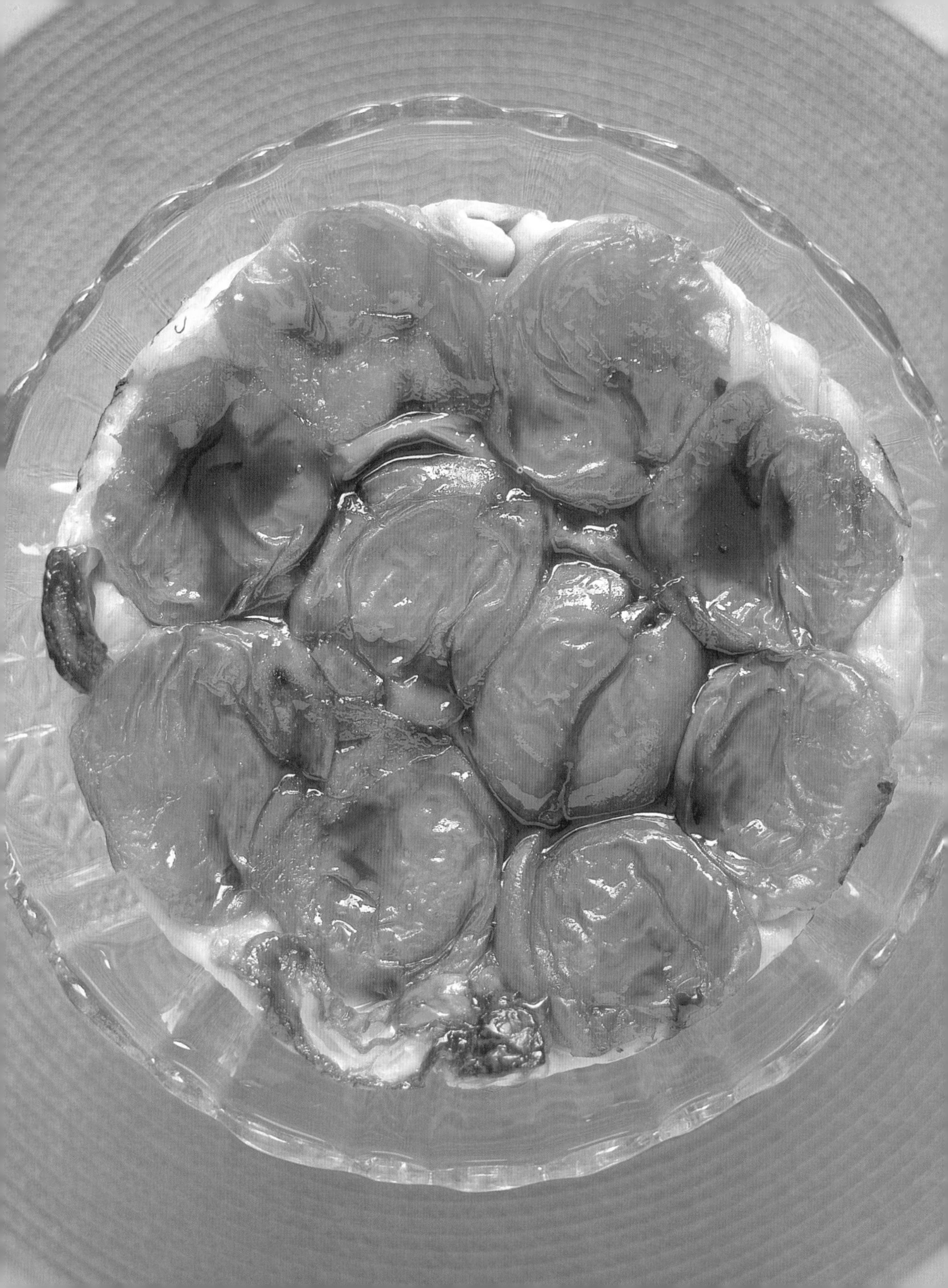

Upside-down fruit pie

600 g/1 lb 3½ oz plums or apricots

125 g/4 oz caster sugar

¼ tsp ground nutmeg

250 g/8 oz puff pastry, defrosted if frozen

Clotted cream or vanilla ice cream, to serve

Serves 6

1. Preheat the oven to 200° C/400° F (gas 6). Loosely line a 23 cm/9 in round shallow cake tin with a piece of baking parchment.

2. Halve the plums or apricots, prise out the stones and set aside.

3. Sprinkle the sugar evenly over the base of a heavy-based saucepan and heat until it begins to melt, tilting the pan to cook evenly and making sure all the sugar is used. Once the sugar is lightly caramelized and liquid, drizzle it over the base of the tin before it begins to set. Dust the caramel lightly with nutmeg.

4. Starting from the centre, arrange the fruit halves to fit snugly over the base of the tin, leaving a slight gap around the edge of the tin.

5. Roll the pastry out on a lightly floured surface to a square about 25 cm/10 in. Place the pastry on top of the fruit and tuck the pastry edges down between the fruit and the paper. Cook in the oven for 35–40 minutes until puffed up, crisp and lightly golden. Cool for 10 minutes, then invert on to a warm serving plate and peel away the paper. Serve warm with clotted cream or vanilla ice cream.

Plum tart with Sambuca crème

For the pastry:

150 g/5 oz flour (strong or plain)

½ tsp baking powder

50 g/2 oz butter, softened

75 g/3 oz sugar

1 egg yolk

1 Tbsp Sambuca liqueur

1 Tbsp warm water, plus 1 Tbsp, if required

For the topping:

8 large plums, preferably Satsuma or Black Doris and icing sugar for dusting

For the Sambuca crème:

1 egg yolk

1 Tbsp sugar

1 Tbsp Sambuca liqueur

100 ml/3½ fl oz skimmed milk

Serves 8

1. To make the pastry mix the flour and baking powder with the softened butter, then add the sugar, egg yolk, Sambuca and water. Work into a dough. Add 1 tablespoon more water if necessary. Roll out the pastry into a square, about 20 x 20 cm/8 x 8 in, cutting and pasting the pieces together until it makes a regular shape. As it gets bigger place it directly on an oven tray lined with baking paper and finish rolling there.

2. To make the tart cut the plums in half, remove the stones, and place the fruit cut side down on the pastry. For a 20 x 20 cm/8 x 8 in base, arrange 4 plum halves down and 4 across the pastry, allowing 1 cm/¼ in around the edge, which can be left flat. Place in the oven preheated to 180° C/350° F (gas 4) for approximately 20 minutes. Remove from the oven, dust with icing sugar and allow to cool on the tray.

3. To make the crème, half fill a saucepan with warm water and set over a medium heat. Whisk the egg yolk and sugar together in a small bowl, then add the Sambuca. Set the bowl over the saucepan of simmering water and continue to whisk the egg mixture, ensuring no water splashes into the bowl. Slowly add the milk and simmer, occasionally stirring until the mixture thickens. It should have the consistency of runny custard. Cool and set aside for serving.

4. To assemble, place a slice of tart on each plate, dust with more icing sugar, if desired, and place 1 tablespoon of crème between the 2 plum halves.

Fresh fig and cherry tart

For the pastry:

Half quantity of brisée pastry, chilled *(see page 17)*

For the filling:

225 g/8 oz plump sweet red cherries, stoned (pitted)

2 fresh purple figs

100 g/3½ oz whole almonds or hazelnuts

100 g/3½ oz butter

75 g/3 oz caster sugar

1 large egg and 1 large egg yolk

2 tsp Kirsch

2 level Tbsp plain flour

For the glaze:

3 Tbsp redcurrant jam

1–2 Tbsp clear, runny, lavender honey

1 Tbsp Kirsch

Crème fraîche or thick cream, to serve

Serves 12

1. Preheat the oven to 190° C/375° F (gas 5). Roll out the chilled pastry large enough to line a buttered 25 cm/10 in round loose-bottomed plain or fluted tin 2½ cm/1 in deep. Refrigerate for 30 minutes. Line the pastry case with kitchen paper and fill with baking beans. Bake blind for 10 minutes, then carefully remove the beans and paper.

2. To make the filling, lay the stoned cherries over kitchen paper to allow as much of the juice to drain away as possible. Slice each fig into four pieces. Remove the skin from the nuts and grind them in a food processor to a fine powder, then set aside.

3. Cream the butter and sugar, then beat in the eggs gradually. Stir in the ground nuts, Kirsch and flour. Spread the mixture over the base of the cooled pastry case, then lightly press the sliced figs and cherries into the mixture and bake for 30 minutes or until the filling puffs up between the fruit.

4. Meanwhile, prepare the glaze. Add the jelly and honey to a small saucepan. Bring to the boil then simmer for 1 minute. Add the Kirsch and stir the jam gently for a further minute to ease out any lumps until it is smooth and has thickened. While still hot, thinly brush over the surface of the tart to add shine and flavour. Serve warm or cold with dollops of crème fraîche or thick chilled cream.

Chocolate almond and pear tart

1 quantity Chocolate pastry *(see page 16)* or 300 g/10 oz ready-made sweet shortcrust pastry

125 g/4 oz unsalted butter, softened

125 g/4 oz caster sugar

2 eggs

125 g/4 oz ground almonds

2 Tbsp cocoa powder

½ tsp almond extract

410 g/14 oz tin pear halves in natural juice, drained

15 g/½ oz flaked almonds

1 Tbsp icing sugar, to dust

Pouring cream, to serve

Serves 6–8

1. Preheat the oven to 190° C/375° F (gas 5).

2. Make the Chocolate pastry and roll out and line a 23 cm/9 in loose-bottomed flan tin. Chill until required.

3. In a mixing bowl, cream together the butter and sugar until pale and creamy. Gradually beat in the eggs and ground almonds. Sieve in the cocoa powder and fold in along with the almond extract. Spoon the mixture into the pastry case and smooth the top.

4. Cut the pear halves in half and pat dry with kitchen paper. Gently press the pear slices into the almond filling. Sprinkle with flaked almonds and bake in the oven for 35–40 minutes until the almonds are lightly golden and the sponge is firm to the touch. Stand for 10 minutes before removing from the tin. Dust with icing sugar and serve hot or cold with pouring cream.

Little apple tarts

450 g/1 lb ready-rolled frozen puff pastry, defrosted

Egg glaze (*see page 19*)

900 g/2 lb or 4–5 medium Bramley (tart) apples

30 g/1 oz butter, melted

4 level Tbsp caster sugar, sifted

Icing sugar, to dust

Crème fraîche, lightly sweetened, to serve

Makes 4

1. Preheat the oven to 200° C/400° F (gas 6).

2. Roll out the chilled pastry so that it is large enough to cut four circles of pastry using a tea saucer as a guide to cut around. Evenly space the pastry circles apart onto a large buttered baking sheet and lightly brush around the edges of the circles with egg glaze.

3. Peel, core and slice the apples as thinly as possible and arrange the slices, rounded side out, from the centre of the tart working outwards and half overlapping the slices. Leave a 1 cm/½ in margin between the edges of the pastry and the apples. Brush the surface of the apples with the melted butter and sprinkle 1 tablespoon of caster sugar evenly over the surface of each tart.

4. Bake for about 15 minutes until the pastry is lightly golden and gently puffed up. Remove from the oven and dredge each tart with icing sugar, avoiding the edges of the pastry. Place the tarts under a hot grill for 1–2 minutes until the apples look richly caramelized around the edges. Serve warm with a dollop of crème fraîche lightly sweetened with sugar or honey.

Chocolate banoffee pie

90 g/3 oz butter

250 g/8 oz double chocolate chip cookies, crushed

3 ripe medium-sized bananas

397 g/14 oz can condensed milk

1 Tbsp cocoa powder

300 ml/10 fl oz double cream

Grated milk chocolate, to decorate

Serves 6

1. Grease the bases and sides of six individual 8 cm/3 in loose-bottomed cake tins or cake rings.

2. Melt the butter in a saucepan, then remove from the heat. Mix the crushed cookies with the melted butter and divide between the six tins. Press firmly into the base of each. Slice the bananas thinly and arrange over the biscuit base. Cover and chill until required.

3. Pour the condensed milk into a saucepan, bring to the boil and simmer over a medium heat, stirring, until the milk turns a toffee colour. Remove from the heat, sieve over the cocoa and add 6 tablespoons double cream and mix well. Spoon the toffee filling over the bananas and biscuit base. Cover and chill for 30 minutes.

4. When ready to serve, remove the pies from the tins and place on serving plates. Whip the remaining double cream and pile on top of each one. Sprinkle with grated chocolate and serve.

Plum and mango tart

- 175 g/6 oz plain flour
- 75 g/2¾ oz butter, chilled and cut into small cubes
- 5 plums, stoned and quartered
- 2–3 mangoes, stoned, peeled and cut into slices
- 2 Tbsp caster sugar
- 1 Tbsp cornflour
- Crème fraîche or natural yoghurt to serve

Serves 4–6

1. Preheat the oven to 200° C/400° F (gas 6).

2. Sift the flour into a mixing bowl, add the butter and rub in with your fingertips. Sprinkle with 2 Tbsp cold water and stir to moisten and gradually bring the pastry together. Knead briefly on a floured work surface then chill for 20 minutes.

3. Place the fruit in a bowl then stir in the sugar and cornflour.

4. Roll the pastry large enough to line a 22 cm/9 in tart tin, with 2 cm/¾ in spare around the edge. Spoon the fruit evenly into the pastry case then fold over the edges of the pastry, leaving the centre uncovered.

5. Bake for 30–35 minutes until the pastry is golden and the fruits are soft. Serve warm with dollops of crème fraîche or natural yoghurt.

Blackberry and apple cobbler

For the filling:

2 eating apples

Juice of 1 lemon

350 g/12 oz fresh blackberries, washed and hulled

60 g/2 oz caster sugar

For the topping:

250 g/8 oz self-raising flour

1 tsp mixed spice

150 g/5 oz unsalted butter

60 g/2 oz golden caster sugar

Approx. 90 ml/3 fl oz milk

2 Tbsp golden granulated sugar

Pouring cream or Custard sauce, to serve ***(see page 21)***

Serves 4

1. Preheat the oven to 190° C/375° F (gas 5).

2. Peel and core the apples and cut into small chunks. Place in a bowl and toss in the lemon juice. Stir in the blackberries and sugar. Spoon into the bottom of a 1.2 L/40 fl oz oval pie dish. Cover with foil and place in the oven for 15 minutes.

3. Meanwhile, make the topping. Sift the flour and spice into a mixing bowl. Rub 125 g/4 oz butter into the flour and stir in the caster sugar. Stir in enough milk to form a soft dough.

4. Turn on to a lightly floured surface and knead gently. Press or roll out to a thickness of about 1 cm/½ in. Using a 5 cm/2 in round cutter, stamp out 16 circles, re-rolling the dough as necessary.

5. Place the rounds, overlapping, on top of the dish. Melt the remaining butter and brush it over the top. Sprinkle with granulated sugar and place on a baking tray. Bake for 25–30 minutes until risen and golden. Serve warm with pouring cream or Custard sauce.

Creamy caramel custard pots

For the custard:

450 ml/15 fl oz semi-skimmed milk

½ vanilla pod, split

2 eggs

1 egg yolk

25 g/2 Tbsp caster sugar

½ tsp cornflour

10 g/½ Tbsp softened unsalted butter or polyunsaturated margarine, for greasing

For the caramel topping:

4 Tbsp light brown sugar

Makes 4

1. To make the custard, put the milk and vanilla pod in a heavy-based saucepan and gently heat until almost boiling. Remove from the heat, cover and leave to infuse for 10 minutes. Lightly grease four 120 ml/4 fl oz ramekin dishes, then place in a small roasting tin.

2. Preheat the oven to 160° C/325 °F (gas 3). Put the eggs, egg yolk, sugar and cornflour in a bowl and whisk together until thick and creamy. Bring the milk back to boiling point, remove the vanilla pod, then pour the hot milk over the egg mixture, whisking all the time. Strain the mixture into a jug, then divide between the prepared ramekins. Pour enough hot water into the roasting tin to come just over half-way up the sides of the ramekins. Bake for 30–35 minutes, or until lightly set. Take care not to overcook – the custards should still be a little wobbly when you take them out of the oven. Carefully remove the ramekins from the hot water and leave them to cool on a wire rack. Once cold, chill in the refrigerator for at least 2 hours.

3. Scatter the light brown sugar evenly over the top of the chilled custards and grill under a preheated hot grill for 2–3 minutes, or until the sugar has melted. Leave to stand for at least 5 minutes before serving.

Fresh orange wobble

600 ml/21 fl oz freshly squeezed or pure orange juice

4 tsp powdered gelatine

2 medium oranges

125 g/4½ oz seedless white or black grapes

Serves 4

1. Spoon 4 tablespoons of the fruit juice into a small bowl. Sprinkle the gelatine over and leave to soak for 5 minutes. Place the bowl over a pan of near-boiling water, leave for 2–3 minutes, then stir until the gelatine has dissolved. Cool for 5 minutes, then stir the dissolved gelatine into the remaining orange juice in a jug.

2. Peel the oranges with a sharp knife, removing all the white pith, then cut into segments between the membranes (do this over the jug to catch the extra juice). Divide the orange segments between four individual serving dishes. Share out the grapes as well, then pour over the jelly (don't worry if the grapes float to the top). Chill in the refrigerator for at least 3 hours, or until set.

Banana rice pudding

15 g/1 Tbsp polyunsaturated margarine

50 g/2 oz dried bananas, broken into small pieces

50 g/2 oz pudding rice

750 ml/1½ pt semi-skimmed milk

A little freshly grated nutmeg (optional)

Serves 4

1. Preheat the oven to 150 °C/300 °F (gas 2).

2. Use the margarine to grease a 900 ml/2 pt ovenproof dish. Put the banana pieces and pudding rice in the dish.

3. Pour the milk into a small saucepan and gently heat until it reaches boiling point (or heat in a jug in the microwave). Pour the hot milk over the bananas and rice, then stir to mix. Sprinkle a little grated nutmeg over the top, if liked. Bake for 1¾–2 hours, or until the rice is cooked and most of the milk has been absorbed, stirring once halfway through cooking. Allow to cool for a few minutes before serving.

Pink grapefruit jellies

150 ml/5 fl oz very hot water

4 level tsp powdered gelatine

2 pink grapefruit

300 ml/10 fl oz unsweetened pink grapefruit juice

150 ml/5 fl oz low-sugar cranberry juice

4 Tbsp thick soured cream

Ground ginger, to taste

Serves 4

1. Pour the water into a heatproof basin and sprinkle over the gelatine. Stir until dissolved and set aside to cool for 30 minutes.

2. Meanwhile, using a sharp knife, slice the top and bottom off the grapefruit and slice off the peel taking away as much of the white pith as possible. Holding the grapefruit over a bowl to catch the juices, slice in between each segment to remove the flesh, and place in the bowl. Cover and chill until required.

3. Once the gelatine mixture has cooled, stir in the grapefruit and cranberry juices along with the juices from the grapefruit segments.

4. Arrange a few segments in the bottom of four cocktail glasses or serving dishes and pour the jelly over the top. Place in the fridge to chill for at least 2 hours until set. To serve, spoon a little thick soured cream on top of each and sprinkle with ground ginger.

Raspberry yoghurt mousse

1 Tbsp powdered gelatine

3 Tbsp cold water

350 g/12½ oz fresh raspberries

1–2 Tbsp caster sugar

300 ml/10 fl oz plain or vanilla low-fat bio yoghurt

100 ml/3½ fl oz whipping cream, preferably half-fat

Serves 4

1. Sprinkle the gelatine over the cold water in a small bowl and leave to soak for 5 minutes. Place the bowl over a pan of near-boiling water, leave for 2–3 minutes, then stir until the gelatine has dissolved. Cool for 5 minutes.

2. Meanwhile, set aside four raspberries for decoration. Put the remaining raspberries in a separate bowl, sprinkle over the sugar and mash with a fork. Stir in the dissolved gelatine, then blend in the yoghurt.

3. In another bowl, whisk the cream until soft peaks form, then gently fold into the yoghurt mixture. Divide between four serving dishes and chill in the refrigerator for at least 2 hours, or until softly set. Decorate the mousse with the reserved fresh raspberries just before serving.

Crème brûlée with nectarines

3 egg yolks

3 Tbsp caster sugar

300 ml/10 fl oz cream (single or double)

2 drops vanilla essence

2 nectarines

4 tsp brown (or Moscovado) sugar

Serves 4

1. Half fill a medium saucepan with warm water and set over a medium heat. Whisk the egg yolks and sugar together in a bowl until pale yellow and foamy. Continue beating and slowly add the cream, then the vanilla essence. Set the bowl over the saucepan of simmering water and continue to whisk until the cream thickens (about 10 minutes).

2. Wash and finely slice the nectarines, then divide between 4 ramekins and cover with the crème. Refrigerate for at least 6 hours. One hour before serving put 1 teaspoon of brown sugar on each dessert, spreading it evenly to the edges. Place under a preheated hot grill for 1–2 minutes. Do not close the grill door and watch the desserts carefully, as they can easily burn. When the sugar changes colour and becomes shiny, remove the dishes from under the grill, cool at room temperature, then return them to the refrigerator. Serve within 1 hour to ensure the top remains crunchy.

Sticky chocolate bananas

4 medium-sized just ripe bananas, unpeeled

100 g/3 ½ oz milk or plain chocolate, roughly chopped

Greek or thick plain yoghurt, to serve

Serves 4

1. Preheat the oven to 180° C/350° F (gas 4).

2. Make a cut along the length of the unpeeled bananas, cutting through the skin, then open up and press the chocolate pieces into the banana flesh.

3. Wrap each banana in foil, keeping the cut-side uppermost, then place on a baking tray and bake for 12–15 minutes, or until the banana is soft and the chocolate has melted. Leave to cool for 5 minutes before serving with Greek or thick plain yoghurt.

Grape syllabub

Finely grated rind and juice of 1 lemon

60 g/2 oz caster sugar

4 Tbsp unsweetened green grape juice

180 g/6 oz seedless green grapes, washed and halved

4 macaroons, finely chopped

300 ml/10 fl oz double cream

Serves 6

1. Place the lemon rind and juice in a small, non-metallic bowl or jug and set aside to soak for 2 hours. Stir in the sugar and grape juice and cover and chill for 1 hour or until ready to serve.

2. When you are ready to serve, divide the grapes and macaroons between six wine glasses. Pour the cream into a mixing bowl and begin whisking. As the cream begins to thicken, gradually pour in the lemon and grape juice mixture. Continue whisking until just peaking and then pile into the glasses. Serve immediately.

3. You can prepare this up to 30 minutes in advance and keep in the fridge. After this time, the juices begin to separate from the cream.

Crunchy oat fruit crumble

675 g/1 lb 8 oz fresh nectarines, stoned and sliced, or apricots, stoned and chopped

1–2 Tbsp caster sugar

50 g/2 oz plain or wholemeal flour

50 g/2 oz porridge oats

50 g/2 oz light brown sugar

50 g/2 oz polyunsaturated margarine

50 g/2 oz skinned hazelnuts, roughly chopped

Serves 4

1. Preheat the oven to 190° C/375° F (gas 5).

2. Put the fruit in a 1.3 L/2¾ pt ovenproof dish and sprinkle with the caster sugar (the amount used depends on the sweetness of the fruit and personal taste).

3. Put the flour, oats and light brown sugar in a mixing bowl, then rub in the margarine. Stir in the hazelnuts. Sprinkle the crumble mixture over the fruit and bake for about 25 minutes, or until the fruit is soft and the topping golden brown and crisp. Allow to cool for a few minutes before serving with custard, yoghurt or ice cream.

Yoghurt raspberry fool

100 g/3½ oz natural yoghurt

50 g/1¾ oz fromage frais

300 g/10½ oz fresh raspberries, slightly crushed

1 Tbsp honey

Few sprigs fresh mint

Serves 4

1. Mix together the yoghurt and fromage frais then gently stir in the raspberries.

2. Spoon into 4 bowls and drizzle with the honey. Garnish each one with a sprig of mint.

Mocha cream jellies

½ quantity Chocolate sugar syrup *(see page 24)*

100 ml/3½ fl oz espresso coffee, chilled

100 ml/3½ fl oz single cream

4 Tbsp brandy (optional)

4 Tbsp cold water

5 sheets fine leaf gelatine

Roasted coffee beans and drinking chocolate, to serve

Serves 4

1. Make up the Chocolate sugar syrup and set aside to cool. Stir in the coffee, single cream and brandy, if using.

2. Place 4 Tbsp cold water in a small heatproof bowl. Using a pair of scissors, snip the gelatine into the water. Leave to soak for about 10 minutes. Stand the bowl over a saucepan of simmering water and heat gently until dissolved. Alternatively, heat in the microwave for about 25 seconds on 'high'. Do not allow to boil as this prevents a proper set taking place.

3. Stir the liquid gelatine into the mocha mixture and pour into four coffee cups or serving dishes. Leave to set in the fridge for at least 2 hours.

4. To serve, top each with a few roasted coffee beans and a light dusting of drinking chocolate.

Birchermuesli

1 banana, peeled and sliced

1 apple, cored and chopped

Juice of ½ lemon

100 g/3½ oz blueberries

100 g/3½ oz raspberries

100 g/3½ oz walnuts, roughly chopped

175 g/6 oz rolled oats

¼ tsp ground cinnamon

400 g/14 oz natural or fruit flavoured yoghurt

Serves 6–8

1. Squeeze the lemon juice over the sliced banana and apple to stop the fruits going brown. Place the fruit, nuts, oats and ground cinnamon in a bowl and mix well.

2. To serve, layer the fruit and nut mixture with yoghurt in glasses or bowls, ending with a small sprinkling of the fruit and nut mixture on top. This can be mixed together completely but looks much nicer served in layers.

Challah French toast with berries

3 eggs
200 ml/7 fl oz milk
1 tsp sugar
8 slices challah bread
125 g/4½ oz strawberries
125 g/4½ oz blueberries
125 g/4½ oz raspberries
100 g/3½ oz blackberries
2 tsp caster sugar
Juice and grated rind of 1 lemon
75 g/2⅔ oz unsalted butter
Dusting of icing sugar to serve

Serves 4

1. Whisk together the eggs, milk and sugar in a large shallow dish.

2. Add the bread slices to the bowl. Leave to soak for about 6 minutes, turning each slice once.

3. Meanwhile place half the fruit in a food processor with the sugar and lemon juice and rind and blitz briefly to break up the fruits. Transfer to a bowl and stir in the whole fruits. Leave to one side.

4. Melt a quarter of the butter in a frying pan and when it is foaming add the slices of bread (however many will fit into the pan). Cook for about 1 minute on either side, or until golden brown. Keep those slices warm while you melt more butter and repeat with the other slices until all the slices are cooked.

5. Serve the warm French toast with the summer fruits spooned over the top – dust with icing sugar if required.

Exotic fruit salad

12 lychees, peeled and stoned

1 small pineapple, peeled, cored and cut into bite-size pieces

2 mangoes, peeled, stoned and cut into bite-size pieces

1 pomegranate, seeds removed

6 Medjool dates, stoned, and diced

5 passion fruit

Crème fraîche and ground nutmeg to serve

Serves 6

1. Place the lychees, pineapple chunks, mango pieces, pomegranate seeds and diced dates in a large bowl.

2. Scrape the seeds from the passion fruits and gently stir through the salad. Serve immediately with dollops of crème fraiche sprinkled with ground nutmeg.

Apricot steam puddings

4–6 tsp apricot jam

50 g/2 oz savoiardi or sponge biscuits

4 dried apricots

150 ml/5 fl oz milk

2 eggs, separated

3 Tbsp sugar

50 g/2 oz ground almond cream, crème anglaise or chocolate sauce to serve

Serves 4–6

1. Grease 6 small or 4 medium individual pudding bowls with butter, and dust with flour. Place a small piece of non-stick baking paper on the bottom of each pudding bowl and add 1 teaspoon of apricot jam.

2. Break the biscuits into a bowl. Chop the dried apricots into small pieces, add to the biscuits and cover with the milk. Beat the egg yolks with the sugar until pale yellow and frothy. Add the biscuit mixture and ground almonds. In another bowl, beat the egg whites into stiff peaks and gently fold into the mixture. Fill the pudding bowls with the mixture, cover with non-stick baking paper or tin foil and secure with a string or elastic band. Gently steam the puddings for 40–45 minutes. These puddings are delicious hot but may also be served cold. Serve with a jug of pouring cream, crème anglaise or chocolate sauce.

Caramelized rhubarb tart

One quantity of sweet pastry, chilled *(see page 16)*

For the filling:

800 g/1 lb 12 oz trimmed and prepared young rhubarb

284 ml/10 fl oz soured cream

2 large eggs

40 g/1½ oz caster sugar

A few drops of pure vanilla extract

2 Tbsp fresh orange juice

Zest of ½ orange, finely grated

Icing sugar, to dust

Vanilla cream *(see page 17)*

Serves 8

1. Preheat the oven to 190° C/375° F (gas 5). Thinly roll out the chilled sweet pastry and use it to line a lightly buttered 23 cm/9 in round loose-bottomed fluted tin. Line the pastry case with kitchen paper and fill with baking beans. Bake blind for 15 minutes, then carefully remove the beans and paper. Reduce the heat to 180° C/350° F (gas 4).

2. Arrange three-quarters of the prepared rhubarb over the base of the pastry case. Beat the soured cream, eggs, sugar, vanilla, juice and zest together and pour the mixture over the rhubarb. Lightly press the remaining pieces of rhubarb into the mixture and bake for about 25 minutes.

3. Serve warm when it is best, or cold lightly dusted with icing sugar. Alternatively, caramelize the tart by dredging the surface with sifted icing sugar and setting under a moderate grill for 1 to 2 minutes, until the icing sugar melts and turns a rich golden colour. Serve in slices with a dollop of vanilla cream.

Pancakes & Waffles

Rocky road waffle stack

1 quantity Basic waffle batter ***(see page 12)*****, sweetened**

1 L/1 3/4 pt tub of your favourite ice cream

100 g/3 1/2 oz mini marshmallows

1 quantity Chocolate sauce ***(see page 23)***

100 g/3 1/2 oz chopped mixed nuts

Serves 6

1. Prepare the waffle batter, then cook the waffles and keep warm until you are ready to serve.

2. Simply layer up the waffles on a serving plate and top with a scoop of ice cream, a few marshmallows, a drizzle of chocolate sauce and some chopped nuts. Serve immediately.

Blueberry and cinnamon silver dollars

250 g/8 oz plain flour
1 tsp ground cinnamon
2 Tbsp caster sugar
2 tsp baking powder
½ tsp salt
4 Tbsp vegetable oil
1 egg
250 ml/8 fl oz milk
90 g/3 oz blueberries, defrosted if frozen
Maple syrup, to serve

Makes 24

1. Sift the flour, cinnamon, sugar, baking powder and salt into a bowl and make a well in the centre. Add 3 Tbsp oil, the egg and milk, and gradually whisk into the dry ingredients to form a smooth, thick batter. Fold in the blueberries. Take care not to over-mix.

2. Heat a large frying or griddle pan until hot and brush lightly with oil. Ladle about 1 Tbsp batter to form a small pancake about 5 cm /2 in in diameter. Cook over moderate heat for about 1½ minutes, until bubbles appear on the surface. Slide a palette knife under the pancakes and flip over. Brown the underside of the pancakes for a further minute until golden. The pancake should puff up and thicken in depth.

3. Turn the pancakes out onto a wire rack lined with a clean tea towel and baking parchment. Fold the paper and towel over the pancakes to keep moist. Repeat the process to use up all the batter and make 24 pancakes in total, re-oiling the pan as necessary and stacking the cooked pancakes between sheets of parchment, until you are ready to serve. Best served warm with maple syrup.

Crêpe and fruit skewers

½ quantity Basic crêpe batter *(see page 13)*, sweetened

12 large strawberries, hulled and halved

1 ripe star fruit, sliced

1 ripe kiwi fruit, peeled and cut into 12 wedges

1 small or "mini" mango, peeled, stoned and cut into chunks

To serve:

1 quantity Tropical fruit coulis *(see page 25)*

Fruit yoghurt

Makes 12

1. Prepare the batter (see page 13) and cook to make six crêpes. Roll up the crêpes and cut into 2.5 cm/1 in thick slices.

2. Thread strips of pancake and pieces of fruit on to 12 long bamboo skewers, cover and chill until required. Serve with the Tropical fruit coulis and fruit yoghurt to dip.

If star fruit are not available, replace with thickish slices of crisp apple or Asian pear.

Banana and butterscotch waffles

½ quantity Basic waffle batter ***(see page 12)*****, sweetened, made up using banana-flavoured milk**

3 large bananas

6 scoops vanilla ice cream

1 quantity Butterscotch sauce ***(see page 24)***

Serves 6

1. Prepare the half quantity of sweetened waffle batter, replacing the milk with an equal quantity of banana-flavoured milk. Cook and keep warm until you are ready to serve.

2. Just before serving, peel and thinly slice the bananas. Place a waffle on each serving plate and top with banana slices, a scoop of ice cream and some butterscotch sauce. Serve immediately.

Apple strudel pancakes

½ quantity Basic pancake batter *(see page 10)*, sweetened

60 g/2 oz unsalted butter

60 g/2 oz light brown sugar

3 dessert apples, peeled, cored and thinly sliced

Finely grated rind and juice of 1 lemon

60 g/2 oz sultanas

60 g/2 oz glacé cherries, sliced

½ tsp ground nutmeg

Icing sugar, to dust

Serves 4

1. Prepare the pancake batter and cook to make four pancakes. Set aside to keep warm while you prepare the filling.

2. Melt the butter and sugar in a frying pan until the sugar dissolves. Toss the apples in the lemon rind and juice, add to the pan and cook, stirring, for about 5 minutes. Stir in the sultanas, cherries and nutmeg and continue to cook for a further 2 minutes.

3. To serve, spoon some filling into the centre of each pancake. Fold two sides into the centre to overlap the filling slightly. Bring the remaining sides over and flip over to form a square-shaped parcel. Cut in half diagonally and serve dusted with icing sugar.

Toasted coconut crêpes

- 180 g/6 oz plain flour
- Pinch salt
- 2 eggs
- 400 ml/14 fl oz tin light coconut milk
- 180 g/6 oz granulated sugar
- 4 limes
- Melted unsalted butter, for brushing
- 45 g/1½ oz desiccated coconut
- 1 Tbsp vegetable oil
- 2 large ripe papayas, peeled, stoned and sliced
- 6 scoops coconut ice cream
- Lime zest, to decorate

Serves 6

1. Sift the flour and salt into a bowl and make a well in the centre. Add the eggs, coconut milk and 300 ml/10 fl oz cold water then whisk, until smooth. Cover and stand for 30 minutes.

2. Meanwhile make the lime syrup. Put the sugar in a saucepan with 180 ml/6 fl oz water, and heat, stirring, until dissolved. Pare the rind from two of the limes and extract the juice from all the limes. Add to the pan. Bring to the boil and boil rapidly for 10 minutes. Remove from the heat and set aside. Remove and discard the lime rind.

3. Whisk the batter again. Heat a crêpe pan – about 15 cm/6 in diameter base – and brush with melted butter. Pour about 50 ml/2 fl oz batter into the pan, tilting the pan to coat the base, and quickly sprinkle over a little coconut before the crêpe sets. Place over moderate heat and cook for about 1 minute. Turn over and cook for another minute. Make a further 11 crêpes and cover to keep moist.

4. Fill each crêpe with a few pieces of papaya and roll up. Top with ice cream, lime zest and lime syrup.

Sweet butterscotch waffle sandwiches

1 quantity Basic waffle batter *(see page 12)*, sweetened

2 Tbsp maple syrup

12 scoops toffee ice cream

180 g/6 oz blueberries, defrosted if frozen

1 quantity Butterscotch sauce *(see page 24)*

1 Tbsp icing sugar

Serves 6

1. Make up the batter (see page 12), adding the maple syrup to the finished batter. Cook as described to make twelve waffles. Allow to cool.

2. When you are ready to serve, place six waffles on serving plates and top each with two scoops of ice cream, a few blueberries and a generous drizzle of sauce. Top with another waffle and press down gently to make "sandwiches". Serve immediately, dusted with icing sugar and accompanied with the remaining butterscotch sauce.

Vanilla crêpes with autumn fruits

1 quantity Basic crêpe batter *(see page 13)*, sweetened

1 tsp vanilla extract

60 g/2 oz unsalted butter

60 g/2 oz light brown sugar

4 dessert apples, peeled, cored and cut into thick slices

1 cinnamon stick, broken

250 g/8 oz blackberries, defrosted if frozen

150 ml/5 fl oz unsweetened apple juice

1 quantity Sweet spiced butter *(see page 26)*, to serve

Serves 4

1. Prepare the crêpe batter, adding the vanilla extract to the batter. Cook the crêpes and keep warm until you are ready to serve.

2. Melt the butter and sugar in a frying pan until the sugar dissolves. Add the apples and cinnamon stick to the pan and cook, stirring, for about 5 minutes. Gently stir in the blackberries and pour over the apple juice. Bring to the boil and simmer for about 5 minutes, until just tender. Discard the cinnamon stick.

3. To serve, carefully fill the crêpes with the apples and blackberries and fold them over. Serve dotted with the Sweet spiced butter.

Almond waffles with cherry compôte

200 g/7 oz caster sugar

625 g/1 lb 4 oz fresh cherries, washed and stoned

1 vanilla pod

1 quantity Basic waffle batter (*see page 12*), sweetened

60 g/2 oz ground almonds

1 tsp almond extract

4 scoops vanilla ice cream

45 g/1½ oz toasted flaked almonds

Serves 4

1. Put the sugar in a saucepan with 210 ml/ 7 fl oz water, and heat, stirring, until dissolved. Bring to the boil and add the cherries. Simmer gently for about 5 minutes, stirring occasionally, until tender.

2. Carefully split the vanilla pod down the centre, and prise open the sides of the pod. Add to the cherries and syrup, and set aside to cool. Discard the vanilla pod before serving.

3. Prepare the waffle batter, replacing half of the flour with the ground almonds and adding the almond extract to the batter. Cook the waffles and keep them warm until you are ready to serve.

4. To serve, arrange the waffles on serving plates and spoon over the cherry compôte. Top with a scoop of ice cream and a few flaked almonds.

Raisin pancakes with tangerine syrup

125 g/4 oz plain flour
2 tsp baking powder
½ tsp bicarbonate of soda
1 tsp caster sugar
2 eggs, separated
250 ml/8 fl oz whole milk
Finely grated rind of 1 tangerine
60 g/2 oz sultanas
30 g/1 oz unsalted butter

For the syrup:
½ quantity Sugar syrup *(see page 24)*
Finely grated rind and juice of 2 tangerines
30 g/1 oz unsalted butter

Serves 4

1. Sift the flour, baking powder, bicarbonate of soda and sugar into a bowl and make a well in the centre. Add the egg yolks, pour in the milk and gradually work into the flour using a whisk. Beat until thick and smooth.

2. In a grease-free bowl, whisk the egg whites until stiff and, using a large metal spoon, carefully fold into the batter together with the tangerine rind and sultanas.

3. Heat a little butter in a large frying pan until bubbling, tilting the pan to coat the sides. Ladle 60 ml/4 Tbsp batter to form thick pancakes about 10 cm/4 in in diameter. Cook over a low to moderate heat for about 2½ minutes, until bubbles appear on the surface. Turn over and cook for a further 2½ minutes until golden, puffed up and thick. Repeat this until you have used up all the batter and made eight pancakes in total, re-buttering the pan as necessary, and stacking the cooked pancakes between sheets of parchment, until you are ready to serve.

4. For the syrup, make up as directed on page 24 but add the tangerine rind to the mixture before cooking. Add the butter and cool for 10 minutes. The butter will melt in the hot syrup. Stir in the tangerine juice and it will still be warm to serve poured over the pancakes.

Lace crêpes with green fruit salad

250 g/8 oz fresh lychees, peeled and stoned

¼ green melon e.g. Galia, deseeded and chopped

125 g/4 oz seedless green grapes

2 kiwi fruit, peeled and chopped

Finely grated rind and juice of 1 lime

2 Tbsp ginger syrup

3 large egg whites, lightly beaten

4 Tbsp cornflour

8 tsp skimmed milk

1 tsp vegetable oil

Yoghurt or fromage frais, to serve

Serves 4

1. Mix all the fruits together and gently toss in the lime rind, juice and ginger syrup. Cover and chill until required.

2. Put the egg whites and cornflour in a jug and stir in the milk, mixing well to form a smooth paste. Brush a non-stick medium frying pan – about 20 cm/8 in diameter base – with a little of the oil and heat until hot. Using a quarter of the batter, pour a thin ring of batter around the outside of the pan and then finely drizzle the batter all over to give a lacy effect. Cook over moderate heat for a few seconds on one side only, until set. Drain on kitchen paper, layer with baking parchment and keep warm while you make the remaining three crêpes.

3. To serve, place a crêpe on each serving plate and top with the mixed fruits. Fold the crêpes over and serve accompanied with yoghurt or fromage frais.

Soured cream waffles

5 eggs

125 g/4 oz caster sugar

125 g/4 oz plain flour

½ tsp ground cardamom

180 ml/6 fl oz soured cream

60 g/2 oz unsalted butter, melted, plus extra to serve

Sour cherry jam, to serve

Makes about 15

1. In a large bowl, beat together the eggs and sugar until thick and pale. Sieve in the flour and cardamom, and carefully fold into the whisked eggs together with the soured cream until well incorporated. Gently stir in 60 g/2 oz melted butter and set aside for 10 minutes.

2. Prepare the waffle irons or waffle machine as directed. Ladle about 3 Tbsp batter over each plate, ensuring that the moulded surface of the lower plate is covered sufficiently. Close the irons and cook until the waffles are just brown on the outside, about 3 minutes. Note: these waffles will be softer than those made with a more traditional batter.

3. When the waffles are ready, remove them with a two-pronged fork or a skewer, taking care not to scratch the non-stick coating. Place on a wire rack lined with a clean tea towel and baking parchment. Fold the paper and towel over the waffle to keep it moist. Continue to make about 15 waffles, stacking the cooked waffles between sheets of parchment, until you are ready to serve. Serve warm, drizzled with melted butter and sour cherry jam.

Ice Cream & Sorbets

Pomegranate sorbet

6 pomegranates
75 g/2½ oz caster sugar
1 Tbsp golden syrup
75 ml/2½ fl oz water
2 Tbsp lemon juice

Makes 700 ml/1½ pt

1. Cut the pomegranates into quarters. Peel back the skin of each quarter and release the seeds into a bowl. Remove any bits of the bitter white membrane. Blend the seeds, then squeeze the pulp through fine muslin into a bowl. Alternatively, push the pulp, a little at a time, through a fine sieve. This should yield approx 700 ml/1½ pt.

2. Meanwhile, combine the sugar, golden syrup and water in a small, heavy-bottomed saucepan. Bring to the boil then simmer for 5 minutes. Remove the pan from the heat and leave to cool.

3. Pour the cooled syrup into the pomegranate juice, then stir in the lemon juice. Cover and chill the mixture for 2 hours. Churn in an ice cream maker, according to the manufacturer's instructions, until frozen. Serve immediately or transfer to a freezer container, cover the surface directly with greaseproof paper or foil and put in the freezer.

4. To serve pomegranate sorbet directly from the skins, cut 4 pomegranates in half, scoop out the seeds with a teaspoon and discard the bitter membranes. Place the bottom halves of skins in the freezer. Cut the remaining pomegranates as directed in the recipe. Spoon the frozen sorbet into the frozen skins.

Raspberry semifreddo hearts

250 g/8 oz white chocolate, broken into pieces

5 large egg yolks

75 g/2½ oz caster sugar

300 g/10 oz fresh raspberries

100 g/3½ oz white chocolate, chopped into chunks

300 ml/10 fl oz double cream

1 tsp vanilla extract

Makes 10 hearts (1 L/35 fl oz)

1. Line the base and sides of the moulds with greaseproof paper or foil (unless you are using flexible silicon moulds). Melt the first quantity of white chocolate and set aside. Using an electric beater, beat the egg yolks and sugar in a heatproof bowl over a saucepan of simmering water until thick and pale; about 5 minutes. Remove from the heat and continue beating until cool. Gently fold the raspberries, cooled melted chocolate and white chocolate chunks into the egg mixture.

2. Beat the cream and vanilla extract until soft peaks form. Gently fold the raspberry-egg mixture into the cream, being careful not to crush the raspberries too much. Pour the mixture into the lined moulds and cover the surface directly with more greaseproof paper or foil before still freezing (see page 29). Serve with fresh berries.

Green tea and ginger parfait

- 400 ml/14 fl oz whole milk
- 3 green tea bags
- 2 cm/1 in piece root ginger, roughly chopped
- 4 large eggs, separated
- 100 g/3 ½ oz caster sugar
- 200 ml/7 fl oz double cream

Makes 600 ml/1 pt

1. Put the milk, tea bags and ginger in a medium saucepan and bring to near-boiling point. Remove from the heat and cool for 30 minutes, allowing the flavour to infuse the milk.

2. Using an electric whisk, beat the egg yolks and sugar in a heatproof bowl until thick and pale. Place over a pan of simmering water and stir in the still-warm strained milk. Stir occasionally until the mixture is thick enough to coat the back of a wooden spoon. Cool completely. When the custard mixture is cold gently beat the egg whites and cream, in separate bowls, until soft peaks form. Fold the cream then the egg whites gently into the custard mixture and transfer to a freezer container. Cover the surface directly with greaseproof paper or foil and freeze overnight.

Chocolate ice cream sponge

- **500 g/1 lb ready-made, good-quality vanilla ice cream**
- **Chocolate trifle sponge (*see page 18*) or 19 cm/7 in ready-made shallow square chocolate cake**
- **150 g/5 oz blueberries**
- **30 g/1 oz white chocolate**
- **1 tsp cocoa powder**

Serves 6

1. Remove the ice cream from the freezer and stand at room temperature until it starts to soften – try to avoid it melting too much.

2. Meanwhile, line a deep 500 g/1 lb loaf tin with clear food wrap. Trim the sponge to fit snugly in the bottom of the tin. Cut another piece to fit the top and set aside.

3. Beat the ice cream to break it up and gently fold in the blueberries. Pack on top of the sponge base and top with the other piece of sponge, pushing down gently. Cover with clear food wrap and freeze for at least 2 hours.

4. To serve, melt the white chocolate. Carefully remove the ice-cream sponge from the tin and peel off the food wrap. Drizzle with the white chocolate and dust with cocoa to serve.

If you want to use other fruits in the dessert, make sure you use other berries or cut larger fruit into small pieces. You could use ready-frozen berries; just crush the bigger pieces with a rolling pin before mixing with the ice cream.

Watermelon and mint sorbet

100 g/3½ oz caster sugar

150 ml/5 fl oz water

30 g/1 oz fresh mint leaves

1.2 kg/2 lb 7 oz watermelon, seeds removed and cut into chunks

Pinch of salt

Makes 1.5 L /2½ pt

1. Combine the sugar, water and mint in a heavy-bottomed saucepan. Bring to the boil, then simmer for 5 minutes. Remove the pan from heat and cool.

2. Strain the syrup and discard the mint. Purée the watermelon chunks until smooth, then stir in the cooled, strained syrup a little at a time. The mixture should be sweet, but this will vary depending on the sweetness of the watermelon. Add a pinch of salt. Chill the mixture for at least 1 hour, then churn in an ice cream maker, according to the manufacturer's instructions. Serve immediately or transfer to a freezer container, cover the surface directly with greaseproof paper or foil and put in the freezer.

3. Alternatively, pour the sorbet mixture into ice lolly moulds and freeze.

Peanut butter chocolate dip

500 ml/16 fl oz whole milk
250 g/8 oz smooth peanut butter
150 g/5 oz caster sugar
2 tsp vanilla extract
150 g/5 oz plain chocolate
30 g/1 oz peanuts, chopped
8 ice cream cones

Makes 8 single scoop ice cream cones

1. Combine the milk, peanut butter and sugar in a heavy-bottomed saucepan over a medium heat. Stir until smooth. Stir in the vanilla extract. Remove the pan from the heat and cool. Churn in an ice cream maker, according to the manufacturer's instructions. Spoon the ice cream into an airtight container and freeze for at least 2 hours.

2. Have a few large glasses (big enough to hold the cones upright) on hand. Melt the chocolate in a bowl over simmering water. Remove from the heat and cool slightly. Working quickly, scoop the ice cream onto the cones. Spoon the chocolate over the top, sprinkle with chopped nuts and place cones in the glasses. Freeze for 15 minutes, then enjoy!

Coffee ice cream

150 ml/5 fl oz espresso coffee or 2 tsp instant coffee dissolved in 150 ml/5 fl oz boiling water

150 ml/5 fl oz whole milk

100 g/3½ oz light brown sugar

5 large egg yolks

300 ml/10 fl oz double cream

Makes 800 ml/1⅓ pt

1. Combine the coffee and milk and allow it to cool slightly.

2. In a heatproof bowl beat the sugar and egg yolks, using an electric whisk, until thick and pale. Stir in the milk mixture and place the bowl over a pan of simmering water. Continue stirring until the mixture is thick enough to coat the back of a wooden spoon. Remove the pan from the heat, cover and allow to cool completely.

3. Stir in the double cream and churn in an ice cream maker, according to the manufacturer's instructions. Serve immediately or transfer to a freezer container, cover the surface directly with greaseproof paper or foil and put in the freezer.

Pumpkin ice cream

375 ml/13 fl oz whole milk
3 large egg yolks
200 g/7 oz caster sugar
1 x 450 g/15 oz tin pumpkin purée
½ tsp nutmeg
¼ tsp cinnamon
250 ml/8 fl oz double cream
1 tsp vanilla extract

Makes 1 L/1¾ pt

1. Heat the milk in a heavy-bottomed saucepan to near-boiling point. In a separate, heatproof bowl beat the eggs with the sugar, using an electric whisk, until thick and pale. Gradually stir the milk into the egg mixture. Place the bowl over a pan of simmering water and continue stirring until the mixture is thick enough to coat the back of a wooden spoon. Remove the bowl from the heat and allow to cool.

2. When cool, whisk in all of the remaining ingredients and cover the surface directly with cling film or greaseproof paper to prevent a skin forming. Place in the refrigerator and chill for at least 1 hour.

3. Churn in an ice cream maker according to the manufacturer's instructions. Serve immediately or transfer to a freezer container, cover the surface directly with greaseproof paper or foil and put in the freezer.

Mini chocolate semifreddo logs

3 large eggs, separated

125 g/4 oz caster sugar

200 g/7 oz mascarpone, beaten

1 Tbsp pure vanilla paste or vanilla extract

Finely grated zest of 1 lemon

60 g/2 oz caster sugar

60 g/2 oz plain chocolate, finely grated

Makes 8 small logs

1. Line the base and sides of each tin with foil. Leave enough overhang to enable you to unmould the ice cream easily once frozen.

2. Beat the egg yolks and 60 g/2 oz of the sugar using an electric whisk, in a heatproof bowl over a pan of simmering water until thick, pale and creamy. Remove the bowl from the heat and beat for a further 1 minute. Add the mascarpone, vanilla paste and lemon zest and beat until just combined. Set aside.

3. Beat the egg whites in a separate bowl until very soft peaks form. Gradually beat in the remaining sugar until it is combined and the mixture looks glossy, still with soft peaks. Fold the egg whites gently into the mascarpone mixture.

4. Fill each loaf tin to half full. Stir the chocolate into the remaining mixture and top up the loaf tins. Cover with foil and freeze for 4–6 hours for small tins (or overnight for one large tin). Unmould before serving and decorate with bought or homemade chocolate curls, if liked.

Coconut ice cream

1 x 400 ml/13 fl oz tin coconut cream
5 Tbsp caster sugar
1 egg white

Serves 4–6

1. Blend the coconut cream with 1 tablespoon of the caster sugar until it has the consistency of a milkshake. Pour into an ice-cream maker and churn.

2. Whip the egg whites into stiff peaks, add the remaining 4 tablespoons of caster sugar, a spoonful at a time, and pour into the ice-cream maker once the ice-cream starts to solidify (about 20–30 minutes). Serve by itself or with berries.

3. To make by hand, pour into a plastic container and place in the freezer. Whisk every 20–30 minutes until the ice-cream is ready, adding the beaten egg white once the ice-cream starts to solidify.

Cranberry cosmo sorbet

315 g/10½ oz caster sugar

500 ml/16 fl oz water

675 g/1 lb 6 oz fresh or frozen cranberries (don't thaw if frozen)

60 ml/2 fl oz lime juice

2 Tbsp fresh orange juice

Grated zest of 1 orange

Makes 600 ml/1 pt

1. Combine the sugar and water in a saucepan over a medium heat, stirring until the sugar has dissolved and the liquid begins to boil. Add the cranberries and simmer until the berries pop and collapse, about 12–15 minutes. Remove the pan from the heat and strain the berries into a bowl, gently pushing on them with the back of a spoon to extract as much juice as possible. Cover the liquid with clingfilm, leave to cool then place in the refrigerator.

2. When the juice is completely chilled stir in the lime juice, orange juice and zest. Churn in an ice cream maker, according to the manufacturer's instructions. Serve immediately or transfer to a freezer container, cover the surface directly with greaseproof paper or foil and put in the freezer.

3. Remove from the freezer 15 minutes before serving to allow to soften slightly. Serve topped with Candied citrus peel (see page 15), if liked.

Nougat ice cream

75 g/2½ oz caster sugar

45 g/1½ oz liquid glucose syrup

60 ml/2 fl oz clear honey

6 large egg whites

300 ml/10 fl oz double cream, lightly whipped

200 g/7 oz dried mixed tropical fruit, chopped

100 g/3½ oz flaked almonds

Makes 1.5 L/50 fl oz

1. Place the sugar, glucose and honey in a saucepan. Bring to a simmer and stir once or twice until the sugar has dissolved. Once the sugar has dissolved, bring to the boil and continue boiling until the mixture reaches 116° C/240° F on a sugar thermometer.

2. When the syrup is nearly ready beat the egg whites, using an electric whisk, until stiff peaks form. With the whisk still running, pour the syrup on to the egg whites and continue beating until cool. Fold the lightly whipped cream into the cool nougat mix, then fold in the fruit and nuts.

3. Pour the mixture into a 2 L/70 fl oz loaf tin lined with baking paper or foil and smooth the top using a spatula. Cover the surface and freeze. When the ice cream is frozen carefully unmould it and serve cut into slices.

Bittersweet cocoa sorbet

275 g/9 oz caster sugar

1 L/35 fl oz water

125 g/4 oz cocoa powder, sifted

1 Tbsp pure vanilla paste or vanilla extract

Makes 800 ml/28 fl oz

1. Put the sugar and water in a medium saucepan and bring to the boil. Add the cocoa and stir until well combined. Bring the mixture back to the boil. Reduce the heat and simmer for 20 minutes over a low heat, stirring occasionally. Cover and cool the mixture completely then add the vanilla paste.

2. Churn in an ice cream maker, according to the manufacturer's instructions, for about 20 minutes or until the mixture is frozen. Serve immediately in small bowls or transfer to a freezer container, cover the surface directly with greaseproof paper or foil and put in the freezer. Remove from the freezer 15 minutes before serving to allow to soften slightly.

Lemon curd ice cream

300 ml/10 fl oz double cream

300 ml/10 fl oz lemon curd, bought or home-made *(see page 26)*

Makes 600 ml/1pt

1. Whip the cream until soft peaks form. Add the lemon curd and continue beating until well combined. Transfer to a freezer container and still freeze (see page 29) for at least 6 hours.

Elderflower and violet frozen yoghurt

200 ml/7 fl oz elderflower cordial

100 ml/3½ fl oz water

300 ml/10 fl oz Greek yoghurt

300 ml/10 fl oz crème fraîche or sour cream

Juice of 1 lemon

75 g/2½ oz crystallized violets

Makes 1 L/35 fl oz

1. Combine the elderflower cordial and water in a small, heavy-bottomed saucepan and bring to the boil, stirring occasionally. Reduce the heat and simmer for 3–5 minutes, or until the liquid has reduced to a thin syrup. Remove from the heat and allow to cool.

2. Combine the yoghurt and crème fraîche in a large bowl. Whisk in the syrup and lemon juice. Chill the mixture for 1 hour, then churn in an ice cream maker, according to the manufacturer's instructions.

3. Chop three quarters of the crystallized violets into smaller pieces, setting the remainder aside to decorate the finished ice. Just before frozen yoghurt has set (usually when 5 minutes remain), stir the chopped crystallized violets into the maker and continue to churn until set.

4. Serve immediately or transfer to a freezer container, cover the surface directly with greaseproof paper or foil and put in the freezer. Decorate with the reserved crystallised violets to serve.

Toasted hazelnut tortoni

- 2 large egg whites
- ¼ tsp cream of tartar
- 60 g/2 oz caster sugar
- 375 ml/13 fl oz double cream
- 1 tsp vanilla extract
- 60 ml/2 fl oz Grand Marnier
- 4 Tbsp desiccated coconut, toasted
- 60 g/2 oz hazelnuts, toasted and chopped
- 100 g/3½ oz plain chocolate (70% cocoa solids), shaved

Makes 6 x 250 ml/8 fl oz servings

1. Beat the egg whites with the cream of tartar using an electric whisk, until soft peaks form. Add the sugar and beat until stiff peaks form.

2. In a separate bowl, whip the cream just until soft. Beat in the vanilla and Grand Marnier. In a small bowl, combine the coconut, hazelnuts and chocolate. Reserve a quarter of the mixture for garnish and stir the remaining mixture into the cream. Combine the whipped cream and egg whites and stir gently until smooth.

3. Place the tortoni in glasses and top with the reserved topping. Freeze for at least 4 hours. Alternatively, freeze the tortoni in a freezer container and spoon into dessert bowls to serve.

Rhubarb and ginger sorbet

600 g/1 lb $3\frac{1}{2}$ oz rhubarb, cut into 2 cm/1 in pieces

250 g/8 oz caster sugar

300 ml/10 fl oz water

2 cm/1 in piece root, ginger peeled and finely grated

Juice of 1 lemon

Makes 600 ml/35 fl oz

1. Combine all the ingredients in a saucepan and bring to the boil. Cover and simmer until the rhubarb is tender, about 5 minutes. Leave to cool slightly before transferring to a food processor. Process until the mixture is combined but still has texture.

2. Churn in an ice cream maker, according to the manufacturer's instructions, until frozen. Transfer to a freezer container and cover the surface directly with greaseproof paper or foil. Freeze overnight.

3. Remove from the freezer 15 minutes before serving to allow it to soften slightly.

Peppermint chocolate chip ice cream

60 g/2 oz caster sugar

3 large eggs, separated

300 ml/10 fl oz whole milk

150 g/5 oz white chocolate, broken into pieces

1½ tsp peppermint extract

1 tsp green food colouring (optional)

200 ml/7 fl oz double cream

45 g/1½ oz chocolate chips, mini chocolate curls or mini chocolate buttons

Makes 600 ml/1 pt

1. Beat the sugar and egg yolks in a heatproof bowl until thick and creamy. Place the bowl over a pan of simmering water and slowly add the milk, stirring occasionally until the mixture starts to thicken. When the mixture just begins to thicken, add the broken chocolate pieces, stirring continuously until the chocolate has melted and the mixture is smooth. Remove from the heat and stir in the peppermint extract and food colouring, if using. Cover the surface directly with clingfilm and allow the mixture to cool completely.

2. When cold, stir in the cream and churn in an ice cream maker, according to the manufacturer's instructions, for about 20 minutes or until frozen. Stir in the chocolate chips and transfer to a freezer container. Cover the surface directly with greaseproof paper or foil and freeze.

Chocolate-dipped ice cream morsels

300 g/10 oz ice cream of your choice

200 g/7 oz plain chocolate

Makes about 16

1. Using a small ice cream scoop or melon baller, shape the ice cream into small balls. Place on baking parchment-lined trays and place in the freezer until frozen hard.

2. Melt the chocolate over a pan of simmering water or in the microwave. Allow to cool but not set.

3. Dip the frozen ice cream balls, using two spoons, into the cooled chocolate and return the balls to the lined trays. Repeat until all the balls are dipped. Freeze until you are ready to serve.

Vanilla ice cream

300 ml/10 fl oz whole milk

25 g/1 oz skimmed milk powder

75 g/2½ oz caster sugar, preferably unrefined

3 egg yolks

1 tsp cornflour

1 tsp vanilla extract

Makes 1 L/35 fl oz

1. Warm the milk, milk powder and 1 tablespoon of the sugar to boiling point, stirring occasionally. Meanwhile, using an electric whisk, beat the egg yolks, remaining sugar, cornflour and vanilla in a heatproof bowl, until thick and pale. Gradually whisk in the boiling milk. Pour the mixture back into the pan and bring back to boiling point, stirring, until thickened. Tip back into the bowl, cover the surface directly with damp greaseproof paper and leave to cool.

2. Churn the mixture in an ice cream maker, according to the manufacturer's instructions, until frozen. Transfer to a freezer container, cover the surface directly with greaseproof paper and store in the freezer for up to one month.

Coffee granita

For the granita:

200 g/7 oz caster sugar or to taste

500 ml/16 fl oz strong espresso coffee, cooled

3 Tbsp water

For the cream layer:

125 ml/4 fl oz double cream

2 Tbsp caster sugar

Makes 6 x 250 ml/8 fl oz servings

1. To make the granita, slowly add sugar to the coffee, tasting all the while, until the coffee is very sweet. Add the water and stir well. Pour the mixture into a shallow metal bowl, dish or even sauté pan – whatever will be easiest for you to break up the ice crystals. Cover with foil and freeze until solid, about 8 hours.

2. Once solid, remove the granita from the freezer and, using a metal pastry scraper, break up the granita into small, irregular shards. Transfer to a chilled, airtight freezer container with a lid, close it and return the granita to the freezer.

3. Half an hour before serving, invert the container to distribute the syrup throughout the shards of ice. Chill glasses or glass bowls – whatever will show off the layers best.

4. Whip the cream and sugar in a bowl until stiff. Layer cream and granita in the serving glasses, finishing with a layer of granita.

Clementine and star anise sorbet

250 ml/8 fl oz water

100 g/3½ oz caster sugar

3 whole star anise

1 vanilla pod

500 ml/16 fl oz fresh clementine juice

Pinch of salt

Makes 500 ml/18 fl oz

1. Combine the water, sugar and star anise in a heavy-bottomed saucepan. Split the vanilla pod lengthwise, and add to the pan. Bring the mixture to the boil, then simmer for 5 minutes. Remove the pan from the heat and leave to cool.

2. When cool, strain and discard the spices. Stir the syrup into the clementine juice and add a pinch of salt.

3. Churn in an ice cream maker, according to the manufacturer's instructions. This sorbet is best eaten straight from the maker. If you are making it in advance however, spoon the sorbet into a freezer container, cover with baking parchment or greaseproof paper and put in the freezer. Remove from the freezer 15 minutes before serving to allow the sorbet to soften slightly.

Ricotta ice cream with pine nuts

4 large eggs

150 g/5 oz caster sugar

150 ml/5 fl oz clear honey, plus 2 Tbsp for drizzling

1 tsp vanilla extract

500 g/1 lb ricotta

500 ml/16 fl oz whole milk

500 ml/16 fl oz double cream, softly whipped

50 g/1¾ oz pine nuts, toasted

Makes 2 L/70 fl oz

1. Beat the eggs, sugar and honey, using an electric whisk, until thick and pale, about 6–8 minutes. Stir in the vanilla, ricotta, milk and whipped cream. Continue to beat for 2 minutes until smooth and thick.

2. Spread the mixture in a 33 x 22 cm/13 x 8 in parchment-lined baking tray with sides or a freezer container. Top with toasted pine nuts and a drizzle of honey. Cover the surface loosely with greaseproof paper or foil before freezing.

Ice lollies

To make the sugar syrup:
350 g/12 oz caster sugar
350 ml/12 fl oz water

Makes 300 ml/10 fl oz

1. Put the sugar and water in a heavy-bottomed saucepan. Place over a gentle heat until the sugar has dissolved, without boiling the mixture. Once the sugar has dissolved, increase the heat and bring to the boil. Boil the syrup for a further 5 minutes. Remove from the heat and cool before using.

2. Mixed berry and orange – put 400 g/14 oz frozen berries, 100 ml/3½ fl oz sugar syrup, and the juice and grated zest of 1 orange in a food processor and process for 1–2 minutes or until liquefied. Strain through a fine sieve then pour into lolly moulds. Freeze.

3. Cantaloupe and lime – Put 400 g/14 oz of melon flesh, 100 ml/3½ fl oz sugar syrup and the juice of 1 lime in a food processor and process for 1–2 minutes or until liquefied. Strain through a fine sieve then pour into lolly moulds. Freeze.

To keep lolly sticks from floating to the top of your moulds, soak them in warm water for an hour before inserting them into the moulds.

Ice cream affogato

8 scoops Vanilla and/or Coffee ice cream ***(see page 259 and 285)***

2 Tbsp coffee beans, finely ground

300 ml/10 fl oz hot espresso coffee

Serves 4

1. Divide the ice cream scoops between four glass cups or small bowls. Sprinkle with ground coffee beans and bring the cups to the table. Once there, pour coffee over each serving.

Mango and yoghurt slush

600 g/1 lb 3½ oz fresh mango flesh

200 g/7 oz caster sugar

200 ml/7 fl oz water

Juice and grated zest of 2 limes

300 ml/10 fl oz Greek yoghurt

Makes 800 ml/28 fl oz

1. Put the mango, sugar, water, lime juice and zest in a saucepan and bring to the boil. Reduce the heat and simmer, uncovered, for 5 minutes. Allow to cool for 10 minutes then purée in a food processor or liquidiser. Cool completely. Stir in the yogurt and and churn in an ice cream maker according to the manufacturer's instructions until soft, slushy and almost frozen. Serve immediately.

Apple and rosemary frozen yoghurt

200 ml/7 fl oz water
300 ml/10 fl oz apple juice
150 g/5 oz caster sugar
2–3 large rosemary sprigs
200 ml/7 fl oz Greek yoghurt

Makes 600 ml/20 fl oz

1. Put the water, apple juice, sugar and rosemary sprigs in a saucepan and bring to the boil. Reduce the heat and simmer for 5 minutes. Allow to cool completely. When cool gently whisk in the Greek yoghurt.

2. Churn in an ice cream maker, according to the manufacturer's instructions, until frozen, then serve immediately or transfer to a freezer container, cover the surface directly with greaseproof paper or foil and put in the freezer.

To crystallize rosemary, remove the needles from the woody stalk. Combine 200 g/7 oz caster sugar with 200 ml/7 fl oz water in a saucepan and bring to the boil, until sugar dissolves. Add needles, reduce heat and simmer for 30 minutes. Remove needles with a slotted spoon and place on kitchen paper. When cool, toss the rosemary needles through another 100 g/3½ oz caster sugar.

Index

Exhibits

Exhibit

Courage does not mean that we have no fear,
but that we don't act out of that fear.

THIN PLACES

SEEKING THE COURAGE TO LIVE IN A DIVIDED WORLD

KIRKRIDGE FELLOWS STORIES

GATHERED BY

SALLY Z. HARE & MEGAN LEBOUTILLIER

INSIGHTS FROM PARKER J. PALMER

Comments or questions: sally@stilllearning.org
Or visit online: www.stilllearning.org

ISBN: 978-0-9895042-6-3

Cover photos by Peter Richardson, a student at Juniata College majoring in photography and visual art. Peter grew up at Kirkridge Retreat and Study Center in the Pocono Mountains of Pennsylvania and captured its beauty in this winter sunrise on the front and back cover.

Book design by Jim R. Rogers

Prose Press
75 Red Maple Drive
Pawleys Island, South Carolina 29585
proseNcons@live.com

DEDICATION

To Sharon Ellies Palmer,
the Godmother of Courage Work, with love and great gratitude
for the ways you hold Parker and all of us.

And to Parker J. Palmer,
our Founding Father, with love and great respect
for your courage and your wisdom and your generosity.

CONTENTS

Section 3 Seeking the Courage to Create a Circle of Trust and Reclaim the Commons

Meeting the Authors

BOOK OPENING

About Thin Places

Thin places have become, for me, a way of naming the space where I have the best chance of nurturing the courage to seek the undivided life I want to live. In a thin place, I see my connectedness to everything around me. I see the wholeness that is my birthright gift.

The idea of thin places goes back to the ancient Irish people, before the Celts arrived sometime after 500 BC, before Christianity came to Ireland. Researchers have uncovered signs and symbols of the beliefs that there was another world, a parallel world, and that thin places were the portals between the two worlds.

For that earliest Irish community, a thin place was an actual physical place. Over the next several thousand years, the definition of thin places expanded to include particular times of seasonal shifts, such as *Samhain*, the Celtic holiday when the boundaries between the material and spiritual worlds were transparent. Some thin places became known for their energy, rather than for being an opening between the worlds; people would go to these places to absorb their power.

Thin places were places of mystery, holy places that allowed humans to connect more easily to their spiritual selves. In thin places, we have easier access to Mahatma Gandhi's "indefinite mysterious power that pervades everything." In a thin place, we would have a better chance of seeing what Thomas Merton called a hidden wholeness in *Hagia Sophia:*

There is in all things an invisible fecundity,
a dimmed light,
a meek namelessness,
a hidden wholeness
This mysterious Unity, and Integrity, is Wisdom, the Mother of all, Natura naturans.

Harvard theologian Peter Gomes writes:

> *There is in Celtic mythology the notion of "thin places" in the universe where the visible and the invisible world come into their closest proximity. To seek such places is the vocation of the wise and the good — and for those that find them, the clearest communication between the temporal and eternal. Mountains and rivers are particularly favored as thin places marking invariably as they do, the horizontal and perpendicular frontiers. But perhaps the ultimate of these thin places in the human condition are the experiences people are likely to have as they encounter suffering, joy, and mystery.*

(http://www.onbeing.org/blog/thin-places-and-the-transforming-presence-of -beauty/6180)

The writers in this book have come to understand that thin places can be created with careful attention to safe and trustworthy space. These authors are all Kirkridge Courage Fellows, which, by prerequisite, means that they are facilitators prepared by the Center for Courage & Renewal (CCR). The Center was founded by Parker J. Palmer -- and what has come to be called Courage Work (it started as The Courage to Teach® – and over the past 20 years, is also The Courage to Lead® and Circles of Trust®) is grounded in Parker's writing and philosophy.

Throughout our book, thanks to Parker's generosity, you will find insights from his writing. He is a writer, teacher and activist who works independently on issues in education, community, leadership, spirituality, and social change. In addition to being CCR Founder and Senior Facilitator, he has authored nine books, including *The Courage to Teach, Let Your Life Speak, A Hidden Wholeness,* and *Healing the Heart of Democracy*. He holds a Ph.D. in sociology from the University of California at Berkeley, and thirteen honorary doctorates. We begin here with Parker's insight on creating space from *A Hidden Wholeness* (p. 56):

- *We know how to create spaces that invite the intellect to show up, analyzing reality, parsing logic and arguing its case: such spaces can be found, for example, in universities.*
- *We know how to create spaces that invite the emotions into play, reacting to injury, expressing anger and celebrating joy: they can be found in therapy groups.*
- *We know how to create spaces that invite the will to emerge, consolidating energy and effort on behalf of a shared goal: they can be found in task forces and committees.*
- *We certainly know how to invite the ego to put in an appearance, polishing its image, protecting its turf and demanding its rights: they can be found wherever we go!*
- *But we know very little about creating spaces that invite the soul to make itself known. Apart from the natural world, such spaces are hard to find – and we seem to place little value on preserving the soul spaces in nature.*

So thin places are places where the soul can show up. The poet Mary Oliver says *"Nobody knows what the soul is"*; nevertheless, we share with you what we mean by the word in our glossary! We began the Kirkridge Courage Fellowship Program (KCFP) out of our yearning to create for ourselves that kind of space Parker writes about, the space we were committed to creating for others. We took to heart Parker's admonition that the natural world was the best place to begin – and we chose the Kirkridge Retreat and Study Center for five retreats over two years from 2014-2016.

We wanted a Circle of Trust for ourselves, a space where we might go deeper into our own inner journeys—and also a low-risk space for practicing new ways to bring our inner work into the outer world. As you read Parker's words about The Movement Way in Section 1, you'll get a sense of our path. This book represents, for us, the step of going public. After all, we are the ones who have been facilitating this Courage Work, who have embedded the principles and practices (the Stepping Stone in the third section) into our lives.

Now we want to share our stories with you. We do so because of our belief in this idea from Frederick Buechner:

> *My story is important not because it is mine...but because if I tell it anything like right, the chances are you will recognize that in many ways it is yours.*

We hope you'll find some of your own story in our stories, that you will find portals to your own thin places.

-- Sally Z. Hare

February, 2017

SECTION 1

Seeking the Courage to Let Our Lives Speak

Before you tell your life what you intend to do with it, listen for what it intends to do with you.

Before you tell your life what truths and values you have decided to live up to, let your life tell you what truths you embody, what values you represent.

--Parker Palmer, *Let Your Life Speak*

Insight from Parker J. Palmer

The Movement Way

I often say that if my ideas never left the pages of my books, they wouldn't be of much use. I celebrate the people who put wheels on those ideas, who find ways to live with integrity, to take their inner work into the outer world.

The Writers in this book have done just that. They share individual stories of deciding to live divided no more and then committing to creating that space for others, by becoming facilitators of the programs of the Center for Courage & Renewal (CCR): The Courage to Teach, The Courage to Lead, Circles of Trust. Their stories offer real-life examples of the CCR mission to create a more just, compassionate and healthy world by nurturing personal and professional integrity and the courage to act on it.

I offer this look at the way of the movement, as a way to gain insight into what sustained them as they took the journey to the undivided life. I began to understand movements when I saw the simple fact that nothing would ever have changed if reformers had allowed themselves to be done in by organizational resistance. Many of us experience such resistance as checkmate to our hopes for change. But for a movement, resistance is merely the place where things begin. The movement mentality, far from being defeated by organizational resistance, takes energy from opposition. Opposition validates the audacious idea that change must come.

The black liberation movement and the women's movement would have died aborning if racist and sexist organizations had been allowed to define the rules of engagement. But for some blacks, and for some women, that resistance affirmed and energized the struggle. In both movements, advocates of change found sources of countervailing power outside of organizational structures, and they nurtured that power in ways that eventually gave them leverage over organizations.

The genius of movements is paradoxical: They abandon the logic of organizations in order to gather the power necessary to rewrite the logic of organizations. Both the black movement and the women's movement grew outside of organizational boundaries--but both returned to change the lay, and the law, of the land.

How does a movement unfold and progress? I see four definable stages in the movements I have studied—stages that do not unfold as neatly as this list suggests, but often overlap and circle back on each other:

- Isolated individuals decide to stop leading "divided lives."
- These people discover each other and form groups for mutual support.
- Empowered by community, they take the risk to "go public."
- Alternative rewards emerge to sustain the movement's vision, which may force the conventional reward system to change.

STAGE ONE: Choosing Integrity

The first stage in a movement can be described with some precision, I think. It happens when isolated individuals make an inner choice to stop leading "divided lives." Most of us know from experience what a divided life is. Inwardly we feel one sort of imperative for our lives, but outwardly we respond to quite another. This is the human condition, of course; our inner and outer worlds will never be in perfect harmony. But there are extremes of dividedness that become intolerable, and when the tension snaps inside of this person, then that person, and then another, a movement may be underway.

The decision to stop leading a divided life, made by enough people over a period of time, may eventually have political impact. But at the outset, it is a deeply personal decision, taken for the sake of personal integrity and wholeness. I call it the "Rosa Parks decision" in honor of the woman who decided, one hot Alabama day in 1955, that she finally would sit at the front of the bus.

Rosa Parks' decision was neither random nor taken in isolation. She served as secretary for the local NAACP, had studied social change at the Highlander Folk School, and was aware of others' hopes to organize a bus boycott. But her motive that day in Montgomery was not to spark the modern civil rights movement. Years later, she explained her decision with a simple but powerful image of personal wholeness: "I sat down because my feet were tired."

I suspect we can say even more: Rosa Parks sat at the front of the bus because her soul was tired of the vast, demoralizing gap between knowing herself as fully human and collaborating with a system that denied her humanity. The decision to stop leading a divided life is less a strategy for altering other people's values than an uprising of the elemental need for one's own values to come to the fore. The power of a movement lies less in attacking some enemy's untruth than in naming and claiming a truth of one's own.

There is immense energy for change in such inward decisions as they leap from one person to another and outward to the society. With these decisions, individuals may set in motion a process that creates change from the inside out. There is an irony here: We often think of movements as "confrontational," as hammering away at social structures until the sinners inside repent and we contrast them (often invidiously) with the "slow, steady, faithful" process of working for change from within the organization. In truth, people who take an organizational approach to problems often become obsessed with their unyielding "enemies," while people who adopt a movement approach must begin by changing themselves. These people have seized the personal insight from which all movements begin: No punishment can possibly be more severe than the punishment that comes from conspiring in the denial of one's own integrity.

STAGE TWO: Communities of Encouragement and Support

But the personal decision to stop leading a divided life is a frail reed. All around us, dividedness is presented as the sensible, even responsible, way to live. So the second stage in a movement happens when people who have been making these decisions start to discover each other and enter into relations of mutual encouragement and support. These groups, which are characteristic of every movement I know about, perform the crucial function of helping the Rosa Parkses of the world know that even though they are out of step, they are not crazy. Together we learn that behaving normally is sometimes nuts but seeking integrity is always sane. But it is clear from all great movements that mutual support is vital if the inner decision is to be sustained and if the movement is to take its next crucial steps toward gathering power.

STAGE THREE: Going Public

The third stage of a movement has already been implied. As support groups develop, individuals learn to translate their private concerns into public issues, and they grow in their ability to give voice to these issues in public and compelling ways. To put it more precisely, support groups help people discover that their problems are not "private" at all but have been occasioned by public conditions and therefore require public remedies.

This has been the story of the women's movement (and of the black liberation movement as well). For a long time, women were "kept in their place" partly by a psychology that relegated the pain women felt to the private realm - grist for the therapeutic mill. But when women came together and began discovering the prevalence of their pain, they also began discerning its public roots. Then they moved from Freud to feminism.

The translation of private pain into public issues that occurs in support groups goes far beyond the analysis of issues; it also empowers people to take those issues into public places. It was in small groups (notably, in churches) that blacks were empowered to take their protest to the larger community in songs and sermons and speeches, in pickets and in marches, in open letters and essays and books. Group support encourages people to risk the public exposure of insights that had earlier seemed far too fragile for that rough-and-tumble realm.

I am using the word "public" here in a way that is more classical than contemporary. The public realm I have in mind is not the realm of politics, which would return us to the manipulation of organizational power. Instead, to "go public" is to enter one's convictions into the mix of communal discourse. It is to project one's ideas so that others can hear them, respond to them, and be influenced by them and so that one's ideas can be tested and refined in the public crucible. The public, understood as a vehicle of discourse, is pre-political. It is that primitive process

of communal conversation, conflict, and consensus on which the health of institutionalized power depends.

The Writers in this book are taking a step towards going public by sharing their stories. Because this activity does not always have direct political impact, some skeptics may call it "mere words." But this criticism comes from an organizational mentality. By giving public voice to our stories, by naming and claiming alternative values, we can create something more fundamental than political change. We can create cultural change.

STAGE FOUR: Alternative Rewards

As a movement passes through the first three stages, it develops ways of rewarding people for sustaining the movement itself. In part, these rewards are simply integral to the nature of each stage; they are the rewards that come from living one's values, from belonging to a community, from finding a public voice. But in stage four, a more systematic pattern of alternative rewards emerges, and with it comes the capacity to challenge the dominance of existing organizations.

8 The power of organizations depends on their ability to reward people who abide by their norms, even the people who suffer from those norms. A racist society depends on a majority who are rewarded for keeping the minority "in its place" and on a minority willing to stay there. But as members of either group discover rewards for alternative behavior, it becomes more difficult for racism to reign. An educational system that ignores human need in favor of a narrow version of professionalism depends on a reward system that keeps both faculty and students in their place. But as soon as rewards for alternative behavior emerge for either group, it becomes more difficult for reform to be denied its day.

What are the alternative rewards offered by a growing movement? As a movement grows, the meaning one does not find in conventional work is found in the meaning of the movement. As a movement grows, the affirmation one does not receive from organizational colleagues is received from movement friends. As a movement grows, careers that no longer satisfy may be revisioned in forms and images that the movement has inspired. As a movement grows, the paid work one cannot find in conventional organizations may be found in the movement itself.

In stage one, people who decide to live "divided no more" find the courage to face punishment by realizing that there is no punishment worse than conspiring in a denial

of one's own integrity. That axiom, inverted, shows how alternative rewards can create cracks in the conventional reward system and then grow in the cracks: People start realizing there is no reward greater than living in a way that honors one's own integrity. Taken together, the two axioms trace a powerful vector of a movement's growth from rejecting conventional punishments to embracing alternative rewards.

These alternative rewards may seem frail and vulnerable when compared to the raises and promotions organizations are able to bestow upon their loyalists. So they are. Integrity, as the cynics say, does not put bread on the table. But people who are drawn into a movement generally find that stockpiling bread is not the main issue for them. They have the bread they need and, given that, they learn the wisdom of another saying: "People do not live on bread alone." We live, ultimately, on our integrity.

UNDERSTANDING THE MOVEMENT WAY

By understanding the stages of a movement, I hope we may see more clearly that many of us are engaged in a movement today, that we hold in our hands a form of power that has driven real change in recent times. At every stage of a movement there is both power to help change happen and encouragement for disheartened souls. Wherever we are on this journey, a step taken to renew our spirits may turn out to be a step towards wholeness, towards integrity—once we understand the movement way.

Parker J. Palmer is a writer, teacher, and activist who works independently on issues in education, community, leadership, spirituality, and social change. Founder and Senior Partner of the Center for Courage & Renewal, he has authored nine books, including *The Courage to Teach, Let Your Life Speak, A Hidden Wholeness,* and *Healing the Heart of Democracy*. He holds a Ph.D. in sociology from the University of California at Berkeley, and thirteen honorary doctorates.

MEETING THE AUTHORS

Janet Files: I feel most alive when I am fully present to the beauty in each moment and when I am part of a vibrant community, discovering and sharing stories of personal significance. I also feel very alive sitting on my back porch in the freshness of morning, enjoying bird songs, coffee, a good read and the delicious tonic of the sounds, smells and feels of the earth and my creatures great and small. And of course, I feel alive when enjoying the zany, warm company anywhere, anytime of the loving heap of my four grown children, my endearing, devoted husband Bill and any beloved friends who are caught up in the links of our loving relationships.

Dianne Baker: *I feel most alive singing in community; being in, on or under water: swimming, paddling or scuba diving; being among the trees; and sharing a meal and laughter with beloved family and friends. I think in song, rhythm and metaphor, fueled by an inventive spirit and quirky imagination. I am deeply in love with my family, and playing in the dirt, making beautiful things grow. Courage & Renewal work has brought out in me love, courage, and compassion and has reshaped my life and much of my approach to work.*

Caroline Fairless: Baseball is my passion, and had I been born a boy, I know I'd have played professional ball (for the Pirates). The banjo is my instrument of choice . . . if only I could play it. For several years I have apprenticed myself to a marble sculptor. After my beloved dog Missy died, I swore I would never have another dog. Now we have two. My book *The Dance of the Caterpillars ~ In a Time Before Texting* is my sweetest and most tender work. The beauty I love takes many forms, with one thread in common – that it takes me out of myself and out of time. I am in awe of the simple walk from our house to a nearby pond. It is pure magic when I can be on the water in a kayak. I love what emerges when I am still and patient; it might be a phrase on a page, or a purple finch at the feeder, or seeing what my hands can shape from a block of clay. I love to garden. I love the knowledge that as I care for the soil, I am making it richer. I love the smell of the seasons just prior to their appearance. I love New Hampshire and the beauty of our home.

Patti Smith: *I feel most alive when the wind, sun, raindrops or snow are touching my face as I walk, ski, or paddle on the water, in the woods, up mountains or along the shore, especially when I am with my most special buddy, my partner Rob. I am a smithy, forging bridges between cultures, religious beliefs, educational philosophies, and the difficult and formed aspects of myself. I wish I were a comedian because I believe laughter is the strongest bridge builder on earth.*

Sue E. Small: I have come to understand that my Work in the world is listening, supporting, and encouraging others and myself to engage in both formal and informal "circle of trust" experiences to hold those difficult conversations within as they listen to others. I am learning to live in the world as well as "to be of use" in it. I am still learning and becoming a Courage & Renewal facilitator as I live the questions within the Kirkridge Courage Fellowship.

Sandra Sturdivant Merriam: *Please call me Sandie. From the time I was in the second grade I have had a love affair with the natural world. I enjoy bird watching, walking my Labradoodle Millie on the beach, and spending time with my family. My Work in the world is fostering hope in those who serve our children, encouraging their voices, creating spaces where they might find their own hopeful voices. I am energized by ideas, paradox, and finding a way forward against great odds, to pay it forward… I learned that from my mother. I am grateful to be a Courage & Renewal facilitator and am passionate about sharing the principles and practice of this approach to living.*

Mardi Tindal: I feel most alive when I am facilitating, cycling along water and hiking wooded trails, baking for those I love, and playing with my granddaughter. My Work in the world is finding hope, sharing it with others, and helping them discover hope, too. Community is core for me: my family, my nascent co-housing community, my community of faith, my Canadian and international communities, including the Kirkridge community. I have been a Courage & Renewal facilitator for about 10 years.

Phoenix Rising: A Season of Loss and Transformation

By Janet Files

There are 44 million minutes in a well-lived life. In three minutes of that collected time, energy, and accumulated material and relational worth, the meaning I had made from those millions of moments crystallized and burst into flame, like a magnifying glass focusing light on dry tinder.

September 26, 2014 was a perfect late afternoon in Myrtle Beach. The sky was blue, and the humidity and temperature so inviting that my friend, Cherie, and I had our 4:00 yoga practice on my back deck. We joked about how we were able to have a deep, restorative savasana in spite of the knocking and clanking of the attic fan above our heads. "I will have to get my husband, Bill, to look at that later as it will keep my friend awake who is staying in the room right under that fan."

It was a warning, but one we had no way to interpret. Yet.

A half-hour later I was enjoying chopping cilantro to add to the mango salsa. Savoring the blended fragrance of the lime, mango and cilantro, I imagined it being the perfect counterpoint for the fresh Murrells Inlet hogfish we would enjoy on the deck for dinner when the smoke alarm interrupted my musings. I put down my knife and followed the sound upstairs to the guest and library wing, wondering what could have set off this false alarm. My smoke alarms had always been false.

As I rounded the top of the stairs, I saw white smoke curling along the ceiling. One second and my body registered full fight or flight—trying its best to help me respond to what was no longer a relaxing evening. My mind was still telling me, "This has to be a mistake!" I ran into the room emitting the smoke. Fire was dropping through the attic air duct onto the floor next to 40 years of collected children's and adult literature. Fahrenheit 451 had been reached!

My body was propelled down the stairs at a freakishly fast pace as all within me cried out to "DO SOMETHING BEFORE IT'S TOO LATE!!" Somewhat confused, my mind told me to grab that trusty fire fighting tool, the handy dishtowel, run back and "save the house" from the invader. After a few powerful but pitifully inadequate swipes at the licking flames, the smoke turning oily and black, my mind finally registered, "Get out now! This is the way people die in house fires!"

I did an about face, slamming the door behind me and any other door I passed through. I grabbed our precious dog Gordito, my phone, and the car keys, and ran out the door. Now all mental, emotional, physical and spiritual systems seamlessly meshed to help me with the real task ahead. What really matters? What is worth saving?

I put my dog in the car and drove it out of the way of potential fire-fighting trucks as I called 911. I tried not to shout..."***YES, I see flames. YES, all animals and people are out of the house. YES, pleeease HURRY***." I didn't learn until later that a house fire doubles in size every 30 seconds. By this time my journals, books and photos were already getting crispy around the edges.

Next call to husband of 37 years: "Our house is on fire."

"Ok, that's not funny."

"No-o-o, it's true. Flames coming out the back window. The real deal!! Do you want me to try to save anything? I have Gordi."

"No, no, there is nothing I want. DON'T GO BACK IN THERE!!"

I could see that the fire had not made it to the other side of the house, or down the stairs, so I ran into the fire-free side and grabbed my computer and a precious handmade brass box the size of a thimble that held a memento of deep spiritual significance to our family and gave the rest to God. Waiting the ten minutes for the fire truck, attempting patience in the midst of heart-racing panic, I struggled to maintain some kind of even breathing while every cell in my body was reaching out to urge those missing firemen with their cooling, water gushing hoses and ladders to HURRY!

My neighbor, Rob, came over carrying a glass of cabernet, and we walked to the back of the house where flames were now licking the siding, reaching out the upstairs window, charring the surrounding walls and illuminating the attic ceiling. My mouth

was too dry to take in more than a sip of wine—but I was deeply comforted by his gesture and found relief in sharing some gallows humor and telling the story for the first time of my fiery surprise at the top of the stairs.

We hurried back to the front of the house as we heard the sweet sound of the very efficient and professional North Myrtle Beach Fire Department fire engine now closing in on our address. Jason was the first to find me. "So glad you are HERE!" I tried not to shout or throw myself in his arms. "The fire is upstairs in the back room!!"

Jason calmly and decisively walked to the back of the house while I tried not to tell him how to do his job. A Minnie-Mouse version of my voice squeaked out, wanting him to see how urgent this was.

"I know, Ma'am," Jason said calmly. "I just have to make sure of what we are going into."

Of course, it was **his** life at stake. I told myself to step back and let the man do his job.

Finally, in what was probably only a few minutes, he and his buddy were in full gear with masks and helmets, dragging four-inch-diameter hoses into my house and up my stairs. I noticed they had little Batman and Robin action figures glued to the top front of their helmets.

"I guess you can't take the boy out of the man," I mused.

Later I learned that the plastic figure has a lower melting point than their helmets and facemasks, so if the figure melts, the partners would know the heat behind the wall they were breaking through was above 1000, and they would need to duck below the heat. Their Batman and Robin came out headless.

More firemen arrived, fire and water restoration reps arrived with their business cards, along with a crowd of other firetruck chasers. Friends arrived and husband, Bill, arrived with bottles of wine and glasses. I reached for him and he for me and we embraced, sharing an understanding that was beyond words.

My friend, Horst, sat in the car with Gordi, our dog who chants Om with our yoga class and loves everyone. Horst wanted to make sure Gordi was not scared, and he knew we had our attention on other things.

We all stood in my front yard watching the coordinated force of firemen rushing into my house with fire hoses, chainsaws and tarps. (Yes, they are so thoughtful they try to cover the downstairs furniture to save it from all the water!)

The young fellow carrying the chainsaw paused and said, "Ma'am, I'm sorry, but I have to cut a hole in your floor to let the water out."

"Of course, do what you have to do!" My heart responded to yet another large act of kindness and civility in the midst of the chaos.

They were blasting water at the now-flaming collection of over 2000 volumes of children's books, many of them signed; my son's framed lithographs; my carefully filed and collected professional notes, notebooks, and videos from 40 years as an educator; and over 46 years of personal and travel journals neatly arranged by year. Strangely, I had already given it all up. In the wonderful clarity of how quickly the elements of air, fire, and water came together to transform my material possessions, I had a chance to let it go...or maybe to realize, it was never that important.

As I sipped wine with my husband and friends, we toasted our abundance in the midst of losses. I felt no anxiety over the material objects that were surely a charred sodden muddle, even as the next few days uncovered how much truly was lost, as well as the miracles of the art and treasures that were saved. (As we made our way through the fire damage three days after the fire, we discovered that all of my son's lithographs were safe, having been covered with sodden insulation when the fireman pulled down walls. One journal that recorded a priceless time and which I felt a pang over losing, oddly appeared in the middle of the floor in the charred room from whence it came.)

Where did this calm come from? I told my husband, Bill, a few mornings after the fire, that it was almost like being dead and having the chance to watch my life as if I were hovering above it and seeing it unfold as in a movie. I had a sense of detachment and objectivity that allowed for a deeper level of reflection.

There is deep wisdom captured best in St. Theresa of Avila's prayer: Let nothing disturb you, let nothing affright you. All things are passing, God never changeth. Moments like these—events like a fire or disaster propelling instant change-- are crucibles for the lesson in that prayer. Lessons for living in the sense that all those "things"--even precious books -- take time and our valuable "life units" of energy in multiple ways. Time to know what books to order—that is delight—one push of the Amazon-buy-with-one-click button and they arrive on my doorstep. Time to read and savor those books--also a delight—and then find a place for them—which is no longer easy in my house, full of burgeoning bookshelves often stuffed two or three books deep. Then, eventually, when needed downsizing arrives, time to decide what to do with all those thousands of volumes on wall-to-wall bookshelves. No longer a problem when, Poof! Solution given in a 30-minute house fire.

Immediately after the fire, friends asked me, "How are you staying so calm?" I suppose it could be that we have excellent insurance which paid for removing all debris, cleaning and restoring our material goods, and could even replace everything that was lost. That certainly helped --though my husband and I occasionally joke that if the fire had burned the entire house, we could have rebuilt a much simpler, much

smaller house and been free of all this abundance of space requires.

I was rather amazed at my attitude toward the losses. I spent a few hours wearing a gas mask and trying to rescue some of my favorite books by authors such as Cynthia Rylant, Jane Yolen, and that mysterious Chris Van Allsburg. A few favorites were put in boxes to try to clean for schools, and some to try to salvage for my personal dwindled collection, saved to read to future potential grandchildren. Dear friends and I sat for hours in my driveway, equipped with Q-tips, latex gloves, and paper towels soaked in alcohol, lovingly wiping and re-reading each rescued book to remove soot and smoke damage, enjoying our time together chatting and appreciating each unique treasure as well as the treasure of our company.

I took odd joy in the dumpster we had outside where we threw not only fire-damaged items but other unused and no longer useful items. (My husband and I long for one to be permanently installed to make excess removal an easy task.)

Where did this calm and detachment come from?

LIFE LESSONS FROM JENNY

I had some time to practice four months earlier when I helped my dearest friend of 44 years pass after a return of cancer. Jenny and I had been roommates in graduate school in Atlanta in the 70's, attended each other's weddings and helped each other through our divorces. She was the godmother of my four children and we spent every Christmas eve enjoying Jenny's childlike joy in giving all of us silly toys—light-up fingertips, impossibly huge chocolate bars, basketball hoops to wear on our heads and try to score, all after wine had been served. We celebrated each other's second and lasting marriages and made it a ritual to go out to birthday lunches, even if we had to wait a month to celebrate; we never missed one.

Before Jenny was released from the hospital, friends cleaned her house where she had stashes of gifts for others and quirky items stacked in the room where her hospital bed would need to find a space. There we brought her home to spend her last days. We prayed with her, sang for her and helped her let go of each of us and her precious husband as we let go of her body. Along with other friends we created a celebration of her life, and friends from near and far crowded our large house and waited for room to view the slide show pictures of Jenny, showing her with those people and places she loved--always with her signature smile, often accompanied by a startling life affirming laugh.

Months after she passed, I asked her husband if he had any of her jewelry left that I had given her over the years, thinking her two god-daughters might like a token. He had given it all to charity. It was easy to let that go, too. It is really just "stuff" that is amusing and often pretty to look at in the moment but in the end, it is just stuff. Jenny

helped me know that nothing of value is ever lost. I have her with me whenever I remember her.

Seeing what really mattered to Jenny as we created her memorial and seeing what really mattered in our relationship must have helped me be ready for the sense of calm after the fire. It could be that age-old wisdom finally burned through all the attachment to stuff and clarified my ability to see that this oddly packaged fiery "gift of God" will free up my time and clear up my own clutter so I can spend more of my life units on the Beauty I love. My job then is to discern and pay attention to what that is.

Where does the calm come from? It could be that the work I have been doing with my life for the last twenty years, consciously allowing myself to attend and to host Circle of Trust retreats set me up to pay attention to what it means to continue to seek joy –to be present to what matters in my life and to spend time on what matters. It is not a goal; it is a practice that is never ending.

THE PHOENIX

A month before the fire I made a trip to New York City to help my daughter, Margaret, move into her new apartment near Morningside Park. We visited the Cathedral of St. John the Divine to see the installation of the six-ton sculpture of the Phoenix by artist, Xu Bing. He created this magnum opus from trash and debris from the construction sites across the rapidly changing urban landscape of Beijing. The monstrous structure hung as if suspended from the thousands of points of light the artist used to outline and illuminate the Phoenix as it rose into the dark-vaulted ceiling over the main cathedral floor. The Phoenix has always been one of my favorite mythological symbols of rebirth and the strength and beauty that rises from seeming destruction.

Kabir told us, "If you have not lived through something, it is not true." The truth of the Phoenix that has risen from the fire and from my life can be glimpsed in small "phoenix" moments I take time in this writing to contemplate. The growing sense of moving toward an undivided life where I return consciously or unconsciously to the question, "What is the action, the thought, the attitude most in line with my inner knowing and the truth my life has revealed to me about taking joy?" You always have a choice—to turn to the ashes or toward the phoenix that rises and is suspended and illumined by infinite points of light.

Four months after the fire I called my 97-year-old father as I always did the morning we were scheduled to pick him up for our weekly Sunday dinner. There was no answer after three tries. We found that he had passed peacefully, like the gentleman he always was, fully dressed with shoes on ready and waiting to go to dinner. We took time to celebrate his life in all the communities he and I touched. My four children left their busy lives and flew in from California and New York and North Carolina to savor and celebrate their grandfather, adding their full participation in his life's celebration.

They each took what they might need or want to remember him. My son, William, wanted his deer-antler pocketknife, Mikey his carefully organized tool bench that he used to repair and build personal mundane treasures for each of us, Margaret took the teacups and etched wine glasses, Daniel made careful selections from his extensive vinyl music albums. It was easy to call Goodwill and Caring Transitions and let them find a use for the rest. I kept his sextant, which he used to navigate by the stars.

Yesterday, calculating mileage for my state job, my worst math word problem ever, I needed a beauty break so I walked up to re-shelve some children's picture books. Touching my old friends, including Cynthia Rylant's *Scarecrow* and Jane Yolen's *Owl Moon,* I noticed my hands were dusted lightly with soot. These beloved book friends were among those that lived through the fire. I imaginatively leapt forward to the stories I would tell my future grandchildren when their fingers came away with a little smudge.

It came to me that this is a defining story that we will tell over and over in our family... A story of survival and wholeness.

Maybe if we see our life story as an allegory—the real meaning hidden in plain sight between the lines—and don't take our own life too literally or too seriously, it will reveal the overwhelming love and light that shine through even the moments that seem darkest. I choose to craft my life around the phoenix and not the ashes.

Author's Note: Life units is a concept I use to think of the amount of physical, mental and emotional energy it takes to do any act. It often helps me make a more mindful choice. I first heard the term when I was working with a mediator to help resolve a legal dispute. In trying to settle the case, the mediator explained that we could try to gain more material restitution over time, but should consider not just the money, but also the number of life units it would take. We might end up with more in terms of financial gain, but did we want to spend the time and energy to be involved with this person and the negative situation over an extended period of time? How many life units would that involve? We don't often think of the time and energy something takes but rather in terms of monetary value, when in reality what is more important is time and how you choose to use it.

Dr. Janet Files has facilitated retreats and workshops that combine Courage principles and writing for a variety of audiences including teachers, hospice workers, and the Franciscan Sisters of Mercy. What travels with her from her Courage facilitator role enlivens the work Janet does for the SC Department of Education with literacy coaches and teachers. She facilitates Circle of Trust retreats using writing as a practice to deepen inner knowing and with her colleague, Dr. Sara Sanders, has written the book, *Writing Along the Mőbius Strip: A Practice to Set the Heart at Rest.* She would like to hear from you and welcomes any writing you are willing to share (janet.files@gmail.com)

A Tale of Two Watches

By Dianne Baker

They tell the best of time, they tell the worst of time!

I own two analog wristwatches that each has rather unique properties, making them far more than simple timepieces. Each watch causes me to pause and reflect, and to open my heart and mind to how I mark time and to the choices I have with the moments, hours, and days that make up my life. One watch is special because of its deliberate design; one I treasure because of an accidental flaw which has come to be a wonderful gift! Let me tell the tale of these two accessories, and the ways they cause me to reflect, with the urgings of the timeless poet, Mary Oliver, on what I plan to do with my "one wild and precious life."

In August of 2009, I traveled with two women friends to the YMCA of the Rockies to attend a five-day Mindfulness Meditation Retreat, which was to have been led by the venerable Vietnamese Buddhist monk and author, Thich Nhat Hanh. At the first gathering of nearly 1200 eager beings, we were told by one of the nuns that Thay (an affectionate name meaning teacher in Vietnamese) was in the hospital in Philadelphia and would not be able to join us for the retreat. The leadership of the event was to

be offered by monks and nuns who had been with Thich Nhat Hanh for years and would be an opportunity for all of us to practice "non-attachment" and letting go of expectations. We were to experience the "continuation of Thay" through their sharing of the Dharma talks and meditation leadership.

In that moment, time stood still. I was really only in attendance because I longed to experience this great master in person; to have the physical experience of being at the feet of someone humble, great, wise and "famous." Another of my traveling friends was also very disappointed. The retreatants were offered that they could have their fees refunded, if they wished to leave. Having driven from Winnipeg in Manitoba for over 20 hours, none of our small cohort intended to depart. So each of us went within our own hearts to "come into the present moment" and simply accept this new now, to enter with freshness and beginner's mind.

The retreat was glorious, powerful, moving, and intimate! Can I call it intimate when there were over 1100 people there? Yes! The silence and the loving regard shared in walking past one another, the intention of creating peace together, felt intimate. I hoped to bring some tangible reminders of the sense of presence and peace into my own life. In the retreat's bookshop, alongside posters, cards and mindfulness bells, I found a watch. The minute hand had the word "It's" written on it, and instead of numerals to mark 3, 6, 9 and 12, was the word "NOW" written in Thay's calligraphy. Thich Naht Hanh's puckish humor had been applied to the development of this watch, so that when anyone asks the wearer what time it is, the person can reply "It's NOW"!

In the spring of 2009, I read *Let Your Life Speak* for the first time. I was deeply moved by Parker J. Palmer's words. I was especially touched by Parker's reflections on depression, as "the noonday demon" has been my own traveling companion in life. I recognized my own inner journey in his words: *"I NOW know myself to be a person of weakness and strength, liability and giftedness, darkness and light. I know that to be whole means to reject none of it but to embrace all of it."* The lessons from a mindfulness meditation practice remind me to value the present moment and to relieve myself from the judgment of comparing myself to others, from living in the anxious place of tomorrow's worry and the acidic rumination of yesterday's errors.

The value of listening to my LIFE and to my moments, supported by mindfulness meditation, brought me to a great appreciation of awareness of "Now," not as imperative or demand, but as presence. This was part of what fueled my interest in attending the meditation retreat in Colorado. As I read more of Parker J. Palmer's work, I began to unearth a sincere longing for community that lived an awareness of integrity, authenticity and presence, in service of the soul's truth and in the value of live encounters with other beings, with our earth and to build sustainable, loving

relationships. I have had moments of this reality in some church experiences of both worship and of justice work, and I knew that it must be possible to nurture this way in more eclectic settings.

I sought out a retreat close enough to drive to (Minneapolis) and began to explore what Circles of Trust meant in "real time." Reading *A Hidden Wholeness* convinced me that skilled leadership, strong boundary markers (group guidelines), evocative questions and generous silence would offer safety and beauty that made shy and tender souls ready to emerge and be heard into speech. This first retreat experience, in a lovely center surrounded by beauty, and with ample time to touch the earth and listen to my heart, felt like a taste of home. I returned to my community and my workplace nourished, renewed, aware of a new community of seekers, and eager to learn more. By the end of 2011, I had begun my journey toward Courage & Renewal facilitation. I lived the experience of embracing the rightness of time, *kairos*, while attending to the marking of days and hours, *chronos*.

When I live knowing "It's NOW," and when I lead from that space as a facilitator, I honor the Courage & Renewal touchstones which support safe community in Circles of Trust, and I won't risk falling into fixing or saving. I commit to "being present as fully as possible," to deep listening that makes space for others to speak their truth. I can enjoy the silence and hold the space for silence, knowing that each participant is capable of receiving what he or she needs from the space, in "the now" we embrace together in these retreats.

My mindfulness watch reminds me of the joy-filled choice to be open-hearted, to welcome surprise and wonder and to trust the inner teacher in me and in others. Courage & Renewal work has opened my heart and mind to the great value of setting apart time to nourish my soul so that my work in the world has compassion, and authenticity. As a participant, I always find that having this retreat from the regular patterns of busy-ness and engagement allows me to drop down into a trusting space of rest, reflection, listening to my inner teacher, hearing the work of integrity engaged by the souls gathered together. There is a special quality of timelessness and spaciousness that pervades a well-designed retreat. Even when, as a facilitator, I need to be aware of the timing around the arc of a retreat, navigating shared leadership and mealtimes, and the group's need for silence, I still find a sense of ease in letting time flow within the boundaries of a good plan. Freedom in the structure, openness within well-defined boundaries: these are some of the paradoxes that hold space well for the soul's work.

My other watch which I want to introduce you to offers me a playful metaphor for the power of retreat. This other watch looks like a run of the mill timepiece; a silver body

and linked bracelet, a white face with gold accents and numbers. In my line of work, I need a simple watch to track the length of my appointment sessions with clients, one that I can read with ease with a simple glance down at my wrist. I have never liked big clunky watches with multiple functions. I just want to be able to read the time at a glance! I bought the least expensive, sturdiest, plainest watch I could find. I did not need this feature, but the watch has a calendar dial; you know, the kind that counts the days of the month, but doesn't indicate the month, and needs to be adjusted between months that end in 30 days and months that have 31 days (you have to pay special attention at the end of February). That amount of fiddling, I could handle.

I bought the watch in January, 2011, and got used to its weight and style. Every morning, I strapped it to my wrist, and carried on with my day. In the first week of February, I was writing a check at a fundraising event and didn't have my datebook with me, and I couldn't see a calendar on the wall in the room I was in. So, I checked my watch calendar for the first time, and saw, to my great puzzlement, that the date was the 35th! I blinked several times and looked again. Yup, 35! As I twisted the dial it counted up, 36, 37, 38, 39.... And then to my great delight, turned over to 00.

I realized that there must be a tooth on an inner cog missing on the calendar dial, surely a defect that might be worthy of getting a refund... and then I thought, "If it is January 35th, no one can find me! I am in an alternate dimension! How freeing!" I decided to keep the watch, embracing its quirk, and allowing myself to relish the oddity for a private giggle now and then.

In my facilitation, several times the dates have slipped across the threshold of a month, and my watch's peculiarity has been observed by me, and then shared, as a grace note, with the gathered group. For each of us, on retreat, we can choose to be in an "alternate dimension of time," in a space set apart from the everyday. We each can choose how deeply to embrace the silence and safety, and to allow the boundaries of the retreat space to extend to the edges of our awareness of the world beyond the edges of our circle. I see people on retreat who hold this space for themselves and others generously, and I see others who are battling with the frequent call of internet, email and messages from home or work. Technology allows us to be, at least digitally, in two places at once, and this seems a manifestation of the challenge to be fully present.

I like imagining that when I am on retreat I am in a separate reality, where time serves the group, rather than being the master of the process. In planning, spaciousness and flow and silence are as important as content. On the 37th of any given month, time expands without the pressure of performance, productivity or evaluation. On the

34th day of April, a live encounter with the land, the trees, and the heart of Rumi, or Wendell Berry, or Margaret Atwood or Chuang Tzu, is a time of alchemy and wonder when one's inner teacher can whisper without interruption.

In *A Hidden Wholeness* Parker writes with clarity and humor about "schedules that possess simple grace," schedules that honor three principles: slow down, do more with less, and pay attention to rhythm. My odd little wristwatch offers me a monthly reflection on being spacious with time, so that I may know a schedule with "simple grace."

I also love that it is the missing cog that has given life to this watch's wise ways. Embracing this unique brokenness allows me the grace to know my own wholeness, and to be more conscientious of creating schedules in retreat that allow others to encounter their own hidden wholeness. Being a wounded healer moves me to a place of less judgment, and invites me to "turn to wonder" at myself, at others, when the going gets rough.

Often, Courage & Renewal retreats are held in places that are imbued with a certain spirit of mystery; magical places, where the veil between the physical and the spiritual are thin, where we walk with a clear awareness of the deep traditions of sacred unity of the human world, the creaturely and natural world. Thin places have a feel that we have come to trust as sacred and nourishing. Thin places are also those places where the sense of time shifts; we become aware that we are in a place where the division between the temporal and the eternal is an illusion. We engage in reflection that takes us to the essence of what it means to be human, and to be a part of the process of making meaning that our species has been puzzling over since we developed language. Our retreats invite us to see ourselves as interwoven with all beings and creatures that inhabit this planet, made from the same elements that have existed since the universe took form. Both figuratively and literally, we are of the eternal, and we are of this unique moment. We are here now! What a miracle and gift. In reminding one another of the boundaries that mark the safety and inclusion of our Circles of Trust we agree to "be here, to be as present, in the present, as possible." We engage "third things" from our literary and poetic ancestors and from contemporary sources. We encounter the wisdom of nature by being in the presence of teachers who speak to us in the languages of millennial wisdom; ancient stones, old growth trees, rivers that run in channels carved into the bones of the earth. These teachers, both temporal and eternal, call us home to our true selves. Time, although a human construct, nevertheless is present to us as we witness the turning of the seasons, the circling of the sun, and the aging of our own bodies. We learn to treasure the gift of this one life as we walk our life journey, and the time taken in a generously,

spaciously-planned retreat can offer us the gift of doing one thing at a time, with our whole attention, in a community of companions.

Since January of 2015, I have been fortunate to be included in the Kirkridge Courage Fellowship with other Courage & Renewal facilitators from across North America. Gathering seasonally over a two-year period in the surroundings of the Kirkridge Retreat Center has been a deeply transformative time for me. I delight in coming to know this landscape as a "thin place," where the wisdom of ancestors is present, is remembered and honored; where the geography speaks of the deep connections to other landscapes, through the shaping of tectonic plate movement and glacial scraping (eternal time); and through the movement of people over thousands of years and over recent times, the Lenape people, the indigenous people of this territory, the connection to the Iona community in Scotland, the early days of creating safe and inclusive space for the LGBTQ communities, for social activists and spiritual seekers. The Kirkridge Fellowship itself has marked a rhythm of gathering in every season of the year, allowing us to see this lovely place change its face and voice, through snow and ice, heat and humidity, autumn color and the abundance of bird and frog life in summer. We have come to know this place and our circle with the trust that forms through repeated encounter, deepening from politeness and kindness to true empathy and love, shaped through puzzle, chafing, conflict and acceptance. This form of being together, in my experience, prepares me to return to my home and my work more joyfully committed to living undivided "in my one wild and precious life."

Two timepieces enrich my life: one designed with a message of invitation to embrace the present moment, one lusciously flawed that creates an awareness that spaciousness is available to me (and to others) when I accept my own woundedness and set time apart to listen to my inner teacher. Courage & Renewal retreats are gracious and nurturing spaces and times to be present in the now, in time set apart from the routines. Courage & Renewal work, at its core, equips us to know our souls' urgings, and to return to our work reinvigorated, to live undivided lives.

These are the best of times, reminding us each day to live wholeheartedly and courageously, even when faced with the worst of times.

Dianne Baker is a therapist, mother, mediator, singer, and peace worker. She has been a Courage & Renewal Facilitator since 2012. Dianne finds joy in friendship, in her garden, as a jewelry maker and recently as a Full Voice Coach. Dianne shares life with her partner, Jim Hatherly, and has roots in both Manitoba and British Columbia in Canada. She invites you to email emergingwholeness@gmail.com

Humpty Dumpty Revisited

By Caroline Fairless

I grew up on Thornton W. Burgess' *Mother West Wind "Why" Stories* and *Mother West Wind "How" Stories.* In volume after volume of short stories, Burgess always constructed his parables in the same way: *How Howler the Wolf Got His Name; How Lightfoot the Deer Learned to Jump; How the Eyes of Old Mr. Owl Became Fixed.* It was Thornton W. Burgess who taught me to read, and it was he who gave me a lifelong love of reading.

The parable that should be here today, however, is not. So, with apology to Thornton W. Burgess:

How White People Lost Their Privilege

A long long long ever so long time ago, maybe as long as 200,000 years ago (depending on which sources . . .), the earliest of humans to be identified as homo sapiens inhabited what we now know as the great continent of Africa. They lived together and shared what they had. They helped one another build their shelters, discern and gather edible plants, hunt their meat. They looked alike and their skin was dark.

One small band, for unknown reasons – perhaps its members were convinced that they didn't have enough; perhaps they were the first

explorers – left their community to wander and fend for themselves. The group grew and grew in number, and split again, and again, and again. Others, too, left the land of their origins. Some of them traveled north and east, some south and east. Others traveled north and west. As they traveled, they lost memory of their origins, and grew inward, engaging only those who looked like themselves and thought like themselves.

The ones who traveled north and west grew tall and mean, arrogant; they also grew lighter skin. White skin was good, that's how they knew their privilege. As such, white and privileged, they had an obligation to assimilate lesser groups, to raise them up to proper standards. But first, they had to colonize them, and they went at it with great fervor.

They colonized lands already settled, and made the inhabitants their slaves. They used their slaves to get rich, and richer, and richer still. They treated the lands and the creatures in the same way they treated the people. They were builders of empires, and nothing could stop them, not even Old Mother Nature.

Old Mother Nature heard the cries of her creatures. She heard the cries of the land and the trees. She sent winds and fire, floods. She made the lands move and the mountains explode. She warned the People of Privilege and warned them again, but they paid no heed.

Finally the People of Privilege went too far. They used up the people and they used up the land. They put sicknesses in the waters and in the air, and no one – not two-leggeds, or four-leggeds, winged, or aquatic - could breathe, or drink, or eat. The People of Privilege could not fix what they had broken.

Old Mother Nature stripped them of their privilege and their vast wealth and power. All that remained was their whiteness. They grew smaller, and smaller, ever so small.

"Please," they begged. "Without our privilege, and with only our whiteness, what will we do?"

*"You will go on your knees to the peoples who've **not** lost their memory, and you will ask them to teach you. And if they say no – which they might - then you have to travel deep deep inside, to where your own memory lives. You will have to do that anyway."*

"But who are these people?"

"You will recognize them. They are the people whom you expelled from their own lands. They are the people whom you enslaved. They are the people you scorned, the people whose cultures you stole. But you couldn't steal their spirit, and you couldn't steal their memory.

"But as for you, your empires have crumbled, you have lost your vast riches. You have compromised your power. You will remain small and white. Others will tend to the healing of the lands and the waters, the air and all who live in them. Others will tend to the healing of the forests, the mountains, and the oceans. The forests, the mountains, and the oceans will heal themselves. In time, perhaps, they will teach you how to live."

SHRINE TO AMERICAN DEMOCRACY?

It is referred to as the Shrine to American Democracy. A more appropriate name for Mount Rushmore might be the Shrine to American Colonization, or maybe The Celebration of Manifest Destiny or the love-child of the Doctrine of Discovery. I've never been to Mount Rushmore but I have seen *North by Northwest* more than once, and so have some sense of what it means to carve a mountain in the likenesses of the four men whose dual roles were to preserve the Republic and continue the expansion westward. To carve a mountain is no less a heinous act than to remove one, and to carve a mountain in the likenesses of these particular four Presidents adds to the desecration.

The Black Hills, site of Mount Rushmore, once belonged to the Lakota Sioux. Some would argue the land still does, and they would be in the right. The Lakota consider this land their spiritual center, "the home of our heart, and the heart of our home." A Lakota story of origin tells of their people's emergence – at the dawn of time – from deep within the mountains, so intimate a connection do the Lakota have with the sacred Black Hills.

They fought the U.S. military to hold onto their land, and from a place of strength signed the Treaty of Laramie in 1868, guaranteeing Lakota sovereignty in perpetuity. Perpetuity lasted for all of six years, until General George Custer came sniffing for gold, and found it.

As I have learned to read this story through the Lakota lens, I can feel my heart breaking again, and at last it plunges me into the deep waters of grief. The breaking open has to do not only with the facts of the truly despicable actions of the U.S. Federal Government, but even more with the realization that I have long stayed asleep to the

many moving pieces of this history, stayed asleep to what this self-congratulatory behemoth carved into the side of a sacred mountain represents to the people from whom the land was stolen and desecrated.

Writing for me often takes an unexpected turn, particularly when I am writing about what baffles me. Sometimes I follow it, sometimes not. This time there has been no such choice, because some months ago I simply stopped writing; I couldn't go any further. It took me two months just to make the decision to dig deeply into this unpredictable territory into which I'd been dropped. During these months I could not write, such was my resistance. Before I could continue, I have had first to face into other kinds of truths.

Russell Means says, *"The Black Hills are not for sale."*

Trebbe Johnson, speaking of a northwestern clear-cut, says, "*Gaze even here.*"

And Ta-Nehisi Coates tells his son, "*You must never look away from this.*"

The Lakota Sioux, the Black Hills of South Dakota, Ta-Nehisi Coates, and a clear-cut forest are on the receiving end of – I want to say unprecedented, but that is not even close to the truth – violence. You must never look away from this. I am struggling to understand what these admonitions mean for me.

From Jeanette Armstrong, Okanagan writer and speaker, who wants to "Okanaganize everyone" and who helps me remember that the Holy Land is the land under my feet, to Ta-Nehisi Coates who tells me that white people ("or at least those who believe they are white") are white by "modern invention," that "democracy is a forgiving God and America's heresies – torture, theft, enslavement – are so common among individuals and nations that none can declare themselves immune," I know that it is time to face into my own blindness.

I have lived under the illusion that I am and have been awakening into consciousness, and I suppose I have. But my reading and conversations over the last three years are giving me a different message, suggesting mine has been a false sense of awakening; the haze was, and no doubt is, still with me. My question is, what do I do with this? Who will talk to me? There are so many things I will never know. What do I do with this? I have no answers.

The grief has been raw and powerful, a seeming bottomless well, which has left me vulnerable and fragile, and, ironically, resolved. It's the grief of waking up to the real meaning and impact of white privilege. It's the grief of what white privilege has cost everyone, has cost all life: the land, the waters, humankind, and other-than-humankind. It's the grief of treaties made and broken. The grief of promises not kept, of greed, of corporate violence, violence of all kinds. The grief of how casually and routinely a Black

life can be stolen by a policeman's fear and hatred. It's the grief of acknowledgement of the gap between what I have thought was my level of consciousness and the blinders I still wear. The grief of shame. It's the grief of being able to enlarge my own footprint whenever it's convenient for me, even as I preach a different challenge. And, of course, it's the grief of "Gaze even here" and "You must never look away from this."

The Black Hills are not for sale.

It's the grief of yearning... Of elusive and heated – even dangerous - conversations in which I don't know how to participate without intruding as a white person. It's the grief of not knowing how to be invited in without inviting myself, or, if inviting myself, doing so without intrusion or worse – cultural appropriation. It's the grief of reading Ta-Nehisi Coates, in a letter to his son (*Between the World and Me*, 2015), tell of an interview with a well-known journalist who kept asking him the wrong questions, and Coates having to tell his son that it was he himself who had failed. The grief of knowing that my questions would have been no better. It's the grief of knowing I am not yet trustworthy in so many ways. It's the grief of having to apply the word "colonizer" to myself.

It's the grief of the woundedness of the land and the waters, the literal extinction of exquisite beauty – four-legged, two-legged, finned, winged, branched, flowered. The grief – I perceive it as visceral pain – of clear-cut forests and vast West Virginia mountaintops simply bulldozed into the valleys.

Above all, it's the grief of knowing that the white privileged will not likely willingly move aside for the leaders and healers essential for this time.

Over the summer, as I was driving home on a dark rainy night, this grief manifested itself in a riotous parade of hundreds of thumb-sized wood frogs doomed on their journey across a macadam road. That night, weeping without even knowing why, I stopped my car, leaving its four-ways blinking, and gently nudged every frog to the other side of the road. The mile and a half took me nearly two hours.

How do I gaze on this?

I see myself as a Humpty Dumpty figure with a different and as yet unsung ending. Cracked, bruised, torn apart, heartbroken, vulnerable, but still here. All the King's horses and all the King's men couldn't put Humpty Dumpty back together again. This is the truth; it was precisely the King's horses and the King's men who couldn't do it. Nor can they do it now. This is the truth for me as well. White privilege cannot accomplish it; white privilege can only hold on to what it knows. Knowing this, just this, is a blessing for me, however. I have no words for this humility and hope, only questions.

Dr. Sherry K. Watt, in *Designing Transformative Multicultural Initiatives*, speaks of the process of deconstruction, a process which must take place before anything else can. I think of it as the essential art of "un-becoming" before it is possible to "re-become." Watt's language helps me contextualize the grief of these years and to understand that deconstruction and reconstruction are lifelong processes... Once begun, never finished.

Statement of fact: this painful and essential process of my own awakening would not have been possible outside the safe and challenging embrace of the Kirkridge Courage Fellowship. Although I would not have envisioned this "rising up from slumber" as a desirable outcome, the irony is not lost on me that what has "become of me" is the direct embodiment of the intention I offered into the universe as I groped with the first awkward attempts to articulate the required Plan for Still Learning.

I wrote this: *When this invitation plopped itself into my inbox, I felt the quickening of my heart in such a way as tells me this is right, this is the next part of my journey. This quickening doesn't come without its fair measure of fear. I have said, and mean it, that I like my "little" life. But I know as well I am reaching for something, and I haven't the courage or the capability to accomplish it by myself.*

I wrote this: *I have known for some time that the next level of my writing requires a new partner for the intellectual part of me, a partnership that I haven't yet dared. I have been writing from my thoughts and ideas alone. The silent "not-yet" partner is my deep visceral creative force which I've not allowed to show up much. I have a shadow need to control creative outcomes (that's an oxymoron) – and because the visceral deep down force is not under my willful control, I rarely dare to access it.*

And I wrote this: *In the writing driven by my intellect, I have been able to slide around my fear of "surprises," by keeping a pretty tight rein on my direction.*

My cerebral function usually works overtime, not so the case with my "entanglement" function. A shadow need to control outcomes is not conducive to collaboration. So, I can write the following statement, and know the truth of it, with embarrassingly little engagement: *Human social justice and environmental (ecological) justice efforts must become entangled; neither can be accomplished without the other. The same is true of human diversity and biodiversity. The rationale, by now, I am hoping has become clear. It is all of a piece. Every life form on this living planet, whether animate or inanimate, is interconnected and interdependent.*

Don Santos Wilca, Peruvian shaman, writes "*. . . all who live in this* pasha *(earth) are persons: the stone, the soil, the plants, the water, the hail, the wind, the diseases, the sun, the moon, the stars, we are all one.*" As I bob up and down in these waters of grief, this statement, true all along, rings with a transfigured pulse and heartbeat.

There are new questions catching hold of me: what are the ethical and spiritual dimensions of continuing to work solo? Can I continue to do this and make it work? Might I be able to learn to collaborate? These questions and so many others cause whiplash! Although I would like to take credit for this inner movement, I can't. The soul of the universe has called me. How can I say no to that? Life is richer as my eyes - which I already assumed were open - begin in truth to open, no matter the pain of it.

Statement of fact: my ongoing awakening would not be possible outside the safe and challenging embrace of the Kirkridge Courage Fellowship. This sense of being held is what allows me to test my still drying wings, my fledgling wings, and I try these wings out by reflecting on the spiritual dimension of third party voting:

As an Episcopal priest (retired), conservationist, and unapologetic progressive, I hear a lot of comments about a Green party vote in November, some of them hostile. My step-daughter asks, *"How can you say mine is a throwaway vote?"* She says, *"I should not feel guilty about voting my heart. I have a moral obligation to vote my conscience."*

The political dimension is fairly straightforward.

The spiritual dimension is more complex.

The United States has always lifted up its individualism, a misguided pride with spiritual consequences. Perhaps there was a time, although it could be otherwise argued, when individualism was an asset, but we are not living in a time such as that. This era cries out for collaboration, cooperation, and partnership. Against that tapestry of the collective citizenry, the personal "I" or "me" is indicative of white privilege. Privileged white people get to vote according to their own self-interest, whether it is economic, ecological, educational, or anything else. The spiritual dimension, however, is about community.

There are two African words which belong in this conversation. One is *ubuntu*. I first heard the word from the lips of the Rev. Michael Battle in a keynote talk at a summer symposium. *Ubuntu – I am because we are*. It is a word of the spirit; we create each other; we belong to each other; we achieve ourselves by sharing ourselves with others. At Nelson Mandela's funeral, President Barack Obama remarked that Mandela was the personification of the word.

The other word is *kwanele*, which, translated from Zulu, means *it is enough*. Like *ubuntu, kwanele* is a word of the spirit. Anything more than enough is in excess; anything more than enough is greed. Together these concepts of respect, dignity, and kindness needed to have formed the spiritual bedrock of this 2016 election. It did not happen.

The tenor of our current political conversation has sickened our country; we seem to have stepped out of our collective soul. We can do better (maybe), I think, if we can release the fear and anger enough to remember what this is about: it's about the collective soul, the world's soul; it's about whole-hearted-ness; it's about our rich diversity; and it's about our dream of justice and our struggle for its fruits.

Today, on this side of my Humpty Dumpty life, I know *ubuntu* to embrace not only the human world, but the non-human, and what Frederique Apffel-Marglin calls the *other-than-human world*, referring to the spirits who were here long before we humans were, and who, I believe, are doing their utter overtime best to open our anthropocentric eyes to the concept of kinship all around. What I have called the *cerebral statement* earlier in this chapter, has become richer by far.

My life, as it enters a reconstructive moment, has allowed me another reflection as well: *It is a Thursday late afternoon, September 8, 2016. Thursday is the day I work long distance, by telephone, with my energy healer whose name is Molly. Molly's training in the traditional medicine practices of tribal peoples has been in partnership with Marcellus Bear Heart Williams, elder from the Muskogee Creek Nation; her mentoring continued until his death in 2005. They co-authored* The Wind is My Mother, *first published in 1996.*

As we spend an hour together each week, I in New Hampshire, Molly in Michigan, I realize I have no idea what she is doing or how she is doing it. I know only that mine has always been an earth-based spirituality, and so I am in familiar territory. She has asked me to set an intention for the session into the universe, and I do. I do not share with her its content. During the session a community grows within me, and I myself am holding connection to all the people who have turned to Molly for healing. Like a copse of trees whose roots travel underground to find one another and exchange nutrients, I am connected in that way. Bear Heart is there, along with the millions of people whose lives he touched. It's quite the gathering.

And then I see myself as part of an endless snaking parade of Native American and First Nations men and women and children. We have come to stand alongside the Standing Rock Sioux. Some are on horseback, in full dress regalia, others in T-shirts and jeans, some with drums; a constant ululation fills the air. A flotilla of canoes are arriving. Many white people are marching. We are in cars, on foot, riding motorcycles. We have come to stand with the Protectors of the waters of the Black Hills, to hold fast against the seventeen banks (and then president-elect) financing the Dakota Access Pipeline, to hold fast against the policing of seven states hired to rid the land of its Protectors, policing which takes violence to creative new levels. We have come to hold fast against those who would bulldoze, dig, and lay pipe. Today, on the other end of a telephone line with Molly my healer, my intention into the universe is to find my place within this Protectorate, and it has been realized. In my vision, I am there,

grateful, as all attendant white people are, to stand shoulder to shoulder. I am as white as ever, but the shift in my presence, my resolve, my commitment, and my knowing is palpable. Spiritually, I am about to enter the ***space between*** *where the indigenous and non-indigenous meet.*

At the time of this writing, I am heading back into my circle of the Kirkridge Courage Fellowship for another year. Someday these embodied gatherings will end, I suppose, and I can hardly stand to anticipate it. But ours is a forever fellowship. I imagine that all of us, at the beginning, thought we knew our deepest desires; I know with some certainty that many or all of us had no idea of how our time together would unfold. I stated in my original learning plan that I wanted to know where I fit in this collaborative. I still would like to know that. Perhaps it is still unfolding. What I do know, however, is that my writing has deepened. On the reconstruction side of a significant process of deconstruction, I turn to wonder each time I share an assumption, or a presumption, or even an opinion. What would this look like, I wonder, if I were looking through the lens of an Issac Bailey who writes for Politico, or a David Archambault, witness to the United Nations about the Dakota Access Pipeline, or an Eduardo Hidalgo, the first Mexican non-military secretary of the Navy under the presidency of George H. W. Bush? What would it look like from the perspective of my Texas niece and her wife? What would it look like through the eyes of the thousands of school children across the country walking out of their classrooms to protest the results of the 2016 election?

The Mobius journey that I have long called mine, has added thickness and depth; it has been and continues to be the gift of this Fellowship.

Caroline Fairless is the author of several books, most recently *The Space Between Church & Not-Church ~ A Sacramental Vision for the Healing of Our Planet,* and *The Dance of the Caterpillars ~ In a Time Before Texting.* She blogs at *www.restoringthewaters.com.* Caroline's vision emerges from the partnership of ecology and spirituality, and she would love you to visit her website. She has been a Courage facilitator since 2008, and a member of the Leadership Core of *Courage Earth ~ Awakening to Place.* Ordained in the Episcopal Church in 1989, Caroline is also the founder and co-director of *The Center for Children at Worship,* a non-profit organization whose mission is to provide strategies for multigenerational worship. She and her partner/husband Jim Sims have offered workshops, conferences, and consultations throughout the United States, Canada, and England. Her email is fairlesscaroline@gmail.com

Letting My Life Speak: The Power of Autobiographical Practices

By Patti Smith

"Let your life speak" is an old Quaker saying that often moves in me as my eyes roam me around each new circle of people to reveal connections, as my breath tumbles me inward to touch myself. Longing often whisks me away to distant wishes as I journey along pilgrimage paths, seeking connections to myself, to others and to the practices that will enable me to find both. Parker Palmer reasserts the meaning of letting your life speak in his book of the same name, writing, *"Before you tell your life what you intend to do with it, listen for what it intends to do with you. Before you tell your life what truths and values you have decided to live up to, let your life tell you what truths you embody, what values you represent."*

My life speaks to me through stories, mapping my autobiography across places I have lived, people who have influenced me, and work I have chosen. In the early 90s, I left a position I loved as a Waldorf kindergarten teacher to enter a world mostly unfamiliar to me because I wanted desperately to work in educational settings serving traditionally "underserved" children. I wanted to make creative, play-based early childhood education available to students attending urban public schools. The path to that end required advanced degrees and unique connections into cultural worlds with

which I had limited experience. Daunting, but I somehow made it possible.

I share this particular story here because it has shaped my life for the past 25 years and allows me to illustrate my reasons for advocating autobiographical studies. One day in 1993, in my 42nd year of life, the parent of one of my kindergarten students told me that she had just attended a fascinating meeting about local education. The program was sponsored by a well-known African American professor who just happened to be looking for a research associate. I asked her if she could connect me to him. She did, and I ended up working for this prominent professor in a university setting that provided entry into the world of underserved students I yearned to serve.

We conducted research studies across the country in urban and rural areas as I completed my graduate studies. I found myself positioned perfectly to meet my goals, as I also worked with a group of educators to develop public Waldorf schools, grounded in the thinking of Rudolph Steiner. A challenge in this work, among many, was to find language that moved past traditional Waldorf rhetoric to build bridges with the public educators. Seeking words that acknowledged the importance of the inner life of the teacher, I turned to Parker Palmer's recently published *The Courage to Teach*. His words touched me through their capacity to lift up the ways the inner capacity of a teacher had to be ignited to release the kind of impactful teaching that led to better experiences for children. I decided to attend the facilitator preparation offered by the Center for Courage & Renewal.

Within a short time of leaving my beloved kindergarten, I had let my life speak through the people it allowed me to meet and the places it enabled me to go. Not to say that I didn't have great challenges, successes and disappointments along the way... As a matter of fact, I completely failed at creating the programs I set out to develop for young children. But now, looking back, I see that I was directing myself forward, inner compass steering me.

In my twenties Steiner's philosophy entered my life as I wholeheartedly embraced Waldorf education. In mid-life continued Courage and Renewal facilitation enriched me, leading me to yet another community committed to spiritual development. Both of these communities continue to be significant to me, as I hope I am significant to them.

DAILY PRACTICE FOR LETTING MY LIFE SPEAK

I have come to understand that my efforts to experience the world from a deeply conscious perspective require active inner and outer participation. Just as riding my bicycle every day strengthens my physical body, so too it is necessary to develop inner muscles so I can attend to inner and as well as outer deeds. Rudolf Steiner's

six essential exercises, the Courage touchstones, and autobiographical studies form the basis of my daily practice that allow me to let my life speak.

Steiner's exercises have been the bicycle for my spiritual body (from Michael Lipson's *Stairway of Surprise: Six Steps to a Creative Life;* also see http://tomvangelder.antrovista.com/pdf/basic.pdf):

1. The Control of Thought
Steiner's first exercise has to do with the control of thinking, designed to keep the mind focused to strengthen meditative work. Select a simple object - a pin, a button, a pencil. Try to think about it for five minutes. Think about the way the object is manufactured, how it is used, and its history. Try to be logical and realistic in your thinking. Catch yourself each time your mind wanders and continue thinking about it. Practice it daily, using the same object or new objects.

2. The Control of Will
This exercise strengthens the ability to take deliberate action at one's own willing. Choose a simple action to perform each day at the same time, one that is doable under a variety of circumstances--wiggling your fingers, touching your shoe, walking up a flight of stairs, watering a flower.

3. Equanimity: Balancing the Life of Feelings
The third exercise is the development of balance between joy and sorrow, pleasure and pain, the heights of pleasure and the depths of despair. Try not becoming angry or annoyed, not being anxious or fearful, nor being overcome by joy or sorrow. Feelings should be quietly felt with composure leading to an inner tranquility.

4. Loving: Working with thinking and feeling
This exercise is the development of a positive attitude toward life. Seek to experience the good, praiseworthy, and beautiful in all beings. This develops the ability to be positive toward others rather than critical.

5. Open Mindedness: Working with feeling and willing
For this exercise, confront new experiences with complete open-mindedness. The possibility of something completely new coming into the world must be left open, even if it contradicts existing knowledge and experience.

6. Harmony of thinking, feeling, and willing
After trying the earlier exercises of thinking, will, equilibrium, positivity and tolerance, try them together two or three at a time, in varying combinations until they become natural and harmonious.

My regular practice of these exercises has made me a better Courage facilitator, able to embody the touchstones of our Circles of Trust. The touchstones are the boundary markers for creating a trustworthy space, to help strangers to feel safe with each other during a retreat. (More about these boundary markers may be found in the Stepping Stone in this section.) I have often marveled at the ease with which people agree to these touchstones, and I recognize that these guidelines have helped me to counter my tendency to feel compelled to problem-solve and judge people. They allow me to meet my inner teacher, rooting me in the everyday reality of the soul/spiritual world that is as real as the physical world.

INVITING THE SHY SOUL THROUGH AUTOBIOGRAPHY

Courage Circles acknowledge the shy soul, with an intentional design to support the emergence of that courageous soul in what is too often a harsh world. As facilitators, we invite the soul toward active participation, using poetry, music, and movement, which we call third things, to create the space for souls to emerge. But I worry that without a sustained practice, individual souls will retreat when that group disperses at the end of a Courage retreat.

For me, it is important to acknowledge the necessity to develop a disciplined practice to bear the "coming out of the soul" on a daily basis, an intentional way of breath tumbling me inward to touch myself. I have found autobiographical studies exercises to be the third thing that lets my life speak/shout/whisper to me from the world within and around me.

Life phases occur across time's natural rhythms. Patterns can be observed, like the movement of ocean waves in sets of seven, the trees across four seasons, moons across months to explore Palmer's question, *"Is the life I am living the same as the life that wants to live in me*?" I find Thomas Cole's four paintings from 1842, *The Voyage of Life*, a strong metaphor for explaining autobiographic studies, as the series depicts four phases of human life: childhood, early adulthood, mid-life, and old age (http://www.explorethomascole.org/tour/items/73/series/). Each painting shows a person in a boat on a river with an ethereal being present, as if a guide, in a landscape that beautifully portrays one of the four seasons.

Living into the paintings, I am clear that each phase of life has particular attributes and expectations for us as human beings. In childhood we make our entry to earth, guidance close at hand. In early adulthood, we are launched from the shore, beginning to navigate our particular destiny, birth family bidding farewell from the shore. In mid-life we weather storms, and guidance seems far away and hard to find in the darkness. Then, in old age, the light grows again as we face upward preparing to exit, guidance ahead rather than lost or behind us.

EXERCISES FOR BIOGRAPHICAL WORK

What is my story across these phases? What can I learn from my family, my name, my place in sibling birth order? From the season into which I was born? Is there something significant about my body type, where I lived, my parents' occupations, that I had no parents? What were my birthright gifts and what skills and characteristics were missing from my backpack when I was launched into my earth vessel? When did I leave my family, why did I leave, who were the first adults that influenced me? What interested me? What made me happy/sad? How did my life of work begin? When were my children born? What illnesses have I suffered? When did important people in my life die? Who were colleagues and foes in my professional life?

Dr. Gudrun Burkhard has explored such questions with her patients, using them to inform her medical practice. Her research, documented in *Biographical Work: An Anthroposophical Basis* (2002), shares a series of questions specific to each life phase. These questions offer a doorway into autobiographical studies, work that develops greater consciousness of the everyday events in our lives and their importance.

Exploring connections in my life confirms my belief that it is no accident that I met certain people and made particular choices. Pondering these specific questions, I began to see myself more actively participating in my life. A few exercises are provided here with the hope that there may be meaning for you:

- Mapping the seasons of my life: Identify events, people, and places across various phases. Begin with the seasons, broad strokes across life phases, as represented in the Cole paintings: birth to 21 (youth), 21-42 (early adulthood), 42-63 (mid-life), 63-84+ (old age). What patterns emerge across these four phases of your life? When did particular influential people enter your life and how did the relationships play out over time? Did patterns in illness appear over time? When were career/professional choices made and how did those choices play out? The table on page 39 provides a way you might want to chart these cycles. What key people, places, and events arise in your heart when you let your life speak to you across years? (To learn more about these phases, you may wish to read Signe Eklund Schaefer's *Why on Earth: Biography and the Practice of Human Becoming.)*

Phase	People	Places	Events	Other
Childhood: Birth to 21				
Early adulthood 21-42				
Mid-life 42-63				
Old age 63-84+				

- Mapping seven-year phases of my life: Explore these seven-year phases represented in the weekly rhythm: birth to 7, early childhood; 7-14, later childhood; 14-21, adolescence; 21-28, early adulthood, finding myself; 28-35, adulthood, becoming myself; 35-42, adulthood, most fully engaged in my life; 42-49, early mid-life; 49-56, mid-life; 56-63, late mid-life; 63-70, early old age, life forces less vibrant; 70-77, old age; 77 and beyond, late old age.

Phase	People	Places	Events	Other
Birth to 7				
7-14				
7th year				
8th year				
9th year				
10th year				
11th year				
12th year				
13th year				
14-21				
21-28				
28-35				
35-42				
42-49				
49-56				
56-63				

- Chance to change: Take a minute to think of an important chance conversation/meeting that ended up having tremendous impact on your life. After identifying that event, follow the thread that linked to the source of the encounter and then follow the thread to this moment in time. Write about the chance meeting that became significant and the important people, places, and opportunities that entered your life as a result.

- Finding my people: Have you ever had the experience when introduced to someone for the first time, that they were no stranger to you; your heart leapt as if to acknowledge, there you are, my old friend, finally! I have had this happen to me many times. My appreciation grows for friends, colleagues, and family, the more conscious I am about the string of events that brought us together and opportunities that entered into my life with each of them. Take a moment to reflect on a first meeting that felt more like a "finding" than an" introduction" and where it has taken you.

- Mine my mentors: Identify a person you consider a mentor. Remember the day you met, the circumstances, the time of year, the location. What were the characteristics of this person that inspired you to seek her/his counsel? Recall the first experience you had together. What other people were there, what ideas were embraced? What tasks did you undertake as a result of meeting this person? Map the threads of the relationships across the years to see what other events, people, and activities were influenced by this person.

- Life Story Dialogues: For the past two years I have been involved in life story dialogues, structured conversations with a colleague for the purpose of sharing our stories across seven-year phases. We developed a three-part process that included preparation, conversation and reflection. Each month we prepared by writing our experiences, based on a series of Burkhard's questions for one of the life phases, beginning with birth to seven. First we charted important events to answer the questions specific to the phase and sent our written stories to each other with a promise to review them before meeting. The second part required our coming together for conversations that included our each having twenty minutes to share, with the listener recording the story and then mirroring it back, with no advice. We agreed that an important aspect of this exercise was to learn how to witness for each other, providing a vessel to hear our stories with higher fidelity. Confidentiality was a cornerstone of the process as we agreed not to share our discussions with anyone. Finally, for part three, we wrote a process reflection to each other a week after the meeting. Each meeting took about two hours, including a few minutes for conversation. After conducting this exercise for 18 months, we acknowledged we had established a unique relationship, grounded in trust and exploration. We know more about each other than we do about many longer-term friends and even family members.

  My colleague has given me permission to share this information here with you, as we feel we have created an exercise that you may use to deepen relationships, practice conversation in its highest form, and learn how lives

unfold differently in service of meeting destiny. We learned that we had extremely different childhoods, different relationships to our parents and siblings and different paths to our professions. I felt deeply loved by my parents and had strong bonds to family. My friend had a lonely childhood, with no strong bonds with her parents or siblings. We learned that her harsh early years led to her deep love of books and writing. My strong sense of family and religiosity likely influenced my love for working in community and strong commitment to spiritual development from an early age. We learned that illness touched each of us, at different times in our lives and with varying degrees of intensity, and yet in both cases, we could see that illness propelled us toward important life changes.

Our career paths are very different: I am an educator comfortable working with groups of people, while she is a psychotherapist, preferring the intimacy of working with individuals, couples, or families. Our sessions revealed the continuing themes of meaning and purpose in each of our lives, allowing a deeper understanding of ourselves. We found it to be important and insightful to work so intimately with another person, to take the time to listen to our lives speak and to hear how differently our destinies spoke through our experiences and relationships. We are still meeting together, working on a series of practices to deepen our capacity. 41

- Cast into the future: Allow the future to emerge in all of its newness. Consider an important event from the past. In quietness, observe the clearest picture possible of the actual situation: the place, time of year, colors, season, number of people involved, even what people were wearing. What smells, what sounds can you remember, and what was the nature of the event; describe the action/drama that was happening. Pay attention to your heart as you develop the picture; invite your brain, shouting in your head to squelch the image rising in your heart, to rest. When the picture is clear, write about it or draw it. Once you are satisfied with your description, let go of the image. Allow it to sink all the way down into the earth. Letting go is important to the exercise. In the emptiness, allow a new image to enter into you and the world... A surprise!

Engaging in these exercises has given me a deep appreciation for how much the people I meet affect the voices of my life, letting it speak to me through them. Noticing the particular circumstances and outcomes of my encounters with people deepens my capacity to experience the deliberateness of my life as it unfolds.

Studying one's life from this observational perspective can become part of a regular

inner practice that grows soul/spiritual capacities. It requires both stepping deeply into the event being observed and disappearing from it. When preparing for life story dialogues or other autobiographical study, it is important not only to consider myself in the situation being described, but to develop the capacity to see it through the eyes of others involved to be less self-centered. Autobiographical studies have not only helped me understand my own life, but have given me insights into my parents, children, colleagues, and friends, leading to greater understanding and respect. For example, when mapping life experiences across phases, I noticed a difficult challenge I faced at 43 when I took on a totally new position. In recalling my childhood, I realized my father faced a crisis at the same age. I remembered the difficulties that developed in my relationship with him at the time, and suddenly I had a much deeper appreciation for his state of being. I realized his anger was likely with his situation, not really with me. I wished he were still alive so I could discuss this insight with him. That made me wonder if I treated my children harshly when I was going through my similar experience? Fortunately, they are still alive, and I have the opportunity to talk with them.

During a recent workshop, my participants were reviewing their 42-49 life phase. One gentleman said, *"I can't believe what new awareness I have into my mother's life as I look at mine when I am at the age she was when I was a teenager! I have to call her about my newfound understanding of her positions at that time."* Another man shared that he asked his mother about her childhood during a phone conversation. She was quite touched, because no one had ever asked her about her childhood or how she felt about her life. He decided to have monthly conversations with her so she could share her life story with him. These conversations were the doorway to a new relationship with his mother.

Dan Wakefield's *Story of Your Life: Writing a Spiritual Autobiography* (1990) affirms that autobiographical studies are both solitary and interactive exercises. He reminds his readers that it is not only important to write your spiritual autobiography, but it is also important to share that story, to make it public. In workshops all over the country, including people in prisons and veterans and writing circles, Dan said his students taught him that in the right situation, one is not only able but is inwardly urged to share the story, to have others witness it, lifting the work to a community engagement realm.

Autobiographical studies demand interaction. Inner capacities are developed; daring to share develops courage; hearing with an open heart develops humility, purging the tendency to judge others. The work deepens the capacity for respecting differences and noticing commonalities. For this reason, autobiographical studies may well be the core social art of the future.

In Courage circles, we invite participants to listen with open hearts. My experience, confirmed by others, is that I hear myself one way when I speak to myself; I hear myself differently when my words are held reverently by another. If someone agrees to listen to me using this selfless gesture, my story is embellished through them as I hear newness in it. My life speaks not only through me, but through the lenses of others around me... Eyes roaming me around a circle of people to reveal connections.

ENTERING OLD AGE

As I grow older, the relationships, connections, and patterns have increased over many fruitful years of living. From an autobiographical studies perspective, past experiences serve as stepping stones as I cast lines of experience forward to guide me towards my future. My many rich experiences and relationships inform my choices for the future, hopefully the seed that connects old age to wisdom. Using autobiographical studies, the attributes of each life phase and viewing myself in each phase, have helped to uncover who I have become, how I have traveled on the earth, and with whom I have agreed to travel.

Not only have I learned from the past using autobiographical studies as a resource, but I am developing the capacity to face the future with excitement. Preparing to re-form myself, I am conjuring my final creative splash to greet mortality with serenity. Allowing myself to move gracefully into old age and the final stage is not easy in this face of a culture that encourages working into my seventh decade. The exciting aspect of this phase is creating the opportunity to pause, look back over my life, gather into my heart all the people, places and activities that ring in me as *I let my life tell me what truths I embody, what values I represent.* My last years are my chance to carry these values, skills, and passions as an elder, living fully as the person my life has enabled me to become.

My challenge now is to carry myself in a new way, one for which there are few models to emulate. How I approach this final chapter, depends on how and what I grasp from the future as well as the past. Can I listen for the needs of the unborn and new ideas needed to cultivate the earth and her people? Can I prepare the space for the younger generation, allowing myself to become a lifeline for them? Have I adequately cultivated the capacity to listen to other lives speak? Can I hear my own future calling me?

Time is a great teacher. Engaging in a daily practice helps me feel more confident that I won't try to fix people, that I will be able to turn to wonder instead of fear, and that I can witness another person's story confidentially and wholeheartedly. The autobiographical studies exercises in my practice let me listen to my life as it tells

me what it intends to do with me, as it reminds me of what I have already done and what I am still longing to do: journeying along pilgrimage paths, seeking connection to myself and to others and to the practice that will enable me to find both. More than once when I least expected it, I had a flash of insight, revealing the role that an encounter played in my life. Pondering the reality of these intersections over and over, I am humbled to experience the multidimensional and complex-but-wildly-sensible way in which my life speaks to me.

Patti Smith, Ed.D., facilitates Circle of Trust® retreats as well as retreats for the Center for Biography and Social Arts, where she also serves as board member. She also serves on the Board of Trustees of the Kirkridge Retreat and Study Center. A former Waldorf teacher, she currently works as a researcher in large urban school districts to increase college and employment opportunities for high school students. She is the co-editor with Signe Schaefer of *More Lifeways*, a book on family growth and development, and the documentary, *Taking a Risk in Education*: Waldorf Public Schools. Please feel free to contact her at pattismith27@gmail.com

A STEPPING STONE

BOUNDARY MARKERS
for the Kirkridge Courage Fellowship Program
To Create a Circle of Trust with Clear Boundaries for Safety and Hospitality

"every circle of trust, regardless of size, requires that everyone in it help hold safe space..." --Parker J. Palmer

- Be here. Be as present as possible.
- Extend welcome and receive welcome.
- Invitation only. It's never demand... Never share or die!
- Speak your Truth into the center of the circle in ways that respect the Truths of others. No fixing!

Tell all the Truth but tell it slant—
Success in Circuit lies...
--Emily Dickinson

- When it's hard, turn to wonder.
- See others – and especially yourself -- with "soft eyes." Hear others – and especially yourself and your own inner teacher.
- Welcome silence, knowing that it allows you to listen to your Life speak, to hear your inner teacher.
- Let the Beauty you love be what you do.

Today, like every other day, we wake up empty
and frightened. Don't open the door to the study
and begin reading. Take down a musical instrument.
Let the beauty we love be what we do.
There are hundreds of ways to kneel and kiss the ground.
--Rumi

- Protect confidentiality; honor the idea of deep and double confidentiality.
- Embrace the possibility that it's possible to emerge from this work with more energy, more openness, with grace, with "soft eyes," with everything you need for this journey.

--Adapted by Sally Z. Hare for the Kirkridge Courage Fellowship Program, 2015-2016, from various versions of Courage & Renewal touchstones and boundary markers and always with gratitude to Dr. Judy Brown for her original touchstones.

Seeing Racism or Setting It Aside: Another Set of Eyes

By Sue E. Small

"You may choose to look the other way but you can never say again that you did not know." *-William Wilberforce*

The video link of Jalen's social studies project, *My Thoughts on Racial Awareness,* arrived in my email one recent fall morning. Jalen is the oldest child of one of my godsons. He was sharing with me his interpretation of an assignment given to his seventh-grade class to create a public service announcement that would include his thoughts and opinions, provide research to support his thoughts, elicit emotional responses from an audience, and stimulate action. Jalen's goal was to know how other people thought about racism so he could know more about it himself. He developed questions:

- *What is racism?*
- *Why is it so difficult to stop racism?*
- *How can we take action to stop racism?*

Then, on video, he interviewed a diverse group of people representing different races, ethnicities, genders, and ages. This project, envisioned and developed by a young man I love, seemed the perfect way for me to review my own journey into living life on the color line. To see racism from my own eyes, I needed do a fearless inventory of my inner journey with the issue. It has required me to go deeper into what I had experienced and learned in my outer environment both explicitly and implicitly, and finally to question my lack of motivation to understand the "tragic gaps" in my own experiences of racism along the way.

I am nearly 65 years older than Jalen. We have had similar experiences, including questioning social situations we observe. What then has made the difference? What has enabled him to see and study racism now? And what is it that enables me only now to publicly express my inner journey of reflection and analysis of my own racism and how I have expressed it in the outer world? I am aware of a shift from seeing only with my eyes, from my limited perspective, to honoring and integrating the perspectives of others to create another worldview, as Jalen sought to do in his research. Making this shift, I feel humbled by Jalen who is my newest teacher, as I hope to join others who have the courage to confront and not to "set aside" seeing racism and to continue to question the motives, integrity, and goals of my actions.

In this story, my story, I explore both the hidden conversations I have with myself and the more public conversations I have had with others who also have been my teachers. I hope to describe the process of the internalization of racism in my identity, my whiteness. It is this exploration into my soul as well as my role as facilitator in conversations about racism and racial justice that compels me to know who I am and the message of my life. Without that understanding I am colorblind in the role of the facilitator and lack the capacity to hold safe space within a circle and with respect to everyone in our racialized society, the wider world, and even myself.

RACISM FROM MY OWN EYES: LEARNING TO SET ASIDE

The topic of racism has become an important and essential theme throughout my adult life. Earlier, as a teacher, a family member, and later, as a teacher educator, that was not always the case. As I envisioned my retirement from the academic life, I wanted to devote time to reflection and to embracing some of the areas of my life I had "set aside" earlier, specifically focusing on the language and literacy as well as the history at the heart of racism. (The term "set aside" is used in conflict communications to refer to an act of putting aside areas of disagreement in order to move forward to achieve a desired outcome.)

I once wrote, "My journey began years ago in my heart," and, in fact, it did. Mine has been a journey of formation and faith, beginning with learning to trust and love God,

others, and myself. This now is the time for me to go public about my journey and the recognition that I need to strengthen my racial awareness and clarify actions for racial justice. I acknowledge Jalen as my new teacher, yet he was not the first.

My initial thoughts and feelings about racial awareness were that I would be able to take off the masks I have worn and go deeper into my heart, mind, soul and role. This I believed would be possible when I no longer needed to hide my real self in order to be successful in my life and career. As I have taken action to go deeper to find my real self, I see the paradoxical and troubling ways in which my eyes were unable to see this "real self" as a person benefiting from racism and the structures and systems that hold it in place, nor could I see that I really didn't want to confront it. It wasn't my career that encouraged my "set asides"; it was both wanting access to success and the fear of losing the hidden privilege of whiteness.

Each time I reflect on my journey with racism, I recognize that I may never understand what peoples of color have endured and face, particularly now at this time in the history of the United States. This does not change my commitment to continue, but it does make necessary another set of eyes, even many other sets of eyes.

Jalen's social studies project and his selection of racism to research made it clear to me that now is a Kairos moment. I may have intellectualized about racism before, but when my precious loved one and his sisters, as well as all of our brothers and sisters, are living in this decisive moment, I can no longer set it aside. Conversations about race, once hidden within our families and like-minded communities, are now bursting forth in an outpouring of many voices with urgent heart-wrenching stories. We are engaging in dialogue about racial awareness and racial justice in schools and universities, books, news media, documentaries, and social media. As I join these conversations, I am faced with new truths about my own learned attitudes.

I now see, more often from other perspectives that which I once could not see at all: racial disparities in the laws, policies, and practices of our racialized society. Yet, there is still much that I cannot see. As a woman of Anglo-Saxon heritage who is now an elder, I can see, hear, and feel emotions of chaos, fear, shame, conflict and change. Nevertheless, I can still, as a white woman, set aside my feelings and go out into the world safely, wearing what Peggy McIntosh named the "knapsack of white privilege," unafraid of losing my life in any given moment (http://nationalseedproject.org/white-privilege-unpacking-the-invisible-knapsack).

It is not just. We need change.

The gifts of this chaos, these escalating conflicts, are the seeds of change. This is a Kairos moment. It is a time when conditions are right for accomplishing the

crucial actions of individuals, communities, corporations, governments, and countries to transform awareness to action for racial justice.

So we must continue. I **will** continue.

LOOKING BACK: MOMENTS IN MY HISTORY

Unearthing my long-buried experiences, stemming from a culture of silence and a history of ignoring the structures of racism, has taken years and active seeking. This process has been facilitated by a shift from seeing the world from my own perspective to seeing the hidden wholeness of life, not only my life but that of others, and knowing that life is ever-changing. This shift is not something I accomplished; rather, it is something I have noticed, named, and nurtured as I have continued to pursue this area in my life's inventory.

Early in my life I was motivated by the ideal of success. I believed in working hard, climbing the ladder of success, and hopefully, relaxing into retirement. Yet along the way, I learned that some of these themes seemed to collide with other themes I valued: family, caring for others, fairness and justice, honesty and truth, loving and wanting to be loved and accepted. When my themes collided, I sometimes used the "set aside."

Growing up in a small town in southern Ohio, I learned about people of the "Heartland," but not about all of the people. I believed we were the face of America, the norm; yet we were all white people. There were no people of color in our town. We had little access to racial or ethnic diversity in the community or in our schools. Throughout my childhood and early adolescence, I was not consciously aware of the need to develop an in-depth awareness of my own heritage or to acquire cross-racial understanding through learning the histories and cultures of people of color, including Native Americans. I thought I was just normal, but in fact this perception has been identified as one of the "two primary privileges of whiteness":

> 1) to assume that whiteness is the norm against which everyone else should be compared and
>
> 2) the privilege to live one's life without ever needing to be aware of one's whiteness and how it might be impacting one's life. (Lyubansky, https://www.psychologytoday.com/blog/between-the-lines/201112/the-meaning-whiteness 2011)

I was a part of the norm in that geographic area. Notwithstanding the fact that I had little opportunity to learn from experience about racial awareness, I was aware, as very young children often are, of differences in people based on the color of their skin. An example was the interracial couple who lived near my mother's sister and

her family in Cincinnati. My mother would take me to their home, and we would be greeted by Mr. and Mrs. Martin. Mrs. Martin was known as an excellent seamstress; her work provided the family's financial support, because Mr. Martin had experienced a debilitating stroke. My mother and the Martins would talk about neighborhood news as well as the repairs and other items to be completed. After we left, I asked my mother about them and noted how they looked different, and her response was that they loved each other. When further pressed, mother told me that Mrs. Martin said, "I would rather be with a black man with a white heart than a white man with a black heart." This explanation of her choice and her relationship with her husband seemed to stop my inquiry, even though I must have been aware that the term black was used to describe a negative aspect of the heart. I had noticed the difference in the Martins' skin color, and that they seemed to be different than the norm I knew. I was ignorant of the complexities of their decisions or the factors and social context involved. It was 1945 and I was five years old.

Awareness of racism was not a constant curiosity or theme in my life as a young child, nor was it a priority. At times during my adolescence when I visited family in other areas of Cincinnati and other states, I was aware of disparities in the gathering spaces and public places where I saw white people, African Americans, and other peoples of color. I noticed that jobs often held by African Americans were as gardeners, domestic workers, farm hands. I saw homes that were in neighborhoods with little grass and few trees. All of that I took in, but I do not recall actively questioning those instances like I did when I was five, or as Jalen is doing at age 12. I had become silent, accepting and benefiting from the structural racism of the time. An unconscious behavior I adopted as a teenager in the 1950's was that of the "set aside." I learned to ignore or at least not talk about racial disparity, and if I did, much of what I heard or said was biased and grounded in fears and discrimination.

BECOMING A TEACHER AT AGE 19

As a young woman in the late 1950's I went to a nearby public university to become a teacher. There I encountered more diversity, not only of people, but also of thought, as I observed a new world. Still, I remained committed to the worldview of the themes of individualism, school success, career mobility, and my primary choices were to pursue those goals. In 1960 at age 19, with just two years of college and teacher preparation, I began to teach on a cadet certificate offered by the State of Ohio to accommodate the severe teacher shortage.

My first two years of teaching were completed in the same town where I attended university. I taught during the day and attended classes two nights a week in order to finish my education and achieve full certification. Emphasis on diversity, specifically racial diversity, was not in the curriculum in those years. Although the 1954 Supreme Court *Brown v. Board of Education* decision had clarified that equal educational

opportunities must be afforded all children and that segregated schools were not constitutional, the teacher-preparation curriculum did not reflect the changes needed to prepare teachers who were, as I was, uninformed in this area.

The issues of race and racism awareness were largely set aside, not only in the area of teacher preparation, but also in my learning pursuits. My themes remained a success orientation and becoming a state-certified teacher. My primary attention to racial awareness was only to be fair in teaching all of my first-grade children, some of whom were African American. This individual focus of racial awareness was actually self-serving; my goals for success and being a good teacher were only peripherally related to understanding implications for noticing and teaching all of the children who were in my classes. I did not focus on including the history and cultural contributions of African Americans in the curricula and classroom conversations.

A significant shift toward recognizing racial awareness was an unintended outcome of my decision to teach in the Cincinnati Public Schools. This decision, based on personal and career advancement, had another, more important benefit. It was movement toward facing the conflict of my own worldview and awareness of others who were racially different with an eye to seeing a broader world.

LEAVING MY COMFORT ZONE

I now had to get out of my comfort zone. I cannot take credit for the decision that resulted in a new developmental task for seeing with another set of eyes; looking back, I now believe it was a gift of God and the Universe. I left the idyllic university town and went to "the city" where my assignment was a large elementary school. All but two of the 1200 students in the school were African American. My work was to teach 27 African American children in the first grade, a task for which I was prepared in knowledge and skills of teaching and learning, yet very much underprepared in the sense of cross-cultural communication and understanding.

This teaching assignment was not yet the end of my mis-education as a white woman, but it was the beginning of a new racial awareness. What did I learn from this experience outside of my comfort zone? I learned that my students were my teachers; that children are children, proximity matters, and learning is not about being comfortable. Learning requires being able to seek and to see other perspectives and to be open to new ways of being and doing.

My learning was grounded in my personal experiences with my students and their families. The families were also my teachers. Two of the children, Carol and Philip, were twins whose parents invited me to a superb dinner at their home. I saw a family gathered around the table, with prayer, inviting me to join their circle of trust. They entrusted me with their children in school, and they welcomed me just as I was, young

and underprepared for the new environment. They wanted to believe I was open in my heart for the task. From them I learned to withhold judgment, to gather information in the moment, and to look into the heart of the matter. I learned to begin seeing others with soft eyes of love, no longer looking largely from a perspective of fear of failure and self-centered focus on success.

There were other children and their parents: Jan, whose father was a doctor; Robert, who in the beginning would not talk in class because he had been told by his parents, probably as a precautionary step to preserve his safety, "Don't talk to white people." There was Alee, who ate his peanut-butter lunch from his shirt pocket because his family did not have bread. I loved the children. I could see them as the precious individual children they were, with diverse gifts, needs, and families. They were open to learning from and loving me. Early in my life I had absorbed the biases and stereotypes common in the environment where I grew up. Now I was beginning to see differently through my human, social interactions with my students, their families, and my colleagues in a new setting.

It was 1962. I was still unaware of the systemic underpinnings of the racialized society in which I lived where race matters so much in the life experiences, opportunities, and social relationships along racial lines. I **did** notice the differences in socioeconomics (including available resources, housing, the city school attendance area patterns), but I did not have any real grasp of the issues. I was noticing some of the results of structural racism that I had not contemplated before, and, intuitively, it made me very uncomfortable. Although I valued learning in this new world, I was not willing to stay out of my comfort zone and take action to confront myself and the realities of racism.

I wish I could say, "I was changed… I stayed and devoted myself and my educational career to changing the systems and teaching my students, all of them, in new ways." I wish I could say I joined in the actions of the Freedom Riders and the Civil Rights Movement devoted to registering African American people to vote or that I walked across the bridge in Selma, Alabama, in 1965, or acted in some other courageous way to join in the movement for recognition of the humanity of all of us, but I didn't. Once again, I ***set aside*** action for racial justice even while gaining new racial awareness.

What else did I learn through this experience? I learned that people are people, we all love our children, and many are open and generous to me as the other. I became more committed to the idea of racial awareness. I began to see through the stereotypes and biases and toward a lens of love, but I "set aside" my newfound awareness, slid back into wearing the "knapsack of white privilege" described by Peggy McIntosh and focusing on individualism and success. I went back to the university to pursue my career and postgraduate education as "a way out" for me, leaving others where they were.

FAST FORWARD: OTHER TEACHERS ALONG THE WAY

One of the lessons I learned from my own upbringing was that education is the key to the way out, the portal toward mobility and access across social divides. It was a guiding principle in my middle years. In the next stages of my life and career development, I moved to a large suburban Maryland school system and became an administrator and later a teacher educator, in both public and private universities. I continued to pursue personal educational goals and believed I was giving back to those from whom I was teaching and learning. My learning came from proximity and experiences with people with whom I worked and shared interests. I learned from those with whom I shared little common background, interests or opinions. In this period, I learned from reading and researching, much like Jalen did in his social studies project. I questioned what I saw and learned from the people I met. Some of the most significant teachers in my new world were different from me and helped me to see with another set of eyes.

In 1968 I met Sharlene, a white woman, raised in economic and religious situations different from my own. She was Jewish and raised Catholic, married at 15 to a lifelong soldier, and deprived of her high school education by parents who believed young women should just get a job and/or marry. In the middle years of her life, she earned her GED, and eventually her undergraduate degree, two masters' degrees, and a Ph.D. She was one of my dearest friends until her death in 2009. What did I learn from her? Pursue the questions with courage. Question biases you learned and that oppressed you as an individual, and go on. Pursue spiritual development as well as professional development and explore the spiritual with an open mind.

I met Marjorie, an African-American physical education teacher, working in the predominantly white school where I was an administrator in 1972. She was the unofficial leader among the faculty, and she did not want to pursue a formal leadership role. We became friends as we proved wrong those faculty members who said she wouldn't like me because I took the place of the previous administrator and because I was a woman. We soon became friends, learning that as much as we were different, we were also alike: both competitive and resistant to authority and control. Later as our friendship deepened, we learned that we grew up in similar families with like values and principles, even though she grew up on a farm in Virginia and I in a small town in Ohio. After 44 years we are still friends and continue to go out together and to talk on the telephone every day. What have I learned from Margie? That each of us must live our own lives, respecting each other and our decisions, hard decisions, about whom you will stand by and how you will stay in close contact even when the conversations are hard. I also learned that we are more alike than we are different!

In 1981 I met Evelyn, who identified herself in most every conversation as the eldest of 15 children. She was a brilliant African American I met while in the doctoral program at a state university. Evelyn was an assertive leader in the group, and it took much persuading by several men who advocated for me to convince her to invite me into her study group. I was struggling with statistics, and, when I was initially reluctant to ask for help, she said, "Trust me." And I did. I later helped her with social exchange theory. In the end, we were the only two in the study group who finished the program. I have on my bookshelf her dissertation, along with the two books she authored and a collection of recipes she collected from her family. Although she is now gone, we were friends for 31 years. Her grandson, Joseph, and I remain in frequent contact. What did Evelyn teach me? She knew who she was and encouraged me to do the same. Her favorite quote was one of Shakespeare's, "This above all: to thine own self be true. And it must follow, as the night the day. Thou canst not then be false to any man."

LeRoy, a single father with three sons, Sean, Stephen, and Sydney, became my neighbor in 1988. We lived across the court from each other; one day when I was pulling weeds in the front of the row house where I lived, we struck up a conversation. LeRoy was a history professor teaching African American history and French at a nearby university. His early experiences with racism in this country as well as the experience of leaving this country to study and work, later returning to complete his doctoral work, provided me with a source of knowledge beyond anything I had previously encountered. He recommended a list of reading materials beginning with Franklin and Higginbotham's *From Slavery to Freedom: A History of African Americans*, as well as many other non-fiction and fiction accounts of the African American experience. Initially, he was curious about the school system where I worked in the Office of Staff Development, Equal Employment Opportunity (EEO) and Human Relations because two of his sons were in middle and high school there. He clearly understood the issues of race and the challenges faced by bright young African American men in the school setting. As we became friends, I learned more and more on a personal level about the ways in which race plays a part in our daily lives as well as in teachers' attitudes and perceptions of students. We confronted commonly-held biases that prevent students of color from placement in high-achieving classes when one son was finally placed in a gifted-and-talented class after we questioned the selection processes. In another live encounter with racism, the second of LeRoy's sons was stopped by police while he was driving my car. He had been "noticed" and stopped without cause except for the curiosity of the officer who asked, "What are you doing driving a white woman's car?" He responded, "It is my godmother's car." The police followed him home to our gated community where they watched him come into the house.

Seeing these examples of injustice up close, as I have come to know and love this family, has changed my life. I see myself as part of their family and I see them as my own family. Now Jalen is the next generation. From all of them, I have learned that facing

racism, not setting it aside, but confronting it through learning, measured discourse, and taking action to dismantle it can produce results and hope in this Kairos moment.

In 1990 I met Marvin when we both participated in a workshop on building coalitions among widely diverse groups comprised of a varied range of race, gender, sexual orientation, ethnicity, age, and ability/disability. He is a lawyer who founded his own organization for providing training and services on alternative dispute resolution and is highly regarded in the field of mediation and arbitration nationally and internationally. Marvin and his family, as well as his staff, have been steady and strong peaceful warriors, consistently raising questions about the day-to-day systemic racism, especially in the area of conflict resolution. In addition, he has taught at several universities as well as at the Center and presented his model of mediation, which enables parties in conflict to engage in conversations and control their own outcomes. I have learned so much about conflict and conflict resolution from the educational opportunities and the myriad ways in which Marvin stands firmly, courageously, in the struggle for racial justice and encourages others to do the same.

I began working for Teach for America (TFA) in 1992 to support new teachers who entered the cadre of teachers in Baltimore. In that context, I met Yolanda who was teaching in City Schools, and we both were selected to go to Los Angeles for the summer of 1993 to observe and mentor new TFA Corps Members as they prepared for teaching in our city. Yolanda did not stop teaching after two years, as many TFA Corps Members do. She continued her education to earn a master's degree and then a doctorate in Teacher Education, and she continues to teach relevant courses on diversity, family and community engagement, and qualitative research to doctoral students at a prestigious private university. Her primary research area is centered on diversity, families and community, honoring the work of African American fathers and families as well as leadership at the intersection of families and teachers. She is recognized as a content expert in the field and serves on doctoral committees for others seeking degrees in these areas. We talk nearly every day, vacation together, and honor each other's lives and efforts to be evolutionary supporters of new ways to deal with the issues of race embedded in the institutions and lives of those we love: our children, families, communities and efforts dedicated to racial justice. One of the many things I have learned from Yolanda as she has become my mentor is that leadership in the areas of diversity is a protracted effort that must continue. In our institutions, priorities shift and new barriers emerge, often imposed by conservative, and perhaps racist, worldviews. Yet Yolanda keeps on leading thoughtfully, fairly, quietly and firmly, while she also supports and mentors her students and others who also are on the leading edge.

Sandy is both my sister and my friend. I have known her most of my life. Now retired from teaching after 36 years, she is another of the important teachers in my

life. We grew up in the same town, same family, and took the same career path. She, however, did it differently. After completing her degree at a small private college in Kentucky, she went on to teach kindergarten, pursue higher education, become a reading specialist, and later, during a bout with cancer, she pursued and achieved certification to teach children who speak other languages. She loves her children, all of them, with, of course, her own son, Travis at the head of the line. Today she is still volunteering to teach children who are learning to speak, read, and write English. What is it that I have learned from Sandy? She is always open to new learning as well as to working hard. She taught her children, "It's ok to make mistakes. Mistakes help us learn. We can always get a helper." She has the philosophy that we start where we are and that is from the heart. Frequently she says to me, "Follow your heart." She has taught me to accept myself and be gentle with myself because she has always loved me just as I am. What a role model she has been for me, and I don't think she even knows it.

My brother, Emmerson, is another significant lifelong teacher who explains that we were born of the same parents, grew up in the same community, but had very different experiences, seeing from another set of eyes. He is twelve years younger, and many things had changed. He left our hometown in Ohio to attend college in Maryland, where he played basketball and continues to support that university's scholar-athlete program. In his professional life he has modeled integrity in the area of investment management and certified financial planning. He is also a Sixth Dan Black Belt Master in Taekwondo and has found a spiritual place there. He continues to teach Taekwondo and its values and principles of perseverance, courtesy, integrity, self-control and loyalty. Both Erica, his daughter, and his son, Stephen, as well as I, have observed these characteristics as he lives his life. Lessons I have learned from him are that accountability matters and deep love of family is a deciding factor in our "spirited discussions" when we each see from our different sets of eyes.

There are many other teachers I have been privileged to know, from all races, ethnicities, and regions of the world. From each I have learned to look from another set of eyes until I could also see from their points of view and shift to see from my own eyes with more clarity. My teachers have helped me to find new courage.

FINDING NEW COURAGE AND LOVE

In 2005, my 65th birthday was a highlight. I gave myself the gift of attending a retreat related to Parker Palmer's work and his book, *The Courage to Teach*. It was glorious. I found a new way to travel my inner journey within a group of others I could trust as the process was so carefully crafted to provide the safe space I needed to go deeper. It was another new beginning, and in 2006 I met Sally who was already a long-time Courage facilitator when I attended her *Circle of Trust: Living the Questions*. As a white woman from her native south, she understood the

need for "Calling All Colors" (a program she had initiated for children about racial healing) and for listening to other voices. From Sally, I learned that where you are born and grow up could be an advantage. I learned that "diversity begins within," and we can only sow seeds, not force new plants to grow. I began to see that, although I am a teacher, no matter what position I hold or even when I am no longer employed, I can only collaborate with others on their own paths as I encourage others to go deeper in the ways only they can. I was able to ***see*** my soul and role as a teacher, and as a facilitator, come together.

Many times I am absolutely out of my comfort zone! I am becoming more aware of myself and the similarities and differences in our so-called races as well as the history and the disparities we in this country and our institutions have created, dating back to slavery and before when we white immigrants settled on Native American land. In a recent Courage retreat specifically designed to bring together facilitators who were committed to "Living Undivided: Explorations of Race, Identity, Soul and Role," I saw once again how so-called white people and people of color see differently. We were all committed to healing the wounds of racism and living in a more just, loving society. At the same time, we had had many very different experiences and been wounded in different and unequal ways. Many noticed that some of the white people "set aside" personal feelings and spoke with historical or intellectualized thoughts, not expressing feelings of shame, guilt, and fear. It seemed to me that people of color (most of the people of color present in this setting were African American) were able to express their feelings of being oppressed, angry, and impatient, while many white people were not.

Having such a safe space for difficult conversations and dialogue is crucial to the healing that is needed. I am grateful to the facilitators, a team both African American and white, who were skilled in holding the safe space and in designing the retreat. It seems to me that this model was effective for moving forward with racial awareness and enabled each of us as participants to determine how we will move forward to take action for racial justice.

Yes, I see that it is one way, a way of non-violence, to stop racism as Jalen asked in his research. Yet it is not the only way. One of the facilitators asked the question, "Is this way to pursue work for racial justice too soft?" Will it take too long to see results? I see this courage approach as a "developmental stage" to prepare us all, especially many of us who are white, to learn about the history of racism and to listen and speak out in a new language for the cause of racial justice. As Ida B. Wells, cited in *The Monastic Way* in December, 2016, wrote:

The right way to right wrongs is to turn the light of truth upon them.

In my pursuit of learning more about the systems of racism, I found that there are many conceptualizations of the idea of race, also called human categorization. One view was created by physical anthropologists who advocated for categorizing human beings into four races. Other views in the scientific community include evolutionary biologists and microbiologists, some who propose evidence that there is no biological basis for race. In race and genomics research, there are questions raised about whether race is real. Further, there is a sociological perspective that race is a social construction, and the learned ways of categorizing people in this way can be erased. These and other topics were presented in a PBS documentary series, Race—The Power of an Illusion (http://www.pbs.org/race/). It seems to me that learning about these various theories, the categorizations, and their origins in our history are important aspects for dismantling the structural racism that exists.

My own learning has been a combination of reading, watching documentaries, and traveling, as well as intentionally joining with others in close proximity who are willing to live the questions of race in our racialized society. I am also learning that I benefited from the laws, policies, and practices that we white people have created; that may be the reason why we so often say things like, "What am I to do? That was a long time ago!" Or even, deny my own "set asides" when confronted with choices of individual, personal success and how the existing benefits of whiteness are embedded in the structures that allow people like me to be in the group that has access to better jobs, more money, safe passage on the streets. I am still looking systemic racism in the face, not only intra-personally, but also seeing interpersonal and intergroup differences of perspective. In fact, for me to be able to see new possibilities for deconstructing systems of racial inequality will require me to do more than dialogue with like-minded others. More frequently I am noticing that the confrontation needed is between my public self and my soul or inner self (hopefully with honesty and openness), taking off the masks I have worn to "go public" in conversations with others who may not be like-minded.

That has been one of the purposes of this work, this search for truth about my capacity as a white woman and as a facilitator, to be able to more effectively see and confront racism. My work is in consistently living the questions and learning about my own culture's emphasis on an individual success orientation, as well as seeing and trusting the good will of others to live their own questions; those are the necessary steps for me to become a better facilitator. It cannot be rushed by learning and knowing more, as I am wont to do. I do need to know and question organizations, support movements like Black Lives Matter, and research efforts to take action politically, systemically, and personally. At the same time, we start where we are, and my greater need is to "see" the working of love in the sphere of human life, relationships, and racial justice. That requires seeking and uncovering reality and willingness to see what has been emerging as I review my response to Jalen's social studies research and reflection.

STANDING FIRMLY IN THE GAP WITH JALEN

Unearthing and telling this story has been important in my noticing and naming new meaning in my life. In *Finding Our Way: Leadership for an Uncertain Time*, Margaret Wheatley (2005) suggests that meaning is what motivates people, that service brings joy, and that courage comes from our hearts. Now I am better able to listen and learn; I am more able to keep moving forward and see different perspectives and recognize not only the struggles, but also the joys and the hopes in the journey toward racial justice; and to look to the future: to Jalen and his mother and father and for all who have the courage to continue this particular journey.

Put another way, my work now is about joining the truth/knowledge in my head and the compassion/love in my heart as a process of spiritual and leadership development to have the capacity to stand my ground when the winds of racial injustice swirl about and to rest, trust, and look up when I am in the trough of the wave and the storm is raging, when I feel I can't go on.

But taking what was inspired by Jalen's work and learned from my life teachers, I will go on. I will know that, in the words of Rev. Dr. Martin Luther King, "One day we will learn that the heart can never be totally right if the head is totally wrong. Only through bringing together of head and heart—intelligence and goodness—shall man rise to a fulfillment of his true nature."

I am no longer envisioning retirement as a resting place, but as Harry Belafonte, singer and activist and also an elder, reflected at the Sundance Festival and recorded in the documentary *Sing Your Song* (2011):

> ***I tried to envision playing out the rest of my life almost exclusively devoted to reflection, but there's just too much in the world to be done.***

I know that I have much to do in order to see racism with another set of eyes…and to take action with hope of making a difference. I may still set aside changes I know are necessary, but not for long! As Jalen's father once said to me in a discussion about matters of race, "It is my life."

It is my life, too.

Although I am an elder, I am still defining myself. I am still learning and experiencing life. I am seeing a new world from other perspectives and developing a new world view. I look to a new future of turning to wonder and joy!

This is a Kairos moment and I want to be part of it. I want to be part of Jalen's life and

contribute to the future of all of our children. Yes, all our lives matter, but it is important that we lift up especially the lives of people of color, who have been too long denied the rights all of us were promised in the founding documents of this country. And yes, it is about the lives of white people too, who have responsibility for acknowledging our part in the institution and aftermath of slavery from which we have benefited. Many of us have been uninformed or misinformed of this history in our families, schools, and religious institutions and have remained silent and set aside the tasks of **seeing** and acknowledging our part in the systemic racism that still thrives.

Yes, all of us will go on, hopefully as allies of change, co-creating a world where we all can live and breathe and support efforts to dismantle systemic racism. This is our chance to see with another set of eyes that our very humanity is at the heart of this "new" worldview where we, black and white and all people of color in America, are interconnected with other peoples of the world and that issues of race are at the intersection of other categories of diversity. This is our opportunity to develop another set of eyes so that we might all see and know that we are interconnected and that intersectionality matters. That which affects one of us affects us all.

60 ***Sue E. Small, Ed.D., Clinical Associate Professor Emerita at University of Maryland Baltimore County (UMBC), is still teaching, learning, and mentoring other faculty as well as facilitating Circles of Trust for People Embracing Equality and Love at a church in Baltimore. She can be contacted at sue17small@verizon.net. She speaks from her heart to you, her Reader:*** "In describing Mr. and Mrs. Martin, I used more formal "titles" or names, as I was young and they were more remote. For the children and other "teachers," I used first names to indicate a more familiar and clear relationship. I make this distinction because honoring people by using their formal titles is an act of respect, and in using first names I am suggesting close relationships, not taking familiarity for granted."

Strokes of Clarity: Meeting Myself in My New Normal

By Sandra Sturdivant Merriam

The space between us is real.
The mud between us is messy.
The silence between us is audible.
How then, do we begin to move in the space between us?
To hear our story of self, of other?
To tell the story of self, of other?
To honor the space between us?
To lift the truth between us?

--Sandra S. Merriam

I know the space between us is real. This work of facilitating Circles of Trust® invites me to meet myself again and again, remembering who I am and hearing the voice of commitment that comes out of knowing and trusting the ground on which I stand.

That voice is an inner voice that has developed from long years of friendship and conflict with myself. It speaks to me from multiple vantage points. My home-voice helps

me remember the familiar knowings from childhood and deep family connections. My self-voice reminds me of the tensions and pressures that have formed, and continue to form, the person I am today, and to foster the confidence that has enabled both my intuition and my resilience. And there is one more voice, which so far has no name. This voice creates my sense of adventure and my desire to explore what is ever-changing. It speaks to me about the Who that informs my responses to my passions and renews my energy.

Hearing my own voice is tricky amidst the world's loud voices, loaded with spin, but all of **those** voices were muted for a moment on July 3, 2016. Mopping our hardwood floors at 4:30 in the afternoon while preparing for our family Fourth of July celebration, I had two strokes, one on each side of my brain! The details of that event, at the end of an ordinary day of house cleaning, food preparation, and grocery shopping, are not the story. The story is my subsequent learning curve – the one that came from listening first to what was outside and then, eventually to my own voice from those inner selves that I have come to know over the past twenty-ish years.

I might have missed this voice if my friend Amy had not said something quite important when she came to visit after my hospital stay. Amy is the CEO and founder of YoungStroke, the first and only American advocacy organization formed to specifically address the unmet needs of young adult stroke survivors and their caregivers. Although I am well beyond the age of "young adult," Amy is a friend, and she knew I needed to hear these words: *"You look just like my friend Sandie, everything looks the same. But dear, you have changed in ways you will now begin to discover. May I suggest you keep a journal? That will be the only evidence of the subtle ways you are different from the friend I used to know. We will have to be reacquainted – and it will be fun – an adventure for yourself and all of us who* ***think*** *we know you."*

So here I am 90 days later, sitting with the most significant questions I have posed to myself in a very long time:

- What if I choose to live as if there are no questions that must be answered?
- In fact, what if no answers exist for any questions?
- What if the real work of my life is **not** to understand the gap between what is and what could be, but instead is to accept the gap itself, allowing myself the freedom to inhabit and even embrace that gap?

My energy is back. The passion to send that energy in a particular direction is not. There is no draw for me from either side of the gap. I am feeling content to simply spend the remainder of whatever time I have bearing witness to the positive energy released by embracing the paradoxes of an ecosystem that defies judgment.

After my strokes, I took the usual and prudent trip through the medical gauntlet. Many

well-educated and well-intentioned medical professionals gave me their best advice, prognoses, and of course, pharmacology. I would be remiss if I failed to thank each and every one of them. In fact my current deeper understanding of my condition is due to my careful listening to ***their*** objectives for ***my*** treatment.

NO FIXING

One paradox in the gap where I now live daily has to do with what is, to me, a precious principle of facilitating Circle of Trust work: NO FIXING. I am now age 68. The chance that I will somehow attain the physical condition of a 40-year-old is delusional. After three months of looking for why my strokes happened and listening carefully to the outcomes the physicians care most about, I am OK with never knowing why this event happened. I don't need to fix or be fixed. I am ready to do some prudent prevention that my doctors and I agree upon and to get on with living.

Achieving homeostasis is no easy trick under the best of circumstances; at worst, heredity and personality can combine for a disastrous outcome for the patient and the physician. My strokes have driven that home again. My physical challenges over many years have helped me gain some wisdom, as I found that I was not always on the same page, related to outcomes, as the physicians who treated me. Along about age 40, I came to the conclusion that I wanted to ***partner*** with any physician who treated my conditions. The skills of deep listening that I have learned in my work as a Circle of Trust facilitator serve me well, as I recognize these critical skills are not taught in most professions, including medical. So I am learning to craft interactions with my doctors to express the outcomes I hold as most important in ways that create the best chance of my being heard.

The most notable after-effect of my strokes was, and still is to some degree, balance issues, and one of the most impactful learnings came from my physical therapist. I'm a *why* person. He has been more than patient with my *why* questions, and he has explained both the inner and outer sources of physical balance. His explanation, simplified for my comprehension, enabled the first reflective shift that took me out of my search for a fix from the strokes. Balance comes from three sources: information from feet on the ground, from perceptions through the eyes, and from perceptions and responses of the vestibular areas inside the head. My own journaling gave me the insight into what I wanted, maybe needed, to live with my growing realization that I would never again be in my pre-stroke frame of mind, that I might never again be completely balanced. I wondered if I could find a different way to be comfortable with this new unbalanced normal.

So now that I have given up the idea that I need to achieve some sort of balancing act, I want to explore the idea of disequilibrium. What would it mean to never again feel balanced in my approach to this Courage Work I know to be my calling? In what direction would I

send my energy? It felt good to have no answers. That was my first clue, although initially I struggled against that what I was feeling was a lack of energy or even laziness.

A NEW NORMAL

In my experience and training as a teacher, I had learned Jean Piaget's theory of cognitive development as a way of helping students with the process of learning. All of us experience disequilibrium when we get information that does not match what we have established as normal, the way our culture says it **should** be. In a learning setting, disequilibrium creates stress. Resolving disequilibrium is desirable to help children avoid or move through periods of discomfort by returning to a state of equilibrium. The return requires new information and the establishment of a new normal.

Now I find myself feeling that **my** new normal is one that is about **NOT** achieving equilibrium. My new desire is to live in a state of **disequilibrium,** and toward that goal, I still require new information as well as a new vantage point from which to integrate the information from those inner voices. I feel fortunate that part of my new normal continues to be following my calling to serve as a facilitator of Circles of Trust. As I begin to experience my own inner voices I am coming to understand that this new image of disequilibrium is also changing the way I facilitate.

Part of my new normal is that the space I imagine for retreat participants must embody my commitment to my own congruence in order to avoid the lack of authenticity I often experienced in those "share or die" spaces from the 60's. Back in those days of the 60's, as a young adult, I would have ongoing conversations about right and wrong with a close childhood friend who is a Jesuit priest. He seemed to have the clarity I lacked as he would note my inability to choose sides in personal and political conversations. One morning he gave me this admonition, *"Sandra, the whole point of keeping an open mind is to close it on something solid."* Listening for this purpose comes up in my thinking now from time to time, and yet I still find myself moving toward some kind of neutral space, a space between, rather than something solid! I want to stand in some middle space. I want to understand every dimension of the spaces in which I stand. Now after many years and two strokes, I find myself questioning the efficacy of my friend's advice for my life.

FIERCE MOMENTS OF CLARITY

One of my favorite book titles this year is L.M. Browning's *Fierce Moments of Clarity.* I know I have had a few of those moments. They push on me in erratic ways that challenge the notion that life is about finding equilibrium. They pick at the idea that equilibrium will give me control and fly in the face of the belief that if I'm in control, my worst fears will never be realized or lived. My energy in these moments of challenge and surprise helps me see the possibility that I might be fully active in a different reality, one that resembles the scientific idea of potential energy... A space charged

by noticing and affirming the reality around me, by understanding the elements that support equilibrium without equilibrium becoming the goal.

And so I go back to that valuable information from my physical therapist, Rich, regarding the three areas from which my body gathers information about *where I am*. My body is trying to stay upright, to somehow keep me safe, and allow me to move through space without bumping into things and causing injury. This new space I have discovered, with his help, is the place where the objective of having three areas of information-gathering is not equilibrium but rather the creation of a neutral zone, a zone of potential energy – one that allows observation without judgment.

My most important awareness in this space is that I am at my best as a person **and** in my role as a facilitator when I keep myself from applying my story to someone else's life. As a facilitator and trustee of Circles of Trust, I engage in the rebellious act of giving up the either/or thinking that is prevalent in our culture. This allows me to understand that authentic growth comes from holding paradox, requiring that I take responsibility for my energy in the world, and that I focus on the ground on which I stand. Only then do I have the possibility of finding my voice in a way that others are able to hear as authentic and hopeful.

I am retired now and fully aware that the challenges I faced while an "in-service" teacher have grown even more complex. In my new normal, I feel the energy to continue to work with teachers and educational professionals who live in that ever-widening gap that I have struggled to name for more than 20 years. I am understanding that my work is in a space between the energy flowing to a world in need and the energy coming back to me. This is a sacred space and is in need of the quiet energy of witnessing and steadfast listening. In order to be of use, I want to give witness to the power of paradox, while continuing to monitor my desire to resist the notion that I must regain my equilibrium. Even now I have to catch myself, to stop the relentless feeling that I must address my energy to what is yet unresolved, in myself, in those I love, and in the world.

Creating space to bring educators together has always been important to me, and paradox has always been a central part of that space. I realize now that my energy in these spaces is different after my strokes, or maybe, as my friend Amy suggested, I am different. I think I felt the tension of the space as anticipation for ... I am not sure of what. Maybe I was holding hope for buy-in or acceptance. It could be that I was wearing a "pleaser hat" – that would certainly have been in my wheel-house. I feel a bit of the letting go of gain and success, and although I never thought those were factors in my preparation, this newest humbling of my own spirit and the shift away from the equilibrium in my own head lets me know something was creating that former tension.

Now as I move to create these spaces for educators in these weeks after my strokes, I know that my own energy has shifted. The tension is different – more like focus than

tension. Being in this space-between gives me the energy to ask hard questions... And the hard questions give me the energy to create a new narrative about what I mean when I stop searching for equilibrium and claim my reality that living is not about balance. Instead, I am free to consider my story, and the story of anyone else, as Truth. I am free to care about a reality (Truth with a capital "T"!) co-created by our individual and collective truths (with a small "t"!).

The diagram below came to me as I have been journaling about this idea. In this reflective space, the Voice of Home, Voice of Self, and Voice of Exploration name three overlapping circles. The middle of the overlapping space creates a neutral place of observation and perspective where disequilibrium is welcome and surrounded by the space-between. This space-between welcomes stories of self and other, not for the purpose of examination and judgment, but to hold the disequilibrium that emerges when

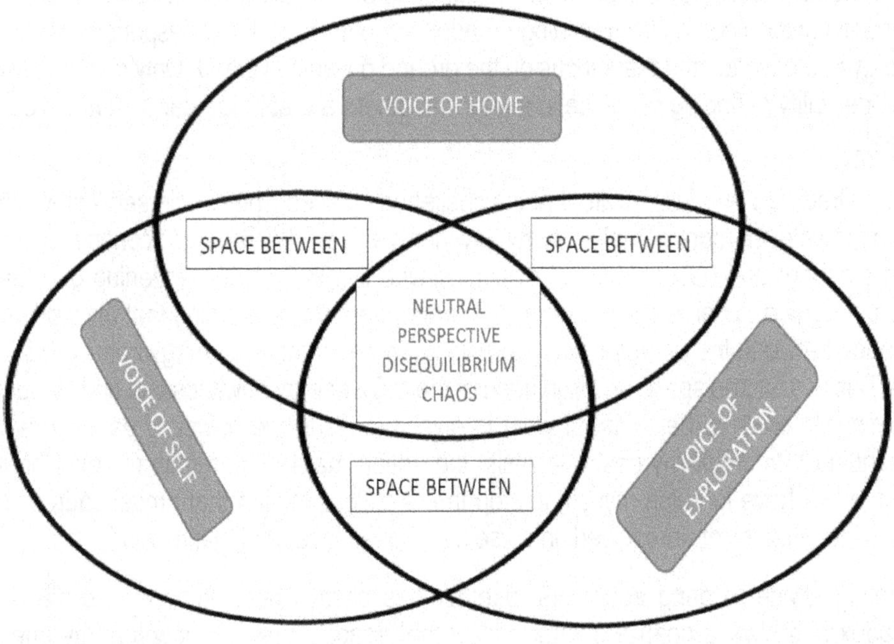

I can honor the tension of a neutral space safe enough for me to be still and allow truth to be practiced. It is a slow space.

The reality of pushing my physical body to regain my ability to stand and move around safely is also a slow space, one that requires a deliberate set of intentional activities. I am confident I will eventually notice that I am safer and trust myself more, but now it is hard some days. Rich's constant mantra is clear: "*Movement that is slow creates more strength than fast, uncontrolled movement – NO POINTS FOR SPEED!*" I always think to myself that these are wise words, and yet I still need the reminders.

THE COURAGE TO TEACH

Twenty years ago, when I participated in The Courage to Teach®, long before I decided to become a facilitator of this work, I was increasingly aware that the profession I was passionate about had become polarized and contentious. I wrote a poem at that time to describe the polarization and to ask some questions about how to create an atmosphere of respect among teachers and other educational professionals.

The No Child Left Behind Act went into effect in 2002 and, like a virus, changed the culture of education: objectivist thinking spread with the predictable outcomes of one-right-way scripted classrooms and teacher competition for test scores and a seat at the decision-making table. Everyone was under enormous pressure. Colleagues seemed to feel comfortable sharing their truths with me and responded in a positive way to my desire that we all speak professionally to the decisions that fostered pressure for teacher and students. I remember thinking, even then, that my responsibility to behave with consistent congruence to the Courage to Teach principles meant that when I sat with other professionals, I insisted we practice deep listening and respect the Boundary Markers from our Courage Work.

Now, as I live into my new normal, I find some lines in that 20-year-old poem speaking to me:

The space between us is real.
The mud between us is messy.
The silence between us is audible.
How then, do we begin to move in the space between us?
To hear our story of self, of other?
To tell the story of self, of other?
To honor the space between us?
To lift the truth between us?

These words from that old poem haunt me as I am constantly trying to parse the sentiment that would embody what my truth is now. These lines feel like the map for living my new normal of an unbalanced life, and I am amused and informed by the notion that I wrote this poem so long ago. I learn from it as if someone else were its author.

And now, I have a glimpse of my own meaning, new clarity from my strokes. I hope for an even deeper connection, as I continue my journaling and my getting reacquainted with myself, especially that voice I thought had no name but seems to have become the Voice of Exploration in my diagram!

Sandra Sturdivant Merriam (Sandie) was a member of the pilot Courage to Teach® on the South Carolina coast from 1996-1998. Since that time, she has known that she wanted to use Courage Work to help teachers hear their own voices, holding space for them to find a hopeful voice from a new vantage point. She can be reached at sandiemerriam@gmail.com

68 Wanna' Know How to Cope with Climate Change? Start with Changing Yourself

By Mardi Tindal

On a gorgeously sunny weekend in the late summer of 2012, I was enroute to a friend's cottage north of Toronto with my husband and two other friends. My term as the elected leader of Canada's largest Protestant denomination had ended just a few days earlier, and I was looking forward to some R&R.

It was a strange feeling to have a whole weekend stretching ahead with no commitments. I'd spent three years at a breakneck pace and the prospect of enjoying some expansive, unscheduled time was both thrilling and, in a way, unnerving.

As our destination neared, my husband signaled for our final left turn and stopped to wait for oncoming traffic. A young man (possibly distracted by the two young women beside him) promptly ploughed his pickup truck into the back of our mid-sized passenger car, crumpling it beyond repair.

An obvious metaphor! But of what?

One of the meanings I've taken from this incident over the years is the challenge of speaking truthfully about what's really going on inside us. As the four of us shook pebbles of shattered safety glass out of our hair and assessed the seemingly miraculous fact that none of us had any visible injuries, we assured each other: "I'm fine. Yes, I'm fine."

But we weren't, of course.

We were in shock. And while we were without serious injury, we would discover many new muscular aches and pains in the weeks ahead. My husband particularly suffered, perhaps because he had glanced in his rear view mirror, seen the truck bearing down on us and, unlike the rest of us, stiffened in anticipation of impact. It took several months of physiotherapy before he felt fully restored. But on that sunny morning, he was as confident as any of us in claiming: "I'm fine. Really, I'm fine."

On a different scale, I was just as bad.

I had thoroughly enjoyed my time in office as Moderator of the United Church of Canada. An extrovert, I thrived on interaction and engagement. Meeting people in church halls, facilitating workshops, presiding at sessions of the church's legislative council, giving media interviews – all of this was a joy to me. Then it ended as abruptly as, say, a rear-end collision. "I'm fine," I said. "Really, I'm fine."

But I wasn't. I was already grieving the loss of the meaningful work and purposeful activity that had defined me for three years. I was wondering how much (if anything) I'd really accomplished. And I was deeply exhausted.

Looking back, I blame Parker Palmer for most of it....

In the United Church of Canada, one doesn't "run" for the position of Moderator. Anyone who wanted the job badly enough to campaign for it would be deemed unfit. Instead, one allows one's name to stand in nomination, and then – apart from a short printed statement and a five minute speech -- keeps quiet until the election.

I'd been asked to let my name stand in the past and had always said no. But by the fall of 2008, a couple of things had come together.

One was the growing urgency of encouraging faith communities to become more actively involved in reducing greenhouse gases. True, in 2008, there were many people who still questioned the *science*, but I'd already become convinced it was more a matter for the *heart*. Climate scientists told me many times: "We can't persuade

people with facts alone. We need your help."

The other was the fact that, after years of participating in Courage to Lead retreats, I had reached a point of no return about "going public." I didn't particularly look forward to public engagement on a controversial issue. I knew it could lead to my being attacked or ridiculed (which it did). But the Courage Work had taken hold in me to such an extent that I couldn't avoid it. If I were to live with integrity, then I had to bring my concern for climate change to offering myself for the role of Moderator.

And so I stood with seven other candidates before the church's General Council and, in my five minutes, I told them that climate change was the greatest moral challenge of our generation. And I proposed that when human beings take an "abundance approach" rather than a "scarcity approach," we can generate the hope to meet this challenge, together.

They elected me anyway.

"Community not only creates abundance, community *is* abundance," says Parker, and these words accompanied me throughout my national and international travels as Moderator, and in "town halls" across the country.

I've learned that when our hearts embrace the truth that abundance is found in community, inner climate change becomes the most powerful resource by which to address outer climate change. And when our understanding of community extends to the whole human community, we gain an even deeper appreciation for our abundant relationships and potential.

There were many opportunities for me to advance this perspective. I attended the United Nations' 2009 COP15 climate change talks in Copenhagen, Denmark, and 2011 COP17 in Durban, South Africa, and was bemused to find myself as the only North American church leader present. I was invited to participate in news conferences and issue statements with other global religious leaders of such stature as Archbishop Desmond Tutu. My words found their way into national and international newspapers on numerous occasions, and more frequently in regional news outlets at home as I traveled the country. I was told that I'd become both a symbol of hope, and a threat, a thorn in the side of our federal government which, at the time, was muzzling climate scientists and blocking constructive global action. I could neither remain silent about that obstruction, nor could I behave in any way other than respectfully, given our practices of Courage and Renewal.

Parker Palmer's language in *Healing the Heart of Democracy* gave me a framework

that sustained me both in the exhilaration of becoming (in the Andy Warhol sense) famous, and in standing firm against the personal attacks my advocacy attracted. I found his Habits of the Heart especially useful in helping me resist the temptation to demonize my critics:

- An understanding that we are all in this together;
- An appreciation of the value of "otherness";
- An ability to hold tension in life-giving ways;
- A sense of personal voice and agency;
- A capacity to create community.

These remind me, in a particular way, of the story about the blind men examining an elephant. In one version of the story, six blind men are asked to determine what an elephant looks like by feeling different parts of the elephant's body. The blind man who feels a leg says the elephant is like a pillar; the one who feels the tail says the elephant is like a rope; the one who feels the trunk says the elephant is like a tree branch; and so on. Each one has felt only his part of the elephant and presents these fragments – true, but utterly misleading – as if they were the whole.

The five habits remind me of this story because it is precisely the opposite. Each of Parker's habits is itself a glimpse of wholeness. They do not contradict each other; they amplify. If we could not value "the other," for example, how could we understand that we are all in this together? If we had no sense of personal voice and agency, what would we have to offer to the creation of community? If we could not hold tension in life-giving ways, how could we see that "the other" has value?

Where the blind men see only fragments, Parker sees only different aspects of wholeness.

When my term as Moderator ended, I returned to facilitating Courage & Renewal retreats, accepted an invitation to be a national magazine columnist, and wondered about other next steps of engagement. But without a formal leadership role, I began to feel disoriented and restless about what more I might do. That's the other way in which, on that August morning when a distracted driver rear-ended our vacation, I was not "all right." I had to find a new way to speak and act with integrity.

In the midst of this struggle, I received Sally Z. Hare's invitation to become a Kirkridge Courage Fellow. At our first gathering, in January, 2015, I heard myself sounding very tentative about the work that was life-giving for me, my ongoing passion for co-creating a livable planet. My hesitation was so pronounced that in response I declared to the circle, "I'm not dead yet!"

In his book, *The Active Life: A Spirituality of Work, Creativity, and Caring*, Parker Palmer writes about "the temptation to think of ourselves as irrelevant, powerless and utterly mundane." Without a given role, I was beginning to fall into that temptation. He goes on to say, *"On the surface, the temptations of the strong ego and the weak ego seem quite contrary to one another. But paradoxically, their origins and outcomes are the same. Both destroy our capacity for right action because both proceed from the same mistaken premise: the assumption that effective action requires us to be relevant, powerful, and spectacular, that only by being so can we have a real impact on the world."*

As embarrassing as it is to admit, I had fallen into the assumption that I somehow needed to be "relevant, powerful and spectacular" to continue with "right action." The Fellowship gave me an opportunity to rediscover my capacity for good work without organizational standing, as I eased into retirement. Just as our principles and practices had readied me to respond with integrity in the past, being in the company of seasoned facilitators would ready me for new circumstances.

Thanks to the trustworthy questions offered to me by the Fellows, I knew how to respond when I received an invitation to lead the United Church of Canada's delegation to the COP21 Climate talks in Paris. I knew in my heart that it was "right work" for me to accept, as an elder of the church.

The challenge was to discern how I would do it in a new way. Elizabeth May, Member of Parliament, and Leader of the Green Party of Canada and a veteran of these talks, says a global UN climate change meeting "is a lot like going through a car wash without the car"! Without the Moderator's preaching stole, a symbol of leadership, I would don instead the role of mentor and guide to the young adult activist and the elder from the Haida First Nation who accompanied me. I could shield my first-time companions from some of the buffeting and help them bring their distinctive voices to the gathering.

It was January 2016 before I'd had a chance to catch my breath after Paris and I was starting to wonder again about what, if anything, I might do now that the talks were over. I had written thank you notes to our Prime Minister and the Minister of Environment and Climate Change, commending them for the courage it took to listen to us at the talks, and take our advice about what will now be difficult commitments to sell to many voters. I secretly hoped that they'd tell me what I could do to help. Our new federal Minister of Science was kind enough to tell me that I'd made a big difference in the progress to date, but there was no clear invitation to play a role from here. And why should there be?

I was slipping back into my own scarcity thinking, “the temptation to think of myself as irrelevant, powerless and utterly mundane.” I was thinking, as I went off to another Fellows retreat, that my capacity for “right action” had dissolved.

Perched on the mountain and buried under a record January snowfall which grew higher by the minute, a number of us cozied up around a toasty wood stove. One of the resource people we’d been expecting was unable to get to us through the snow, so our leader asked if I would share something about the climate talks. As it turned out, this was the first chance I’d had to speak of my experiences in Paris, and I was grateful that it came in such a setting. Our Fellows had by now developed a mature level of trust amongst each other, and this invitation represented an opportunity to go deeper, to reconnect my soul’s truth with the significance of those talks, and to think further about the inner climate change that would determine right work from here. I was surprised to hear myself humming, and then singing the chorus of a favorite hymn as I began this impromptu presentation:

My heart shall sing of the day you bring.
Let the fires of your justice burn.
Wipe away all tears
for the dawn draws near
and the world is about to turn

My Soul Cries, also known as The Canticle of the Turning, is sung to a stirring traditional Irish melody. I sang what I knew to be true: that I had witnessed the world turning, the fires of justice burning, and great momentum growing in a movement of which we are all part. And that movement is turning the world.

I spoke about how Courage Principles and Practices had guided my approach and contributions to the talks. In daily briefings with the Canadian negotiators, for example, we grew to understand that we truly were “all in this together.” In consulting broadly with others in the civil society sector, we learned to value the other. Each of us spoke with our own voice, and in the speaking, helped to forge community.

At earlier talks, nations of the Global South had argued that the nations of the Global North had caused climate change and benefited from the dirty economy; therefore it was solely up to them to change. It’s an understandable perspective, but if the most catastrophic climate change is to be averted, both North and South together will need to reduce greenhouse gas emissions. Emerging economies cannot rely on fossil fuels for development. This seemingly intractable issue was resolved creatively. Northern nations will provide significant help to meet the challenge of adapting to the ravages of climate change in the South, and will support pre-industrial economies to leap-frog

to clean energy. Nations in the South will do their share, and all nations will abide by transparent mechanisms to track action. It was a remarkable demonstration of holding the tension in life-giving ways.

As I told the Fellows about these things, it became clearer to me how important it is that we go public with what Courage and Renewal can offer to the healing of the planet. We create the conditions for inner climate change which are critical for addressing outer climate change.

All of us have a stake in this. A democratic government will risk only what its voters support, so citizens will need to actively support positive risk-taking, and challenge their elected officials when they retreat from their "better angels." Political capital will be risked, and courage must be rewarded. We must guard our own integrity, and resist the temptation to withdraw our support when decisions require our personal sacrifice.

I shared with the Kirkridge Fellows words from Sanjay Khan, the futurist-in-residence at the Toronto Symphony Orchestra. In an article for the United Church Observer, he lands on the primary importance of small circles in local communities:

> *I doubt that hope and opportunity will arise from social protest; traditional rabble-rousing is unlikely to prompt a response from business and government that's commensurate with the scale of the coming changes. Rather, I anticipate our best source of hope for adapting to the future will be in the quiet and determined resolve of communities to organize around exigencies we're likely to face — independently of, and together with, business, government and not-for-profits.*

The quiet and determined resolve of communities is the strongest lever in the turning that I see. As a community of practice, courage facilitators who "go public" offer transformative work on the ground. Individuals in our retreats hear their own heartsongs and choose to live with greater integrity between their inner change and the outer changes they seek.

I also shared with the Fellows the story of Yeb Saño. In the two months preceding the talks, he and his fellow pilgrims took enough steps, enroute to Paris, to circle the globe seven times. They became a resilient traveling community, calling upon ordinary citizens and national leaders to be people of hope, on every continent. Two years earlier, as head of the Philippine delegation at the COP talks in Warsaw, Saño had broken down in tears of sorrow as he addressed the global forum. Hurricane Haiyan, whose ferocity was likely amplified by climate change, had just clobbered his homeland. When his words were not enough, he invited a global movement of citizens to join him in walking, talking, and engaging in heart-deep practices that would call leaders

to their better selves. His witness, and that of those who joined him, made a palpable difference to global leaders. Christiana Figueres, the then-Executive Secretary of the UN Framework Convention on Climate Change (UNFCCC), responded with tears of joy when the pilgrims presented her with petitions from citizens around the world, as the Paris talks began. She affirmed the importance - spiritual and material - of ordinary citizens offering their solidarity.

When, after sharing some of these stories, I invited the Kirkridge Fellows to complete the sentence, "I wonder...." I was moved by their wisdom. Here's some of what they said:

I wonder how to honor traditional and indigenous knowledge in visible ways in our work.

I wonder about other opportunities we may have for dialogue with our governments.

I wonder how we can help affect the shift from power to partnership, from mastery to mystery.

I wonder about the nature of the scope of the shift we're in. There is a spiritual movement behind everything, and I wonder about the collective life-force that is coming through us in Courage Circles, and about what we bring to the collective soul.

I wonder what would happen if we listened to the depth of the grief in all of us.

I wonder about how my individual soul is inseparable from the soul of this planet, how our culture of individualism poisons and disconnects from the biosphere, and how that's killing us. How can we broaden our circle and not diminish soul-safety?

In the months after that conversation I had another opportunity to work with Parker's Habits of the Heart when, with Dan Hines who is another Fellow, I led a circle titled *The Politics of the Open Hearted: Courage and Climate Change*. Over the course of a week at the beautiful Sorrento Centre in British Columbia, Canada, we took one habit as each day's theme. There is a sense in which, as we came to realize, we are all in shock from the threat climate change poses to our world, perhaps especially those of us who have seen it coming. But we are learning to speak the truth, and helping others do the same. We are no longer in denial saying: "I'm fine. Really, I'm fine."

My own need to practice a non-violent vocabulary about climate change has become clearer. I am learning how it feels very different to speak about "climate health" and "climate peace" more than "climate disaster" and "climate justice." The latter terms

have often sounded hyper-charged, antagonistic, and out-of-sync with reality to me. So now I'm exploring language that can better motivate us toward a low-carbon society, and I share news of hope-filled change wherever it's to be found. What words are more likely to bring us into a creative, dynamic, and organic relationship with one another, with other beings? Which contribute to a more whole-hearted reconnecting?

In order to stay true to my best contributions for this stage of my life - and support others in theirs, I'm inviting old and newer friends into fresh conversation. Plans that my husband and I are making to live communally are reinvigorating, as one way for us to live with greater integrity and within the limits of Earth's resources.

Listening, speaking and facilitating as an elder, and resisting thoughts that the only kind of "right work" for me is the over-active kind, provide me with a guideline. I will continue to encourage and accompany others, including those elected to public office, without pursuing such an office.

When I was invited by my Member of Parliament to help him "set the tone and context" for a Town Hall about Climate Change in our neighborhood, I knew it would be a tough room. However, I also now knew what my "right work" would be. I had witnessed a similar climate change forum in another part of the city, so I knew some of the activists who would arrive without much interest in developing an appreciation for "the other" or '"holding tensions in life-giving ways." I had reason to believe that there would be plenty of anger hurled toward government, but would there be enough humility for something constructive to be born of the encounter? I would describe the change of heart and the corresponding practices that would get us where we needed to go, as community.

In part, I said: *My granddaughter is 3 years old. By the time she's the age of her Dad, we will need to be living in a decarbonized economy, a society that can continue to sustain life.*

Getting there requires a combination of humility and chutzpah from us all. I hope that's what each of us will bring tonight - both the humility to listen to those with whom we disagree and the chutzpah to present our strong views.

I hope we will challenge our government to fulfill the commitments it made in Paris, and support it when taking steps to do so.

Because we're all in this together.

I then witnessed 200 people, with varied views, have a civil, constructive conversation.

It appeared to be deeply heartening for us all, including our Member of Parliament.

Going public in new and different ways such as this will continue to be "right work" for me, thanks to the community of mature practice and support reflected in our Kirkridge Courage Fellowship. We're each on a long road of taking Courage and Renewal to places that call to us to bring our best for the sake of our healing and uncovering our hidden wholeness. Our work is slow and steady. It won't be done before we are, but the movement will continue to pick up speed.

As Desmond Tutu once said: *"Do your little bit of good where you are; it's those little bits of good put together that overwhelm the world."*

Practices of Courage and Renewal are starting to overwhelm the world.

Mardi Tindal is a writer, presenter and facilitator, and a past Moderator of The United Church of Canada. She lives in Toronto, Ontario, with her husband Douglas Tindal and delights in being the mother of two adult sons and daughters-in-law and in being a grandmother. She can be contacted through email: mardi.tindal@gmail.com

SECTION 2

Seeking the Courage to Live in A Community of Strangers

Community does not necessarily mean living face-to-face with others; rather, it means never losing the awareness that we are connected to each other. It is not about the presence of other people – it is about being fully open to the reality of relationship, whether or not we are alone.

--Parker Palmer, *A Hidden Wholeness*

Insight From Parker J. Palmer

13 Ways of Looking at Community (...with a 14th thrown in for free)

- Whether we know it or not, like it or not, honor it or not, we are embedded in community. Whether we think of ourselves as biological creatures or spiritual beings or both, the truth remains—we were created in and for a complex ecology of relatedness, and without it we wither and die. This simple fact has a critical implication: community is not a goal to be achieved, but a gift to be received. When we treat community as a product that we must manufacture instead of as a gift we have been given, it will elude us eternally. When we try to "make community happen," driven by desire, design, and determination—places within us where the ego often lurks—we can make a good guess at the outcome: we will exhaust ourselves and alienate each other, snapping the connections we yearn for. Too many relationships have been diminished or destroyed by a drive toward "community-building," which evokes a grasping that is the opposite of what we need to do; relax into our created condition and receive the gift we have been given.

- Of course, in our culture—a culture premised on the notion that we must manufacture whatever we want or need—learning to relax and receive a gift requires hard work! But the work of becoming receptive is quite unlike the external work of building communal structures, or gathering endlessly to "share" and "solve problems": receptivity involves inner work. Community begins not externally but in the recesses of the human heart. Long before community can be manifest in outward relationship, it must be present in the individual as a "capacity for connectedness"—a capacity to resist the forces of disconnection with which our culture and our psyches are riddled; forces with names like narcissism, egotism, jealousy, competition, empire-building, nationalism, and related forms of madness in which psychopathology and political pathology become powerfully intertwined.

- We cultivate a capacity for connectedness through contemplation. By this I do not necessarily mean sitting cross-legged and chanting a mantra, though that may work for some. By contemplation I mean any way one has of penetrating the illusion of separateness and touching the reality of interdependence. In my life, the deepest forms of contemplation have been failure, suffering, and loss. When I flourish, it is easy to maintain the

illusion of separateness, easy to imagine that I alone am responsible for my good fortune. But when I fall, I see a secret hidden in plain sight: I need other people for comfort, encouragement, and support, and for criticism, challenge, and collaboration. The self-sufficiency I feel in success is a mirage. I need community—and, if I open my heart, I have it.

- The most common connotation for the word "community" in our culture is "intimacy," but this is a trap. When community is reduced to intimacy, our world shrinks to a vanishing point: with how many people can one be genuinely intimate in a lifetime? My concept of community must be capacious enough to embrace everything from my relations to strangers I will never meet (e.g. the poor around the world to whom I am accountable), to people with whom I share local resources and must learn to get along (e.g. immediate neighbors), to people I am related to for the purpose of getting a job done (e.g. coworkers and colleagues). Intimacy is neither possible nor necessary across this entire range of relationships. But the capacity for connectedness is both possible and necessary if we are to inhabit the larger, and truer, community of our lives.

- The concept of community must embrace even those we perceive as "the enemy." In 1974, I set off on a fourteen-year journey of living in intentional communities. By 1975, I had come up with my definition of community: "Community is that place where the person you least want to live with always lives." By 1976, I had come up with my corollary to that definition: "And when that person moves away, someone else arises immediately to take his or her place." The reason is simple: relationships in community are so close and so intense that it is easy for us to project onto another person that which we cannot abide in ourselves. As long as I am there, the person I least want to live with will be there as well: in the immortal words of Pogo, "We has met the enemy and it is us." That knowledge is one of the difficult but redeeming gifts community has to offer.

- Hard experiences—such as meeting the enemy within, or dealing with the conflict and betrayal that are an inevitable part of living closely with others—are not the death knell of community; they are the gateway into the real thing. But we will never walk through that gate if we cling to a romantic image of community as the Garden of Eden. After the first flush of romance, community is less like a garden and more like a crucible. One stays in the crucible only if one is committed to being refined by fire. If we seek community merely to be happy, the seeking will end at the gate. If we

want community to confront the unhappiness we carry within ourselves, the experiment may go on, and happiness—or better, a sense of at-homeness—may be its paradoxical outcome.

- It is tempting to think of hierarchy and community as opposites, as one more "either-or." But in mass society, with its inevitable complex organizations, our challenge is to think "both-and," to find ways of inviting the gift of community within those hierarchical structures. I am not proposing the transformation of bureaucracies into communities, which I regard as an impossible dream. I am proposing "pockets of possibility" within bureaucratic structures, places where people can live and work differently than the way dictated by the organization chart. The most creative of our institutions already do this; e.g., those high-tech companies that must organize efficiently to protect the bottom line and get the product out the door, but must also create spaces where people can collaborate in dreaming, playing, thinking wild thoughts, and taking outrageous risks, lest tomorrow's product never be imagined.

- Contrary to popular opinion, community requires leadership, and it requires more leadership, not less, than bureaucracies. A hierarchical organization, with its well-defined roles, rules, and relationships, is better able to operate on automatic pilot than is a community, with its chaotic and unpredictable energy field. But leadership for community is not exercised through power (i.e. through the use of sanctions) that is the primary tool of bureaucratic leadership. Leadership for community requires authority, a form of power that is freely granted to the leader by his or her followers. Authority is granted to people who are perceived as authentic, as authoring their own words and actions rather than proceeding according to some organizational script. So the authority to lead toward community can emerge from anyone in an organization—and it may be more likely to emerge from people who do not hold positional power.

- Leadership for community consists in creating, holding, and guarding a trustworthy space in which human resourcefulness may be evoked. A critical assumption is hidden in that definition—the assumption that people are resourceful. Standard organizational models assume that people have deficits and scarcities rather than resources; people do not want to work, so the organization must surround them with threats; people would not know what to do with the unexpected, so organizational life must be routine; people will try to cheat if given half a chance, so the organization must build walls of security. When we act on the scarcity assumption, it becomes a

self-fulfilling prophecy through a process called resentment (small wonder!), and people are rendered incapable of community, at least temporarily, sometimes permanently.

- Ironically, we often resist leaders who call upon our resourcefulness. We find it threatening when leaders say, "I am not going to tell you how to do this, let alone do it for you, but I am going to create a space in which you can do it for yourselves." Why is that threatening? Because many of us have been persuaded by institutions ranging from educational to industrial to religious that we do not have the resources it takes to do things, or even think things, for ourselves (which, to the extent that we believe it, expands an institution's power over our lives). Many people have been convinced of their own inadequacy, and any leader who wants to invite them into a community of mutual resourcefulness must see this invisible wound and try to heal it.

- Seeing and treating that wound takes courage and tenacity; while the leader is calling followers to fullness, the followers are accusing the leader of not doing his or her job. Every teacher who has tried to create a space for self-sustaining learning community knows this story: students resist on the grounds that "we are not paying tuition to listen to John and Susie talk, but to take notes from you, the person with the Ph.D." It takes a deeply-grounded leader—a leader with a source of identity independent of how popular he or she is with the group being led—to hold a space in which people can discover their resources while those same people resist, angrily accusing the leader of not earning his or her keep.

- In the face of resistance, an ungrounded leader will revert to the bureaucratic model, the teacher will revert to lecturing rather than inviting inquiry, the manager will revert to rule making rather than inviting creativity. In the face of resistance, leaders will do what they are taught to do—not create space for others, but fill the space themselves—fill it with their own words, their own skills, their own deeds, and their own ego. This, of course, is precisely what followers expect from leaders, and that expectation prolongs the period during which leaders of community must hold the space—hold it in trust until people trust the leader, and themselves, enough to enter it.

- There is a name for what leaders experience during this prolonged period of patient waiting. It is called "suffering" (which is the root meaning for the word "patience"). Suffering is what happens when you see the possibilities in others while they deny those same possibilities in themselves. Suffering is

what happens when you hold in trust a space for community to emerge, but others lack the trust to enter the space and receive the gift. Suffering is what happens while you wait out their resistance, believing that people have more resources than they believe they have. But leaders do not want to suffer. So we create and maintain institutional arrangements that protect leaders from suffering by assuming the worst of the followers and encouraging leaders to dominate them by means of power.

- I have yet to see a seminar in suffering as part of a leadership-training program. I can think of three reasons why. One, we train leaders for bureaucracy rather than community, no matter what we say we are doing. Two, the idea of leadership is still so steeped in machismo that we do not want to acknowledge a "weakness" like suffering. Three, suffering is a spiritual problem, and we want to keep leadership training in the orderly realm of theory and technique, rather than engage in the raw messiness of the human heart.

But leadership for community will always break our hearts. So if we want to lead this way, we must help each other deal with that fact. We might begin by viewing the problem through the lens of paradox, that spiritual way of seeing that turns conventional wisdom upside down. Here, "breaking your heart" (which we normally understand as a destructive process that leaves one's heart in fragments) is reframed as the breaking open of one's heart into larger, more generous forms – a process that goes on and on until the heart is spacious enough to hold a vision of hope and the reality of resistance with tightening like a fist.

If we are willing to embrace the spiritual potential of suffering, then community and leadership, human resourcefulness and the capacity to hold it in trust, will prove to be abundant among us – gifts we have been given from the beginning, but are still learning how to receive.

Parker J. Palmer is a writer, teacher, and activist who works independently on issues in education, community, leadership, spirituality, and social change. Founder and Senior Partner of the Center for Courage & Renewal, he has authored nine books, including *The Courage to Teach, Let Your Life Speak, A Hidden Wholeness,* and *Healing the Heart of Democracy*. He holds a Ph.D. in sociology from the University of California at Berkeley, and thirteen honorary doctorates.

MEETING THE AUTHORS

Joanne Cooper: Teaching, leading Circles of Trust, hanging out with my grandchildren, being in the Fellowship.. these are what make me feel alive, My Work in the world is creating space for others to learn, grow ,and listen to their own inner teacher --- and also, being in true community with others. I have been a Courage & Renewal facilitator for over 10 years. I am a passionate journal keeper, having kept a journal for over 40 years. I want you to know, Readers, that I love my family, my friends and my life – and that writing my story for you has been empowering!

Diane Petteway: *What makes me feel most alive are honest conversations, holding hands with my husband, being "in flow," being with my journal, singing in community, opening night at the theater, the energy of adolescents, mountains, books, and Flair pens. My Work in the world is about creating safe, creative places for the soul; fighting for social justice; gathering stories, sharing music. I have a very shy soul. I wish I could live more "out loudly," like my daddy did. Writing my story to share with you has made me feel like I was claiming a birthright gift, naming truths that had been long dormant.*

Sally Z. Hare: My passions are teaching and learning. What makes me feel alive: walking on the beach; making love; being in nature; being in the Fellowship. I am a passionate reader, which also means I have to climb over the stacks at the bedside to get into bed! I love my e-books too! I have been a Courage & Renewal facilitator for over 20 years, and I am still becoming a facilitator. I have the world's best life, living in a nest, co-created with Jim, that feels a bit like a thin place.

Karen Noordhoff: *Envisioning, creating, and facilitating Courage & Renewal Circles of Trust makes me feel alive... So does conversation with my husband, David, over a glass of wine; being by the Metolius River in central Oregon; time in the Kirkridge Fellowship, and listening to French music and any time in France! I am coming to know that my Work in the world is supporting others as they grow into the deepest core of who they are, and becoming a witness, particularly in Circles of Trust. I value deep listening and try to offer it to others. My middle name is Joyce, which reflects my soul of quiet joy. I tear up easily. Although not a Facebook person, I'm invested in my family and friends, making deep friendships. I am a serious Francophile and love the language, although I don't speak it well or fluently.*

Carol Kortsch: I like to be called by my name, Carol - Song of Joy. Here's what makes me feel alive: wilderness solitude, dirt under my nails, the drumming of pileated woodpeckers, 45 years of canoe trips with my man, dancing to an African beat. I know my Work: it is to stop, look, and listen – together. I relish creating safe and challenging communal circles that bring us home to ourselves and our wildest connections in earth. Writing from the heart of our circle has reminded me how essential it is to creatively tell my story in words and images. I will keep writing from this fresh beginning!

Veta Goler: *I'm most alive when I'm moving. That could mean I'm moving my body, as in walking my dog in nature, walking a labyrinth, drawing or coloring, or dancing in the kitchen. It could also mean moving within the terrain of my inner landscape while meditating or chanting. The Beauty I love is accessing and expressing the divine within me and helping others to do the same. My purpose on the planet is to know my divinity, which I do through creativity, spending time in nature, contemplative practices, and listening to and following my intuition.*

Elaine Sullivan: I feel alive when I am listening to stories, playing with my grandchildren, and being in nature. I value quiet and meditation AND connections with friends, family, and colleagues. I am a Seeker. I have spent over 40 years working with written life stories and inviting people to mine the depths of those stories. Yet, even after inviting so many others to write their story, I was surprised by the challenge to write my own for this book! I discovered layers of my inner world that make me even more curious about my soul journey.

Longing and Belonging

By Joanne Cooper

This is the tale of community longed for and found, the story of a fractured life made more whole. It is also the story of my growing understanding of the quality of community, whether in a retreat setting, in academia or in a family situation. What I have found in community is my own hidden wholeness, glimpses of which came from sharing parts of me I've never shared with anyone. And the key to this sharing, wherever it is taking place, is trust.

Every time I tell someone in Oregon that my husband and I split our time between Oregon and Hawaii, they sigh and go, "OHHHH! You are so lucky!" But the truth is that even though Hawaii is a place of beauty and wonder, it is also an isolated place in the middle of the Pacific Ocean. In fact, space shuttle photos show it as the most isolated population center on earth. It is roughly 2,400 miles to the closest land mass (California).

Yes, it is beautiful and yes, I have had a dream job there (being a tenured professor). I love my students, my friends, and my church community, but higher education is an island unto itself, a rather cold and lonely place that worships rationality. No one talks about the soul, only the intellect. I found there a lack of conversations that matter, much posturing and little that allows the soul to show up.

In short, higher education can be soul crushing. Alexander and Helen Astin affirm this in their study, *Meaning and Spirituality in the Lives of College Faculty: A Study of Values, Authenticity and Stress* (1999). They found little to feed the spirits of professors. Through a series of interviews, they explored issues of spirituality, authenticity, meaning, wholeness, and self-renewal in higher education. The researchers shared that some faculty wept in their offices when they were interviewed, as research questions gave participants an opportunity to honestly confront the desert in which they worked.

Looking back through my journals, I remember my own feelings. In 2007, I wrote about my life in the university:

> *Yesterday my department chair told me that when the dean's office called to ask who our personnel committee chair was, he said it was me, but that I was too busy to come to the training session. OK, there are several things wrong with this picture. First, not only did he neglect to tell me that I was chairing the committee this year, he didn't even ask me. Second, he neglected to tell me there was a training meeting. I found out because I was in a meeting with the dean, who was heading out the door to attend. Third, he decided without asking me that I didn't need to go to the meeting. So what if I screw up the procedures and my colleagues sue us. No big deal, right?*

LONGING FOR COMMUNITY

Is it any wonder, given these circumstances, that I was longing for a trustworthy community? I tried to construct that kind of community in my classes, carefully creating safe spaces where students could share their thoughts with each other. Even before I moved to Hawaii, I had been teaching a journal-keeping course which also combined reflective writing with honest conversations in small groups, but I figured that my new academic colleagues might think Journal Keeping was too "touchy feely." So when I started teaching in Hawaii, I re-named the seminar *Critical Reflection in Educational Administration* and continued to teach the same reflective journaling courses I had always taught. In these classes I would work to create the kind of community I needed, each semester starting with a new group that would eventually become a place of truth and honesty, where it was safe to laugh, to dig deep, think hard and then articulate those thoughts. These encounters always made my heart sing. One Samoan doctoral student told me she was going to quit the program until she took that course.

I shared Parker Palmer's *The Heart of a Teacher* with students in my courses and longed to experience the *Courage to Teach* retreats he described, but I couldn't because of my isolation in Hawaii. So I was propelled across the Pacific to the Northwest when a sabbatical opened the opportunity to attend two retreats in the

state of Washington. During that sabbatical I felt even more drawn to this work and to the Center for Courage & Renewal.

The Center's philosophy fit hand–and-glove with my love of journal-keeping, and especially my Critical Reflection course. The retreats gave me access to my inner teacher and to the realization that, all my life, I have been trying to create the community for which I longed. At the end of the second retreat, I invited the two facilitators, Terry Chadsey and Yarrow Durbin, to come to Hawaii to lead a retreat. This began a ten-year journey that included my becoming a facilitator and then inviting one of my students to do the same. I offered retreat opportunities to those who were place-bound in Hawaii, serving teachers, college faculty, principals, ministers, nurses, and, of course, students. At one point, we had participants who came from both Los Angeles and Korea in the group, so our community stretched across the Pacific.

Despite its isolation, Hawaii is a place of deep soul-nourishing beauty that gives itself naturally to this work. After my minister attended our year-long retreat series, he told me: "*Joanne, I've been to a lot of retreats in my life, but never anything like this before.*" Another participant, a faculty member who was a former Jesuit priest and grew up on a tiny island in the Pacific, wrote of his retreat experience: "*Thank you so much once again for such a wonderful gift of the weekend. I will forever remain grateful to you for loosening my heart to re-discover all the treasures buried deep within from ancestors past and winged spirits ahead. I can only promise what I am able to do within my control and that is to remain grateful and keep on dialoguing he alo ahe alo* (face-to-face) *with the endless possibilities of fullness ahead...*"

Ironically, it was I who needed my heart loosened and these retreats did just that. The hidden wholeness that Parker Palmer writes about was becoming more evident in my life. My journal allowed me to reflect on my life, then to step back and examine the pieces of this life in privacy and safety. I had written of my higher education experience:

> *I struggle each day in my journal to pick up all the pieces of my life, like the shattered slivers of a mirror that are reflecting my life back to me. Some pieces are jagged and painful to hold. Some are simply too small to handle and some are too big to lift. Together they make up the totality of my existence.*

What I didn't know at the time was that I could go even deeper in that reflection when I was able to share these pieces in a safe and trusting community that would allow me to feel much more whole.

YOU CAN'T GIVE WHAT YOU DON'T HAVE

When I applied for the Kirkridge Fellowship, I wrote in my application that I was isolated in Hawaii and in need of community. I had had a glimpse of this kind of community when I attended a Circle of Trust retreat at Zapata Ranch in Colorado with facilitators Sally Z. Hare and Jeff Creswell. I knew right away that I wanted more. As a very thirsty person, I had only taken a tiny sip of water---totally refreshing and yet just a hint of the possibilities that lay ahead. But the depth of my need and the rich rewards that lay ahead in the many opportunities to be in community with other facilitators were still unknown to me.

The truth is that it was hard for me to think that I deserved this blessing. As a facilitator, I was supposed to be giving retreats, not partaking of them. I was supposed to be giving water, not drinking it myself. But in that first gathering of facilitators at the Kirkridge Retreat Center, I heard others say that they were also questioning their role as a facilitator. Many were not actively offering retreats at that time and were concerned about whether they even met the requirements of the fellowship program.

I wondered how it could be OK to be in retreat and not be leading it myself. I saw others doing this, but I was almost afraid of my hunger for community. I felt like a starving person; if I started eating, I might never stop. And so, I was strangely hesitant. I had a whole state of people back in Hawaii who needed my services. How could I spend my time soaking up the blessings of community for myself? And yet---maybe I could. The truth is we all needed that kind of trusting community, one that allows us to be our true selves and to be accepted for whoever shows up. I was beginning to believe that you can't give what you don't have.

THE CLEARNESS TRIAD: WHERE I COULD SPEAK THE UNSPOKEN

One of the most powerful aspects of these Fellowship retreats was the Clearness Triad. Instead of the traditional Clearness Committee where there was one focus person, we met in the same group of three over three days, and each of us had time as the focus person. The format was the same as for Clearness Committees: deep listening, open and honest questions, taking notes. I found that continuing the process each day with the same people built trust over the course of the retreat, creating a space in which we dared to speak of things in our lives that we had never shared with anyone.

In one retreat, our triad had built a "nest" in a round room, surrounded by windows and a view of the scenic Delaware Water Gap Valley below. We became so engrossed in the process that we lost track of time and missed the group photo. We vowed to get together at the next retreat and make time for this tight, safe community. The next time we found a quiet room and had just started sharing when a guest poet from the retreat

poked his head in the door and said, *"I am so tired. I just need to lie down in a corner and rest. I promise I won't listen or bother you. Please, can I come in?"*

There was a stunned silence. Neither of my dear friends said anything. I felt desperate for some time alone with them and knew it would not be the same with this stranger in the room. I hesitated only a moment and then said, *"I'm sorry. That's not going to work for us."*

Later I heard he complained he could "get no respect" at the retreat, that we had rebuffed him. I felt badly for him, but still glad I had protected our privacy and our community. I was willing to risk being rude to preserve the precious trust we had slowly built. What I found in that community was the ability to share parts of me I'd never shared with anyone. Sharing those pieces meant I could incorporate them into the totality of my being, that I could be more whole. I could welcome parts of me that had been unspeakable, shut off and alone in a tiny corner of my being. This was a huge gift, one I was willing to fend off even requests of guest poets to preserve.

IMPORTANT ENOUGH TO MOVE HEAVEN AND EARTH

To attend my last Kirkridge Fellowship retreat, I needed to fly all the way from Honolulu to Newark, New Jersey, and then travel by car to Kirkridge in Pennsylvania. My daughter and her family were visiting us in Hawaii for a week's vacation, and I really wanted time with them, so I booked a red-eye flight that allowed me to see my family and get to the retreat on time. My granddaughters looked stricken when they found out I was leaving the next day and asked, "You mean this is the only night we get to see you?" My daughter and her husband said they were too old to take overnight flights anymore and looked at me like I was crazy. What was I doing? Finally, my daughter looked at me and said, *"You must really want to be there."*

"Yes," I said, feeling heard, understood. This fellowship and this sense of community are so important to me that I am willing to move heaven and earth to be there.

My idea of community extends to my family, which is unraveling. My daughter and son-in-law are in the middle of a divorce, and we are stepping in to care for our grandchildren. We struggle to support both parents as we help our grandchildren make sense of what is happening to them and to their family. The kids' counselor says our job is to help them continue to lead normal lives in the midst of the chaos and pain... Not an easy task.

Loving community, I realize, extends to family as well as to our Kirkridge Fellowship and the university classrooms I oversee. A powerful lesson for me is that everything changes. Just when you have adjusted to a new reality, everything begins to morph. My beautiful grandson, at 14, sprouts up and is suddenly taller

than me. His voice drops as he rises, so that he ends up taller and more deep-throated than my memories of him from just three weeks ago. And I need to remind myself that this is normal. Everything is always in the midst of great change, even as time seems to be standing still.

We often move into our grandchildren's house and take care of them while their parents are out of town. We literally and figuratively hold community for this household that includes a large dog that will eat anything he can find or steal (like the roast off the kitchen counter) and a cat that stays out all night and returns with dead birds in his mouth or rat bites on his paw. All of this is normal but I feel a little like the canvas seat on their outdoor furniture that gave way as I sat down and suddenly I was sitting on the ground!

I am trying to reach my own new normal, juggling Courage work, my university teaching, and my family's great pain. Frequently I ask, "What am I doing here?" I am trying to be glue to a wobbling community, but I feel like I could topple any minute without a little shoring up of my own! What feeds me are the times when I am nourished by my various communities. It is the moments with my grandchildren when we sit and talk after dinner about our dreams, who we want to be when we grow up; the moments in our Kirkridge Fellowship when we are deep in conversation about the things that matter most to us.

TRUST IN COMMUNITY

I recently traveled to the Baltic Capitals and Russia with a group of 15 people. One of the things that was most unsettling was the amount of time we spent in small talk about where we'd been and what we'd seen, about where we were going that day and what we would see (the Estonian capital and its gardens, the towers of the Kremlin and the changing of the guard, etc.). Even though the places were interesting, I ended up thirsty for conversations about things that really matter.

I realized that the essence of trust in a community is what matters. A group of strangers traveling together and making small talk at breakfast each morning is not the same as a community of trust, a group of people willing to create the safe space that allows talk about what really matters. I have been deeply moved by that quality of community in our Circles of Trust, and I can see that trust is the key to any community. Even families come with different levels of trust. If you are getting beaten up every day by someone bigger than you, there is little trust in that family/community.

I remember research I conducted with faculty women in higher education around "Finding a Home in the Academy." When we asked them about the meaning of home, I was surprised by one woman's response that home for her was a dangerous place,

not one of comfort and safety. That gave me pause; I had assumed home meant only positive things. Just so with community... A community can be dangerous, like a gang or cult. The sad thing is that everyone longs for community, some so much that they are willing to join a dangerous pseudo-community rather than having none at all. Some communities take advantage of that longing and our own vulnerability, cults, gangs, even some families.

So I need to qualify what I am saying here. I was longing for a community of trust, whether in a family or in a group of professionals. I think this is what the faculty that wept in their offices were longing for, that kind of trust. Trust is needed to speak your truth, and as Parker Palmer says, trust is needed for the shy soul to show up.

So often we grope our way through our lives, feeling lost both inwardly and outwardly. Mark Nepo says the root of the word lost means to be divided or cut apart, the very opposite of whole. But when we are lost, he says we are "ripe for transformation" (*Seven Thousand Ways to Listen,* p. 41). He tells of a Jewish philosopher who said we are often like someone in the midst of a very dark night, over whom lightning flashes again and again. *"When lightning flashes in our mind or in our heart, we glimpse the hidden order and our changing place in it"* (p.42).

Those flashes will come whether we are alone or with others. But struggling alone as I have for most of my life, often acutely aware of my own confusion and pain, is not nearly as healing as being in the good company of others who are also struggling. Being in community with the Kirkridge Courage Fellows has provided a safe place to share my confusions and struggles. The lightning flashes come brighter and faster in that community, as well as the understanding and acceptance of how lost I sometimes feel, without anyone's trying to fix that condition.

Nepo writes that *"we can only gain strength from sharing our experiences, without second-guessing any of it, just putting what we've been through into the small fire between us that has kept us warm for years."* He tells of two women crossing a frozen lake, who came upon a moose that had fallen through the ice. They could not pull the animal out; so they simply put their tent over him and stayed with him through the night until they could go for help in the morning. This, he says, is a metaphor for how to listen and be with those who have fallen: *"Stay close and keep them warm, resisting the urge to prematurely solve the situation. If nothing can be done, sit with them, and withstand the urge to abandon those who seem stuck. Offer a tent and stay 'til the way out presents itself, not forcing a rescue"* (p.188).

I realize this is what we are now attempting to do with our grandchildren, to stay close and keep them warm until a way forward presents itself. Make no mistake; this kind of encounter is rare and precious and hard work to create. But the work is so very worth it.

I remember the poet who wanted to rest in our room. I realize he did not understand the hugeness of what he was asking us to give up for him. But I did.

Dr. Joanne E. Cooper is a professor emerita from the University of Hawaii and now teaches graduate courses at Portland State University and for the University of New England. She splits her time between Portland, Oregon and Honolulu, Hawaii. She can be contacted through email at jcooper304@gmail.com

An Invitation to Dance

By Diane Petteway

Dance when you are broken open
Dance, if you've taken the bandage off
Dance in the middle of the fighting.
Dance in your blood.
Dance when you are perfectly free.
--Rumi

It is the end of August. A new teaching year is just around the bend. Teacher workdays begin tomorrow. Students arrive in a few short days.

Time will fly quickly---many hours of training for a new school initiative, the latest "magic recipe" to ignite student engagement, stimulate critical thinking, prepare students for the 21st century (although we are already sixteen years in) and, of course, to ensure solid performance on End-of-Grade tests next spring. The annual walk-through of policies, the famed Bloodborne Pathogens and Sexual Harassment videos, grade-level meetings, team meetings, department meetings, Individual Educational Plan meetings, mentor meetings, the creation of the Professional Growth plan, setting up gradebooks and attendance rosters---the list of tasks seems endless for my job

of teaching music to middle school students. There will be a few hours, far too few always, to prepare the physical space of my classroom and wrap my head around what really matters to me----my students.

DANCE WHEN YOU ARE BROKEN OPEN

I think about the faces of my students a lot. Their eyes. Their bones and flesh and blood. This is what I dream of. This is what fills me with wonder. Who are they? How can I, with one forty-five-minute class for forty-five days, even scratch the surface of who they are? I spend a lot of time imagining them, individually and collectively. Who will make me crazy? Who will make me laugh? Who will make me weep?

Even those kids that I've known before come back re-formed after the summer, shaped and shifted by extended time with their families, summer camps, new tensions and worries, new fears, new chinks in their adolescent armor, new reasons to hide. And they hide with such feverish intention. They hide behind electronic devices; behind a rush of prattling, excited words, behind their hair and the newest, trendiest clothes and shoes; behind their sagging pants and their just-above-the-dress-code skimpy shorts and spaghetti straps. They hide behind their anger and their nonchalance and their sarcasm.

No matter how desperately they hide, no matter how elaborate their camouflage, I see them. My old eyes are so hungry for their palpable heart beats, for their vulnerable, shy souls.

I see you. That's what I want to say to each of them.

DANCE IN YOUR BLOOD

I know something about hiding. I was born into a working class family in the late 1950s. My daddy was a salesman for Sears Roebuck. My mother stayed home with me, my older sister, and my younger brother. My daddy played in a southern string band with his brother and several other family friends. Every Saturday night, they played around town; bluegrass tunes, country music covers, and music for community square dances. Whenever they jammed at our house, I stood at my daddy's knee, dancing and singing along. Music and dancing were in my blood.

I was five years old when my father was killed in a car accident, coming home from work. Life became different. The music was gone.

My mother, broken and grieving, got a job at a local mill. She moved us to a nearby town where my father's mother and siblings lived. Many evenings and weekends, I

spent the night with my grandma and my aunt. On Sundays, my brother and I would accompany them to the local Pentecostal Holiness church.

My mother, a proud Southern Baptist, did not approve. In my childhood and adolescence, navigating between the Baptist and Pentecostal practices, I learned the harsh realities of racism and cultural bias. Though the demographics of the town were a third African American, a third Native American, and third Caucasian, all of the political and social power was controlled by white citizens and businessmen.

My mother's story was consistent: our family was white. But I knew that my daddy's family---my grandmother and her children---were Lumbee Indian. Native-American blood danced through my veins.

By the time I was the age of my current students, I could effortlessly conceal the truth of my identity. I didn't even have to think about it---whiteness was artfully entrenched. I carried my mother's shame about being Native American, and I loved my daddy and wanted to hold onto his memory.

I learned about racial inequities in public schools. Native-American children were poor, trashy, and worthless. They would never become as good as white people. Although I didn't know it consciously, I knew on a soul level that I could be discovered as poor, trashy, and worthless, if anyone looked too carefully. So I didn't allow anyone really to know the truth about Diane. I became enculturated into white society, holding close the secret of my tainted blood, never allowing the secret of my heritage to be known.

DANCE, IF YOU'VE TAKEN THE BANDAGE OFF

Watching my students, I see myself.

"If you knew who I am, you would not love me." The familiar ancient whisper of the adolescent. Old habits die hard, and I still keep a safe distance between me and the rest of the world. This will be my last full year of teaching before retirement. Ready access to hundreds of relationships will soon be changing.

Instead of greeting this year with curiosity and wonder, instead of allowing grief for this chapter of my life that is ending, I have been fully immersed in safe tasks… planning my planbook (yes,it's true); writing each date, each holiday, each early release date, each meeting; writing each student's name, alphabetized by their first name since this is how I know them; creating seating charts, sub plans, welcome letters; creating and printing posters. Though none of these tasks speaks to teaching music to middle school students, all of them help manage the chaos of public school teaching.

But none of them addresses other ancient questions that haunt me: Who am I? Right now, at this moment, who am I? Why does this, any of this, matter? My journal entry reflects my state of mind on this first workday:

8/19 /16 Oh, God,
As I begin this dance, this year,
Let me be a full part of the narrative.
Let me be open and whole.
Let me <u>see</u> my students, really see them.
Let us be, together.
Let us find and hold, together, what really matters.

In meetings before school begins, as I step into my work with students, in small conversations in the hallways and in teachers' meeting-spaces, I often feel shy and small. I keep conversations and my own vocal investment succinct. My model is the quiet person at the party who, when least expected, speaks one sentence that blows everyone away with its insightful power. Short, sweet and BAM! It doesn't surprise me that this was the wise Native model of my youth, the way that Indians on TV and in movies communicated their message. This is the image I choose for my Native-American voice.

But when I think of the voices of Native Americans in the classrooms of my youth, it saddens me that the true voices of real live Indians were either silent or surly. The Lumbee Diane that I create in my imagination is not the Lumbee that my classmates and their families experienced. The painful truth is that my white privilege allowed me the choice to romanticize my hidden heritage.

DANCE IN THE MIDDLE OF THE FIGHTING

I think about this issue of voice. Because of the cultural stigma associated with having Native-American blood in a white-dominated culture, I have never, until now, considered the connections between my small voice and the Silent Indian voice that I still love to watch on *Bonanza* reruns.

Difficult questions rumble within me. Does my voice matter? Does what I say really make any difference? Most often, deepest in my soul, I de-value my voice.

I teach voice.

My core belief that each person has a right to their own truth has led me to this

awkward space with my voice. Music is what I do, every day, with a room filled with awkward voices. My students, like me, are so very tentative about their true voices.

Speaking in my own voice requires risking discovery as a fake, an imposter. What if my voice cracks? What if I don't speak in the current "hip" vernacular? What if my voice doesn't match the voices of others—is too loud, too quiet, too nasal? What if my voice is misconstrued, then resurrected to challenge my credibility? What if my words offend someone? And these issues reference only the speaking voice.

What if I sing a note that doesn't match the other notes in the room? What if I accidentally sing when everyone else is silent? What if someone tells me---verbally or nonverbally—that my voice is not contributing to the beauty of the sound and I should "mouth the words" or not participate at all? Does my voice, active and alive, make a difference? These are crucial questions. But the question beneath all of these: am I willing to be vulnerable enough to speak my truth, in my own voice?

Hovering over these questions around voice and vulnerability is the issue of authority. In these millions of minutes spent in August meetings, these are the voices that rise consistently:

"The district strategic plan requires that each teacher ____________________."
"When administration comes in to observe
they will expect to see ____________________________."
"This year we are adopting ______________."
"Our growth targets are ____________________."

There are multiple bosses to please, each with their own measurable standards. The 4 C's, critical thinking, communication, creativity and collaboration, must be addressed in every lesson. Global connections must be clearly articulated. Literacy and math standards must be evident in all classes. 21st-century skills must be included in daily lessons. Technology must be implemented. Professional Learning Teams must clearly map out steps towards yearly growth. Students must be measured quarterly by these standards. Grades must be updated every two weeks.

How do I find, in all of these clearly articulated expectations, the voice of my own authority? How do I connect what I believe---that the voice of each person's soul speaks the truest authority, with the multiple authorities piled upon my plate each day?

I know what is true for me---that the voice of authority is a deeply resonant inner song. And I stand as a daily witness to the chasm between the imposed authorities and the authority that I speak in my own true voice. I sit quietly with this truth: my voice is

small because there is no longer space for her wisdom. She is silent because she is not invited to speak. The Lumbee within me nods. She knows this truth. For so long, I have lied about the strength of her voice within me. My journal entry from more than ten years ago tells me I have known this truth for a very long time:

9/5/05
I am afraid I will not be seen.
I am afraid I will not be valued.
I am afraid my needs—my essence, my values—won't be known.
There is so much strength and wisdom within me that no one here honors.

DANCE WHEN YOU ARE PERFECTLY FREE

And so, here I am. Small. Quiet. Yet my heart, in these last months of teaching, is so large.

In my best hours, I can approach this dilemma with curiosity. What are the gifts of this season? How can I stand in this space, with full intention and full heart? As I listen for the quietness of my small inner voice, there is a sadness that reverberates. I am standing in what we call in Courage Circles the Tragic Gap. This is a place I know well.....the space between the way things are and the way I dream them to be. I am noticing that, standing in such a wide, spacious cavern, the voice of my truth bounces off the walls. I can feel the power of the reverberation. As I root down into my truth, my voice, the echo of what I know to be true, calls back to me again and again. When standing in the ground of my truth, my voice is surer and stronger. It is my Native Voice, Lumbee Diane.

My students arrive and all of the fake truths fall away. Standing before them, just me with them, I know why I am still here. It's only a mystery when I take my eyes off the children. I have often struggled to love this calling. Teaching adolescents was never my first love.

So much was so hidden and so wrong in my privileged, white adolescence. I have resisted walking this ground again.

But standing in front of my students, I am aware that my experience with holding deep secrets about my identity has nourished my inclination towards silenced voices. My experience of hiding who I am has attuned me to a seeing and being in the world that is exactly what my students crave. My students' voices are silenced. Many authorities negate what they know to be true in their souls. There are few spaces in the vast tragic gap of public schools where adolescents can stand in their own beauty and wrestle with their own truths.

My job is to extend an invitation to dance. I, too, have stood by the sidelines, trying so hard to be invisible. I, too, have stood with my feet frozen, glued to the floor, unable to move. So, here I stand. Around me there is exuberant energy, loud, explosive voices. I know they are hiding, uncertain of what will happen if they claim their own power, speak their own truth. These struggles are timeless. I have known them in my bones, as powerfully so many years ago as they are now. These questions are a deep, resonant rhythm that shakes the ground. We step to the rhythm, together. In the circle of my classroom, we learn to dance in new ways that honor their questions and mine, our hidden brokenness and our emerging wholeness.

And so, as August bends into September and January and May, this is the invitation: To listen to the deep rhythm, to move together in a dance that will never happen this way again and is, paradoxically, always the same. Like my Lumbee ancestors, I claim that false voices do not speak to my truth or to my work. My work is to create spaces where students' voices are honored and their shy souls are held gently. Standing before them, my work is simply to extend an invitation to dance to the rhythm of all of our questions and our fears again and again and again.

AN INVITATION TO DANCE

From my journal 1/17/04: Autopoiesis. We are always self-organizing, continually making and re-making ourselves. How do I honor autopoiesis in my work? In my life? The acorn knows about becoming an oak.

The end of my teaching career will arrive in just a few months. I will be ready to begin a new dance.

I claim my voice. My voice matters. And my dreams matter. I have long dreamed of creating the space where teachers in my state can encounter their truths and speak from their own authority about who they are. Nurturing the *who* above the *how* and the *what* and *when* of our profession feels imperative right now. Providing and sustaining a space where teachers can be invited to dance with their inner wisdom: this is the legacy that matters most to me. I have heard the drumbeat of this call for many years; it has taken great patience to wait for the ending of my work in public schools before launching into this grand dream.

The time is almost here.

My work now is to create spaces where teachers' voices are honored and their shy souls are held gently.

I will still teach voice, but in a very different way. I will teach teachers, as I have taught myself, to hear their voices, to value their voices. Standing with them, my work will be to simply extend an invitation to dance to the rhythm of our questions and our fears and our dreams again and again and again.

Diane Petteway is a teacher, a leader, a dreamer, a musician, a writer, a thespian and a southerner. She is a facilitator of Courage Work and a Kirkridge Fellow. She lives in Raleigh and Blowing Rock, North Carolina, with her husband Bernie and their cocker spaniel, Andy. She can be reached at dpetteway@me.com

A STEPPING STONE

What is the Clearness Committee, the Clearness Triad?

By Sally Z. Hare

As we gathered the stories for our book, the editors noticed the topic of the Clearness Committee and the Clearness Triad as threads in several of the stories. So we decided to add this stepping stone to lift up the Clearness Committee, a practice that has been used in the Quaker community for over three hundred years, and the special adaption we often used in our Kirkridge Courage Fellowship, the Clearness Triads.

My introduction to this practice more than 25 years ago changed my life. Or perhaps it would be more accurate to say that with the help of the Clearness Committee, I changed my life. The basic idea behind the process is that each person has an inner teacher, and with the help of our communal resources, we can more clearly hear that inner teacher. That certainly happened for me as I struggled with a career decision.

As Parker J. Palmer so insightfully writes in *The Clearness Committee: A Communal Approach to Discernment*, "On the one hand, we know that the issue is ours alone to resolve and that we have the inner resources to resolve it, but access to our own resources is often blocked by layers of inner 'stuff' – confusion, habitual thinking, fear, despair." The Clearness Committee process allows us to tap into our inner wisdom by using the community to run interference, to help us through our own inner maze.

Parker adapted the traditional Quaker clearness process for our use in Circles of Trust, and it quickly transformed the nature of our being together. We adapted the format of Clearness Triads as a way of extending the clearness process over three days – and going even deeper.

I admit to being awed by the power of the process of the Clearness Committee. It is a simple process – and a sacred one. Parker cautions that the Clearness Committee is not for everyone – or for every setting. The process invites a level of vulnerability that requires a space of safety and trust. It is not a process to be entered into lightly.

Entered into with care and intentionality, the process offers a valuable means of finding clearness in a world that often feels muddy and chaotic. The rules of the Clearness Committee are critical to its success. They create and hold the boundaries for the safe space. Even when group members are familiar with the process, I teach

the rules at the beginning of each session. I want to remind myself as much as anyone of their importance, because the behavior required in Clearness Committees is counterintuitive. The Clearness Committee demands that we suspend our normal ways of doing business, our typical ways of being in our society, in order to be in community in a way that is virtually unknown to us.

Perhaps the most crucial rule is that of confidentiality. We go beyond the familiar confidentiality to what we call deep confidentiality, meaning that committee members would not only never speak to each other or anyone else about the issue when the Clearness Committee ended, but they also would not speak with the focus person about the problem unless she or he requested the conversation.

In most retreat settings, the facilitators invite persons who seek clearness on some issue to volunteer to serve as focus persons. Committees of five or six people are carefully put together by the facilitators, with important input from the focus persons. In the Fellowship Program, we self-selected groups of three – and everyone had the opportunity during the three days to serve as both focus person and committee member.

Time is critical to the process; it can't be rushed. During that scheduled time, committee members practice the discipline of giving the focus person their total attention. They are fully present to the person and his or her issue, listening deeply, creating a space of deep respect. The function of the committee is not to "fix" or give advice, but to help the focus person hear her own inner wisdom, claim his own authority (to literally be the author of her own story).

The committee begins with the focus person sharing his or her issue. *That is when the other critical rule comes into play: Committee members are forbidden to speak to the focus person except by asking open, honest questions.* Since authentic questions are not the norm in our society, the practice of asking open, honest questions requires discipline and self-monitoring. We so easily slip into advice disguised as a question, judgment disguised as a question, sharing our own experiences disguised as questions. "Have you thought about seeing a therapist?" is NOT an open, honest question. Neither is "Have you ever tried to lose some weight?"

What is an open, honest question? Perhaps the best answer to that is that it's a question to which the questioner could have no idea of the answer. The pacing of the questions is as important as the wording of the questions. The Clearness Committee is not a grilling of a suspect or a dissertation defense or a cross-examination; questions should be asked at a gentle, humane pace. Time to reflect on the answers, moments of silence, "wait time" are vital to inviting in the focus person's inner teacher.

The focus person usually responds to the questions. The questions – and the answers – then often lead to deeper questions. The focus person should be brief but full in her

answers, resisting the temptation to tell his entire life's story. Sometimes, for whatever reason, the focus person may choose not to answer a question or may ask to have a question reframed. *The focus person always has the right NOT to answer a question.*

The exception to the rule of asking only open, honest questions may come about ten minutes before the end of the Clearness Committee. At this time, a committee member asks the focus person if he or she would like to have the "question only" rule suspended and to invite committee members to mirror back what they have heard from the focus person. Mirroring is exactly that: the committee member serves as a mirror, holding up for reflection the focus person's own words or body language. Mirroring is not an opportunity to give advice or pronounce judgement.

For the last five minutes, the Clearness Committee members share affirmations and celebrations. As with the other aspects of the process, this is important, as the focus person has been very open and vulnerable with the group. Group members find much to celebrate after a glimpse into the gifts and grace of a human soul.

I said earlier that the behavior required in Clearness Committees is counterintuitive. This means suspending our normal ways of being together – no small talk, no jokes to break the tension, no noisy laughter, no attempt to fix or reassure or comfort the focus person, no patting or touching. The only task for members of the Clearness Committee is to listen deeply and ask thoughtful questions. They are not trying to impress the others by their grasp of the situation or by their ability to ask clever questions. They are charged with holding the space for the focus person, not filling that space with their own egos. The reward for the committee members is often being surprised by some clearness on their own issues, by some insight they weren't expecting.

The Clearness Committee is not about fixing anyone or solving anything. In fact, with a good clearness process, the answers, the insights, continue to come for hours, days, even weeks after the actual meeting. In my own case, I find that I sometimes go back to questions from that first Clearness Committee more than 25 years ago; sometimes I review the notes and have yet another "ah-ha."

Parker first introduced me to the Clearness Committee during that weeklong retreat on leadership and spirituality more than two decades ago. I will never forget Parker's charge to the committee members: he used the metaphor of holding the focus person (me) as if she were a small bird. Your responsibility, he told the group, is to hold the bird safely in your cupped hands rather than giving in to our all-too-human tendencies to either suffocate the bird by closing our hands too tightly or by putting the bird down prematurely or pushing her to fly before she is ready. The success of the clearness process, he told us, is not measured by whether the bird flies, but in how we hold the bird.

Claiming the Birthright Gift of Community: The Work of a Lifetime

By Sally Z. Hare

Geese appear high over us,
pass, and the sky closes. Abandon,
as in love or sleep, holds
them to their way, clear
in the ancient faith: what we need
is here. And we pray, not
for new earth or heaven, but to be
quiet in heart, and in eye,
clear. What we need is here.

--from ***Wendell Berry's*** **Wild Geese**

We come into the world knowing that what we need is here. We are born into community, interconnected to everything in the Universe. Quantum physics now confirms the undivided wholeness that every child is born into, the innate sense that we **are** community. And then we become disconnected, and we forget. Finding it again is the work of a lifetime.

Remembering who we are, our sense of community, is the purpose of education. From the Latin word *educare*, to lead forth that which is within, education creates the space for recovering our birthright gift. So the work of **my** lifetime has been not only finding my own sense of community, but learning how to create a space in which my students could find theirs. Now as I reflect back on my life's work as a teacher, including the last two decades as a facilitator of Courage Work and Circles of Trust®, I am grateful to come full circle; to discover, or perhaps recover, that what I need is here.

I know firsthand that there is no quick fix for remembering what Thomas Merton called a hidden wholeness, to living from a place of integrity, to being the person we each came to be. Early in life, we begin to forget that community is our birthright gift, that we are an integral part of Earth and connected with all other living creatures. And yet the national Commission on Children at Risk, an independent, jointly sponsored initiative of the YMCA of the USA, Dartmouth Medical School, and the Institute for American Values, says we are "hardwired to connect." The group of 33 children's doctors, research scientists, and mental health and youth service professionals, headed by principal investigator Dr. Kathleen Kovner Kline of Dartmouth Medical School, has concluded that the mechanisms by which children become attached to others are biologically primed and can be discerned in the structure of the brain (see *Hardwired to Connect: The New Scientific Case for Authoritative Communities,* http://www.americanvalues.org/search/item.php?id=17).

So community begins in the human brain. And the current research in early childhood shows that the human brain begins in community. More than half of brain development occurs in the first two years of life, requiring nurturing, loving connections with adults. There is a four-year critical period from conception until about the third birthday during which the child is learning language and the other physical, social, and emotional skills to be a competent community member.

Too often, in those important first years of life, we don't get what we need to nurture that inborn sense of connectedness. Developmental psychologist Erik Erikson famously theorized that the sense of basic trust must take root in the first year of life – and is multi-faceted and depends heavily on our caregivers and our environment. If trust doesn't develop in healthy ways, our sense of connectedness, our very ability to be in community, becomes deformed.

We speak of community as if it exists outside of the individual – but in fact, it is an integral part of the self. We have no adequate English words for describing the wholeness: the integrated form that is the self and the community, the inner and the outer. Community is.

We exist in community. Community exists in us. We can't exist without community, as

Rene Spitz's study of institutionalized orphans dramatically illustrated in the 1940's. These babies and young children literally turned their faces to the wall and died, although they had no discernible problems. The foundling home provided the babies with adequate food, clothing, and medical care, but there was only one nurse for every eight infants, and except for brief feedings and diaper changes, each baby was isolated in his or her crib, its sides draped with sheets to prevent the spread of infection. With a bare minimum of human contact and affection – and no contact with nature, these babies suffered devastatingly, with most dying before the age of two years. Those who lived were physically stunted, highly prone to infection, and severely cognitively and emotionally disabled. By three years of age, many of these children were unable to walk or talk and were described as withdrawn and apathetic.

I realized as a young teacher that community would be essential to creating the space for learning in my classroom, a necessity for my students to thrive. We need relationships with others; we need love; we need touch; we need community. We are communal creatures. We **are** community. Yet we see community as something outside of us, something separate. How could I create that sense of interconnectedness, a feeling of belonging, for my students? How could I create that for myself? Now, at the end of my career of teaching, I am coming to understand that what I need is here.

WRAPPING MY HANDS (AND MIND) AROUND COMMUNITY

Creation myths offer human attempts in every culture, in every time, to explain community, to reduce it to its least common denominator, to make it something around which we can wrap our hands.

Lynn Margulis and Dorion Sagan, in *What Is Life*? (1995), remark on the observation of researchers Eugene d'Aquili and Andrew Newburg that human beings appear to have "*no choice but to construct myths to explain their world.*" I love the Balinese myth of creation that was shared with me when I spent time exploring that culture: God fashioned figures of clay, but left them in the oven too long, and they were an over-baked black. With the next batch, perhaps overly cautious, God didn't leave the figures in long enough, and they were an underdone white. The last batch of people was just right, a golden brown, and they were the Balinese.

In another sense, the sciences (particularly biology, physics, psychology, sociology) are other human attempts to find meaning, to reduce the idea of community to a definition, an explanation. One fascinating example is *autopoiesis*, the term coined by the Chilean biologists Humberto Maturana and Francisco Varela, from the Greek roots meaning self (*auto*) and making (*poiein*, as in "poetry"), which refers to life's continuous production of itself. Lynn Margulis (1995) postulates that all of Earth is community, a living system, of which we humans are a part. Her theory of symbiogenesis emphasizes the importance of cooperation over the Darwinian explanation of competition, of community

as the essence of all life. "We are coming to realize that we are part of a global holarchy that transcends our individual skins and even humanity as a whole." I love that word *holarchy*, created by Arthur Koestler to mean the coexistence of small beings in larger wholes, especially because Koestler's coinage is free of implications of "hierarchical" or "higher" or that one of the constituents in the holarchy is somehow controlling the others.

The mathematical cosmologist Brian Swimme sees community as the solution to the crisis of mass extinction he feels we are facing today. He says we need to *"reinvent ourselves, at the species level, in a way that enables us to live with mutually enhancing relationships… Not just with humans but with all beings—so that our activities actually enhance the world. At the present time, our interactions degrade everything… What's necessary is for us to understand that, really, at the root of things is community. At the deepest level, that's the center of things. We come out of community. So how then can we organize our economics so that it's based on community, not accumulation? And how can we organize our religion to teach us about community? And when I say 'community,' I mean the whole earth community. That's the ultimate sacred domain—the earth community"* (http://www.wie.org/j19/swimme.asp).

As I wrap my hands and my mind around community, I have moved from seeing community as something to be created ***out there***, external to the individual, a perception of a whole of which the individual is a part, through seeing community ***within*** the individual, not only confined to the body but also our inner experience of the world, to now seeing community as ***both inner and outer***, as not only an entity of which the individual is part, but a holarchy.

community comes to those who empty

a day at brookgreen
of friendship, of writing, of seeing.
a day of community, of clarity,
of paradox, of fullness and fallness.
a day of tears, shared frustrations,
inviting in the dark
as well as the light.
it's so clear community
is not a goal to be achieved –
it takes time and space
and emptying.
it takes slowing down, being
intentional, being gentle.
i can't make community –
but I can revel in it.

--- Sally Z. Hare

NAMING COMMUNITY IN A CIRCLE OF TRUST

My experience in the Kirkridge Courage Fellowship has affirmed for me that trustworthy community is a space where my soul can show up, where I can connect with the seed of true self and can hear my own voice and recover my sense of interconnectedness. Deforming experiences with religious patriarchies cause me to resist that language of soul or true self, and I struggle to find a way to name this voice within that is not owned by any particular creed. It has helped to discover that these concepts exist across every culture and have many names and forms. Thomas Merton calls it true self; the Buddhists, original nature; Quakers, the inner light; Hasidic Jews, the spark of the divine; Humanists, identity and integrity; various Native American traditions use the language of the Great Spirit or Grandfather or Sacred Spirit or the Great Headman.

The language of "hidden selves" in a Writing Circle of Trust with Dr. Sara Sanders and Dr. Janet Files helped me move beyond my stuckness around religious hierarchy. Grounded in their book, *Writing Along the Mobius Strip: A Practice to Set the Heart at Rest,* Sara and Janet created a playful space that freed me to connect with my gifts and their inevitable shadows—and to name for myself those inner guides. These past two years in the Kirkridge Courage Fellows Circle of Trust have offered me the space to encourage those guides to show up.

Parker Palmer defines the way a circle of trust invites this hidden wholeness to come forth: "*Here is one way to understand the relationships in a circle of trust: they combine unconditional love, or regard, with hopeful expectancy, creating a space that both safeguards and encourages the inner journey. In such a space, we are freed to hear our own truth, touch what brings us joy, become self-critical about our faults, and take risky steps toward change.*"

Thomas Merton calls it wisdom, the feminine face of all that is sacred, in *Hagia Sophia*: "There is in all things an invisible fecundity, a dimmed light, a meek namelessness, a hidden wholeness. This mysterious Unity, and Integrity, is Wisdom, the Mother of all, *Natura naturans.*"

What I name it does not matter as much as **that** I name it, that I recognize that circle of trust, that *"mysterious Unity and Integrity,"* to be community.

THE LAST OF LIFE FOR WHICH THE FIRST WAS MADE

As I approach my seventh decade, I am grateful to be able to say I love my life. I know the ground on which I stand, and I am able to live, most of the time, from a place of abundance and joy and contentedness and the sense that what I need is here, even when clouds of negativity swirl around me. I remember reading, as a young college student, lines from Robert Browning:

Grow old along with me! The best is yet to be,
The last of life, for which the first was made

Now I am remembering those lines I loved at age eighteen and realizing that it has taken another 50 years to live into them! I am embracing aging as a privilege. I am understanding the first of life as the work before the Work, and I am embracing the last of life as a time for that Work of integrating the outward and the inward journey to wholeness. I am seeing the relationship of teaching and learning and community with a new clarity, deepened by my work as a Courage facilitator.

Now I am living into a knowing that what I need is here, that I **am** community. Community is not an end to be achieved or a project to be created; it only requires opening our hearts to recognize and receive our birthright gift. As I claim this privilege of aging and becoming an elder, I am finding this time of life to be one of recovery as well as discovery of knowing community as both inner and outer, of my sense that we **are** community, that what we need is here.

Another gift of this age is recovering the joy of learning, of reading whatever I choose; no grades, no requirements. I read Chief Seattle: "*This we know: the earth does not belong to man, man belongs to the earth. All things are connected like the blood that unites us all. Man did not weave the web of life, he is merely a strand in it. Whatever he does to the web, he does to himself.*"

I discover Margaret Wheatley's valuable perspective for looking at community through the lens of quantum physics, chaos theory, and the science of living systems in *Leadership and the New Science: Learning about Organization from an Orderly Universe* (1994): "*How do you understand a world in which the only material form is that of relationships, and where there is no sense of an individual that exists independent of its relationships? That was the gift of the quantum worldview. It said there are no independent entities anywhere at the quantum level. It's all relationships. That was something that made a lot of sense to how we were starting to think about organizations — as webs of relationships. But the real eye-opener for me was to realize how control and order were two different things, and that you could have order without control. That was a major shift in my own thinking that I certainly discovered through the science.*"

Order without control gives me a new and vibrant frame for life at this stage, far more accurate than *retirement*. In fact, I find the word *retirement* to be of no use -- and even, at times, to be a damning and limited naming for this creative stage of life. I love hearing Gloria Steinem say that "*People often ask me at this age who am I passing the torch to? First of all, I'm not giving up my torch, thank you! I'm using my torch to light other people's torches. … If we each have a torch, there's a lot more light.*"

I don't want to give up my torch. I want to be of use, to go even deeper into this work of my lifetime, into claiming this birthright gift of community. I am drawn to the labyrinth as a metaphor for seeing my life now. The labyrinth, unlike the maze, has no dead ends and is not a place where one can get lost, although the path may meander and seem confusing. There is only one way in and one way out – and all paths lead to the center and then back to the beginning. With a labyrinth there is only one choice to be made -- the choice to enter or not. A receptive mindset is needed; a labyrinth is not a goal to be achieved. At its most basic level the labyrinth is a metaphor for the journey to the center of one's deepest self and back out into community.

Some days internet and newspaper headlines and TV news seem to defy my knowing of community as our national consciousness is bombarded with a growing sense of disconnectedness and isolation. From the Oklahoma City bombing in 1995 and the Columbine shootings in 1999, the 21st century was ushered into the United States with violence that has continued with the Mother Emmanuel Church massacre and the Boston Marathon bombings and the Orlando murders and too many others. Robert Putnam's *Bowling Alone* was one of the first books in a long line of 21st century bestsellers to attempt to find ways to understand social change in the United States. Putnam's detailed graphs and tables point to his belief that we are looking for ways to create or re-create social capital as the antidote for the so-called loss of community.

I say "so-called" because I don't believe we lose community any more than I believe we can create it. Humans can't exist without community. If we've lost anything, it's our own hearts – and our own capacity to **know** that what we need is here, around us and within us. And our system of education is failing miserably in creating the space for recovering our birthright gift.

No, we haven't lost community, and yet we cite the breakdown of community as the cause for everything from children murdering each other in schools to racism and ethnocentrism to drug overdoses to the high rates of suicide. The disappearance of community gets the blame for why we are destroying the planet – and it is Brian Swimme's answer to what he calls the crisis of mass extinction.

ARRIVING WHERE I STARTED

We shall not cease from exploration
and the end of all our exploring
Will be to arrive where we started
and know the place for the first time.

--T. S. Eliot (from *Little Gidding*)

This place of knowing community feels familiar. Yet, to use the poet Eliot's words, I am knowing the place for the first time. Much of my career in higher education has been about community and the critical relationship of community and learning. I understand, as I wind down a lifetime of teaching, that the purpose of education is to rid ourselves of the illusion of separation between the individual and the community, the internal and the external.

Teacher: A Definition

Facilitating, teaching, guiding, learning,
Weaving connections,
Listening to unspoken as well as spoken;
Using silence to hear herself, to hear her students into their voices.
What is the teacher anyway but guide on the inner journey,
A kind of human compass, always pointing toward north?

She's a weaver
Of connections inside, outside, over, across,
down, under, through, between—
Of connections that hold space for the learner
To construct her own knowing.

She's a mirror
Of the student's reflection,
Of the light to better hold the student
So he can see his own gifts, name himself,
Create himself in his own image.

She's a creator
Of space in which the growing can happen,
Of silence in which the learner can hear herself;
Of her own knowledge about how to tend a garden,
Whether to use ladybugs or Sevin dust, to water or wait for the rain,
To plant the seed just beneath the surface or deeper still.

She's a seeker
Of her own Truths
Of her own gifts
Of who she is and whose she is.
She may never know.
But it's her life's work anyway.

--- Sally Z. Hare

Even as I still struggle with the language, these past two years with the Kirkridge Courage Fellows have deepened my experience of the power of a trustworthy community to a level beyond any I had previously experienced. Growth and transformation happen in ways that seem tangible, and I have a strong sense that individual change is vital to community transformation. I embrace that trust is the essential element of knowing community, and my experience affirms research findings that respect is the key to creating trust. In fact, trust and respect seem to be the true north of my compass on this journey of a lifetime.

Parker Palmer, with his gentle but fierce manner of safeguarding the Courage Work, insists that the space in a Circle of Trust is only for the purpose of the individual's inner work and is never the means to any other end, including community. Yet in my years of experience with two-year seasonal groups and even in one-time three-day retreats, I watch community happen; I see community become visible.

I realize that I have always known that community is more important to learning than any technique or method. When I first came into the role of facilitator, I spent a lot of time talking with Parker and the other pilot facilitators about the difference in teaching and facilitating. Now, after twenty years of Circles of Trust and especially the recent Kirkridge Courage Fellowship, I know there is a seamlessness between good teaching and good facilitating, between creating the space for others and creating the space for myself. As I glimpse the hidden wholeness, I celebrate that what I need is here.

Dr. Sally Z. Hare, Singleton Distinguished Professor Emerita at Coastal Carolina University, is president of still learning, inc. (www.stilllearning.org). She lives in Surfside Beach, South Carolina, where she is happy to share her ocean with her husband Jim R. Rogers, and dog, TBO. She can be contacted through e-mail: couragetoteach@sc.rr.com

On Becoming a Witness

By Karen Noordhoff

The most beautiful thing we can experience is the mysterious.

-- Albert Einstein

In the summer of 2015, I found myself in the middle of many nights praying fervently, even feverishly, for the physical safety of my then 95-year-old mother who lived alone in her house of 38 years, supported by some daytime care. Some weeks later in the middle of the night, she fell and broke her collarbone. In my journal I wrote with a sense of knowing from who-knows-where, "This must be the beginning of the end." At this time, I was called to move even more deeply into the practice of "being a witness" to my mother's completion of this earthly life and her passage from it. And, in the aftermath of her death, I was to experience others witnessing me.

In this story I want to share reflections about my ongoing, transformative journey toward being more strongly connected to the wholeness of my soul. When I sense moments of this connection, I feel more fully human. And, just as importantly, the more firm this connection, the more capable I am of offering my best self with authenticity, integrity, courage and faithfulness to others through my roles, responsibilities and relationships.

I'll share with you experiences surrounding my mother's death and of community in that period and how my search for my life's soulful purpose is being deepened and re-formed – all of this in the context of my exploration of being and becoming a "witness." Still, I continue to struggle, in the most positive sense, to find language that describes and names these beautifully mysterious experiences and ruminations.

I use "witness" in my story and reflections to suggest an active yet tender practice in presence, rather than referring to the usual and more specific legal or religious meanings. (I hope that those readers who may feel injured or deformed from their experiences with "witnessing" in the more traditional senses will read on!) As significant and valuable as acts of witnessing in the legal and religious senses can be, for me the idea of "being a witness" is more encompassing and perhaps, more blurred or mysterious. A working definition I've developed is: A tender, non-anxious witness contains the space for truth, as well as for possible healing and wholeness, to emerge – particularly an inner truth to be expressed in one's life.

From my perspective and experience, witnessing is a participatory way of being. It is more than mere observation, more than acting as a disinterested spectator or voyeur. Rather, I see witnessing as a way of being in relation with others and with oneself that comes from first-hand knowing on the part of the witness. (The root of the word *witness* derives from the Old English "wit," referring to one's own knowledge or knowing and is also related to "wisdom.") It involves deliberately giving over oneself to profound awareness and attention.

True witnessing honors and provides companionship to others on their journey toward greater connection to their innate wholeness. Respectful deep listening to words and actions as well as what is left unsaid or not enacted – without interruption and/or agenda – plays an important and necessary part in witnessing, as does silence (interesting to note that the words **listen** and **silent** are both composed of the same letters). Both listening and silence can sometimes be taken as an absence of talk. Instead, to me, witnessing through listening and silence shows itself as a kind of live existence and an encounter of present energies.

Sometimes being a witness happens in the setting of one-on-one conversations and at other times in group facilitation, as well as in the context of social justice and peace work. For instance, during a recent conversation with a long-time friend, I came to "know" that what she truly wanted from me was not just my listening keenly to the stories of her daily activities, but my witnessing the condition of her life. Similarly, in a Circle of Trust I facilitated, I listened as a participant spoke of the disconnection between his values and the kinds of decisions he was pushed to make by his work

organization. In his struggles, I was called to witness his broken heart. In these instances, I felt wakeful, alert, and attentive. I felt both centered and on the edge. I felt fully there and not there. Given my personal explorations and experiences, I focus here on witnessing in the context of more intimate relationships, rather than in regard to larger socio-political systems and cultural dynamics. No matter the type of interaction or context, witnessing each other embodies holding or steadfastly standing with each other with compassion and the courage to hear the truth.

David Hagstrom, in his poem, describes for me what I experienced every weekend during intensive hour-long phone conversations with my mother:

Witness

Standing watch
With her, with him
Keeping the vigil
Listening carefully

Remaining steadfast
Deliberately waiting
Cherishing the quiet
Embracing silence

Resting together
One being heard
The other, a witness
To truth, to what's real

-- David Hagstrom

Over the years, these opportunities to practice witnessing with Mom were usually on Saturdays, always 9 a.m. my time, noon hers, given that we lived on opposite coasts of the continent. We could count on each other's presence, and I particularly wanted to offer her deep listening, a wholehearted connection, and a space for truth. Not surprisingly, all such gifts returned to me manyfold.

Particularly during the last year of her life, my mother questioned "why am I still here?" She declared that no one knew what it was like to be her at her age. I agreed and added, "But we can be with each other." Speaking about the power of friendship and connection, Mom passionately remarked, "When everything is taken away, what you

want is to have a friend." At the same time, Mom's realistic hope and her deep faith brought her each morning to ask, "What are God's priorities for me right now?" just as she also stated, "We only have the present." As well, she often spoke of others' suffering; she described the world as both "devastating and delightful." Looking ahead, my mother even said that she thought she'd "still be learning, even up in Heaven." We often spoke about the nature of paradox – living with two apparent opposites held in a both/and relationship – such as the gifts of dependence *and* freedom, questioning or struggling *and* acceptance or submission, attending to the present *and* anticipating dying and heaven. I found her to be creatively trying to live in the inevitable tragic gap between "what is," or reality, and "what can be," or possibility, as she reflected on her end-of-life preparations and choices. I was reminded of what I now understand to be the practice of Wei-wu-wei, "the action of nonaction," the central paradox of Taoism. My challenge as a daughter and witness in this place of nonaction was to be, as much as possible, a non-anxious presence.

HOLDING THE LABYRINTH

Before carrying on with my story, I need to look backward a bit to explain and explore how I came to use the language and practice of "witnessing" in my life and work. It is a part of my own journey toward greater connection to my soul's wholeness, toward living my life in the most authentic, integrated, courageous, and faithful ways possible. My focused, intentional exploration of "being/becoming a witness" began in earnest in May, 2014, but this search may well be the continuation of a longer thread in my life, one that has been further stretched and strengthened by the death of my mother.

I've always felt myself to be a kind of reflective observer; other folks also have noted over the years that this quality is essential to how they know me. It seems to be a birthright gift of mine. Yet, being a witness seems to call into play something beyond sensitive watchfulness. That's what I had the unexpected opportunity to explore when I was asked to "hold" the labyrinth as part of the 2014 Global Gathering of Courage & Renewal Facilitators.

As I interpreted this invitation, doing so meant introducing its journey-based metaphorical and meditative practice to those persons new to it, providing a small handout of background and resources, leading folks in silence to the labyrinth and remaining outside it to support their experience of a bounded and safe space for their embodied inner work. In addition, as I stood at the threshold of the labyrinth and people walked its curving paths, I found myself observing and praying for the so-called pilgrims ("may her journey be safe," "may this journey bring him guidance"), carefully

watching the birds and clouds and feeling the changing winds, and blessing each person as they emerged from the walk – all things I had not planned.

As the participants exited the labyrinth or sought me out during the rest of the day, they shared their experience of being "held" and what it had meant to them. For instance, they used language such as "invisible but palpable, steady presence," "loving, grounded encourager," and "a shepherd tending." One labyrinth-walker wrote me after the Gathering to say: "Thank you for your faithful and generous holding of the space as people walked the labyrinth at the Gathering. I have never had the experience of turning and turning and seeing someone standing at the entrance and tending the pilgrims. It was **lovely**, and for me, added an important element of being 'witnessed' and honored in my walk." Both at the Gathering and later, I felt greatly touched and moved. When thanked, I found myself spontaneously replying, "It was my true **joy** to hold you in that way." Indeed, in holding the labyrinth, I was granted an embodied experience of the poet William Stafford's words in *You Reading This, Be Ready*: *"How you stand here is important. How you / listen for the next things to happen. How you breathe."*

I write about these responses not to convey my "goodness," but rather to share my own experience, which was the door opening widely onto the concept and practice of witnessing. I've come to realize the several layers of witnessing that seemed to be present in this mutual experience of the labyrinth. First, I was being a witness to others on their journeys. I was providing a kind of non-intrusive, non-anxious companionship, even as I did not move from the threshold of the labyrinth. Second, it seemed that a part of me witnessed myself as I held those travelers on the walk to the center and out again. It might be said that my inner Self witnessed the self who was attending to the walkers. (Exploring the idea and activity of an "inner witness" is calling me these days.) And then, finally, I received witnessing by those pilgrims putting one foot in front of the other along that circular path. They said they experienced and witnessed my inner gifts in the context of that moment-in-time's expression of my Work in the world, my role as "holder" of the labyrinth.

Even at the time, I wrote in my journal that my own experience of this particular holding of the labyrinth felt like another and deeper level of recognition and sense of a birthright gift, a kind of deep core quality of who I am. Even then, I named my felt-presence as "witnessing/being a witness." I was (and am) in new territory, even though I've felt a vague but persistent attraction to the idea of "witnessing" in the sense I suggested above since sometime in my late 30s or early 40s. This labyrinth experience and now my experience of my mother's death, as well as the attendant experiences of community, have come together to evoke this statement around my

gifts, Work in the world, and quite possibly, my life's purpose.

After the time of holding the labyrinth at the 2014 Gathering, I began to read and write about what being and becoming a witness might mean, such as ideas about what a witness does (or not) and the qualities called for in a witness. Although I sought out and made lists of resources to research and people to talk to, my usual strategy into a project, what I found myself doing instead was following my nose, making the path by walking, simply following where my energy and interest wanted to go. This adventure was exhilarating and non-stressful!

At about the same time, I also began to participate in the Kirkridge Courage Fellowship Program, an ongoing group of 27 Courage & Renewal facilitators attending a series of retreats to foster our personal wholeness, and in the process, deepen our facilitation of Circles of Trust and our use of the Courage principles and practices in other settings (e.g., consulting, coaching, health care and non-profit organizations, educational institutions). In this community, focused conversations and activities helped me approach the concept and practice of witnessing "at a slant" through poetry, fairytales and the visual arts. Hearing others' stories of life and work encouraged me toward more deeply understanding witnessing in terms of social action.

But my understanding and practice of being a witness remained limited. Until I received more personal and heightened experience, I wasn't fully prepared or able to move in the direction I was feeling called.

BEING WITNESSED

Then, my concerns about my mother, as I shared at the beginning, began seriously in the summer of 2015. Her fall and collarbone break in late August called for 24/7 in-home attention, a real strain on her finances and nerves, as well as for my brother and me, even though we all felt immensely grateful for the exceptional care she received. I began to experience an overriding and ominous sense of heaviness and increasing dread. My husband and I canceled our three-month autumn sabbatical in France.

My phone-witnessing intensified. As in previous year's in-person visits and over recent phone calls, I noticed the need for what I came to call "focused flexibility." I needed to be completely focused and fully flexible, in other words completely attentive (often to the particular), while being as absolutely open and receptive as possible, able to shift without effort.

In late September my brother and I visited Mom at her home. As a small family of three, we all spoke candidly and Mom gave us children the blessed gift of volunteering to move to an assisted-living setting. I further explored such options and imagined that she and we could make a move in November so that she wouldn't have to pass

another worrisome winter in the house, as much as she loved that private, quiet, comforting space looking out onto the woods, now beginning to turn yellow-orange-red. I left on September 30th, heading toward one of the Fellowship retreats, tearfully choking my good-bye with the words, "I'll be back."

And I did come back on October 18th.

Having spent a couple of weeks trying to hone in on an assisted-living situation that was available, affordable, and would fit Mom's needs, I then attended the 2015 Gathering of Courage & Renewal Facilitators in Minneapolis in mid-October. I was agitated, anxious, deeply discontented, even disoriented. In response to a journal-writing prompt in one session, I wrote, *"Am I brave enough to* ***invite*** *what is coming?"* I felt the ocean swells coming my way.

As the Gathering concluded two days after my journal writing, I picked up a text message from the nurse with my mother's home-care service that Mom had been taken to the emergency room that morning. Within minutes, I learned from the ER doctor that my mother was dying and in accordance with her wishes, I communicated that she wanted no extreme measures but only comfort. In fact, I was told she would not have survived any extreme measures. She was given two or three days to linger in transition. I was catapulted out of the practicalities of being a care partner and into deep mystery.

My friend and co-facilitator, Celine, accompanied me from the conference site to the airport and stayed by my side until my ticket was changed, and I moved through the security line. I felt her guardian spirit even as I knew that I was on my own. Still, I knew she would have sat vigil with me, right there in the pre-formed, plastic seats as long as I needed her with me. I traveled from Minneapolis toward western North Carolina, where my mother had lived and was to die. I had to make a change of planes in Chicago. This poem tells the story of this part of my journey:

For Elizabeth – in 12B

You, in your twenties,
Gray sweater
Blondish hair
Playing solitaire
And reading your book
For the hour it took
To fly into O'Hare.

I, huddled, up against
The fuselage

Short on time
Encased in unknown paradigm
And short on breath, it being shallow
Tears constant yet still gentle
Headed toward a bedside vigil.

My phone, on landing in the night
Trills, carries voice and heart-rending news
From the calm, plain-spoken hospice nurse
At the Four Seasons Elizabeth House:
"I'm sorry to bring you this word,
Your mother will probably die" I heard
"In these next few moments."

And into the deepest silence
Of the dark vast Universe
I fell
With audible gasp inhaled
As my mother exhaled her own at last
Tell her "Karen loves you" I asked.
"I will, but she may have already gone."

Hunched over my lap
Hugging belly like hers from which I'd come
Head on the seat before me, eyes a-blur
Keening such sobs I did not know whose they were
I feel the young woman lean toward my shoulder
"Do you want a hug?" she offers to enfold me.
But I couldn't accept at that time.

Crying still, but softer now
Abruptly and so utterly alone,
Now on my back I sense a gentle hand
And with me a kind spirit in this sudden anguished land
Later raise my head, turn toward her side
With quivering mouth say, "My mother has just died."
I receive her hug and tissues, try to dry my eyes.

Then I ask, "What is your name, please?"
With soft, peaceful and calm whisper
"It's Elizabeth," she replies

I sense it's my open soul she sees.

Nonetheless, I am so alone
Yet not completely as I breathe
Grateful for her presence to my sorrow, attentiveness
To my suffering – a quiet, loving, tender witness.
I must walk now into the airport's frenzied pace
The bright, glaring fluorescence of this place,
Enlightened in this passage of my own:

Who else is in pain, here in this space?
For whom am I now called to bear
Witness to their woundedness
With generous, compassionate grace?

Elizabeth, Elizabeth:
Accompanying angel and a place of death
Both witness to surrender, to release
Into the arms of deepest sorrow and of peace
Carry us in transition below and above
So that into the depths of the Great Love
We rest.

-- Karen Noordhoff

In those profound moments, Elizabeth – sitting next to me in seat 12B – held me; in a sense she rested with me in my distress. So I call her my witness.

As my companion, she witnessed my truth, my reality. Although as I've written, I felt "utterly alone," I also felt her deliberate, compassionate and wholehearted presence, fully within my sphere, just as I'd felt Celine's earlier. I was not in this space entirely alone. With her witnessing of me, Elizabeth created an intimate community, even communion, between us, ultimately without intrusion or interference into my experience.

As it turned out, a kind of community-of-the-moment also gathered around me in our part of the plane. It manifested in the form of multiple packages of tissues! When I left, Elizabeth gave me four packets that had been passed over the seats and aisles, touched by many hands connecting their hearts to mine. As I exited, passengers smiled gently and lovingly at me and wished me well.

I entered the community of the Elizabeth House hospice well after midnight. Margo, the hospice nurse I'd spoken with on the phone on landing in Chicago, along with her

assistant, quietly greeted and welcomed me. In the waiting room, I received soothing chamomile tea in a china cup. Then, I sat with my mother, just the two of us, into the deepest part of the night, although her spirit had already left her body.

During the days and weeks that followed – what even then I called a period of "sorrow and grace" – facilitators from the Courage & Renewal community reached out to me in waves of witnessing. I felt astonished, saturated, and at times overwhelmed in the best sense by the magnitude and generosity of their acts of kindness, words of comfort and courage. Courage facilitator-friends I knew well and others I did not stepped into my circle of grief to gather me up in their arms, literally and at a distance. Anne and Tom drove hours to pick up my husband at the airport and deliver him to my doorstep. Karen opened her heart and home to me during a snowstorm later in the year when I returned to clear out my mother's home. Sally called at just the right moments.

As well, the Kirkridge Fellows confirmed the necessity and power of community as a space for witnessing. During each of the retreats I subsequently attended, I checked in with the full circle, sharing the story of dispersing my parents' possessions, readying their home for sale, donating my mother's original paintings, working intensely with my brother – and all the accompanying feelings and learnings. The Fellows held it all, steadfastly standing **by** and **with** me, yet without trying to fix me or make it all better. Individually and as a collective, they witnessed my emotional and spiritual condition and accompanied me on my journey as a daughter and as a person becoming more wholly connected to her soul.

Finally, how very fortunate I am that my mother continues to be a witness to me, as well. During the Christmas holidays following her death, I came upon the birthday card she'd given me just six weeks before she died:

Dear Karen

Wishing you a Birthday of beautiful moments,

wonderful memories and nothing but happiness

for all the days ahead.

Your Mom loves you so very much

Reading it again then was a numinous moment as I literally heard her voice speak to me. Reading her message again, now, I hear her wishes for the rest of my life, of which she will always be a part and a witness, but not in the same way as we'd known each other for 68 years.

The whole set of experiences I've related here – holding the labyrinth, my initial exploration of witnessing, hoping to be a witness honoring my mother, and then in the

aftermath of her death my having been offered others' tender, healing companionship as witnesses to me – and so much more, has called me to live more wholeheartedly, with more authenticity, integrity, courage, and faithfulness. Even in and because of this time of loss, I have become more connected to my soul's wholeness. This wholeness is touched by my mother's spirit.

RECEIVING GIFTS

The further gifts I've received from these experiences are personal, communal, and vocational. These are the gifts I know of; no doubt there are others that have yet to come to my awareness.

First, and personally, I've ridden the waves of emotion in the months since the summer of 2015. When I was in the trough of those waves, I couldn't see the horizon of my life. I floundered although I also knew in my own depths that my boat was a safe one; I felt upheld in these turbulent times by a Source, a Love greater than myself.

And because I've experienced what at times felt like little control over events, others' actions, evolving situations, and sometimes even my own responses, I've also found myself of necessity or inevitability letting intuition, rather than reflection, take the lead. It's not that my inclination toward thought and reflection left me; I knew and used both expressly in this time. As a result, what I've come to call "focused flexibility" became required and called into play.

Just as focused flexibility came forward in witnessing, listening, and responding to my mother and her circumstances, I also recognized its simple-yet-complex, unexplainable company and support as I mourned my mother and responded to the practical needs of selling her house, clearing out her earthly tent of material goods in the resulting storage units, and dispersing her life's creativity. In so doing, I received guidance from both mind *and* spirit, thought *and* intuition.

Yet, and this is a second gift, I was not solely on my own, then – or now, as I continue to approach firmer ground, emotionally and spiritually, and have the possibility of again seeing a horizon in my life. In terms of community, as I rode those waves, others accompanied me in the boat, particularly my husband and brother (both my "Davids"), and especially those in the community of Courage & Renewal facilitators, particularly our Kirkridge Courage Fellows. Being a witness or being witnessed by another is essentially an act of community, perhaps communion. We commune with each other. This story began in community with the holding of the labyrinth, carried on in an airplane, then became visible in the community of facilitators who gathered around me. And, in my "going public" with this story and my reflections, I am reaching out to an unknown community.

Finally, in terms of my vocation – especially as expressed in my work facilitating

Circles of Trust in the context of Courage & Renewal retreats – I continue to explore the intersection of soul and role, both mine and yours. The condition of my soul manifests in my roles and relationships. Who I am intermingles with who you are. Our gifts, shadows, and stories interrelate. Yet, the space of witnessing is more than one of interaction.

It is "thin."

It is a space where the human or earthly/physical and the eternal, some would say divine or the Divine, come together, collaborate and co-create. Perhaps witnessing as a thin place can be described as porous, permeable, and penetrable. Might it be a space where one absorbs another, like a sponge, yet remains appropriately non-attached? Indeed, it is a space of integration and transformation. I do not sense this space of witnessing as a thin place with my five senses; hence, I find myself only able to use language like "mysterious" and "energetic."

As well, I've come to realize through the process of being witnessed myself that I have been initiated, am being initiated, into a deeply meaningful, consequential, even mystical practice. In a sense, I've traveled through a rite of passage with my mother's death. I am coming back from that experience having been transformed into a new way of being, emerging into a deeper stage of life or sense of role. In other words, it has not been enough to intellectually understand the idea and practice of witnessing. To profoundly experience it myself – as a recipient – has given me a clearer window on and more compelling perception of the practice of being a witness.

Thus, my significant, perhaps – at least for me – momentous, experiences holding the labyrinth (being a witness) and those surrounding my mother's death (being witnessed by others) are leading me toward a deepened sense and practice of being a witness for others – both in one-on-one situations and also as a facilitator in a group setting. What is required of me now in this practice? I am called to be receptive, fully openhearted, indeed broken-openhearted.

Witnessing another demands of me that I allow my vulnerability, without imposing it. My own soul must be given space to come forth. Being a soulful witness in these ways also creates space for another's soul to show up. Witnessing creates an ill-defined but palpable space for healing and wholeness to emerge for both the one(s) being witnessed and the witness.

FINISHING, FOR NOW

My experiences of the past few years have shown and taught me what it means to let my life speak, rather than my telling my life what it is or is to be. Whereas I first mentioned "reflective observation" as a central birthright gift of mine, I no longer believe that language adequately describes or names the form of the gift that is now

seeking to emerge in me. This gift is more than being renamed; it is being re-formed. Perhaps I am actually growing into, living more deeply into (if those aren't contradictory metaphors) the gift that has always been there. I would now say that my life's purpose is to become and be a witness. It takes more than a bit of courage for me to make this declaration, to claim this gift and practice!

So, what might such a bold statement mean to my Work in the world – to my roles, relationships and responsibilities – both in my daily life and in my facilitation of Circles of Trust? I don't quite know yet, but I do know that standing in the ground of fertile questions is helpful to my growth. Here are mine, for now:

- Is "witnessing" the place where my soul and role come together most deeply?
- Moreover, if witnessing is to be a way in which I serve others – not something to be accomplished or achieved, but rather a gift to be received – how might I make myself available to witness?

I'm further guided by the desire to welcome, co-create and hold transformative spaces, ones in which witnessing plays an essential part, inspired by Shannon Huffman Polson's words:

> *There is no greater intimacy than sitting with someone traversing the tenuous boundary between worlds, sitting vigil with a spirit trembling on the border, reaching toward the new and releasing the old*
> (http://www.goodreads.com/author/quotes/5304504.Shannon_Huffman_Polson).

Although Polson may well be referring to the space between life and death, her words, for me, might also refer to the way I can be with – can witness – another person involved in any transformative change.

During the week that I completed this story, I received word from a long-time friend that he may die of brain cancer. He is reaching out, sharing the living questions of his inner life. As for me, I am being offered a clear response to the question from a stanza of my poem "For Elizabeth – in 12B" and I am utterly and overwhelmingly moved by his trust in me:

Who else is in pain, here in this space?
For whom am I now called to bear
Witness to their woundedness
With generous, compassionate grace?

I began this essay with Albert Einstein's words: *"The most beautiful thing we can experience is the mysterious."* My mother's life and death have brought such incredible

mysterious beauty into my life, as did the holding of the labyrinth and my being held in community. To have others be a witness to me and to witness others will always be an experience of mystical grace.

Having journeyed through these times, I'm becoming more powerfully aware and genuinely moved toward my true gift and the practice of being a witness. May I bring all of this mysterious beauty and the wholeness of my soul to my life, to my family, friends, and others I do not know well, and to my work as a facilitator of Circles of Trust. May I do so with authenticity, integrity, courage and faithfulness.

Karen Noordhoff is a facilitator of Courage & Renewal offerings with 18 years experience, having served educators from PreK-12 and university settings, leaders in spiritual communities and non-profits, and cross-professional groups. She is a professor emerita at Portland State University (Portland, OR) with interests in spirituality and education. As well as living in Portland, she and her husband, David, spend time in central Oregon where they walk the labyrinth at their cabin in the high desert called "The Clearing." Karen can be reached via email at karennoordhoff@yahoo.com

A Love Story about Pangolin and All Wild Beings

By Carol Kortsch

Tender warmth permeated our group conversation that morning. We had just returned for our fourth three-night retreat; twenty-four hearts spilled gratitude to once again sit together in our Kirkridge Courage Fellowship meeting room. The expansive Delaware River Valley horizon spread out below and above us, completing some infinite circle that echoed the mystery of our traveling as a community of seekers.

"*I feel like a pangolin,*" I blurted out, surprising even myself. "*I realize that part of me is curled up tightly, hidden inside an armored ball of scales. Today I feel very hesitant and fearful to show up, to come out and expose what is inside.*" Tentatively, I continued with this inner dialogue, speaking to the center of our circle from my heart. "*I sense I am carrying some deep grief that is too much to bear alone.*"

In the open space that followed, as my companions listened, as my tears softened my fears of speaking, I was recalling the memory of my unique childhood pet – a great pangolin. I had named him Chantilly Lace, because he was anything but delicate and see-through. Raised in Central Africa, I had the privilege of being up close and personal with many wonderful creatures, but in my mind, the pangolin was a creature straight out of the mythic past, out of the back-end inferno of God's creation. Chantilly was so utterly weird that he gave me goose-bumps being alone with him, but I also recall he felt particularly "mine" in some dark way. Sixty years later, it was clear that we were still becoming acquainted, still connected, still living in relationship. How curious.

Have you ever struggled with feelings that seemed bigger than words, or remained silent in a group, aware of a desperate need to communicate but sincerely concerned that no one else would understand you? On this morning I recall how overwhelmed I felt after a decade of living on a financial roller coaster. Our family life had always lived outside of many cultural norms that bring material security - that had been a conscious choice we made following in the radical steps of our parents - but this past season had shattered my confidence, and I was clearly lost in the void between feast and famine. Too much and/or too little of anything tends to flood our human psyche; so I arrived "flooded" into our community group.

So you, like me, may be wondering,

Why did this image hold so much energy?
How it is that childhood experience leaves such a mark on psyche and spirit?
How does each of us as individuals, organizations, or nations carry stretch marks, shadows, and gifts from all the past connections of our lives?
How can we access the power trapped in our shadowy inner world?

It has been my practice in my adult life to circle around questions about the real-life effects of our human "outer" and "inner" community. The complex interaction of my private and my public world-views often have left me standing alone, divided inside myself while struggling to keep my head high with the understanding of my mind. I have fought in goal-oriented ways up many mountain paths, leaped across contrasting water-sheds, only to consistently discover skeins of dualistic and/or myopic vision.

What do I see with clarity -- and what is hiding?
Who or what do I cherish, get close to – or am I repulsed by?
Why as a human do I have so many ways to run from the painful struggle towards change and growth?

Questions like these have been food for years of reflection. How good to journey with courageous circles of individuals who are committed to living in the authenticity of the undivided life. My journey keeps descending into the depths, into the shadows, and in this circle at Kirkridge, the word "community" had taken on fresh meaning. What joy to feel more energized by my work and my relationships than ever before. How remarkable that to walk in more wholeness gave me opportunity to keep searching for those parts of me that are waiting in hiding, longing to be found. As I seek daily for more whole ways to live in a broken world, I am deeply grateful for a trusting community within which to practice these new ways of being.

In the shadow-lands my soul searches for images, and as a writer today - for words. Like the pangolin, darker, more hidden aspects of my being are scrabbling around below the surface. Some just need the light of consciousness; others become fodder for my creative life force. As we sat together that morning, I realized how urgently, almost explosively, a darker, less social part of me needed to move into the light of awareness. In discovering that, like the pangolin, my soul is mostly a night animal, this gift of metaphor opened an underworld of meaning. I could name many other creatures in the same breath, but Chantilly and I are so much more alike than first appearances!

This shy being, the pangolin, staggers around clumsily on two back legs and uses extraordinarily sharp claws to dig burrows and tear apart rock piles while searching for ants. When under threat, this scaly creature will curl up into an impenetrable ball. I recall that as curious children we attempted to prove who might be the strongest. Who could pull Chantilly Lace apart without cutting their fingers on his razor-sharp scales? We wondered what was inside. What was he hiding so zealously – maybe we might find his belly button, or catch a glimpse of some juicy genitalia? Poor Chantilly. No wonder he clawed his way out of his cage one night!

I remember being very sad and yet somehow also cherishing his freedom and his need to escape. As a child in boarding school, with my missionary parents hundreds of miles away in another country, unconscious parts of me resonated deeply with this scaly creature. And years later, it was not unlike the resonance I was feeling in this circle of kindred spirits.

Thus it was that I sat in our circle of facilitators, troubled and challenged with another iteration of the age-old question: "*At this season of my life - who am I, and what gifts do I offer into the world*?" I felt like Rilke's wonderful lines: "*I am circling around God, around the ancient tower, and I have been circling for a thousand years, and I still don't know if I am a falcon, or a storm, or a great song.*"

When Chantilly resurfaced in my mind that day, he brought with him a flood of awareness that continues to inspire and challenge me. In that moment I was able to admit publicly that I was feeling ornery, aggrieved, and imprisoned. I recognized my own sharp claws that itched to hurl around stones and throw dirt and make a big mess of this loving, kind circle. A part of me felt very alone and despite the good company, I was hungry for the deepest kind of soul food that this world can offer – that of my innate and often hidden wildness. In a lifetime of good service, I have learned to shield others from this unruly self and have grown a tough, protective, and shining armor; my ego skills are well-honed, finely-tuned, and in good working order. I still wasn't sure that all of me was acceptable or wanted, but I knew that somehow I had to move this volcanic energy beyond the neat circle of chairs and gentle conversation.

Do you know that pangolins dive headfirst into an anthill because they have no chink in their system where ants can attack? A pangolin is invulnerable when they hunt their food supply and unappetizing to their foes. Even the eyes and ears of pangolins have tough nictitating membranes that wipe away and close off access to the invading hordes – other than humans.

Have you noticed that certain stories, people, or sayings haunt you? How they keep popping up, grab a thought, or some deep sense of knowing, and then disappear into an elusive shadow? Parker Palmer has taught us well, saying often, "*The soul is a shy wild animal. It shows up at the corners of our awareness.*" It was like that too with this wild visitor - Chantilly. He had already been agitating to be recognized as part of my own shadow; my soul was burrowing up from the darker and less penetrable places of my being.

Curiously, a few days before our Kirkridge Courage Fellows meeting, I had been shocked to read an article about the giant pangolin by Jeff Flocken, "*The shy, nocturnal creature is the most trafficked mammal in the world. Almost a million pangolins were*

trafficked in the past 10 years. We are finding crates filled with pangolin scales, entire boats with bags of live, or frozen and dead, pangolins that are being taken from the wild." It used to be for the value of their countless scales, but now pangolin meat is considered a luxury item in parts of Asia, where "*the body is actually being eaten as some sort of celebration when a business deal is done.*"

This story of yet another endangered being brought me great grief, not only for the species loss of such a precious, peculiar animal, but that somehow, once again, the violent cycle of monetary power and consumptive acquisition has birthed such a destructive ritual – the sacrifice of one of the most helpless creatures of our globe. How curious to now be "feeling like a pangolin," surrounded by some of my closest friends on a sunny winter morning in the picturesque mountains of Pennsylvania. Somehow I felt the suffering of making soulful choices to live out of my own wholeness, and yet still be left, skinned alive by bankruptcy and the cultural shame and criticism that brings. The experience of helplessness had become intolerable to bear alone.

For years our family had been caught up in an international monetary business deal that was bankrupting us, freezing our assets, and us, and our precious home now belonged to the bank. How curious that although I felt trapped in the cage of poverty, at the same time I was enjoying endless benefits for my mid-to-upper class creature comforts. And even more curious, consider the reality that once I was able to muddle through and speak about all of this, once I had been witnessed by others who had no need to fix me, pull me apart, or drown me in their sympathetic attention, it was as if I escaped an invisible cage of my own making. Like Chantilly escaping his cage, I was free to be all of me – especially the wild and untamed animal-self. What a gift to be seen and known for who we are, free from shame. Free to be naked, natural, wild beings in a vast cosmic order of exquisite beauty and complexity

Wild beings are my family. I know this to be true. Maybe it is my DNA from African soil, but Chantilly was a personal messenger in a long line of earth voices. Over the past decades I have learned more from sister snake and brother bear than either of my flesh-and-blood siblings. I've hunkered on the ground and been taught by grandmother oak and granddaughter wren through every season at the home we share at Stonehaven. We are a commons there – I have discovered this reality. Together we have become a place where owl and turtle arrive as my teachers, offering their wisdom from their scat and shell, where the lotus queen first wove her sultry magic in my water-garden.

Stonehaven Commons is a place where the rocks cry out when nobody listens or pays attention. Frankly, even great-grandmother lion, who has been prowling around my bedroom windows since birth, is around here, still stalking me. She used to offer me nightmares that my terrified child had no idea what to do with, now I am not so

afraid of that underworld of fear and fantasy. In fact, this underworld story is the world of soul that calls my name and is guiding me. I am reminded of this favorite promise from Isaiah 11:16, aware I live in this promise today: "*The wolf will live with the lamb; the leopard will lie down with the young goat. The calf and the lion will graze together, and a little child will lead them.*"

I am aware that my soul's "inner community" is rich in the diversity from early life in Angola, Zambia, and Uganda. I am also forever changed by decades of meaningful work as a spiritual leader in international faith communities, and as a healer in our Western psychological community. Now as an elder, I can say proudly and with humility that I am a global citizen. I share this planet with beings of all kinds – in a deep and complex web of relationships with both human and other-than-human community. It seems my journey has been that of an edge-walker, an adventurer around the fringes of many kinds of communal experience. To be clear though, it is in the consistent practice of showing up wholly and grounding myself in intentional circles of trust, with both human and non-human voices, that I have been given on-going clarity as to my soul's deepest name and calling.

We suffer from the confusing babble of too many voices in our era. I have followed many other voices, listened to the heartbeats of others as if they were my own, and eventually I am coming to know and recognize the "golden shadow" of my own being; she is dancing and singing to be recognized for who she is, that which she was born to be. It is clear now that, hiding in the deep underbelly of my armored pangolin being, lays the most precious treasure of darkness. It is only in showing up whole and vulnerable in all my relationships, in all my work, will I find "She Who Waits."

Thus I write today with a fresh confidence, an earthy call from this place of hidden wild energy where my passion and creativity springs. What awe – to be aware that we are all in and of this Circle together. The more I let go of my human ego story and allow the deeper and more unknown soul story to emerge, the more I find it is not just about me. It is all about us. Truly, we are all in this together.

Carol Kortsch is the author of a novel about this work, *The Retreat*, as well as a Circle of Trust facilitator. She and her husband Uli see themselves as global partners, born in Germany and Angola, together now for over 40 years. Uli and Carol moved from Canada into Stonehaven in 1992, and with the help of a team of loyal friends, bought the property from Eastern University in 2001. See that special thin place at stonehavencommons.org and reach out to her at ckortsch@global-partners.com

Soul Journey: Living a Spiritual Life as a Black Woman in America

By Veta Goler

Watching the 2016 presidential election results the evening of November 8 was painful. It was difficult to believe what I was seeing. Eventually, I went to bed, hoping that I would awake the next morning to a miracle—a disaster averted. Instead, I awoke to what felt like a strange, yet familiar, new world, a world in which there was no longer any pretense that I, a black woman, held any value in my country.

I grieved deeply that day.

I also began searching for words that would help me make sense of this reality. How would I navigate living in a country in which so many people believed that only white, male, heterosexual, wealthy, and (probably) Christian men were deemed worthy, that they voted for someone whose words and actions were clearly vile, racist, sexist, homophobic, hostile, bigoted, small-minded and mean-spirited – decidedly not Presidential? This was especially painful after the compassionate and intelligent Presidency of Barack Obama.

I felt vulnerable in this hostile world and sought sources of peace and courage. Most of those to whom I turned for solace in my internet browsings were spiritual leaders. These included Michael Bernard Beckwith, Kryon (channeled by Lee Carroll), Deepak Chopra, Neale Donald Walsch, Lenedra Carroll, and Adironnda (channeled by Marilyn Harper). I also turned to visionaries like Sharif Abdullah and Barbara Marx Hubbard. Some referred directly to the election results. Others did not. While I found all helpful in some way, I realized that I most wanted to hear from those who could relate personally to what so many of us were facing. Beckwith, Abdullah, and Chopra are people of color; the others are not.

For a long time I've been looking for a book on new thought spirituality that includes people who look like me – that takes into account the realities of embodied life where race, gender, age, class, and ability seem to matter. I am clear that all spiritual paths and religions ultimately lead to the same place, and that the Divine (God, or whatever one wants to call the Supreme Being) is in all beings and all things and has no gender or color. However, the absence of any reference to the lived experiences of those of us who are not white, male, affluent, able-bodied, and Christian offers a not-so-hidden message that our daily realities, and therefore, our lives, are not important. And while I know that the experiences we have on the earth plane are fleeting and of less importance than our soul's journey, in order for us to devote our attention to the inner journey, which we must do for individual and planetary evolution, we must navigate and negotiate various "isms"– racism, sexism, ageism, heteronormativity, etc.– in the external world.

In other words, to attain the inner spiritual development that enables us to live as if the outer world doesn't really matter, we must face the challenges of that external world, as if it does matter. This means that for black women and other people of color, there is one more step required for spiritual growth and development. In addition to the regular challenges that all humans face as incarnated beings, black women and others must also face the various forms of oppression.

I can accept that this additional physical step provides additional opportunities for spiritual growth. And I know the journey of a spiritual being in a human body is arduous. We are required to remember again and again and again why we are here. A community can be very helpful with this. I am fortunate that I have several communities to support my journey: the meditation center I attend in Atlanta; two organizations that hold contemplation, compassion, and diversity as core values-the Center for Courage & Renewal and the Center for Contemplative Mind in Society; several online groups of new thought spiritually-minded people; and several friends with whom I regularly reflect and share are all important to me. Nevertheless, I still seek texts that address experiences of people like me directly.

Therefore, I am writing what I want to read. Hopefully, by capturing my own experiences and approaches, I will help myself—and others—to walk a spiritual path in 21st century America.

A BRIEF BIOGRAPHY

I grew up in somewhat unusual circumstances for my time as a black girl in the U.S., with educated and professional parents (lawyer father and kindergarten teacher mother), in a small Midwest town. In my middle-class life, I had enough food to eat, a free-standing home with front and back yards, and summer vacations in northern Michigan. And I always I knew I would go to college.

Religion was and wasn't important in my upbringing. My family belonged to the African Methodist Episcopal (AME) church for most of my childhood, until a disagreement with the minister led my parents to join the local Presbyterian church. There were only a few black families in the church; and while in some ways we were welcomed, in other ways, it was clear that black people didn't really belong. No one said anything hateful to my family, but during a teen workshop question and answer session, when I asked about interracial dating, I was told that I should stick to my own kind.

This was a politically powerful time in the world. The Civil Rights, Black Power, and Women's Movements were in full swing. Protests against the Vietnam War continued. Woodstock happened. On one hand, there was such hope for a changed world. On the other hand, there was such resistance to change—like now.

I knew people were working and agitating and fighting for something—for a better world for black people, women and others. But Martin Luther King, Jr., and Malcolm X were killed, as were John F. and Bobby Kennedy.

At the time hippies were talking about love. Something about love resonated with me. I came to see myself as a black hippie, a flower child, and a bridge between black and white worlds.

The moment I can identify as the dawning of my search for God took place during the summer between high school and college. By the time I graduated from high school, like many young people, I was disillusioned with so much of my daily experience, which I attributed to the immaturity of my classmates and short-sightedness of some of my teachers. I remember wondering if the whole point of life was just to accumulate experiences. I couldn't see anything beyond that. But merely accumulating experiences didn't seem very fulfilling. At the time, I didn't realize my question was spiritual; what I was really searching for was meaning. The feeling of being unsettled, of knowing there was something else going on that I couldn't identify, would return to me over the years. And later, I would see it as a search for God.

During and after college, my search manifested in decidedly "unspiritual" ways—in seeking through sex, drugs, and drama. These offered moments of feeling intensely alive. Some of these were quite vivid, yet they were always followed by a let-down. Nothing seemed to stick.

There were also some fleetingly beautiful moments that, while not sustainable, didn't have the same sense of futility. I discovered the awe of nature on my first backpacking trips, gazing at mountains, drawing pictures of the wildflowers I saw in a meadow, or simply listening to the water as I sat on a riverbank for a moment of rest.

Making music (playing piano and flute) and creating visual art (silk screening and pottery) had a similar effect. These may not have led to such awe-inspiring moments as the mountains, but the act of focusing intently and creating something beautiful was deeply fulfilling.

Eventually, I discovered modern dance. I began dancing in college and dedicated myself to it as a graduate student. Later, I came to see dance as a contemplative practice. From the moment warm-ups began, I could release whatever problems I had; I could let go of what was going on out in the world and focus my attention on the studio, my body, and the emotion or energy needed at a particular moment. Before performing, I prayed to be a vehicle for the truth and beauty of the Divine. And I believed my dancing was characterized by authenticity, forthrightness, and openness.

My first formal experience with contemplative practices took place during my sophomore year of college, when I took a Transcendental Meditation workshop just before spring-semester final exams. I began meditating right away, but I kept falling asleep when I needed to be studying for finals, so I stopped meditating almost as soon as I started. Over the years, I would try to kickstart my meditation practice, but never seemed able to sustain it, until I discovered an eastern spiritual path almost 25 years later.

My free-spirit, flower-power life led to various kinds of substance explorations. For a while, this was quite moving and a lot of fun. Eventually, however, it became clear that my drug of choice, marijuana, controlled me more than I controlled it, and I found my way to Alcoholics Anonymous. Perhaps the most important thing about attending AA meetings was the focus on a higher power. I had long ago stopped going to church, but AA brought me back to thinking about meaning. If God existed, then maybe life wasn't about feeling good or racking up experiences, after all. And this time, God wasn't in a white church, where I was tolerated, but not truly welcomed. This time, God was around people who looked like me, as well as those who didn't.

A few years after committing myself to sobriety and attending AA meetings regularly, I found my spiritual path. Once I realized that I really was a seeker of God, I dove in enthusiastically. Meditation, chanting, selfless service, and

scriptural study all consumed me. During most of my spare time, I was meditating, attending programs at my local meditation center, or traveling to ashrams in upstate New York, California, and India.

At the same time, I started reading new-age books and listening to channelings of ascended masters, anything focused on the evolution of human consciousness. Eventually, I came to see that the answers to all problems are spiritual. And I brought spirituality in the form of contemplative practices to my work. I began incorporating breathing, meditation, journaling, labyrinth walking, and other contemplative practices in my classes, offering meditation sessions for the college community and leading daylong contemplative retreats.

With this focus on contemplative practices at home and at work, I felt like I was living a spiritual life. I reminded myself to see God in other people, to recognize and challenge my own judgmentalism, and to do what I could to be an anchor of light.

But the recent presidential election shook me to my core. Immediately after the election, I sensed my personality change. I felt afraid, vulnerable, and unwelcome wherever I went, and contracted into a shell. As I moved about, I avoided making eye contact with white people. I didn't feel I could trust them.

However, two months have passed since the election and I have come to realize that nothing has really changed. The hatred and bigotry that characterized the Presidential campaign were already present and very active. And the spiritual leaders I've turned to have offered the same teachings that I already knew in my heart to be true. So I no longer feel the need to do anything new to deal with the change in leadership in the country. I simply need to remember that everything is not always as it seems and to intensify what I already do.

SOME PRACTICES FOR TODAY

Since the election, many of us have been asking the question, How then shall I live? Some people have been offering ways to become more politically active, and others, ways to spend our money more consciously by boycotting businesses and organizations that support hatred and bigotry. I am committed to those approaches as well, but am drawn to focus most on living a spiritual life. So much of what is happening today doesn't make sense to me intellectually. Humanity is making greater and greater strides with improving the lives of people through technology, legislation, and increased compassion. Consequently the right-wing bigotry, hatred, and radicalism point to a regression of human development, not evolution.

They don't make sense.

Therefore, I conclude there must be spiritual reasons for so much of what is happening

these days. And because of this, it makes the most sense for me to focus on spiritual development. To this end, I have intensified my spiritual practices. Sitting meditation is my main contemplative practice. One of the simplest, clearest definitions of meditation I've seen is that it is "substituting another object of attention for your thoughts." I may focus on my breath, a mantra, a teaching, or the inner energy I experience. But the act of returning my focus to that object of attention over and over throughout my meditation transports me to a place of connection with the source of peace, insight, creativity and strength. In addition, I am often practicing metta meditation, also known as loving kindness meditation. As I meditate, I shower others and myself with love and blessings. Perhaps most importantly, through daily meditation, as I connect again and again with the Divine, I increase my sense of self worth. My ability to love and treat others with compassion is enhanced when I can do the same for myself. Thus, whatever kind of meditation I am practicing, I am contributing to the upliftment of others, as well as myself.

Political activism is extremely important at this time, but spiritual evolution is equally, if not more, important. So, I'm committed to meditating every day. I use the Insight Timer app to time my meditation and have signed up for the 365-day meditation commitment for 2017. It is important to have a personal practice, whatever that is. Meditation works best for me because I can do it alone or with a group of people; there are lots of different ways to approach meditation, and whether I do a long meditation or a short meditation, I am able to feel my connection with God.

Another practice of mine is breathing consciously. This almost always helps me to slow down. As expected, it is as if the election gave people permission to disregard civility. Since the election, hate crimes have increased, and it seems to me that people are moving about more quickly, driving more aggressively. In part as a reaction to this, I have been focusing on my breathing and slowing down. I am moving about with more calmness and intentionality and am not giving in to frenzied ways of being. If drivers rush past me in ways that don't seem the safest, I am also reminding myself to avoid judgmentalism and to maintain my state.

I love practicing random acts of kindness. My goal is at least one random act of kindness each day. This could be holding the door for someone, paying for the drink(s) of the car behind me in the Starbucks drive-thru, giving money or food to a homeless person, or something else. At first, I was focusing my efforts on other people of color, in an effort to say, "You are valuable." Now I am including all others in my efforts.

Being on retreat is one of my most important practices. Taking time away from the daily grind to focus on reflecting, with like-minded souls, rejuvenates me. Some retreats I offer as daylong retreats for interested folks at my work. I also attend retreats for Courage & Renewal facilitators. And I am planning a series of longer retreats for

faculty of color, whether they teach at Historically Black Colleges and Universities (HBCUs), predominantly white institutions (PWIs), or other institutions. My experience has been that, no matter where they teach, they appreciate the opportunity to take time out for their own personal well being, which helps them when they return to work.

And finally, I firmly believe that what we consume—whether food or media—is important. Where we place our attention matters. That is why, long ago, I stopped watching violent movies and television shows. However, a few years ago, I was caught up in watching some very popular—and very violent—network television shows with black female leads. These were juicy roles for African American women and I delighted in seeing versions of myself on the small screen. Although I stopped watching these shows a year or so ago, I am recommitting myself to taking greater care of myself—and sending my own message to Hollywood—by avoiding violent television and films.

WHAT ELSE HAVE I LEARNED?

Even as I continue to walk the spiritual path, I find it helpful to reflect on the lessons I have learned. The first lesson is that human consciousness is evolving and everything is not what it seems. Scientists tell us that evolution requires challenges, difficult situations that motivate change. And while things may look a particular way on the surface, perhaps the evolutionary impulse has allowed or enabled things to happen in a certain way to create the impetus for deep change.

We are a young—and immature—species. In *New World New Mind*, Robert Ornstein and Paul Ehrlich imagine Earth's history as if it has taken place in one year. With each day representing 12 million years of actual history, the origin of the Earth would have taken place at midnight, January 1, and homo sapiens would have emerged around 11:45 PM. Amazingly, all that has happened in recorded history would have occurred in the final minute of the year! This gives me a valuable perspective on current and past events.

We have been like bratty toddlers who don't know how to play together. We are now poised to grow up a bit. And some of us are doing this more quickly than others. Some of us have developed enough to embrace higher evolutionary characteristics (like love and compassion beyond our individual families or "tribes"), while others are still focusing on survival and lower level characteristics. Eventually, we will all develop fully to enlightenment. But we are on different time frames. Those who are evolving more rapidly are helping others to evolve, through their spiritual practices and how they live their lives.

This brings me back to how to live. It is critical that those of us who are able engage in some kind of spiritual practice each day. In her wonderful book, *We Are the Ones We Have Been Waiting For*, Alice Walker reminds us that this is not a time to live without

a practice. I feel that so clearly; some kind of daily practice in which I connect with God is essential for my well-being and for what I can offer the planet. It doesn't matter whether or not I feel like I've connected with the Divine deeply or only superficially in my practice. It is important to do it anyway.

Love everyone. Period. I don't have to be best friends with everyone. And I may not like what someone has said or done, but viewing someone with anything but love is viewing them with fear. And fear hurts me, not them.

Ultimately, it does seem that color, gender, and other characteristics of particular individuals don't matter. However, by doing my practices and engaging in efforts to be in the present moment, without judgment, I am better able to face the challenges of living as a black woman. In this way, I become more and more free within myself, no matter what is going on in the external world. And through my own spiritual evolution, I contribute to the evolution of humanity, which will diminish and eliminate the hatred and bigotry that seem to surround us.

For me, there are no other options.

Without hope and contemplative practices, I see myself sinking into despair and depression and losing my sense of purpose. The world makes less sense if I succumb to negativity. So, even as I see and work to change the actions and systems that do not support all people, I turn within to see the divinity within me, knowing that that same divinity exists in all others.

In the October 9, 2016 episode of Oprah's *SuperSoul Sunday*, Michael Bernard Beckwith said these words that affirm the importance of living a spiritual life:

> *When you believe more in what you don't see than in what you do see, then what you* ***do*** *see, you* ***won't*** *see, and what you* ***don't*** *see, you* ***will*** *see.*

To me, Dr. Beckwith is saying that by focusing on the inner journey, we are able to look beyond the dramas that play out in daily life to the underlying spiritual realities and reasons behind them. With this foundation, we can avoid getting stuck in the daily dramas and can begin to envision a more wonderful world. And this is an important first step in making that world a reality.

The most critical thing I can do is to know my worth—deeply, from within. If other black women and I can know our value, if we can release the internalized oppression that we have consumed all of our lives, then even though racist, sexist behaviors may continue to exist, they won't have the same effect on us. We will be able to respond to them in more response-able ways—in contrast to reactive ways. And this has the power to shift things dramatically. As Neale Donald Walsch says, someone *"who walks through the world holding the Identity of Divinity deep within changes the*

exterior experiences of everyone else, everywhere she or he steps…"

As I reflect on my spiritual journey and the lessons I have learned, I realize that I already have access to what I want to read. The teachings and practices I have learned may not always have been presented to me in a way that is specific to my own cultural identity, but they are simply reminders of what my soul already knows.

That knowledge is within me.

By accessing that knowledge and honoring who I am as a person, I value myself. And as my worthiness reveals itself to me, I am able to be authentically myself. My being directs my doing so that I stand tall, live my truth, and help usher in a new world, a world that works for all.

Veta Goler, PhD, has served as Arts and Humanities Division Chair and Associate Professor of Dance at Spelman College. A dance historian and former modern dance artist, she has been a national Circle of Trust® facilitator since 2007 and can be reached at vetagoler@gmail.com

Living Alive on the Frontier

By Elaine Sullivan

Sometimes it takes darkness and the sweet
confinement of your aloneness
to learn
anything or anyone
that does not bring you alive
is too small for you.

--David Whyte

I heard the poet David Whyte speak about living on the frontier of life, being at the frontier of your identity. The image touched me and helped me reawaken my imagination and reflect on my life at this time of challenge as I watch my beloved husband slowly slip away from me.

Whyte uses the image of the frontier to mean that place on the edge of our identity where we meet the Self we didn't know we knew. He said that when he began to realize that *"my identity depended not upon any beliefs I had, inherited beliefs or manufactured beliefs, but my identity actually depended on how much attention I was paying to things that were other than myself. And that as you deepen this intentionality*

and this attention, you started to broaden and deepen your own sense of presence. And I began to realize that the only place where things were actually real was at this frontier between what you think is you and what you think is not you. That whatever you desire of the world will not come to pass exactly as you will like it.

"But the other mercy is that whatever the world desires of you will also not come to pass. And what actually occurs is this meeting, this frontier. But it's astonishing how much time human beings spend away from that frontier, abstracting themselves out of their bodies, out of their direct experience, and out of a deeper, broader, and wider possible future that's waiting for them if they hold the conversation at that frontier level" (interview with Krista Tippett, http://www.onbeing.org/program/david-whyte-the-conversational-nature-of-reality/transcript/8581).

I reflected in my journal on what it means to live fully in and on that frontier:

Living on the frontier of life

I can refuse to be myself - I can step out on to the edge
I can fully incarnate in the frontier I find myself
I can stand on solid ground and reach for the intangible nature of this frontier
I can discipline myself and seek a language that supports my darkness
I can find a courageous way of living in this beautiful and difficult world
My home is so close to me, everything a numinous call to the depth of this frontier.
Courageously I place my identity at the edge of discovery and remembering.
On the new frontier I hear myself speak about things I did not know I knew
I reimagine myself - I renew myself - I rediscover myself - I hear my own truth.

After more than 80 years of living, you would think there would be no more new frontiers. But I find myself at one of the most difficult edges so far as I am literally losing my dear husband of forty-four years after severe memory loss from several mini-strokes. ***On the new frontier, I hear myself speak about things I did not know I knew. I reimagine myself. I renew myself. I rediscover myself. I hear my own truth.***

Much of the work of my life has been helping others find the power and meaning of their own stories. Now, as I remember the many frontiers of my life, I am making meaning from my own story. And I realize that, this time as I navigate this difficult world, I have a gift that wasn't as evident on early frontiers: the trustworthiness of my Kirkridge Courage Fellowship community.

The invitation to the Kirkridge Fellowship was a surprise in my 80th year, when I wasn't really anticipating a new frontier. Arriving at Kirkridge Retreat Center in the Pocono

Mountains of Pennsylvania, I again experienced what I had felt at this special place many years before: a profound peace, a sense of being at home. The spirit of a man I loved and admired, Dan Berrigan, seemed pervasive as did the spirit of this place where many have found renewal, hope and community. This commitment to a community who would be together over a two-year span was indeed a blessed frontier.

Words from Joyce Rupp's poem, *Old Maps*, shared in that first retreat, linger in my soul:

No map, no specific directions,
no "this way ahead" or "take a left."
How will I know where to go?
How will I find my way? no map!
But then my midlife soul whispers:
"there was a time before maps
when pilgrims traveled by the stars."

It is time for the pilgrim in me
to travel in the dark,
to learn to read the stars
that shine in my soul.
I will walk deeper
into the dark of my night.
I will wait for the stars.
Trust their guidance,
And let their light be enough for me.

In this challenging new frontier, I was truly a pilgrim letting go of old maps and traveling more deeply into the dark of my night. Supported by a loving, caring community of colleagues, I made discoveries about myself, was invited to share my approaches to this work, learned incredible wisdom from our community, and found myself alive with the sounds of the soulful space of Kirkridge. The poet in me was reawakened, and I discovered bread for my journey. As I traveled this frontier I reflected on what this work has done for me. Now, re-reading parts of my journal, I know that what I need is already here.

Community is a gift to be received,
It begins in the recesses of my heart,
Community is my crucible,
my commitment to be refined by fire.
I know what I have to do
though voices around me keep shouting bad advice.
It is late –
the darkness is deep –

a wild night –
the road is full of strewn branches and stones.
Little by little I leave those voices behind.
The stars begin to burn through sheets of clouds
and there is a new voice.....
I am in the crucible of my community
with people who have collaborated in dreaming,
in thinking wild thoughts
about funding and invitations,
about creating safe spaces,
about facilitation of this work,
with people who have taken courageous risks,
inviting me to be a castaway on my own island,
discovering my own inner teacher,
my own drum, my own heartbeat.
I will remember that community is found
in the recesses of my heart,
in the recesses of your hearts.
Out beyond ideas of wrong doing and right doing
there is a field.
I'll meet you there.
Bring your Wilson – I'll bring mine
As we travel together, with the Great Spirit
on the Mobius Trail.

MY FIRST FRONTIER

The Texas Panhandle was my first frontier eighty-one years ago. There under the wide open spaces and the brilliant stars I lived through many seasons: brutal winters when the cold reminded me of the rope tied to the barn, surprising springs when the new green shoots came through the muddy earth, long summer days of watching crops grow and gardens bear fruit, and the most fruitful falls when the harvest was gathered. As children we lived by the seasons. Though we were very poor we were extremely rich. At night the vast sky was ours as we lay on the ground finding our stars, and during the day the earth offered many opportunities for our playful imaginations. Living in that frontier, the relationship to family, to the church, to God, and to our small community was the essence of my life.

During this time I heard the small still voice in my soul calling. At the very young age of fifteen, I entered a Benedictine convent, even though that meant leaving my home,

my community, and my security. Words from my journal speak my truth:

If I can let go as my tree lets go its leaves,
So casually, one by one
If I can take the dark with open eyes
And call it seasonal
If I can find within me a silence –
A silence as vast as a universe,
If I can find that silence
And remember who I am.
Silence is my deepest nature, my home.
Silence reveals – silence heals,
Silence brings me to the real work –
the roots of my being.
Silence invites me to hear the voice within
So that I know what I have to do.

Being called to a new frontier at such a young age presented me with many challenges. I felt the utter loneliness of being five hundred miles from my family: Mom, Dad, and eight siblings whom I dearly loved. Part of this new frontier was learning to live the disciplined life of a nun. Over time I learned the art of deep meditation, the meaning of silence (very difficult for me who was a chatter box), the chanting of the Divine Office throughout the day and evening, simple recreation, simple foods, hours of spiritual reading and the challenge of living in community which is the heart of the Benedictine Way. I lived my way into the questions concerning this vocation. In very dark times I wondered what I was doing with my life and at times I considered leaving. My journaling speaks to the seasons I experienced:

Seasons of my soul, rich in paradox,
What is growing in me will die,
What is seeding will blossom.
My work, my willingness to go into my deepest dazzling darkness,
To visit the unknown spaces in my heart and soul,
To be willing to embrace my hurt, my fear,
My saboteur, my victim, my healer,
My magician, my seasonal gifts.
To know that in that embrace I am whole.
To visit in autumn the seeds of my true Self.
As I am willing to let go of things so dear to my ego,
To embrace my winters
Where I experience the darkness and the dormancy.

To dance my springs –
The inevitable seeds of new life yearning to be born.
To celebrate my summers aware of the abundance
In my life as I acknowledge my fears of scarcity.
Yes, there is in me a deeper Self
That loves paradox even as I seek comfort in certainty.
My seasonal paradoxes invite me
To do my inner work –
To get past my ego into the deep dazzling darkness within.
Remembering, recalling the power of the mobius
What is inside me – my darkness and my light
Always being projected on to my world.
What is outside of me is always affecting my inner world.
I stand grounded on the earth
As I listen to the deep waters of my soul.

ANOTHER FRONTIER: THE CALL OF SOCIAL ACTIVISM

At age eighteen I was thrust into a new frontier which demanded so much growth and so much maturity. I was sent to an African American school to teach. It was pre-civil rights. Having grown up in an all-white community, I had no idea what I would learn in this new environment. I had forty children in grades three, four and five and no training around teaching. I knew in that first year I was born to teach and relished what each new day taught me. My children used separate bathrooms and were isolated in balcony seats because of the color of their skin. I was devastated. How could this be? It was during this time that becoming a social activist to right these injustices took center stage of my life. Words from my journal remind me of my deep gratitude for the call to this new frontier:

I am living my life.
I will make a difference.
I have stood on the silent river of ice.
I have listened to the currents of my life coming from miles away.
I have asked myself whether the life
I'm living is the one that wants to live in me.
I know that what I strive for in perfection is not
what turns me into the lit angel.

What disturbs me and what nourishes me has everything I need.
Time to go into the dark
where the night has eyes to recognize its own.
The night gives me a horizon further that I can see.
The dark is my womb.
I own my weakness and my strength,
my liability and my giftedness,
my darkness and my light.

Wintering through my story, I'm discovering my voice.
I am becoming fierce with reality.
I hear the sprout hidden in the seed.
I am learning I can be everything by simply listening.
Like the woodcarver, I guard my spirit,
do not expend it on trifles.
I slow down. I pay attention.
If I am not so single-minded about keeping my life in motion,
if I make peace with the wars inside me,
if I for once would do nothing,
perhaps a great silence – a winter's silence –
a compassionate connecting silence,
a silence that would lead me to otherness,
would be enough for the new life I must and will call my own.

I left that school at age twenty-one when I was sent to be principal of a small school in Arkansas. Martin Luther King was sounding his powerful message in the media. I was deeply moved by his work and sought to bring his message to our school.

Resistance was all around me.

I was fearless due to remembering my students from my first school. I spoke out in public meetings in this community and challenged the status quo. Because I had good relationships with the parents in my school, I found the courage to challenge. During this time our country experienced the marches in Selma and many other non-violent protests. The mood was tense, and I felt it in the very fabric of my being. Again my journals reminded me of my feelings on that frontier:

I know a deep commitment to making the world more beautiful
is growing in me.
I recognize my coward and my procrastinator.
I know my garden of flowers – one clearly lopsided –
another half nibbled away.

But what in this world is perfect?
I want to be whole, not perfect.
My world is more beautiful, more dazzling
because I see the hidden wholeness in me and in another.
I commit to guarding my spirit against trifles –
To make the world more beautiful
by believing that imperfections are nothing – that light is everything –
That it is more than the sum of each flawed blossom rising and fading.
I will become god to even the palest of flowers within.
I will honor and nurture the green stone – my heart energy –
the greening of my heart.
My soul looks into the white fire of a great mystery.
My heart is pounding.
I will not die an unlived life.
A perfect sweetness has blossomed in the depth of my own heart.

MEETING MYSELF ON THE FRONTIER

"So in other words, whatever you want to happen, will not happen," David Whyte says about being on the frontier. *"But equally, whatever the world wants to happen for you will not happen either. And what happens is this meeting. And it's in that meeting that you overhear yourself being surprised by your reality, by the larger context that you haven't yet explored. So you're trying to overhear your Self whom you didn't know you knew. And you're trying to speak it out loud in the world so it can be known consciously. There should be a lovely sense of surprise when you're working at that edge and a sense of being gifted."* (from Tami Simon's interview with David Whyte, http://www.soundstrue.com/store/weeklywisdom/?page=single&category=IATE&episode=1641)

That lovely sense of surprise came when I was given an opportunity to take a break from teaching and go fulltime to school at Loyola University in Chicago to become a social worker. I was there when Martin Luther King was assassinated. The next day, on Palm Sunday, I took the bus into the inner city of Chicago which was awash with fire and protests. With many volunteers I worked among the very poor giving out food and clothing.

That incredible experience changed my life, and I went back to the University and changed my major to education and entered a new frontier. I heard the call deep in my heart: Do what you can to change attitudes, open hearts and help people see with new eyes. That day in Chicago my heart was broken, broken open to seeing new possibilities. I promised to live non-violently and to give voice to what I knew:

I don't have to be good;
I want to be whole – embrace my hidden wholeness.
What I have become
Is the country where I live.
The world offers itself to my imagination.
Some seed in me awkwardly awakens,
Stirs to life.
Terrible and instinctive
It touches my guts.
I fear and resist it.
I run madly, busy myself, overload my plate.
What I fear and desire
Pokes up its head.
The root struts from the seed
In the earth's darkness, my darkness, my Shadow.
I confirm in my very marrow the paradoxes of my inner life –
Strengths and weaknesses, wounds and gifts.
I cannot see the shape of what wants to be born.
I don't know its nature.
But just underground is the long avoided latency.
It may be that when I no longer know what to do
I have come to my real work.
That when I no longer know which way to go
I will have come to my real journey.
I have fewer answers now – more wonderings.
I wonder about my harvest
And the feast at the edge of my sleep.
I wonder in silence,
In solitude in nature, in relationship.
I know I have a place in the family of things.
Darkened, I am carried out of need, deep
Into the country I have married.
I am home.

When I graduated with a Masters in Counseling and Education, I was invited into the PhD program but decided I wanted to go study with teachers and leaders who would offer me the opportunity to know myself, to discover who I was. For years I have studied with incredible teachers and have never regretted not having a doctor before my name because I realize what an incredible inner journey I was invited to take with so many mentors. I loved synthesizing the specialties of so many in the field of transformational work. I was invited to step on the edge of many internal frontiers:

Above these Taos mountains the blue skies hold
the silhouettes of white moving clouds.
I search for the one line inscribed across the heavens so I can find the one line written inside of me.
It took this great New Mexico sky to find that small, bright indescribable wedge of freedom in my heart.
That line rediscovered and reclaimed – you have within you a hidden wholeness
holding the fire of passion – the groundedness of earth,
the water of life, and the breath of the spirit.
Sifting through the ashes when the fire has gone out,
Sifting through so many layers this week in Taos,
I have found new creative parts of myself.
I am not leaving this experience – I am arriving at another way of knowing that who I am speaks louder than anything I say.
I recommit to my soul-work, to the lines already written in my heart,
that ancient place where my will, my intellect, my emotions converge.
This is my journey.

After grad school I went to work at the University of Wisconsin in Stevens Point, where my frontier shifted. During this time I left the convent and began to find my way as a single thirty-three-year-old in a world I had never known. It was truly a time of living in the in-between.

It was there that I became involved in the Wellness Movement. The University hosted the first Wellness Conference in this country. Last year we celebrated our fortieth anniversary. I served on the Board of Directors for years and worked on the integration of mind, body and spirit as the core of wellness throughout the US and Canada. My gift to this conference was my work with the power of knowing and owning our own story. This was back in the seventies when there was nothing written about story.

Some of my fondest memories of these years were being called *touch/feely* and *out of touch* and *crazy lady*. I never minded because I had learned the power of story from my own beautiful students. I started story-telling workshops with the students at the university. I offered three-hour sessions where the students would share in small and large groups. We had problems with eighteen-year-olds at bars trying to meet folks. My workshops became well-known, and soon I was offering them three evenings a week. I was deeply moved by the openness and the sharing that occurred.

MARRIAGE: THE NEW FRONTIER

At the university I met Joe, who was the leader of the Catholic Newman Center on campus. We led many retreats together. Later he left the priesthood and a few years

later we were married. Marriage was the new frontier in 1972 in Chicago, Illinois, where Joe and I were both employed in education.

While in Chicago we were blessed with two beautiful children, a joy beyond our deepest imagination. (And now we have four delightful grandchildren who are our greatest gifts). We loved being parents and balancing our work life with our marriage and our new family. This new frontier offered many possibilities for personal growth and development. Living in intimacy opened up the hidden caverns of my soul. We each had our own baggage, and as we moved down the road of marriage, we sought help to heal the old and deepest wounds we carried. This frontier offered shadow work as well as claiming our light:

My summer tree – full of abundance
the dead leaves are gone
green – shiny – stately.
The sun strokes your leaves with
his old buttery fingers.
I have hurried into this place
to be with you, to exclaim your dearness,
to reflect on my journey,
To remember my dark, underground cities,
to remember it is there where the beauty,
the exemplary are waiting to blaze open.
Down there in my depths
I have struck a great thing.
I sit here in silence
with my summer tree abundantly full.
Has everything happened
and I am now standing, quietly, in a new life?
Unfinished tapestry –
stories in thread – my history
Images of yesterday –
my tree in autumn colors, winter's dead leaves –
spring's budding and today
I stand on holy ground – the wind sings through my tree
like a breath of God awakening me to the sacred present,
This abundance – I have more than enough
to be all I can be.

In Chicago I was blessed with a career at a community college where my vice-president asked me to do something to help women who wanted to return or come to college. I took a course that was on the books called Psychology of Personal Growth and

designed it for women who would come and spend sixteen weeks writing and sharing their life stories. By my fourth semester I was offering twelve sections of the class, and I was training faculty to hold safe space for this work. Little did I know what I was embarking on: the depth, the pain, the repression, the secrets, the joys, the dreams, the emotional abuse, the sexual abuse, the loss and grief... No one had prepared me for these encounters.

What I learned is that when women felt safe they shared what was deep in their hearts and souls and somewhere in that experience became more authentic with who they were. Deep and abiding friendships were made and kept through the years. I was being challenged to grow in every aspect of my being: emotionally, spiritually, intellectually and socially. Every fiber of my being was alive and I became passionate about the work. I was criticized by colleagues who believed education was about objective reality and that my class was fluff. When two faculty went to the Board to get me to drop that course, my women students helped unseat the Board member. I never had any more problems.

I have taught that class for over forty years and read and studied over 2500 written autobiographies. Here I learned what lies hidden in the hearts and souls of many incredible people. This frontier opened my heart and soul to the depth of my own story and to the importance of deep inner work, and I reflected in my journal:

I, like Adam, part the veil to see with
New eyes this garden entrusted to me.
Flowing water circled with scum and debris,
Multiple bluebonnets decorated with specks of pink
Lay by dead weeds and enormous dandelions.
Redbuds bursting into green, green leaves
Trees in every shade of green – pale
Newborn green – dark, deepened green.
Grasses covered in tiny pink flowers and multiple dandelions
Rocks, stones, covered with green, green moss in my inner garden.
Debris and scum swept away in the art of forgiveness
My trees' dead leaves and limbs – only a few – to invite deeper
awareness of the deadness in the garden of my soul.
Let the wind call for my jasmine – I will not weep.
This garden entrusted to my care – I will till, water, weed and embrace.
My tree dripping with seeds of possibility
I will not sacrifice to the wind.
The garden of my heart is opening to receive and to give
Is open to join with other hearts across this larger garden –To know and own the
violence, the warring parts of myself – the paradoxes of my soul –

to bring peace to my world.
To see the world from the eye of my heart,
To hear the world from the ear of my heart,
To be unafraid of the relentless teachers of my heart.

My next frontier was Dallas, Texas, where my husband became vice president of a college. The transition to Dallas was the most painful in my life. In Chicago I had just finished eleven years of teaching a class entitled *Women in Transition.* Now I was a woman in transition; lost, grieving, hating the move, no friends or family, two small children, new doctors, new neighbors. I suddenly realized that what I had been teaching from my head was now being felt deeply and powerfully in my soul. Now I personally experienced the power of transition to open my heart to new possibilities.

Through the grief and darkness, through the tears and struggles, through slowly moving forward, I found myself again. I was, again, blessed with a career at another community college where I continued my work with written stories. Working at my college offered me the challenge of deepening who I was and speaking my truth. At the college we had what we named an "un-committee," which was established by our president as a way of inviting connections across all disciplines. We read one book a month. The greatest gift from that experience was to meet Parker Palmer in his book, *To Know As We Are Known.* I felt I finally had a friend, someone who understood the value of subjective knowing and the importance of balancing both objective and subjective knowing. I carried his book like a bible, reading and reading what he wrote. I knew I had a colleague in higher education who would understand and appreciate the work I had been doing against all odds for many years. I made up my mind that, if I ever had a chance, I would go study with Parker.

AGE 55: A SPECIAL FRONTIER

A special frontier appeared at the college when I turned 55. I was working with a program for people from age 25 to 55. Suddenly I realized I was not close to death and neither were many folks in our community. With the support of a wonderful president I started a program for folks 55+ called the Emeritus program. It took on a life of its own, and I quickly realized what it meant for older people to write and share their life stories, to have the opportunity to study and learn with younger people.

Perhaps more than any other frontier, this one taught me about attitudes toward aging, the importance of meaning for older adults, the value of learning and stretching. I watched folks in their seventies walk across the stage at graduation having completed their first degree. What joy!

Several years later when I was presenting a workshop at the National Wellness Conference on the power of story where I mentioned Parker Palmer's work, I met a

woman from the Fetzer Institute who wanted me to know that Parker was working with the Fetzer Institute and would be offering workshops. I was thrilled! As the universe works I was invited with a group of my colleagues to go to a retreat with Parker at the Fetzer Institute. From that workshop we wrote a book, *To Teach with Soft Eyes*, essays on how we would bring Parker's ideas to the classroom.

This was the beginning of one of the most significant frontiers of my life. Nothing I had ever done compared with what I was learning from the work of Parker Palmer. I was being invited to enter the labyrinth of my life, to take the journey down into the paradoxes of my own identity and integrity: wounds and gifts, shadow and light, strength and weakness, limitations and possibilities. I found myself standing on solid ground, knowing I was truly home. I read, studied, discussed, meditated-just could not get enough of this approach to the inner journey.

Then another miracle and another opportunity presented itself. I was invited to the Fetzer Institute to participate with 30 others from across the country in a retreat offered by the Center for Courage & Renewal. I went home so grateful but with a somewhat heavy heart because the Center would be selecting ten people to continue training with Parker and staff for a year, and I knew I would not be one of them. I was totally astounded when I received an invitation to become part of that training, allowing me to study for one year with ten colleagues who would meet at Parker's home in Madison, Wisconsin. This was, indeed, a new frontier, an invitation to engage in soul work in ways I had never encountered. I cherished the challenge and slowly grew into the principles and practices of what we then called formation work.

Somewhere I am awakening to something deep within myself.
The images of spring have so much to tell me about my life.
I am the black bear. I come down from the mountain each morning.
How do I love the world!
How do I let go of the praise and order of my life
in new and different ways?
How will I take the images of spring
and make them real for myself?
I know my tree is still holding on to its leaves –
Afraid of letting them go –
And yet new life is bursting on this same tree.
Where are my cracks?
How do I find new perspectives in the paradoxes of spring?
I must take time for silence and prayer.
I will miss the dazzling darkness of my own life
If I refuse to take time to sit with my victim –
Sometimes I play such a great martyr.

Oh, leaf that is one that must go – must be released.
I forget to love the world – to love what is –
To remember how a flower becomes what it is meant to be –
How it opens itself to the sun, rain,
How it bends with the wind.
Crack me open!
Crack open my heart!
Let my lips caress the taste of life.
Let my eyes see and my ears hear
The spring of my life.

Though I had retired from the college, I was invited, at Parker's suggestion, to work in the newly-created Center for Formation in Community Colleges, which had received a grant from Fetzer to continue this work with teachers in higher education. Opening up a new frontier with many challenges, many unknowns and many possibilities, we prepared facilitators to hold formation retreats at their colleges.

This frontier, perhaps more than others, demanded that I do my own inner work, that I become clear about my own identity and integrity. Story, poetry, metaphor, and imagery became my bread and nurtured my soul. I had the opportunity to work with John O'Donohue and David Whyte, who opened my imagination and offered me opportunities I never knew existed. The more I engaged in the work, the more I realized how I and many others had been schooled out of our imagination. All the other frontiers of my life seemed to have led me to this work I have now loved for more than 18 years, preparing facilitators and mentoring them in this work.

And then, when I turned eighty, I was surprised again by the invitation to apply for the Kirkridge Courage Fellowship Program. After reflecting and meditating, I decided to apply. I was thrilled when I received the news of my acceptance. This was indeed, a new frontier, a time for me to step back and pay attention to my own life. How authentic am I really? How is my life speaking? In my journal I wrote:

You don't have to be good, you can be whole,
A leaf with life and death – a leaf in full bloom
Yet severed from the tree.
In this autumn of your life you can celebrate
And thank God for your life.
Simple leaf, among thousands of leaves,
I chose you to remember.
Remember the strong life-line that courses through you –
Never broken – my own deep faith even in dark times.
I see your brokenness and I remember times of letting go –

Feeling broken – finding my way through.
You hold for me the deep memories of childhood –
Convent, marriage, career and moving into the last part
of my life on this earth.
I notice the curl at the end even though you are still green.
Teach me the art of wonder, of mystery in these years.
I feel my age - with hearing loss, eye problems, stiff joints –
And I want to continue to live in this world, not merely visit.
Teach me to hold on for dear life
And gently let go when the time comes.
In this last quarter of my life I want to walk in the rain,
Ride more rapids, climb a mountain – see more clearly.
I want to live the life that wants to live in me.
I want to know more clearly what the river says.
I want to lose what I need to lose, to keep what I can keep.
I want to take the dark with open eyes and call it seasonal.
I want to hold you, precious leaf,
As you lend yourself to my imagination.
I don't want to be good – I long to be whole –
Accepting all of who I am.
You are just what you were created to be – a leaf –
A special leaf, among thousands of leaves.
So be it.

Elaine Sullivan is a licensed professional counselor and licensed marriage and family therapist. She is a consultant and has been a facilitator of Courage Work for almost 20 years. She prepares facilitators for this work through the Center for Renewal and Wholeness in Higher Education. Elaine lives in Dallas, Texas, and can be contacted at elainemsullivan34@gmail.com – and she invites you to visit her website, www.sullivanconsultingandcounseling.com

SECTION 3

Seeking the Courage to Create a Circle of Trust And Reclaim the Commons

Here is one way to understand the relationships in a circle of trust: they combine unconditional love, or regard, with hopeful expectancy, creating a space that both safeguards and encourages the inner journey. In such a space, we are freed to hear our own truth, touch what brings us joy, become self-critical about our faults, and take risky steps toward change—

--Parker Palmer, *A Hidden Wholeness*

Insight by Parker J. Palmer

Why We Need Circles of Trust

Like a wild animal, the soul is tough, resilient, resourceful, savvy, and self-sufficient: it knows how to survive in hard places. I learned about these qualities during my bouts with depression. In that deadly darkness, the faculties I had always depended on collapsed. My intellect was useless; my emotions were dead; my will was impotent; my ego was shattered. But from time to time, deep in the thickets of my inner wilderness, I could sense the presence of something that knew how to stay alive even when the rest of me wanted to die. That something was my tough and tenacious soul.

Yet despite its toughness, the soul is also shy. Just like a wild animal, it seeks safety in the dense underbrush, especially when other people are around. If we want to see a wild animal, we know that the last thing we should do is go crashing through the woods yelling for it to come out. But if we will walk quietly into the woods, sit patiently at the base of a tree, breathe with the earth, and fade into our surroundings, the wild creature we seek might put in an appearance. We may see it only briefly and only out of the corner of an eye - but the sight is a gift we will always treasure as an end in itself.

Unfortunately, community in our culture too often means a group of people who go crashing through the woods together, scaring the soul away. In spaces ranging from congregations to classrooms, we preach and teach, assert and argue, claim and proclaim, admonish and advise, and generally behave in ways that drive everything original and wild into hiding. Under these conditions, the intellect, emotions, will and ego may emerge, but not the soul: we scare off all the soulful things, like respectful relationships, goodwill, and hope.

A circle of trust is a group of people who know how to sit quietly "in the woods" with each other and wait for the shy soul to show up... In such a space, we are freed to hear our own truth, touch what brings us joy, become self-critical about our faults, and take risky steps toward change - knowing that we will be accepted no matter what the outcome.

Parker J. Palmer is a writer, teacher and activist who works independently on issues in education, community, leadership, spirituality, and social change. Founder and Senior Partner of the Center for Courage & Renewal, he has authored nine books, including *The Courage to Teach, Let Your Life Speak, A Hidden Wholeness,* and *Healing the Heart of Democracy*. He holds a Ph.D. in sociology from the University of California at Berkeley, and thirteen honorary doctorates.

MEETING THE AUTHORS

Caryl Lea Menkhus Creswell: I feel most alive when I am being with my twin sister, my children, grandchildren, and husband; when I am sharing Godly Play and Courage Work with others and being in one of those circles myself; on hikes in the Northwest and daily walks; with Beauty and Creativity. I say that my Work in the world is paying attention and helping others pay attention. I am a Quaker seeker. I have been a Godly Play practitioner and trainer for almost 20 years nationally and internationally. I am so fortunate to be able to do both Godly Play trainings and facilitate Courage Work together with my husband, Jeff Creswell.

Debbie Stanley*: I feel most alive when I am teaching and learning; sailing and snorkeling; singing and praying. My work in the world is to be a witness to life in the roles of teacher, minister, and friend. The commandment "Love thy neighbor" saves me daily. My neighbors, in all their forms and in all their places, amaze me and cause me to turn to wonder and practice loving in the most unique ways. Writing my story to share with you has provided the safe space for me to find words to utter what my soul has been telling me all along... I laughed, cried, felt angry, and received peace.*

James R. Sims: Please call me Jim. I feel most alive when I am given the opportunity
for intimate conversation. The chance to talk about important things with people is life-giving to me. I long to hear about what matters to folks and share with them what matters to me. At this point in my life, my "Work" has become acting and responding with Love in every moment. I fall short of that intention so often, but I believe that it is the nature of Love to forgive me while encouraging and challenging me with more and more opportunities to live out my longing. Whether it is through my writing, or my music and lyrics, I hope that my readers and listeners get a sense of common ground – of comfortable familiarity – whether I am in the midst of hope or despair, of sadness or joy. And I also think it would be OK if they come away with the feeling that I am a fairly nice person and, given the opportunity, they would like to get to know me better.

Megan LeBoutillier: *I feel alive walking in nature with my dog, learning new things, making things, creating beauty, being in this Fellowship, teaching, exploring with color. I am a writer and an artist as well as a facilitator for Circles of Trust. I am a curious observer of this world. I am an independent learner and avid reader. I am a shy introvert and like to see myself as having a strong spiritual aspect. I am a writer so the process of writing my story for this book felt familiar, but as always I was surprised by what showed up on the page. I always say that I write what I need to read and often I don't know what that is until it has emerged. The process is mysterious and thrilling.*

Jeffrey M. Creswell: I feel most alive when I am outside in the natural world paying attention with reverence. I also feel most alive when I am with people who are open and vulnerable. My Work in the world is teaching and learning and loving the people and the world around me. I have an amazing loving family consisting of my wife, Caryl, and eight children, four grandchildren, and lots of siblings and their families. I feel honored to be invited to share my story in this book about a retreat experience that was significant and life-changing for me.

Vicki Metzgar: *I feel most alive when I am in nature, with friends and family, and enjoying an active endeavor, like hiking or a campfire conversation (like a Circle of Trust). My Work in the world is changing as I enter retirement from a formal career in education to an informal, but no less important, role as "responsible citizen of Earth." This role takes on many manifestations, from serving as president of my HOA to political activism on behalf of minorities of all kinds, including the Earth and its plant and animal inhabitants. I am, like you, curious and open to ideas and thoughts that challenge me to examine myself and the world around me, find my place among all things, and work to bring justice and peace to this imperfect and wounded, yet wonder-filled world.*

Linda Pololi: My research and work with the professional and personal development of faculty in academic medicine, including women and members of underrepresented minority groups, make me feel alive. I believe strongly in an evidence-based collaborative group approach to mentoring and leadership development for medical faculty - I feel personally fulfilled when facilitating these programs, where I get in close with the faculty and witness them being authentic and thriving. I am honored that my recent multi-institutional research on the academic medical environment showed the importance of the "culture" to faculty vitality, challenging academic leaders to be change agents. Both my work and my personal life sustain my aliveness. I love to spend time with my two sons and my husband, and relish walking in the countryside and on the beach with them. I also experience deep pleasure when listening to music and painting, and most of all, I find loving and learning exciting.

Jean Richardson: *I feel most alive when I am being with friends and family, enjoying a good meal at our dining room table, kayaking in the early morning, pondering how to change the world just a bit toward kindness, and being a part of the Kirkridge Fellowship. As the director of a retreat center, I hold and create space for individuals (and myself) to do creative, loving justice work in their communities and the world. I love to create. I love to create safe space, ideas, possibilities, food, art, and ways to play. Writing my story for this book has helped me clarify my thoughts about my Work and why I feel so passionately about my life as the director of Kirkridge Retreat Center.*

Susan Nodurft: What makes me feel alive is living in relationship with self and the world around me. I especially love spending time with my family, hiking and kayaking in wild places, and sharing my home with three spoiled dogs. At this stage of life my Work has increasingly become listening and acting on what calls my heart. Courage Work and teaching tai chi are expressions of the heart that bring great joy. I live in gratitude for each moment of life. Though I don't consider myself a writer, composing this essay turned out to be a gift received, as well as offered.

The Dance of Creating Safe Space

By Caryl Lea Menkhus Creswell

One of the many gifts of the Kirkridge Courage Fellowship has been to be in the Circle with some of the original facilitators, having their perspective and hearing their stories of the beginning days of this work. We have heard and need to hear over and over our founding story of how this work was birthed and nurtured.

One of the pilot facilitators, Sally Z. Hare, has periodically shared her memories of those very first Courage to Teach Circles and given us a glimpse of those fledgling and formative times. I have especially found it interesting to hear the story of how the Touchstones came to be essential guidelines for this work. I remember being quite amused and surprised the first time Sally told us the story of the different perspectives regarding the inclusion of the touchstones, first offered by Judy Brown, another of the pilot facilitators in those beginning days. In those first Courage circles there was actually some uncertainty as to how important they really were and even whether they were all necessary. And yet, in Sally's first two-year retreat series, she found the Touchstones in particular (which she re-named Boundary Markers) to be of huge importance to those first participants.

Over the ensuing years, the Touchstones have been revised and edited and modified

but never lost. They have remained a critical component of Courage Work. I personally have often experienced and witnessed a communal sigh of relief when these are presented at the beginning of a Courage Circle. Participants have said that it was when the Touchstones were read that they were able to let go of their apprehensions and were assured that this time together would be a safe place.

Some lists have been condensed and name just the essence:

- *Extend and receive welcome.*
- *Be present as fully as possible.*
- *What is offered in the circle is by invitation, not demand.*
- *Speak your truth in ways that respect other people's truth.*
- *No fixing, saving, advising, or correcting each other.*
- *Learn to respond to others with honest, open questions.*
- *When the going gets rough, turn to wonder.*
- *Attend to your own inner teacher.*
- *Trust and learn from the silence.*
- *Observe deep confidentiality.*
- *Know that it's possible to leave with whatever it is that you need.*

Other lists fill up several pages with explanations and definitions of each Touchstone. Regardless of the length or format, facilitators believe they are essential for building the container in which we do this work. We always, **always,** begin with these. They serve as the guideposts and boundary markers to show us the way and keep our circles safe. In my own journey working with these markers, I have come to recognize their value and contribution in other settings as well. Any work that respects the need to provide safe places where people are invited to listen deeply to themselves in community can benefit from using these Boundary Markers. These Touchstones have become an integral part of other work that I do, ensuring its health and integrity.

One of the areas where Courage Touchstones have made a significant contribution is in the work I do with *Godly Play*, a Montessori-based program that deeply respects and honors the innate spirituality of children. It is not unlike Courage work in that its core philosophy is that we (especially children) already have "that of God" within us. What we don't have is the language (or the space) to speak about it. Both in practicing *Godly Play* personally and in the training of adults nationally and internationally, the Touchstones have become an integral part of noticing, naming, and nurturing what is essential in this work. They help to create a safe place for children (and adults) to be encouraged to pay attention. These boundary markers make it safe for the inner teacher to show up.

Following is a brief outline of a Godly Play session side by side with the Touchstones showing how they support and inform what is happening.

"Are you ready?" I'm asked as I'm greeted by name, welcomed and invited by the doorkeeper to cross the threshold into the Godly Play room. I recognize with this question that I need to prepare, to slow down and open my heart and check myself to see if I am ready. "Yes, I am ready." I step across the threshold and enter another space. I am greeted again by the storyteller and invited to join the circle. There is a calm anticipation and a familiar comfort to the forming of the circle. I take my place and make room for others to take their place. There is room for everyone... a place just for you...a place for who you really are...and a community that welcomes you.

• ***Extend and receive welcome.***People learn best in hospitable spaces. In this circle we support each other's learning by giving and receiving hospitality

This invitation is about bringing my whole self to the circle and choosing to be present as authentically and accurately as possible.

• ***Be present as fully as possible.* Be here with your doubts, fears and failings as well as your convictions, joys and successes, your listening as well as your speaking.**

Narrative: The storyteller opens a box and places an ancient story in the middle of the circle – everyone has equal access. The universal value of story (through narrative, poetry, art, music, etc.) is that it allows me to listen to my own story. There is an economy of words and an economy of gestures so that there is uncluttered and open access to the story. No eye contact from the storyteller allows me to focus on and enter the story. There are frequent and comfortable spaces of silence, held without filling them with words and gestures. It takes a courageous storyteller to not fill up the spaces.

• ***Trust and learn from the silence.* Silence is a gift in our noisy world, and a way of knowing in itself. Treat silence as a member of the group. After someone has spoken, take time to reflect without immediately filling the space with words.**

• ***No fixing, saving, advising or correcting each other.* This is one of the hardest guidelines for those of us in the "helping professions." But it is vital to welcoming the soul, to making space for the inner teacher.**

I'm not told what the moral or the point of the story is. There is no interpretation, advice, or correcting – trusting each of us to find and make our own meaning.

At the very heart of all of this is the deep conviction of and respect for that inner light in everyone, however one chooses to name it: soul, true self, inner teacher, spark of the divine, that of God...however it is understood.

From that primary and fundamental conviction I, along with the other members of the circle, are asked open, honest questions that encourage us to hear ourselves and our own inner teacher. There is no coercion, only invitation.

The first question that comes is, "I wonder what part of this story you liked best?" What a safe question! No right or wrong answer required. And whether I am aware of it or not, I am paying attention to what I liked -- not what someone else expects me to like. It is followed by, "I wonder what part of this story is the most important part?" and "I wonder where you are in this story?" Questions again that help me hear and pay attention to my own self and not what someone else expects.

The final question, "I wonder what we can leave out and still have all that we need?" results in a lively disagreement which is simply acknowledged and hosted.

• ***What is offered in the circle is by invitation, not demand.* This is not a "share or die" event! During this retreat, do whatever your soul calls for, and know that you do it with our support. Your soul knows your needs better than we do.**

• ***Learn to respond to others with honest, open questions** instead of counsel, corrections, etc. With such questions, we help "hear each other into deeper speech."**

*an open honest question is one that you have no idea what the answer could be. It is respecting that each person has their own inner wisdom and the questions are asked to help the person pay attention to and listen to that within themselves.

• ***Attend to your own inner teacher.*** We learn from others, of course. But as we explore poems, stories, questions and silence in a circle of trust, we have a special opportunity to learn from within. So pay close attention to your own reactions and responses, to your most important teacher.

• ***When the going gets rough, turn to wonder.*** If you feel judgmental, or defensive, ask yourself, "I wonder what brought her to this belief?" "I wonder what he's feeling right now?" "I wonder what my reaction teaches me about myself?" Set aside judgment to listen to others—and to yourself—more deeply.

After the story is put away, I am invited to choose my work and respond to the story in whatever way I choose. There is a variety of simple but top quality response materials. I choose my work and find a place where undisturbed or monitored I am free to continue wondering with my hands. There is no interference, no hovering, no judgment. We are not asked to share our work. It is work we do for ourselves not for someone else. Silence is intertwined throughout while each person deeply engages in her or his own response.

After a generous amount of time, we are invited to put our work away and come back to the circle. We are invited to share our joys and concerns. We take turns listening and speaking. Each of us is invited individually to receive a blessing as we leave and again cross the threshold.

- ***Speak your truth in ways that respect other people's truth***. Our views of reality may differ, but speaking one's truth in a Circle of Trust does not mean interpreting, correcting or debating what others say. Speak from your center to the center of the Circle, using "I" statements, trusting people to do their own sifting and winnowing.

- ***Know that it's possible*** to leave the Circle with whatever it was that you needed when you arrived, and that the seeds planted here can keep growing in the days ahead.

Does this work of Godly Play sound familiar? Like Courage Work, it is soul work. It is about being alone, together. It is about creating a safe place.

I have taken the Touchstones and used them to establish guidelines for *Godly Play* trainings with adults using the parts of a *Godly Play* session and the language of the Courage Touchstones. They are included in every training when we first gather and guide the three days we are together:

Getting Ready - We recognize that we need to prepare, to slow down, open our hearts and anticipate that of God in each other and in our coming together. We check ourselves to see if we are ready.

Crossing the Threshold - We choose to leave one space and enter another, bringing our whole selves to the circle and choosing to be present as fully as possible. We come with our doubts, fears and failings as well as our convictions, joys and successes, our listening as well as our speaking.

Building the Circle - We extend and receive welcome. We do best in hospitable places. In this circle we support each other's learning by giving and receiving hospitality. We take our place and make room for all to take their place.

Telling and Listening to stories - We need and use story to listen to our own story. We use an economy of words and an economy of gestures so that we provide uncluttered and open access to the story.

Wondering - We invite dialogue with open, honest questions. No fixing, saving, advising, or correcting each other. When there are differences and we feel judgmental or defensive we turn to wonder. "I wonder what brought them to this belief - I wonder how they are feeling now? I wonder what my reaction teaches me about myself?" We strive to put aside judgment to listen to others and to ourselves more deeply.

Silence - We trust and learn from silence. Silence is a gift in our noisy world and a way of knowing in itself. We treat silence as a member of the group. After someone speaks we take time to reflect without immediately filling the space with words. We only speak to improve on the silence.

Response - We practice attending and responding to our own inner teacher as we explore stories, questions and silence in the circle. We pay close attention to our own reactions and responses, to our most important teacher and give freedom to express that in a variety of ways. We trust our minds, our hearts, our emotions, our hands and our bodies. We play together.

Prayers and Feast - We take the time to express what is most deeply true and important (prayer). We recognize that feasting is who we are with (relationships) - not what or how much we get (product).

Blessing - We both give and receive blessing. We look for and call out the best in each other and affirm who each person most authentically is. We each are called to have the courage to be who we most authentically and uniquely are.

Goodbye - We have all the time we need. We believe that it is possible to leave the circle with whatever it is that we needed when we joined the circle and that what we receive will continue to grow in the days ahead.

Both *Godly Play* and Courage Work have tapped into a primal stream of ancient understanding that has flowed throughout the history of humankind. It is present in all wisdom traditions and in the ways we wrestle to make sense of ourselves and our world. It has to do with story, with play, with listening, with asking questions, with community, but primarily and fundamentally, with deep respect for the inner teacher in every person, however one chooses to name it: soul, true self, inner light, spark of the divine, that of God. Courage Work and *Godly Play* are both about creating a safe space to provide access to that stream of ancient knowledge. It is challenging and deeply rewarding work. The Touchstones are critical components to help create the space where this work can happen.

Caryl Lea Menkhus Creswell, a recorded Quaker minister, *Godly Play* trainer (in both English and Spanish) and Courage & Renewal facilitator, lives in Portland, Oregon and can be contacted at carylcreswell@me.com

The Practice of Loving Others

By Debbie Stanley

Love your neighbor as yourself.

Does anyone really understand what this type of love involves?

On June 15, 2014, at midnight, my life changed from being a beloved only adult-child to an orphaned adult. My mother died.

After eighteen months of actively listening, gently caring, releasing assumptions, prayerfully begging and pleading, death came. How could this be? The person who loved me more than life itself was gone from life as I knew it. At the moment of death, as I steadfastly looked at my mom, a question provided by a dear friend dropped into my psyche: Can you befriend sadness? Sadness was right beside me with all its characteristics: uncontrollable wailings, feelings of loss and despair, heartbrokenness, loneliness, and woe. Who would want to befriend such an entity that causes the light of the sun to dim and takes your breath away? But I am finding out that sadness has been with me throughout my life and especially during the precious time when I provided care for my dying mother.

Sadness is a gift like time, which the poet William Stafford penned "wants to show me a different country." While taking care of my mom I experienced how to listen deeply because each word/phrase from her lips was like a jewel. As my mom lost her ability to move, I carried her, probably as she had carried me so many years ago. As her illness advanced, my mom began to call me "mom." What a privilege to be given such an honorary title. As her eyes grew dim, I remembered her bedtime stories from days of long ago, and I then read those stories to her.

Throughout these dark days with hints of light, my mom continued to teach me how to love. Yes, love is demanding, but so worthy of emulation. This gift from my mom prepared me to provide care for my cousin who, now at age 54, has dementia and is in the process of dying. My mom's love lessons continue in a new form. So the daunting question lingers with me through the precious moments of writing this chapter. I am learning how to befriend sadness in myriad ways. It has become such a master teacher in my life. I am so grateful to have the opportunity to pen my process of befriending sadness as a way to authentically practice loving others.

Growing up as an only child, in retrospect, was so paradoxical. As an only child, I lived alone but not lonely in various forms of community, including church, school, extended family events. I loved having friends come over to play, but I never longed for a baby sister or big brother. In elementary school, my favorite place was the library, a place where I could read alone and in the company of strangers. One Christmas my dad bought me a bike with an attached basket on the handlebars. The basket was designed to carry up to ten books. Dad was so proud that I had earned the privilege of being able and responsible enough to check out **ten** books at the Brooklyn Public Library! My friends laughed with scorn and said my bike was a truck. You know what? I didn't care because my dad bought it and that's all that mattered!

Speaking of Christmas...my mom and dad had to leave a letter from Santa stating that he would not be returning until I had children of my own. I never really got over this and never taught my children about Santa because I felt betrayed. This was an important lesson for me. My take-away: never lie to those you love, tell the truth even if it hurts.

Though events in our family were not always ideal, my mom, dad, and I were the perfect family of three. I was the beloved daughter who knew I was loved and learned how to love and be loved. For many years, I thought my life was like the lives of other children. Whenever I returned home from any outing lasting from a few hours to a couple of months, I was greeted, welcomed, and received by two people who were genuinely happy to see me and I them. I believe the way my parents loved me created a "fearless" place in my psyche. The love that blanketed me throughout my childhood afforded me the space to not be fearful, although there were and are fearful places in the world around me. I do believe my parents practiced "loving" with me.

In my current work as a Courage & Renewal facilitator I have found the values of my upbringing are underscored by the core values of the Center for Courage & Renewal (CCR). Two of the values that resonate deeply within my soul are love and diversity. CCR defines these values as such:

- **Love:** Our work is grounded in love, by which we mean the capacity to extend ourselves for the sake of another person's growth. Our work in community stretches us to understand, respect, and support each other, teaching us why learning to love is one of the most demanding disciplines we can choose.

- **Diversity:** Diversity is a deeply valued source of strength, richness, and wisdom for us and for the communities in which we live and work. The capacity to welcome and make space for diverse voices and multiple perspectives is critical to the creation of Circles of Trust, and to the healing and wholeness needed in our world.

How does one not only value love but practice it fully? As CCR states in its core values, practicing love is a "demanding discipline." As a receiver of this love, I must say that my parents practiced it seamlessly and authentically. The lessons I learned, especially from my mom, are evident in my work as a minister, consultant, parent, relative, and friend.

My first realization of the impact my parent's love had on my professional and personal life roles and work was noted when I applied for the Kirkridge Fellowship for Courage & Renewal facilitators in September, 2014. I was invited to write a plan with goals toward some form of self-actualization in a specific area of deep interest. I found the invitation evocative, perplexing, and intriguing. As I pondered my goals for the fellowship, the questions I entertained were laced with my ongoing and baffling question around befriending sadness. The framing of the questions and goals included my experiences both professionally and personally.

My overall life has been enhanced and assaulted in the social arena as a university professor, classroom teacher, minister in a non-denominational Christian church, and single parent (while married) of three very busy, challenging, and bold children. How have I held sadness in these roles? I wholeheartedly know that I sustained myself through the power of love. In my Fellowship application I wrote:

> *As a Lead Facilitator of the Center's Facilitator Preparation Program, I usually create space for potential facilitators to uncover their understanding of "otherness." I am learning so much from others as I extend genuine invitations to journey inward to see what one knows or seeks to know. Being with others at Kirkridge will allow me to, once again, seek deeper understanding of how to connect with those who are so like and unlike me. I expect the experience will be transformative. My role of Pastor of Children's Church provides an opportunity to engage children in the various ways to "Love your neighbor*

as yourself." Does anyone really understand what this type of love involves? I think the concept of ***ubuntu*** *offers a most illustrative and concrete way to express the meaning. The Fellows program provides the opportunity for me to engage with others looking for love in all the right places!*

During the time of the Kirkridge Fellowship, I was gifted by my colleagues, in honor of my mother, with a trip to Chiang Mai, Thailand. This bucket-list trip, *Finding Your Elephant Self*, was facilitated by renowned cellist Jami Sieber. The trip had many "leading up to" live love encounters. The first encounter was the love between my students and me. The words of revered educator Paolo Freire, *"Education (teaching) is an act of love, thus an act of courage,"* served as a truism and mantra for my classroom pedagogy. I wrote about this in the book, *Let the Beauty We Love Be What We Do,* and I stated my yearnings to practice love:

I wanted a classroom full of independent learners who were fully engaged in the teaching/learning community. I wanted to hear them deeply into speech. I wanted to be known as a teacher who cared, who shared, and who listened. This is the beauty that I love. My classroom was the place where I loved and was loved; listened and was heard; was seen and saw. My deepest teaching desire was to provide a classroom designed like an oasis; better yet, a refuge for the souls of children... A place where they could receive what they needed emotionally, intellectually, and socially.

It takes courage to love others. My live encounters with people who shared neither my race nor culture have been, I feel, the best indicator of loving others. These encounters are undergirded by what Dr. Parker J. Palmer, CCR founder, defines in *Healing the Heart of Democracy* as "faithfulness":

We must judge ourselves by a higher standard than effectiveness, the standard called faithfulness. Are we faithful to the community on which we depend, to doing what we can in response to its pressing needs? Are we faithful to the better angels of our nature and to what they call forth from us? Are we faithful to the eternal conversation of the human race, to speaking and listening in a way that takes us closer to truth? Are we faithful to the call of courage that summons us to witness to the common good, even against great odds? When faithfulness is our standard, we are more likely to sustain our engagement with tasks that will never end: doing justice, loving mercy, and calling the beloved community into being (192–193).

My trip to Thailand showcased my ability to faithfully practice love to unfamiliar humans and an elephant named Tantawan. I wane poetic when I think of my "once in a lifetime" trip. I used George Ella Lyon's poem *Where I'm From* as my writing prompt to articulate my musings while in Thailand:

Where I'm From or My Now and Then Story

I have been to Chiang Mai, Thailand in the Mae Ping River Basin. Located near water like my Myrtle Beach, SC where the Atlantic Ocean invites the inlander to enjoy "fun in the sun." I have been to Lampang, Thailand, with its undulating hills, dense forests, grasslands, brooks, streams and rivers. I am from Little River, SC, where the river supplies fresh clams, spots, and oysters to locals and visitors.

I have been to Sukhothia, Thailand, named by its rulers "the dawn of happiness." I am from Brooklyn, "City of Churches" the dawning place of my journey as a Christian minister. I am from the question "What is awakening in me?" I have seen Thailand's historic Buddhist temples built on the mountains, the Dharma and koans displayed on placards in the wildwoods, the covenant of grace realized.

I have been to Thailand where I met Peun, the mahout, and Tantawan, an elephant...a herd's matriarch-- fearless and present, intentional and tender, quick to laugh. Or speak silence. I turn to wonder as Peun sings to Tantawan. A song of freedom is what I hear. I am a learner.

I am from South Carolina, a state whose geography has the blood of my ancestors traced throughout, from a quiet river town where I am continuously challenged by bigotry, a longing for inclusion, hatred and love... my own andmy neighbors .I know why the caged bird sings.

From "Sawadeeka," "Kawp koon ka," and "Mai Pen Rai." A language as gentle as the people who speak it. This is my story. This is my song. I am from "What's love got to do with it?" and "Stop the Love You Save." I have been to the land of free and chained elephants. I am from that paradox where true mahouts live and dance in love with their families both human and elephant.

I am from John 3:16. From God's Love on display. I am from the place where Dr. Jenn cared for the animals (dogs and elephants) and humans. I grimaced as she placed acupuncture pins in Mahout John's head. I am from the Lampang Elephant sanctuary where the Boon Lot elephant had an infection in his rear humongous leg and the mahout assistant washed and bathed it daily. I am from love manifested in Thailand.

I'm from the tragic gap where I hold intellectualized confusion and intriguing insight, where I'm less concerned with bitterness and pain, and more interested in compassion.
From Brooklyn's suburbs of my Jewish Godfather, Farragut Housing for the low to no income (race not a factor).

From Little River and Myrtle Beach where some children have never seen the beach. I'm from the Thai Elephant Conservation Center where the children played with the elephants and fished where the elephant bathed. I am from the mahout community where the pond's substance served as a communal meal.
I learned the way of a mahout and an elephant.
I am from what I have witnessed in Thailand. Boundless love.

I'm from a walk in Prospect Park to visit the elephants with my dad who died in 1983. From a recently deceased mother who loved flowers (we visited Brooklyn's Botanical Gardens a lot). I am from the place where she planted them meticulously and strategically on her land in Little River, SC. I am from my granddad, who "accidently" drowned after he purchased this land for his family in 1949 through sharecropping.

I am from that land. I am from the legacy of my parents and ascribe to them my love of nature's beauty and my unyielding stubbornness to honor it. I uncovered this knowing in Thailand. I am from a new place. A place of renewed hope for the diversity I long to know.
Hope found on the back of an elephant named Tantawan. I am from the Thailand mountains where Tantawan and I walked along the dusty path with her mahout, Peun. The faint smell of Poo Pond and the pond where mom planted her azaleas are presenting hope across waters.
If I had not met this particular elephant among the trees in the mountains of Thailand, there would be no heartbreak at all.
I am still learning.

When I met Tantawan, not only was I mesmerized by her bigness but captured by her graceful welcome. I wept. Tantawan "stooped" down so I could climb up onto her massive neck. She stood and we began a journey into the experience of my uncovering and discovering my elephant self.

There are many lessons I reclaimed from "Tantee" (our secret code name). I reclaimed my right to live fearlessly, even in unfamiliarity. Tantawan was so different from me. No language. No kindred species. No cultural affiliations. We had one similarity; we live on the same planet. This is where we began.

I placed all of my assumptions aside and began practicing love...for an elephant. It was just that simple. I fed Tantee naturally, she fed me soulfully. I would sing to her, and she would bob her enormous head as if she were singing too. When I was on her neck, I would brush the trash of the forest out of her bristled strands of hair. Her maternal presence soothed the sorrowing segments in my soul. She would give me elephant kisses with her massive trunk.

I wondered if everyone were experiencing this elephant joy? No...this was my experience and it was real. I wept many times because I remembered the days with my mom, her loving silence, her singing Porgy and Bess' *Summertime*, her gigantic presence in my life. In some unexplainable way, Tantee and I were practicing some form of love for each other. Believe me, I am not romanticizing this experience: a live encounter with an elephant deepened my understanding of diversity. As our guide Jami explained, "If this great communication and this great connection can be made between different species, how can it not be made between humans? How can we not continue to work to make that connection?" (You can see and hear her: *https://www.youtube.com/watch?v=duSglcEqUzQ)*

Now, as I continue in my work as a facilitator of Circles of Trust, I look for Tantee in human form. I seek ways to enter the conversation and sustain the yearning to know and be known by others. One way that my interaction with Tantawan is being honored is in my sessions on diversity in the CCR Facilitator Preparation Program. I call my session Beloved Community -- and I offer this premise with great gratitude to Tantawan as I continue to make connections to others:

> *I desire to live a life free from the labels of others. I don't want to be known as a part of a "marginalized" group as defined by our society. I long for the freedom to be my truest self and remain committed to stand up for this freedom, for myself and others. My angst, my longing, is holding the question of how one can create an equitable, inclusive, and fair people-space when the creation of that space can mean very different things to different people? Therefore, I am continuously and intentionally seeking to know how to create spaces where courageous honesty, open-minded acceptance, authenticity and consistent integrity are valued and honored. I can belong in a diverse group of people who seek social justice and equitable policies if the group genuinely enjoys diversity and doesn't need me to conform to their standards, nor them to mine. Where is my Beloved Community? We are the ones we've been waiting for...*

Sometimes making connections is extremely challenging. It is during tumultuous times, such as the recent Presidential election campaign of 2016. I am a minister in a multi-ethnic congregation in rural South Carolina. The majority of the people I minister

to and with are staunch Republicans; I am not. In our Circles of Trust we have "rules of engagement" called touchstones or Boundary Markers. One of the touchstones that support my quest to practice love with others is *Turn to Wonder:*

> ***When the going gets rough, turn to wonder***. Turn from reaction and judgment to wonder and compassionate inquiry. Ask yourself, "I wonder why they feel/think this way?" or "I wonder what my reaction teaches me about myself?" Set aside judgment to listen to others—and to yourself—more deeply.

Before I was introduced to this touchstone, my mom's rule of life was "If you can't say something nice, choose silence until you can." My mom's rule helped me as a minister to turn to wonder. I was in what my friend Parker calls a "tragic gap" between my Christian principles and practices. There were times when my church brothers and sisters would utter opinions that would literally remove the air from the room. I allowed myself to feel invisible and voiceless, once again. I alluded to this state of being in *Let the Beauty We Love Be What We Do* when I wrote about my experience as a graduate student in education:

> *Although my classes were relevant and teacher-education courses were content specific, I remember, very vividly, feeling invisible and voiceless in my college classroom. The invisibility which I experienced in third grade was more pronounced and made more explicit through the actions of my professors. I was a lost soul in the academy of higher learning. I had neither advocate nor empathetic ear to help me process these churning feelings of inadequacy. One professor told me, "You are a diamond in the rough." To me that meant, for right now, you are useless.*

This time, unlike my years in graduate school, I didn't have my mom to help me process these feelings of inadequacy. I was saddened by the church family and their seeming unwillingness to be kind as we disagreed and experienced differing political persuasions. The opportunity to befriend sadness was making itself known... again.

I chose to use words of others to strengthen my decision to love like Langston Hughes quipped "*in the dark where there ain't been no light.*"

I chose to respond like Dr. King when he declared, "*Darkness cannot drive out darkness; only light can do that. Hate cannot drive out hate; only love can do that.*"

I chose to cling to the words of Jesus when he urged us to "*Love thy neighbor.*"

I also remembered my grandma, especially as her death was approaching and she would sing, "*Better days are coming by and by*" and "*You keep on living, you'll learn.*" These words and a few others are what sustained me in my quest to practice loving

others when love wasn't readily available from the others.

It's one thing to speak lovely words but living within those lovely words is "demanding." Yes, Dr. King, I too "*have decided to stick with love. Hate is too great a burden to bear.*" Sadness, once again, had me in its embrace, teaching me how to lean into love rather than resist it.

An important lesson that I had to remind myself not to ever lose sight of is about the power of forgiveness when practicing love is demanding. It helped to read Sharon Salzberg, meditation teacher, author and cofounder of Insight Meditation Society, especially her column for Krista Tippett's *On Being*: *"Forgiveness is a way of loosening the grip of fixation, but I've seen over and over again that it is a process. It is not a decision, and it does not come about by force of will."*

As I sought clarity in my role as a minister, I knew I had a choice to make: leave the church or stay. Forgiveness isn't easy, **and** it is complicated. By choosing to forgive those who seemed to me to have violated many of the teachings of Christ in their choice of Presidential candidate, I had to release myself from feelings of rightness. I remember the words of Rumi, an ancient mystic poet translated by Coleman Barks:

> ***Out beyond ideas of wrongdoing and right doing,***
> ***there is a field. I'll meet you there.***
> ***When the soul lies down in that grass,***
> ***the world is too full to talk about.***
> ***Ideas, language, even the phrase "each other" doesn't make any sense.***

I believe the field in which Rumi invites us to meet is Parker's tragic gap. Parker asserts, ***"****By the tragic gap I mean the gap between the hard realities around us and what we know is possible — not because we wish it were so, but because we've seen it with our own eyes."*

I had the opportunity during this election year to hold the paradoxical nature of practicing love. Love is paradoxical because it negotiates. "*Love and negotiation are inextricably connected,*" writes mediator Robert Benjamin. *"Both love and negotiation require in equal parts a passionate commitment and dispassionate calculation"* (http://www.mediate.com/articles/benjlove.cfm).

I understand Benjamin to mean that, in any relationship, an intentional calculation must be made for how I will extend myself for the sake of another person's growth. This personal belief was actualized when I chose to stand faithfully in the pulpit of my church and speak lovingly to my church family, saying I could not partake in the behavior I had observed during election year 2016. I told them I could not agree to antagonize others because their political persuasion was different from mine.

I think I had a John Woolman moment, as I drew on a favorite story of the minister who advocated against slavery in the midst of his slave-holding Quaker Friends. Woolman never directly attacked slave-holders, but instead, he stressed equality and urged against the buying and keeping of slaves. John Woolman's faithfulness in the practice of love was observed through his refusal to purchase goods produced by slave labor. Four years after Woolman's death, slave ownership among Friends was finally prohibited. To my point, I didn't leave the church; I stayed because I found value in my relationship with the people to whom I ministered and loved, but on this one grave point, I happened not to agree.

I also more fully understood my friend Parker's beautiful writing about a broken heart: *If I keep my heart supple by "exercising" it — allowing my suffering and the suffering around me to stretch that spiritual muscle — heartbreak will open my heart, bringing me more peace and adding to the world's vital store of compassion.* This 2016 election year helped me, as a minister, practice love by allowing my heart to be broken and reveal my hidden wholeness.

Yes, love negotiates. The gift of sadness showed me a different country. I continue to seek the courage to live in a divided world, as the gifts of sadness that repeatedly break my heart are my great teachers and guides.

Dr. Debbie Stanley, a longtime public educator, is now Children's Pastor and Church Evangelist and Courage and Renewal facilitator. When Debbie is not in a Circle of Trust, she is present in the journey with her very dear "sister" Demetra who has dementia. Debbie learned, from her amazing mom, to take time for self-care so she walks a mile a day with her dog, Cabeau. Debbie can be reached by email joyfulone120@gmail.com

A PLACE AT THE TABLE

By James R. Sims

If there has been a consistent theme in the struggles of my life, it has been in recognizing, calling attention to, and serving the ones at the margins, the ones I feel many of us would just as soon remain invisible. I have a strong awareness of who is not at the table and why and how are they being excluded.

The greatest suffering in my life has come from my failure to raise awareness, both my own and others, to the presence and conditions of those who are marginalized. And when the consciousness of individuals and communities **has** been raised and we can open our arms wider, or move over just a little bit and set another place at the table, it has been the source of my greatest joy.

Since my first experiences as a participant in a Circle of Trust, I have been drawn to being a facilitator of Courage work. I have the sense that I would gain skills that would improve my effectiveness and deepen that joy that flows from helping individuals and communities become more accepting, inclusive, and open. But something has been tugging at me, even from the beginning of facilitator preparation. As its pull increased, I realize that I cannot and must not ignore it.

Because I am a visual learner, I will describe the scene that I see with the eyes of my heart. I find myself seated at a gracious banquet – a Circle of Trust filled with an

amazing array of healthy and delicious choices. As I look about at the others who have a place at this table, I recognize that we have achieved considerable socioeconomic and educational advantages, occupational and influential positions that imply that we are "qualified" to be here. And, indeed, we are.

But there is more to this scene. Next to our table is a window with a view of the world beyond. Through this window I can see hungry, frightened children with their faces pressed against the glass; adults, young and old, faces lined with worry and regret. Our eyes meet, and I yearn to create a place at the table for each and all of them.

I think part of what drew me to Courage Work initially, and inspired me to become a facilitator, has been the certainty that I would gain tools and skills needed to create safe spaces where all are welcome and where everyone is included. That also motivated me to apply for the Kirkridge Courage Fellowship. So, let me tell you the story I shared as part of my application for that program:

It is the summer of 1961. My family and I have been in Louisville for two years. My teachers have been noticing that I am a bright, inquisitive, and enthusiastic student. My parents have been encouraged to have me evaluated for placement in the Advanced Track, an experimental accelerated learning model that is new to Kentucky. The model is not new to my family; my older brother John has been benefiting from it and has skipped a grade. I am aware that this is an exceptional opportunity for which I have qualified, and I am eager to see what it has to offer.

I soon discover that the eagerness and excitement I am feeling is thoroughly justified, and I soak up all the stimulating and complex subject matter that is being handed to me. I am not alone in my enthusiasm. My classmates are also ready for the stimulation that the program offers, and we thrive individually and synergistically. My teacher, Mrs. Stratton, is wonderful.

Because my father is a musician, I have been given exceptional encouragement, training, and opportunities in music. My extra-curricular activities reflect this during my third-grade year. I am one of the three child spirits in Mozart's Magic Flute, *offered by the Kentucky Opera Association.*

Mrs. Stratton comes to see one of the performances and afterwards makes her way backstage to see me. She finds me, administers a huge hug, and bursts into tears while telling me how proud she is of me. I am stunned. Having touched my teacher's heart so deeply intensifies my appreciation of my educational experience and my desire to excel in my schoolwork.

My success in music at such an early age was to have a profound influence on the direction of my life. But my love of and yearning for artistic expression were about to expand. I developed a deep commitment to understand the influence of the arts when

fully integrated into the educational process. Through this commitment, I discovered my love of the visual arts. I experienced my first instruction and encouragement in those skills, and I was enchanted. Through the generous allotment of time dedicated to art, and the wide variety of media available, I began to broaden my abilities and interests. The enchantment of this connection would influence my life and livelihood in the same ways that my musicianship would.

But I could not recognize or control the seductive power of it and the ways it would draw my attention from less interesting but critically important tasks.

For the most part, my grades were good throughout the year. There were inconsistencies – a characteristic that would follow me throughout my schooling and into adulthood – but I would always bounce back. As I moved through elementary school into middle school and on to high school and college, the inconsistencies became more and more extreme. Excel, fail, excel, fail. (It was not until my mid-forties that I would be clinically diagnosed with Attention Deficit Disorder which – in retrospect - explained a lot of things.)

I am coming to the end of the year and it is time for standardized testing. Number 2 Pencils. Filling in the circles. Mrs. Stratton has suggested that we bring a book to class in order to have something to do if we finish before the time is up for each section. I have checked out a book on drawing cartoon faces – a skill that I have an intense interest to develop.

Perhaps you can see where this is going. And if you have ever been either an educator or a student, you might have a strong sense that this is not going to turn out well. You will be correct.

I am in the third grade, and it makes sense to me that if I simply go through and mark the circles in a random pattern that I will probably get a bunch of them right. And then I could read my book and draw. This is what I proceed to do.

When the test results are passed out to the class, I do not receive anything. I am confused. I am thinking, "Surely it can't have been that bad..." My growing sense of impending doom is confirmed when the Jefferson County school system superintendent, Dr. Richard VanHoose, shows up at our classroom door, and I am summoned into THE HALL (a place of shame and degradation where one is sent to be ostracized and humiliated) for questioning. His dark gray suit, nondescript tie and obvious frustration stay in my mind. He is perplexed when he asks me, "Jim, what happened?!"

At this point I must say that I have never been one to show great personal courage in the face of such authority. Truth-telling has been a lifelong struggle for me in the best of situations. I take no consolation in the fact that it is for others as well.

When Dr. VanHoose asks, I am unable to explain my reasoning – which by this time I have determined is completely absurd – and so I hang my head and do not say a word.

I was back in my former school the next year. The decision to remove me from the Advanced Track was made without any further discussion with me. The assumption the school authorities shared with my parents was, "We believe Jim was sending us a message: that the work was too hard - that the stimulation or the stress of complex studies was more than he could bear."

While I am aware of what I have accomplished in spite of this unfortunate episode in my young life, I will never know what might have been achieved if I could have summoned the courage to blurt out to Dr. VanHoose, "I really just wanted to draw! And I thought that guessing a pattern of dots on the page might just work. I know it sounds silly, and I cannot believe that I thought it might work! May I please have another chance?"

It was not until I was in college that I ever told anyone what I had done.

I take responsibility for my silence. Even at that tender age, I knew that I should have owned my foolishness and called for a "do-over." In letting go the opportunity to own my fallibility, I took on a burden of guilt and shame. As an adult, I realize, with great sadness, just how onerous this burden has been. Suffering beneath this load was at least as damaging, and possibly worse than the lost opportunities that the advanced education might have provided. Moreover, experiences of this weight that transpired at early age set a pattern of response that has been self-replicating.

As an adult, I also realize that the system failed me. I was nine years old. Some attempt on the part of those educators – from the teacher in the classroom to the superintendent of the school system – to work with a nine-year-old heart until they could discern what had transpired would not have taken a huge effort on ***their*** part.

I have worked with children and adolescents, as well as many adults, who are struggling to recognize their limitations, identify foolish choices, and engage their highest selves as the path to achieving their potential. (Incidentally, I am on the same quest.) I have proven to myself many times that this can only be accomplished by engaging the other, regardless of age or station, with the kind of respect that honors the dignity and uniqueness of their journey. This kind of respect grounds fears, guilt, anger and shame. This kind of respect honors the power of creativity and encourages self discipline. This kind of respect encourages the other to recognize and follow his or her own source of deep wisdom.

For me, the ability to access and demonstrate this kind of respect for others does not come easily. For me, it requires that I set aside my pride, my solutions for their problems, and that I avoid anything that puts me between them and their discovery

of and trust in their own deep knowing. The other person is every bit as worthy of this kind of respect as I am. The commitment to this kind of respect requires intense practice and patience with one's self.

This led me to Courage work.

One of my sister Courage facilitators, Sally Z. Hare, says of herself that after more than twenty years of extensive experience of Circles of Trust, she is ***still*** "becoming a facilitator." So if she embraces this process, then I will also state gladly that I, too, am still **becoming** a facilitator. In claiming that, I have a great sense of relief from that part of me that says I should know everything by now. I am further relieved by owning the fact that I seem to know so little. But I am not discouraged, nor do I despair, for I am relieved of the huge task of maintaining the facade of knowing everything.

My honesty allows me to set aside my ego and glimpse my true self. So, having written my third-grade story for the first time in my life, and particularly in the context of this Fellowship that has provided such intense, safe experiences with an array of seasoned facilitators, my eyes begin to leak. I am startled by the realization that there is a person in this story who is on the outside looking in, who qualifies for the title of "Least of These." His name is Jimmy.

And in an instant, three streams of insight emerge:

- First, in identifying the points in my life in which I find myself on the outside of the "Safe Place" or the "Circle of Trust" (insert any of those thin places where the shy soul appears), I am finally able to re-examine and re-frame those events in ways that allow me to lay down those burdens of guilt or shame or anger.

- The second stream I name *Creating A Circle of Trust around Any Conversation.* I long to open the circle wide enough to include every person with whom I will ever have a conversation. Conversations with people unfamiliar with Circle of Trust principles and practices or our Touchstones or Boundary Markers happen so fast. Even in conversations with experienced facilitators when we are not "encircled" or have not "set the stage" or reminded ourselves of our commitments, I find - more often than not - that I am unable to access those principles and ground myself in those practices. And I slip and slide inexorably into my default position of "I know what everybody needs to solve their problems at any given moment, or if not, gimme a couple o' seconds and I'll figure it out."

  (I hope you're laughing at this. I also hope you recognize the universality of this tendency, and perhaps have seen yourself in this position upon occasion ...)

But this second insight comes from the recognition of my complicity in these kinds of moments, and knowing that I have the capability to hold a safe space, that I will be able to be present to the insights of others, bearing witness to the appearances of other shy souls.

- The third insight gradually comes into focus out of the deep respect that I have learned to offer in Circles of Trust. My heart imagines a transformation of Jimmy's/my experience:

> *We, Mr. Sims and Jimmy, are not out in the "Hall of Shame and Alienation," but have walked out the door at the end of the hall and are somewhere on the playground – perhaps under a tree – with a cool drink. After we have been seated for a few minutes, I suggest, "I wonder if we could play a sort of game. I would tell you some of the things that I really like and then you could tell me about some of your favorite things. Would you try that with me?"*

Maybe creating a place at the table for my Self, young and old, is a step in the right direction. Now that I have extended an invitation to Jimmy **and** Mr. Sims, perhaps my arms are open wider and I can move over a bit and set another place.

James R. Sims (Jim) has been a musician all his life. He is also a potter and loves to create with his hands. A Courage & Renewal Facilitator for almost seven years, Jim is married to Caroline Fairless, who is also a CCR Facilitator AND a courageous writer of great skill and depth. They live with three rescued dogs (Callie, Carson the BubbaDog, and Althea) in Wilmot, New Hampshire. You can reach Jim through email: jarosims@gmail.com

A STEPPING STONE

Principles of the Circle of Trust Approach

If we are willing to embrace the challenge of becoming whole, we cannot embrace it alone—at least, not for long: we need trustworthy relationships to sustain us, tenacious communities of support, to sustain the journey toward an undivided life. Taking an inner journey toward rejoining soul and role requires a rare but real form of community that I call a "circle of trust."

—Parker J. Palmer, A Hidden Wholeness (adapted)

- **Everyone has an inner teacher**: Every person has access to an inner source of truth, named in various wisdom traditions as identity, true self, heart, spirit or soul. The inner teacher is a source of guidance and strength that helps us find our way through life's complexities and challenges. Circles of Trust give people a chance to listen to this source, learn from it and discover its imperatives for their work and their lives.

- **Inner work requires solitude and community**: In Circles of Trust we make space for the solitude that allows us to learn from within, while supporting that solitude with the resources of community. Participants take an inner journey in community where we learn how to evoke and challenge each other without being judgmental, directive, or invasive.

- **Inner work must be invitational**: Circles of Trust are never "share or die" events, but times and places where people have the freedom within a purposeful process to learn and grow in their own way, on their own schedule, and at their own level of need. From start to finish, this approach invites participation rather than insisting upon it because the inner teacher speaks by choice, not on command.

- **Our lives move in cycles like the seasons**: By using metaphors drawn from the seasons to frame our exploration of the inner life, we create a hospitable space that allows people of diverse backgrounds and perspectives to engage in a respectful dialogue. These metaphors represent cycles of life—such as the alternation of darkness and light, death and new life—shared by everyone in a secular, pluralistic society, regardless of philosophical, religious, or spiritual differences.

- **An appreciation of paradox enriches our lives and helps us hold greater complexity**: The journey we take in a Circle of Trust teaches us to approach the many polarities that come with being human as "both–ands" rather than "either–ors," holding them in ways that open us to new insights and possibilities. We listen to the inner teacher and to the voices in the circle, letting our own insights and the wisdom that can emerge in conversation check and balance each other. We trust both our intellects and the knowledge that comes through our bodies, intuitions, and emotions.

- **We live with greater integrity when we see ourselves whole**: Integrity means integrating all that we are into our sense of self, embracing our shadows and limitations as well as our light and our gifts. As we deepen the congruence between our inner and outer lives, we show up more fully in the key relationships and events of our lives, increasing our capacity to be authentic and courageous in life and work.

- **A "hidden wholeness" underlies our lives**: Whatever brokenness we experience in ourselves and in the world, a "hidden wholeness" can be found just beneath the surface. The capacity to stand and act with integrity in the gap between what is and what could be or should be—resisting both the corrosive cynicism that comes from seeing only what is broken and the irrelevant idealism that comes from seeing only what is not—has been key to every life-giving movement and is among the fruits of the Circle of Trust approach.

Practices of the Circle of Trust Approach

In this culture, we know how to create spaces that invite the intellect to show up, to argue its case, to make its point. We know how to create spaces that invite the emotions to show up, to express anger or joy. We know how to create spaces that invite the will to show up, to consolidate effort and energy around a common task. And we surely know how to create spaces that invite the ego to show up, preening itself and claiming its turf! But we seem to know very little about creating spaces that invite the soul to show up, this core of ourselves, our selfhood.

—Parker J. Palmer, ***A Hidden Wholeness***

- **Creating spaces that are open and hospitable, but resource-rich and charged with expectancy**: In a Circle of Trust, we are invited to slow down, listen, and reflect in a quiet and focused space. At the same time, we engage in dialogue with others in the circle—a dialogue about things that matter. As this "sorting and sifting" goes on, and we are able to clarify and affirm our truth in the presence of others, that truth is more likely to overflow into our work and lives.

- **Committing to no fixing, advising, "saving," or correcting one another**: Everything we do is guided by this simple rule, one that honors the primacy and integrity of the inner teacher. When we are free from external judgment, we are more likely to have an honest conversation with ourselves and learn to check and correct ourselves from within.

- **Asking honest, open questions to "hear each other into speech"**: Instead of advising each other, we learn to listen deeply and ask questions that help others hear their own inner wisdom more clearly. As we learn to ask questions that are not advice in disguise, that have no other purpose than to help someone listen to the inner teacher, all of us learn and grow.

- **Exploring the intersection of the universal stories of human experience with the personal stories of our lives**: Guided conversations focused on a poem, a teaching story, a piece of music or a work of art—drawn from diverse cultures and wisdom traditions—invite us to reflect on the "big questions" of our lives, allowing each person to intersect and explore them in his or her own way.

- **Using multiple modes of reflection so everyone can find his or her place and pace**: In Circles of Trust, we speak and we listen. We explore important questions in large group conversation and dialogues in small groups. We make time for individual reflection and journaling. We respect nonverbal ways of learning, including music, movement and the arts. We honor the educative power of silence and the healing power of laughter. Together we weave a "tapestry of truth" with many and diverse threads, creating a pattern in which everyone can find a place that both affirms and stretches them.

- **Honoring confidentiality**: Participants in Circles of Trust understand that nothing said in these circles will be revealed outside the circle and that things said by participants will not be pursued when a session ends, unless the speaker requests it.

For more about the principles and practices of the Circle of Trust approach in theory and in practice, please see the Center for Courage & Renewal (www.couragerenewal.org) and Parker J. Palmer, *A Hidden Wholeness: The Journey Toward an Undivided Life* (San Francisco: Jossey-Bass, 2004).

Moving at the Speed of Guidance

By Megan LeBoutillier

Let yourself be silently drawn by the strange pull
of what you really love. It will not lead you astray.

----Rumi

My fourth grade teacher, whose name was Fred Weirdsma, looked like Alfred E. Newman from the cover of MAD magazine. One day he gave the entire class the assignment to take a pad of paper and a pencil to the library, look something up, and write a paper about it. It was such a departure from the customary blackboard lecture, note-taking model of day-to-day classroom education that the entire class sat stunned for a few moments. I remember immediately scanning my imagination, trying to find that place where liveliness was trying to catch its breath.

I was a curious kid. I liked learning. I loved school, especially the library. Anything you could think of, you could find in the library. So this invitation from Mr. Weirdsma arrived in my mind as an unanticipated dream come true. As I passed through the

doors of the library with my fresh pad of lined paper and finely sharpened pencil, I could feel the excitement surge into my body. The library was filled with interesting books, stories, facts and discoveries to be made. I was delighted with the invitation to explore and delirious to be released from my passive seat in the classroom. In this moment the world of independent learning and learner-directed education opened for me, and I was ruined for classroom education forever thereafter.

The year was 1964. Maybe I had seen Angie Dickinson on *Perry Mason, Mike Hammer*, or *The Fugitive*. I was a big fan of those television programs. I cannot remember what brought her to mind or if she was even what led me to look up the fact that Lloyds of London Insurance Agency insured her legs for one million dollars, but that detail was sufficiently interesting to me that I wrote my assignment about it. My curiosity was permanently piqued from that moment onward. Teachers willing to invite exploration outside the classroom remained harder to find.

During my sophomore year in high school I did battle with my English teacher, Mrs. Katz. I was in school outside of Washington, DC, and there were race riots taking place in the district. I'm not sure how I even knew about them because surely we were not being taught about racial tension -- quite the contrary. I had a strong urge to educate myself, and toward that end I created a curriculum and bibliography which I presented to Mrs. Katz as an alternative learning plan, adding that there would be plenty of time in my life to catch up with Victorian literature. Looking back on my proposal, Mrs. Katz herself, and the sort of school I was attending, I am surprised I didn't wind up in the Headmistress' office, or flat-out expelled. Needless to say, Mrs. Katz did not agree to my proposal, and I conducted my Black History course independently.

The experience convinced me that I needed to seek out alternative forms of education for myself. Once again the library held the answer. I found a college preparatory handbook that listed "alternative education." I sent off for catalogs. By the following year, with much determination and equal parts of guile, I had enrolled myself in Colorado at a co-ed college preparatory high school that afforded a much wider and, for me, more relevant scope of education. In addition to all of the academic classes, there were arts and crafts, outdoor activities like hiking, kayaking and gardening; and whole-school camping trips. I was in heaven, but I still struggled to get out of the classroom. Luckily for me when I proposed alternative or accelerated learning plans to my teachers at this new school, they were receptive and allowed me to move at my own pace through their curriculum. An unexpected outcome resulted in my going to college after my junior year and earning my high school diploma after completing a full year of college English.

Despite what I had been told about the rigors of college, my experience was that of being sent back to third grade. I remember only one professor who allowed me to write a paper on pseudo-hermaphrodism for extra credit in a class on human sexuality.

Otherwise the battle was on once again and my starts and stops in college finally ended when I found a completely learner-directed college program in Vermont and proceeded to graduate at age 30.

My intention after graduation was to never enter the halls of academia again, but when I heard of a graduate degree program that was entirely learner-directed, it spoke loudly to my heart. I applied and was accepted. I did not have any problem convincing them that I was the ultimate poster child for independent learning. Writing a learning plan, selecting my own doctoral committee members, and then conducting and documenting my new learning was a more sophisticated invitation to go to the library, look something up and write a paper about it. Thank you, Mr. Weirdsma, for planting this abundant seed of possibility.

> ***We have all a better guide in ourselves, if we would attend to it, than any other person can be.***
>
> *---Jane Austen*

So, what is the point of writing about all of this? I have been thinking lately about guidance and invitation and the importance of paying attention. In Circles of Trust® I am frequently invited to notice, name, and nurture. It is through this quiet practice that I often receive guidance and perhaps even the notion of making some changes in my life. What I have come to notice while writing this chapter is that I have long had a resourceful, resilient inner guide who looks after my survival, happiness, and well-being. Most of what I have learned, and the various paths I have taken in this life, have not followed a very clear-cut plan.

When people ask me what prompted a decision to move or to undertake such and such, I never seem to have a logical answer. I used to think this was a liability and that I was some sort of loose screw that couldn't find a place to become attached, but I have come to recognize that I have always been informed from the inside and have never found it easy to express this reality to those who are not. I used to be ashamed of my intuition, but I have come to see it as my closest ally. The inner prompts that guided my studies and insisted on more appropriate educational outlets literally saved my life and led me to find my true self, an inner peace, and perhaps even put me in closer touch with my soul. Lately I have been calling it guidance, though even the dictionary seems to think that guidance comes from the outside, and has something to do with missiles.

I believe that to squelch curiosity or impede learning in any way is to violate the integrity of an individual. I learn every day about the power and mystery of invitation. I am not sure it is true for everyone, but in my case being invited into learning was a great and lasting gift.

Therefore, when I was first introduced to the *Courage to Teach* with its premise that we all have an Inner Teacher, I was intrigued. I felt the same enthusiastic rush of possibility I felt walking toward the library with pad and pencil in fourth grade. The respectful recognition of an Inner Teacher, combined with the gentle practice of invitation, has taken me for a long journey with Courage & Renewal work.

> ***Inner guidance is heard like soft music in the night by those who have learned to listen.***
> ---*Vernon Howard*

In 1995 I was invited by Sally Z. Hare to attend a weekend retreat with Parker Palmer. Sally is masterful at invitation, so I accepted, even though I didn't think that Parker Palmer or his work with public school educators had anything to do with me and I was reluctant to spend three days in a hotel conference room. Sally's gentle invitation and assurance that I would not be disappointed, combined with my boyfriend's parents visiting from out of town, convinced me.

I didn't know it at the time, but my life would be changed forever by Sally's invitation and my brief introduction to Parker Palmer. The following year I became the scribe for Sally's two-year seasonal *Courage to Teach* which, along with three other national pilot groups, launched the Courage Work that has now evolved into Circles of Trust and other forms of Courage & Renewal work. In my role as note-taker, trying to accurately catch the words being spoken, I was listening in a very different way than one listens when in conversation. When I got home and began transcribing my notes after the four-day weekend retreats, the impact of the words began making their impression on my mind and in my heart. I often found myself weeping in front of my computer screen because I was so moved by the honesty, vulnerability, and whole-heartedness of what was being shared within the circle. I didn't even have words to describe what I experienced within the group when I was not busily taking notes. I just knew that my affection for all of those people was exploding and I felt immensely alive in their presence. I have come to call those rapturous sensations "community."

When the two-year retreat series ended, I applied for the first facilitator preparation cohort because I had glimpsed the cultivation of an inner life, and I wanted more. More importantly I felt my inner yearning aligning with something larger than myself for perhaps the first time in my life. I could not have articulated it then, and I am having some difficulty now, but my actual self and my desired self were becoming aware and curious of one another. This may be when I began to consider naming what I was noticing as *guidance* because I was watching myself ask for and do things that were genuinely surprising me.

By 1999 I was "prepared" as a facilitator with about a dozen others, and the presumption was that all of us would start facilitating two-year retreat series for public

school educators. Funding from the Fetzer Institute had supported the pilot groups, but now the new facilitators were faced with the daunting task of raising their own funds. Fetzer had generously fully funded these early retreats for teachers, and to follow this model would require raising approximately $100,000 per two-year series. I felt desperately unprepared for such an undertaking and frustrated by my lack of confidence. In short, I got stuck and couldn't seem to find a way to move forward.

> ***...have patience with everything unresolved in your heart and try to love the questions themselves as if they were locked rooms or books written in a very foreign language. Don't search for the answers, which could not be given to you now because you would not be able to live them. And, the point is to live everything. Live the questions now.***
>
> ***Perhaps then, someday far in the future, you will gradually, without even noticing it, live your way into the answers.***
>
> ---Rainer Maria Rilke from *Letters to A Young Poet,* translated by Stephen Mitchell

From my beginnings with this work we call Courage Work I have been attracted to these words the poet Rilke wrote as advice to a young poet – and the invitation to me to "live the questions." This, to me, is much like moving at the speed of guidance. Living the questions involves not being in too much of a rush to get to the answer, but rather to sit patiently until one arrives.

In retrospect I now see that I sat with the question for many years about how to fund this work. I also sat with the questions of where and how Courage Work truly intersected with who I am as a person and who I am as a facilitator. After quite a few years the answers are quietly beginning to show up.

For the past two years I have been one of twenty-seven Kirkridge Courage Fellows. As Fellows we were invited to step more deeply and genuinely into our facilitator selves. Unlike a typical assignment, such an invitation provokes uncertainty, confusion and honest self-reflection. I now realize that Mr. Weirdsma didn't give us an assignment that day; he issued an invitation to allow our individuality and our curiosity to inform our learning. So, with lined tablet and sharp pencil I sat with the question of what I might have to offer our community as a facilitator who was stepping more fully into her facilitator self.

The initial guidance came from my own questions about fundraising and my frustration with how facilitators were, or were not, equipped in this crucial area. I pushed back

against guidance. I did not want to read and write about money, but guidance persisted, as guidance often will, and I began reading and exploring the topic. It seemed I was being moved to become part of a solution rather than continue to bemoan a problem. I share some of the learning that has come for me from what I have come to call "***Navigating the Mobius Strip of Money":***

> ***Money is something we invented. We invented it to facilitate the transfer of goods and services when bartering became difficult to manage. But since we invented money we have imbued it with all sorts of powers and meaning that were never intended. Money has no inherent meaning in and of itself. The meaning we imagine money to have has actually been assigned to it by us. What if we were able to step back a bit and take an honest look at our culture? What if we were able to rethink our relationship with money and get back in touch with who we truly are and what really matters? What if we could take off the Lie of Scarcity that blurs our vision?***

I was talking about the metaphor of scarcity being a pair of glasses that distort our vision with a friend recently and he said, "I have several pairs of glasses that I have been trying to claw off my face for a while." He was not happy that despite his efforts, the glasses continue to blur his intended better vision in the areas of sexism, racism, and white male privilege. Before he went too much further with belittling himself for being a mortal human being, I asked him whether his glasses prescription had changed any over the years. He looked somewhat relieved and answered yes; as his eyes have gotten stronger, his eyeglass prescription has been able to become weaker. We agreed that this might be the best we can hope for.

Much of what we tell ourselves about money is a lie, or a justification for wrongdoing. We give money more meaning than life, the natural world, and even ourselves. Many people will do almost anything to garner more money. We pollute for money. We kill for money, and we disregard our souls when it comes to money. We live in a culture that encourages us to do this. Unless we admit this and shift our consciousness regarding money, we will forever operate without conscious awareness of our values, our assumptions and our worldviews when it comes to financial matters.

Lynne Twist, in *The Soul of Money*, presents the Three Toxic Myths of Scarcity:

- **There is Not Enough**
- **More is Better**
- **That's Just The Way It Is**

The first two myths probably come as no surprise. One doesn't need to look very far to convince oneself that those two myths fuel our economy, our overindulgences, our

fear of missing out, our competitiveness, and our fears that, in fact, we are not enough. The third myth is possibly the most toxic because it keeps us from questioning the first two. When we "buy into" the third myth we become effectively powerless. We become mindless consumers and forget what it means to be a citizen.

Without some conscious awareness of that part of ourselves that is involved, one way or another, with money, we run the risk of bringing only a diminished aspect of ourselves to bear in any circumstance. It isn't so much a question of how to get money or how to distribute it, but rather the question is more about our attitude about money.

Money can be a great divider. In order to bridge the gap we need to look with wide-open eyes and a wide-open heart for that place between what we are and what we hope to become.

> ***Without consciousness of the part of ourselves that is involved with money, we run the risk of becoming moral and spiritual beings with only one half of our nature—and therefore not really moral or spiritual at all.***
>
> ---Jacob Needleman, *Money and the Meaning of Life*

To navigate the Mobius strip of money with grace and understanding we need to examine our attitudes about money and where those attitudes originated. Money plays a strong role in our inner and outer lives. It's time to bring that role into clearer focus by looking closely at what we think and feel about money, and maybe even why we think and feel what we do.

The Clearness Committee, a Quaker practice of discernment, is important in our Circles of Trust for its use of open, honest questioning to assist the Focus Person in hearing his or her Inner Teacher. I offer the following questions to invite you to be the Focus Person and explore, perhaps through journaling, the light and the dark places along **your** personal Mobius strip of money. Remember, you cannot get to the truth if you are telling yourself what you want to hear rather than what is true.

These questions are invitations for you to use to explore more closely what you may have simply taken in without any conscious awareness at an earlier time in your life. Not all of the questions will resonate with everyone. Choose the ones that speak to you and seem to lead you toward self-discovery. Skip the rest, but notice if and where you experience inner resistance.

- What were your family's financial circumstances when you were born?

- When did you first learn something about money? Was it from your mother or your father? How old were you? What were the circumstances surrounding this learning event?

- How could you acquire money as a child? Did you do chores to earn money or were you given an allowance? How do you handle money with your own children?

- Do you remember the first time you bought something with money you had saved? What did you buy? How did you feel? Was it money you earned, or money that was given to you?

- What do you remember about your first paycheck?

- Did you dream of having a particular job or career when you were a child? Have you achieved this? Was the amount of money you could earn a factor in your choice of career?

- If your relationship with money were a personal relationship, how would you describe it?

- How do you relate to people who have more money than you?

- How do you relate to people who have less money than you?

- Do you recall your mother's or father's relationship with money? (Use your primary caregivers if mother and father are not appropriate.)

- What did you hear said about money?

- What did you **not** hear said about money?

- Have you ever given or received a gift of money? If yes, how much? For what reason(s)? How did you feel about this?

- Regarding money, for what do you want to be known?

- Regarding money, for what do you **not** want to be known?

- How does money correspond with your spirituality?

No man is great enough or wise enough for any of us to surrender our destiny to. The only way in which anyone can lead us is to restore to us the belief in our own guidance.
---Henry Miller

My husband asked me recently to be more specific about what guidance is and where it comes from. I found myself talking about background noise. It is there all of the time, but every now and then, the volume gets turned up and something comes through louder and clearer. It's not just auditory though; guidance can be visual or visceral or just plain intuitive. Some call it "trusting your gut" or "following your bliss." I have been known to describe myself as being moved beyond reason to do something. We live in a culture that promotes and rewards a sharp, successful-looking veneer, and that leaves us inarticulate about how to cultivate a meaningful inner life. Learning to recognize and follow guidance helps to nurture a wise heart.

As I wind down this chapter on moving at the speed of guidance, I want to take a moment to explore shadow and speed. Guidance sometimes tells us that plans need to change, relationships end, or decisions be revised. We may not always welcome guidance or want to do what we are being prompted to do. We may want to push back against guidance and many of us do just that.

Any path forward is not always well lit, hospitable, or even desirable. Sometimes guidance requires a lot more time and patience than we may be willing or able to expend. Just because we are receptive to and wish for guidance is absolutely no guarantee that it will show up.

Things do not always turn out the way we might have wanted, and sometimes we have to question whether guidance has our best interests at heart. I don't believe there are guarantees that accompany guidance. The challenge is not to assign labels like "right" or "wrong," "good" or "bad," but rather to hold the paradox of "both/and" and try to learn from all of our experiences.

To do so, we need only move at the speed of guidance.

Dr. Megan LeBoutillier is an artist and writer who lives outside of Charlottesville, Virginia, with her husband, Bruce Gordon, and their Weimaraner, Chance. She has a doctorate in creative non-fiction and is a national Center for Courage & Renewal facilitator. You may email her at mlboots@earthlink.net

Learning to Be Vulnerable: A Courage & Renewal Men's Retreat

By Jeffrey M. Creswell

Breitenbush Hot Springs is the ideal place for holding a Courage & Renewal retreat for men. Located deep in the ancient Cascade forests between Mt. Hood and Mt. Jefferson in Oregon, where for hundreds of years, Kalapuya, Wasco, and Molalla people used the springs for medicinal and spiritual purposes, Breitenbush offers a sheltering, safe space for men to come together to experience the land, the healing waters, and the fellowship of one another.

As a Courage & Renewal facilitator for the last sixteen years I have always been curious about the fact that our work is dominated by women. In a circle of twenty people it would be unusual to have more than two or three men in addition to myself.

- Was there something about the work that made men uncomfortable?
- Would a retreat designed specifically for men be any different?
- Could we create safe space for men to be vulnerable and to show up with their true selves?

These were some of the questions I was holding as I began planning with Dan Hines for our men's retreat. We were happy to have fifteen men sign up for the retreat. It was a diverse group ranging in age from 24 to 74. We had two father-and-son pairs, three business partners, a climate scientist, and a sculptor. About two thirds of the men at the retreat had found us through the Breitenbush website, not through our traditional Courage & Renewal networks.

Our meeting space was a yurt down by the river; a lovely, warm, open space that felt comfortable and welcoming. Although we had arrived early in the afternoon, Breitenbush hosts many different groups so we would not meet our group until after dinner. As we set up our meeting space and formed our circle, we imagined who would be sitting here with us for the next three days. We went to a Breitenbush orientation meeting after dinner before our first session, and Dan and I both looked around at the men present, wondering who would be a part of our group? I made mental notes of the men I was sure would be in our circle and the ones that I was sure would not be.

I was wrong almost every time. So much for my stereotypes of men who would come to a Courage retreat.

A man needs to love and to hate at the same moment,
to laugh and cry with the same eyes,
with the same hands to throw stones and to gather them,
to make love in war and war in love.
And to hate and forgive and remember and forget,
to arrange and confuse, to eat and to digest
what history
takes years and years to do.

-Yehuda Amichai

Here we were, seventeen men sitting in a circle and reading these words as Dan spoke them aloud. The silence in the room was full. We looked at each other. We looked down. We closed our eyes. As for me, I took a deep breath and wondered if I could trust the process. Could we come together as a group of men to create a safe space where our souls would show up? Would I be able to hold this space with a group of men?

We gave each person a printed copy of the Touchstones and read them out loud. Here were the agreements we were making with each other. I have learned over the years of facilitating Courage Circles that these boundary markers are key to establishing safe space. But I wondered if they would work in a men-only retreat.

Trust the process, I said to myself. I know that it works and I know that I can rest into this offering. But it's not easy.

I have grown to deeply appreciate the concept of paradox in my Courage & Renewal work. One of the paradoxes I always hold as I begin a retreat is that I am responsible for holding the safe space for participants at the same time that I am holding a space for me to do my own inner work. I have always struggled with an image of masculinity that I didn't fit into very well. Here I was in a group of men who collectively represented all the things that I saw as traditionally male and that I didn't live up to. I wanted to be able to rest into this paradox and allow the work of our circle to work on me just as I wanted it to work on the men present.

After our first session Dan and I went to the hot springs for a soak before bed. We had so much anticipation, so much humility. We had already discovered that our preconceived ideas of who these men might be were completely wrong. This was a group of guys who were ready to show up. We were looking forward to the next morning when we were going to spend our time together on a hike in this beautiful mountain wilderness.

The next morning we started the day with a soak while we watched the sunrise on a misty, drizzly morning. I was aware of the sheltering, softening presence of the hot springs waters which seemed to be literally holding us, nurturing us, caring for us. There is a vulnerability to sitting naked in hot springs and relaxing in the warm waters. I could see that this was an essential part of our retreat, even though we all weren't going to the springs together. Yet the healing waters, which had been cradling and healing people for hundreds of years, were supporting us as we came together in our Circle of Trust.

Our morning hike began in a light drizzle. We hiked up to a beautiful rock outcropping that overlooked a valley with a river below. Much of the walk was done in silence. Silence was literally the ground on which we all stood throughout our time together. Silence was the space where we met each other, man to man, face to face. We didn't have to prove anything. We didn't have to be anything other than ourselves. And best of all we didn't have to try and live up to some unrealistic image of what it means to be a man. We walked in silence. We sat in silence. And we were able to be ourselves.

Dust in our eyes our own boots kicked up
Heartsick we nursed along the way we picked up
You may not see it when it's sticking to your skin
But we're better off for all that we let in

-The Indigo Girls

As we gathered in the afternoon after lunch and a soak, we listened to this song by the Indigo Girls. It seemed a fitting song following our morning walk. We had a time to journal and one of the prompts that we were offered proved powerful and transforming for me personally, the paradox of doing my own work while holding the space for others to do their work.

Having spent the last day and a half with this group of men it was so clear to me what was sticking to my skin. It was my image of what it means to be a man, an image that I now knew so clearly was wrong and no longer served me.

It was time to let it go.

In the safe space of this circle I knew I didn't have to live up to any image of what it means to be a man. I was already a man, fully, completely, beautifully a man just like all the rest of the men in our circle. I didn't have to prove anything to anyone because I was already accepted for who I was. It was time to let go of a struggle I had lived with since I was a teenager. It was time to live into my true self as a man.

We ended this session before dinner by reading *A Ritual to Read to Each Other*, a poem by William Stafford. We read it out loud together. The final stanza spoke deeply to me of the transformation happening in this group of men, and in me:

For it is important that awake people be awake,
or a breaking line may discourage them back to
sleep;
the signals we give - yes or no, or maybe -
should be clear: the darkness around us is deep.

That evening we had a short session and then invited anyone who wanted to come and have a soak in the silent pool. Pitch dark with only the stars for light, there was a closeness that didn't need words for those of us who went. It was enough just to know we were there together. Words were unnecessary.

The next morning was sunny and we spent it outside, letting the natural world speak to us in the silence. We each had an hour and a half to create something with the natural world around us, to let it speak to us, draw us out, inspire us. When we came back together, we walked around on a gallery walk to see each other's creations. I was most impressed by the variety of expressions.

Each man had created something that uniquely expressed his personality, his strengths, and his passions. There were works that were large and required a lot of physical effort to create. Then there were works that were delicate, simple and spare.

Some of the men took the entire time and barely finished. Others spent a lot of time in silence waiting to be inspired and finished early with time to just be and enjoy the sunshine. There was a great freedom in knowing that each of us could pay attention to our own inner teacher and do what was right for us.

The gallery walk was powerful. One of the men had a good camera and volunteered to photograph each work. Somehow this honored the work in a way that increased its stature. We walked through the forest, the meadow, down by the river, and were startled, surprised, amazed, delighted, and quieted by the different expressions we saw.

In the afternoon we held Clearness Committees. At this point in the retreat the group was ready for this process, the deepest and most powerful part of Courage & Renewal work. We had three committees. Again, spacious silence held each group and we sat with each other deeply listening. There was a sense of something profound in these clearness committees. I believe that for most of us this was a completely new experience. Men do not show their vulnerability to each other easily, if at all. This felt like sacred time.

After dinner we paired up and sat facing each other. We looked into each other's eyes. I was startled to realize how rarely I had ever looked directly into another man's eyes. It felt right in this circle where we had come to trust one another. We had one partner ask the question, "Who are you?" Without thinking about it, the other partner would answer; then the question was repeated. This went on for five minutes. Then, after a time of silence, the roles were switched. There were tears for many of us. For me, they were tears of gratitude and wonder. Being able to be myself in the company of men was so freeing. I felt great love for these men, my brothers, who had given me this gift.

On our last morning we had time to reflect on our experience together and share a walk and talk with a partner. It was good to listen to another man on the retreat and to hear his experience. I was able to talk about the transformation that had occurred in me. My partner shared a similarly profound transformation for him. We walked in the beautiful woods around Breitenbush and felt so held, by the place and by each other.

We allowed extra time at the end of the retreat before lunch, which was a good thing because the closing circle took two hours. Each man took the time to share from his heart about the retreat and how it had changed him. There was a lot of silence. There were silent tears. There was talk of change, of transformation. We had all been changed as men, as individuals, as fathers, sons, friends, brothers. Many of the men expressed the fact that they had never experienced this kind of vulnerability before and certainly never with other men.

I left this retreat changed.

I had helped to hold the space for this group of men and I had been able to do my own work. I left behind my old image of what it means to be a man, an image that had never served me well. I took with me a new sense of wholeness that came from the experience of being fully myself in a group of other men. Courage & Renewal work provides a safe space for men to encounter their own inner teachers, and in so doing, to encounter other men. We were able to share our vulnerability, our dreams, as well as our strength and our passion. We were able to be tender with each other and powerful with each other.

One of the men in the group, the youngest at 24, shared a song with us, which he taught us on the second day and we sang together. We sang it often after that as it expressed so much of what we experienced together. I believe that our world needs men who can sing these words with conviction, humility, and power:

I am a strong man. I am a loving man. I am a peacemaker; my soul will never die.
I am a strong man. I am a loving man. I am a peacemaker; my soul will never die.
I honor you and empower you to be who you are.
I honor you and empower you to be who you are.
I honor you and empower you to be who you are.

We decided that the song needed to be shared, so we organized a flash mob in the dining room. The man who taught us the song stood up and began to sing. We all joined him, and the room was filled with the strong, loving voices of seventeen men singing their truth to the people present. We made a point to turn to someone near us and sing the line ***"I honor you and empower you to be who you are,"*** as we looked them in the eyes.

There were cheers and applause when we finished. Afterwards a woman came up to Dan in tears. She shared that she had been in a workshop in the morning with women who had experienced sexual abuse. It had been a very emotionally painful morning for them.

I came into this retreat holding three questions. Reflecting back on these questions helped me to glean some of what I learned from this experience:

- ***Was there something about the work that made men uncomfortable?***
  I don't think this work itself made men uncomfortable. I think that the lack of a space where it feels safe to be vulnerable, particularly with other men, is what makes men uncomfortable. We do not have much experience of being vulnerable with one another and so we don't know how to create that kind of space for each other. The Touchstones which we put in place at the start of the retreat offered that kind of safety, allowing the men to be vulnerable with one another in such a bounded space. Being in nature added to our sense of creating a thin place where the soul was invited to show up.

- ***Would a retreat designed specifically for men be any different?***
  Having now been involved in two different retreats for only men, I do think that there are some differences than groups of men and women together. I believe that men need more spacious amounts of silence in order to settle into the space and show up with their whole selves. Men are used to being much more task oriented and taking charge so the silence provides a conscious way to slow down and disengage from the need to be in control.

  I also think that men need to spend more time together in the natural world interacting with each other while interacting with nature. Both the hike we took and the morning we spent creating Andy Goldsworthy inspired creations allowed us to be together while doing something. This seemed to provide a kind of intimacy that felt safer and more secure.

- ***Could we create safe space for men to be vulnerable and to show up with their true selves?***
  Our long and heartfelt closing circle was evidence of the fact that men could be vulnerable with one another. It also showed that men are hungry for this kind of intimacy with one another. I think that men lack the skill to create the safe space.

Each man who spoke at the closing circle spoke from a deep, vulnerable place. Men spoke of never having experienced this kind of vulnerability with other men. They spoke of the power of being in the presence of other men who shared their desire to live a life of integrity and purpose. The men who were focus persons in the clearness committee were deeply moved by the opportunity to listen to themselves in such an intimate way, an experience they said they had never had before.

One man who was the last to speak shared his difficulty with speaking up in a group. He said that he was often paralyzed when he had to speak. But he couldn't keep silent because the experience of the retreat had been so powerful for him. He felt like our time together had given him the courage to claim and use his voice.

There are so many good men in the world. Courage & Renewal Circles of Trust provide a way for good men to come together to support one another, to share with one another, to grow together. I am grateful for the opportunity to offer these circles to men. I am grateful for the way these circles have changed me.

Jeffrey M. Creswell (Jeff) lives in Portland, Oregon where he was an elementary school teacher for 32 years. He continues to share the Scottish Storyline method of curriculum integration with teachers worldwide. Jeff and his wife, Caryl, co-facilitate Courage and Renewal retreats in Oregon with Karen Noordhoff. The website for this work is www.couragecircleoftrust.org His email is creswell@me.com

Finding Myself in the Space Between

By Vicki Metzgar

I believe in synchronicity. For most of my life, I have had a dim awareness that when I had a need for something specific, there was usually a manifestation of some sort that filled my need. I always appreciated having my needs met in unusual and unforeseen ways, and I feel very fortunate to have had so many blessings.

I find myself reflecting on the Kirkridge Courage Fellowship and noticing a collection of small synchronicities, that, when added together, form a profound sense of meaning. These incidents surely were not accidental! I must pay attention to them, for together, they inform my experience of Kirkridge and the Courage Fellowship itself. These synchronous events point toward a spiritual epiphany.

Like many people, my spiritual journey has been, at times, twisted, and at other times, disconnected. Born into a family with deep ties in rural Southern culture and tradition, I was raised in a very evangelical tradition. Church was as important as breathing. It was where you went each week, and so did your extended family. I have come to treasure that experience, as it taught me many important lessons of life, but it has taken a lot of time and reflection to give that experience meaning in my life.

I was always headstrong (stubborn some might say). I thought that church was a waste of time, and I did not like being made to attend. Church just did not make sense to me. As a teenager, I rebelled and told my parents that, "as soon as I am old enough to make my own decisions, I won't attend church at all." I left church and all those God-fearing people behind once I began college.

However, all of that changed with the birth of my own children and my desire to rear them in a more rational spiritual tradition. After much "church shopping," my young family decided to join a small inner city Episcopal Church that had a rich tradition of outreach and reconciliation. I was attracted to the way people were able to approach religion rationally, while at the same time, they were welcoming in a broad open way. I thrived in that place and was deeply involved in all aspects of the parish, including several leadership positions. I studied and read widely of the many religious traditions as part of the Church's training for adults and as part of my own curiosity about the state of this world.

Once my children were grown, my life changed in some dramatic ways, and suddenly my relationship with the rational, reasonable, God-loving church with which I had become so involved became one of dissonance. I began to question the Church and its policies, which seemed more and more in conflict with my own beliefs. After 25 years of faithful attendance, I separated from the Church completely. I was disillusioned with Church leaders, whom I saw as greedy and power hungry, not to mention much more conservative socially than I could ever imagine myself. I suddenly found myself (stubbornly?) afloat in a sea of uncertainty about what I believed.

A DIFFERENT SPIRITUAL DIRECTION

In the early 2000's, I became involved in work that spoke to my heart in ways I had not experienced since my early adulthood. Parker Palmer's *The Courage to Teach* led me to become part of a movement that values connecting the soul and role of individuals. In my work as a retreat facilitator, I met and came to know amazing educators who were dedicated to working for the good of all children and were, simultaneously, broken-hearted by the "systems" within which they were forced to perform in ways that were the antithesis of their deeply held beliefs about how children should be educated. I felt as if I had finally found my calling, and I felt more connected to this movement than to any religious tradition. I saw the teachers in my Circles of Trust and my colleagues in facilitator preparation as my "spiritual" family. The people of this movement came from all traditions and religious backgrounds, and we found common ground in the work of the heart and in Circles of Trust.

As my professional career was coming to a close, my thoughts were not about continuing to do retreat facilitation, but an interesting synchronicity entered my life. I received an intriguing invitation to join a group of Circle of Trust facilitators in the

Courage Fellowship at the Kirkridge Retreat Center in Pennsylvania. I looked over the application and found all of it simple to follow, but then I came to one question that completely stumped me. As much as I was drawn to this Kirkridge program and the opportunities it offered for me to continue doing the work I love, there was one question that set me on edge: What is your religious identification? It had been many years since I claimed any religion. My earlier experiences set me against most religions for what I thought would be a lifetime.

So I called the program leader, Sally Z. Hare, as I felt I needed to come clean and admit as much to her, in light of this generous offer of Fellowship with valued Courage colleagues. I should have known, really; Sally always finds a way to open a path to trustworthy spaces. Her response was that the question was a way of looking at diversity in the selection process, and *no religious identification* was a perfectly appropriate response.

Then she turned the question to me: "Have you read Caroline Fairless' book, *The Space Between Church and Not Church?"* I admitted that I had not and immediately ordered a copy. In those pages, I found a description of sacred space that I could embrace with all my being. For over 20 years, I had wrestled with feeling extremely disconnected from my Episcopal roots and faith, and as I read *The Space Between*, I was struck by Fairless' description of "the space":

> **There is a space between things, between all things. The space is sacred and it is rich with blessing...that space between church and what the church refers to as "the world"... I talk to people from churches who, although they continue in their congregations, are nonetheless articulating a longing for a depth of sacred connection that lies beyond their Sunday morning experiences. ...people outside churches want the sacredness of the natural world without the Jesus overlay. (Preface, page xiii)**

The concept of "space between" resonated with me in a way that few ideas had in my lifetime. Not only was it refreshing to me conceptually, but it was calling to another deep belief of my own about the state of Earth and our sacred duty to preserve it for the future of humanity. Here, I had found a deep description of my own spiritual dilemma.

I applied for the Fellowship. Now that I am nearing its end, I am noticing other synchronous events that speak to my longing for finding a "space between" for us all. It seems, everywhere I turn, **SPACE** has found its way to my consciousness.

Working with a group of Kirkridge Courage Fellows on a potential grant proposal, we shared the article *Into the Field* from Orion Magazine. The author, Amanda Giracca, recounts her experience visiting her alma mater, Prescott College in Arizona. She

relates her experience with an undergraduate ecology professor, Bob Ellis. As she visits Professor Ellis on a class field study, Giracca recounts how he seeks to take students into the field in order to "ground truth" the concepts and theories his students have been studying in the textbook and classroom. For Giracca, "*it felt more like reflective conversation: What do you notice? What do you think? What do you make of all this information you're steeped in, and what are you going to do with it? (p. 2)*"

Then, as Giracca thinks about her own freshman writing course and the students she teaches, mostly biology majors seeking their way into medical school, she laments that they do not have any undergraduate experience that requires field studies in natural settings. Instead, *"their curriculum is comprised of large lectures and labs held inside."* She writes:

> ***It's experience in its purest form that seems to be missing, for my students and for many college students in the United States---exposure to the world, whether it's the wilderness, a city neighborhood, or a polluted stream trickling through campus. What's increasingly lost is the chance to be brought out into the huge, wild mess of it and be asked, "So, what do you make of all this?" (p. 5)***

MY OWN GROUND TRUTHING

As a high school Biology teacher, I felt that "ground truthing" was invaluable in teaching students about the beauty, complexity, and interconnected character of the natural world. I count among my most cherished memories of teaching those that were experienced outside, on the 40-acre campus where I taught. In building our own nature trail, students discovered amazing animals, like the flying squirrel that occupied the hollow of a tree on campus. On bleak winter days, my students could cross the road and search the bare woods for downed logs. We found termites inside dead logs and took them back to the lab to reveal the mutually-beneficial lifestyle enjoyed by the termites and microscopic inhabitants of their gut, which made digesting all that wood possible. These fascinating creatures could not survive without each other.

For me it feels a lot like the work of Circles of Trust (COT) that my fellow Kirkridge facilitators and I have been practicing in order to create the space for people to bring their lives into congruence with their deeply-held beliefs. Much of the COT work is done in natural settings, and for a reason. In small and large groups, COT facilitators ask similar questions as Professor Ellis:

What do you notice?
What do you think?
What do you make of all this?
What are you going to do about it?

Such questions prompt silent reflection, journaling, and discussion to allow participants to hear the wisdom of their own "inner teacher" that can guide them to understanding their place in the world and their priorities for living congruent lives.

THE SPACE BETWEEN ALL THINGS

Synchronicity once again brought important ideas to my attention as I listened to an *On Being* podcast with Krista Tippett interviewing Frank Wilczek. Dr. Wilczek is a Nobel laureate and MIT professor of theoretical physics and mathematics. Their discussion was about Wilczek's recent book, *A Beautiful Question*, which opens with a single question: Does the world embody beautiful ideas? I was so caught up by the interview that I got the book. Here again, in yet another format, was an inquiry into the "space between."

In the quest for finding the answer to this overarching question of beautiful ideas, Wilczek takes the reader on an historic journey through the development of the fundamental ideas of mathematics and physics, from Pythagoras and Plato to Newton, Maxwell, Faraday, and Einstein. Wilczek credits Pythagoras with discovery of "*a most fundamental relationship between numbers....and sizes and shapes*" in his Pythagorean Theorem. Wilczek writes, "*because Number is the purest product of mind, while Size is a primary characteristic of Matter, that discovery revealed a hidden unity between Mind and Matter.*" He also notes that Pythagoras discovered the relationship between numbers and musical harmony, which he contends "*... completes a trinity, Mind-Matter-Beauty, with Number as the linking thread.*" *These discoveries led Pythagoras to propose that "All Things Are Number."* Thus, for Wilczek, the Beautiful Question arises!

Wilczek goes on to remind his reader that Plato is celebrated for his metaphor of the Cave, *"raising important emotional and philosophical aspects of our relationship…with reality."* Plato "*imagined a mediating demiurge…who rendered the realm of perfect, eternal Ideas into its imperfect copy, the world we experience. Here, the concept of the world as a work of art is explicit"* (p. 5).

Mathematical ideals form the guideposts in Wilczek's search for answers. He proposes, *"Two obsessions are the hallmarks of Nature's artistic style: Symmetry---a love of harmony, balance, and proportion, and Economy--satisfaction in producing an abundance of effects from very limited means"* (p. 11). So the quest proceeds.

The search continues for Wilczek as he approaches the topic of Space. He notes that "*Newton's physics left space empty, but he was not happy about it*" (p. 118). As I am not a physicist, I had really never pondered the actual nature of space. For me, space has always meant that there was no thing there, but as I read more, I came to understand that "space" is something more than a void. Apparently, Newton was aware that this concept of Space as a void was inadequate to explain his theory of gravity and its properties, but he was unable to find another explanation to explain the observable properties of objects. I am suddenly confronted with a conceptual understanding of Space as a Medium, not a void. My mind is blown! Now I see Space so differently, as if, all of a sudden, I am able to see ultraviolet light, and I am able to see a whole new world and understand my own better.

SPACE AS A BEAUTIFUL MEDIUM

As if to confirm my new understanding of Space as a Medium, I had another synchronous event right around the corner. A trip to the Berkshires took me to the Massachusetts Museum of Contemporary Art, and as I walked into the building, I noticed that, in the pavement of the parking lot, shiny golden filled each of the cracks. It seemed a bit strange, but I did not think much about it.

Once inside, I found a brochure describing an exhibit called *The Space Between.* I could not ignore such a blatant synchronous signal as this! Inside the brochure I found a picture of the very cracks in the pavement I had noticed in the parking lot. Come to find out, the cracks were actually part of The Space Between exhibit. A quote from the artist, Rachel Sussman of Baltimore, Maryland, described the work as *Sidewalk Kintsukuroi.* Sussman's installation restores the cracks in the pavement by adapting the Japanese art of *kintsukuroi,* in which gold is used to repair broken ceramics. Japanese tradition treasures these restored ceramics as more valuable for having been broken. This was bringing ever more clarity and resolution to my concept of the space between.

KIRKRIDGE AS THE SPACE BETWEEN

Finally, I am able to more fully describe how the experiences of Kirkridge and the Courage Fellowship have changed my perception of so many things. Kirkridge is described in one brochure in this way:

> ***Kirkridge sits on the Kittatinny Ridge of the Pocono Mountains, part of the Appalachian Range. Located in eastern Pennsylvania, less than two hours from New York City, Kirkridge is often, like the island of Iona, called "a thin place," a place where the distance between heaven and earth collapses, where the soul might show up.***

There it is! That "thin place." It is the place where one might encounter heaven and earth. It is about that space between where I now see energy and motion, not emptiness and void.

> ***For the past 75 years, [Kirkridge has] served a thriving Christian and interfaith community. Looking ahead, we plan on serving an even wider community of people of good faith, no faith, and interfaith – and providing safe harbor to all. Our historic motto of "picket and pray" has now extended itself "to protect, tend, and embrace." From the peak of the ridge to the clear waters in the valley below, the new century calls for stewardship, nurturing, and embracing inner stability with outer sustainability.*** (http://www.kirkridge.org)

Now this synchronicity makes sense to me. All along, I have been experiencing Kirkridge without the ability to translate my experience of the place to others. Now I can see that Kirkridge IS the ***space between***. It is that thin place between heaven and earth. It is the place that makes me able to take my reality and see meaning and purpose that is somehow reconnecting my soul and my role in the world. It is the space that, like a beautiful question answered, is not void of action, but full of energy, motion, and matter. It is harmony and beauty alive with everyday experience. The people of Kirkridge, as well as those in the Fellowship, are meeting in that space between church and not-church to attempt to bring ourselves and others into congruence with the inner teacher and voice of conscience. We are all broken, but mended with golden fillings that make us more valuable for having been broken and able to relate more readily to a broken world.

I continue my search at Kirkridge, which has become, for me, the embodiment of the space between. Here I have found a place that is not part of my everyday job or working life routine. Here, there is space for ground-truthing the meaning of creation and my place in it. Here, there is for me a deep spiritual connection and experience. And if I stop and look deeply at the world from this place, I can see through to new dimensions, new visions of possibility, and new understandings of things unknown until now. And so, my quest continues.

Vicki H. Metzgar, Ed. D., is an educator of 42 years. She lives and works in an intentional Cohousing Community in Nashville, Tennessee. She may be contacted at: Germantown Commons, 1325 5th Ave. N. Apt. #23, Nashville, TN 37208-2970 or by email at vicki.metzgar@gmail.com

Engaging in Culture Change in Academic Medicine

By Linda Pololi

I am a physician and I have spent most of my career in medical schools and their teaching hospitals. My last such affiliation was as Professor of Medicine and Vice Chancellor for Education at the University of Massachusetts Medical School. Currently, I work in the Women's Studies Research Center at Brandeis University. My work efforts have always focused on the personal and professional development of medical school faculty and, in extension, on the overall culture of academic medicine. I have been fortunate over the past 20 years to have had many opportunities to design, develop, and implement professional development and mentoring programs for physicians and scientists. For the most part, these programs - and particularly the dimensions that draw upon the principles and practices of the Center for Courage & Renewal are countercultural to the usual offerings in academic medicine; as such, it has been a source of great personal gratification for me and for the medical faculty participants in my courses to be able to participate in such work.

One overarching aim for my work is to help academic physicians and scientists focus on the work that is most meaningful to them, that is congruent with their own deeply held values, and that allows them to preserve a compassionate approach

to patients. How can these talented and hardworking individuals address best the needs of our nation's healthcare while sustaining their own humanity and vitality in roles that are very demanding, both intellectually and emotionally? These have been the compelling reasons for me to persist in this work.

I believe that what started me on this road was the wrenching experience of looking after a dear acute leukemia patient in Chicago. I was then a young physician and assigned to my care was an elderly, dignified, and poorly educated African American woman, Mrs. Y. We treated her intensively and plied her body with chemotherapy, platelets, red blood cells and white blood cells, as her life waned. I eventually married the physician who alongside me had cared for this patient and shared the same deep sorrow I felt when our patient eventually died. Shortly after, we moved to Providence, RI, where my husband was offered a position at Brown University. I made the decision to temporarily give up the practice of medicine to look lovingly after our two small sons. I determined then that I didn't want to return to the practice of Hematology and Oncology. I felt that my efforts would better serve our societal needs by focusing in preventive medicine.

When I did return to medicine after a few years, I chose to take a position in General Internal Medicine. In that capacity, as a faculty member in the School of Medicine at Brown, I practiced medicine and supervised physicians in training. I became fascinated by medical education and how one might be able to facilitate behavior change in one's patients to aid their wellbeing and prevent illness. I found out that our physicians and medical students lacked, for the most part, insight into their own behavior.

As part of the education modules I developed, I incorporated the opportunity for medical students and residents to change their own behavior as a way for them to understand better this complex process.

At the same time, I learned about the American Academy on Physician and Patients (AAPP), a group that aims to improve effective communication between physicians and patients. I joined the organization and was drawn into its mission to improve interviewing skills - that is, the words to say to patients to form therapeutic relationships with them and to alleviate their fears, which would also be helpful in promoting behavioral change. A major focus of AAPP training programs was the development of personal awareness by physicians, since many of us have difficulty in handling the emotional toll of medicine as evidenced by our poor communication skills with patients. I became part of the facilitator-in-training program of the AAPP (now called the American Academy on Communication in Healthcare) and eventually was certified as a facilitator for its national faculty development programs to teach interviewing skills and effective relationship formation skills for physicians.

RECOGNIZING THE NEED FOR A CHANGE

Out of these experiences, I came to hear about the lives of physicians and the daily effects of the practice and professional organization of medicine on their souls. This cycle was repeated for me at my subsequent job in North Carolina where I was given responsibility for "curriculum reform" of medical student education at the school. What I learned there was that students were enthusiastic about more humanistic ways that facilitated their learning in medical school. Many faculty, however, didn't understand why they should, or how to, teach differently as they had only experienced traditional and somewhat abusive forms of medical education themselves. To address this, I started programs for faculty that offered them the experience of learning in ways that involved the development of personal awareness, trusting communities embodying relationship formation and the type of culture that I thought would better serve not only our faculty but also their medical students and patients.

At some point, when I was myself deeply hurt and traumatized by the organizational culture at my last position in a medical school, I moved to Brandeis University and started a research project, the National Initiative on Gender, Culture and Leadership in Medicine – frequently called "C - Change" for culture change. I passionately wanted to change for the better the existing culture of academic medicine as I had become increasingly aware of many faculty in academic medicine who were also being wounded and changed adversely by this culture. Faculty were becoming cynical, with lowered vitality, or they left academic medicine altogether.

Through my various medical school responsibilities earlier, I had become familiar with the personal lives of the faculty from the stories they told me about their own experiences. However, we also needed rigorous scientific data to document the effects of this stressful culture and understand what could be a foundation for possible future change. After my arrival at Brandeis University, I managed to secure a very generous grant from the Josiah Macy Jr. Foundation to do this work and I was able to gather a talented, interdisciplinary team of experts to work on the project. We launched a national research program, conducting initially and recording a set of 100 in-depth interviews of medical school faculty from across the country. The findings of the interview study were very sobering and uncomfortable to read. For example, faculty described feeling very isolated and depersonalized in their roles:

> *"This is a place that doesn't recognize you as an individual; no one is interested in what a fun, interesting person I am. There is nobody who is interested in that. They're interested in the work I do, perhaps. But nobody cares what makes me tick here. I'm completely invisible – as a human – as a person."*

"I couldn't pick out anybody that I corresponded with by email or letters out of a line-up. I knew very few people in different divisions. It was very much an isolated situation. Go to your clinic, do your thing, go back to your office, go to the medical suite, do your procedures, go back to the office..."

"Check your humanity at the door, that was how it felt. Any sign of... this is going to sounds harsh, but... any tendency towards kindness was viewed as weakness."

Faculty, physicians in training (residents) and medical students frequently reported a sense of not belonging in their work environments, of not being able to express their opinions freely without fear of retribution, of ethical and moral distress, of feeling disrespected, and unsupported.

"Well, I think the hardest thing for me was to be in a department where you couldn't express yourself [your opinion] without feeling that you were jeopardizing your career. The hardest thing was that I wasn't honest to myself sometimes and because I was afraid earlier on that I would lose my job - I would get kicked out of the department."

We found a significant gap between the values held personally by the faculty and those they observed being prevalent in the organization.

"So while we have this emerging technology and the ability to treat patients, we have no sense of social purpose or social policy."

"But in an academic institution that doesn't value community, culture, partnerships, collaboration, I wouldn't have wanted to stay there. That's where I was going and what I valued, it was a dead end."

Some faculty described being adversely changed by the culture:

"And there were colleagues of mine to whom power meant a great deal and I watched them become people I didn't like as they dealt with this hostility and grabbed for power, and they achieved a great deal and I don't take it away from them, but in the course of it, they lost their humanity. They became people I could no longer respect. They became dishonest and manipulative and I just wasn't willing to go there."

Discrimination on the basis of race and ethnicity and gender was widely felt:

"What I struggled with for a long time was my being an African American woman, in a male, white male dominated institution and the feeling that I was invisible. My opinion didn't matter, what I was feeling didn't matter. There were people who I passed every single day who were chairmen of departments, and I mean, good God, after five years you've got to see a person."

"I sent my resume for something and when I showed up someone said to me, 'Your resume didn't look black.' Can you imagine someone saying that?"

We decided then that we needed to find out how representative the perspectives of the initial 100 faculty we interviewed were, so we turned their words into an extensive survey. We surveyed faculty nationally in a balanced but random selection of 26 U.S. medical schools and have published many of our research findings. Through these qualitative and quantitative research studies, we documented that the culture of academic medicine is fiercely individualistic, competitive, harshly non-relational and discriminatory.

DOCUMENTING THE NEED FOR A CHANGE

When we have continued to survey medical schools in the U.S. and Canada and Europe, we are finding the same results. For example, in the U.S. 38% of male and 46% of female faculty say they feel burnt out. Twenty-nine percent of faculty agree with the statement, "I feel isolated here." Twenty-one percent of male faculty and 31% of female faculty say they feel ignored or invisible. Only 54% of the faculty agree that their values are well aligned with the values exhibited by their respective institutions. Fifty percent report that "the administration is only interested in me for the revenue I generate." Eleven percent of the faculty find work to be "dehumanizing," and 25% of the faculty say "the culture of my institution discourages altruism." Twenty-two percent of the faculty agree with the statement "I find myself being more aggressive here than I like." Just 64% of faculty feel confident that they can overcome whatever professional barriers they encounter.

Faculty turnover in academic medicine is huge, there are significant ethical issues in the professional behaviors of physicians and medical scientists, and the existing culture provides big challenges to faculty of color, as well as to the advancement of women into leadership roles. I am not a survey statistician like some members of my research team, but more of a change agent, and I am excited to be able to use our research findings to inform the development of new programs for medical school faculty that aim to cultivate the experience of a humanistic, relational and inclusive culture – small communities of learning for diverse groups of faculty. Thus, creating humanistic, relational and inclusive environments for faculty and students has become the overarching goal of my career in medicine for the last 25 years. To experience such a culture is the prime aim of the programs that I now offer to medical schools. An additional prominent theme in the programs is an appreciation of differences, particularly of cultural and racial nature.

In these C - Change faculty development programs there is intense focus on enhancing each person's understanding of their own deeply held-values and beliefs, helping them decide what is most meaningful to them. We focus on the realization

of a person's humanity and how that can manifest in their work. The structure of the programs is essentially relationship–based and facilitates the formation of relationships between participants. The programs aim to nourish the "deeply human" in the faculty participants and help them develop self-awareness. With this comes the ability to bring all of oneself to one's work, to be authentic, find work meaningful and more energizing. Below are a couple of comments written by former participants in such mentoring programs I have implemented:

> *"The program provided the opportunity to think about and define clearly my core values, and to redefine the idea of career and success with core values in mind."*

> *"What was most meaningful was the license and protected time/space to perform self-reflection. In doing so, it allowed me to understand more fully where my ambitions lay and in what way I was not being true to myself."*

> *"Relationships absolutely are the magic of the program. I can actually see a lot of potential collaborations and relationships moving forward and so I'm excited about that."*

In our courses, we structure time for reflective practices, authentic conversations, appreciation of differences, and then we help participating faculty think through how this experience applies to their careers and choices. Faculty learn how to develop practices at work to support these dimensions in colleagues and learners so that they might become habits and an integral part of the day.

In these group-mentoring programs, I have mostly designed and facilitated on my own. Over the years, I have become more confident in anticipating that this solo practice will have good results. Recently, program attendance has been a marvelous 95% in five cohorts of faculty over four years who met for monthly daylong retreats, and the participants wrote moving accounts of their experiences in the programs. Once one understands the power, trustworthiness, and value of the group, attendance becomes a priority. Even so, I have felt lonely not having partnership for myself in preparing, presenting and debriefing the sessions.

FINDING MY OWN SPACE

When I first read the description of the Kirkridge Courage Fellowship, I immediately recognized the Fellowship as such a wonderful opportunity, along with the promise of new friendships, perspectives, and learning. I hoped that in the Kirkridge Courage Fellowship, I would be able to focus on developing my own deeper understanding and humanity, as well as understanding others in the group and being there for them. I would be able to enhance my facilitation skills and expand the types of programs that I might offer in the future. While I am facilitating, I often have to put my own needs aside

and prioritize the needs of the group. I have found it difficult to take the necessary time and develop the ways to attend to the personal awareness part of my practice. I have always hoped to find a trusted group to enrich this aspect and to help my work and me.

In former years when I was based in medical schools, I had easier access to medical colleagues with whom I could partner. During both the AAPP and Center for Courage & Renewal facilitator preparation programs, I enjoyed and valued the opportunity to learn with and from my colleagues, but now I am considered mostly an instructor for such training.

I have found it difficult to know where to find the encouragement that I need in my work. As Leonard Cohen said when asked about where he found the inspiration for his songs, "*If I knew, I'd go there more often.*" I have tried to create similar relationships with colleagues, and I do have many friends in medicine that I could call on, but without the structure of a fellowship I find that it's really difficult for a group to maintain this purpose due to everyone's multiple responsibilities and calls on their time.

The Kirkridge Courage Fellowship offered me the learning and friendships to enrich my practice and my work. I have felt fully accepted by the group of fellows, whereas in medicine I usually felt like an outsider. Participation has helped me be more self-aware and reflective about myself. Something else that attracted me to the Fellowship was that throughout my career in academic medicine, I have usually found myself working in groups that are majority male; I am one of few women who have landed in leadership roles in U.S. academic medicine. Now the Fellowship offers a space for me to enjoy having a good number of women in a working group.

The Kirkridge Fellowship provided me with the deep generosity and sense of belonging I had such difficulty finding in organized academic medicine. The program structure allowed me time, space, and support, to access my inner self and for listening to my inner voice. This teaches me how to live in my work.

It is this deep well of generosity, trustworthy relationships, and sense of belonging that I also try to recreate in the programs I offer for groups of medical school faculty. At Kirkridge Fellowship meetings, within this most thoughtful of environments, we participated in structured approaches to explore our "shadow selves," based on Jungian psychology. I found this area of inquiry fascinating. I became more aware of my own competitive nature, and of other aspects of my personality/self that react differently in various situations and that had been molded at least in part during my time in organized medicine. It's hard to know whether these attributes of myself were cultivated within the academic medicine culture, or were part of what led me there in the first place. It probably doesn't matter, but acknowledging these traits in myself allows me to make better choices regarding collaboration and to offer better experiences within the programs I facilitate. Intuitively, I know that for me a lot of

this work revolves around the issue of true collaboration. What is that, under what circumstances can true collaboration be felt and accomplished? Is it just with true love and abundant generosity? I don't come from a background that practiced generosity, but I do want to practice and receive it. What is the shadow side of generosity? I find that I am more drawn to this work than to medicine.

Just as I have benefited from my own experiences in the Kirkridge Courage Fellowship, I continue to hope that through the C - Change program experiences of a different culture, medical faculty will return to their medical schools and teaching hospitals invigorated and with a clearer sense of their own values and self-worth. In turn, faculty will be able to model these attributes and program methods for their own colleagues, trainees, and students.

Linda Pololi, MBBS, FRCP, is Senior Scientist Brandeis University and Resident Scholar, Brandeis Women's Studies Research Center. She is Director of The National Initiative on Gender, Culture and Leadership in Medicine: C – Change and is nationally recognized for her research and innovative contributions to the professional and personal development of faculty in academic medicine, including women and underrepresented minority groups. A graduate of the University of London Middlesex Hospital Medical School, she has held faculty and administrative positions at the Universities of Illinois, East Carolina, Brown, and Massachusetts, where she was a professor of medicine and vice chancellor for education. Dr. Pololi is the recipient of the 2011 Association of American Medical Colleges Women in Medicine and Science Leadership Development Award, and is a fellow of the Royal College of Physicians (UK). She has published numerous research articles on the culture of academic medicine and a book: *Changing the Culture of Academic Medicine: Perspectives of Women Faculty (Dartmouth College Press)*. Dr. Pololi is a certified facilitator for the American Academy on Communication in Healthcare and the Center for Courage & Renewal. Her email is lpololi@brandeis.edu

Reclaiming the Commons
By Jean Richardson

> ***I only went out for a walk, and finally concluded to stay till sundown, for going out ... was really going in."***
>
> ***John Muir, 1938***

I have always loved the outdoors. Like John Muir, going out for me is really going in.

Years ago, when trying to explain to my parents why I made a radical move from San Francisco to the very rural setting of Ghost Ranch in Northern New Mexico, my father stopped me in mid-sentence and said, "Face it, Jean, you always were a camper at heart." He was exactly right then and the same is true now.

I have been following my camper heart for many years. My camper heart calls me out into the quiet mountains, invites me to the waters of the river, and encourages me to sit in silence listening to the sounds of the seasons. After I was rejected by the church I loved because I was a lesbian, it was my camper heart that healed my soul, reminded me of the inclusive wholeness witnessed in nature, and provided me a wider theological landscape to explore my own spiritual questions and inner life. From years of work in pastoral ministry I had truly come to embody the words of Leonard Cohen's song, *The Future*:

The blizzard of the world has crossed the threshold and it has overturned the order of the soul.

That blizzard guided my camper heart to Kirkridge Retreat and Study Center more than a decade ago. It is my camper heart that speaks to me still on this ancient mountain as the executive director of this "beacon on the hill." Over the years I have learned many lessons here and have come to understand the value of this natural sanctuary.

By the time I arrived at Kirkridge in 2005, the blizzard of the world had crossed the threshold into my life and my soul had been turned over. It is said that you do the work you most need to learn in life. Like many others, I have found this to be true. As a pastor, more often than not, I wrote sermons that I most needed to hear. I declared forgiveness to others that I needed to offer to myself. I worked for radical inclusion in the church because of the deep exclusion I experienced in my own life.

Arriving at Kirkridge, I had little idea of how deeply I needed to restore my soul. At Ghost Ranch in New Mexico and now as the director of Kirkridge Retreat Center in Pennsylvania, for well over 23 years, I have witnessed the change that takes place with individuals when nature's quiet and beautiful abundance are mixed with a generous portion of hospitality and acceptance. I believe Robert Raines, author and former director of Kirkridge, got it best when he would offer this welcome to Kirkridge visitors:

> *Like Chaucer's pilgrims we are stopping over for a couple of nights of rest in this inn and to tell each other some of the stories of our lives. ...If you brought some of your demons with you, remember that your angels are with you too. This mountain welcomes you. ... This ancient rock has been here for 300 million years. Whatever sin or sorrow, grief or anger, you've brought, the mountain is not appalled. It's seen and heard it all. It is one of the arms of God where it's safe to lean awhile.*

For some divine mysterious reason, it is safe and good for our souls to lean on ancient rocks over 300 million years old. As I write this piece in my Kirkridge office, I am observing women and men from a New York City seminary as they stand below my window, taking in the vista and breathing in the common landscape. Placed on an ancient mountain where we believe the earth first crested, Kirkridge holds steady and proclaims the hospitality of our earth that offers abundance in every season. Here we are reminded of what Thomas Merton called our individual and communal "hidden wholeness":

> ***This mysterious Unity, and Integrity, is Wisdom, the Mother of all, Natura naturans.***

Kirkridge is a gift, left in trust by those who went before us so we and future generations might remember our wholeness and listen for our true names as individuals and as a

community, surrounded by the healing gift of natural beauty. Like a national treasure or park, there is no claim on the ownership of Kirkridge. This is a radical reality. There is no denominational ownership or shareholders with financial investments at stake. Rather, over the years, Kirkridge has hosted a parade of supporters who come and go, donate and volunteer, serve on the board, work and care for this place based on a common understanding of its contribution to our world.

Since its conception, Kirkridge has been rooted in embracing the sacred and honoring the common good in our lives. If Kirkridge had a "mother church," it would be the Iona Community of Scotland founded in 1939. The Iona Community was, and still is today, a movement built upon a deep understanding of establishing a religious community based on working for the common good. George MacLeod, the founder of the Iona community, stated that for any community to survive it needed to come together around a "common demanding task"... A task that would take everyone's skills, and need everyone's gifts and talents, to accomplish.

Heather Menzies in her book, *Reclaiming the Commons for the Common Good,* writes:

> ***The word common originally meant "together-as one," "shared alike" and "bound together by obligation."***

Since the beginning, the great and demanding task of establishing and maintaining Kirkridge has been invitational. Survival through the years has been no one person's job to accomplish or take credit for accomplishing. We work and volunteer here because at our core we believe that it is for the common good of all that places like Kirkridge survive. Just like our national parks, retreat centers are good for our common soul.

Soul work is not easy and indeed takes courage. My mother used to say, "Life is not for the faint of heart." Her words ring true for me, and equally true is the fact that when we allow others to hear and hold our hearts, the journey of life takes on a new possibility away from an individualistic challenge to a gift of the common.

Knowing the critical gift of undeveloped land Kirkridge offers to our world, the board recently acted to place more than half of the property, 107 acres, into permanent land easement with The Nature Conservancy. The Board acted to assure that a portion of this land would never be vulnerable to private development or acquired for personal gain. This act guaranteed a contiguous watershed from the top of the ridge to the Delaware River, offering clean water to future generations, a gift for the common good.

The Kirkridge Governing Board is living into Rachel Carson's words from 1956: *"Those who contemplate the beauty of the earth find reserves of strength that will endure as long as life lasts."* We need "reserves of strength" to face the complexities threatening our planet. As elders we must assure that future generations will have places where

they too can discover "reserves of strength" and be reminded of our common task to seek justice and work for kindness.

We also need places that honor the divine Spirit of this life. Terry Tempest Williams in *The Hour of Land,* celebrating the centennial birthday of our national parks, describes Acadia National Park in Maine as "another breathing space." Williams goes on to say, *"Perhaps that is what parks are – breathing spaces for a society that increasingly holds its breath."*

Kirkridge is not only a place where individuals are invited to breathe; it is a place that honors our very breath. The Hebrew word for **breath**, *ruach, also* means **wind** or **spirit**. I believe Kirkridge is what George Macleod, founder of the Iona Community, described as *a thin space*. The Celts, have a saying that *"Heaven and earth are only three feet apart, but in the thin places that distance is even smaller."* Thin places offer a rare light that reveals the divine in our natural world, in us and in one another.

When I interviewed for my position as executive director of Kirkridge, I carried Parker Palmer's book, *A Hidden Wholeness*, under my arm. I knew then, as I know now, that Courage Work was critical for our time and the right partner for our retreat center. From its beginning Kirkridge has honored our deep need to live seamlessly, in the way Parker Palmer describes as life on the Mobius strip. "Picket and pray" has been the historic motto of Kirkridge, as from its beginning, pilgrims at this retreat center have been invited to take time out from the demands of the world for prayer, silence, and reflection, restoring their commitment to go back out into the world and work for the common good. The essential DNA has remained the same for 75 years.

Over the years I have learned to live into the simple paradox I first learned as a congregational pastor and now as the director of this sacred place. When I focus on healing the wounds and divisions in my own life, I allow space for others to do the same. When I offer grace to myself, it is easier for me to offer grace to others.

As I learn to trust my own inner teacher, I can trust and not judge when others follow their own hearts. When I deeply appreciate my own gifts and value my own unique contributions in the world, I can encourage the gifts and contributions that each individual offers to the whole. Gathering in Circles of Trust, both as a participant and as a facilitator, has offered me this gift. It is the paradox that the restoration of one's own soul allows space for others to do the same. My work in retreat settings heals my heart, calls me inward, tests my passion for justice, and challenges my commitment for inclusion.

There is a room at Kirkridge named the Lenape Room, in honor of the First Nations people who lived in this region of the Eastern American continent. The room is filled with photos of founders and famous leaders who led theological and justice revolutions

in decades past. There is one poster that stands out for me personally more than any other. It is a portrait of Rosa Parks sitting on a bus. Although many Civil Rights leaders came to this mountain, as far as I know, Rosa Parks never found her way to Kirkridge. Her story reminds me daily of why I engage in and am so passionate about my work as a director of this retreat center.

I deeply believe that lives are changed here.

When women and men dare connect to their truest selves and experience a deep connection with one another, a new energy emerges. Courage is found and courage is acted upon. Rosa Parks symbolizes this metamorphosis for me. Yet her life took on new meaning as she sat in circles at the Highlander Center in Tennessee during the Civil Rights Movement. She found the courage to sit down in the front of the bus because she knew that her act was for the "common good." Not only was she not willing to participate in her own diminishment, as Parker Palmer writes in *The Courage to Teach*, but she knew that her action was connected to the "common good."

Rosa Parks was able to find the courage to sit down because she knew that she was not alone in her act of public disobedience. Miss Parks trusted that she was supported by a larger circle of courageous people who would never abandon her. Retreat centers build such communities. I have always held the truth close to my heart that the Civil Rights Movement was a success in large part because of the relationships forged between blacks and whites in circles that inspired common dreams. Dreams were made into reality in large part because of seeds planted in a small retreat center called Highlander in the Tennessee mountains.

Over the years Kirkridge has played a major part in both the underground of American history and carving the future of movements. Weekends at Kirkridge have inspired many actions of civil disobedience related to anti-nuclear movement, the Viet Nam war, Latin America and LGBTQ civil rights. Since 1977, Kirkridge led the way in the church by providing hospitality to Gay and Lesbian Christians and their allies who gathered here annually for support and affirmation.

Daniel Berrigan, the only Catholic priest ever to be placed on the FBI's most wanted list for his actions against the Viet Nam war, was a regular at Kirkridge for decades and found one of his spiritual homes here. In his own words:

> ***Let us imagine a time when the whole world seemed to have gone mad, when there was heard throughout the land a huge slamming of doors like cannons going off.***
>
> ***Suppose, though, something else. In a distant place, quite off the beaten path, a few people went counter to the cultural ruck and wrath. They continued to welcome guests, kept them in***

heart, feeling, memory. Cherished them, beckoned them in, spread the board, cleared time and place for the widest (and wildest) variety of the human. No outsiders, no pariahs, no stigma- an utmost, unforced spirituality. A place shaped like a heart.

No supposition this. But plain, steady, consistent, surprising. And humming like a hive, secreting years of sweetness and lavishly giving it all away.

Kirkridge. Dear Friends, innkeepers of the open door, multitudes shall arise and call you blessed.

We are in such a time in our nation and in the world: a time when division in our communities and the language of "the other" is evident in our vocabulary. At Kirkridge we offer space for conversation and dialogue as we gather around common tables for breakfast, lunch, and dinner. There is no special room service for presenters. We gather together, sharing our common stories.

Together we become what Terry Tempest Williams describes as an "*ecotone,* ... the border area where town patches meet that have different ecological composition." She continues, *"Call it a mete of creativity where the great diversity of species meet."*

Not long ago I heard an older woman say, "This weekend has been so wonderful; I have never spoken with a convicted felon before, and this weekend I have heard his story, and now I understand the need for prison reform." Over meals and good food, her table became an *ecotone*.

We meet as companions on our common life passage at Kirkridge. People who might never find reasons to connect outside of Kirkridge find reasons to share their journeys here. We meet across class, economic barriers, cultures, and race. We meet across sexual orientation, faith beliefs, political ideologies, and generational understandings. Trust is formed and commonalities of the human experience are discovered.

Never doubt the power of a small group of committed citizens to change the world. Indeed it is the only thing that ever has.

--Margaret Meade

The Kirkridge Courage Fellows embody one of the recent incarnations of individuals who understand the DNA of Kirkridge. Each Fellow is an experienced facilitator of Courage & Renewal Work. They understand that Courage Work emerges from the same deep stream as Kirkridge. They value the need of balancing our inner need for quiet and reflection with our call to be involved working for a more just and kind

world. The Fellows understand that this is a "courageous" solitary journey that, paradoxically, must be done in the companionship of others. Over several years this group has developed a deep trust in one another. Exciting ventures and partnerships are emerging. Ideas are being birthed for the "common good" that are based not in competition, but rather on a trust and deep appreciation for the gifts each has to offer to the world. Trust, appreciation and inclusion are radical concepts in our world that, when honored, allow for deep creativity and innovation.

Kirkridge and other retreat centers like it are committed to returning "order to the soul." Together we drop pebbles into the ocean of our shared lives as humanity and proclaim that valuing the good of the common has a critical place in our survival. Together we learn to honor the unique contributions of each person and encourage gifts of creativity and imagination to be our companions into a new day. Trusting in the gifts of each season of life, relying on the universal message of abundance in nature and the healing power of ancient mountains, our souls find rest and restoration in the midst of chaos. Dreaming dreams of inclusion and justice that carry us to the edge of what has never been done before can be accomplished with the courageous companionship of others.

Other exciting conversations are emerging across the Kirkridge family. As we approach our 75th anniversary, there are conversations emerging about interfaith programs that expand our spiritual connections to the world, questions about inclusion for adults with autism and intellectual disabilities, wonderments of how to ethically live in this world with diminished resources. We are asking what does it mean to live "non-violently today" and how do we support one another creatively pushing the edge of innovation and new ideas to serve the common good.

This weekend at Kirkridge brought a program on Thomas Merton and Peacemaking. Merton's words hold a sacred thread that speaks to what I experience as the director of Kirkridge. It is here that I feel a hidden wholeness in my life, work and community. Here is where I experience the threads that weave in directions I never expected or imagined and yet, have always been in plain view, valuing "the commons." My experience is shared with many others through decades on this mountain. Who can truly explain "the hidden wholeness" of life? It is for each of us a gift, to be discovered, shared and honored for in the end, it is a mystery only to be experienced and never to be claimed.

My camper heart found its home at Kirkridge. I can breathe here. As my feet touch the forest floor in every season, I am aware of the deep lessons offered by the natural world. Walking well-worn paths in the woods, I am reminded daily that I walk on lands where many have walked before. Here I have been held through the blizzards and droughts of my life. Over the years on this land, my theology has become more gentle and inclusive, as I am able to hold paradox.

Living on this ancient mountain, I have experienced valuable lessons about our common humanity. As I learned many years ago in scouting, I know that it is dangerous to wander too far alone in life. Over years I have found trustworthy companions who care passionately about the common world in which we live. I have met women and men who honor their need to live in balance honoring both their souls and the call to offer their gifts to the world.

I come back to Menzie's words: "***The word common originally meant 'together-as one,' 'shared alike' and 'bound together by obligation.'*** " With the community formed around Kirkridge, I have been deeply blessed to gain insight on what it means to be part of "common." Over the years, here on these ancient rocks, my camper heart has learned it is safe to lean awhile, journey with others, share my soul, honor my heart, and work for the common good of our world.

Dr. Jean M. Richardson, is the director of Kirkridge Retreat Center. She lives with her partner Pat and together they have 4 grown children and 2 not-so-grown Labrador retrievers. They live in the Pocono Mountains of Pennsylvania at Kirkridge. Jean can be reached at jeanr@kirkridge.org or 610-588-1793.

Home is Here and Not Here

By Susan Nodurft

We shall not cease from exploration, and the end of all our exploring will be to arrive where we started and know the place for the first time.
~ T.S. Eliot ~

The summer morning air is slightly cool, typically still, and pleasantly breathable in southern Mississippi. That pleasantness begins to fade as the humidity rises with the sun. Although an early riser by nature, it is now, as it was as a child, also by choice. I rise early to greet that morning freshness with anticipation. The child rose anticipating a day companioned with dog and imagination exploring the wildness surrounding our small farm. Today, from the perspective of seventy-five years, I rise anticipating a quieter exploration. Still companioned with dog and wonder, I rise to watch the sun rise and begin its slow progression southward into the day.

Of course, as the poet T.S. Eliot says so well, our exploring never ends, but what he is saying is every true exploration brings about a new seeing as if for the first time. My experience as a Kirkridge Fellow was that kind of exploration, one that brought about a new seeing of self and possibilities for sustaining our lives as facilitators and bringing this work into the world.

This is that story.

It is being told through the voice of someone who has called Courage Work home for over fifteen years. Through those years, this blessed work has time and again opened new paths for "unceasing" exploration. In varied and often unexpected ways, each played a role in forming and transforming this explorer. However, none has been more significant than my experience as a Kirkridge Fellow. What I know now, unimagined at the trailhead, is the depth of realization and transformation possible when traveling over time within a community of deeply committed seekers in communion with Place.

In the pages that follow, I share with you some of the features of this Kirkridge Courage Fellowship Program (KCFP) with the hope that, even if you can't be a Fellow, you can take away some new possibilities for your own unceasing exploration. First some background...

Born free, as free as the wind blows
As free as the grass grows
Born free to follow your heart

-- "Born Free" lyrics by Don Black and John Barry

Born in Minnesota and transplanted in southern Mississippi in the 1940's, I have called that Place on the planet home for the majority of my seventy-five years. It is a place for which, in spite of its complicated and traumatic history, I have abiding affection. My dad, son of Swedish immigrants, was an agronomist by vocation. He inherited his ancestor's love of the land, and so, to my good fortune, did I. That love and growing up in the midst of wildness shaped my sense of the world. This world was experienced as whole, workable, and wise. Forever fascinating, it was a world in which exploration was irresistible. Wildness was home.

It takes courage to grow up and become who you really are.

~ e.e.cummings ~

As with every child, my early years were the beginning of my learning the steps of the culture's dance of division. It began in school, moving in slow motion toward adulthood, and dancing the jig. All part of the exploring, but then there is always that call, that "thread" as William Stafford describes it in *The Way It Is:*

There is a thread you follow. It goes among the things that change.
But it doesn't change.

It was following this thread, perhaps unconsciously, that I felt my way into Courage Work and found myself standing at the door of the Kirkridge Fellowship program. The invitation to the Kirkridge Courage Fellowship Program (KCFP) for facilitators, a series

of five retreats held over a span of two years, came framed within the context of the Mobius journey. This was to be an opportunity to live more deeply into the "knowing" that we do our best work as facilitators when we "facilitate who we are." In thinking into the work ahead, we were asked to develop a Plan for Still Learning (PSL), a field guide of sorts; outlining and shaping our hopes for personal development, gaining insights to be shared with the larger collaboration in sustaining this work, and importantly, how this experience might inform our personal commitment for "going public." The guide and these intentions were swirling in my head as I created a somewhat sketchy vision of what I hoped might evolve through the series.

Making its creation a bit more difficult, however, was the fact that since retiring from teaching, I had been living a life more in the rhythm of an almanac than a field guide. But as a biologist, I appreciated the value of a good field guide. What I know about such guides is they can be indispensable roadmaps to life and land. They are wonderful to use, but not easy to create. Undertaking such a task requires both passion and an intimate "knowing" of subject and territory – who or what is there (and what is not), relationships, details of distinction, habits, sounds, quirks and on and on. People I know who do this work often possess an innate sense of curiosity, wonder, and notice things – they pay attention. And (I might add) love their subject! Having tried my hand at a few of these, the jewel in the work was a closeness, a sense of kinship one begins to feel with the beings and place, far beyond name and form. Of course, I always hoped to end up with a usable guide, but that jewel was in the process, not the product. This surely would be the hallmark in creating my PSL.

Kirkridge is located on the Kittatinny Ridge of eastern Pennsylvania near the Delaware Water Gap and the Pocono Mountains. It was built in 1942, a vision of the late John Oliver Nelson who drew inspiration from the Iona Community off the coast of Scotland. It houses three main meeting facilities (lodging and dining): at the base is the original Farmhouse; ascending the mountain, Turning Point is midway; at the peak stands Nelson Lodge. Each has its own aura and personality, and during the series we had the opportunity to gather in, and come to love, each. However, Kirkridge as Place is much more - deeply embedded in Soil and Spirit.

In its rich and storied history, Kirkridge has often been described as one of those "thin places" on the planet particularly welcoming to soul. If you've visited this mountain Place, you have experienced the magic and mystery embodied in its ancient rocks and the sacredness of its Celtic roots. My history with Kirkridge, prior to the Fellowship series, was short. I had only stepped foot on its sacred soil a time or two prior to the series. However, I brought with me a "knowing of" going back to the 1960's. It was "The Place" I knew Daniel Berrigan, a Jesuit priest whose commitment to peace and justice I deeply admired, returned time and again to draw sustenance for his good work in the world. It was a place I was longing to know.

In preparing for the journey, my wish was to go light, paring things down to the essentials- curiosity, openness, and an intention to be awake. I hoped to hear what this mountain community might have to say about embracing more fully this stage of life. What were the guiding questions to be asked, to hold? The field guide had a title, but the pages were blank.

THE TRAILHEAD AND WALKING IN THE DARK

Inscribed on the trailhead marker was a quote by the American writer, Rebecca Solnit, *"Leave the door open for the unknown, the door into the dark. That's where the most important things come, where you yourself came from, and where you will go."* It was an invitation to get lost. This was reinforced by Joyce Rupp's advice in *Old Maps No Longer Work* to toss old maps away...be pilgrims, walk deeper into the dark of our night, wait for the stars and trust their guidance. So we began, waiting for the stars to appear – the questions. The questions appeared in that night sky – questions of home. *What exactly IS home as we commonly reference the destination in our work? Is wholeness home? If so, what does it feel like, look like? What will I know about this place "for the first time" when I arrive?* It was in Clearness Committees that the light began to shine from these stars.

If you come to a fork in the road, take it.

~ Yogi Berra ~

Being a family of facilitators, familiarity with the clearness process could be an advantage or disadvantage, but as Yogi's fork in the road, this path is *both/and*, not *either/or*. Admittedly, it can be a slippery slope if a committee of facilitators gets too "relaxed" with the guidelines. However, if members are vigilant in up-holding the boundaries, it offers a unique opportunity to listen more deeply and gain fresh insights into how the teaching of clearness might be done more effectively in retreat facilitation as well as gaining personal clarity.

And having a community of skilled facilitators also provided an opportunity to try different approaches to traditional practices and evaluate their effectiveness. An example in this series was the convening of Clearness Triads composed of the same three individuals, meeting each day of retreat (total of three). I found participating in this novel experiment of clearness work to be powerful and insightful. In the first committee, issue explanation and inquiry began to attune the "focus" person to listening, and each successive gathering picked up at a new depth that enabled the focus person to go ever deeper. It almost goes without saying, being relieved of "re-explaining the issue" in following committees was a distinct advantage in allowing more time for inquiry. Another significant feature was a format alternating Circle sessions with committee gatherings. Clearness deepened sessions, and sessions deepened clearness.

The result was a retreat space that held a hub of silence at its center.

I am reminded of Elie Wiesel's response to the question, "*Why do you pray?*" posed by his spiritual teacher, Moshe, during their concentration camp ordeal. His answer was simply, *"I don't know why."* Wiesel goes on to say, in his book *Night*, that after that day, Moshe explained to him with great insistence that every question possessed a power that did not lie in the answer. I found this patient, consistent, alternating processes of "question holding" created space for accessing that kind of power. There were questions I held through a single retreat and those held through the entire series. This experience gave me much to think about as I construct future retreats and approaches to teaching the process more effectively. As an example, I share a learning...

Having participated in many committees through the years, I noticed in myself as a focus person, and as a committee member, that if each question was *always* held in silence before a response was given, it was more likely the voice speaking would be that of the soul. In teaching clearness we emphasize the importance of holding spaces for silence in the circle, some even holding its place with an extra chair. However, more importantly, is the holding of each question in silence within. The mind, of course, is always first in line, eager to field the question and share its thinking (old and known), but we've covered that ground before. If we wait in the dark unknown allowing time for the question to drop into the heart, the wisdom voice of the shy soul may speak the new into our lives.

I share this example of sitting in committee as a focus person over eight years ago exploring the question of retiring. I received these questions: "If retirement was a door I was passing through, what does the door look like? And, if opened and stood in the foyer, what would I see?" Holding that question in silence and waiting resulted in an image of a very specific type of door, and upon opening, a scene that changed the trajectory of my life. I have revisited those questions many times, and they continue to "open doors" of possibility. All this is not to say that the mind has nothing to offer; there is value in its efforts, but clearness offers so much more – the opportunity to unleash that power Moshe speaks of, the power that lies beyond the answer if only we sit quietly under the tree.

Rumi the poet was a scholar also.
But Shams, his friend, was an angel.
By which I don't mean anything patient or sweet.
When I read how he took Rumi's books and threw them
into the duck pond,
I shouted for joy. Time to live now,
Shams meant.
I see him, turning away
casually toward the road, Rumi following, the books
floating and sinking among the screeching ducks,
oh, beautiful book-eating pond!

~ Mary Oliver, *The Return* ~

This is professional development of a different kind! It is the kind of development we engage in each and every time we participate in a Circle facilitated by a Courage colleague. We are always participant-observers, continually learning from one another. In such a gathering as the Kirkridge Fellows, in which gifted facilitators led our Circle, this was professional development at its best. Yet, there is more and speaks to the important role of retreat design in creating powerful spaces for accessing our deep inner resources.

One can hear Mary Oliver's delight in *The Return* (in her book *What Do We Know?)* at Shams' dramatic act of throwing poor Rumi's books in the duck-pond. I can only imagine how I would feel if Shams dispatched my books. Aghast comes close. But I, too, can delight in his wisdom and message, *Time to live now* – learning IS life, a live encounter. It can't be lived in the head. Shams, the mystic, understood there comes a time when the books must be put away and we walk into the dark, engaged and awake, watchful and reflective. In the design of this retreat series, there was a weaving of *head or book space* (thinking and imagination) with *live encounter* (interactive and experiential) with *reflection* (clearness committee) that powerfully invited the voice of soul.

As an illustration of this interactive design, I share a description from our first retreat, while holding the questions of "home":

- **The Head: A Book**
  I'm one of those fortunate beings who wholeheartedly embraces the notion emblazoned on the plaque sitting on my computer desk, "*Dogs are not our whole life, but they make our lives whole.*" So it is not surprising one of the provisions I carried for our first retreat was John Muir's small book, *Stickeen*. Stickeen was a scrawny, black, worthless-looking dog, as Muir described him, who was a stowaway of sorts on a trip he made in the 1880's to explore the glaciers of southeastern Alaska. Stickeen had been so named because of his enthusiastic adoption by the Stickeen Indians as a good luck totem. As Muir tells it, this little dog was destined to share (and survive) one of the most perilous nights of either of their lives. Their story was animating my imagination, as I sat in Circle contemplating my questions about home. Was my sense of "home" related to curiosity, living wholeheartedly this adventure of life? Was it about risk-taking or staying attuned to the world around me, responding without thought? Muir and Stickeen, as Shams would recognize, *lived now*. Not surprisingly, after spending a storm-battling night traversing crevasse-laden glaciers, there existed a bond between the two, not of words, but of knowing. From that time forward, Muir wrote, the little dog stayed close to his side and often would catch his eye, as if to say, "*Wasn't that an awful time we had together on the glacier?*" Their story stirred my imagination with thoughts of home – curiosity, being "at home" as they say, in their own skin, literally walking into the dark unknown, and bonds of connection. These impressions stayed with me in an experience the following day.

- **Live Encounter: An Experience**
  The next morning we meandered from the Farmhouse a short distance up the mountain to a small glass fusion art studio known as the TIP Glass Studio. TIP - *Together It's Possible* - is an initiative of the Kirkridge Retreat Center. It is composed of a group of families working toward new possibilities for cognitively-challenged young adults in the area. Along with educating parents and providing support for families, the group advocates for change in old thinking about people with intellectual disabilities. Day-to-day they provide opportunities for recreation, work experience, and social engagement. If the walls could speak in that small studio, they would say love happens here.

  Once settled in the studio, a relaxed excitement was in the air as we anticipated the invitation to create our own "glass fusion" art. In the center of the room were several large tables with small baskets containing various colored glass chips and rods. Next to two walls were displays of glass pendants and nightlights created by members of the TIP family. Each was beautiful, unique, inspiring, and a wonderful model as we envisioned our work. This placing of a hands-on experience (one of many in the retreats) created a new spaciousness in which the head lets go into the hands, a spaciousness welcoming to the voice of soul. Ever the participant-observer, we simply notice - what shape/s do the hands choose, the colors, the pattern being formed? I chose a dark green rectangular glass piece for the base of a pendant. Then – two thin red rods placed at angles on the corners much like furniture rounds off corners of a room. An orange rod down the center with two small beads, one red, one orange, placed in the center on either side of the orange rod like bright eyes looking out at me. In time with this tangible work of my hands, in my hands, I will explore questions of home: what the colors, the arrangement, the bright eyes may say? But for now, those meanings were to be held in the spacious gift of time.

- **Reflective Exploration: Clearness**
  In Clearness Triad, holding each thoughtful question from my committee partners in silence, I listened for clues of home. I began by following Muir and Stickeen who had a sense of the direction toward home. There were many more companions on this exploratory journey; adding to hints from the pendant's teachings were my childhood love of wildness, life experiences, and everything and everyone that was "my" world in the moment – my courage community, the mountain's dynamic wildness, the love and labor that is the life of TIP – nothing was excluded from the conversation. It was just the beginning of a journey, and it was, as the saying goes, going to be a trip.

And so it went, weaving of life and learning, giving and receiving within a rich community of gifted facilitators. The container of topics was varied and vast – social justice, understanding personality and shadow, music, shadows of money, poetry, bearing witness, wildness, and our proper Place within the family of things (to name a few). All unfolded as professional development of the transformative kind.

Wasn't that an awful time we had together on the glacier?

~John Muir's projection of Stickeen's thoughts ~

Deep and abiding friendships formed during our time together in retreat over the two years. Those relationships sustained us then and will certainly continue to sustain our lives and work well into the future. From this time forward, when we catch one another's eye, in the same wordless way of Stickeen, we will be saying, *"Wasn't that an incredible time we had together on the mountain at Kirkridge*?"

The bond will forever be. Anyone who has participated in Courage Work knows the gifts of "inner knowing" possible in a Circle of Trust. These gifts are available whether a single stand-alone retreat or a series. But beyond doubt, a series over time (usually a year or two) offers so much more. There is not only a greater opportunity to discover "true self," but to actually experience the power and possibilities of a **Community** of Trust. The greatest of my insights of "home" did not come from exploring questions, but from the *lived experience* of being a Fellow. It is the live encounter – the whole of it. This has much to say about how we might sustain this work.

When we try to pick out anything by itself, we find it hitched to everything else in the universe.

~ John Muir ~

If you sense this "hitching," then you too have felt the tugs and ripples in the vast network of universal connections. For most of us, it has been the tugs that changed us, sending ripples through our lives and beyond. The gathering of Kirkridge Fellows was a tug. For many, it was the first time since facilitator preparation there had been an opportunity to participate in a Courage series simply as participants (rather than facilitator-participants) and "do our work." As a facilitator working in a more remote part of country, the Fellowship was a gift I had long "longed for." As soon as the call went out, without hesitation, I answered. As it turns out, this longing was echoed throughout our gathered community. From retreat to retreat, as friendships and trust deepened, understanding of self and work became clearer. We came to understand what we had been missing – a sense of real connection to the courage community.

Marge Piercy in *The Seven of Pentacles* encourages us to "***Weave real connections, create real nodes, build real houses.***" Real connections come from real encounters in real time - a Place where transparency, vulnerability and realness can be practiced

– a house that trust builds. If we want to sustain this work, offering more retreat opportunities for facilitators to "live community together" is the greatest support we can provide. It is our foundation, joy and hope as we strive to bring this good work into the world.

At the 2015 Center for Courage & Renewal Global Gathering, I both experienced and observed the energy of the Fellows rippling through the larger collaboration. There was a more palpable sense of connection to the whole, more reaching out and more sharing of gifts. Enlivening the part had enlivened the whole. The tug had pulled us closer as Fellows while pulling us closer to the collaboration of facilitators and our common work. It was hitching made visible.

Reach out, keep reaching out, keep bringing in.
This is how we are going to live for a long time: not always,
for every gardener knows that after the digging, after the planting,
after the long season of tending and growth, the harvest comes.

~ Marge Piercy, *The Seven of Pentacles* ~

Stepping off the trail, I reflected on what had come from this exploration of "home" – this journey of reaching out, bringing in, planting and tending...

It may be my Scandinavian heritage and the farming blood running through my veins that I first staked my claim of home in soil and family. On *this* soil and to *these* people, I belonged. The roots ran deep. It was my Place of belonging in which I never felt "home alone." I was born connected to universal net (not to be confused with electronic). My solitary childhood wanderings were well populated by life around me and imaginings within; other was a paradox, both me and not me. Although my early years spent in wildness could best be described as parallel play, wildness held teaching of home. Seeds of a knowing were blowing through the needles of those long leaf pines - home is here, and not here.

Since then, I have called many places "home," but questions rooted in the pines lingered. Reflecting on my life, I realize I have been seeking the answer to this question, in one form or another, most of my life – in relationships and vocations of choice. It was in communion with the people, the mountain, and spirit of this thin place that I was prompted to ask this question again.

I love that John Muir and Stickeen were companions on this journey looking expectantly with me for what exploration might be waiting around the bend. I, too, wanted to live as they lived, one foot (or two) among the domesticated, and the other(s) in the wild.

The story's end is almost too simple... Perhaps the kind of simplicity Eliot must have

known when he wrote "*to arrive where we started and know the place for the first time.*" By tucking the question away in a backpack and living the adventure, home reveals itself everywhere... In the beauty of the mountain and the faces of the Fellows and Kirkridge family who welcomed us with a hospitality that said "we're glad you're here." From the rocks and the rooted to the walking and the winged, all said **home**. It's simply seeing with new eyes right where we're planted. Living among the wildness of Kirkridge was not unlike living among wildness on the childhood farm – same wind, same voice, same words, "home is here and not here."

Home is in the beauty of everywhere and we're it.

Home is where the heart is. The harvest had come.

Dr. Susan Nodurft is a retired biology teacher who has been a Courage & Renewal facilitator for over 15 years. She lives in rural southern Mississippi. In addition to her courage work, Susan is a Tai Chi practice leader. She can be contacted at snodurft@bellsouth.net

BOOK CLOSING

Arriving Where We Started

We shall not cease from exploration
and the end of all our exploring
will be to arrive where we started and know the place for the first time.

----- T. S. Eliot

Twenty-five years ago I was invited by a casual acquaintance to attend a women's book group. Not being generally attracted to such gatherings, I went with a touch of hesitation. I was a newcomer into a group that clearly had been meeting over an extended period of time. I felt out of place and awkward. The only thing that prepared me for the evening was that I had read the assigned book. As it turned out, the book never entered the conversation and I spent the evening feeling like an out-of-place eavesdropper. On the drive home I thought about the university professor I met named Sally. She was a quiet observer like me and I felt drawn to her. I wondered how I would approach or manage getting to know her. There seemed no point of intersection besides the book club, and the book club was not going to become part of my life.

I don't remember the timing, but I invited her to have lunch. Then she invited me to work with some teens in a leadership development program at the university. She invited me to a retreat with Parker J. Palmer. I invited her to serve as adjunct faculty on my doctoral committee. She invited me to serve as "scribe" for her two-year pilot program, *The Courage to Teach,* grounded in Parker's writing and funded by the Fetzer Institute. Today, many years later, our lives are deeply entwined in ways I would never have imagined. We accepted one another's invitations and the intersections began weaving themselves into a brilliant tapestry.

I approached the position of "scribe" as a job that would fulfill a graduate school requirement for an Internship, but from the moment I arrived at the first retreat for 24 public school educators, I knew I was in rare company. Sally filled our circle with artifacts, books, flowers, poetry and gently binding silence. When group members spoke I wrote as fast as possible to capture the essence of our time together. Poetry invited group members into conversation with themselves, and if they wished, into the

center of the circle. People were real. There were tears. There was no chit chatting. We were instructed not to "fix" one another, but rather to learn to listen deeply. I cried as I transcribed the notes I had scribbled after each three-day retreat because it wasn't until I was home that I really heard with the ear that is at the center of my h**ear**t what was being said.

Eight three-day retreats over a two-year period is a significant period of time to share with people who have been skillfully invited to go deeply inside of themselves and hear their inner teachers. Not to mention the fact that we met in places that were beautiful, places that invited us into nature. We laughed and cried together. We ate great food. We sang and danced and learned to see one another with soft eyes. We revealed ourselves to one another and to ourselves. We were carefully and capably held. Truly, it was a life-changing experience. One I never expected to experience—ever in my life.

One of the questions we were always holding for ourselves was how could we take these ways of being back out into the world which is typically not as safe a place to be real. As time progressed each of us felt ourselves becoming stronger in our convictions to live with integrity, and the question began to lose its urgency. At the end of two years I know I was profoundly and forever changed by the experience. And since our original group convened last spring for a 20-year reunion, I think it is safe to say that we were all deeply moved by our time and experience together. We stepped back into our circle as if twenty years had not passed.

Because I was so moved by my experience in that two-year Courage to Teach retreat series, I applied and was accepted into the first cohort of facilitators being prepared to take Courage Work further out into the world. The Center for Courage & Renewal's first cohort of facilitators in 1998 was also generously funded by The Fetzer Institute.

I arrived at facilitator preparation with three specific questions that seemed to me to be crucial to the successful implementation of future programs. I knew that Fetzer was not going to be funding this Work in the future (they often planted and nurtured seeds for new work in the world), so I had questions about how to raise funds, and how the Center would be involved with supporting facilitators in those efforts. My questions were not answered in the way I hoped, and I left facilitator preparation without a strong concept for how to fund future programs. Between 1999 and 2014 I facilitated very

little, but I regularly attended Circles of Trust to keep myself close to the work that meant so much to me. As the Center grew and evolved, and the number of facilitators grew worldwide, and the format for retreats branched into many other forms, funding remained a daunting question for me. I began asking other facilitators about their experience and learned that lack of funding was an impediment.

When Sally conceived of a Fellowship for facilitators, I raced toward the opportunity to work with and surround myself with other facilitators. The invitation to take my inner work deeper spurred me to stop asking questions about fundraising and to come up with some answers. I researched and wrote a fundraising guide expressly for Courage & Renewal facilitators called *Navigating the Mobius Strip of Money* in order to empower them and myself. When I tested my ideas within the Fellowship, people told me their perceptions shifted. Fellows told me they think and act differently about money issues and cultivating support for their work.

My experience of being in a second two-year retreat series, this time with other CCR facilitators, has been a second life-changing experience I never expected. Ending the isolation I felt for most of my time as a facilitator has had a catalytic effect. It took some time and a fair portion of patience, but my questions have found answers. I have arrived where I started, and I have been transformed in the process.

This book tells part of each participant's story: how the invitation to "take our work deeper" has translated through each of us. But this book does not tell the story of how this invitational Fellowship has invigorated and catalyzed each of us as facilitators. Multiple new retreats and series have grown out of this Fellowship, this amazing thin place that is both the Place that is Kirkridge and the power that is community. People who have never worked together before are combining their skills and interests. We have intuitively developed a self-regulatory system that improves who we are individually and how we work collectively.

I echo Sally's hope from the Book Opening: We hope you'll find some of your own story in our stories, that you will find portals to your own thin places.

Megan LeBoutillier
February, 2017

AFTER WORDS of INVITATION and APPRECIATION

As we come to the end of gathering the stories for this book, we are overflowing with gratitude for the Kirkridge Courage Fellows for daring to go where no woman or man has gone before – and for taking us with you. That includes each writer in the book – AND Donna Bivens and Kathy Gille and Dan Hines and Fred Monteith.

And we have gratitude for you, dear Reader, and some invitations... We would welcome you into an email exchange or a phone conversation – AND into a retreat. We are creating Circles of Trust going deeper in thin places and in the ideas we've shared in our book, hoping you might find them portals to your own thin place. Come walk with us at this very special thin place that is Kirkridge Retreat and Study Center. Join us for a Circle of Trust – and/or invite us to your neck of the woods. You have our contact information at the end of each story –or you can go to the Kirkridge webpage or www.stilllearning.org.

To Kirkridge, we share our gratitude for your radical hospitality – and your stewardship of this thin place that made it all possible. Janet and Rob and Stacey and Gail and Jean and Pat and Peter and Alek. TIP and Judy and Jeff and the Glass Studio. Happy 75th Anniversary. (Reader, go visit them at www.kirkridge.org)

We thank Sara Sanders and Joe Sullivan and John Fenner and Terry Chadsey and Fisher! and Tantawan and Denise and the faces in the trees, for your willingness to be our Third Things and to enrich our experience. Jonetta Moyo, your beautiful handcrafted journals and your loving care have been an integral part of this journey. Reader, meet Jonetta at http://myinspirationstudio.com/

We have deep appreciation for the many poets and authors and seekers we have quoted in our stories and who have enhanced our journey. (We intentionally made the decision to forego footnotes and bibliographies and to gently embed their names and the sources within our stories. Knowing how deformed we have been by academic writing—and realizing that today's technology has changed our understanding of access to information, we debated whether to use APA or MLA style or some other – and decided instead to create our own! Each writer has shared her or his email or

website in the hope that you will reach out with any questions or comments.)

Words feel inadequate to thank Jim (Sally's husband and forever-love) and Bruce (Megan's husband and traveling partner on this journey of Life) for always being there, for support and encouragement and design skills and honest words and, most of all, for love.

And we thank each other... For saying yes... For always trusting that together, we could be more than either of us could be alone.

With love and courage,
Sally and Megan

THE NAMING OF THINGS
BECAUSE WORDS MATTER

glos·sa·ry: a collection of textual glosses or of specialized terms with their meanings (**gloss:** a surface luster or brightness: shine)

---Merriam-Webster Dictionary, 2014

Naming things is a political act, an act of power. So we are naming the things that are important to us – and sharing with you, our Reader, what we mean with the words we use. Words matter, and we want to be inclusive in our language.

We refuse to give up words that are important to us because Others demean them or misuse them or label them as jargon. Instead we are claiming them here. As you read the stories in our book, we hope you'll visit this glossary again and again; bathe in our names for things, delighting with us in knowing what we mean, and seeing the gloss of our words, the shine, the luster.

Birthright Gifts:
We come into this world as unique individuals, each with our own **birthright gifts**. They are hard for us to see, because they have always been there. Often if something comes easily for us, such as the gift to see with an artist's eye or the gift to remember poetry or the gift to see how to arrange a room with beauty, we devalue it. **Birthright gifts** are evident from the moment of birth; we only have to pay attention to an infant to understand that. Babies do not show up as raw material to be shaped by their environment and culture; they come fully formed, with the seed of true self. Yes, we are born with identity and integrity, and even as young children, we know what we like and dislike, what we are drawn towards and what we feel resistance to, what makes us feel alive and what drains our energy. But over the next decade or two, as we move through adolescence and schooling, we too often become **deformed**. We spend the first half of our lives abandoning our **birthright gifts**, Parker Palmer writes in *Let Your Life Speak*, or letting others disabuse us of them. The purpose of education, at its best, is to create the space for each of us to recognize and deepen our unique **birthright gifts**, to honor them and learn to use them in fulfilling our life's purpose.

Boundary Markers, Touchstones:
These are the covenants by which members of a Circle of Trust agree to accept shared responsibility for holding safe and trustworthy space. The Stepping Stone in Section 1 gives the version of the Boundary Markers used by the Kirkridge Courage Fellows. Another version may be found at http://www.couragerenewal.org/touchstones.

Chronos:
Ancient Greek word describing the marking of days and hours. See *Kairos.*

Circle of Trust®, circle of trust: The **Circle of Trust®** (capital C, capital T)is a registered trademark of the Center for Courage & Renewal, and the programs can only be offered by facilitators prepared by the Center. For a bit more of an explanation, see Parker's insight in Section 3, or go to the Center's webpage (www.couragerenewal.org). Perhaps even more important, a **circle of trust** (lower case c and t) could be two people or ten or twenty, who create a safe space for the soul to show up. Although you will find other meanings for a **circle of trust** if you search the Web, the best place to understand the phrase as it we use in this book is in Parker's writing, especially *A Hidden Wholeness.*

Clearness Committee, Clearness Triads:
The **Clearness Committee** has been adapted for the Circle of Trust program from the Quaker tradition. It is a focused microcosm of a larger circle of trust, a safe and trustworthy space, where we have an intense experience of gathering in support of someone's inner journey. In the Kirkridge Courage Fellowship, we often used an adaptation we called Clearness Triads. For a bit more of an explanation, see the Stepping Stone in Section 2.

Confidentiality, Deep or Double Confidentiality:

Most of us know the concept of confidentiality, of not sharing anything that is said in a particular setting with anyone outside of those present. **Deep or double confidentiality** is used in the context of the Clearness Committee/Clearness Triads, meaning that committee members would not only never speak to each other or anyone else about the issue when the Committee ended, but they also would not speak with the focus person about the problem unless she or he requested the conversation.

Courage:
From the Latin, *cor,* heart. Courage does not mean that we have no fear, but that we don't act out of that fear. See **heart**.

Courage Work, Courage and Renewal:
An affectionate way of talking about the various forms of Courage to Teach, Courage to Lead, Circles of Trust, and other work, grounded in the writing of Parker J. Palmer, offered by facilitators prepared by the Center for Courage & Renewal.

Hearing into Speech:
This wonderful way to describe a sacred deep listening that honors silence is credited to theologian Nelle Morton from her experiences in the early 1970's. She writes in *The Journey Is Home*, "If one can be heard to one's own speech, then the speech would be a new speech and the new speech would be a new experience in the life of the speaker – that is, the one heard to speech." She describes this kind of deep listening

as "a depth hearing that takes place before speaking – a hearing that is more than acute listening. A hearing that is a direct transitive verb that evokes speech – new speech that has never been spoken before."

Heart:
The heart is important in our Courage Work, as it is literally where courage begins. The word courage comes from the Latin word for heart, ***cor***. So we are reclaiming the word **heart** from its too-often sentimental use in our culture, to "the core of the self," as Parker writes in *Healing the Heart of Democracy*, " that center place where all our ways.,, of knowing converge – intellectual, emotional, sensory, intuitive, imaginative, experiential, relational, and bodily, among others. The heart is where we integrate what we know in our minds with what we know in our bones, the place where our knowledge can become more fully human."

Hidden Wholeness:
"*There is in all things...a hidden wholeness. This mysterious Unity, and Integrity, is Wisdom, the Mother of all,"* writes Thomas Merton in Hagia Sophia. *"This is at once my own being, my own nature, and the Gift of my Creator's Thought and Art within me, speaking as my sister Wisdom. I am awakened at the voice of my Sister."* Courage Work invites individuals who want to live an undivided life into a Circle of Trust, creating a safe space for the soul to show up, to make that hidden wholeness a bit more visible, to awaken to that inner voice.

Identity and Integrity:
These two words are at the root of Courage Work, as we talk about creating space where participants can name and claim and nurture their identity and integrity. We share here Parker's beautiful explanation in *The Courage to Teach*: " By ***identity*** *I* mean an evolving nexus where all the forces that constitute my life converge in the mystery of self: my genetic makeup, the nature of the man and woman who gave me life, the culture in which I was raised, people who have sustained me and people who have done me harm, the good and ill I have done to others, and to myself, the experience of love and suffering—and much, much more. In the midst of that complex field, **identity** is a moving intersection of the inner and outer forces that make me who I am, converging in the irreducible mystery of being human. By ***integrity*** I mean whatever wholeness I am able to find within that nexus as its vectors form and re-form the pattern of my life. **Integrity** requires that I discern what is integral to my selfhood, what fits and what does not—and that I choose life-giving ways of relating to the forces that converge within me: do I welcome them or fear them, embrace them or reject them, move with them or against them? By choosing **integrity**, I become more whole, but wholeness does not mean perfection. It means becoming more real by acknowledging the whole of who I am."

Inner Teacher:
The voice of the authentic Self in each of us. Thomas Merton calls it Wisdom (see Hidden Wholeness above). Sandie Merriam also goes into more detail in her story in Section 1.

Kairos, Kairos Moment:
An ancient Greek word meaning the right or opportune moment. The ancient Greeks had two words for time: *chronos* and *kairos*. *Chronos* refers to chronological or sequential time; *kairos* signifies a period or a season, that particular moment in time in which an event of significance happens.

Listening, Deep Listening:
The theologian Paul Tillich said the first duty of love is to listen. A kindergartener named Alec carefully explained to me that the words **listen** and **silent** have the same letters – just in a different order – and you can't do one without the other. Both listening and silence are essential elements of a Circle of Trust, and that is where deep listening comes in. Deep listening requires the listener to be fully present, with no necessity to respond or to fix. The purpose is to create the space for the speaker to hear his or her own inner truth. Deep listening may include open, honest questions, which are explained below. A result of deep listening is often feeling heard into speech, as explained above.

Mobius, Mobius Strip, Mobius journey:
The dictionary tells us that the Mobius strip, named for the German mathematician A. F. Mobius, is a one-sided surface made by joining the ends of a rectangle after twisting one end through 180 degrees. Parker Palmer talks about the stages of growing into who we are, of developing our birthright gifts, as growing towards "life on the Mobius strip," a seamless flow of our inner life and our outer world. We often talk about our journey to the undivided life as a Mobius journey, a kind-of thin place where inner and outer feel seamless.

Movement Model:
See the Insight from Parker Palmer in Section 1 on the Movement Way.

Paradox:
The ability to understand paradox, to hold two seemingly opposite truths, to embrace both/and rather than either/or, is another important element of the journey toward the undivided life. As the scientist Niels Bohr said, "The opposite of a correct statement is a false statement. But the opposite of a profound truth may well be another profound truth."

Questions; Open, Honest Questions:

We have found that questions offer us a much more fertile ground for this journey to living undivided than do answers. The words that Rainer Maria Rilke wrote to a young poet in 1903 still serve as important touchstones for us: "...have patience with everything unresolved in your heart and try to love the questions themselves as if they were locked rooms or books written in a very foreign language. Don't search for the answers, which could not be given to you now because you would not be able to live them. And, the point is to live everything. Live the questions now. Perhaps then, someday far in the future, you will gradually, without even noticing it, live your way into the answer." Honest, open questions have become a practice in our Circles of Trust, one that we learned in the Clearness Committee. Parker defines and teaches the asking of honest, open questions in *A Hidden Wholeness*. He writes that an honest question is one to which the asker cannot possibly know the answer. An open question is one that expands rather than restricts your area of exploration, one that does not push or even nudge towards a particular way of seeing or responding.

Soft Eyes:

The idea of soft eyes often feels countercultural in a world that emphasizes sharp focus. In our Circles of Trust, we have come to understand that soft eyes are another important practice in the journey toward the undivided life. We encourage participants to see not only each other with soft eyes, but especially, to see themselves that way.
Sally often explains soft eyes by sharing a story from her Kellogg fellowship in Bali: "When I asked the Balinese elder who was my mentor while I was there to help me understand the Balinese childrearing practices that result in gentle, compassionate young people, she explained to me that they saw their children with soft eyes. The Balinese consider their children holy. The younger a person is, the closer her soul to heaven and the purer her spirit. Babies have just come from God, so they are not permitted to touch the impure earth before their first birthday and are carried everywhere. Balinese children are never left alone, nor are they ever physically punished, and rarely are they upset. So, this wise woman told me, we see them with soft eyes, like you would see someone you love... It's not that you don't see the imperfections; you just don't see their sharp edges."

Soul:

"Nobody knows what the soul is," says poet Mary Oliver in her poem *Maybe*: "it comes and goes/ like the wind over the water." The soul has many names (Thomas Merton calls it true self; the Buddhists, original nature; Quakers, the inner light; Hasidic Jews, the spark of the divine; humanist, identity and integrity)– and Parker writes in *A Hidden Wholeness* that it doesn't matter *what* we name it, but *that* we name it matters a great

deal. We have come to know in our Circles of Trust that the soul is shy, making the creation of safe space very important if we are going to have a chance to hear that inner voice.

Thin Places:
Thin places are the way we are naming the space where we have the best chance of nurturing the courage to seek the undivided life we want to live. In a thin place, we see our connectedness to everything around us. For a bit more, see the Book Opening on Page 1.

Third Things:
Another important practice in our Circles of Trust is the use of third things so that we don't scare that shy soul away by approaching it too directly. To achieve that indirectionality we approach topics and themes in our Circles metaphorically, by using a poem or music or art or quote or object that embodies it. Parker names these embodiments as third things – and again, we send you to A *Hidden Wholeness*, if you want more details!

Touchstones:
See boundary markers. Also see Caryl Creswell's story in Section 3 and the Stepping

Stone in that Section.

Tragic Gap:
Parker writes in *A Hidden Wholeness* that "violence of every shape and form has its roots in the divided life." He offers the insight that the heart of nonviolence requires that we acknowledge that we live in a tragic gap – a gap between the way things are and the way we know they might be. In our Circles of Trust, as we learn to embrace paradox, we also learn the practices that allow us to stand faithfully in that tragic gap, holding the tension between reality and possibility.

Ubuntu:
This Nguni Bantu word literally means human-ness and is often translated as "humanity towards others." Since Nelson Mandela's presidency in South Africa, the term has spread from that region to other places, often through the writing of Desmond Tutu, who uses it to express the philosophical belief that we are all connected. In our Circles of Trust, as we come to understand the paradox that the inner journey can only be undertaken by an individual, and yet it is too hard to take alone, Tutu's writing on Ubuntu helps us find language for this seemingly countercultural concept, another way to name the idea of solitude in community.

CPSIA information can be obtained
at www.ICGtesting.com
Printed in the USA
FFHW021646270519
52593778-58061FF

9 780989 504263

Acknowledgments

Our thanks to:

Catherine Atkinson - p.50–51, 64–65, 120–121, 186–187, 188–189, 190–191, 194–195, 198–199, 202–203, 284–285

Pippa Cuthbert and Lindsay Cameron Wilson - p. 32–33, 34–35, 36–37, 40–41, 42–43, 44–45, 46–47, 48–49, 52–53, 54–55, 56–57, 58–59, 60–61, 66–67, 68–69, 72–73, 78–79, 80–81, 82–83, 246–247, 248–249, 250–251, 254–255, 256–257, 258–259, 260–261, 262–263, 266–267, 268–269, 270–271, 272–273, 274–275, 276–277, 278–279, 280–281, 282–283, 286–287, 288–289, 290–291, 292–293, 294–295, 296–297, 298–299

Kathryn Hawkins - p.62–3, 74–75, 76–77, 92–93, 94–95, 98–99, 100–101, 102–103, 104–105, 106–107, 118–119, 124–125, 162–163, 164–165, 166–167, 168–169, 170–171, 176–177, 180–181, 184–185, 192–193, 200–201, 206–207, 220–221, 222–223, 224–225, 226–227, 228–229, 230–231, 232–233, 234–235, 236–237, 238–239, 240–241, 242–243, 252–253

Sue McMahon - 122–123, 126–127, 128–129, 130–131, 132–133, 134–135, 136–137, 138–139, 140–141, 142–143, 144–145, 146–147, 148–149, 150–151, 152–153

Carol Pastor - p.84–85, 86–87, 114–115, 116–117, 118–119, 120–121, 122–123, 154–155, 156–157, 158–159, 174–175, 178–179, 216–217

Joy Skipper - p.182–183, 204–205, 208–209, 210–211, 212–213

Alessandra Zecchini - p.38–39, 70–71, 96–97, 172–173, 196–197, 214–215, 264–265

Preface

This book originated from the request of a friend for advice on starting a business. Observing that he was a bright and educated individual, I sent him to the bookstore to buy a "how to start a business" book. When I reviewed the material with my friend, I could see two things were needed: (1) information that applied specifically to Hawaii and (2) actual cost references.

I have attempted to supplement other books on starting a small business by including costs and subjects of special interest applicable to Hawaii. This book is directed to people like my friend who have no business background but plenty of intelligence and hope, as well as to those who have already tested their business knowledge.

Because there is no single way to succeed in business, I have included actual quotes presenting, at times, varying opinions. Readers should be prepared to form their own opinions. That is the purpose of this book—to help you develop your own business attitude.

One word of caution. This book was updated in 1995 and reflects cost estimates and laws in that year. Readers should modify their estimates accordingly.

My gratitude to my wife Jill whose suggestions and encouragement added balance and perspective, to Norma Gorst whose copy editing gave my material readable structure, to Doug Chun for his excellent graphics, and to the Production Department staff of the University of Hawaii Press for their patience, helpfulness, and expertise. My special thank you to Jim Proctor of The Chamber of Commerce of Hawaii for his support. Finally I wish to thank all those people who gave willingly of their time for interviews and discussions so that others might have a better opportunity.

Introduction

Starting and operating a business is like preparing for and taking a hike into Haleakala Crater. My personal experience on such a hike might provide insight into what it is like to start your own business.

Standing at the trailhead in the cold at 10,000 feet on Haleakala, I hoped I had made the right choices among all the information I had gathered over many months. Advice from other hikers who had been to Haleakala was especially vivid.

> **Hiker:** It is cold in there; it may dip to 40 degrees at night. Take warm clothing.
>
> **Hiker:** Check to see if the water level is satisfactory by calling the park headquarters before you go. You may have to take your water in.

I was glad I knew some experienced hikers who had tried to prepare me for the trip. On the one hand I felt uneasy that what I had in my backpack was all I had to sustain me for the next couple of days. On the other hand, I was excited about this new experience and my sense of adventure and accomplishment overcame most of my immediate anxiety.

Something new and exciting can make us temporarily suspend our objectivity. A sense of euphoria hung over the entire hiking group during the planning process; nothing appeared difficult.

Unfortunately, only one hour into the hike we experienced our first major problem. Another hiker's boots came apart going over a rocky ledge. I panicked—the hike was over before it had even begun! Should we hike back to the trailhead and drive to Wailuku for a new pair of boots? Fortunately, the hiker had some running shoes and could complete the hike. At that point, I realized that no matter how well we had planned the hike, we could not have foreseen the broken boots—we had to be flexible to solve these unexpected problems.

Confronting unexpected problems can be made easier if you develop a mental toughness similar to that which I noticed developing in some of the other hikers. These hikers seemed to handle the same problems with quiet determination and a certain "grittiness" which one might find in more experienced hikers.

When we finally reached the compound at Holua at the bottom of Haleakala Crater, I was surprised at how tired I was. The hike was much harder than I ever thought it would be. Everything took much longer than I expected; problems and surprises abounded. It was a thrilling but humbling experience.

Your business venture, like my hike, will be thrilling and humbling. While words cannot replace experience, I hope this book may help you develop a winning business attitude and a realistic perspective which will smooth the trail as you begin your business journey.

PART I

Developing a Winning Business Attitude

1

What Does It Take?

As we talked across the coffee table, you could see the excitement in Jay's motions. He shuffled a stack of booklets and different colored papers. Jay had come for some business advice. His business was to be a new venture —wholesaling a new type of biodegradable industrial cleaner.

Jay was a college-educated 26-year-old with no previous business experience or background in industrial cleaners. He had worked in Hawaii for four years as a flight attendant with a major airline. Jay had heard about this business opportunity through a friend and, very taken with the idea, had visited the manufacturers on the mainland.

As soon as Jay was able to get the colored papers in presentation order, he asked a flurry of questions. "How much money do you think I will need?" "How big a warehouse should I get?" "Should I hire employees right away?"

Jay is typical of most people who start in business. He is bright, enthusiastic, hard working, and ambitious, and, like them, he is also filled with untested optimism. Jay has many qualities that can help him succeed in this venture but he lacks a major one—business experience. Unfortunately, there is only one way to get business experience, and that is by owning your own business or by operating one for someone else.

In lieu of acquired business experience, however, a prospective businessowner can still solve business problems as an experienced person would by approaching situations with a business attitude. That is, people with no business experience can review a situation in a businesslike way if they know how an experienced businessperson might handle the same situation. This book will provide inexperienced business people with the framework to develop a proper business attitude.

We can see that Jay has two major goals:

1. to learn about industrial cleaners (the industry, the competition, the market, etc.)—a product aptitude; and
2. to learn how to turn that product and service into a business—a business attitude.

If we were to relate Jay's status to the hiking experience in the introduction, we might say that Jay is in the initial planning stage of the hike. At this point in the hike too much enthusiasm impaired our objectivity to assess all the potential obstacles, and everyone was too optimistic. Consequently, it is not surprising to hear Jay's description of the venture in superlatives. According to Jay, not only is it a gold mine, it is also going to be easy (a great new product and the competition is nonexistent). Jay's language reveals his lack of a business attitude. He has few concrete pieces of information, and his presentation is based solely on the merits of the product with no attention given to potential problems and how he plans to address them.

Unfortunately, Jay had already placed some money to secure a franchise. Emotionally, he was beyond return. Jay relied only on sales materials from the manufacturer, and, without any other knowledge about the industry, the competition, how he might sell the product, or cost estimates, he had already started hiking down the trail.

Jay did not make it in his new venture and is again a flight attendant. The business world welcomes the fit and is unmercifully brutal to the unfit. Like a majority of new businesses, Jay's failed in the first year (seven out of ten new businesses fail within the first three years according to current estimates by the Small Business Administration). Jay survived the experience, although a bit battered and much more humble. It was small consolation that along the way he acquired a business attitude.

Your Journey Begins

Fran Tarkenton, a star professional football player was asked in an interview what it takes to succeed in the National Football League. His reply echoes the reply given by many people who have been in business when asked what it takes to succeed: It is not the most talented who succeed, but the most persistent.

Statistics indicate that going into business is not easy and not everyone is suited for it. It takes a special kind of person to give up the luxury of a paycheck every month, who is willing to mortgage everything to work 11 hours a day 7 days a week at half pay and then to say he wouldn't have it any other way.

Print-shop owner: I think everyone thinks you have to be smart to start a business. I think you have to be tough and a bit insane.

What is it that sends thousands of people each year to start their own businesses?

New businessowner: For me, it was knowing that it was something I always wanted to do. Being my own boss and being able to set my own direction is important to me.

Graphic artist just starting out: I wasn't going to make money working for someone else.

These answers are common reasons people have for going into business. The reality seen by some established business people, however, is different from the visions of these new entrepreneurs, just as the untested views of the hikers differed from their actual experience.

Electronics wholesaler: It is nice to be your own boss, but I have spent more time at this business than I ever anticipated and I don't consider myself a workaholic. It's just that there is always so much to do. You never get completely away from it even when you are on vacation. In that way, you are more a prisoner of the business than its master.

Retailer: I always laugh when someone tells me since I have my own business I have it made. The businessowner is the hardest working and least understood worker. We are also the lowest paid. I make less per hour than my employees. In fact, sometimes I think that I work for my employees. In the first year of operation, it was a luxury for me to get paid. Even now I am the last person to get paid and that is after everything else like rent, insurance, phone.

A fabric manufacturer: A new business is like a baby; you have to keep feeding it for a long time. That means you can't take any money out. I don't think a new businessowner should be able to draw a salary for the first year. This is particularly tough to explain to other family members who just see the business sales. They think, making sales—great. So why can't you take some money out?

These revelations show a difference in perspective between the prospective businessowners and the current businessowners. Could it be that the current businessowners have a more realistic business attitude?

Do You Have What It Takes?

A consultant from an accounting firm: The initials W.I.T. stand for the formula that makes a winning entrepreneur. A good entrepreneur or businessperson does WHATEVER IT TAKES to get the job done.

Do you have that same grittiness we saw in some hikers, that dogged persistence?

Retailer: Yes, doing whatever it takes to keep the business going is a good way to put it. I never realized how resourceful I was until I started my own business. You have to learn fast and be willing to take the risks. That is what the average employee never experiences—taking the risk. One day I was a manager running a department in a company and the next day I was a businessowner. I did not realize that these were two different worlds.

Food manufacturer: The best advice I can give someone starting out in business is to make their mistakes on someone else's time. By that I mean, if you want to open an ice-cream shop, go and work for a year in an ice-cream shop. After a year you will have learned industry policies, shipping procedures, cash handling, and purchasing.

Assuming that you have the grittiness and some background in the industry in which you hope to start your new venture, are you willing to take all the risks? Although most people are willing to assume some risk, the extent and depth of the risk is what separates the hikers from tour bus riders. Are you willing to assume the financial and emotional risks of a businessowner? Here are some questions to ask yourself.

Financial Risks

Will I be willing to invest my life savings or mortgage my house? If I fail am I willing to lose it all?

Am I willing to assume personal liabilities on behalf of the business that will follow me if the business fails?

Am I willing to make some drastic changes to my life-style which will include limited income for a couple of years?

Personal Risks

Physically, am I going to be able to handle the long hours of work? Emotionally, can I handle the stress? How will my family handle these problems?

How will I be able to handle the separation from my family that the long hours with the business will require?

If I fail can I still retain my self-esteem?

The prospective businessowner is willing to answer yes to all these questions and mean it.

Assuming risk does not mean throwing all caution to the winds, however. In fact, the benefit of experience is to allow the entrepreneur to minimize risks from the very beginning.

Talk to someone with some business experience. You will find that they know they have to assume some risk, but they know the difference between good risk and bad risk and just how much of each they can live with. Just as an experienced hiker will know when to discontinue a hike, professionals will understand the probability of success or failure in exact relationship to their risk exposure and potential return.

Retailer: When we first started this clothing business, we had no business experience and didn't know what to look for. We did, however, try to isolate the risks involved and talked to a lot of people in this type of business who were not our competitors. Everyone was very helpful especially in pointing out how much we could lose. That was a good viewpoint because all we were looking at was how much we were going to make.

Print-shop owner: We have just pulled out of a deal that I have been working on for over a year. The other party was just not living up to some of my expectations and I had a gut feeling that, as much as I wanted it, I had better pull out.

Owning your own business will bring out qualities you never knew you possessed. It's that survival instinct. Don't sell yourself short. You will find that shortcomings in one area can be outweighed by talents in another. It will be important, for example, to know when to seek help. Above all, the grittiness and persistence required of business hopefuls will soon develop as business pressures mount.

One of the first things you will need to learn is how to make realistic assumptions when starting a business. Chapters 2 and 3 give guidelines for making sales and cost estimates.

Additional Reading

Hawaii Dept. of Business and Economic Development. 1988. *Starting a Business in Hawaii.* Rev. ed. Honolulu: DBED.

Hawken, Paul. 1987. *Growing a Business.* NY, NY: Simon and Schuster.

Prescott, Eileen. 1987. "What It Takes to Be an Entrepreneur." *Working Woman* (August): 34.

Tanouye, Elyse. "Taking the Plunge." *Hawaii Business* 32 (3): 17–20.

2

The Sales Estimate: You Need a Crystal Ball

Jay, whom we met in chapter 1, started his wholesale industrial cleaner company without the benefit of a market plan. His mistaken optimism was the result of inaccurate sales projections. Since the lifeblood of a business is its sales income, the first step in any business venture is to estimate how much the business plans to sell. That sales estimate will determine the size of the operation, the number of people needed, and the amount of money required.

> **Potential shoe store businessowner:** I have no idea how much we will sell. But we have picked out the styles of shoes we will sell and the best location.

To relate the importance of sales revenue to a business, consider the sales revenues a business receives as equivalent to your monthly paycheck. Just as you will use the income you receive to pay your living expenses, a business will use the income received from its sales revenue to pay its operating expenses. The major difference between your paycheck and the sales revenue of a business, however, is that, unlike your paycheck, you do not know with any certainty what your sales may be each month. Because no one can guarantee how many people will purchase your product or service each month, the best one can do is estimate future sales. This estimating process is especially difficult for a new business venture with no past record.

For a proposed business venture, a common method of estimating sales revenue is to multiply the proposed selling prices of the products or services by the number of units you plan to sell each month. Using this method, a hairstylist might estimate monthly sales as

Number of customers per month × Average price of a haircut.

A swimsuit retailer might use the same process:

Number of swimsuits sold per month	×	Average price of the swimsuit.

It is easy to see how the scope of two hairstyling businesses would be vastly different if one estimated 160 customers per month at $12 each and the other estimated 3,000 customers per month at $45 each. Based on these estimates, we would expect differences in the amount of money needed to start each business, in the number of employees needed, and in the marketing of each business. All of these major decisions are based on the sales estimate. Yet many businesses will use only a hastily prepared sales estimate for making these other decisions.

Obtaining Early Sales Is Difficult

Our Haleakala hikers taught us that hikes are much more difficult than first imagined. Although you may think otherwise, the world is not going to beat a path to your door for your product or service just because you start a business. The grim reality is that all too often sales are not as high as you estimated.

Attorney: One of the biggest fallacies people believe is that just because you have a product that is cheaper or better it is going to sell—that is bunk!

Ice-cream shop owner: I have learned that it is not enough just to have the best product.

The reality of the market is that it is extremely difficult to get customers to see the value of your business or service. The problems encountered by Chester Carlson serve as an illustration. Carlson felt that his invention was going to revolutionize business. Although he was an attorney, he so believed in his product that he quit his practice to devote full effort to his project. With technical help he completed the design and took it to all the major companies. They all turned him down. For ten years, Carlson persisted and finally convinced a company, Haloid, that he had a useful product. The machine that Carlson developed was the dry paper copier. The Haloid Company is now known as the Xerox Corporation.

Businessowner: I have been in on the start-up of several businesses. My experience is that it takes a couple of years for a business to establish itself in the marketplace. Most novices expect that to happen in a couple of months—a true mark of inexperience.

Travel service owner: For us to get a new client to sign on the dotted line often requires 6 to 18 months of sales presentations.

Chester Carlson's experience shows that persistence and time are important ingredients in the success of marketing a service or product. In addition to patience, a successful businessowner needs to know the market for a particular product or service.

Market Research

Since all sales estimates must use preconceived ideas of the number of customers and what each customer will pay for a product or service, *these estimates are only as valid as the assumptions from which they are derived.* Jay made several assumptions about his customers, and he was very much in error. With millions of dollars in costs associated with each new product or business venture, a large business may spend hundreds of thousands of dollars in market and buyer research to ensure the accuracy of its assumptions. Unfortunately, few small businesses can afford that level of market research. However, with the same concerns of larger businesses, the owner of a small business must still identify the market by conducting market research.

Market research is not as difficult as you might first imagine. The fact is that every new business conducts some market research—even if it is nothing more then a wild guess. Good market research attempts to take the "wild" out of "wild guess."

Although you may not be a market expert, you can at least say that you are a shopping expert. For most of your adult life you have made the personal buying decisions that affect your clothing, food, transportation, and entertainment. If you do not know what everyone else buys, you at least know what *you* like. But this fact contains both a blessing and the seed of a problem. The blessing is that you share in common the experiences of the market audience. The potential problem lies in confusing the market "likes" with your personal "likes." The first step in developing a business attitude toward marketing is to understand the difference between your likes and market likes. Good market research attempts to determine what your customers like.

A certified public accountant: My experience is that most people think just because they feel their product is a good idea, everyone else feels that way too. It just does not work like that. There is a real distinction one has to make between what one feels is good and what the market is willing to spend money for.

Stereo retailer: I look at myself as a businessman. In that regard, I don't mind selling whatever the market wants, even though I am not too wild about it.

Steps to Market Research

Professional market research includes statistical samples, specially designed questionnaires, and computer programs. But without access to these aids, the owners of a small business can still conduct a limited survey by following these steps:

1. Describe your typical customer.
2. Determine your geographic area.
3. Identify the number of typical customers in the geographic area.
4. Determine your share of the market.
5. Confirm your estimate.

Describe Your Typical Customer

Every business has a "typical" customer. This customer may be identified by age, sex, income level, and geographic area. Even businesses that sell to other businesses can describe their typical customer in terms of type of business, number of employees, or by the geographic location. Let us see how three retail businesses in Waikiki might describe their typical customers:

Criteria	Surfboard Rental	Swimsuit Shop	Macadamia Nut Shop
Age	13–25	13–50	25–50
Sex	Male	Female	Couples
Annual income	$10,000	$20,000	$50,000
Geographic origin	US tourist	US tourist	Japanese tourist

We could refine this description by adding other criteria that would further identify these typical customers.

1. Is the purchase spontaneous or planned?
2. Do the customers come to you or does the business approach the customers?
3. Where do the customers live?
4. How long does the customer stay in Hawaii?
5. Where do the typical customers stay while in Hawaii?
6. What are their occupations?
7. Are they first-time or repeat visitors?

A customer analysis for the surfboard rental shop might read: US male tourists between the ages of 13 and 25 years. These customers are students and/or young adults with annual incomes of about $10,000. Their average stay in Hawaii is about five days, and they normally stay in one of five major hotels. These customers visit the business on their first or second day. The average rental is from $30 to $50.

Every businessowner is able to clearly describe a typical customer. A potential businessowner needs to develop such a description and keep it close at hand during all planning.

Determine Your Geographic Business Limits

Once the typical customer is identified, the next step is to establish the geographic limits of your market.

Although all businesses would like to have a product or service that has no geographic limitations, establishing that type of market reputation usually takes a number of years. Consequently, if you plan to have customers visit your business, start by drawing on a map a circle with a three-mile radius around your proposed business location (Exhibit 1). This circle will contain the probable geographic area of the majority of your customers. You can then adjust this circle to take into consideration traffic flow, population concentration, and the type of business. For example, a gas station may be concerned only with the traffic pattern on the streets that front the business. Customers may come from any geographic area, but future gasoline sales estimates will more than likely be based on traffic counts on those streets. If the station does repair work, however, it will probably be derived from the surrounding neighborhood. For that estimate, the station owner will need to know the extent of potential business within an estimated area. The important point is to establish a realistic geographic boundary for your probable market.

If you plan to visit customers instead of having them come to your business, then your geographic market will be limited to those areas or clients you decide to service. You can start to identify this market by preparing a list of all the potential customers. For example, a new furniture wholesaler could make a list of prospective customers by looking in The *Yellow Pages* under furniture retailers.

> **Retailer:** Except for some of the bigger shopping centers or specialty stores, most people are going to shop where they live or work. You don't see too many people who live in Kaneohe shopping in Waipahu. That's understandable, but most new businessowners think that everyone on the island is going to come to their store. Actually, they are not even going to get everyone from their own neighborhood.

Determine the Number of Typical Customers within the Geographic Limits

How many potential customers are included in your geographic area? If you are able to describe your typical customer and identify the geographic limits of your market, then there is information available that will help you estimate the number of these typical customers in your geographic market area. Both the Hawaii Department of Business and Economic Development (DBED) and the Hawaii State Library (main branch) are good places to start your information gathering. For instance, in 1980, Pearl City had a resident population of 42,577 with a median age of 27.6 years and 11,140 households with a median income of $29,345 (from the *Hawaii*

EXHIBIT 1

DETERMINING THE GEOGRAPHIC BOUNDARIES OF A BUSINESS LOCATION

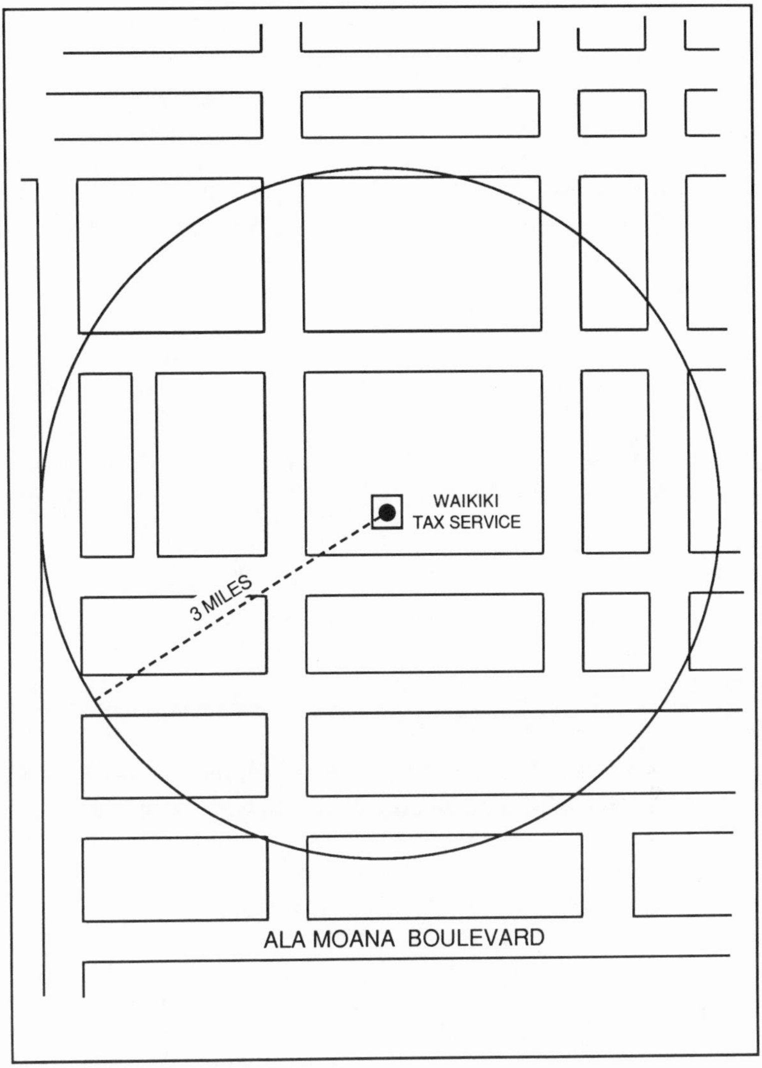

Data Book, 1986). Or did you know that 28,731 microwave ovens were sold on Oahu in 1987?

A wealth of information is available about Hawaii's traffic patterns, population areas, income levels, and items sold. For example, Exhibit 2 gives the profile of the Fort Street Mall shopper obtained from the DBED. Besides the *Hawaii Data Book* mentioned above, other sources of business information are: *Hawaii Facts and Figures,* published by The Chamber of Commerce of Hawaii; the annual *All About Business in Hawaii,* published

EXHIBIT 2
PROFILE OF THE FORT STREET MALL SHOPPER

Age	%	Geographic origin	%	Annual household income	%
18–24	14	Windward	25	Less than $15,000	19
25–34	17	Hawaii Kai	9	$15,000–$25,000	16
35–44	24	Aiea/Pearl City	18	$25,000–$35,000	21
45–54	19	Town	19	$35,000–$45,000	20
55+	19	Leeward	11	More than $45,000	23
		Kaimuki	12		
		Kalihi	32		
		Manoa/Punahou/ Waikiki	20		

SOURCE: From a survey conducted by the Hawaii Newspaper Agency, March 1984.

by Crossroads Press; economic forecast newsletters from the major banks; and *Hawaii Business* magazine.

Retailer: If you are starting a new business, do your homework before you start because once you get started it will overwhelm you. You can never plan too well.

Once you determine the size of your market, you must calculate your share of that market.

Determine Your Share of the Market

Unfortunately, all your potential customers will not be purchasing customers. For instance, it would be unrealistic to assume that every US male tourist between the ages of 13 and 25 who stays in the five target hotels of the surfboard rental business will be a purchasing customer. Your potential customer sales might look more like the example in Exhibit 3. This exhibit shows that of the entire market for a product, only a small percentage of the potential customers are interested in a purchase at any one time. This small percentage is the *buying market* your business will share with your competitors. Your portion of this buying market is known as *your market share* and will equate to how much you will sell (Exhibit 3).

Every industry has market share breakdowns. Exhibit 4 shows the market shares of several manufacturers in the national doll market in 1986.

But how do you determine how much of the buying market you will sell? The percentage of the market that will be purchasing your product or service will depend on the answers to three questions:

1. Who is your major competition?
2. What is the maturity of the industry?
3. What makes you special?

EXHIBIT 3
Your Share of the Market

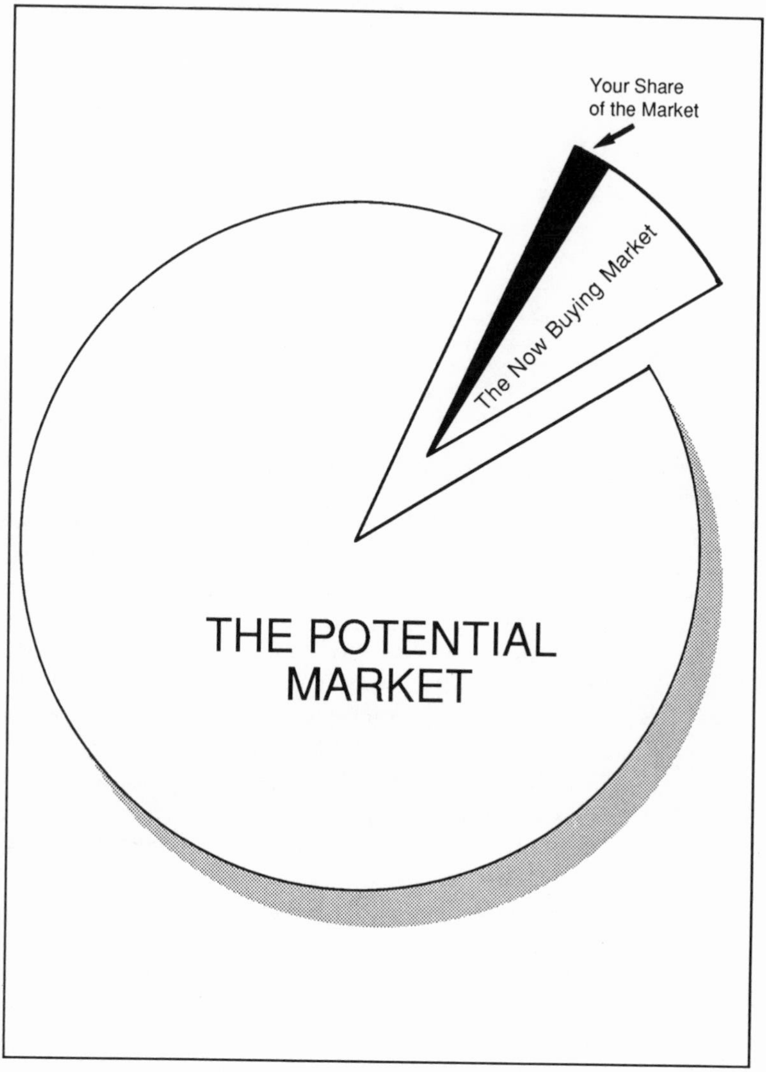

Who is Your Competition?

If you are the only one providing a product or service, then the entire share of the buying market may belong to you. More commonly, however, you will share the buying market with other businesses.

The first step in analyzing your market niche is to assess your competition. Where does your typical customer presently purchase this product or service? This may appear to be the easiest part of developing your marketing plan. Your competition is normally very visible, and you have had time

EXHIBIT 4
NATIONAL DOLL MARKET, 1986

Manufacturer	Doll	Market (%)
Mattel	Barbie	36
Coleco	Cabbage Patch Kids	20
Hasbro	Jem	9
Mattel	Baby Heather	7
Playmates	Cricket	6
Mattel	Lady Lovelylocks	6
Hasbro	Moondreamers	5
Other		11

SOURCE: *Toy and Hobby World* survey of more than 3,000 retail accounts.

to assess their strengths and weaknesses. But have you considered *all* your competition?

Although there are thousands of businesses in Hawaii, each business falls into a specific category of industry. A Chinese restaurant is in the restaurant industry, the broadest category. But it is also in a finer category, a *Chinese* restaurant. This category, Chinese restaurant, is a small, specialized part of the entire restaurant industry. However, the category of Chinese restaurant can be subdivided even further by type of Chinese restaurant. For instance, a Chinese restaurant that specializes in Cantonese food is different from another which specializes in Szechwan cooking.

If you subdivide your prospective industry into unique specialties, you will have a clearer view of your actual competition. A Chinese restaurant has general competition from other restaurants within its geographic area, direct competition from any Chinese restaurants, and specific competition from any other Chinese restaurant with the same type of food preparation.

As a rule the more competition there is for a product or service, the smaller the market share for all competitors. A businessowner will adjust the market share estimate depending on the number and strength of the competing businesses.

What Is the Industry Maturity?

Will your business be part of a growing industry where most of your sales will come from the introduction of a new service or product, or is your business in a more mature industry where you must "steal" customers from competitors?

Most industries are like people, they grow and mature. For example, when car stereos first came on the market, they were novel and required customer acceptance. Initially, only a very small portion of the potential market was interested in the product. During this time the car stereo suppliers were able to charge full prices, for little competition existed. As the popularity of car stereos increased, demand outpaced supply and suppliers experienced tremendous growth and profit. As consumers became more familiar with the reliability of car stereos, however, they became more price conscious. As more suppliers entered the high growth market, prices had to be cut to remain competitive. Finally, as the market matured, price became an important criteria, forcing profits down and some suppliers out of business.

This same scenario can be repeated for many products. Just replace the words *car stereo* with color televisions or nylon stockings and you get a similar history.

Business and trade magazines are good sources if you wish to determine the maturity and growth of your industry. Some common general business magazines are *Business Week, Inc., Forbes, Working Woman,* and *Entrepreneur.* The library has these magazines.

For the most part, the more mature the industry, the more competing businesses will have to share the same customer. On the other hand, if the industry is in its growth period, a businessowner might increase the estimate to take into account untapped demand.

What Makes You Special?

To a large extent the success of your business will depend on how well you determine your *market niche.* The market niche can be defined as those qualities your target customers see as the reasons to buy your service or product instead of that of your competitors. What makes you different is the hardest question for a business to answer. The best approach to an objective self-analysis is an honest assessment. Although there may be many differences, for the sake of this analysis assume that the customer perceives only these differences:

1. Your cost is cheaper;
2. Your location is more convenient;
3. Your selection is broader;
4. Comparable service or product is unavailable elsewhere;
5. Your sales staff is better;
6. Your service is measurably superior to that offered elsewhere.

Retailer: When I started in business I felt that my advantage was that I was going to work harder, have better service, and have a more efficient operation than my competition. I later found out that my competition works just as hard, has just as good service, and is just as efficient. In fact, he is a guy just like me.

If you look carefully, you can see how different businesses have created special market niches all around you. At one time in Honolulu only one automobile dealership existed where you could buy a Chevrolet. A department store may create an image of high quality and wide selection. A certain hotel may cater to the high income tourist, while another tries to attract the discount traveler.

Within each industry different businesses choose to establish a certain market image and to sell customers in a certain market niche. If a business does not know its market niche how can it expect its customers to know it? Generally speaking, the better defined the market niche, the greater the probability of a business capturing that target market.

Confirm Your Estimate

Once you have accomplished all this paper research, you need to confirm your estimate by interviewing some businesses and customers in the area.

> **Stereo retailer:** Our first store was located in Wahiawa, 25 miles outside of Honolulu. We opened the store without any market research; things seemed to happen too fast. In fact, we spent most of our time researching the lease, although I did drive up to see our competitor's store. After we had opened, to my surprise, most of our customers were military with only a few local Wahiawa residents. Only sometime later after I talked to another local storeowner did he comment: "The residents in this area may take a long time to warm to a new business." Had we planned to sell the residential local market we would have been in for a surprise.

This businessowner should have confirmed the market estimate by

1. talking in depth to merchants in the area to get some detailed information on customers, traffic, and market trends (It is surprising how much one can gather from simple face-to-face meetings. Most merchants are extremely helpful once they know you are a noncompeting business.);
2. checking with the state and city planning agencies to see what plans are anticipated for the area (new highway?);
3. interviewing local community or business associations;
4. meeting with the local bank branch managers. Most will be pleased to give you valuable insights in hopes of acquiring your future business;
5. interviewing some typical customers;
6. interviewing similar businesses in other geographic areas. One way to see if your estimate is realistic is to compare it with actual results from similar stores in other geographic areas. For instance, if you plan to open an ice-cream shop in Kailua, compare your estimates to actual sales of other ice-cream shops in Honolulu or on the outer islands. You may be surprised how helpful some of these businessowners will be.

A large business performs these basic steps in its market evaluation and spends thousands of dollars for the information. A less elaborate market analysis can be conducted by the owner of a small business and time may be the only cost. But time is the best initial business investment when you consider that the information uncovered will either confirm or deny your preconceived market opinions and could lead to the commitment of thousands of dollars to your business.

A Practical Example

Here is an example of how a new specialty furniture business estimated its possible market share.

Assume that there are currently two stores selling this specialty product to all ranks of the active duty military. A prospective businessowner plans to open a similar business and needs to estimate the possible market share. The original estimate is that monthly sales would average $60,000.

Step 1. Describe the typical customer. All active duty military personnel stationed on Oahu.

Step 2. Estimate the geographic market limits. The island of Oahu. But because the military buyers may be scattered over the entire island, this store will concentrate on the navy market based at Pearl Harbor.

Step 3. Estimate the market universe. State data show that there are 58,000 active duty military in Hawaii. Of this total the navy has 23,000 active duty personnel.

Step 4. Estimate the buying market. After interviewing some typical customers, the businessowner, using his best judgment, assumes that 15 percent of the potential market will be a buying market:

23,000 potential sales × 15 percent = 3,400 estimated sales.

Step 5. Consider market maturity. From business magazines the businessowner finds that this specialty market is considered a growth market. As a result the businessowner arbitrarily increases the estimate by 10 percent to 3,740 (3,400 + 340).

Step 6. List all the competitors. The businessowner estimates that Military Furniture is the dominant store, because it advertises extensively and has a good sales force with good servicing. However, its prices are high and its location inconvenient. A1 Furniture has the best selection and the best prices. Quality Furniture is the new business. It hopes to have the most convenient locations.

Step 7. Allocate points among the competitors. From the market survey the businessowner determines a probable scale of the important criteria a typical customer would consider in making this specialty purchase.

Reason customer would buy	Market (%)
Best price	25
Most convenient	10
Best selection	15
Dominant business	25
Best sales staff	15
Best service	10
Total buying market	100

Based on this estimate the businessowner rates the three stores as follows:

	Market share (%)		
	Quality Furniture	A1 Furniture	Military Furniture
Best price	5	20	
Most convenient	10		
Best selection		10	5
Dominant business		5	20
Best sales staff	5		10
Best service			10
Market share	20	35	45

As you can see, the businessowner projects that the new store, Quality Furniture, will have 20 percent of the market.

Step 8. Calculate your market potential. Once the market share is determined, the businessowner estimates how that will equate to actual sales dollars:

Estimated buying market × Share of the market

or

3,740 customer sales × 20 percent = 748.

Step 9. Estimate your individual sales.

Total estimated sales × Average sales price

748 customer sales × \$500 = \$374,000
or \$31,166 in average monthly sales

We have done this market analysis to confirm the original sales estimate. The new businessowner's initial estimate of sales of \$60,000 per month has been revised to about $32,000 per month. The businessowner also learns that a similar size store on Maui averages monthly sales of $28,000. Estimates now range from $28,000 to $60,000. This businessowner will now make an optimistic or pessimistic estimate of potential sales. Only time will prove which estimate was closer to the truth. But without the use of a crystal ball, this potential businessowner has done the next best thing to seeing the future.

Now that you have the sales estimate you need to put that into a market plan.

The Market Plan

A market plan is a written guide designed to explain what you expect to sell, in what time frame, and how you plan to accomplish it. It can be a one-page or a one-hundred-page report.

The first order for any business is *to get to a comfortable level of sales as fast as possible.* You can be very sloppy in many other parts of your business and still have a good chance at business success if you have the sales you need. Because it normally takes a business a number of years to reach a comfortable sales level, the market plan will be revised many times. Here is an example of how to approach developing a market plan.

Miles and Beverly are artists. They started their handcraft business as a part-time venture selling at craft fairs. After they had reached a certain level of sales, they decided to try it as a full-time venture. Their market strategy involved three areas:

1. Craft fairs in Hawaii and on the mainland;
2. Art galleries; and
3. National gift catalogs.

For each of their market areas, they developed a market plan with sales projections, budgets, and a plan of action. Over the next two years, they experienced mixed success. Their national catalog plan did not return the expected sales and ended up costing the most money. They have since replaced that market program with a new one—working with local designers. Of all the Hawaii galleries, only a few accepted their pieces, but two of those produced surprising sales. They have now redirected their marketing program to include more visits to these galleries.

We can see how Miles and Beverly looked at several ways to market their product and developed written market plans for each strategy. They did not hesitate to modify these plans—eliminating those which did not work and concentrating on those that were successful. It would be unrealistic to expect any business to get everything right from the start. A more sensible approach would include a built-in means for modification of the market plan. A simple statement of their market plan for catalog sales looked like this:

Market Plan for Catalog Sales

Overall goals:

1. Test the national catalog market.
2. Develop a new sales area.
3. Achieve sales of $3,000 per month within a year.

Sales goal:

Monthly sales of $3,000.

Time Frame:

1. Place first catalog advertisement by June.
2. Place second advertisement for Christmas issue.
3. From June to March.

Budget:

1. $2,000 for the June ad.
2. $3,000 for the December ad.

Steps:

1. Decide on media by February.
2. Submit first ad by April.
3. Produce 100 items in May to cover the first two months of anticipated sales.
4. Rework billing system to handle catalog sales.
5. Assess first ad results in August.
6. Place second ad in September.
7. Increase inventory in November for December ad.
8. In February assess the program.

Miles and Beverly were willing to commit up to $5,000 over a one year period to try to enter a new market area. They had a plan which included time frames and concrete dollar estimates. They are artists with a good business attitude.

In the introduction our hikers had to visualize their journey and the problems they would encounter. The businessowner must do the same thing in two areas. The first is sales, which we have covered in this chapter. Without a crystal ball, the businessowner must conduct a market analysis and assess the target customers, the industry, and the competition. The second area in which the businessowner needs a crystal ball is costs.

Additional Reading

Baty, Gordon B. 1981. *Entrepreneurship for the Eighties.* Reston, VA: Reston Publishing Co.

Breen, G., and A. Blankenship. 1982. *Do-It-Yourself Marketing Research.* 2nd ed. New York: McGraw-Hill.

Hawaii, State of. *Data Book.* Honolulu: Dept. of Business and Economic Development. (Published annually.).

Holtz, Herman R. 1982. *The Secrets of Practical Marketing for Small Business.* Englewood Cliffs, NJ: Prentice-Hall, Inc.

3

What Is This Thing Going to Cost Me?

New business ventures start from a position of optimism. Similar to excited hikers planning their next trip, entrepreneurs are often oblivious to potential business problems when market research suggests promising sales. One difficulty for prospective businessowners is accurately determining how much a business will cost to start up and to operate on a monthly basis. Because starting with too little money is a common error of new businesses, a successful entrepreneur must temper his market optimism with realistic cost estimates.

Two categories of costs associated with starting a business (or expanding a current one) are start-up costs and monthly operating costs.

Start-up Costs

Start-up costs are the monies you will need just to open your doors for business. These costs vary with the scope of the operation and the type of business. Although the amounts and types of start-up costs may vary among businesses, there are some common expenses that most new businesses will share. Here are some of the more common start-up expenses:

1. Lease rent—a one-month deposit and the first month's rent for the office, store, and/or warehouse.
2. Salaries—employee or owner salaries during the preopening period.
3. Special equipment—this includes store fixtures, counters, refrigerators, test equipment, and any piece of equipment needed to operate.
4. Office equipment—common office equipment, such as desks, typewriters, phones, calculators.

5. Renovation—both the labor and material costs for new lights, walls, painting, signs, flooring, as needed.
6. Office supplies—typing paper, stamps, pens, computer paper, folders.
7. Vehicle—delivery or salespersons' vehicles.
8. Legal fees—for the establishment of the business structure or a lease review.
9. Accounting fees—for the design of the accounting system.
10. Insurance—initial premiums.
11. Government fees—for business registration and permits.
12. Materials or inventory—depending on the type of business.
13. Association dues—if joining any business associations.

To illustrate how these typical start-up costs may vary with the type of business, let us look at two fictional examples—a service and a retail business. The first company, Waikiki Tax Service, will do tax returns in the businessowner's home and will have no employees other than the owner. This is similar to a free-lance or part-time business. Exhibit 5 summarizes possible start-up expenses for this service business.

The major estimated start-up costs of Waikiki Tax Service are office equipment and insurance.

Now let us take a look at a retail store example (Exhibit 6). The Windward TV Shop will be located in a commercial building, and, besides the owner, will require one full-time sales person, a part-time clerk, and a part-time technician. They plan to sell new televisions and video equipment and provide service for the Kailua and Kaneohe area. Based on the estimate in Exhibit 6, Windward TV will need at least $27,631 to open its doors. The major start-up expenses are:

1. Rental and deposit. Before moving into new office or store space, you will incur up-front costs equal to two-months rental (the first month and the deposit). Because it may take you from two weeks to six months to complete your improvements and open for business, this is a major start-up expense.

2. Salaries. If you will need personnel to help you get set up, then this payroll item needs to be considered a start-up cost. A fine line exists between waiting to hire employees until you are ready for business and the benefit these employees may contribute before you open. Finding a quality employee and providing adequate training takes more time than most small businesses realize. On the other hand, you do not want to pay staff when there is no work to perform.

3. Improvements. Depending on the type of business and the image desired, improvement costs vary. The more expensive improvements are normally associated with retail businesses, where public contact is important, or in cases where government requirements must be met, as in the

EXHIBIT 5

WAIKIKI TAX SERVICE
ESTIMATED START-UP COSTS

	Cost
Rent (home-based)	$ 0
Salaries	0
Office equipment	780
Calculator $60	
Typewriter $300	
File cabinet $150	
Phone instrument $70	
Desk/chair $200	
Office supplies	150
Vehicle	0
Office renovation	0
Professional subscriptions	200
Legal fees	0
Accounting fees	0
Insurance	500
Inventory	0
Business phone service	164
Connection charge $125	
First month rental $39	
Miscellaneous	
Business cards	20
Stationery	60
Logo prepared	50
Post office box	25
Government fees	25
Advertising	0
TOTAL	$1,974

restaurant industry. But, generally, all businesses need some type of improvement—no space seems exactly what is needed.

4. Equipment. The equipment needed to conduct your business can be considered improvements. As with other improvements, this equipment is necessary to the business. For Windward TV that necessary equipment may be test equipment used in the repair service. For an accountant it may be a computer and the software programs needed to process a client's financial reports.

5. Insurance. Insurance includes yearly premiums for the policies required by the Hawaii state government, such as workers' compensation and temporary disability, as well as for liability, fire/theft, and use of a commercial automobile.

EXHIBIT 6

WINDWARD TV SHOP
ESTIMATED START-UP COSTS

	Cost
Rent (first month plus rental deposit)	$2,250
500 sq ft at $2.25/sq ft = $1,125	
Rental deposit $1,125	
Salaries	1,580
Owner $800	
Part-time clerk $320 ($5/hr)	
Part-time technician $460 ($6/hr)	
Part-time salesperson (not hired yet)	
Office equipment	926
2 desks $338	
2 chairs $178	
File cabinet $160	
Typewriter $200	
Calculator $50	
Improvements	8,000
Sign $300	
Electrical $1,500	
Office partition $1,000	
Display shelves $5,000	
Painting $200 (painted by owner)	
Service equipment	5,000
Office supplies	200
Vehicle (will use own car)	0
Legal fees	500
Accounting fees	500
Insurance (one-year premiums)	1,500
Medical insurance (first month)	100
Government fees	75
Inventory	5,000
Display models (10 @ $250) = $2,500	
Back-up stock (10 @ $250) = $2,500	
Miscellaneous	2,000
TOTAL	$27,631

6. Inventory. For retail businesses (those selling products to the general public) or for wholesalers (those selling products to retailers), inventory stock will be a major expenditure. How much inventory to buy so that you can meet sales demands is both an art and a science. If you purchase too much, you may have tied up your cash in inventory needlessly. But pur-

chase too little and you may lose sales because you do not have the stock readily available.

Although these two example estimates illustrate some of the more common start-up costs experienced by most new businesses, there are many other types of expenses related to each business. For a simple perspective, consider these estimates to be minimum estimates.

> **Giftshop owner:** You cannot imagine all the costs that are associated with opening a business. We planned things down to the last detail and were still over the estimate. Unexpected problems with the contractor doing the renovations cost us plenty we had not counted on.

> **A certified public accountant:** Most people planning a new business seriously underestimate what the start-up costs will be. Few plan for the unexpected expenditures that always come up.

Start-up costs let you open your doors, but your operating costs will determine how long you can keep them open.

Operating Costs

If you pay the monthly bills for your family, you are already familiar with estimating business operating costs. A family has monthly costs such as rent, phone bills, and a car loan payment. Some of these costs, such as a mortgage payment, are fixed and do not vary from month to month. The monthly grocery or electric bills, however, may vary considerably.

A business has monthly operating costs similar to those of a family. Some of these costs are fixed, such as rent; others are variable costs such as advertising or wages. Many people find working with these numbers scary. They seem to relate better to a customer problem or to the failure of a manufacturer to ship a product on time.

> **Retailer:** Listen, I am no good with numbers. I would rather spend all my time in sales and leave the number side to someone else.

That retailer is encouraging disaster. Good business people are well-rounded generalists with enough common sense to realize that what they do not know can hurt them.

Our sample companies, Waikiki Tax Service and Windward TV, will have quite different monthly operating costs. Let us look at those for Waikiki Tax Service, the free-lance situation, first (Exhibit 7). With estimated sales of $5,000, salaries of $1,350, and miscellaneous expenses of $100, Waikiki Tax Service needs $2,339 to operate each month. The fixed costs are rent, medical insurance, phone, and an office equipment lease. These costs do not vary from month to month.

The variable costs are taxes, salaries, electricity, and gas for a vehicle.

EXHIBIT 7

WAIKIKI TAX SERVICE
PROJECTED MONTHLY OPERATING COSTS

	Cost
Rent (operating from home)	$0
Salaries (owner)	1,350
Office equipment	50
Lease of copy machine	
Utilities	20
Electric	
Office supplies	50
Vehicle	200
Lease $150	
Gas $50	
Medical insurance	100
Professional	50
Training seminars	
Phone	89
Business line charge $39	
Yellow Pages advertising $50	
Taxes	330
General excise tax (4% of sales; assume sales of $5,000/month = $200)	
Employment taxes (estimate 9% of payroll; 9% of $1,400 = about $130)	
Miscellaneous expenses (estimate)	100
TOTAL	$2,339

These variable costs are somewhat controllable. Just as you might reduce your personal entertainment expenses if other costs increase, a businessowner will cut variable business costs to adjust to sales income.

Let us look at the projected monthly operating expenses for Windward TV (Exhibit 8). A close examination of Windward TV's monthly projected expenses shows that, given the assumptions listed,

1. we can anticipate that the major expense categories will be rent, salaries, payroll taxes, general excise taxes, and possibly the lease of the vehicle and other equipment.

2. Windward's fixed expenses are rent, vehicle lease, office equipment lease, medical insurance, alarm, phone (except long distance calls), and taxes. These total $2,893 or 44 percent of the monthly total. This percentage of *fixed* expenses means that total *variable* costs—those costs the businessowner has control over—represent 56 percent of the operating budget. Although the rent cannot be changed, something can be done about salaries and wages if business slows.

EXHIBIT 8

WINDWARD TV SHOP
PROJECTED MONTHLY OPERATING COSTS

	Cost
Rent	$1,125
Salaries	2,580
Owner $1,000	
Part-time salesperson $800	
Part-time clerical $320	
Part-time technician $460	
Office equipment	50
Office copier lease	
Utilities	100
Office supplies	50
Vehicle	200
Lease $150	
Gas $50	
Medical insurance	200
2 employees (only 2 employees covered)	
Professional fees	300
Accounting $275	
Legal $25	
Freight	200
Alarm	30
Repairs and maintenance	50
Advertising	300
Payroll taxes	260
(estimate 10% of payroll)	
General excise tax	800
(4% of retail sales; assume $20,000 of sales per month)	
Interest	100
Anticipated bank loan	
Phone	278
Business line (2 lines @ $39 each) $78	
Phone system lease $100	
Telephone book advertising $100	
Miscellaneous expenses	100
TOTAL	$6,723

But How Much Do We Need to Start?

To determine how much money we might need to start a business, let us first estimate what it would cost Windward TV to start up and operate for six months (Exhibit 9). We will have to make some assumptions to do this. They are:

EXHIBIT 9

WINDWARD TV SHOP
ESTIMATED START-UP COSTS
AND THREE MONTHS OPERATING COSTS

	Month 1	Month 2	Month 3
Rent	1,125	1,125	1,125
Salaries	2,580	2,580	2,580
Office equipment	50	50	50
Vehicle	170	200	200
Medical insurance	200	200	200
Professional fees	300	300	300
Freight	200	100	200
Alarm	30	30	30
Maintenance	50	50	50
Advertising	1,000	700	500
Payroll taxes	260	260	260
General Excise Tax	320	400	600
Interest	0	0	100
Phone	278	278	278
Miscellaneous	100	100	100
TOTAL	$6,663	6,373	6,573

1. Higher than normal advertising costs for the first three months.
2. It will take one month to renovate the store and get merchandise before the store can open.
3. Average monthly operating costs for months 4, 5,and 6 are $6,700.

If we were to estimate the total costs for the first six months of set-up and operation for Windward TV we might calculate:

Start-up costs (from Exhibit 7)		$27,631
Operating costs		
Month 1	6,663	
Month 2	6,373	
Month 3	6,573	
Month 4	6,700	
Month 5	6,700	
Month 6	6,700	
Six months operating costs		$39,709
Total		$67,340

Later chapters will show the significance of managing the monies needed to run a business. In the meantime, for a rough estimate of the amount of money you might need to start your business use this simplified formula:

Money required = Start-up costs + Six months of operating costs.

Does this mean that you need $67,340 to successfully run Windward TV? Unfortunately, it is not that easy. In fact, because the exact amount needed is directly related to the unknown of sales income, we could estimate anywhere between $27,631 and $120,000 as the "correct" amount. This estimate is only an arbitrary guide for the money needed to start and operate the business for the first year. Some new businessowners would start with less money and some would start with more based on personal judgments of risk and how optimistic they are.

Using this guide we might estimate the minimum amount of money required to start Waikiki Tax Service as a full-time business:

Start-up costs (from Exhibit 5)	$ 1,974
Six months operating costs (from Exhibit 7; 6 × $2,339)	14,034
Total	$16,008

Certified public accountant: I think that most people starting a business have a rough idea about preparing start-up and operating estimates but do not go to the extent of actually writing it down. These costs are all somewhere in their head. I think it is a very high-risk way of starting or running a business to just keep all the numbers in your head.

Travel services businessowner: I would recommend someone have one year's cost in the bank before they start a new business. That is start-up costs plus twelve months of operating expenses. The reason is that no matter how well you plan for costs, there are always some that are unforeseen.

Retailer: When we first started our business we prepared a cost estimate for the bank. We really did not know what we were doing and, looking back on it, the banker must have tried hard not to laugh or cry. But the saddest part of it is that we never realized just how important a tool it was. Instead of looking at it as a bank requirement we learned how it could help us in our business. Once we understood how to use these estimates as guide lines, we felt much more in control of our business. Take it from me, if you are not doing it you are in trouble.

Retailer: When I was just starting out, a banker recommended that, after I made all my estimates, I cut my sales estimate in half and double my cost estimates. You know, he was right.

Starting a new business can be compared to having a baby or purchasing a new house. You start with a wonderful concept and end up with a money pit. Of course, in a business you eventually hope to earn enough money to make that investment worth your time. However, since it takes time to develop your business concept, you need enough money to carry you to the point where you can realize some return.

The next section will introduce you to some of the advisers who will help you refine your cost estimates, decide on a business structure, and deal with the registration and licensing requirements for a new business.

Additional Reading

Bank of America. 1984. *Steps to Starting a Business.* Small Business Reporter Series. San Francisco, CA. (Dept. 3120, P.O. Box 37000, San Francisco, CA 94137.)

"How to Start a Business." *New York* 20 (24) (June 15, 1987): 45–57.

Robert Morris Associates. *Annual Statement Studies.* Philadelphia, PA. (Published annually.) (1616 Philadelphia National Bank Bldg., Philadelphia, PA.)

PART II

Laying the Goundwork with Your Advisory Team

4

Structuring Your Business: Do You Need an Attorney?

One of the first decisions you will need to make when starting a business concerns the form that business will take. Will it be a sole proprietorship, a partnership, or a corporation? Another decision will need to be made about accounting methods in order to apply for a general excise tax license. Then there are questions about money. Who might give you financial support and advice? Running a business is a lonely venture. You can easily get lost in a maze of options. To assist you in your decisionmaking, you should assemble a team of advisers. These advisers will give objective and experienced guidance. Although your spouse, a friend, or even a next-door businessowner may help you, a better plan includes a professional team of advisers, which will include an attorney, an accountant, and a banker. In this chapter we will look at choosing advisers and how an attorney might help with your business structure.

Choosing Advisers

Choosing your advisers is an important task. In fact, during the course of your business career, you may change individual advisers several times. Because these advisers will influence your business a great deal, it will be worth your time and effort to find ones that are suited to you.

Selecting each one of these advisers is like selecting your family doctor. You certainly will want someone who is competent and someone with whom you can establish a comfortable rapport. You will also want to consider the cost of the service. The same considerations apply to the selection of all your advisers.

The Need for an Attorney

One of the first advisers you may choose is your attorney. A good way to start to find someone with whom you will be comfortable is from your current experience. If you have a family lawyer, you might have him recommend three business lawyers. Another source of ideas is friends or other business people. If you obtain a recommendation from another business, ask why they feel the attorney is so good. Sometimes other professionals, such as your accountant, may be able to provide a good recommendation. If all else fails, ask some of the business associations, such as a chamber of commerce.

Once you have several recommendations, call each attorney and explain your current business or plan for a new business. Most attorneys do not charge for the first visit. This gives you an excellent opportunity to get some advice and see if you can develop a good rapport. As you will see in a moment, you may not need the services of an attorney to set up your business, but when you eventually do need one—to review a lease, for example —that is a poor time to start looking.

> **Attorney:** Most people have a mistaken impression of the role of the attorney. They think that all they need us for is to sue or to be protected from suit. In actuality, very few of my clients ever get to that situation.

> **Pet service businessowner:** I got the attorney reference through a friend and found out later it was a social reference not a business association. I don't recommend that.

> **Attorney:** There is a wrong way to look at an attorney and that is as a heart surgeon—to be used only in a life or death situation. The right way to use an attorney is as someone who assists you in avoiding problems.

The current rate for business attorney services in Hawaii averages from $125 to $150 per hour. The estimated attorney's fee to set up a standard business format can range from $500 to $1,500.

Although any new business can be established without an attorney, the need for an attorney's services will increase as the complexity of the business increases. For instance, if the business resembles the Waikiki Tax Service example—a single owner working out of a private home—the need for an attorney to set up the legal business structure might be limited. On the other hand, the principals of Windward TV, who plan to have several owners, a lease in a shopping center, and a bank loan, may find an attorney useful to provide legal advice on the advantages of different business structures, lease options, and partnership agreements.

One measure of the value of these advisers is their ability to suggest options never considered by the businessowner. For instance, a typical unforeseen legal concern which an attorney might address is the buy-out provision of one of the principals in a business. How will the remaining principals or partners buy-out a partner who decides to call it quits? In most cases, potential businessowners do not even consider this problem, for who thinks of leaving when the business has not even started? An adviser for a new business should be looked upon as an insurance policy against the future pain of the unforeseen.

Here are some of the things you might consider in selecting your attorney:

1. Rapport—either you like his style or not. Is he too pushy? Does she take the time to explain things you do not understand?
2. Responsiveness—an attorney is a businessperson just like you. A good attorney will be very busy. Do your calls to her remain unreturned? Does he take too long to get a project done?
3. Experience—has the attorney dealt with this type of problem or handled this type of business before? What other businesses does he represent?
4. Good advice—the attorney's business product is information. As with any product for sale, are you getting the appropriate value for your money? Does the attorney make common sense?

If you do visit an attorney for a business start-up, one of the first items to discuss is your legal business structure.

Three Business Structures

One of the first steps in starting a business in Hawaii is registering the business name with the Business Registration Division, Hawaii Department of Commerce and Consumer Affairs. One of the first choices this form requires you to make is among the three types of business structures: (1) sole proprietorship, (2) partnership, and (3) corporation.

The legal structure of a business will affect how it will pay its taxes, assume legal liabilities, and maintain certain administrative forms. The legal structure will not have any direct effect on the business operations. Therefore, both of our fictional businesses, Waikiki Tax Service and Windward TV, could choose any one of the three legal business structures.

The Sole Proprietorship

A business created as a sole proprietorship is owned by one person. Consider a sole proprietorship as similar to a parent with the legal obligations of a dependent child. If you have a dependent child, you can deduct certain expenses from your income tax for the upkeep of your dependent.

At the same time you are responsible for all liabilities that this dependent may incur.

Simply stated, a sole proprietorship is a business owned by one individual who pays all the income taxes (or takes the income tax losses) for the business on a personal tax return. In addition, the owner is legally responsible for any liabilities the business incurs. A sole proprietorship is by far the simplest business structure. But that does not mean that a sole proprietorship has to be small, for the designation merely stipulates the legal and tax reporting structure of the business. A sole proprietorship may have any number of employees or may grow to any level in sales revenue.

As a business becomes larger, however, it may be less advantageous for an individual to operate as a sole proprietorship. For instance, let us say that the sole proprietor would like someone else to share in the ownership of the business. By definition, the business would no longer be a sole proprietorship. Some other type of legal business form must be chosen.

The Partnership

A partnership is similar to a sole proprietorship but two or more owners or principals are involved. The income and losses from the business are now shared between or among the principals in either equal proportions or under some prearranged formula.

For example, let us assume that the sole proprietor of Waikiki Tax Service wants to take another person into the company as an owner. One method would be to form a partnership. Under the agreement between these two principals any combination of ownership can be established. Depending on the money or expertise contributed to the business by each partner, they may divide the ownership in any way, such as 60 to 40 percent or 50 to 50 percent. This percentage allocation between the partners affects how any profit (or loss) from the business will be distributed. If the agreement is for 60 percent and 40 percent ownership, then the first partner would get 60 percent of the profits and the second partner would get 40 percent unless otherwise negotiated.

The liabilities of the business, however, are shared equally and severally in a partnership. This means that any or all of the partners many be liable either individually or jointly for any liabilities incurred by the company. Each partner, regardless of the distribution of ownership, would be 100 percent liable for any legal obligations incurred by the partnership. Consequently, as a partner, if your business suffers losses and your partners cannot pay, you may be liable for the entire amount. Under certain conditions the liabilities of one or more partners may be limited. However, even in these limited partnerships there has to be at least one general partner who will assume the liability of the entire partnership.

Attorney: Partnerships can become very complicated and, because of the risk exposure, need to be well conceived.

A disadvantage of a sole proprietorship, and to some extent of a partnership, is that the existence of the business is tied directly to the principals. A sole proprietorship with a hundred employees will have to be dissolved at the death of the sole proprietor. To resolve this problem, a new type of business structure was conceived—one with a life of its own. This is a corporation.

A Corporation

There are several misconceptions about the corporate business structure. One common mistaken belief is that the term *corporation* is synonymous with the term *business*. Not every business is a corporation. Another mistaken impression is that corporations are only big businesses. The fact is that many corporations in the United States are small businesses, and it is not uncommon to see a one-person corporation.

Corporations are similar to children who reach the age of majority. Adults are responsible for their own actions and also for their own income taxes. You as a parent are no longer able to deduct expenses from your tax return for the upkeep of a dependent, once the child becomes an adult.

A corporation gives notice to the world that it is a corporation and not a sole proprietorship or partnership by stating in its business name, "Corporation" or "Incorporated" (Inc.). Consequently, if Waikiki Tax Service, our sole proprietorship, decided to incorporate, the new name would be Waikiki Tax Service, Inc. Its method of operation would not change except in its method of tax reporting. But other significant conceptual changes do take place.

Stockholders as Owners

A sole proprietorship is owned by the proprietor. A corporation is owned by its stockholders. To understand the role of the stockholder, let us say that three people start a business by putting in $500 each. The corporation has $1,500 and each of the three people owns one third of the corporation. To signify this ownership accurately, the corporation issues three stocks worth $500 each, one to each of the stockholders (in corporate terminology, we have three stocks with a par value of $500 each). The stock represents the portion of ownership.

Let us now assume that after the first year the corporation makes a profit of $300 (after all expenses). Now each stock is worth $600 ($500 + $100). This is a simplified example because the true value of a business is difficult to assess. For example, what if this small corporation, in its second year, invented and was granted a patent for a new process to grow hair naturally that was approved by the Food and Drug Administration? The anticipation of future earnings might change the value of that stock. Would you be willing to sell your one third share with a stated value of $600 for $3,000? That is a healthy profit and a terrific return on your original investment of $500. How about $30,000? Welcome to the stock market.

The concept of stockholders as the owners of the business also makes it easier to raise more investment money or to have more people participate in the ownership of the business. For example, if the corporation needed to raise money for the purchase of equipment to manufacture the hair-growth product, it might sell more stock.

A corporation has the additional advantages of ease of ownership transfer and limited liability. Since the corporation's ownership can be represented in stock ownership, the sale or transfer of that stock can change the ownership of the business—the business continues but with different stockholders as the stock is sold.

Corporate Owners' Liability

As a separate entity a corporation may also protect the owners from certain liabilities and it may limit the owners' loss to the amount of the stock investment. There are several exceptions. For example, the corporate shell may not be able to protect the major stockholder in certain types of businesses, such as the medical profession. Consequently, Dr. John Doe, Inc. may still be personally liable for certain professional liabilities, even though the business is a corporation. In addition, banks, as you will see in later chapters, often request personal guarantees from the major stockholders to secure loans made to a small corporation. These personal guarantees are not protected by the corporation's limited liability.

Disadvantages of a Corporation

Generally speaking, however, with the advantages of limited liability and perpetuity of ownership, why shouldn't all businesses incorporate? The disadvantages of a corporation are in the tax rules that apply to it. Income for tax reporting in a sole proprietorship or partnership is included on the income tax report of the owner or partner. The proprietorship or partnership does not pay any taxes. But a corporation does. And because a corporation is a separate entity, you are considered an employee of that corporation even if you are the sole stockholder and the only employee. Consequently, you will be subject to payroll taxes that you would not have been subject to as a sole proprietor.

Furthermore, any profits withdrawn from a corporation are subject to taxation. If the company made money and you would like to distribute this profit to the stockholders as a dividend, the corporation will have to pay a tax on the dividend and you will have to declare it as ordinary income and eventually pay income tax on it also.

Here is an example. If Waikiki Tax Service, the sole proprietorship, made $300 in profits at the end of the year, that profit would be reported as additional income on the owner's personal tax return. The business files no tax return. Assuming that the owner is in the 30 percent tax bracket, he would pay \$90 (\$300 × 30 percent) in taxes on the profits he made. If Waikiki Tax Service, Inc., the corporation, earned the same \$300, it would file a corporation return listing that as income. It would pay say 20 percent as income tax or \$60 (\$300 × 20 percent). Assuming that the rest was then distributed to the sole stockholder as a dividend, the stockholder would receive the \$240 as income and then have to pay 30 percent on his individual tax return or \$72 (\$240 × 30 percent).

The net return to the stockholder is \$168 compared to \$210 as a sole proprietorship. This "double taxation" is not a problem in sole proprietorships or partnerships since profits are considered income only to the principals.

The S Corporation

Someone must have convinced the government of the need for a business structure that had the advantages of a corporation but the tax payment capabilities of a partnership. The S Corporation (named after its subchapter in the tax code) is a hybrid business structure that allows the businessowner to incorporate, but also to take the corporation's profits or losses on a personal tax return similar to tax payments of the sole proprietorship or partnership.

In actuality, the S Corporation is a corporation that *elects* to pay its taxes like a partnership. Some restrictions to an S Corporation exist, one of which is that it is limited to no more than 35 stockholders. In all other respects it is just like a regular corporation.

This has been a very simple description of the basic legal business structures. There are many other accounting and tax considerations that apply to all the business forms. A professional should be consulted for further clarification.

Certified public accountant: Those people going into business should recognize that you are not stuck with a certain business type. In fact, I know several businesses that have changed several times. Good planning, however, in the selection of your business type will avoid all the extra paper work required in these transitions.

Here is a brief summary of the advantages and disadvantages of the various business structures.

Business type	Advantages	Disadvantages
Sole Proprietorship	1. Easy to set up 2. If owner in low tax bracket, all profits income	1. Only one owner 2. If owner in high tax bracket, can not defer income 3. Accepts liability

Partnership	Same as proprietorship although more complicated to set up	1. Accepts liability 2. More complicated tax reporting
Corporation	1. Limited liability 2. Continued life	1. More complicated to set up 2. Double tax
S Corporation	1. Limited liability 2. Continued life 3. Net operating loss deductible by shareholders	1. More complicated to set up 2. Limited to 35 stockholders

Once you have chosen the business structure for your business, you can take the two steps needed to register the business with the Hawaii state government: (1) registering your business name and (2) applying for a general excise tax license (certain types of professions and businesses, such as a contractor, may require other types of licenses in addition).

Steps in Registering a Business

1. Registering Your Company Name

To register your company name you will need to submit a Trade Name Application to the Bureau of Business Registration, State of Hawaii, 1010 Richards Street. Even if you checked to see if your business name was being used in the telephone book and did not see it, it may still be on reserve for someone who is contemplating a business.

At the Bureau of Business Registration office, your next step is to scan the computer name files for any similar names. The Bureau of Business Registration processes your name request under the following guidelines:

a. Names that are successfully registered are valid for a period of one year, at which time they must be reapplied for. If that is done, then the name is good for 10 years.
b. If you find a name that you would like and you believe that it is not being used, you may attempt to contact the holder of the name and ask that it be released.
c. Registering the name with the state does not in itself constitute any legal guarantee of use of the name.

Once you have selected your name, you must complete a registration form and pay a $25 registration fee (Exhibit 10). The state will inform you within four to six weeks if you can use the requested name. You may want to pay an additional fee to rush the processing to three days, since you cannot open a bank account or order stationery until the name is registered.

EXHIBIT 10

Application for a Trade Name

Nonrefundable Filing Fee – $25

Submit Original and One True Copy

STATE OF HAWAII
DEPARTMENT OF COMMERCE AND CONSUMER AFFAIRS
Business Registration Division
1010 Richards Street
Mailing Address: P. O. Box 40, Honolulu, Hawaii 96810

APPLICATION FOR REGISTRATION OF TRADE NAME

(SEE REVERSE SIDE FOR GENERAL INFORMATION AND INSTRUCTIONS)

PLEASE TYPE OR PRINT LEGIBLY IN BLACK INK

1. APPLICANT'S NAME: JOSIE AKANA
   Address: 92-1244 KUHIO HWY. City HONOLULU State HAWAII Zip Code 96728
2. Check one: Registration is: [✓] New OR [ ] Renewal
3. Status of applicant: *(Check one)* [✓] Sole Proprietor [ ] Corporation [ ] Partnership [ ] Unincorporated Association
   [ ] Other (explain) ______
4. If applicant is a corporation or partnership, list state or country of incorporation/formation: ______
5. Trade name is WAIKIKI TAX SERVICE
   (This form is not to be used to register the name of a new corporation or partnership.)
6. Applicant is *(check one)*: [ ] Originator of name OR [ ] Assignee *(one to whom name was assigned by another)*
7. Nature of business for which the trade name is being used:
   TAX PREPARATION SERVICE

I certify, under the penalties set forth in Section 482-3.5, Hawaii Revised Statutes, that

CHECK ONE: [ ] I am the applicant OR [ ] I am the ______ (office held) of the applicant

named in the foregoing application, and that the statements made in the application are true and correct to the best of my knowledge and belief.

Josie Akana (Signature) OCTOBER 12, 1991 (Date)

This application must be certified by the applicant if an individual, or by an officer if a corporation, or by a general partner if a partnership. Signature must be in black ink.

(DEPARTMENTAL USE ONLY) Certificate of Registration No. ______

CERTIFICATE OF REGISTRATION OF TRADE NAME

In accordance with the provisions of Chapter 482 of the Hawaii Revised Statutes, this Certificate of Registration is issued to secure to the aforesaid applicant the use of the said TRADE NAME throughout the State of Hawaii for the term of ______ year(s) from ______ to ______.

DEPARTMENT OF COMMERCE AND CONSUMER AFFAIRS
STATE OF HAWAII

Dated: ______

REGISTRATION OF A TRADE NAME WITH THE DEPARTMENT DOES NOT GRANT YOU OWNERSHIP OF THE TRADE NAME

______
Director of Commerce and Consumer Affairs

T-1
1/92

B48 (Fee)
S18 (Act 153)

2. Corporation Registration

If you plan to establish your business as a corporation, a Hawaii corporation registration must be completed. Remember, a business may be incorporated at any time. It is not necessary to do so at start-up. The Hawaii incorporation registration form is submitted at the same Bureau of Business Registration (see Exhibit 11). The cost of filing is $50.00. When your incorporation is approved, you will receive an approved copy of your registration with an incorporation number and the date of incorporation.

EXHIBIT 11

Filing Articles of Incorporation

Nonrefundable Filing Fee - $50
Certified copy, if desired:
$10 plus 25¢ per page

Submit Original and
One True Copy

State of Hawaii
DEPARTMENT OF COMMERCE AND CONSUMER AFFAIRS
Business Registration Division
1010 Richards Street
Mailing Address: P. O. Box 40, Honolulu, HI 96810

DOMESTIC PROFIT

ARTICLES OF INCORPORATION
(Section 415-54, Hawaii Revised Statutes)

PLEASE TYPE OR PRINT LEGIBLY IN BLACK INK

The undersigned, for the purpose of forming a corporation under the laws of the State of Hawaii, do hereby make and execute these Articles of Incorporation:

I

The name of the corporation shall be:

____

Note: The name must contain the word "Corporation," "Incorporated," or "Limited," or an abbreviation of one of the words.

II

The mailing address (must be a street address) of the initial or principal office of the corporation is:

____

III

The purpose or purposes for which this corporation is organized shall be:

(a) ______________________________

(b) The transaction of any or all lawful business for which corporations may be incorporated under Chapter 415, Hawaii Revised Statutes.

D1-3
10/89

B13 (Fee)
B23 (Certification)

The a

The i
follows:

Name

Note:

The i
are duly elec

All th
otherwise pr

The c
appointed by

The f

Office Held

President

Vice-Preside

Secretary

Treasurer

-2-

The r
of capital pa

Names of S

(Opti

We c
belief.

Witn

(Type/Print Name of Incorporator)

(Type/Print Name of Incorporator)

(Signature of Incorporator)

(Signature of Incorporator)

Please sign in black ink.

-3-

If Your Disagreement Leads to the Courtroom

You will probably need your attorney only for the review of a lease or contract. But you may at some time have to retain an attorney's services to rectify an injustice or to defend yourself against the legal claim of another. Normally both parties to a lawsuit will have been aware of the problem for some time—a dispute in the payment of bills or a misunderstanding of an agreement between two parties. Eventually the disagreement reaches a point where one of the parties retains an attorney to solve the problem. The other party will then want to answer through an attorney also.

Here are some points made by attorneys and a retailer concerning what might follow from this confrontation.

Attorney: Attorneys rarely advise for long drawn out legal battles.

Attorney: In my opinion, only five out of one hundred disputes ever go to trial and perhaps two out of one hundred in business situations.

Attorney: Too few clients are willing to confront reality to solve a problem. They don't sit down beforehand to see how it should be solved before they get emotionally involved.

Retailer: In the eight years I have been in business, I have been in two legal suits. Both never went to court. The first one was with our landlord, a disagreement over the payment for improvements to the building when we signed the lease. After two years of our attorneys writing letters back and forth we settled for what we had almost agreed to before we took the matter to our attorney.

Attorney: If the parties to a legal problem agree on the facts but not the legal aspects, then one might expect a resolution to take one and a half years and cost $25,000. If they agree on the legal aspects but not the facts, then the sky's the limit.

Attorney: It is very unrealistic for small businesses to hold a belief that it is possible to solve long-festering business problems cheaply and quickly. It is like going to a doctor with cancer. It is not going to be fun, cheap, or easy.

Most potential businessowners look at a business venture solely from the standpoint of sales and income. Yet their business, whether it is an auto body shop or a medical practice, is a legal entity governed by laws tied to the choice of business structure. Since the consequences of these laws directly affect the businessowner, a general appreciation of the legal structure of a business is important.

Your attorney is an adviser who can help structure the legal framework of your business. An attorney is of greatest value in helping to avoid potential problems rather than in resolving those problems after the fact.

Once you have registered your business, the next step is to complete your application for a Hawaii General Excise Tax license. We will take that step in the next chapter in which another adviser, your accountant, will be discussed.

Additional Reading

Jessup, Claudia, and Genie Chipps. 1979. *The Woman's Guide to Starting a Business.* New York: Holt, Rinehart and Winston.

5

Your Accountant Will Help You Learn a Foreign Language

All businesses in Hawaii are subject to the General Excise Tax (GET). Since a business cannot even take out a business checking account without a general excise tax license, most new businessowners apply for the license before they understand all the choices that are required on the form. What appears to be a simple, single-sheet form has serious tax and business implications.

At the end of this chapter we will discuss the GET licensing process, but to do that you will have to know something about accountants, their language, and what to look for when selecting one.

Accounting Language

The language used by accountants (and all business people) is unique as is the language of any profession. For instance, a cook will use a recipe to bake a banana cream pie that might call for 2 c of sugar. All cooks would know this means 2 cups. By looking at the recipe, a cook can visualize the end result and change the recipe to suit particular tastes. The recipe provides a means of precise communication so the cook can duplicate the pie. It also allows the cook to visualize the end result.

Like a recipe, financial language allows the accountant and the businessowner to discuss the status of a business in the abstract. Without having to make every sale, both will be able to visualize what was sold, when it was sold, what months the business made money, and which expenses seem too high.

Accountants are very much technicians who view your entire business in the abstract. This means that while you are emotionally involved with the operation of your business, the accountant is not. To you, picking the right color shirt to sell in your shop is important, but to the accountant the shirt is just inventory or sales.

Before we begin, let us define some of the terms the businessowner at Windward TV will need in order to communicate with an accountant.

Purchases: the dollar amount of what was purchased to sell.

In our example, Windward TV purchased 42 televisions at a cost of $250 each. Therefore, purchases for the month totaled $10,500:

42 televisions × $250 = $10,500.

Not every business will purchase goods or material that it will resell. But every business will have sales.

Sales: the dollar amount of what you sell.

Sales are the merchandise which you sell or those services you render that someone pays for. Using the Windward TV Shop as an example, let us say that for the month of June they sold 20 televisions at a price of $500 each which equaled $10,000:

Sales for June = $10,000 (20 televisions × $500).

Cost of Sales (or Cost of Goods Sold): the cost of what you sold.

The 20 televisions Windward TV sold cost $250 each:

Cost of sales = $5,000 (20 televisions × $250).

Unfortunately, most businesses do not sell everything they purchase for resale.

Inventory: what you have purchased but did not sell.

Windward TV purchased 42 televisions but sold only 20. Consequently, they have 22 televisions in current inventory at a cost of $250 each:

Current inventory = $5,500 (22 television × $250).

Gross Profit: sales less cost of sales.

Gross profit = $5,000 ($10,000 − $5,000).

Operating Costs: all the costs needed to run the business. (We saw these in our examples in chapter 3.)

In our example in chapter 3 (Exhibit 8) for Windward TV, total costs equaled $6,723 for June:

Operating costs = $6,723.

Operating Profit or Loss: gross profit less operating costs.

Operating loss for June was ($1,723). (Numbers in parentheses are negative numbers.):

$$\text{Operating loss} = \$5{,}000 - \$6{,}723 = (\$1{,}723)$$

Net Profit or Loss: operating profit less income taxes and other expenses.

Assuming no other income or income taxes, the net of ($1,723) is the net loss for the month.

Profit and loss statement: a summary of these transactions for a particular month or year.

The profit and loss statement reflecting Windward TV's June transactions would look like Exhibit 12. The profit and loss statement is a numeric representation of what Windward TV did financially during one month. Large businesses, such as Sears and Amfac Corporation, use the same method to assess and review their operations.

Since other people, such as accountants and bankers, do not know your business as intimately as you do, it is through these numeric representations that they picture your progress. The profit and loss statement is a picture in numbers of a business. Considering all the variables related to the net profit or loss, it is surprising how any company can operate successfully without preparing a monthly profit and loss statement. Without this statement how would Windward TV have known it lost $1,723 when sales looked fairly promising at $10,000?

> **Retailer:** The goal in our company is to get the end of the month profit and loss statement within three weeks of the end of the month. We are always surprised at how some cost affected our bottom line or how some cost is way out from what we expected. Of course, with a profit and loss statement within three weeks of the end of the month we are able to check our figures or immediately implement some corrective action. I knew a business that had only a yearly profit and loss statement. I don't know how they knew what was happening month to month and whether they were even making money.

> **Retailer:** Most accountants are too busy to spend the time to train you about accounting. Consequently, you have to do a lot of self help. In my case, my wife took care of all the books with our accountant giving guidance. I have got to admit that this part of the business is a full-time job, and my wife really took it upon herself to learn all the details. But our first accountant was too busy to help us so we checked around and got one who had the patience and was willing to work with us.

But where does the accountant or the business owner obtain all the information for the profit and loss statement? If you have ever been an employee, chances are much of your job entailed completing paperwork. Much of that paperwork would eventually be used by the employer's accountant to keep track of expenses, inventory, and sales. The concept of

EXHIBIT 12

WINDWARD TV SHOP
PROFIT AND LOSS STATEMENT
JUNE 19__

Total Sales		$10,000
Returns (none)		0
NET SALES		$10,000
Cost of Sales		5,000
GROSS PROFIT		$ 5,000
Operating Expenses		
Rent	$1,125	
Salaries	2,580	
Office equipment	50	
Utilities	100	
Vehicle	200	
Medical insurance	200	
Professional fees	300	
Freight	200	
Alarm	30	
Maintenance	50	
Advertising	1,000	
Payroll taxes	260	
General excise tax	400	
Interest	100	
Phone	278	
Miscellaneous	100	
TOTAL OPERATING EXPENSES		$ 6,723
Net operating loss		$(1,723)
Other income		0
Income taxes		0
NET LOSS		$(1,723)

recordkeeping will be covered in more detail in chapter 15. For the time being, consider that every major transaction (sales, purchases, payment of expenses, etc.) in the business must be documented with paperwork.

Your accountant can help you set up a good record-keeping system to ensure that you have the correct paperwork.

What Your Accountant Will Do

Initially your accountant will:

1. advise you on your record-keeping system;
2. establish your accounting system;
3. review and submit all required government filing forms;
4. advise on and establish your periodic tax filing;
5. give you advice on your market plan;
6. help you prepare a bank loan proposal (if necessary).

Afterward the accountant may:

1. prepare your financial statements (such as the profit and loss statement);
2. prepare your year-end income tax return for the business;
3. submit all quarterly government tax payments;
4. review your accounting ledgers;
5. reconcile your bank checkbook.

You can do many, if not all, of these tasks yourself. If you decide to do some or all of these tasks, however, you should have an accountant review your work periodically. As you would expect, the more you have the accountant do, the higher the bill. This is the major reason that most small businesses start by doing as much as they can themselves. A good accountant will assist by teaching you how to handle many of the routine functions.

Some of the questions that may be discussed with your accountant on your initial visit are:

1. Can you advise me on the basic record-keeping systems I should have for my type of business, such as sales receipts, purchase orders, and so on?
2. What basic bookkeeping systems should I have, such as a sales journal and a cash receipt ledger?
3. What special forms do I need to file with the government to start this business?
4. Can you show me the taxes I will have to pay and when?
5. Can you provide me a monthly profit and loss statement?
6. How much will this cost me if I try to do most of the routine bookkeeping?

What You Should Look For in an Accountant

There are three types of accounting firms: national CPA firms, local CPA firms, and bookkeeping services. A CPA or Certified Public Accountant is, by training and state examination, considered to possess certain qualifications.

Certified public accountant: The distinction between the services is in the level of sophistication. The CPA is a highly trained professional who can service the technical, financial, and tax aspects of a small business.

Accountant: The level of expertise of the businessperson is important in determining the type of accounting firm to use. There is a wide range of accounting expertise in this area.

The primary distinction among accountants is based on the types of service each kind of firm performs. Two possible types of accounting services a business could require are day-to-day bookkeeping services and accounting advice to include tax planning.

The CPA firms concentrate on providing accounting system design, audits, tax planning, and tax preparation services. The bookkeeping services offer more services related to the day-to-day accounting needs of a business, such as checkbook reconciliation, monthly profit and loss statements, customer billing, and payroll tax forms submissions. In recent years, however, the lines between types of services have become blurred, with more CPA firms offering bookkeeping services and some bookkeeping services offering tax planning.

Most small businesses perform some internal bookkeeping functions and use the outside bookkeeping service or CPA for guidance and for areas that prove too complicated or time consuming for the business to handle itself. For example, a small business might be able to balance its own checkbook every month, bill its customers, maintain its sales records, and even do a monthly profit and loss statement. The business might need professional accounting assistance only in such black-and-white areas as preparing its year-end tax return and reviewing its accounting ledgers, or in deciding how to handle gray areas, such as an inventory loss due to water damage. The CPA or accountant earns money by helping you interpret these gray areas and by analyzing your numeric picture. Advice on how to handle certain expenditures with tax considerations in mind will save you money. Her ability to accurately assess your business will draw attention to possible faulty areas of operation or expose potential liabilities. If you are not getting this service from your accountant, you are underutilizing her true potential.

As with your attorney, you would be wise to shop around for your accountant. In addition to considering all the factors used in selecting your attorney, you might want to look for an accountant who is familiar with your type of business. Do not be afraid to ask to speak to some of her clients. Only time will tell how well you have chosen, so be critical.

Printshop owner: My accountant is very important. On a daily basis he is more important than my attorney or banker. But the main problem with all accountants is you have to wait too long to get information. If I have complaints about my accountant I go and get another.

CPA: Timeliness with a CPA is a big problem. Generally speaking, accountants have a bad reputation for getting information back to the client. This problem can be overcome by providing the information to the accountant on a timely basis and in turn requesting a timely response.

Accountant: The big problem is often with the businessowner. They don't respond quickly to our requests for more information in the maintenance of their system. Either they don't get back to us or they say "make something up." Businessowners need to realize that although we provide a service the end result is their ultimate responsibility.

Costs of Accountants

The accountant or accounting service, like the attorney, will quote you hourly rates. In Hawaii, the current rate for a bookkeeping service is $20–$60 per hour, $55–$125 per hour for a CPA, and $100–$175 per hour for a senior partner CPA. A bookkeeping service may cost approximately $200–$350 per month, depending on the services performed. A CPA firm might cost slightly more.

CPA: Generally, our fees are approximately $500 to $1,500 to set up an accounting system including the year-end tax return.

Since there is a wide choice of available accounting services, it is advisable that you have an idea of how you will help your accountant. This information will give your accountant a clear view of what will have to be done and the cost for that service. For example, you might inform your accountant that you plan to do the payroll, GET forms, checkbook, and monthly profit and loss statements. You would like the accountant to do employees withholding tax forms; review every three months the general ledgers and profit and loss statements; assist you in setting up your general ledger and accounting system; a year-end financial statement; and the year-end federal and state tax returns for the business. What would the estimated cost for each of these services be? Your accountant might respond: "I think you are looking at a cost of $200 every three months, plus $400 for the year-end tax return and financial statements." That is the type of cost estimate you need.

CPA: You should ask the accountant for an engagement letter which will include an outline of the estimated fees and of the services to be performed.

CPA: Generally, small businesses do not know what they need. Artists don't want to know about financial statements. They are just interested in creating artwork. Doctors have a significant receivables problem with uncollectable patient invoices. These are highly educated and intelligent people who just want to practice medicine. Who can fault either of them? Who wants to do the drudgery of running a business?

The Hawaii General Excise/Use Tax License

Your accountant will help you with the next step in registering your business with the state. After registering the business name (see chapter 4), you must apply for a general excise tax license. This tax is a gross sales tax that applies to all businesses (full-time or part-time) in Hawaii. We are going to review several accounting decisions you will have to make when filling out the application form for this tax license (Exhibit 13). Some background in these accounting areas, such as choosing your accounting method, will be helpful before you complete the application and meet with your accountant.

A complete discussion of the tax itself is covered in chapter 17. For your meeting with your accountant, however, this review will be limited to the two choices you will have to make on the application: "Filing for Employee's Withholding Tax" and "Accounting methods."

The GET: Filing for Withholding

Do you plan to have employees in your business? If you pay these employees wages, you will have to deduct state (and federal) payroll taxes and estimate the amount of the withholding. Although you are still only filling out the GET form, you are making decisions about the future of your business. If you intend to hire employees, you will need to complete another form to apply for an Employer's Withholding Identification Number (see Chapter 17). Your accountant or the Hawaii Department of Taxation will help you file this form. (The Internal Revenue Service will assist you in filing the complementary federal withholding form for your federal withholding number).

The other major decision you will make is outlined in "Accounting methods." Your choices are "Cash accounting" or "Accrual accounting." (see the reverse side of this form—not shown here.)

The GET: Accounting Methods

Your accounting method, cash or accrual, is one of the areas you will want to cover in some detail with your accountant.

EXHIBIT 13

Application for General Excise Tax License (GET)

This Space for Date Received Stamp

STATE OF HAWAII
DEPARTMENT OF TAXATION
APPLICATION FOR GENERAL EXCISE, USE, EMPLOYER'S WITHHOLDING, TRANSIENT ACCOMMODATIONS, AND RENTAL MOTOR VEHICLE & TOUR VEHICLE IDENTIFICATION NUMBER
WALK-INS: SUBMIT TWO FORMS
MAIL-INS: SEND ORIGINAL ONLY

This Space For Office Use Only

02

Identification Number

Form GEW-TA-RV-3
(Rev. 1992)
TYPE OR PRINT LEGIBLY

1. MAILING ADDRESS	BUSINESS ADDRESS
Taxpayer's Name: Last, First, Middle/Corporation, etc.	DBA Name: (i.e., Your Business Name)
C/O	
Address	Address
City / State / Zip Code + 4	City / State / Zip Code + 4

2. TYPE OF OWNERSHIP (Check One)
1☐ Individual 3☐ Corporation 5☐ State Agency 7☐ Other (Explain)
2☐ Partnership 4☐ Federal Agency 6☐ City Agency

3. PHONE NUMBER
(a) Business ( ) -
(b) Residential ( ) -

4. (a) Your Social Security Number	5. (a) Federal Employer's I.D. Number (FEIN)	6.(a) Contractor's License Number
(b) Spouse's Social Security Number	(b) Parent Corporation's FEIN	(b) Parent Corporation's G.E. I.D. Number

7. OWNERS, PARTNERS, PRINCIPAL CORPORATION OFFICERS: (Note: Attach a separate list if more space is required.)

Social Security Number	Name (Last, First, Middle)	Title	Business Phone Number	Residential Phone Number
			( )	( )
			( )	( )
			( )	( )
			( )	( )

8. APPLICATION IS HEREBY MADE FOR: (Please check all that apply) STARTING DATE, AND LICENSE/REGISTRATION FEE

		Line	Fee
1 ☐ General Excise License	Date Business Began in Hawaii __/__/__ (If Box 1 is checked, enter $20.00 here)	1	$
2 ☐ Employer's Withholding Identification Number	Date Withholding Began __/__/__	2	-0-
3 ☐ Transient Accommodations Registration	Date Transient Accommodations Began in Hawaii __/__/__ (Code 05) ☐ $5.00 (1 - 5 units) (Code 06) ☐ $15.00 (6 - more units)	3	
4 ☐ Seller's Collection	Date Began in Hawaii __/__/__	4	-0-
5 ☐ General Excise License for One-Time Event	Date Began in Hawaii __/__/__ (If Box 5 is checked, enter $20.00 here)	5	
6 ☐ Use Tax Only	Date Imported in Hawaii __/__/__	6	-0-
7 ☐ Rental Motor Vehicle & Tour Vehicle Registration	Date Began in Hawaii (Not Before 01/01/92) __/__/__ (If Box 7 is checked, enter $20.00 here)	7	

Total Amount Due (Add items 1 thru 7)
Pay in U.S. dollars on U.S. Bank to "HAWAII STATE TAX COLLECTOR." Attach check to this form $

9. FILING PERIOD FOR: (check your filing period for the applicable taxes)

(a) General Excise Tax ☐ Monthly ☐ Quarterly ☐ Semi-Annually
(b) Employer's Withholding Tax ☐ Monthly ☐ Quarterly
(c) Transient Accommodations Tax ☐ Monthly ☐ Quarterly ☐ Semi-Annually
(d) Rental Motor Vehicle and Tour Vehicle Surcharge Tax ☐ Monthly ☐ Quarterly ☐ Semi-Annually

For items (a), (c), and (d): Check monthly if you expect to pay more than $2,000 a year of taxes in the respective taxes;
Check quarterly if you expect to pay $2,000 or less a year in the respective taxes; or
Check semi-annually if you expect to pay $1,000 or less a year in the respective taxes.

For item (b): Check monthly if you expect to pay more than $1,000 a year in withholding taxes; or
Check quarterly if you expect to pay $1,000 or less a year in withholding taxes.

FORM GEW-TA-RV-3 **02**

CPA: Most people do not realize the significant implications of Box 14 when they complete the GET form. That is because the GET form is one of the first forms they are expected to prepare. Few recognize the tax elections made with this simple form.

Cash Accounting

Cash accounting requires that you report all sales and income when you receive the cash for them. At the same time you will declare all expenses when you pay for them. It almost seems that that goes without saying.

It would be very straightforward if we handled all business transactions like a supermarket checkout counter. That is, when we buy the goods we pay cash for them right then and there. It gets a little bit more complicated when credit or terms come into the picture. Then it is like using charge cards. We may purchase a television from Windward TV and, instead of paying cash, charge it on our credit card. We take the television home today, but when did we pay for it? At the time we charged it at the store or 45 days later when we pay the charge card bill?

The cash method of accounting says you paid for your purchase 45 days later when you wrote a check to pay off the charge. The accrual method of accounting says that you paid for the television when you charged it.

Your choice of either the cash or accrual method will be influenced by the tax implications assigned to each way of viewing income. Certain businesses, such as doctors or lawyers, in which services are rendered but cash is not received until some time later, may benefit from a cash method accounting system. For example, let us say that you are on the cash accounting method and you have had a good sales year. You may decide to defer receiving some of your sales in December until January of the following year. Although the services have been rendered in December, you did not receive the income until the following year. Therefore you will pay no taxes on that income until the following year.

Unfortunately the cash accounting method cannot be used for any businesses that have inventories or sell products instead of services. These businesses, as well as those others which do not choose to use the cash accounting method, must use the accrual method.

The Accrual Method

Accounting by the accrual method simply means that a sale is made at the time of invoice and not when the cash is received. It also means, that "accounts receivable" exist as well as a potential for a "bad debt" if the bill is not paid, since the customer may not pay immediately.

For example, a carpet cleaning company cleans the carpet of a hotel on February 1 and sends an invoice for the $2,000 fee with payment expected in 30 days. That payment is now due on March 1 even though the work was completed on February 1. The carpet cleaning company has recorded sales of $2,000 in February and must pay all the taxes on the sales, although they have not yet received any cash for the services rendered. Until the hotel makes a payment for the services, the outstanding amount is an account receivable (money owed to the carpet cleaning company). When the hotel makes a payment the account receivable is reduced by that amount.

As you can see from the foregoing, two additional questions you will have for your accountant are:

1. If I have employees in the business, what tax withholding forms do I need?
2. Based on my business structure and type, should I use a cash or accrual accounting system?

Every profession has a unique language. The businessowner has to understand two different types of languages that will relate to his specific type of business. The first language is "shop talk" unique to his industry. The other language needed by the businessowner is the business language used by accountants, bankers, investors, and other business people. It is by using this language that the owner of Windward TV will be able to explain to his banker that, although sales for March were up from February, higher than expected operating expenses reduced net profit. Did you understand that? The accountant is the key adviser in helping you understand this second business language.

Up to this point, you have some background for a meaningful discussion with both your attorney and your accountant. You will need many legal and accounting questions answered before you see your next adviser, the banker.

Additional Reading

Hawaii Dept. of Planning and Economic Development. 1985. *Hawaii Business Regulations*. Honolulu: DPED.

Hayes, Rick Stephen, and C. Richard Baker. 1982. *Simplified Accounting for Non-Accountants*. New York: John Wiley and Sons.

6

Bankers: When Do They Want Your Business?

Most new business people, once they obtain their GET licenses, head for the bank for a business checking account and a business loan. By all means, get your checking account, but wait to make that appointment with the bank manager for a business loan. Postpone this meeting until you are fully prepared to discuss your complete operation.

In the case of the other two advisers, your attorney and your accountant, you went to scrutinize them. It was up to them to sell you on their abilities and services. In the case of your banker, you must sell *yourself.* The sales presentation is on your side of the table. While you will be assessing your mutual rapport, the banker will be judging your abilities. The banker's first impression of you will influence your future. If the impression you make is to be a good one, your presentation should be well prepared.

Bankers would not be considered part of your advisory team if all they did was loan you money. As with accountants, they have seen the internal operations of many businesses. Their experience can help you to succeed if you know how to use it. The banker's experienced advice will be especially evident if the bank lends you money. At that point, it has a vested interest in your success—the return with profit of the bank's money. In this case, you may get advice on your business whether you like it or not. Neither of the other advisers have that much at stake or will become as emotionally involved in your business. If a bank lends you money, consider it more than a bank—consider it a partner.

Choosing Your Bank

1. Location. If possible your bank should be near your business. At the very least, a branch of it should be available for fast access in deposits or to secure special bank services, such as a cashier's check.

2. Bank's responsiveness. A bank is a business and, as in other industries, each has its own marketing style. With the deregulation of the banking industry, savings-and-loan companies and out-of-state banks now have entered a market for the business account that had previously been the exclusive reserve of the local commercial banks. This has forced the local banks to compete for your business. All things being equal, you should prefer to work with a bank that aggressively seeks your business. You can tell how much they want your business by how they handle your request for a loan. Were you treated with respect and speed?

3. The banker. In dealing with the bank you will be working with one person. This person will give you advice and present your proposal to superior officers in the bank to win approval for a loan. If you are working with a branch office, that person will most likely be the branch manager. All the considerations which applied to the selection of your attorney and accountant apply to the selection of your banker.

4. Past personal relationship with the bank. A happy past personal relationship with a bank may be the best starting point for a business account with the same bank.

5. Special services. Each bank has special services for small business accounts. These services may include: business charge cards, an international section, and so on.

Banker: First impressions are very important. And personalities also. In looking for a banker I would recommend a business not just pick the closest bank but look for a banker who you can communicate with, who is creative, open-minded, offers alternatives, and explains things, especially when a loan is denied.

Retailer: I think I spend more time with my banker than I do with my accountant. He has been a source of excellent managerial, as well as, financial advice. When I go in for a loan I really feel that it is he and I against the rest of the loan committee at the main branch. I guess he has a tough job trying to satisfy both sides.

The Banker's Viewpoint

Almost every businessowner can tell some horror story related to his dealings with a bank.

Pet service owner: My initial experience with a bank was horrible. They were very shortsighted and rude. I understand they have rules, but I felt they only knew the words "yes" or "no" and no in betweens.

Garment manufacturer: Many banks are not interested in new small businesses.

Car stereo retailer: I am so disgusted with my bank. They dragged out our loan request. What should have taken three weeks took four months. I am looking for a new bank.

The banker is a business professional who walks to a different beat from the entrepreneur. The first problem most entrepreneurs have in dealing with a banker is they think the banker thinks like they do. In many cases, a banker will approach the business proposal with concerns entirely opposite to those of the entrepreneur. Often when the entrepreneur is optimistic, the banker is pessimistic. When the entrepreneur wants to talk about terrific sales potential, the banker wants to look at costs.

To provide you with a better appreciation of the banker's perspective, let us say that a friend comes to you and asks: "I have this great idea and just need a few bucks to make it work. How about lending me $30,000?"

You: Well, tell me about it.

Friend: I am going to open an ice-cream parlor. It is going big on the mainland and I can get the franchise for Honolulu.

You: Do you have any written specifics?

Friend: Sure. Here is a prospectus about the franchise, including franchise fees.

You: Okay. Now, have you done any thinking about how this relates to Hawaii and how much this might cost all together?

Friend: Yes, I have this written market study about the ice-cream industry in the United States and here in Hawaii. I did the research myself over a three-month period. I think if you look this over you will see how I conclude that this product has a market niche. This separate business plan outlines the start-up costs in detail. I have taken the franchise estimates and worked with my accountant and a contractor to refine the estimates. I have laid out total start-up costs, as well as projected profit and loss statements for the first year of operation. Finally, I have projected our total cash requirements for this period using fairly conservative estimates. I have listed all my assumptions in the beginning of the business plan.

You: Well, I must say that you certainly seem to know what you are doing. Have you selected a site yet?

Friend: Our market study put a lot of thought into the best locations. For that, we worked with a commercial realtor and we have several possible locations as listed in the business plan.

You: I am glad that you included a resumé. However, it does show that you never operated an ice-cream shop before. How do you feel about that?

Friend: That is true. But I have been a manager of a shoe department for the last five years and I feel that the management skills I acquired will be useful in this new venture. In addition, I have spent the last three months visiting several ice-cream shops on the mainland and on the outer islands, talking to these owners to get a better background. In fact, I will be hiring as the general manager a guy who has been running a very successful shop on Maui for the past two years.

You: Is this going to be a sole proprietorship?
Friend: Yes.
You: Are you going to work at this full-time?
Friend: Yes, it is going to take a full-time commitment.
You: I know this is in the package, but how much do you need in total and how much are you putting up?
Friend: Our estimates call for $50,000. Of that amount, I have $20,000 and plan to borrow the remaining $30,000. Our estimates call for $30,000 start-up costs, and we would like to have enough for six months of expenses—$20,000.
You: How about your living expenses?
Friend: I have budgeted that out carefully. Since my wife is working I won't need to take a salary for the first three months. Thereafter, I plan to draw about $500 per month for the first year.
You: Well, what are the terms and my possible return from this loan?
Friend: I have written all that out in this loan request, but to highlight, we would like to borrow $30,000 for five years at 16% interest.
You: It all looks good, but what type of collateral might I have just in case things do not work out.
Friend: You will have the first right as a creditor to proceed against any assets of the company.
You: That is okay but what about any other personal collateral like real estate or stocks and bonds.
Friend: My car and some personal property.
You: How about a guarantor like your father?
Friend: I do not think so.
You: Well, you have given me a lot to look at and consider. I will probably want to see more information on your franchise with special emphasis on the training you will receive. Since I can only lend you up to $10,000 on my own, give me a few days to go over your proposal with my wife and we will see if we can commit $30,000.

What other questions might you ask? What are the major problems you foresee? What did you think of your friend's presentation? How are you going to present this to your spouse? Your thoughts on reviewing your friend's proposal will be influenced by several factors:

1. The size of the loan request. If you had $1 million dollars in your bank account, $30,000 might not be such a major investment. But if it represented your life savings, you would be a lot more careful.

2. The past track record of your friend. A first venture is very risky. But had he come to you having successfully owned and operated a similar store in California, or had he successfully owned some other type of store, you would have more confidence in him. Even if he had failed at a similar project with lessons learned on how to succeed, he might be more appealing than someone with no prior background.

3. His analysis and plans. Are they realistic? Is there substance in the

plan or just a lot of paperwork? Does he really have the market niche he claims? Can he capture that market niche before he goes broke? Has he calculated a worst possible scenario?

4. Where is he going to get more money when he needs it? Has he exhausted all his future borrowing potential? If things go bad will I have to lend him more funds? Has he made an accurate projection of his borrowing needs? Has he overestimated sales?

5. Am I properly protected? If he goes broke, how much can I get back through his collateral pledged?

6. His character. Is his word good? How does he handle his personal finances? What about his business knowledge?

Applying for a Bank Loan

As you might have guessed, the preceding factors are the same ones the banker will consider in dealing with you. Just change the "friend" to you and "you" to the banker. Now that you understand how the banker thinks, let us consider how the banker can be of most help to you—by lending you money.

> **Banker:** Most new small businesses are often angry and disappointed in their initial exposure to banks. That's because they expect the banker to hand over tons of money. Isn't that what a bank's supposed to do? This misconception may arise from their experience as a consumer. Consumer loans and business loans are totally different. Businessowners are disappointed when we can't help them because they expected the same treatment as for a consumer loan. Bankers view new small businesses as totally high risk. Most people don't have an idea of all the things that can go wrong in a business.

> **Retailer:** A bank loan is something you get if you have a lot of assets to use as collateral or if you have a proven track record, preferably both. Since most people starting out normally have neither, a bank loan is a long-term goal, or it means a terrific selling job to the bank.

The key person in getting your bank loan is the bank lending officer, whether it is the branch manager or a loan officer in the main office. Although loan officers vary considerably in what they like in projects and people, their primary concern is whether the loan will be repaid. Since many business loans do become problem loans, it is a legitimate bank concern. Consequently, when you apply for a business loan, the banker will consider the probability that you will be his next problem loan. Can you fault the banker for being conservative and skeptical?

How to Inspire Confidence

If the first concern is your ability to repay the loan, you can expect your banker will want to be convinced that you know what you are doing. If you come to him with a past business track record that fits neatly into your new venture, the banker will start to feel more comfortable. But past business or industry experience is only a start. Even with a good track record, what strengths do you have that will help you in this new venture?

If you have been operating the business for some time, you have a proven track record of sales and profitability. However, in lieu of an actual track record you will need a convincing business plan. The quality of your business plan will determine how much you impress your banker (see appendix A).

A written business plan accomplishes a number of things, but to your banker it demonstrates that you have business expertise or the proper business attitude. If you have been operating the business for a time, then your business plan is used to explain your past performance and your current position.

Banker: Not even 10 percent of new business loan requests come as a written proposal.

Banker: A new businessowner would impress a banker with a written business plan. The most important parts of this plan are: First, does the market plan seem reasonable? Second, do the market plan and the financial plan match? Finally, does the businessowner understand it? Many business plans are prepared by a CPA for the businessowner. But as impressive as these plans may be, if the owner who will have to implement the plan doesn't understand it as written, it's a no go.

Just writing a good business plan will not get you a loan. The banker will still be skeptical. Most experienced business people understand that having a plan and being able to implement it are two very different things. A sure way to show the banker that you can implement your business plan is to demonstrate a successful operating business. Consider the difference in your perspective if your friend of the ice-cream-shop loan pointed out that he was not asking for a new loan, but rather for a loan to expand his successful operation.

The realistic banker, knowing that any business plan will take a long time to implement, believes a business has several key operating periods. The first key operating period is from the day you open until your first anniversary. National records indicate that more than 50 percent of all businesses fail within the first year. If you can show the banker that you have survived this first year, you have at least demonstrated you are better than most of the new business start-ups.

The next significant period encompasses the time up to the end of your third year of operation. A business with three years of operating history has a reasonable track record. Although still considered to be a high risk, the banker will give you a more reasonable probability of success, even if the business has not been profitable.

Only after five years in business does the bank start to take you seriously. Five years! At this point, the company has a proven track record (both up and down) and the owners have had enough experience to handle most ordinary problems. From this point on you have the banker's full attention.

Therefore, if you are just starting out, your banker really does not want to see you for a loan (unless you have a previously successful track record) until at least after the first year. But that does not mean he will not give you a loan. It just means you have to be better prepared and do a terrific sales presentation.

Even if you are not planning to take out a loan until after the first year of operation, prepare a business plan and visit the bank soon after you open. The banker will be delighted that you are not applying for a loan but have instead prepared a business plan to keep him abreast of your progress.

Two reasons for visiting your banker when you are not applying for a loan are: First, you will be establishing a rapport and track record up to the time when the business plan turns into a loan package request. If you have provided your bank with regular updates before the request date, they will know your operation quite well when you finally ask for a loan. Your processing time will be faster and your chances of getting the loan will be much improved because you are indeed a friend and not a stranger. (Replace the word *friend* with the word *stranger* in our loan request example and hear how it sounds.)

Second, providing your banker with regular updates is a way to get feedback from one of your advisers. The banker has an extensive business background and can be a source of valuable local information, as well as of specific information on your business. A banker might be able to provide the same insights as your CPA, at no cost to you. Of course, you do not want to intrude on the banker's time, but if you have established a good rapport, the banker knows the work done now may save hours later when you come in for a loan.

> **Banker:** I see businesses in two main categories: those thinking about going into business and those requesting financing. When a customer comes in to see me with a "thinking about it" approach, I look at the concept—does it make sense. If they come in with a financial request, then I look at the completeness of the package.

Developing a good rapport means being candid with your banker. You must point out the good with the bad. In fact, if you do not point out potential problems, the banker will start to get a little suspicious. Every business has problems. Bankers would prefer to know these up front or at least know that you are aware of your problems. Therefore, the way you handle the potential problems is as important as how you handle your sales estimates. So that your banker can give the best advice, lay out your problems and their possible solutions. By providing both problems and possible solutions you will gain the banker's confidence in your problem-solving ability.

The first step, then, in applying for a loan is to develop your banker's sense of confidence in you. The second step is to assess your collateral position.

Collateral

Understand that although the banker seems to be in a very strong negotiating position, your business is wanted. In fact, the bank wants all of it. Do not think that you will be able to get loans from several banks. That happens only when your sales reach more than several million dollars.

> **Retailer:** After a couple of years with one bank, we thought we would try to establish a borrowing position with another bank too. We were especially worried that if we needed a loan fast, that we were too dependent on one bank. Unfortunately, the other banks did not like the idea. In effect, they said choose one bank for all your borrowing.

> **Banker:** When we look at a business account, we do take into account a businessowner's personal business with us. For example, if we have her personal checking account, personal savings, and IRA, that represents an attractive package for the branch. Of course, if she has had personal loan experience with us that is a big plus.

Consequently, assess your total collateral position to include your past personal relationship with the bank. Here are some strong collateral options:

Real estate—the best collateral; has assignable title and assessable value.
Stocks and bonds—publicly traded stocks and bonds have readily assignable value.
Life insurance—any cash value portion.
Personal savings—any type of savings or pension account.
Past personal credit history—a strong credit history of past borrowing and repayment.
A guarantor—someone with a strong net worth position to guarantee your loan.
The assets of the business—the lease or improvements or inventory of the business itself.

> **Banker:** From the banker's point of view, most businesses are unsecured credit. If a shoe repair store that we give a loan to goes under, what is the bank going to do with 20 pounds of leather?

> **Stereo retailer:** When I first started in business we had a little capital and no real assets. Although the bank asked for a guarantor, we asked if they could make the loan without one. They finally gave us a small loan without any real collateral. I think they did it on our personal record. In essence, they gave us a personal loan for the business.

Of all the factors that influence a banker's loan decision, the character of the businessperson is by far the most important.

Banker: One of the things we are interested in is the character of the individual. How does he handle his personal money. To find that out we may pull a credit check to look at how he pays his bills and at how many overdrafts he may have in his checking account.

Banker: If everything else looks good, but the character is not there, the loan is no go.

Banker: Banks have a standard set of criteria to evaluate loan requests. However, it is not unusual for a banker to make a loan that does not meet all the required standards. Good character is so important. This often happens after we get to know someone. If you feel that this guy is the type to pay you back before he will spend money to go out to a fancy dinner, then, although the loan should not be approved under normal bank standards, it may go just because you know it has a good probability of being repaid.

Having assessed your collateral position, you have a range of alternatives open to you in which to negotiate a loan. Although the bank will want all your possible collateral, your hope is to be able to retain some collateral for future borrowing needs. You will be able to determine how far you can go in preliminary negotiations, and this is best accomplished well before you need the loan. If you have to select your banker one day and ask for a loan the next, all your negotiating will be done under duress.

A much better method is to review your business with your banker a couple of months prior to your loan request. During this time you will "inquire" how a certain dollar loan request might be received by the bank and what the bank might accept in collateral. This same scenario can be used for starting a new business when you need the loan as a condition for opening.

It is always a good idea to remind yourself that the only reason the bank wants collateral is to minimize its potential losses. It does not want to repossess your house if your business loan fails. It is not in the real estate business, at least not in that way. Furthermore, the banker realizes that the full value of the collateral may not be regained in the event of a repossession.

A bank looks at loan collateral at liquidation value. Its feeling is that, if the loan fails, any collateral will not bring its full value under forced sale. Let us look at some different types of collateral and how your banker may value them.

Real estate. You can expect to borrow up to 75 percent of the market value less the mortgage owed. For example, say you and your husband own a condominium in Hawaii Kai and similar units have been selling for $165,000. The balance on your mortgage is $100,000. Seventy-five percent of the market value is $123,750. From this value we subtract the mortgage outstanding of $100,000 and we get $23,750 of collateral value.

Negotiable stocks and bonds. The collateral value of publicly traded stocks and bonds depends upon the security of the stock. If they are high grade stocks and bonds, one might expect to use 60 percent of the stock value as collateral. If the stock value declines, however, the bank may reserve the right to request that additional stock be supplied as collateral to bring the collateral relationship back in line. Bonds are normally collateralized for 90 percent of the face value of the bond.

Business assets. These assets may look good on paper, but the banker usually thinks that, as collateral, they are not worth very much, and with good reason. If the business fails, any inventory will have been depleted, and what type of market is there for your used ice-cream equipment? The banker may be justified in feeling lucky to get 10 cents on each $1 of cost of liquidated business collateral.

When you do finally negotiate your collateral in exchange for a bank loan, attempt to keep some collateral in reserve for future loans. For example, if you were applying for a bank loan on the ice-cream shop, an ideal position would be to secure a $30,000 loan on a pledge of business assets alone without having to take a second mortgage on your home. In this way, if you need future bank loans, you have the option to offer a second mortgage on your home as collateral for that second loan. If you have to pledge all your collateral, you will have no further bargaining chips when you need more money later.

If the bank insists on taking all your collateral on your initial loan (in most cases, they will), then try to get the maximum commitment of a loan, even if you do not plan to use it all. For example, if you need $30,000, you might request $50,000. You can then use the $30,000 you will need as planned and save the other $20,000 as a reserve.

The length of the loan repayment depends on the size of the loan and on the amount of confidence the banker has in you. You can anticipate small, short-term loans until you establish some track record with the bank. Start to establish that track record as soon as possible.

Generally, a short-term note is anything that has a maturity of less than one year. The banker would rather give you the same amount of money in small increments more often than all at one time. These shorter loans are preferred if for no other reason than that they force you to visit the bank more often to review your progress.

Retailer: We started off with 90 day notes to finance our inventory. These were specific dollars tied to specific orders. Everything was really tightly controlled. We went down and signed for each loan every 90 days even if we were going to roll it over for another 90 days. After doing this for a year, we asked for a three-year fixed loan that would cover much of this and give us some extra working capital. I know we got it based upon our track record with the short-term notes. I think it would have been hard to get the three-year loan if we had not done the small loans.

Banker: One of the most important areas is: How is the loan going to be repaid? Most people believe that the only type of business loan is a monthly payback type. I guess this is based on our consumer loan experience. If you take a car loan out, you borrow the entire amount and pay it back monthly. All business loans are not like that. In a business loan we need to know how you plan to pay back the loan. If you borrow $10,000 for 90 days to buy some inventory, by the 90th day were you able to sell the product, collect the payment, pay for the product, and then pay the bank?

Banker: Most people fail to define the need for the loan and its repayment. They want a working-capital loan that ought to be paid back in 90 days paid back in 12 months. For example, they might say they need $30,000 to meet payroll next week but would like to pay it back over three years.

Each banker has a certain loan limit. If your loan request exceeds the limit, your banker will have to sell you and your loan request to his boss and/or to a loan committee. Ask your banker what you should emphasize in your loan package that might sell the loan and then write it accordingly. Remember, your banker will become your salesman in winning higher approval, so make the job easier.

A sample loan proposal is given in appendix B. It is just one in a number of steps needed to achieve a loan. Assuming you have the appropriate collateral, the real question is whether the bank has confidence in you.

After You Obtain Your Loan

Obtaining a bank loan is quite an achievement. If you do get a loan, you should congratulate yourself for more than just getting the money. It also means that professional business people see things the way you do and have confidence that you will be able to accomplish your goals. But be prepared for close supervision from the bank. It now has a vested interest in your success or failure. It will monitor your progress. You can expect to prepare numerous financial reports for review. These reports will multiply if you start to have problems.

Very few businesses operate without problems. When they occur, be able to identify them and show your banker you have a plan of action to resolve them. For instance, if sales are lower than anticipated, submit revised sales estimates along with reasons for the decline, and a plan for reducing costs to compensate for the lower sales. Your candid actions instill confidence. It is what you would expect from your friend if you were the lender.

When your loan goes bad, the banker has a nightmare on his hands: unpleasant calls from his superiors; endless reports to complete when you miss your monthly loan payments. If that happens, your banker needs support from you. Most businesses do just the opposite—they run away from the situation.

Banker: What I hate is when people try to cover it up (late payments) and try to talk around you. I think we are understanding people. Any business is not going to be smooth sailing all the time. We would like to work together with the businessperson. Maybe they forget that the banker can help them too.

Banker: Remember, when you borrow to start a business, you will have a higher break-even cost, so you do not have the luxury of coasting. The bankers are no longer shy about taking your property.

Banker: I feel I have a personal stake in every loan request I grant. If someone is delinquent, I take it personally because I had faith in that person.

The Small Business Administration (SBA) Loan

If the banker views a new small business as a high risk, a loan guarantee from the government might diminish that risk. The Small Business Administration is an agency of the federal government. As such, it provides a number of services for small businesses most notable of which are its loan programs. There are two types of loan programs: (1) loan guarantees and (2) direct loans.

SBA Loan Guarantees

For a loan guarantee, the SBA works with a bank to provide a guarantee of up to 90 percent for the loan made to the small business. Consequently, it is the commercial bank that makes the loan. That means you must first place a loan application with your current banker.

Your banker will probably be the first to suggest the possibility of an SBA guaranteed loan in preliminary discussions concerning your loan request. This suggestion will normally come after review of your loan request to the bank. If the bank feels that your package is not strong enough to be granted as stated, then your loan request will be returned to you with a suggestion that you resubmit it as an SBA guaranteed loan. Before accepting the recommendation, however, explore all your possible options. Could you reduce the size of the loan? How about more collateral?

A good banker will take the time to explain the bank's position. It may be to your advantage not to go with the SBA if you can work something out with the bank. After looking at all the possible alternatives (and do not forget to talk to your accountant for a second opinion), you may decide that you have no other option but to attempt an SBA guaranteed loan. Then have your banker explain all the possible consequences. It might also be advisable to find out if the banker has ever done one before, for as you will discover, the process is very cumbersome.

Most banks do welcome the SBA loan program. The major disadvantage of this program to the banker is that the loan processing time is normally long and requires much documentation (remember you are dealing with the federal government). The responsibility for all the documentation rests with you, the businessperson. Fortunately, your accountant may be experienced in putting an SBA package together, or there are other services that may help with an SBA loan application.

If you do get an SBA loan, be prepared to have restrictions placed on the operation of your company. You will have reports to submit, and you will have to ask permission of the SBA for all major financial changes, such as applying for a new loan or changing your salary. (In many cases, these restrictions are not unlike those that might be placed by your bank.)

> **Retailer:** When we first received news that we had got an approval for our SBA loan, we were elated. However, when we received the list of restrictions, such as getting SBA approval on all future loan requests, we were pretty upset. Even though our bank said these were standard procedures, we could really foresee a nightmare with the SBA holding up the operations of our business. We went ahead and fortunately never encountered any problems. Both the bank and the SBA were very professional to work with.

SBA Direct Loans

A second type of SBA loan is an SBA direct loan. In this case your bank and one other lending institution first must have turned you down for any loan (outer island businesses only need one bank turndown). When this happens, you may apply directly to the SBA for a loan.

Needless to say, you are considered a high risk by other financial institutions, and the SBA knows it. The documentation procedure will now be completed between you and the SBA directly. You no longer have the luxury of a banker to sell your program to the SBA.

> **Banker:** Most businesses don't know about SBA loans, or they have heard a lot of negative things about them, so they don't want to try going that way. These negative things relate to more documentation required and the hard questions that the SBA asks.

Having sources of funds available is a never ending responsibility of the successful businessowner. In addition to being a primary source of money for your business, your banker is an experienced business adviser who should be fully utilized by a business.

With your advisory team—attorney, accountant, banker—complete, your business name registered, and a general excise tax license applied for, let us now look at some Hawaii business basics.

Additional Reading

Blaine, Devon. 1986. "When the Bank and I Broke Up." *Venture* (November): 132.

Greene, Gardiner G. 1983. *How to Start and Manage Your Small Business.* Bergenfield, NJ: New American Library.

PART III

Some Hawaii Business Basics

7

Suppliers: Are They Better Than Bankers?

In the excitement of opening their small barbeque-rib restaurant, the young couple from Texas had not realized that meat prices from their supplier had been seasonal. Unfortunately, when they held their grand opening, the menus, which had been printed using lower meat prices, no longer applied. For each meal they sold at the grand-opening introductory price, they lost money. The restaurant soon printed new menus reflecting the new meat costs, underscoring the importance of their food supplier.

The meat this restaurant was using represented a *cost of goods* it planned to resell in the form of meals. In chapter 5, we saw how the televisions represented a cost of goods for Windward TV. Although the cost of goods is more commonly associated with retail, wholesale, and manufacturing businesses, even service businesses may use certain types of supplies that generate costs of goods or services. For example, a janitorial service would consider the cost of cleaning solutions a direct cost of goods. These costs of goods are important because they influence the final cost of the goods or services provided.

The supplier will be valuable to a business for many more reasons than just supplying the raw materials at a competitive price. An alert business-owner will utilize the supplier as a source of industry information, product training, advertising support, and trade credit. Fortunately, if you are starting a new business, your suppliers are going to be anxious to see you because you are a potential customer.

Artist: I was surprised how our packaging supplier helped us. We are real small, but they spent a lot of time with us the very first time we went in.

Types of Suppliers

The three major types of suppliers are the manufacturer, the distributor, and the sales representative.

The manufacturer is that company which makes or is ultimately responsible for the distribution of a product. Buying directly from the manufacturer entails finding the regional office that includes Hawaii in its territory and contacting their sales office. The sales office will then forward you their price list, shipping instructions, and payment requirements. If the manufacturer has a Hawaii branch office, they may send a salesperson. Most manufacturers, however, do not have the resources to establish regional offices in Hawaii. Many manufacturers may then contract with a local distributor to sell their products in a particular geographic area. Unlike a branch office of a manufacturer, a distributor is an independent business which buys, warehouses, and sells many manufacturers' products.

By using distributors the manufacturer is able to warehouse a product in many more geographic areas throughout the country than it could alone (Exhibit 14). A Hawaii distributor offers the customer immediate warehoused stock and service where a manufacturer located in Ohio could not. In exchange for this service, however, the distributor normally charges a higher price than the manufacturer.

Distributor: The primary role of the distributor is to provide local stock to the retailer or user. Traditionally, the distributor was supposed to fill the need of the small accounts which could not meet minimum manufacturer order requirements or which did not want to risk carrying large inventories in their stores. The retailer, in using the services of the distributor, was willing to pay slightly higher prices for the convenience of local stock and service.

Appliance retailer: Since there are several local distributors in Hawaii for appliances, most retailers keep very little stock in their own warehouses and just ask the distributor to deliver as often as they need it. In this way, the retailer is not tying up all his dollars in inventory which is sitting in his warehouse.

TV retailer: The retailer rides a fine line between being out of stock and being overstocked. The customer who is willing to buy may not be willing to wait for the delivery of the product if your competitors have something he can get right away.

Another way that a manufacturer can extend representation into an area where it does not have its own sales force is by contracting with an independent sales representative company. The sales representative, unlike the distributor, is not the actual supplier. You still will purchase your goods from the manufacturer, but you will receive sales, ordering, and technical support from the sales representative. The sales representative may represent many manufacturers, and is basically an extension of the sales force of the manufacturer.

Finding Your Supplier

To the uninitiated, product suppliers are not very visible. Where does one go to find the suppliers in an industry?

EXHIBIT 14

Typical Product Flow for Consumer Goods to Hawaii

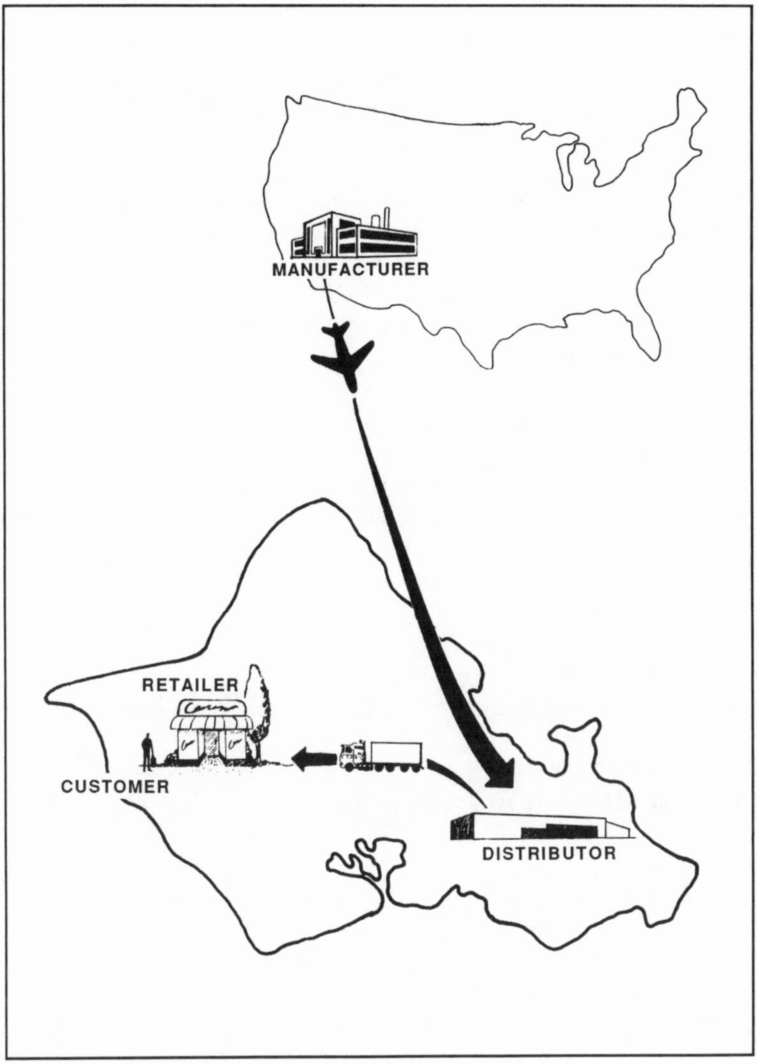

1. Other Businesses. Similar types of businesses can be a ready reference to a wide range of suppliers. If you are planning to open a restaurant, other restaurants would be a good place to start to look for your supplier. If you are in a small industry and the other similar businesses are all competitors, you might consider gathering supplier information from similar businesses on the other islands. For example, if you were planning to start a swimsuit specialty shop on Oahu, it might be difficult to get a swimsuit shop on Oahu to give you industry information, since they may consider you a competitor. However, if you were able to convince a swimsuit shop

on Maui that you were only interested in staying on Oahu, that owner might be willing to tell you all about local suppliers and how they compare with mainland suppliers. In addition she might tell you which suits sell for her, what seasonal sales' swings she has, and what her costs are.

Waipahu retailer: When we first started we got a wealth of information from some of the bigger retailers in our industry in the Honolulu area. I guess they never considered us a threat and they were very helpful in a lot of areas.

2. Trade Magazines. Each industry has specific trade magazines which provide product information, selling ideas, and general trade background. These magazines are not distributed to the general public and are often free to businesses in the industry.

The main branch of the Hawaii State Library has a list of references to different trade magazines by industry. The library also has some of these magazines available.

3. Trade Shows. Almost every industry has a national trade show at least once a year at which businesses in that industry can meet suppliers. These shows and conventions are advertised in the trade magazines.

4. Local Associations. Many industries have local associations. These associations can be an excellent place to receive supplier information. Some examples of these associations are:

Retailers—Retail Merchants' Association
Artists—Arts Council of Hawaii
Food Processors—Hawaii Food Manufacturers' Association

Getting Credit from Your Supplier

This chapter is titled "Suppliers: Are They Better Than Bankers?" for good reason. Although the quality of the supplier's product, the price, stock availability, freight charges, and other services offered are all considerations in your selection of a supplier, this section is going to concentrate on the *trade credit* the supplier may extend.

Trade credit is to a business what a charge card is to an individual. When a business makes a purchase on trade credit, it does not have to pay for those goods or services immediately.

Common Types of Credit Terms

1. "COD"—Cash On Delivery. Payment for the goods or services is due at the time of delivery or on completion of the service. This is the most stringent credit term because it offers no option to delay payment. In your personal life, the supermarkets give you COD credit terms on your purchase of food.

2. "Net 30"—This credit term simply means that your payment is due 30 days from the date of the invoice. Any number may be substituted for 30 as in Net 60 or Net 10. Your personal credit card purchases might be considered credit terms of Net 30. If you make a credit card purchase, you may not have to pay for the purchase until you receive your statement the following month.

3. "2/10 Net/30"—This type of credit term gives you an incentive to pay sooner. In this case, you are entitled to take a 2 percent discount from the total invoice if you submit payment within 10 days of the invoice date. If you do not take the discount, then the entire bill is due by the 30th day.

Retailer: Terms are very important to us. We know it takes us about 60 days to sell each piece of merchandise we receive. If a company offers us Net 30 terms, that means we must pay the entire bill when only half of the merchandise is sold. Right now we have changed our supplier to one that has slightly more expensive products but offers us better terms of Net 60. We feel that if we can turn our inventory every 60 days, the sale of the goods will pay for the products, our cashflow will be greatly improved, and the only thing we did was change our terms.

Wholesaler: Most businesses need some type of terms to survive.

Getting trade credit terms is equivalent to getting a bank loan. For example, if Windward TV buys ten televisions at a cost of $250 each, the total bill due is $2,500 (10 televisions × $250). On terms of COD, the owner must come up with all $2,500 before receiving delivery.

With Net 30 terms, on the other hand, the owner can take delivery of all the televisions without making any payment at that time. If it were possible to sell five of those televisions at $500 each by the 30th day, the sales would generate the necessary $2,500 (5 televisions × $500) to pay for the suppliers invoice of $2,500. This is a very simplistic example, for it is rarely that easy. What is important is the understanding that the extension of trade credit is, in effect, a short-term loan from your supplier.

Sales representative: I remember this stereo shop started by a local guy. He couldn't get a bank loan or even a small line of trade credit when he started. Now he has a $500,000 line of trade credit with just one supplier!

It took this retailer ten years to build that line of credit with a supplier. Like the banker, the manufacturer and distributor are going to want to see a track record before they are willing to expand that credit line. But, unlike the banker, suppliers are in a more open position to grant you some type of credit terms. In addition to being more open to the granting of credit than a banker, a supplier will usually require a minimal amount of collateral, no written loan proposal, and a short time for approval. Isn't this easier than applying for a bank loan?

Wholesaler: The things that weigh in our consideration for the extension of credit are: length of time in business, amount of assets, credit lines from other

> suppliers, and the size of the store. Generally, our sales representative will come back with a recommendation. For us, almost everyone can get at least $300 to start. From that point, we really monitor the first couple of payments. If they are prompt or take the discounts, then it is easy for us to take it to $1,000 or higher. You would be surprised how many people screw up on their first payment with a bounced check or have us chase the first invoice.

The other consideration for trade credit is the credit limit. Think of your credit limit as being similar to the credit limit on your charge cards. Your initial charge card limit might have been $300. If you are the same as many other people, in a short period of time you had charged up to your limit and could no longer use your credit card. After some good experiences, the bank sent you an unsolicited note saying that as a valued customer your credit limit had been raised to $1,000. The same practices that apply to your personal credit limit also apply to how your business credit is extended by your suppliers.

For example, Windward TV is given a credit line of $2,500 and Net 30 terms. They purchase ten televisions and use their entire credit line. In the first week, one model sells out. If they try to place an order on terms with their supplier, the order will be held up or rejected in the credit department because they are "over credit limit." They are not past due, in fact, they still have three more weeks before the invoice is due. But unless they can obtain a higher credit limit, they are in effect on COD for any new orders.

In large companies, the credit department is separated from the sales department for good reason. If they were not separated, the sales department might make credit extension too easy in their pursuit of higher sales. The sales department is on your side. They want you to have a higher credit line, for that should mean more sales. But it is the credit department and, more specifically, the credit manager who you will have to convince to increase your credit line. The credit manager views your business in terms of how well you pay your bills. If you are prompt in your payment and take the discounts, you are liked. But credit managers are very cautious in extending credit limits.

Because most growing businesses need increased lines of credit, one approach to increasing a supplier's credit line is to enlist the aid of your sales representative. By paying your bills on time, you can request higher credit lines. Most credit managers want to work with you, and if they receive some assurance from the sales representative, they will generally take you at your word until you prove otherwise.

Once you have established your credit with at least one supplier, that supplier will then become the reference for future suppliers. There is nothing that will get you credit faster with other suppliers than having one tell another that you pay promptly or "take the discount."

The process of increasing your credit limit and your terms is never ending. The stronger your sales position becomes with a supplier the more you should press for increases in terms and credit lines. Most businesses just concentrate on getting the best prices from suppliers and completely miss the importance of terms and credit lines.

> **Distributor:** I don't think our dealers ask enough about terms. For the most part we initiate those offers as sales programs. In some cases, we need to move some stock and are willing to make some real exceptions, like Net 90, to clear it.

> **Retailer:** One method that works for us to increase credit terms with mainland manufacturers is to point out the difference in shipping times to Hawaii. Remember, it helps to give the credit manager some credible reason for making an exception for you.

Your relationship with your suppliers can become a classic love-hate situation. On the one hand, you are entirely dependent on them to complete your product line or service. You will thank them for that service and for accepting your excuses when payment is delayed. On the other hand, you will raise your voice when they forget a crucial delivery. But as important as suppliers' products and services are, their credit extension is critical. A business is always short of cash, and suppliers' credit is a major source of funds.

8

Location: Where Is Paradise?

Ralph had just bought a new ice-cream shop located in a Waikiki condominium. Considerable foot traffic existed on both streets of the condominium. Unfortunately, the ice-cream shop was located in the building on the second floor and was not visible to the street traffic. The only major traffic on the second floor seemed to come from the building's tenants. Recognizing this, Ralph implemented the only plan he could—an ambitious advertising program to draw in business. That did not work, and within six months he was out of business.

A couple of years later Ralph purchased a coffee shop. Like the ice-cream shop, this new business was located in a high traffic area, but unlike his previous venture it was located at street level. Although there are a number of other reasons that may have contributed to Ralph's current success, his improved location for the type of customer he was attempting to attract was a significant factor.

Everyone realizes that the location of a business is important, but not everyone considers all the factors that relate to location selection. While we might agree with a realtor who says that the three most important things in buying a home are location, location, and location, we must also realize that a businessowner must take into consideration several site factors that a home buyer may not.

What made you choose your current residence, the neighborhood, the monthly rent, or the pool? These considerations are not unlike the ones you will use in the selection of your business location.

Questions to Ask

To help in this analysis, let us ask eight questions about a business location that would not apply in the selection of a home.

Type of Business

Question 1: What is your business image?

Is the business in retail, professional, wholesale, or manufacturing? What is the image that this business is attempting to convey? Every business has an image. The type of building, the geographic location, and even the surrounding businesses will either support or detract from the business's intended image. To determine business image, you must ask yourself the following:

- Is the business in retail, wholesale, service, or manufacturing?
- What types of facilities are comparable businesses using?
- Will your business be upscale, similar to, or lower scale than these businesses?

Our hypothetical business, Waikiki Tax Service, might classify its business image as professional and lower scale than most of the similar businesses operating from business office space. In the future, the business might look for a small office space and move out of the residential office. Windward TV would consider itself a retail operation with a more upscale image than its competitors.

Location of Your Competition

Question 2: Does the location of your competitors affect your location? If so, should you locate farther away or closer to those competitors?

One way to look at the location of your competition is to grant your competition a certain geographic advantage and select a different geographic area where that competition may not be as visible. The theory is that, other things being equal, a store or service located in a specific area has a closer tie to the customers in that area. Another view on location is to look at your competitor as dominant in the market and to position yourself next to that competition to share the competitor's traffic. This is illustrated by the clustering of fast-food restaurants. For many other businesses the location of competitors may be of no consequence. A tree trimming business that serves the entire island of Oahu may not care about the location of its competitors.

Location of the Majority of Target Customers

Question 3: Where are the majority of the target customers and are these customers coming to you or are you going to the customer?

Are customers going to seek you out or are you going to seek the customer? If the customer is coming to you, is customer traffic flow-through traffic as in an ice-cream shop, or is it destination traffic such as that found in a doctor's office?

Need for High Visibility

Question 4: What is the need for high visibility?

High visibility equates to a location that receives high foot or vehicular traffic. Unfortunately, high visibility also means higher lease costs. Not every business needs high visibility. A sales representative company which calls on its customers may not need to be seen. A dentist who relies on referrals may not need to be located on the main street. A manufacturing company which does not sell directly to the public does not have to be in a high traffic area.

Retail businesses, however, need high visibility. High visibility means ease of access. If your business is not convenient to your customer base, then you force the customer to seek you out. To succeed this way, you must have a good reputation or do more advertising.

To summarize, your ideal location will be a site that is convenient to the majority of your customers, takes into consideration your strategy with your major competitor, has addressed the need for high visibility, suits the image you are trying to convey, and fits your price range. This type of broad analysis will point the way to your specific site selection. Specific site locations can now be compared by looking at the following areas.

Space Required

Question 5: What are the minimum space requirements?

To determine the correct amount of space needed for your business, start with some advice from other businessowners, preferably ones in a similar type of business, and with a commercial real estate agent.

A fine line exists between need and want. We all want more space, but the question is, do we really need it. A good way to approach this problem is to determine the *minimum* requirements for your space, parking, and storage needs. Then compare the *ideal* space requirements calculated on three-years growth. Your true space requirements will probably fall somewhere between these two estimates.

Although space requirements are relative to the size of the company and to the type of operation, we might still generalize on some minimum space requirements in Hawaii.

Type of Business	*Estimated Minimum Space*
A one- to two-person office	100–300 square feet (sq ft)
A three- to five-person office	300–700 sq ft
Small restaurant	500–1000 sq ft
Small retail shop	300–750 sq ft
Small warehouse space	300–1000 sq ft

(If you have a difficult time visualizing 400 sq ft, start by measuring your living room. A living room that measures 20 ft by 20 ft is 400 sq ft.)

Renovations Required

Question 6: What renovations does each site need? Is the site functional?

Except for small office spaces, very few sites escape the need for some renovation to customize the work area or store presentation. Renovations include: painting, lighting, carpeting, plumbing, walls, or work necessary to meet governmental regulations as for a restaurant. Any semipermanent or permanent improvement can be considered a renovation.

The real question is: Does the space do what you want it to do?

Realtor: I had a client who was ready to sign a lease and at the last minute realized they needed 24-hour air conditioning. Since the site they were about to lease did not meet that requirement, we were back looking for a new site.

Cost

Question 7: What are the costs of the different locations?

Space costs are normally quoted in dollars per square foot. This dollar amount can be quoted in several ways, as shown in the following discussion on types of leases.

There are five major items that affect the cost of a lease:

1. Space rent—the actual space to be leased.
2. Common area maintenance fees—the prorata cost charged to your leased space for the maintenance of elevators, security, and other common areas.
3. Property taxes—the prorata portion of state property taxes.
4. Building insurance—your prorata share of the general building, fire, and liability insurance. Not to be confused with your own liability and fire insurance, which you have to secure separately.
5. Utilities—generally electricity and water.

Each of these costs will be discussed in relation to the different types of leases.

Types of Leases

A Gross Lease

All five components—space, common area maintenance, property taxes, building insurance, and utilities—are included in the rate for a gross lease. The rate may be given for the entire space (as $500 monthly gross rent) or on a square foot basis (as $1.50 per square foot monthly gross rent).

A Net Lease

The rate for a net lease (or a triple net lease as it may sometimes be called) applies only to the actual space rented. A net lease assumes that the tenant will bear the additional prorated charges for common area maintenance, property taxes, utilities, and even building insurance. Consequently, a rate quoted at $1.50 per square foot will mean two different things depending on whether it is a gross or net lease. Unless one can quantify the additional costs which complete a net lease, any comparison with a gross lease is difficult.

Here is an example. Let us assume that you are looking at two possible locations. Location A has a gross rate of $1.50 per square foot for 500 square feet. Your total cost will be $750 (500 × $1.50) plus 4 percent tax per month. Location B is $1.15 per square foot at a net rate for a similar 500-square-foot site. You are able to confirm that the space is charged $.30 per square foot for maintenance. You then estimate that utilities will cost you $.20 per square foot (an estimate of $100 per month divided by 500 square feet), and that the property tax and building insurance portion charged to you will be $.15 per square foot. Given these estimates, the total cost per square foot of location B is:

Space rent	$1.15 per sq ft
Common area maintenance	.30
Utilities	.20
Property tax	.15
Total	$1.80 per sq ft

The total cost can now be estimated for location B at $900 ($1.80 × 500 sq ft) plus 4 percent tax.

Dressshop owner: I did not know there were all these extra charges on top of the square foot cost after I signed the lease. It surprised me.

Realtor: Ask for a definition of the net lease. Everyone's interpretation is different.

A paragraph from a standard net lease might look like this:

This is an absolute net lease. Tenant is to pay all property related costs including tenants own utilities, personal property and liability insurance plus all other costs of operating the tenant's business. Tenant shall also pay their pro-rata share of the property's net operating expenses including, but not limited to: real property tax, common area maintenance, management, building fire and liability insurance, conveyance tax, assessments. The net operating expenses are currently $________ per square foot monthly. 4.167% general excise tax and recovery shall be added to the base rent and net operating expense reimbursement.

Percentage of Sale Lease

Under the percentage of sale lease arrangement, the lessor (the property owner) will assess you a percentage of your gross sales or a minimum fee, whichever is greater. In this case the landlord gets to participate in a higher rental if the tenant performs well. This type of lease is more common at shopping centers.

Other Considerations in a Lease

Question 8: What other considerations like parking, option to sublease, improvement restrictions, and insurance requirements does the lessor have in the lease?

Option to renew. Some leases may be negotiated with an option to renew the lease after the initial lease period expires. This renewal option will often result in a price increase. For example, you might negotiate an office space at $1.50 per square foot gross for two years and have an option to renew the lease for an additional three-year period at the going fair market rate.

Option to sublease. Whether you plan to or not, you might want the option to sublease part or all of your space. This option in a lease is dependent upon the approval of the lessor. It offers the opportunity to decrease your overhead expense by sharing space, or to move to another space before the lease has expired and subleasing that space to someone else.

Parking. Parking for your customers and your staff is more a necessity than a luxury. Unless otherwise negotiated, employee parking is normally a separate cost. Parking rights need to be addressed in the lease.

Improvement restrictions. Improvement restrictions are dependent upon the type of building and the attitude of the lessor. Generally, if the improvement will enhance the leased space, most lessors are fairly accommodating. On the other hand, if you are planning to make extensive improvements, it might be advisable to review these plans during your lease negotiation with your lessor.

Insurance requirements. The lessor will request that you carry a minimum liability and fire insurance policy and that the lessor be named as an additional insured party under your policy.

Finding the Location

You will increase your chances of finding a location that is ideal if you start with a lot of patience. It will probably take you as long to find a suitable business location as it would to find a new house. It would be unusual for you to find a business location that satisfies all your requirements. In most cases, there will be compromises as you narrow your possibilities. You can look for your location by yourself or with the help of a commercial real estate agent.

> **Downtown office specialist realtor:** The business decisionmaker should always have an agent to represent him. The landlord will most often pay the real estate fees, not the lessee. But even in the rare instances where the business-owner ends up paying directly for the real estate broker's commission by prior agreement, I have normally assisted the tenant in negotiating something favorable in the lease that more than makes up for my fee.

> **Realtor:** In most cases, our fee will be the equivalent of one or two month's rent, depending on the length of the lease.

Maximize your real estate agent's efforts by providing a detailed guide. If nothing else, provide the agent with the answers to the numbered questions in this section. A good real estate agent will be able to fine-tune these guidelines within current market availability.

> **Commercial real estate broker:** Rent per square foot is determined by supply and demand. If the availability in an area is low and there is high demand, then rents will rise. Since that status will change as new building space is developed, the going rate in an area will change accordingly.

Finding the right location may take a few days, a couple of months, or more than a year for large organizations. An often overlooked consideration is that the landlord may be seeking a certain mix of tenants and may not want you because of your type of business.

> **Realtor:** Ninety days is an average time to find a location. But I have taken as long as thirteen months with one client.

> **Real estate agent:** Landlords are cautious. A wrong tenant added to the building may make it difficult to rent other space.

A normal lease term is three to five years. If there are major improvements, then the landlord might consider a longer lease with an option to renew.

> **Realtor:** The landlord wants a lease length of a minimum of three to five years. But if the space has been vacant for a while, you can probably negotiate a shorter lease of one to three years. Someone wanting retail space usually wants two to five years with options for additional years. Some landlords stay away from options—they see them as benefits to the tenant only.

As of 1995, the cost of space in Hawaii was approximately as follows:

Office space	$1.50–3.25 per sq ft gross
Retail space	$2.00–6.00 per sq ft gross
Warehouse space	$ .60–1.25 per sq ft gross

Negotiating the Lease

What you are able to negotiate in the lease with the landlord will depend on the market supply and demand for that space. If the space is in high demand and space is tight, the landlord may not have to negotiate, because he will have a waiting list of possible tenants. If, on the other hand, there is space that has been vacant for some time, your position is improved. The most common concession a landlord might make to a new tenant is a month or more of free rent. This concession is granted to accommodate the tenant during the moving and renovation period. Sometimes the cost of painting the interior or of new carpeting is assumed by the landlord.

Finding a suitable business location is similar to finding a new place to live. Factors in both decisions balance what is available for lease with what you hope to spend. In addition, consideration must also be given to renovation costs, parking, and future growth needs. But there the similarities end, because a business has one other consideration that a home location does not—the customer. To complete its marketing strategy, a business will have to decide how its location will affect its target market and its market plan. An error here will have more serious consequences than an error in selecting the wrong color for a bathroom.

9

Freight: One Cube or Two?

The old adage, "What you don't know won't hurt you," did not have freight costs in mind. Living in Hawaii, we are accustomed to having many items shipped or flown into the state. We assume that freight expenses added to our cost of living are just part of the cost of paradise. If freight costs are so much a part of our lives, why is it that we are so unfamiliar with them? One of the reasons appears to be that the freight industry, in establishing rates, has done so in what could easily qualify as advanced mathematics. Consequently, if your business plans to use mainland or overseas suppliers, or if you plan to ship products to the outer islands, now is the time to take out your calculator.

Domestic freight rates are regulated by either the state or federal governments under a tariff system. This tariff system covers the maximum charges for certain types of service and for product shipment.

Shipper: The tariffs are rates and procedures for all shippers to follow. But because there are so many options, and the procedures are somewhat complicated for the uninitiated, I can understand why most people are lost when it comes to freight rates and options.

Retailer: Our freight expense is significant, and we used to take everything at face value on the billing. Especially since it looked so complicated. But a very conscientious bookkeeper on our staff took the time to sort things out and to our amazement found some significant billing errors on the part of the shipping companies.

The two primary freight methods in Hawaii are air freight and ocean freight.

Air Freight

Air freight rates are determined by "cubes," weights, and density. A "cube" is an abbreviation for *cubic volume measurement,* and density relates to the weight of a package relative to its volume. In freight, those are the two major considerations, the size (dimensions) and weight of a package or shipment.

To calculate the cubic measure of a package, multiply the outer dimensions in inches and divide by 1,728. For example, let us assume that a package to be shipped to you will measure 36 inches long by 12 inches wide by 14 inches deep (36 in × 12 in × 14 in). Multiplying these dimensions will give the result: 6,048 cubic inches. Most freight rates, however, are determined in cubic feet not cubic inches so we divide our total cubic inches by 1,728 (1 cubic foot = 12 in × 12 in × 12 in) and find that our package is 3.5 cubic feet or 3.5 cubes (Exhibit 15).

For most of the products shipped surface or ocean, all you now need is the destination or where it will be shipped from (if the destination is Hawaii), and the freight company will be able to quote you a rate.

There is, however, one other factor for most air freight companies—density. Density takes into consideration the weight of the package relative to its volume (Exhibit 16). Consequently, shipping 3.5 cubic feet of foam seats versus 3.5 cubic feet of steel brackets may call for different rates, although both require the same cubic space. To calculate the density of the package:

1. Calculate the cubic feet; then
2. Divide the actual weight by the cubic feet (cu ft).

Here are two examples: for foam seats weighing 30 pounds, calculate

1. 36 in × 12 in × 14 in = 6,048 cu in; 6,048 cu in/1,728 cu in = 3.5 cu ft
2. 30 lb ÷ 3.5 cu ft = 8.57 or 9 lb/cu ft.

For steel brackets weighing 100 pounds, calculate

1. 36 in × 12 in × 14 in = 6,048 cu in; 6,048 cu in/1,728 cu in = 3.5 cu ft
2. 100 lb ÷ 3.5 cu ft = 28.57 or 29 lb/cu ft

The density of the foam seats is 9 pounds per cubic foot and, for the same box with steel brackets in it, it is 29 pounds per cubic foot.

As you might guess, the cost for the shipment by air freight will be based upon the cubic feet, density, shipping distance, and how fast you want the shipment delivered. For now, let us simplify things by saying that there are overnight, next day, and space available types of air freight deliveries, each with its own rate structure. One of these categories is used in the example in Exhibit 17, Sample Air Freight Rate Structure. The example is for air freight in a density/space available category. Let us calculate our estimated freight from Akron, Ohio, for each of our sample shipments. The rate chart is partially re-created in Exhibit 17.

EXHIBIT 15

Estimating Cubic Feet

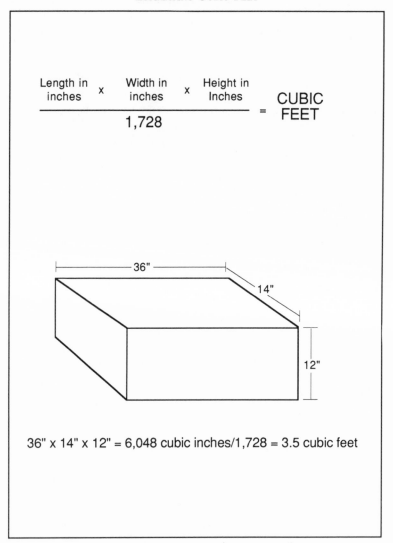

$$\frac{\text{Length in inches} \times \text{Width in inches} \times \text{Height in Inches}}{1{,}728} = \text{CUBIC FEET}$$

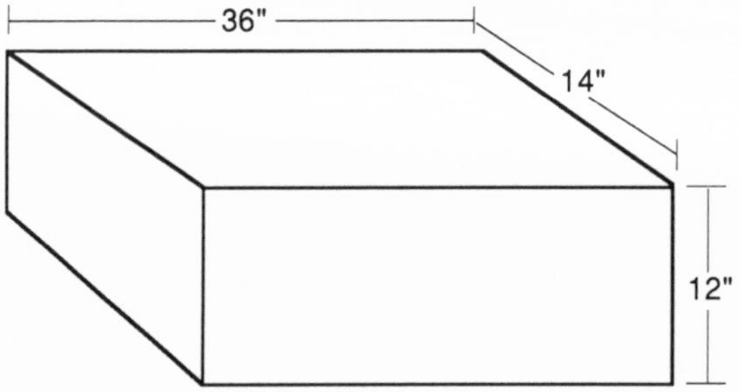

36" x 14" x 12" = 6,048 cubic inches/1,728 = 3.5 cubic feet

The foam seats have a density of 9 pounds per cubic foot. In the section "When the density is," we find the line for a density of "At least 9," "But less than 12." We then go across that line and learn that our shipment of 30 pounds will fall in the first category because it is under 100 pounds. The rate per pound in that category is \$1.62. Our estimated cost will be \$48.60 (\$1.62 × 30). Notice there is a minimum charge of \$30.

To ship our other example, those steel brackets, we discover that at a density of 29, we are in the category of "At least 25," "But less than—." At

EXHIBIT 16

Estimating Shipping Density

HOW DENSE IS YOUR FREIGHT?

Density is usually defined by pounds per cubic foot. To determine density you must first establish the volume of a shipment.

$$\text{VOLUME} = \text{LENGTH} \times \text{WIDTH} \times \text{HEIGHT}$$

$$\text{CUBIC FEET} = \frac{L'' \times W'' \times H''}{1728} \text{ or } L' \times W' \times H'$$

Once you have the number of cubic feet, you divide the weight by the number of cubic feet to derive the density.

$$\text{DENSITY} = \frac{\text{WEIGHT}}{\text{CUBIC FEET}}$$

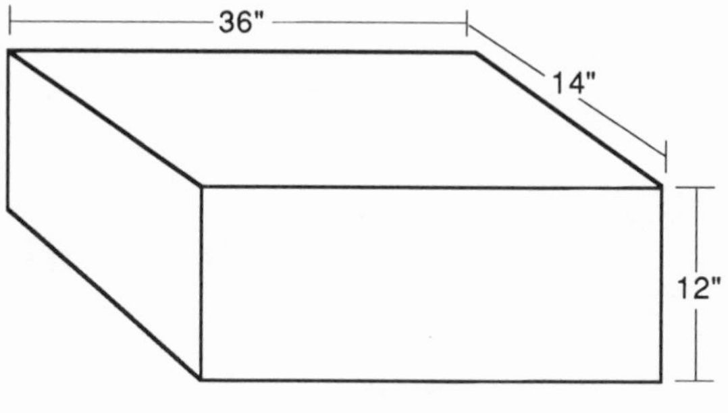

EXAMPLE: $\frac{36'' \times 14'' \times 12''}{1728} = \frac{6{,}048}{1728} = 3.5 \text{ ft.}\ \frac{30 \text{ lbs.}}{3.5} = 8.57 \text{ lbs./ft.}$

Therefore the density of the package shown above is 8.57 lbs. per cubic ft.

100 pounds, the rate is \$58.75. Not as bad as you might have expected. The reason is that this air freight rate structure is designed for dense items. The delivery rate is on a space available basis, so we might expect delivery in three to five days. If the brackets weighed 163 pounds, we would calculate \$58.75 × 1.63 = \$95.76.

Air freight manager: Often shippers do not specify which type of service they are requesting. In these cases, we send the shipment regular air. If the shipper wanted a cheaper, slower service, like space available air freight, he may get upset.

EXHIBIT 17

SAMPLE AIR FREIGHT RATE STRUCTURE
TO HONOLULU FROM AKRON, OHIO (SPACE AVAILABLE BASIS)

When the density (lb/cu ft) is:		Rate ($)				
At least	But less than	1 lb+	100+	500+	1000+	2000+
25	—	0.90	58.75	55.85	52.95	50.05
20	25	1.02	66.10	62.90	59.65	56.40
15	20	1.21	78.45	74.65	70.85	67.05
12	15	1.36	88.60	84.35	80.10	75.85
9	12	1.62	105.60	100.60	95.55	90.50

NOTE: Minimum charge $30.

Often, when a manufacturer is shipping the same packaged product over and over again, cubic and density calculations are readily available. Some even include them in the product brochures. If nothing else, a call to the manufacturer should give you an estimate. With these estimates you can discuss your different options and cost alternatives more intelligently with your air freight sales representative.

What do you think the freight factor (the percentage freight cost to the total cost of the shipment) for the foam seats might be? Let us assume that each foam seat costs us $7 and that there are 20 in a box. That means:

Cost per seat		$7.00
Total invoice cost ($7 × 20 seats)	$140.00	
Freight cost	48.60	
New total cost	$188.60	
NEW COST PER SEAT ($188.60 ÷ 20 seats)		$9.43

Sometimes, in the course of business, a product needs to be sent "rush." If consideration is not given to increased freight costs, what you don't know will hurt you.

> **Retailer:** We do about 50 percent of our purchasing from local distributors and the other 50 percent from the mainland. We have tried to work out freight arrangements with the suppliers where they cover some of the freight costs if we order a certain amount. These suppliers have some freight allowance for mainland dealers, but you would think they consider Hawaii as part of Borneo by the way they approach any type of similar freight discount for Hawaii.

Hawaii is fortunate in having a wealth of air freight carriers. You can be selective in choosing the best freight forwarder for your needs. Although prices vary and are a major consideration, service that is satisfactory to your needs is equally important. Shop carefully for a carrier and establish a good working relationship. Contact your suppliers on the mainland and indicate who your air freight carrier of choice is and provide the local contact for the supplier (you can get that from the air freight carrier).

Retailer: We once had a supplier send us a shipment by another carrier with similar sounding names. The cost was 30 percent higher. We now make sure that all our suppliers know the exact name of our air freight carrier and even the local number in their area.

Distributor: There are many cases where we or the manufacturer have held up an order but then need it "rush." It is nice to have a good relationship with our air freight carrier so that I can call their representative and ask if they could tag the shipment and give special handling. They will do that at no additional cost if I don't abuse the request.

Air freight sales representative: The actual shipping time will depend on the location and the type of service. We try to get our high priority shipments here the next day, especially from the west coast. But most businesses ship using our density rate, which is our deferred service. The rate is about 20 percent to 70 percent cheaper and takes about three to five working days. I think most businesses think of air freight only for high priority shipments.

US Ocean Freight

At present there are two steamship lines serving Honolulu from the mainland: Matson Navigation Company and Sea Land. Each is a separate company operating independent shipping schedules. Both are primarily concerned with container-sized shipments. Matson uses both 24-foot and 40-foot containers which carry 1,415 cubic feet and 2,398 cubic feet, respectively. Sea Land uses a 20-foot container with 1,187 cubic foot capacity and, like Matson, a 40-foot container.

At present Sea Land provides only full-container service, while Matson offers less-than-full container shipment. A sales representative from either line will help review cost and shipping instructions.

Although shipping full containers directly from a supplier may be the most economical method to ship by ocean, most businesses do not usually have that type of volume, at least in the beginning. Consequently, many use the services of a freight forwarder. The freight forwarder orders containers from the steamship companies and loads them by consolidating a number of smaller orders. Freight forwarders also provide delivery to your warehouse or shop at an extra fee. Shipping times are the same as with the steamship companies because the freight forwarders ship the containers on the same vessels operated by the steamship companies.

Costs for using a freight forwarder on less than a full container shipment are sometimes lower on a cubic foot basis than when using the steamship company directly. Here it pays to shop around for terms, rates, and service because all vary significantly. A typical rate chart from a freight forwarder might look like this:

Ocean freight charges from Los Angeles:
0 cu ft to 399 cu ft = $2.20/cu ft
400 cu ft to 799 cu ft = $2.10/cu ft
over 799 cu ft = $2.04/cu ft.

This freight forwarder has a minimum charge of $28.00.

Two other charges related to ocean freight are:

1. Wharfage charges of $.19/cu ft from Los Angeles ($.17/cu ft from Oakland);
2. Delivery charges to your store or warehouse.

Wharfage charges are those miscellaneous charges assessed by the ports of origin and discharge related to the handling of your merchandise. These charges apply whether you use the shipping company or a freight forwarder.

Let us now look at an example of shipping some chair seats from Los Angeles for a furniture store in Honolulu. Your supplier reports that your freight terms are FOB. LA, which is a polite way to say that, from Los Angeles on, you pay the freight. If the shipment is coming from New York, then the supplier will pay for the freight from New York to Los Angeles and you will pay it from Los Angeles to Hawaii. If it is coming from Los Angeles, you pay all the freight. You are told by the supplier that there are ten boxes of equal size in the shipment and that each box is 9 cubic feet. So your total shipment is 90 cubic feet. You can then estimate your ocean freight as follows:

Ocean freight charge = (90 cu ft × $2.20/cu ft)	$198.00
Wharfage charge = (90 cu ft × $.19/cu ft)	$ 17.10
Delivery charge = (based on geographic area)	$ 46.00
TOTAL FREIGHT ESTIMATE	$261.10

Freight forwarder: Special tariffs apply to each industry. For instance, corrosive material has a higher rate. Car batteries fall into this category. So you still need to check if you have any special tariffs that apply to your product which will affect your shipping cost.

Both Matson and Sea Land have ships that leave the west coast weekly. To ensure that a shipment makes a scheduled departure time, it is recommended that the order be at the west coast terminal at least three days before the sail date.

Retailer: Since we order consistently from our supplier in Los Angeles, we have a system where I call him every Thursday with my order to go out on the vessel sailing the next Wednesday. Our staff then knows to receive a shipment at our Honolulu warehouse on the following Tuesday.

Foreign Ocean Shippers

Shipping from the Orient to Hawaii is handled by several steamship companies. Three such companies are N.Y.K. Lines, Columbus Lines, and Sea Land.

There are three types of charges for foreign ocean freight that are similar to mainland ocean freight: (1) ocean freight charges (done internationally in cubic meters); (2) the wharfage charges; and (3) an optional destination delivery charge. Since the ocean rates vary between countries and these fees also may vary with currency fluctuations (some fees, such as the receiving fees, are handled only in foreign currency), a close examination of all possible costs should be made with the shipping agent for each line.

The length of time needed for shipments from the Orient to Hawaii varies with the destination and steamship line, but here are some average sailing times:

- Yokohama, Japan to Hawaii: 6–10 days sailing time. Ship leaves every week.
- Kaohsiung, Taiwan to Hawaii: 14 days sailing time. Ship leaves every week.
- Pusan, Korea to Hawaii: 14 days sailing time. Ship leaves every week.

Shippers advise that merchandise be at the loading dock at least one week prior to the vessel's departure to better ensure timely processing.

When dealing with ocean time from both the mainland and overseas, it is very important to work closely with your supplier and shipper to minimize the time your order is in transit. If your order misses sailing, then it must wait for the next departure. As you can see in both foreign and mainland shipping schedules, your order could be sitting on the dock quite awhile, thereby diminishing the value of your credit terms. It is not uncommon for businesses to aggressively negotiate good terms from their suppliers, only to lose those terms to poor shipping management on their part.

Retailer: We never paid too much attention to our mainland shipments until we really needed an order. Because the manufacturer got the order out late, it missed the ship by one day. We got that order a week later than we needed it.

There are two lessons about freight to be learned up to this point: (1) understand your freight costs and options and (2) set up controls to review your ordering procedure to minimize transit time.

Furniture retailer: It's amazing, but because furniture is so bulky to ship in many cases, the freight charges are up to 30 percent of the cost of the item. On very inexpensive pieces, I have seen where the freight per piece is even more than the cost of the item.

Interisland Ocean Freight

Although the bulk of the business and population in the state is on the island of Oahu, the outer islands (Maui, Kauai, Hawaii, Molokai, and Lanai) represent a substantial market for Oahu-based businesses.

Matson ships cargo from mainland ports to some neighbor island destinations at the same rate as to Honolulu. Only Young Brothers, however, handles "intrastate" surface shipments which originate within Hawaii between islands.

Here is a sample schedule of service between neighbor island ports and the island of Oahu. As a rule, heavier items will need a weight standard and bulkier items will need a cubic foot measure. The weight standard is 2,000 pounds and the cubic foot standard is 40 cubic feet. Once you determine which measure you will use (either weight or volume), you find the exact rate by dividing the actual weight or volume by either 2,000 (for weight) or 40 (for cubic feet). You should call Young Brothers for exact schedule and rates.

- To Hilo—Monday and Thursday with a general cargo all inclusive (tax, insurance, wharfage) rate of $25.70/lb or cu ft;
- To Maui—Sunday, Tuesday, and Thursday, general cargo rate of $24.17/lb or cu ft;
- To Kauai—Monday and Thursday, general cargo rate of $24.17/lb or cu ft;
- To Lanai—every Wednesday, general cargo rate of $24.30/lb or cu ft.
- To Molokai—every Sunday and Wednesday, general cargo rate $22.40

An example might be easier. Let us say that you are shipping some furniture dressers to your branch on Maui. You determine that volume is the measure to use, because the dressers are bulkier than they are heavy. Each dresser is 5 feet by 3 feet by 2 feet for a total of 30 cubic feet. The estimated cost to ship each dresser would be:

1. 30 cu ft divided by 40 cu ft = 3/4;
2. 3/4 times the rate of $22.93 = $17.19.

The cost to ship each dresser from Honolulu to Maui is $17.19. If you were shipping ten dressers, your estimated interisland ocean freight cost might be $171.90. There is a minimum charge.

Other Freight Services

Interisland Air Freight

Interisland air freight service in Hawaii is one of the most competitive anywhere. In addition to the major interisland airlines who offer airport-to-airport service, there are several interisland air freight forwarders that offer door-to-door service at competitive rates.

Airport-to-airport service means that you take the package or shipment to the interisland cargo terminal. The airline will ship it to the destination interisland airport terminal and then call the addressee. The addressee is then responsible for pick-up of the package at the airport terminal.

With door-to-door service the shipper picks up the order at your location and delivers it to the door of the addressee. These services are normally a little more expensive, but recently, surprisingly competitive.

Any of these services also handle priority shipments at priority rates and will take COD shipments. Certain size and weight restrictions apply.

US Postal Service

The US Postal Service is often overlooked in favor of the other shippers. With them, certain weight and size restrictions apply.

Retailer: We have had good experience with the Postal Service, especially when there is no major time requirement on the shipment.

United Parcel Service (UPS)

The United Parcel Service is a private company used by many businesses for air freight shipments. Certain weight and size restrictions apply. UPS also ships interisland.

Sooner or later you will use one of these freight shippers. All of them have excellent sales representatives who will help you select the right service for your needs. Get to know your freight program and monitor it for inaccuracies. What you don't know will hurt you.

10

Merchandising and Advertising: Having the Best Fishing Pole

In chapter 2 we saw the importance of the sales estimate and the market plan. Now we must take the market plan and develop an advertising program to fit it.

Will you plan a grand opening advertising promotion for Windward TV? If you don't mind could you choose the media, get the layout, and estimate the costs. I will need it by the end of this chapter.

> **Retailer:** Every business has to advertise. It is just the type or amount that differs.

Let us revise the retailer's statement about advertising by saying: "Every business has to merchandise. One way is to advertise, and the type and amount of advertising may differ."

Many people confuse merchandising and advertising. Advertising is better defined as the use of media to attract attention to yourself or your product, while merchandising relates to the entire product presentation of which advertising is but one part.

Merchandising

Merchandising encompasses your philosophy of doing business, the image your business wants to project, your appeal to a particular market, your facilities, how your employees handle your customers, your pricing, and your advertising. In short, merchandising is how both you and your customer see the business and the products and services that you offer.

You can see how this theory works in reality by the image you visualize when someone mentions Liberty House, Sears, Shirokiya, or Hyatt Hotels. All of these companies have spent a lot of money creating a certain image in the market place. On closer inspection, we might discover that the advertising in the newspaper and on television only helps to reinforce an impression each has already created.

> **Sales representative company:** When we first started our sales representative firm, none of the accounts knew who we were. We just tried to provide the best service we could. Eventually, when the stores and buyers recognized that we did follow through and that they could count on us, our sales took off. I guess without thinking about it we developed a good image. We never had to do the traditional type of advertising because we called on all our customers, but I guess you can say that our advertising was our reputation.

A veteran retailer once said that the best way to determine the image of your business is to stand on the outside of your store and to ask customers as they leave the store if what they saw inside was what they anticipated. Since customers anticipate certain products and a level of service from Liberty House and the Sheraton Hotel, why should your customer not expect a certain level of product or service from your business? They do.

Factors in Merchandising a Small Business

The Philosophy of the Business

The philosophy of the business will reflect the personality of the major operating principal, the owner or manager. Whatever is important to this person will be reflected in the business. For example, an owner who feels customers will appreciate the product just by seeing it will have a different attitude toward merchandising than the owner who feels the customer must be educated as to the benefits of the product.

The Value to the Buyer

Buyers will spend money for a product or service only to the extent they see value. Good merchandising creates a level of value in the mind of the buyer. For example, a Mercedes and a Ford are both automobiles, but some people will place a different value on each car. Some common factors that create this value judgment for small business products and services are: price, convenience, uniqueness of product, and level of service. Your product or service can create value in the buyer's mind if:

1. It is less expensive and of the same quality as what is now being bought.
2. It is more convenient in terms of location and selection.
3. There is no other comparable product or service available.
4. The level of service or quality is measurably superior to what is now offered.

The Level of Competition

Established businesses are similar to incumbent politicians. Just by being there and offering products and service they command a certain loyalty from their existing customers. A new business needs to prove itself before it can hope to take customers from its competition. The level of competition and what that competition will do when a new business enters the same market will determine how the new business might merchandise itself.

Advertising

Advertising is the most visible form of merchandising. It is a quick means to get your merchandising message to the buyer. There are many ways to sell the same product, however. Not every one of the advertising methods will be equally successful. Moreover, what works once may not be as successful a second time. Good advertising is an art.

Advertising Basics

Once you understand the difference between merchandising and advertising, your first questions in advertising planning should be: What is the image of the business and how can we project that image to our target customers?

The best type of advertising gives you high visibility and costs very little, such as word of mouth recommendations. When she first started, Mrs. Field's of Mrs. Fields Cookies would walk around the shopping mall handing out samples when sales were slow—very effective and inexpensive advertising. Not all businesses have a product or service like Mrs. Fields Cookies, however. You may try a number of different types of advertising before you find what works best. If you know your market, it will be easier to decide which advertising medium is worth trying.

A good place to start developing any advertising plan is a look at what your competition is doing. For instance, a major department store provides its management clippings of all competitors' advertising. Not only does this store's management know what products the competition is advertising, they also know which media are being used.

Retailer: There is one thing I have learned in advertising and that is you never know what is going to work. Some of the hottest promotions were off the simplest ads and some of the promotions that I thought would be terrific were flops. A lot depends on just hitting the right product with the right price and media, and the right buying mood. As you can see, there is an element of luck here.

Furniture store owner: Of the entire population, I believe that only 10 percent may be interested in purchasing furniture at a given time. Maybe half of them or 5 percent are my market customers. But the problem is, that 5 percent is constantly changing so I have to keep my store in their thoughts.

Types of Advertising Media

The major types of advertising media are: newspaper, radio, direct mail, the *Yellow Pages,* and television.

Newspapers

Newspaper rates are based on what is known as a *column inch.* The actual dimensions of a column inch may vary with different newspapers. For the major daily Oahu newspapers, the *Honolulu Star-Bulletin* and *Honolulu Advertiser* (collectively referred to as the Hawaii Newspaper Agency), a column inch is 2 1/16 inches by 1 inch. Exhibit 18 illustrates this format. The 1994 open rates (general rate) for one column inch for the *Advertiser,* the Star-Bulletin, and for the combination of the two papers or the Sunday paper were:

Inches/Month	*Advertiser*	*Star-Bulletin*	Combination	Sunday
open	$44.73	$42.50	$65.45	$69.54

(The difference in pricing is based on the circulation of the papers. Different rates may apply for certain businesses. Discount rates for frequent advertisers are available.)

Suburban Newspapers

A number of regional and suburban newspapers cater to specific geographic regions in Hawaii. Some of these papers are mailed directly to homes and others are left at distribution points in retail outlets. None of these are subscription newspapers.

Midweek—direct-mailed to residences once a week. The 1995 open rate was $56.71 per column inch.

Other newspapers—these cater to specific residential areas; delivered to some homes or placed in pick-up bins. Advertising rates vary for these papers but are generally $5 to $7 per column inch.

Constructing a Newspaper Ad

To illustrate how to size and cost a newspaper ad, you must understand that a full page in the Hawaii Newspaper Agency papers is equal to 6 columns across (each column being about 2 1/16 inch wide) and 21 1/2 inches deep (Exhibit 19). This gives a total of 129 column inches (6 × 21 1/2) for one full page. Exhibit 19 shows the more common space advertising sizes and the corresponding column inches. Knowing this, let us estimate the cost of advertising a one-quarter page ad in the Sunday paper at the open rate.

EXHIBIT 18

SAMPLE COLUMN INCHES MEASUREMENT

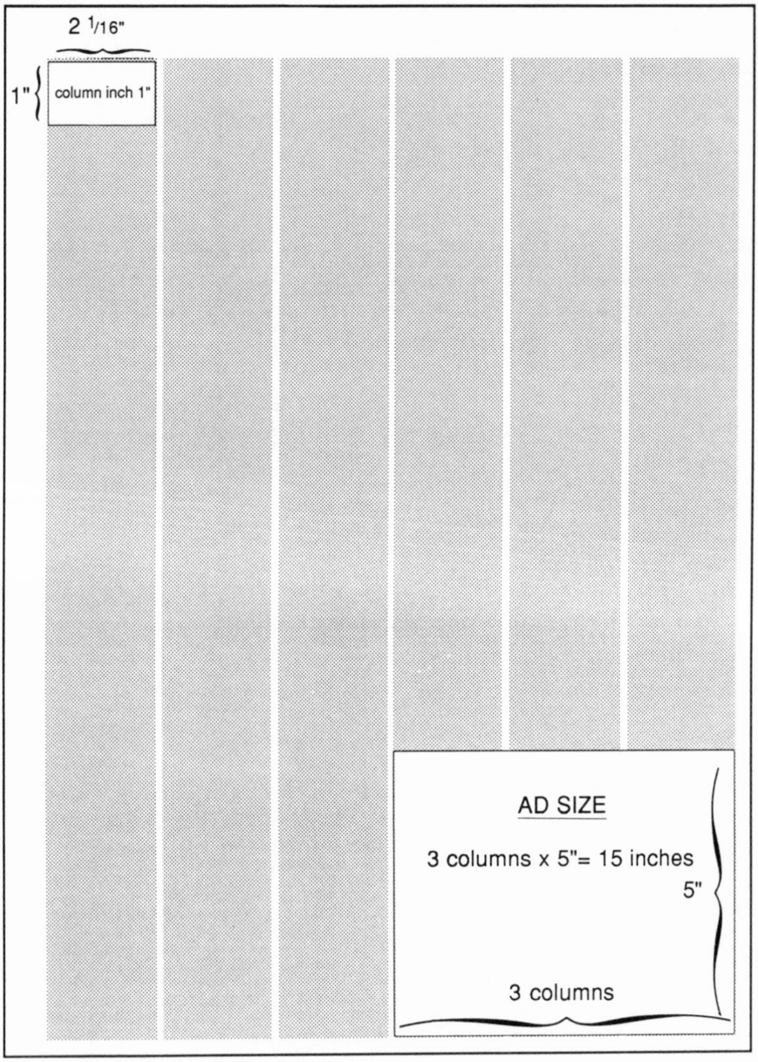

1. Column inches to advertise = 32.25 column inches (one-quarter page)
2. Rate/column inch = $69.54
3. Total estimated cost = $2,242.66 (32.25 column inches × $69.54) plus tax.

(Note: This rate is used for illustration only. Actual rates will vary.)

EXHIBIT 19
SAMPLE NEWSPAPER AD SIZES

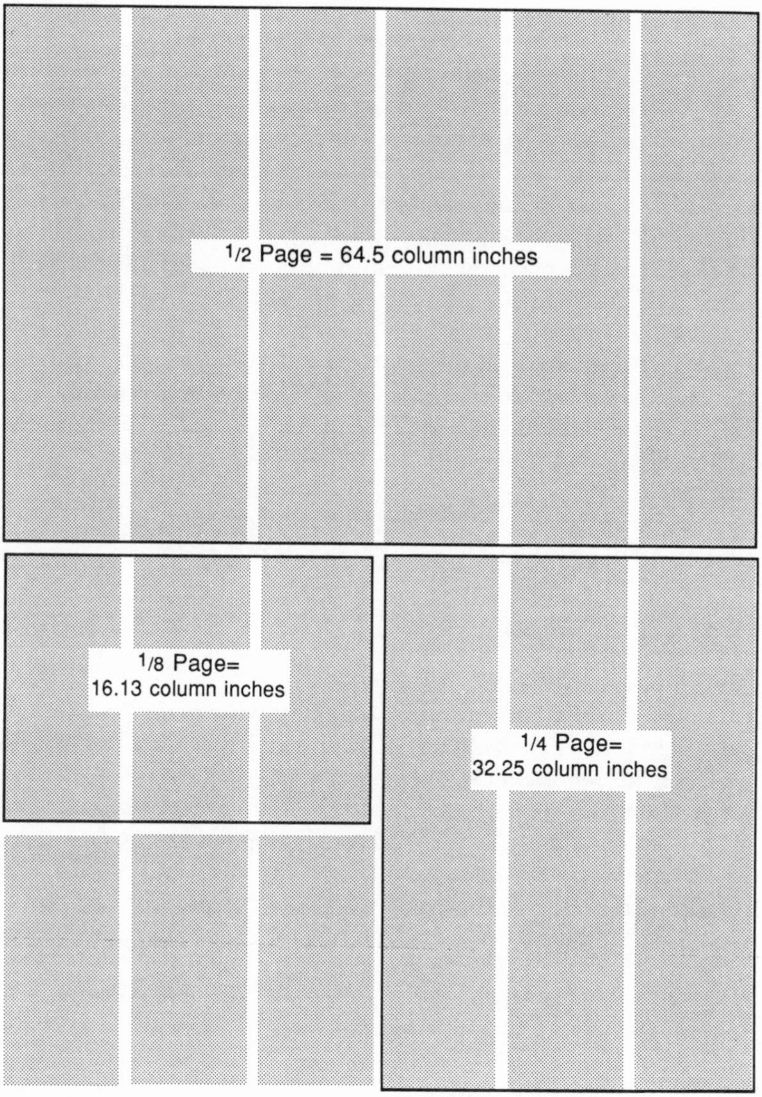

Ad Layout

On an average, people spend but a few seconds reading a newspaper advertisement. If you are going to spend a lot of money on a single day's newspaper advertisement, you will want to do everything possible to ensure your intended customers see it and spend some time reading it. Some factors that influence a person's perception of a newspaper ad are:

1. the size of the advertisement;
2. the layout design; and
3. the placement in the paper.

A tremendous amount of effort goes into the design and artwork of any large ad. A typical department store ad will start with the selection of the products and prices to be advertised. Then the rough draft of the ad is designed. This layout process may take several weeks. The ad is next sent to the managers for final approval. Any revisions are subsequently made and the copy is sent to the newspaper three days in advance of publication. For a large department store, this entire process may take two or three months.

Although most small businesses have a less elaborate ad preparation process, even small ads need the same steps. Newspaper sales representatives (account representatives) will provide a liaison between you and the newspaper's graphics department. This process, called the layout of your ad, is normally provided free of charge by the newspaper.

Steps to a Newspaper Ad

Here are the steps you might follow for a newspaper ad:

1. You contact the newspaper account representative, reserve a tentative date, and negotiate a rate.
2. You work out an ad size.
3. You provide the representative a rough drawing of the proposed ad in as much detail as possible. The representative will assist you. You provide the representative with prices for the advertised items, the sales theme, and any artwork or pictures that might be available.
4. The representative will then take the proposal to the newspaper's graphics department for layout.
5. The representative will deliver a copy of the proposed ad for your "proofing" (review). You will make any corrections and improvements.
6. The corrections will be made. You may request a second proof.
7. The ad is run in the paper.

Newspaper account representative: The newspaper account representative has more to do than just reserve space. Our biggest problem is businesses who wait until the last minute, then want us to rush an ad and proof it within a couple of days. I would like to get the rough draft at least two weeks before the run date. That leaves enough time for the graphics department to do a good job and time to get it back to the business to proof.

Another option is having an independent graphic artist prepare the layout to your specifications. Why do this when the service is already free? You might consider using an independent layout service for some of the same reasons that the big companies do. Although a newspaper's graphics department is very professional, they often lack the time to create a unique style for you. You know a Liberty House ad even before you read it. If you are going to spend $1,000 for an ad, it might be worth an additional $100 for a layout that is a knock-out or at least establishes a certain image.

The newspaper will not object if you have an independent graphic service layout your ad. In this case, all your coordination with the layout of the ad will be with that graphic art service, and only your newspaper space reservations will be with the newspaper's account representative. The graphic artist will then produce camera-ready copy that only needs to be delivered to your newspaper account representative a couple of days before the print date.

> **Graphic artist:** I think we offer much more flexibility in the design of the advertisement than can the newspaper. We can also turn around an ad faster. In many cases, the retailer will come to us with a rush job that we can get out within 24 hours.

The final consideration on the visibility of your newspaper ad is the placement within the paper. The newspaper is divided into sections—sports, financial, and entertainment. If you know that your target market can be pegged in one of these sections, then it will increase the effectiveness of the ad. It is no coincidence that all bar advertisements are bunched in the sports section. Although the newspaper may not be able to guarantee exact placement, you can request that your ad be run in a particular section.

Radio

We now move from the column inches of the newspaper to a "spot" on the radio. Hawaii has one of the highest numbers of radio stations per person in the United States. Having so many stations allows an advertiser to target a market for specific listening audiences. In fact, radio stations set up their formats to target specific audiences. If your market is the teen-age group, you might select certain radio stations that cater to that group.

Radio stations derive their rates in a manner similar to that of the newspapers—they are based on listenership (as opposed to readership in the newspaper). To determine the proportion of listenership for each station, an independent survey is conducted every six months which ranks each radio station's listenership by age category. The higher the rating the higher the listenership and the rate charged per spot.

A radio "spot" is one commercial. Normal spots are either 30 or 60 seconds in length. Since the spots are included in the radio station's regular format, there are a set number of spots, depending on the length, that can be run in a day's programming. Although the radio station may air programs 24 hours each day, they recognize that there are certain times when their audiences are larger. These times may be referred to as peak times or "drive" times (assuming that more people are listening to their car radios going to and from work). In addition, those stations that have different "shows" at different times of the day may have different ratings on the popularity of each show.

All this really does not concern us until we get down to rates. The rate for each spot depends on:

1. The overall rating of the station in the independent survey;
2. The length of the spot;
3. The time of day each spot will run; and
4. The number of spots you plan to buy.

Here are some sample "open" radio rates:

Radio Station	30 Sec Spot	60 Sec Spot
Station A	$40.80*	$51.00*
Station B	$14–$34	$22–$60
Station C	$33	$42

Note: All these rates are estimates.
*Lowest package rate. This station charges over $100 per spot for some of its drive-time spots.

At this point, the only thing we want to determine from this chart is a rough scale of potential radio advertising costs. A knowledgeable advertiser knows running just one spot might not be very effective. How many spots should be run?

Retailer: When we use radio, it is often in conjunction with our newspaper advertising. Our target market is the younger market, and we feel we get better market coverage supplementing it on radio. We found that the best number is 5 spots per day and 20 spots per week. Depending on the promotion, that may be either one or two weeks.

Radio station account representative: If the advertiser is attempting to build or rework an image, then we recommend a long-term program of a number of spots over several months. If they are looking for immediacy to move some product or create some sales, a better program is over a one- or two-week period.

We can now make an estimate using our sample rates on the cost of a radio advertising program. Let us say that we think that 20 spots of 30-seconds each over a one-week period might work for us. We can then anticipate our cost.

Station A	$40.80 × 20 = $816
Station B	$34 × 20 = $680
Station C	$33 × 20 = $660

Similar to the newspapers, radio stations offer a frequency discount if you agree to advertise a number of spots over a given time period. Another way that radio stations reduce the cost of a spot is in the design of creative advertising packages. The concept of these packages is to offer the advertiser a number of spots at a reduced rate. These spots, however, are dispersed over various time slots, some of which are in very low listenership periods.

For example, let us say that the open rate is $25 per spot. You would like to run 20 spots. At the open rate that will cost you $500, ($25 × 20). These spots will all be run between 7 AM and 6 PM, the stations peak period. On the other hand, they offer you a package of 20 spots at $18 per spot. Your total cost is $360, a saving of $140 or 28 percent. These spots, however, will run as follows: 10 spots in peak times, 5 in evening hours, and 5 in the midnight to 7 AM period.

One advantage that radio has over other types of media is that production is easy and quick. As with the newspapers, the account representative will be a liaison between the station's production department and you. Here is how it might work.

Steps to a Radio Ad

1. You meet with your account representative to negotiate the rate, spot placement, and number of spots.
2. Determine the dates your ad will run.
3. You provide a rough copy or idea with specifics as to product, prices, and tone of the spot.
4. The account representative will make some suggestions to polish the ad.
5. The representative will take the ad to the station production department and cut a copy.
6. You will proof the ad by listening over the phone or to a tape and give approval.

Account representative: The advantage that radio has is it can convey image or excitement in the advertising. One feature not too many people use is to cut several copies to use as the sale progresses. Instead of using the same ad over and over we could have a second ad near the end of the sale announcing "last two days."

Account representative: Many people come to us expecting that all they are going to run are a couple of spots and sales are going to double. Advertising is a long-term process, and I believe that you get your best results when there is a real commitment to advertise over a long period of time—say at least three to six months. Then you can honestly say that it didn't work.

Direct Mail

In both radio and newspapers a high probability exists that the object of your advertising may "tune you out" or never see your ad. Direct mail works on the assumption that something sent directly to potential customers will be opened and get their attention. Making direct mail effective advertising and not junk mail is an art.

Most businesses will attempt some type of direct mail. Two ways are: (1) using a direct-mail service and (2) doing it yourself.

Let us first look at doing it yourself. Assume that your business is in Waipahu and that you are interested in mailing a special promotion to the local area. The steps for doing a local bulk mailing would be as follows:

1. US Postal Service Bulk Mail Permit. You must apply at the main post office of your city for a bulk-mailing application. There is a $75 annual charge for this permit and a one time permit imprint fee of $75. You will be given a packet of rules and regulations (and there are many).

2. Labels. Once you have determined your target area, you will need to get the addresses. You might be surprised to discover just how many households there are in your area. For example, the potential mailing list for Waipahu and surrounding areas is:

	Waipahu	Barbers Pt.	Ewa Beach	Makakilo
Households	7,791	2,340	4,023	2,726
Total: 16,880				

To obtain these mailing lists, you might look under "Mailing Lists or Services" in the the *Yellow Pages*.

3. Layout the Flyer. Next, you would go to a graphic artist with a rough drawing of the proposed flyer and its dimensions. The graphic artist will give you camera-ready copy of your flyer.

4. Print the Flyer. The next step is to take the layout of the flyer to your local printshop and have it printed and folded.

5. Labels Affixed to Flyer. Once you get the flyers from the printer, then you or the mailing service will affix the mailing labels.

6. Prepare Postal Forms and Mail. Finally, when the flyer is ready to be mailed, you will prepare the bulk-mailing forms and mail the flyers. (Meet with your post office prior to the mailing to review the rules and regulations. They may be confusing initially.)

This process will soon become familiar. But we must still discuss the cost.

The advantage of using a bulk-mailing stamp is that the cost to mail each piece may vary between 16.5 to 19.8 cents for profit business (the reasons for different rates are covered in the US Postal Service rules and regulations on bulk mailing). But even at 19.8 cents, that is quite a savings from the 29-cent first-class rate. Remember, in bulk mailing we are not talking about 10 or 20 pieces but thousands!

The bulk rate fee is not the only cost. Here are the others:

1. Label cost—average cost per label affixed to flyer is 3 cents per label.
2. Layout cost of flyer (graphic artist)—estimate $100.
3. Printing of flyer—varies with stock of paper, color of ink, size of paper, and number to be printed. For simplicity, let us assume that an order of 10,000 copies printed both sides on standard paper might cost $500.00 or $.05 per copy. Folding charges equal $100.00 or $.01 per flyer.
4. Postage—assume 11.4 cents per piece.

For a direct mailing of 10,000 pieces we can estimate the cost as follows:

Labels	$ 300	
Layout	100	
Printing	500	
Folding	100	
Affixing labels	0	(included in label charge)
Postage	1,140	
Total	$2,140	

For a single mailer to 10,000 addresses, our estimated cost would be $2,140.

If that cost is too high, we can decrease the number of pieces in the mailing to fit our budget. We could delete streets from the mailing list least likely to contain customers and ask the mailing service not to provide labels for these addresses.

The other way to handle direct mail is to let a mailing service handle everything except the layout and the printing. Costs will be higher per piece.

Retailer: I have had mixed results with direct mail. The experts say that you should expect a 2 percent return in the form of customers from your mailer. Sometimes I am lucky to get that. It really depends on the layout. I find that creating a sense of immediacy helps, but since bulk mail is the lowest mailing priority for the post office, I have to be careful with the dates I use since it may take five days to deliver the mail.

Retailer: I have had my best results inserting a flyer in some of the regional papers. Of course, my market is very regional. My costs are running about 7 cents per piece which is lower than just the mailing cost it would take me to do it myself.

The Yellow Pages

Once you apply for business phone service from Hawaiian Telephone Company, they will forward a request to GTE Directories and a sales representative will call you for a *Yellow Pages* directory listing.

Since the *Yellow Pages* is published only once a year, you might want to ensure that your listing is included if it is close to the cut-off date. The cut-off date for each year's directory is generally sometime in September of the previous year.

For many businesses, *Yellow Pages'* advertising is the most expensive and most consistent advertising they do. *Yellow Page* advertising adds a monthly charge to your telephone bill. Current rates run from a couple of dollars to a couple of hundred dollars per month.

> **Retailer:** We have a small business with just three phone lines and our phone bill averages over $500 each month. If you break that down we pay about $150 for the three lines; $90 for the lease of the phone equipment; $275 for *Yellow Pages'* listings; and $50 for long distance charges.

Television

Television advertising is very similar to that of radio in both terminology and structure. Again, we are talking about a "spot," time slots for the spot, number of spots to run, cost per spot, time-slot viewership, and production. Consequently, if you understand the radio advertising format, you will find the television format almost identical in nature.

As with the radio stations, a television station is able to determine its rates based on independent surveys which publish the viewership at different times. One major difference between radio and television is the programming format. Radio will generally format its entire station programming for one market segment. This means that no matter what time of the day you plan to run your advertising, you would be targeting only that market. On the other hand, television stations plan their programming to capture a wide range of the market and do so by varying the programming each day. As a result, the audience for Saturday morning cartoons may be different from that for Sunday morning football. The television station account representative will help you determine the best program for your market.

Another difference is, television production does cost extra. Most of the major television stations provide their own production departments. The fees may vary considerably depending upon the extent of the production. Estimates may range anywhere from $500 for a simple production to $2,500 for something more substantial. Here are some sample television open rates:

Daytime series:	$50–275 per 30-sec spot
Prime time:	$350–1,200 per 30-sec spot
Late evening:	$30–150 per 30-sec spot

Package rates vary considerably with daytime spots averaging $50 and some prime-time spots at $375.

These are the highest rates at the open rate. As with radio, the television stations may offer advertising packages with a broad mix of time slots or frequency packages with lower rates per spot.

Retailer: I think you have to have a product or service that can draw from all over the state to really get the best mileage out of television advertising. For me I am just too small a regional store to use television.

Television account representative: Most people think that all television advertising is expensive. At certain time slots we are just as competitive as radio and newspaper.

Cooperative Advertising

Cooperative advertising is used primarily in product retailing. Here the manufacturer sets aside a certain amount of money to help in the the local advertising of the product. The way this works is that the manufacturer or the local distributor will have a cooperative advertising policy that will allocate a certain percentage of purchases (normally 3–5 percent) for advertising reimbursements.

For example, let us say that Windward TV is making purchases from a distributor that has a cooperative advertising plan which calls for a 5 percent cooperative advertising allowance on paid purchases. During the month, Windward TV may purchase 20 televisions at $250 each for total purchases of $5,000. At 5 percent cooperative advertising, Windward TV can expect a credit from the distributor of $250 for the advertising of the distributor's televisions.

Let us assume further that Windward TV does not advertise that month but continues to purchase televisions at the rate of $5,000 per month. After one year, Windward TV would have accrued $3,000 in cooperative advertising from this one distributor.

Distributor: I think that manufacturers plan on a great many of their dealers not fully utilizing the cooperative advertising allocated or earned by them.

Planning an Advertising Promotion

Now that we have discussed the major advertising media, we can plan a Windward TV grand-opening advertising promotion.

Many businesses advertise as painlessly as possible by putting low-effort advertising in the newspapers or on radio. By advertising in this manner, they are doing a poor job of merchandising when a little more effort might increase their probability of success. By understanding how to put together an advertising promotion, you will understand how to maximize your advertising effort.

Items to consider in an advertising promotion are:

1. The Theme. A theme will provide you, your advertising account representative, and your customer a framework for quickly understanding your message. Remember, good merchandising is not selling on price alone. Common themes are: "Grand-Opening" sale, a "12-Hour" sale, or an "Introduction" sale.

2. The Product or Service for Sale. What makes this special? The more special it is the better. Is it the first time that it is available in Hawaii? Is it the cheapest it has ever been? Is this the first service in this area?

Account representative: When I meet with new businesses, they often don't have an idea of what they might use as a leader in their advertising to attract the customer. Most think, well here I am. I try to find out what makes them special and work the advertising around that.

3. Total Estimated Sales. How many units do you plan to sell? What will be the total estimated sales at the end of the promotion?

4. The Advertising Budget. Based upon the estimated sales, what is the advertising budget? Most businesses use from 3 to 8 percent of estimated sales as their advertising budget. As a result, if we estimated total sales of $15,000 for this promotion and used 5 percent as an advertising budget, we might allocate $750 to advertising. If we felt that this promotion would be all the advertising we would do this month and we anticipated total monthly sales of $30,000, then our total advertising and promotion budget would be $1,500.

Consultant: I am amazed at how few businesses work with an advertising budget. For the most part they advertise by the seat of their pants. A typical response will be, well, sales are down so how much extra do we have so we can advertise. Very poor planning.

5. Media to Use. You would then have to decide on the media or mix of media to use for this promotion.

6. Other Promotion Costs Not Media Related. If you were planning to have a "tent sale" in your parking lot and needed to rent a tent, then that cost would have to be considered as part of the advertising costs. Or if you were planning to hold a seminar for your clients, the room rental and the refreshment expenses would be considered advertising expenses.

7. Estimated Cost of Media. Once all nonmedia related promotion costs are deducted from the advertising budget, then the total media dollars become evident. Rough estimates can then be made on the scope of the advertising before the advertising account representatives are contacted.

8. Cooperative Advertising. Any cooperative advertising funds available?

The Windward TV Grand-Opening Advertising Promotion

1. Theme. "Grand-Opening" sale. Three weeks only. Free portable television to be given away.

2. Product or Service for Sale. The lowest priced 25-inch TV in Hawaii while supplies last. To introduce the service department, free TV inspection during sale.

3. Estimated Total Sales.

Model 1243: 10 units at sale price of $599 =	$5,990
Model 1245: 5 units at sale price of $399 =	$1,995
Model 1213: 10 units at sale price of $199 =	$1,990
Total sales estimated for sale pieces	$9,975
Other sales estimated	$3,000
Total sales estimated	$11,975

4. Advertising Budget. Normally 5 percent but for the grand opening, using 10 percent. Advertising budget is $1,197 ($11,975 × 10%).

5. Media to Use. The competition seems to be using the daily papers. After looking at the customer base, it is felt that the daily papers, the suburban newspapers, or a direct flyer might be the best media. After some thought it is decided that the first option is to have 10,000 flyers printed. From these, 3,000 flyers will be direct-mailed to the surrounding area and the additional 7,000 will be inserted in a suburban newspaper.

6. Other Promotion Costs, Nonmedia Related. The cost of the give-away television will come to $100.

7. Estimated Cost of Media.

To layout flyer	$ 100
To print 10,000 flyers	475
To direct-mail 3,000	450
To insert 7,000 in a suburban newspaper at $45/1000	315
Total estimated media cost	$1,340

This estimate compares favorably with our budget of $1,197.

8. Cooperative Advertising. The distributor will issue credits of 50 percent of the advertising cost up to $600. At the current budget that brings the advertising expenses down to 5 percent from 10 percent on estimated sales. It is determined that the advertising is adequate as it stands and that no new expenditures should be made.

Now we can call the printshop, graphic artist, direct mail organization, and the newspaper account representative for more detailed information.

You may have a great product or service, but unless you merchandise it well you will not have a business. Good merchandising is able to get customers or clients to try a product or service. Thereafter, real success will be validated with continual sales. Customers vote for their choice with their dollars.

Unless your sales confirm otherwise, you are the only one who thinks your product or service is really good. Most people do not do enough to tell their story, and this does not necessarily mean using expensive media.

There are no rights or wrongs in merchandising—the only question is does it work or not. Have you accurately identified the needs of the customer and designed your entire business personality to enhance the satisfaction of those needs? Or put another way, what makes your business special? Successful businesses ask that question often and spend a lot of time analyzing the answer. From that answer comes their merchandising strategy.

Retailer: I can see that if you have the best product but do not have the right merchandising program, it is like having the best fishing pole but not knowing how to use it.

Additional Reading

Drucker, Peter F. 1985. *Innovation and Entrepreneurship.* New York: Harper and Row.

Holtz, Herman. 1982. *The Secrets of Practical Marketing for Small Business.* Englewood Cliffs, NJ: Prentice-Hall.

Klein, Ted, and Fred Danzig. 1985. *How to Make the Media Work for You.* New York: Charles Scribner's Sons.

McCormack, Mark H. 1984. *What They Don't Teach You at Harvard Business School.* New York: Bantam Books.

11

Insurance: Protecting Your Business

The insurance industry is like any industry in that it experiences cyclical changes. These cyclical changes become a concern for other businesses when they cause fluctuations in the rates charged as insurance premiums. For the first five years of the 1980s rates were low and insurance coverage was fairly easy to obtain. Starting in 1985, however, that trend reversed itself with premiums skyrocketing and coverage becoming scarce. During a period when premiums are high, the question is not whether you can obtain the best rate, but whether you can afford or can get the coverage at all.

Just as an individual needs automobile insurance, life insurance, or fire insurance for a home, a business needs a number of different types of insurance. Some of these insurance coverages are options for the business-owner and others are required by law. Some of the more common types of insurance are:

1. Employee Medical Insurance
2. Commercial General Liability (CGL)
3. Workers' Compensation Insurance
4. Temporary Disability Insurance (TDI)
5. Fire Insurance
6. Theft Insurance

Insurance agent: Most businesses view insurance as a necessary evil and are only interested in how much it is going to cost. But a good agent looks at a business to measure the potential exposure and what type of protection might be needed to prevent a catastrophic loss.

Employee Medical Insurance

Employers are required by state law to provide medical insurance for all employees working at least 20 hours per week. As stated in Hawaii Form

DC-1 (Rev. 10/92), *Hawaii Workers' Compensation, Temporary Disability Insurance and Prepaid Health Care Laws:* "[The law applies to] all employers with one or more employees, working part-time or full-time."

The law requires that you provide: "Medical and hospital care for non work related illness or injury by: (1) purchasing an approved health care plan from a health care contractor such as Kaiser, HMSA, or a Hawaii-licensed insurance carrier, (2) by adopting an approved self insured health care plan, or (3) negotiating a collective bargaining agreement which provides health care benefits at least equivalent to that mandated by this chapter."

Workers excluded from coverage: "Federal, State, and County workers; workers employed for less than 20 hours per week; agricultural seasonal workers; insurance and real estate salesmen paid solely by way of commission; individuals working for son, daughter or spouse; children under age 21 working for father or mother; workers covered as dependents under a qualified health care plan; workers covered by State-governed medical assistance; workers receiving public assistance."

Eligibility requirements: "Workers in covered employment must have worked four consecutive weeks of 20 or more hours a week and earned monthly wages of at least 86.67 times the Hawaii minimum hourly wage, rounded off to the next dollar. Coverage must be provided at the earliest enrollment date of the prepaid health care contractor selected to this chapter."

Premium costs: "The employer may pay the entire premium cost or share it with the workers. You can deduct one-half of the cost but not more than 1.5 percent of the worker's wages. You pay the remaining portion exceeding the prescribed limitation."

There are more provisions in the advisory and it is recommended that you call the Hawaii Department of Labor and Industrial Relations, Disability Compensation Division, for a copy.

What does all this mean? Again, the State of Hawaii requires that all employers have a state-approved health plan for each regular employee working at least 20 hours per week. A few exclusions from this basic stipulation do exist, however.

One common exclusion for the employer is an employee who is covered under another plan. For example, if you hire someone who is a military dependent or already covered under their spouse's plan with another employer, they may decide that they do not want the coverage that you have. It is their option. If that is the case, the state form, HWC-5—Employee Notification to Employer, must be signed by the employee requesting a waiver of medical coverage from your medical plan.

If in doubt about some provision of the law, contact the Hawaii Department of Labor and Industrial Relations office. The penalties for noncompliance are stiff, and the potential liabilities could be catastrophic.

Although your insurance agent can help you select a health plan, Hawaii is dominated by two such health plans mentioned in the state informational advisory—Kaiser Medical Plan and the Hawaii Medical Service Association (HMSA). Since these health contractors have a number of different employer plans, it would be wise to investigate all your options.

The monthly rates for the basic employer plan in 1995 were:

	Monthly rate ($)	
No. of people	HMSA (PPP)	Kaiser
Single	133.64	132.98
Couple	267.28	265.96
Three or more	492.00	398.94

(Please note that the coverages and benefits of both plans are different and these rates are provided to give the businessperson a cost perspective.)

The amount that the employee can be made to pay toward the monthly medical premium is a maximum of one-half the premium, except if the salary is so low that this amount would be greater than 1.5 percent of the gross salary. Here is an example. Suppose you have a part-time employee who is working 20 hours per week at $5.00 per hour. The monthly wage is $400 (20 hours × $5.00/hour × 4 weeks). You will be able to deduct only $6.00 ($400 × 1.5%) from the wages for payment toward medical premiums. Assuming that you subscribed to the HMSA plan listed above and using the single rate of $133.64, this means that you will pay $127.64 and the employee $6.00 toward that employee's monthly medical insurance.

The legal responsibility of the employer is to provide coverage for only the employee under the basic medical plan. Because the health plans charge higher premiums for family plans, the employee is responsible for that additional charge, as well as for any supplemental programs such as dental or vision plans.

Once an employee is covered with a medical plan and visits a doctor or hospital, doctor's claims are submitted between the doctor or hospital and the medical carrier. The business has no responsibility to complete any forms. That is not true with the other type of medical claim—Workers' Compensation Insurance.

Workers' Compensation Insurance

Worker's compensation insurance—another state-required insurance—provides both medical insurance and wage reimbursement for work-related injuries or illness.

The following exerpts are from the Hawaii Department of Labor and Industrial Relations *Digest of Chapters 386, 392 and 393, Hawaii Workers' Compensation, Temporary Disability Insurance and Prepaid Health Care Laws,* Form DC-1(Rev. 10/92):

The law requires you to provide for your employee(s): "Wage replacement benefits and medical/hospital care for *work-related* illness or injury by purchasing insurance from a Hawaii-licensed insurance carrier or adopting an approved self-insured plan."

Workers excluded from coverage: "Federal government workers; certain domestic workers earning less than $225 a calendar quarter; domestic workers or public welfare recipients; unpaid or volunteer workers for religious, charitable or non profit organizations; students working for a school or university in return for board, lodging or tuition; duly ordained or licensed ministers or rabbis."

Eligibility requirements: "The only requirement is that the worker is in covered employment and the injury or illness is work-connected."

Benefit provisions: "For work related injury or illness—all required medical, surgical and hospital services and supplies including drugs; weekly benefits from the fourth day of disability to replace wage loss, representing 66 2/3% of the worker's average weekly wage but not more than the maximum weekly benefit amount annually set by the DCD; additional benefits if injury results in permanent disability or disfigurement; funeral and burial expenses if work injury results in death; and additional weekly benefits to surviving widow and other dependents."

Premium costs: "The employer pays the entire premium cost; sharing it with workers is prohibited."

Workers' compensation insurance is different from medical insurance in that: (1) it covers injury or illness that is only work-related; (2) it may reimburse the employee for wages lost as a result of that illness or injury; (3) provides for other benefits such as funeral and burial benefits; and (4) the premium cost cannot be shared by the employee.

The employer takes out the workers' compensation insurance policy with an insurance carrier and not the medical contractors (like HMSA or Kaiser Medical). A simple request to an insurance agent for workers' compensation insurance will start this policy request.

The premium rates for workers' compensation insurance are set by the insurance companies. Individual rates are set based upon the job classification and on a rate per hundred dollars of gross pay. Here are some example rates in 1993 from one insurance company:

Job classification	Rate/$100 gross pay
Tree trimmer	$39.12
General clerical	$ .93
Outside salesman	$ 1.75
Sales manager—retail store	$ 3.61
Delivery person—furniture	$ 9.52

Since rates will vary among insurance companies, it is advisable that you obtain several quotes.

These example rates provide an indication of the total estimated premium. Consequently, if you planned to hire one clerk and one outside salesperson at salaries of $1500 and $2000 per month, respectively, you might anticipate an annual premium of $587.40 for the two employees. (Clerical = rate of $.92/$100 × annual salary of $18,000 = $167.40. Outside sales person = rate of $1.75/$100 × annual salary of $24,000 = $420.00.) We would then have to compare this estimated premium against the minimum premium for each of the categories. (For new businesses, these rates are estimated at the start of the business based on the estimated salaries and are adjusted at the end of the year.)

Often a small business will have one individual handling several functions (i.e., as both a manager and an outside salesperson). The insurance industry will rate a person who may perform several work classifications at the highest rated category even if the employee does not spend the most time in that position. The exception is in the construction industry which allows payroll to be split between several job classifications if records are kept to support it. Properly classifying each employee may lower workers' compensation insurance premiums.

Insurance agent: Each type of business is rated individually. There is a separate rate for retail clothing, wholesale clothing, restaurants, etc.

Insurance agent: In some businesses the job classifications are cut and dry. But I often try to assist my client by trying to get a proper classification for each employee. This is an area where the insurance agent and the insurance underwriter who sets the rate for the business have to do some talking.

Unlike the medical insurance claim process, the employer will help to complete the workers' compensation claim form. This employer responsibility often surprises new employers.

Retailer: When the business had it's first major workers' compensation claim, we were completely unprepared for the processing requirements. The result was the employee was caught in between the hospital asking for payment and our office holding up the claim. It took more time than it needed to.

Because the primary concern of the employee at the time of injury or illness is for immediate medical treatment and not whether the insurance claim will be paid under employee medical insurance or as a workers' compensation claim, it is easy to confuse how medical treatment should be claimed. If the doctor or hospital suspect that the claim should be filed as a workers' compensation claim, they will ask the employer for the name of their workers' compensation insurance carrier. Bills for the medical services will then be forwarded to that insurance carrier and not to the employee's medical plan. In the meantime, the employer will need to request that the insurance carrier forward a three-part claim form (Exhibit 20). The first part of this form is completed by the employee receiving the service; the second part by the doctor or hospital that performed the service; and the third part is completed by the employer.

EXHIBIT 20

SAMPLE WORKERS' COMPENSATION CLAIM, EMPLOYER PORTION

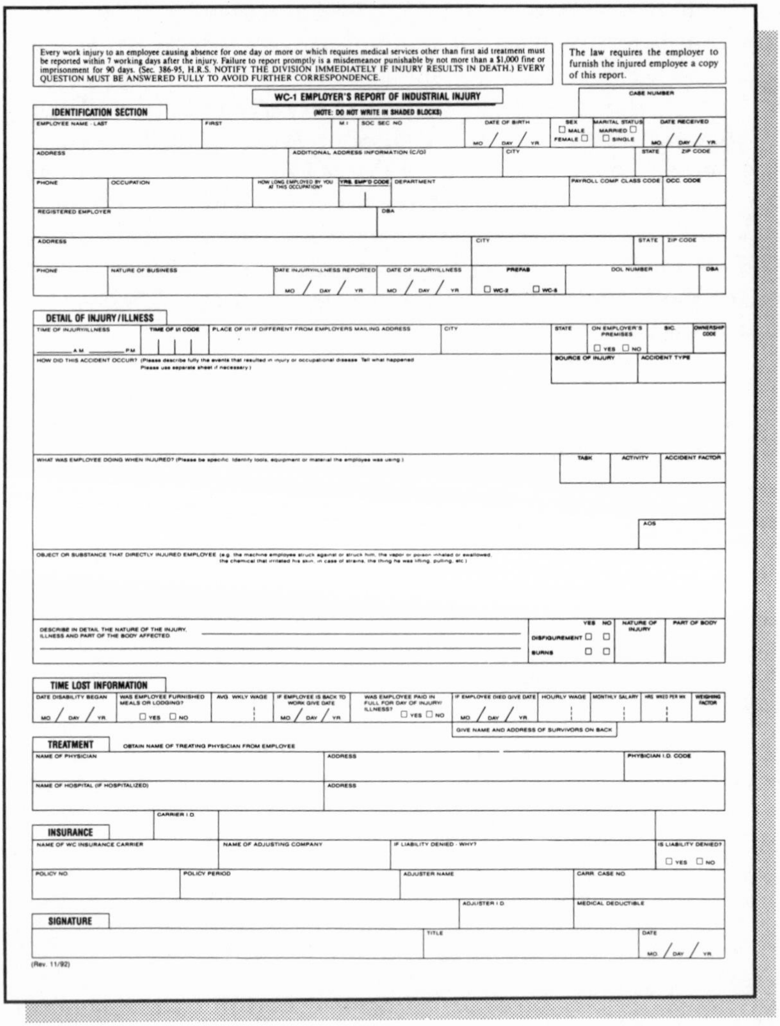

In addition to medical coverage for work-related injuries and illnesses, the workers' compensation insurance policy provides for loss of wages benefits, death benefits, and survivor benefits.

Temporary Disability Insurance (TDI)

The following exerpts are from the Hawaii Department of Labor and Industrial Relations *Digest of Chapters 386, 392 and 393, Hawaii Workers' Compensation, Temporary Disability Insurance and Prepaid Health Care Laws,* Form DC-1(Rev. 10/92):

The law requires you to provide for your employee(s): "Wage replacement benefits for *nonwork-related* disabling illness or injury by the same methods listed above or by negotiating a collective bargaining agreement which provides sick leave benefits as favorable as required by this chapter."

Workers excluded from coverage: "In addition to the above exemptions [the same exemptions for workers' compensation], insurance agents remunerated solely by way of commission; individuals under 18 years of age in the delivery or distribution of newspapers; individuals working for son, daughter or spouse; children under the age of 21 working for father or mother."

Eligibility requirements: "Worker must have been in covered employment with any Hawaii employer for at least 14 weeks with remuneration of 20 or more hours in each week and earned wages of at least $400 during the four completed calendar quarters immediately preceding the first day of disability."

Filing a claim: "Your employee obtains claim form (TDI-45) from employer and completes Part A—Claimant's Statement. Employer completes Part B—Employer's Statement. Worker must then have Part C—Doctor's Statement—certified by a licensed doctor, dentist, chiropractor, osteopath or naturopath. Completed claim form must be filed with insurer within 90 days of disability date."

Benefit provisions: "For nonwork-related injury or illness—wage replacement benefits representing 58 percent of the worker's average weekly wage rounded off to the next higher dollar with the maximum amount correlated with the State unemployment insurance maximum, payable from the eighth day of disability for a maximum duration of 26 weeks in a benefit year. A plan providing benefits deviating from the above must be reviewed and adjudged equivalent by the DCD."

Premium costs: "The employer may pay the entire premium cost or share it with the workers. You can deduct one-half of the cost but not more than .5 percent of the worker's weekly taxable wages up to the maximum set annually by the Division. You pay the remaining portion exceeding the prescribed limitation. If a worker does not meet the eligibility requirements, you cannot withhold any deductions until such time the worker meets the eligibility requirements. No premium payments required for employees who are not eligible for benefits."

There are more provisions on the form.

Although TDI is very similar to workers' compensation in design, it is meant to address a separate problem. Temporary disability insurance is intended for long-term, nonwork-related disabilities and workers' compensation is for work-related disabilities.

As with workers' compensation insurance, temporary disability insurance (1) is contracted with an independent insurance company; (2) is entirely employer paid; (3) has premiums that are calculated as a percent of gross payroll; and (4) requires employer participation in the claim process.

Commercial General Liability

Commercial general liability (CGL) provides for business insurance against injuries caused by negligence or willful conduct on the part of your business as it may involve customers or other businesses. As with any insurance, there are specific exclusions. For instance, even if you have CGL and you slander someone, your CGL policy may not be responsible for that type of liability. Or if you operate a restaurant and your food spoilage results in a customer getting food poisoning, your CGL will not apply. (In this second case, a separate rider, "Product Liability," would apply.)

Because every business faces different types of liability, your insurance agent should explore with you both the limits of coverage and other options you might have to consider.

Fire Insurance

Fire insurance is purchased for: (1) building protection, (2) inventory protection, and (3) business interruption.

Often the limits for your building fire insurance may be dictated by the terms set by the lessor in the lease agreement. For example, the lessor may request as a condition of the lease that you maintain $200,000 of building fire insurance.

Every building and structure in Hawaii has its own rate of insurance. Factors considered in fire insurance premium rates are building construction, type of sprinkler system, and age of the building. Other factors may even involve the tenants in the building. What if one of the tenants stores volatile chemicals in the building? The fire insurance premium will be determined by your exact business location.

Fire insurance may cover only the building and may not include any coverage for inventory or inside property. Because inventory insurance premiums are based on the value of the inventory, the temptation is to value your inventory low. Besides the obvious disadvantage of not having enough coverage for your loss, there is an additional consideration called *coinsurance.*

Coinsurance is a common provision which allows for rate discounts in inventory insurance that may result in the insurance company not covering the entire loss, even though the loss amount is below the stated policy limit. This is best illustrated with an example.

How you might get reimbursed $10,000 on a $20,000 loss even if you have $40,000 of fire insurance.

Let us say that you have $100,000 of inventory in your store and $40,000 of insurance. You suffer a fire loss of $20,000, which is well under your $40,000 limit. You expect an insurance payment of $20,000. If your policy had a stated 80 percent coinsurance provision, however, then the insurance company might argue that you should have been insuring 80 percent of $100,000 and not had a policy of only $40,000. In effect the insurance company might say that you were underinsured for the premium you were paying. As a result, the $20,000 loss would not be completely paid.

In this example:

$$(\text{Actual insurance}) \div (\text{Insurance you should have had}) \times (\text{loss}) = \text{actual payment}$$

or

$$\frac{\$40{,}000}{\$80{,}000} \times \$20{,}000 = \tfrac{1}{2} \times \$20{,}000 = \$10{,}000.$$

If this is the insurance company's position, then you might receive a check for $10,000 to cover your $20,000 loss even though you had $40,000 of insurance.

If your business experiences seasonal inventories, then you should alert your insurance agent to significant shifts in your inventory. Such reporting practices provide for more accurate insurance coverage.

Wholesaler: I remember once receiving a call from one of our manufacturers that he was going to send us a large shipment with super terms and prices to move some overstocked merchandise. Where we usually sold about a hundred pieces each month he was sending us three thousand pieces! It was the largest single dollar shipment we had every seen and it increased the total dollar inventory by four times. Our plan was to use special promotions to clear these units over a three month period. One of the first things we did was to call our insurance agent to notify them of the increased inventory. They requested that we provide them monthly inventory figures until we were back to normal levels. Had we not done that and suffered a loss, our portion not insured would have put us out of business.

A final consideration in fire insurance is related to the down business time after a fire. How will the business pay monthly operating expenses with diminished sales? Business interruption insurance is intended to provide funds to sustain a business during this disruptive period.

Rates

Insurance agent: Make sure that you are comparing apples with apples. Policies may differ in deductibles, coinsurance, requirements, and additional coverage. Like any good product, I don't think that you can shop on price alone. Other things to consider are: claim processing, lost control service, and installment premium payments.

Retailer: I am not a big business—just five employees including myself and I pay $15,000 of insurance premiums each year. That does not include medical insurance, just workers' compensation, TDI, fire, liability, and auto. It's a killer.

Since insurance premiums can be expensive, most insurance companies have installment payment plans. Each plan varies, but most allow a business to pay monthly premiums after an initial downpayment. Insurance costs are too large an expense to be inaccurately estimated by a prospective businessowner or ignored by a current businessowner. Your agent or prospective agent can assist you if you provide the following information:

1. Actual site (to include the address and type of building);
2. Square footage of lease;
3. Total dollars of payroll;
4. Number of employees and job descriptions;
5. Type of business;
6. Estimated gross sales.

Some insurance is required by law, some may be required as a condition of your lease, and some will be required as a matter of prudence. All of it is expensive and difficult to understand, but none of it can be ignored.

Additional Reading

Hawaii Dept. of Labor and Industrial Relations, Unemployment Insurance Div. 1984. *Handbook for Employers on Unemployment Insurance.* Honolulu: DLIR.

12

Importing and Exporting: A Brave New World

What do wicker baskets from the Philippines and Toyota automobiles from Japan have in common with chocolate-covered macadamia nuts shipped from Hawaii to Hong Kong? The answer is foreign trade. In 1985, the United States traded with more Pacific and Far East countries than with Atlantic and European countries.

Hawaii's central geographic location and unique cultural mix makes foreign import and export a definite business opportunity. In addition to new business opportunities, exports add new dollars to our economy, while imported goods and services benefit Hawaii in new products and services.

Because Hawaii is a very small market for most of the world's products, far more products and services are available worldwide than are businesses to handle them here. Many a successful entrepreneur has identified saleable new products or services and simply introduced them to Hawaii before anyone else. Although many of these entrepreneurs found opportunities on the mainland, some business opportunities were created with foreign countries.

> **Retailer:** We were not looking to get into this type of furniture, but one of our managers saw a copy of the Chamber of Commerce's bulletin about manufacturers looking for distributors and sent a request to this manufacturer in Taiwan. Before we knew it, we had set up a tentative program for Hawaii.

> **Executive, computer company:** We now have branch offices in Hong Kong, Japan, and Australia. We got involved with the Far East solely at the request of a bank. When they had a major expansion into the Orient, they needed the services we provided and we piggybacked their operations wherever they opened an office.

Some of these companies were able to secure business relations with foreign companies, and others extended their services to US companies doing business in a foreign country. In addition, many foreign companies are interested in developing Hawaii ties.

Australian manufacturer: For our products, Hawaii is an ideal test market for the United States. Our climates and lifestyles are somewhat similar and that helps.

Importing from a Foreign Country

1. Find a reputable foreign business. The respective foreign embassies and consulates provide periodic listings of foreign businesses looking for US ties. In addition, trade shows for your industry in the United States bring together many US and foreign interests.

2. Check with the Bureau of Customs on any country restrictions and precautions. The Bureau of Customs will be able to advise you on any restrictions in dealing with a particular country. Unlike ordering goods from within the United States, goods from foreign countries may be subject to import duties, tariffs, and US import restrictions.

3. Check with a customshouse broker. A customshouse broker is a business that specializes in handling the customs and document processing of foreign goods. These agents are knowledgeable about customs requirements and duties for different classes and types of merchandise.

4. Check with your banker on how they handle letters of credit. Because many foreign transactions are handled in foreign currencies, you cannot simply write a check as you might for goods received from the mainland. Most foreign funds' transactions are handled interbank using a letter of credit. A letter of credit is a financial agreement between the seller and the buyer's bank for the payment of goods transferred between countries at specified currency amounts and under exact shipment procedures.

To the seller a letter of credit is a financial instrument outlining how payment is to be made for a certain order. The letter of credit also serves the purpose of protecting the importer, because payment cannot be made unless the manufacturer can satisfactorily complete all of the documentation requirements set out in the letter of credit. Once these conditions are met, your bank will pay the foreign bank. All this is handled between your bank and the shipper's bank, and funds are wired from one to the other. You will want to discuss this procedure with your bank's international department.

(**A note of caution:** With respect to letters of credit, banks deal only in paper transactions. The bank does not inspect or guarantee shipment, or insure that what was ordered was indeed shipped.)

5. Negotiate an agreement with a foreign company.

Retailer: When we first negotiated arrangements with a foreign business, no formal written contract was drawn up. Almost everything we did was verbal. Our US arrangements were always followed by 10-page contracts. Now we are concluding a deal with a company in a foreign country over a handshake and a few scribbled notes.

Wholesaler: I think it helps if the foreign business is already doing some business in the United States. That means that they have some experience in US procedures.

Wholesaler: I would recommend that you check to see if the product you plan to import is admissible. For example, there are quotas on some materials and some items are prohibited. Get a good customshouse broker for some advice.

Negotiating an agreement with a foreign business is not entirely different from what one would experience in dealing with a US supplier. Prices, delivery times, minimum quantities, and freight allowances will have to be negotiated. However, several major differences will be encountered in the consideration of foreign currency fluctuations, language, and customs restrictions.

Wholesaler: We had negotiated with our Japan manufacturer a rate of 220 yen to the dollar as a standard for our price list. After a while, the yen dropped to 185 to a dollar meaning that our dollar would buy less. Then we successfully negotiated a new rate.

Former wholesaler: It takes a lot of experience to deal with foreign manufacturers. Not only language barriers and currency differences are potential problems, but also different types of laws and customs. And it's not as if you can just pick up the phone and call as you can with mainland manufacturers. I would verify any foreign business credibility with some other US company.

A Foreign Trade Example

Here are steps a Hawaii electronics distributor used to import car stereos from a Japan manufacturer:

Step 1: Estimate the order and delivery dates from an agreed price list of the Japan manufacturer.

This distributor had made prior agreements with this foreign manufacturer on the price of merchandise, shipping requirements, and payment terms. For instance, the distributor could purchase a model 3100 car stereo for 20,000 yen; had a minimum order requirement of US$5,000; needed to place the order three months ahead of schedule; and had to pay with a letter of credit in yen through a certain Japan bank. Based upon this prior agreement, the distributor estimated the following order:

Model 3100
Cost per unit: 20,000 yen
Order quantity: 200 units
Total cost in yen: 4,000,000 yen
Total cost US$ at conversion rate of 185: $21,622

Step 2: Arrange a short-term bank loan.

The distributor then arranged a short-term inventory loan with a Hawaii bank for $21,622.

Step 3: Place an order with the foreign manufacturer.

The distributor then telexed the order to the Japanese manufacturer. The telex listed the model numbers and quantities requested, shipping instructions, and purchase order numbers. In addition, the distributor requested that the manufacturer send a proforma invoice to confirm the order.

Step 4: Receive a reply from the Japan company.

Within a few days, the distributor received a telex reply acknowledging the receipt of the distributor's order.

Step 5: Receive the proforma invoice from Japan company.

About a month later, the distributor received the proforma invoice from the manufacturer. This tentative invoice outlined all shipping instructions and the quantities and cost of the order. The distributor checked this proforma invoice for any discrepancies with his original order.

Step 6: Prepare a letter of credit (LC) with the bank.

The LC is somewhat similar to a certified bank check. By using an LC, the manufacturer is assured payment for the order. The LC also provides some safeguards for the distributor so that the shipment will be received under the conditions listed in the LC. The process of payment by LC is accomplished with the help of both banks. The distributor, in this case, would arrange with the international department of a Hawaii bank that a LC be sent to the specified Japan bank "in favor" of the manufacturer. Before the distributor's bank will issue the LC it must be assured that the distributor has the necessary funds to cover it. In this example the distributor is able to show an approved short-term loan for $21,622. When the bank sends the LC to the Japan bank for the distributor, the US bank is assuming responsibility to pay under the LC.

Step 7: The LC is accepted.

When the LC is received by the manufacturer's bank in Japan, the manufacturer is "advised."

Step 8: Receive invoice and copy of shipping documents from Japan manufacturer.

At the time the goods are shipped from Japan, customs documents will be mailed to the distributor. These documents should arrive sometime before the actual goods reach the dock.

Step 9: Send one copy to the customshouse broker.

The distributor will send the customs broker one set of these documents and the customs broker will start the customs processing.

Step 10: The original *bill of lading* is received from the bank.

The bill of lading is the title to the merchandise. It is sent to the distributor's bank with other documents as required in the LC and shows the actual merchandise, value, and shipping instructions. The original copy of the bill of lading is the title document for these goods. Some of the other documents often required are:

1. a commercial invoice
2. packing list
3. certificate of origin
4. insurance policy
5. inspection certificate

The exact forms required for any shipment can be clarified with a customs broker or a banker.

Step 11: Bank pays the letter of credit.

If all the conditions outlined in the LC have been complied with, the US bank pays the Japan bank. The distributor's bank will then release the bill of lading to the distributor.

Step 12: Clear customs.

The distributor has the goods inspected by US Customs.

Step 13: Pick up the merchandise.

The distributor receives a call from the freight company to pick up the shipment. The distributor takes the freight bill (received from the freight company) and the original bill of lading to the freight company with a check to pay for the freight.

Step 14: Pay any customs duties.

The process as outlined here appears more cumbersome than it really is. The assistance of the customs broker and the international department of the bank will ease much of the process. The main point is that the distributor (importer/buyer) had to make separate arrangements with the bank and with the foreign manufacturer (shipper/seller). To arrange for the letter of credit, the distributor had to show the bank funds were available to cover the amount that the bank would eventually have to pay. The bank is only acting as an intermediary. The distributor also had to arrange pricing, shipping, and payment terms with the foreign manufacturer.

Other Provisions of the Letter of Credit (LC)

The LC is a useful method of payment for foreign transactions. Each LC can be tailored to suit the conditions of the shipment. Here are some of the provisions in the LC used between this distributor and manufacturer:

1. "Marked Freight Prepaid"—Freight is prepaid by shipper.
2. "CIF Honolulu"—The manufacturer will pay all insurance and shipping charges to Honolulu.
3. "Partial Shipment Prohibited"—Shipper must send entire shipment.
4. "Irrevocable"—Once the credit has been accepted by the manufacturer it cannot be altered by the distributor without the permission of the manufacturer and it cannot be canceled by the issuing bank prior to expiration.
5. "Sight Draft"—Payment is due at the time all the required documents are provided by the manufacturer to the distributor's bank.

Instead of payment terms of "Sight Draft," which calls for payment before the actual physical possession of the merchandise, the distributor might negotiate better payment terms of "Sight Plus 30 Days." Under these terms, the manufacturer would not be paid until 30 days after the documents are received.

Banker: Letters of credit are fascinating because you can structure them any way that you want. I don't think any two letters of credit are ever the same.

Other Payment Methods

Using a letter of credit is the most stringent method of coordinating payments. There are two less stringent—but riskier—methods: document against payment (DP) or document against acceptance (DA).

The DP is instructions from a manufacturer or shipper to the bank that papers transferring title to the goods should be released to the distributor or buyer only upon the buyer's payment of draft. This method of payment provides the buyer more flexible payment options. There are fewer restrictions on the buyer.

The DA is instructions given by the manufacturer or shipper to a bank that the papers transferring title to goods be delivered to the distributor or buyer only upon the buyer's acceptance. In essence, the distributor would receive the goods on credit terms.

Payment terms of DP and DA generally are negotiated after both the seller and the buyer have developed a satisfactory long-term relationship.

Exporting to a Foreign Country

Exporting is not for everyone. To export a product or service a business should have: a suitable product selling well in the United States; a commitment from the businessowners to export; and extra products to sell. The two most common questions are:

1. How do you know where the market is for your product?
2. How do you find customers in a foreign market?

For starters, the answers to these questions can best be discussed with the International Trade Administration Office of the US Department of Commerce. There you will find a variety of programs and services to assist you in developing your overseas operations.

As an exporter you reverse your role and perspective from that of an importer. Instead of a distributor seeking suppliers in foreign countries, you become the Hawaii supplier or manufacturer seeking a distributor outside your own country. In addition to the usual problems inherent in any business transaction, when exporting there are the problems of language, cultural differences, currency, and tariffs.

An export program usually is based on a successful sales program close to home in Hawaii and in the familiar surroundings on the US mainland. This success will give you credibility when you present your sales program in a foreign country. Do your research well. Each foreign country has tariffs which restrict or discourage the import of certain products just as the United States does. Many foreign consulates provide assistance in reviewing their tariffs and paperwork requirements. Establishing an export program requires a real commitment in time and money from the business.

Most businesses will have no need or desire to import or export products or services from or to a foreign country. Those who are able to successfully develop foreign connections earn the praise of the entire community. Our overall economic quality of life may well be dependent on the success of the Hawaii business people who develop new foreign and mainland markets to supplement our dependence on tourism.

Additional Reading

Kephart, Linda. 1986. "Going Abroad." *Hawaii Business* 31 (8) (February): 20–26.

US Dept. of the Treasury, Customs Service. *Importing into the United States.*

US Dept. of Commerce, International Trade Administration. *A Basic Guide to Exporting.*

13

Employees: What They Really Cost

The businessowner wears several job hats, not only as the owner but often also as the salesperson, bookkeeper, secretary, manager, and delivery person. With all these job assignments, owners of new businesses should not be surprised to find that their work day never ends. Sooner or later a businessowner may need an employee to help with some of these tasks.

To help us understand the employment process, let us hire a clerk/receptionist for our hypothetical Waikiki Tax Service. The first question will be: Can you afford to hire an employee?

Can You Afford to Hire an Employee?

If Waikiki Tax Service decides to hire a secretary at $2,000 per month, what will the total cost be to the business, and how much additional income will have to be generated to cover this new expense? We have already seen that in addition to the gross salary of each employee there are additional expenses such as medical insurance and workers' compensation insurance which add to the monthly costs per employee (see chapter 11). Some of these additional expenses can be estimated as:

Gross monthly salary	$2,000.00
FICA (employer's portion 7.65%)	153.00
State Unemployment Tax (4%)	80.00
Federal Unemployment Tax (.8%)	16.00
Est. Temporary Disability Insurance (.2%)	4.00
Est. Workers' Compensation (.86%)	17.20
Employee medical insurance (5.0%)	100.00
Subtotal monthly cost	$2,370.20

The estimated \$370.20 per month equals about 18 percent of additional costs besides salary. Adding other benefits like sick leave and vacation time might bring these costs to 20 percent of salary. Another way to look at it is, for every dollar of salary there will be \$.18 to \$.20 of additional employee costs (depending on the industry and company, these additional costs may be as high as 35 percent of gross salary).

Given our estimated employee costs, Waikiki Tax Service will need \$2,400 of additional sales each month to cover this new employee cost and remain at current profitability. If Windward TV were hiring the same receptionist they would need new monthly sales of \$4,800 to offset this new cost, because a portion (assuming 50 percent in this case) of their sales dollar goes to their cost of goods leaving \$2,400 to apply to employee costs. At \$4,800 of increased monthly sales, Windward TV would need to generate \$57,600 (\$4,800 of monthly sales × 12 months) of additional sales per year to cover this one employee.

Other things being equal, the decision to hire a receptionist at a salary of \$2,000 is justified if Waikiki Tax Service can consistently generate \$28,800 of new income (or is willing to lose \$28,800 of current income).

By the way, to convert a monthly salary of \$2,000 into an hourly salary the State of Hawaii currently uses the following formula:

$$\frac{\$2{,}000 \times 12}{52} \div 40 \text{ hours per week} = \$11.54 \text{ per hour.}$$

If you hire an employee, you will want to develop a good personnel program from the very start. With a little thought you can have a program that is as good as that of any large company. A good personnel program treats three areas: (1) the employee selection process, (2) training, and (3) employee retention.

The Employee Selection Process

Every employee is an expensive choice. Unfortunately, many small businesses approach the task of adding employees haphazardly. Often very little consideration is given to selection or to the contributions and problems an employee brings to the enterprise. On the other hand, many successful businesses attribute their success to their employees.

Telephone interconnect businessowner: One way to be successful is to have key employees who support you 110 percent. These employees do not put in eight hours a day and go home. With them we can make a job commitment and know that the personnel can deliver. Although good people are hard to find, management has some responsibility too. Management must relate to the needs of the employees and set a good example. If I ask them to work twelve hours a day, then so do I.

But successful or not, managers and businessowners often decry the heartache of finding and managing employees.

Restaurant owner: I was the least comfortable with handling employees. I was not prepared for all the different personalities and problems.

Company president: A real headache is finding good people. If your business is in Sacramento, you can go to San Jose or San Francisco to hunt for qualified employees. There is no other place to go in Hawaii.

Employment counselor: Some young people, especially those right out of high school, have an unrealistic view of what the real world is like. They often have no skills, yet are unhappy to start at the bottom or to put in the time with a job and learn some real skills.

The hiring of a new employee may require a week to a couple of months, depending on the type of job and how you recruit for it. But before we get to that, one thing that will help to speed up the selection process is a job description.

The Job Description

A simple job description similar to that in Exhibit 21, besides providing a more detailed definition of a position, will give the job interviewer a clear picture of the ideal person for the job. From this job description we have a good idea as to the duties and work schedule for the position. Furthermore, we have an idea of the types of skills this person should possess. The next step is to outline all the qualities and skills our ideal applicant should have. Here is a sample list:

Education:

1. High school graduate or equivalent but preferably a business school graduate.
2. Ideally, with past computer input training.
3. Ideally, someone with past bookkeeping training.

Past Work Experience:
This is an entry level position but preference would be given to someone with at least one year clerical experience.

Required Skills:

1. Pleasant phone voice.
2. Able to handle customer complaints.
3. Type at least 40 words per minute.
4. Demonstrated skill at handling money.

EXHIBIT 21
SAMPLE JOB DESCRIPTION

Job title: Receptionist/General Clerk
Employee reports to: Josie Akana, Owner
Direct supervisor for: None

Major duties:

1. Answer the phone—will handle incoming calls to include customer inquiries and complaints. Will make return calls on behalf of the owner.
2. Typing and filing—type all correspondence (approximately 10 letters a week). File all invoices, correspondence.
3. Receive mail—receive and sort mail.
4. Petty cash—maintain the petty cash fund.
5. Bank deposits—make out daily bank deposits.
6. Computer input—input invoices in the computer.
7. Other duties as assigned.

Estimated time per week:

Phone calls	20%
Typing and filing	43%
Mail	1%
Petty cash	1%
Bank deposits	5%
Computer input	30%

Skills needed:

1. Must type 40 words per minute.
2. Trainable for computer data input.
3. Able to handle incoming phone calls.

Equipment used on the job:

1. Typewriter
2. Computer terminal
3. Xerox machine

This position carries the authority to:

1. Make petty cash disbursements of less than $20.
2. Make a customer refund.

Training responsibility: This employee will train new clerical hires on the filing system, mail receiving, and petty cash.
Comments: Should be a high school graduate or equivalent but preferably a business school graduate.

With this description of the ideal applicant and the job description, you can now conduct interviews. Interviewing applicants for a new job is like going fishing—you never know what is out there or what your bait might bring in. But one thing is certain, your notice of a job opening will attract a wide range of people.

Because of the diversity of the applicants' job qualifications, the interviewer is often confronted with people who have some, but not all, of the desired qualifications. For example, this clerical opening may produce two somewhat qualified candidates. One applicant may be a high school graduate with the required typing skills and phone personality but no other work experience. The other applicant may be a business school graduate with good work and bookkeeping experience but lacking in phone skills. Businessowners usually consider themselves fortunate when faced with a choice among many ideal applicants. But the more common challenge for these personnel interviewers is making a good selection from applicants that do not fit the ideal job qualifications.

Office secretary: When we advertise for a new clerical position, our phones ring off the hook for three days. Forget about getting any work done. And we get everything from high schoolers who just graduated to mothers returning to the work force after 15 years.

Retailer: I think when you are hiring people you try to replace yourself where you can't be. So you look for someone you hope will have the same values and the same concerns for the business or products.

Personnel interviewer: I am of the opinion that it is better to leave a position open rather than hire the wrong person for that job.

Advertising the Position

The next step in the selection process is to advertise the position. One way to advertise for new employees is to place a help-wanted ad in the newspaper. The wording of the ad is crucial to attracting the type of person you desire. Let us write the help-wanted ad for the clerical position in our example, keeping in mind the Hawaii Newspaper Agency guideline of 33 spaces per line for help-wanted classified advertising.

General clerk. Experienced with
pleasant phone voice. Prefer bus.
school grad w/computer and
bookkeeping exp. Call 836-1400.

Other points the applicant might want to know are: pay, location, type of business, and benefits. If you want to appeal to a more specific applicant, the advertisement might be worded like this:

General clerk for accountant.
Experienced with pleasant phone
voice. Type 40 wpm. Prefer bus.
grad w/ computer and bookkeeping
exp but will train. $8/hr. 836-1400

Employment Agencies

Employment agencies recruit employees for businesses. Most of these agencies charge the prospective employee for the service and can be helpful in screening applicants. The State of Hawaii and the military (Joint Employment Management Systems) maintain employment services that are free of charge and can be a source of new hires.

Once the newspaper help-wanted ad appears or a listing is placed with an employment agency, you will start to receive inquiries. You may attempt to screen these inquiries on the phone, but eventually you will have to schedule interviews.

The Employment Interview

Most of us have been through some type of employment interview. The purpose of the employment interview is to:

1. Determine the personality and compatibility of the applicant to the organization.
2. Determine the qualifications and interest in the position of the applicant.

The interviewer has only the benefit of the prospective employee's application (Exhibit 22) and the results of an interview on which to base a decision. Therefore, a good interview is essential to a good hiring decision.

The best location for an interview is one that minimizes interruptions and will allow the applicant to talk openly. In a small business, however, it is not uncommon for the businessowner to conduct an interview while waiting on customers or answering the phone. Hiring temporary help during the interview period might be well worth the expense.

Anyone can conduct a good interview if they have the right questions to ask. Let us use the following questions based on the job application in Exhibit 22:

Interviewer: Thank you for coming in this morning. Were we hard to find? Excuse me for a moment while I read your application.

1. Could you tell me about your last job?
Applicant: As you can see from my application, I worked for East West Savings and Loan as a teller for about one year. I received cash and posted savings to customer accounts. I also handled some phone inquiries.

2. What did you like about working there?
Applicant: The people were very nice to work with.

3. How was the previous job at Tech Industries different from East West Savings?
Applicant: Tech Industries was a manufacturer and I was a bookkeeper/receptionist there. I posted accounts receivables, answered the phone, and typed letters and reports.

EXHIBIT 22

Application for Employment Form

Date: 5/1/9_

Name: Marianne Rego

Social security number: 574-49-3500

Address: 98-088 IPO STREET, AIEA, HI 96872

Position applied for:

Date you can start: immediately

Telephone: 488-5400

Can you work: [X] Full-time [ ] Part-time [ ] Temporarily

Employment History Begin with most recent position

Date of Employment Month — Year	Name and Address of Employer (include military service) Name and Telephone of Supervisor	Job Title and Responsibilities	Salary	Reason for Leaving
From: 9/85 To: 8/86	East West Savings & Loan 931 University Ave.	Bookkeeper Posting / phones	# 850	
From: 8/85 To: 12/83	Tech Industries 501 Sumner St.	Bookkeeper Accounts Payable	$ 700	Took position at East West
From: To:				
From: To:				
From: To:				
From: To:				

May we contact the employers above? [X] Yes [ ] No

Are you currently employed? [ ] Yes [X] No

Education	Name and Location	Type of Diploma	Years Completed	Did You Graduate?
High School	Aiea High, Aiea, HI	High School	3	yes
Trade or Technical School	Alpha Business sch., Hono.	Business School	1	yes
College				

List any special skills or training:

10 Key, computer

Important — Please Read and Sign

As an 'equal opportunity employer' this company's policy, as well as Federal and State Law, prohibits discrimination in employment based on race, color, religion, sex, national origin, physical handicap, or age with respect to individuals who are at least 18 years of age.

As part of this application for employment, I hereby authorize the company to investigate my references and to make an independent investigation of my character, conduct and employment records.

I further agree that failure to reveal any prior employer, or the giving of false or misleading information by me will be grounds for termination of employment.

Signature: Marianne Rego Date: 5/1/9_

For Company Use Only

Interviewer:

Date:

Comments:

Hired

Department:

Position:

Starting date:

Location:

Salary:

Approved:

(Note: This exhibit is not recommended for use by any business but is only presented for illustration.)

4. Of the two jobs which one did you like the best?
Applicant: Tech Industries because it was more varied. I especially liked handling the phone calls.

5. What didn't you like at Tech Industries?
Applicant: I did not like their end of the month posting which required a lot of rush work.

6. You only worked a year at East West Savings but two years at Tech Industries. Could I ask why?
Applicant: I did not like being a teller. I much prefer working in a small office rather than in a big one where there are strict rules such as, when you can go to lunch.

7. Have you had schooling in bookkeeping?
Applicant: Yes. I took one year at Alpha Business School.

8. What area in bookkeeping do you enjoy the most?
Applicant: I enjoy posting accounts ledgers.

9. Why do you think you enjoy that the most?
Applicant: I guess because I like working with numbers.

10. How many words per minute do you type?
Applicant: 40. But I haven't been tested recently.

11. What was it about this job that made you apply?
Applicant: It is close to home and I do not have to drive into town. I am also looking for a clerical job, and your ad seems to be just what I am looking for.

12. If I asked your best friend, what one word would she use to describe you?
Applicant: That's a good question. I guess she would say that I am reliable.

13. You have read our company background information sheet and the description of the job you are applying for. Do you have any questions?
Applicant: No. It was very complete. But I would like to know when you might be making your decision?
Interviewer: We will be interviewing the rest of this week and then we will pick the top three applicants to come in for a short written and typing test. We should notify these three people by Friday. Thank you for coming in.

Although the names on this application are fictious, this was an actual 20-minute, 13-question interview. From it the businessowner was able to determine the job skills, communication skills, personality, job interest, and potential job stability of the applicant. Other questions this interviewer could have asked are:

1. Having read the job description, in what area do you think you could help us the most? Why?
2. Is the pay satisfactory?
3. How do you think your past supervisor might describe your work there?

Application forms and interview questions should avoid areas that might be interpreted as a basis for discrimination. Some of these areas are ethnic background, age, physical disabilities, or marital status.

After conducting 24 interviews over a week's time, the businessowner was able to narrow his choices to two applicants—Betsy and Margret. He then called both in to take a short employment test.

The Employment Test

The test results of these two applicants are shown in Exhibit 23 and 24. Both Betsy and Margret did well in the interview, but based on this written test, Betsy was eliminated as a candidate.

The employment test can be any simple test of the basic skills required for the position. Exhibits 23 and 24 are actual test results for a clerical position in a business services company. This business simply chose common words and calculations it uses in its operation to prepare the test. This employment test supplements the interview, and a similar test can be developed by any manager or businessowner.

Now that the owner has found the most likely applicant, one additional function to perform is verifying prior employment.

Verifying Prior Employment

Always verify prior employment. To start you should obtain a signed release from the applicant authorizing you to verify references and the information provided on the application. This release statement is commonly found on the job application (see Exhibit 22).

Common questions asked about prior employment involve verifying the dates employed, the salary listed on the application, and positions worked with previous employers. But the employment verification does not have to stop there. The following questions are recommended for employment verification by the employment agency, Robert Half International, Inc., in its booklet, *How to Check References When References Are Hard to Check* (reprinted with permission. Copyright 1986 by Robert Half International, Inc.):

1. How does she compare to the person who is doing the job now?
2. If she was good at her job, why didn't you try to induce her to stay?
3. When there was a particularly urgent assignment, what steps did she take to make sure it was done on time?
4. None of us is perfect at everything. Please describe her shortcomings.
5. Have you seen her current resume? Let me read you the part that describes your company.
6. She indicated her salary was $________. Is this correct?
7. Did she have problems with a particular type of person?

EXHIBIT 23
New Hire Employment Test

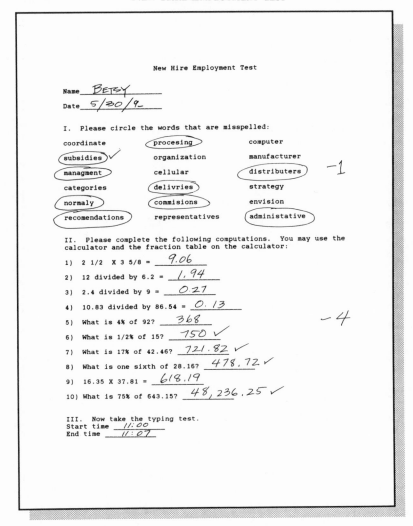

New Hire Employment Test

Name BETSY
Date 5/30/9_

I. Please circle the words that are misspelled:

coordinate	procesing	computer
subsidies ✓	organization	manufacturer
managment	cellular	distributers
categories	delivries	strategy
normaly	commisions	envision
recomendations	representatives	administative

−1

II. Please complete the following computations. You may use the calculator and the fraction table on the calculator:

1) 2 1/2 X 3 5/8 = 9.06
2) 12 divided by 6.2 = 1.94
3) 2.4 divided by 9 = 0.27
4) 10.83 divided by 86.54 = 0.13
5) What is 4% of 92? 368
6) What is 1/2% of 15? 750 ✓
7) What is 17% of 42.46? 721.82 ✓
8) What is one sixth of 28.16? 478.72 ✓
9) 16.35 X 37.81 = 618.19
10) What is 75% of 643.15? 48,236.25 ✓

−4

III. Now take the typing test.
Start time 11:00
End time 11:07

8. How many times a month did she take days off for personal and sickness reasons? How many times did she come in late?

One other question that might be added to this list is:

9. Would you rehire this individual?

If at all possible, attempt to verify an applicant's prior employment over the telephone even if that requires a long-distance call. There are personal voice inflections that cannot be conveyed in writing that may influence

EXHIBIT 24

New Hire Employment Test

New Hire Employment Test

Name Margret

Date 5/30/9_

I. Please circle the words that are misspelled:

coordinate	(procesing)	computer
subsidies	organization	manufacturer
(managment)	cellular	(distributers)
categories	(delivries)	strategy
(normaly)	(commisions)	envision
(recomendations)	representatives	(administative)

−0

II. Please complete the following computations. You may use the calculator and the fraction table on the calculator:

1) 2 1/2 X 3 5/8 = 5 7/16 ✓
2) 12 divided by 6.2 = 1.94
3) 2.4 divided by 9 = .27
4) 10.83 divided by 86.54 = .13
5) What is 4% of 92? 3.68
6) What is 1/2% of 15? .08
7) What is 17% of 42.46? 7.22
8) What is one sixth of 28.16? 4.69
9) 16.35 X 37.81 = 618.19
10) What is 75% of 643.15? 482.36

−1

III. Now take the typing test.
Start time 10:27
End time 10:34

your decision. In the case of Margret, the manager called a mainland employer and received the following enthusiastic recommendation from the department manager:

> **Department manager:** Yes, I remember Margret. Yes, she worked for us during that period and for that pay. She got along very well with others. She did take a little longer to learn something new, but when she did she rarely made a mistake. We would have loved to have her stay with us but her husband got reassigned. She had no attendance or other problems and we would gladly rehire her.

Margret was hired.

The estimated cost involved in the selection process was:

Advertising	$100.00
Manager's interview time (20 hours × $20 per hour)	400.00
Long distance calls	2.00
Reference/testing (3 hours × $20 per hour)	60.00
Total cost	$562.00

Employee Training

The second requirement of a good personnel program is an employee training program. There are two types of training programs: (1) initial hire and (2) continuing training.

Having spent over a week receiving phone calls and interviewing applicants, this businessowner now has a work backlog. The tendency might be to get back to the work piling up on the desk and to let the employee learn "on the job."

Clerical employee: After I was hired my training consisted of reading some product brochures, being assigned a desk, and getting to work.

Salesman: My training consisted of the owner talking to me for about an hour and then I went on the sales floor. I learned by asking a lot of questions and by making mistakes.

How long does it take to make an employee fully productive? To put it in a personal perspective, how long would it take for someone to learn all the facets of your job?

Consultant: It is one thing to learn the technical skills that go with each job, but to learn all the little do's and don'ts takes a long time. My guess would be that it takes three months to a year for a clerk or salesperson to be fully productive and two or more years for a manager.

We might guess that it will take our new clerical employee the first week just to learn how to use the typewriter and refill the copy machine. Although the clerk will be working during this time, she will be far from fully productive. Let us assume that, even if she asks a lot of questions, she will not be fully productive for at least three months.

The goals of an initial training program are:

1. To get the employee to full productivity faster;
2. To provide a less frustrating transition for the employee; and
3. To assess the skills and potential of the new hire.

To meet these three goals we are going to use the training outline in Exhibit 25 for our new clerical hiree. Because the employee will learn the job information one way or another, you would prefer that it be the correct way from the start. All that is required of you is a commitment and time invested up-front in employee development.

A businessowner who hires an employee is now a manager, and a good manager works with and through the employees. A good way to do this is by providing continual training and guidance. This training program is the start. By participating directly in the initial training, the businessowner can assess immediately the potential of the new hire within the probationary period.

Using our sample training program, let us estimate the cost, assuming Josie's salary is $20 per hour and Sally's is $8.00 per hour. This training cost is:

Josie	20 hours × $20 per hour =	$400
Sally	12 hours × $8 per hour =	$ 96
Total training cost		$496

Employee Retention

Because employee selection is both costly and disruptive, the goal of an employee retention program is to keep desirable employees. The best method of retaining employees is to create the right work environment. While it would be unfair to expect all employees to remain with the business forever, a good business will attempt to minimize the disruption caused by frequent employee turnover.

Large companies generally have more attractive lures for a prospective employee than small companies:

1. Higher pay ranges;
2. Better benefits;
3. Company name recognition;
4. Excellent training programs.

To combat these big company advantages, small businesses need to offer unique work benefits. Some of these are:

1. More opportunity for growth;
2. More flexible work conditions;
3. More participation in decisionmaking;
4. Part ownership in the business.

EXHIBIT 25

Training Outline for Clerk/Receptionist

Monday		
8:00–12:00 (with Josie)	1. Complete employment forms, W2, etc.	
	2. Explain parking, show office	
	3. Review job description	
	4. Phone procedures	
	5. Typewriter, copy machine operation	
	6. Typing letter training	
1:00–5:00 (on own)	1. Read Employee Manual (see appendix C for sample)	
	2. Type actual letters	
	3. Read copier and typewriter manuals	
Tuesday		
8:00–12:00 (with Josie)	1. Mail handling	
	2. Filing and file system	
	3. Bank deposits	
	4. Review typed letters	
	5. Special forms introduction	
1:00–5:00 (on own)	1. File	
	2. Type new letters	
	3. Type special forms	
Wednesday		
8:00–12:00 (with Josie)	1. Special forms	
1:00–5:00 (with Sally)	1. Special forms	
Thursday		
8:00–12:00 (with Josie)	1. Special forms review	
1:00–5:00 (with Sally)	1. Continue work on special forms	
Friday		
8:00–12:00 (with Josie)	1. Review special forms	
	2. Petty cash	
	3. Computer input	
1:00–5:00 (with Sally)	1. Computer input	

Carpet company employee: I know I can make more money elsewhere, but I like where I am working now. This is a small company and the boss is very nice to work with. He has given me a lot of decision-making authority that I wouldn't get elsewhere at my level.

It is fortunate for small businesses that people work for more than just money. The secret of good management is to find the right mix of benefits and working conditions in your working environment that encourages employee retention.

Employee Termination

If the employer is not satisfied with the work performance of an employee, the employee should be informed of the employer's dissatisfaction. Often the employee may be unaware that something is amiss. If the problem is a serious or repeat problem, however, the employer should spell out expected performance changes and possible disciplinary consequences. An employee manual should explain general company policies (see appendix C). To avoid the possibility of misinterpetation, all disciplinary action should be documented in writing.

Government Reporting

Both the state and federal governments take a keen interest in your employees. All new hires must be reported to the state. The Hawaii "Report of New Hire(s)" form is used to report all newly hired employees (Exhibit 26). Although the state no longer requires a report when an employee leaves employment, one company maintains its own report (Exhibit 27). The first part of their form is completed when the employee is hired. Upon termination, the remainder of the form is completed as a quick summary for future reference. Questions about the state form should be directed to the Hawaii Department of Labor and Industrial Relations. In addition, the federal government requires that the employer complete an "Employment Eligibility Verification" (Form I-9) report on each employee (Exhibit 28). After June 1, 1987, all employers are required to hire only US citizens and aliens lawfully authorized to work in the United States. As a result, the employer is required to complete and maintain such files for all new hires for a period beginning on the date of hire and ending either three years after the date of such hiring, or one year after the date the individual's employment is terminated, whichever is later. Inquiries about Form I-9 and the requirements of the law should be made to the US Immigration and Naturalization Service.

The total estimated first month's costs to hire the clerk/receptionist for Waikiki Tax Service is:

Salary	$2,000
Additional costs	370
Selection costs	562
Training costs	496
Total cost	$3,428

But more than just costs, it took this businessowner a period of three to

EXHIBIT 26

Hawaii Report of New Hires

UC-BP-5(A) (Rev. 9/87)

STATE OF HAWAII
Unemployment Insurance Division
REPORT OF NEW HIRE(S)

TYPE OR PRINT ALL INFORMATION

The Hawaii Employment Security Law requires that employers report all hires to the Unemployment Insurance Division on Form UC-BP-5(A), REPORT OF NEW HIRE(S). This information enables the Division to detect fraud in cases where applicants continue to file for benefits after starting employment. Therefore, it is important for employers to properly complete and file timely reports as required below.

INSTRUCTIONS

Prepare each form in duplicate. Submit the original to the Division and retain a copy for your file.

Under the appropriate columns, enter the employee's name, social security number, type of work performed, status (either fulltime (F) or parttime (P)), the number of hours the individual is employed per week, and the date started.

At the bottom of the form, in the appropriate spaces, enter your signature, title, date, telephone number, ten-digit Unemployment Insurance Account Number, company name and address.

After completing the form, fold and staple it with the address side up. Place the proper amount of postage on the form and drop it in the mail. A report that is returned to you for completion and/or for insufficient postage may be considered untimely so be sure that all items are complete and the form properly stamped before mailing.

WHEN TO FILE FORMS

To report the hire of a single employee, the REPORT OF NEW HIRE(S) must be completed and submitted within five (5) working days from the date the employee began work. To report a list of hires, the form must be completed and submitted within five (5) working days from the earliest date of hire.

Failure to submit a timely report will result in assessment of $10.00 for each hire that is reported late unless the department determines that the failure to file was excusable.

WHERE TO GET FORMS

If you have questions, or require an additional supply of forms, contact the nearest Unemployment Insurance Office whose address and telephone number is listed below:

OAHU	HAWAII	MAUI	KAUAI	MOLOKAI
P.O. Box 1200	P.O. Box 652	P.O. Box E	P.O. Box 911	P.O. Box 806
Hon., HI 96807	Hilo, HI 96720	Wailuku, HI 96793	Lihue, HI 96766	Kaunakakai, HI 96748
Phone: 548-8750	Phone: 961-7461	Phone: 244-4377	Phone: 245-4485	Phone: 553-3281

EMPLOYEE'S NAME			SOCIAL SECURITY NO.	TYPE OF WORK PERFORMED	FULL (F) TIME PART (P) TIME	HOURS PER WEEK	DATE STARTED
LAST	FIRST	MI					
Floyd	Margret		555-23-4123	Clerical	F	40	7/9/91

I certify that the above information is true and correct to the best of my knowledge and belief.

Josie Akana — EMPLOYER REPRESENTATIVE
Owner — TITLE
7/9/91 — DATE
836-1400 — TELEPHONE
0000197220 — EMPLOYER ACCOUNT NUMBER
Waikiki Tax Service — EMPLOYER NAME
2828 Paa St., Honolulu, HI 96819 — EMPLOYER ADDRESS

**SUBMIT THIS FORM WITHIN FIVE (5) WORKING DAYS FROM DATE EMPLOYED.
LAW PROVIDES PENALTY FOR LATE/NON-COMPLIANCE.**

four weeks to find and train this new employee. A good employee is a scare commodity, and if found should be cultivated like a prized orchid. Yet, too few small businesses actively develop and refine employee selection and retention programs. In a sense, small businesses need to have an even more efficient employee selection, training, and retention program than their larger competition because they work with a smaller employee base. In addition to the job hats of businessowner, salesperson, and bookkeeper, a businessowner must wear the full-time hat of personnel manager.

EXHIBIT 27

Employment Summary Report

EMPLOYMENT SUMMARY REPORT

Employee Name: ______________________

Social Security No.: ______________________

Start Date: ______________________

Starting Pay Rate: ______________________

Starting Job Title: ______________________

Last Day Worked: ______________________

Ending Pay Rate: ______________________

Ending Job Title: ______________________

Reason for Termination: ______________________

Other Comments: ______________________

Signature ______________ Date ______________

Additional Reading

Bank of America. *Personnel Guidelines.* Small Business Reporter Series. San Francisco, CA. (Dept. 3120, P.O. Box 37000, San Francisco, CA 94137.)

Dessler, Gary. 1980. *Human Behavior: Improving Performance at Work.* Reston, VA: Reston Publishing Co.

Robert Half International, Inc. 1986. *How to Check References When References Are Hard to Check.* New York.

EXHIBIT 28

Employment Eligibility Verification

EMPLOYMENT ELIGIBILITY VERIFICATION

1 EMPLOYEE INFORMATION AND VERIFICATION: (To be completed and signed by employee.)

Name: (Print or Type) Last	First	Middle	Maiden
Ramos	Rosario	S.	

Address: Street Name and Number	City	State	ZIP Code
1060 Malana St.	Honolulu	HI	96818

Date of Birth (Month Day Year)	Social Security Number
5/20/60	571-44-1130

I attest, under penalty of perjury, that I am (check a box):

- ☐ A citizen or national of the United States.
- ☐ An alien lawfully admitted for permanent residence (Alien Number A ____________).
- ☐ An alien authorized by the Immigration and Naturalization Service to work in the United States (Alien Number A ____________, or Admission Number ____________, expiration of employment authorization, if any ____________).

I attest, under penalty of perjury, the documents that I have presented as evidence of identity and employment eligibility are genuine and relate to me. I am aware that federal law provides for imprisonment and/or fine for any false statements or use of false documents in connection with this certificate.

Signature	Date (Month/Day/Year)
Rosario S. Ramos	July 16, 199_

PREPARER/TRANSLATOR CERTIFICATION (If prepared by other than the individual) I attest, under penalty of perjury, that the above was prepared by me at the request of the named individual and is based on all information of which I have any knowledge.

Signature	Name (Print or Type)		
Address (Street Name and Number)	City	State	Zip Code

2 EMPLOYER REVIEW AND VERIFICATION: (To be completed and signed by employer.)

Examine one document from those in List A and check the correct box, ***or*** examine one document from List B ***and*** one from List C and check the correct boxes. Provide the ***Document Identification Number*** and ***Expiration Date,*** for the document checked in that column.

List A Identity and Employment Eligibility	List B Identity	**and**	List C Employment Eligibility
☐ United States Passport ☐ Certificate of United States Citizenship ☐ Certificate of Naturalization ☐ Unexpired foreign passport with attached Employment Authorization ☐ Alien Registration Card with photograph	☒ A State issued driver's license or I.D. card with a photograph, or information, including name, sex, date of birth, height, weight, and color of eyes. (Specify State) ____________ ☐ U.S. Military Card ☐ Other (Specify document and issuing authority) ____________		☒ Original Social Security Number Card (other than a card stating it is not valid for employment) ☐ A birth certificate issued by State, county, or municipal authority bearing a seal or other certification ☐ Unexpired INS Employment Authorization Specify form # ____________
Document Identification # ____________	***Document Identification*** # 576-42-7138		***Document Identification*** # 576-42-7138
Expiration Date (if any) ____________	***Expiration Date (if any)*** 10-2-9_		***Expiration Date (if any)*** ____________

CERTIFICATION: I attest, under penalty of perjury, that I have examined the documents presented by the above individual, that they appear to be genuine, relate to the individual named, and that the individual, to the best of my knowledge, is authorized to work in the United States.

Signature	Name (Print or Type)	Title
Josie Akana	JOSIE AKANA	OWNER
Employer Name	**Address**	**Date**
WAIKIKI TAX SERVICE		7/16/9_

Form I-9 (03/20/87)
OMB No. 1115-0136

U.S. Department of Justice
Immigration and Naturalization Service

14

Recordkeeping: Not Just Bookkeeping

Dressed in an aloha shirt and carrying a briefcase and a calculator, the visitor did not look ominous. Why had this proposed visit caused the business-owners three months of anguish and sleepless nights? A State of Hawaii tax auditor and this dreaded moment had been announced in a form letter requesting documentation of sales receipts, canceled checks, paid bill receipts, past tax returns, and payroll records for the past three years. During the next two weeks, the auditor occupied an unused desk in the small office and politely asked the company owners to explain sales totals and to document certain expenditures. In many cases, the auditor's requests were greeted by sheepish grins and shrugged shoulders.

Although tax audits are not that common, a good record-keeping system is maintained as if one were expected next week. A good record-keeping system accomplishes two things:

1. Documents accurately the transactions of a business, and
2. Provides a means to check on its operations.

The more common business record-keeping systems are:

1. The purchase order system
2. The accounts payable system
3. The cash control system
4. The accounts receivables/sales system
5. Inventory control
6. Personnel and payroll

Ice-cream shop owner: The record-keeping system is just as important as your product and your service. All three areas should be treated the same.

Business services owner: I have two full-time jobs in my business: my regular work and my paperwork. I do my regular customer work in the day and my paperwork at night after the business is closed.

The Merchandise Process

The general merchandise process is illustrated in Exhibits 29 and 30 for a retail and a service business. The first step in a retail business is to order the merchandise you plan to sell. Once that decision is made, the first paperwork needed is a purchase order. The purchase order provides a written record of what was ordered, the quantities, and prices.

The Purchase Order

To illustrate the purchase order let us have Windward TV purchase some television sets.

Office supply stores sell blank, serial numbered, purchase order forms like that used in Exhibit 31. The purchase order form provides space to record from whom you will be purchasing the service or the items, the quantities ordered, the unit prices, freight cost, shipping method, dates of shipment, and payment terms. Once the purchase order is completed and approved, it authorizes the purchase under the conditions listed on the purchase order. Exhibit 31 shows the Windward TV purchase order. Can you tell what the payment terms are on purchase order 7260 (on page 156)?

Wholesaler: We have often experienced problems in receiving goods from our suppliers. Either they inadvertently bill us the wrong cost or charge us for freight they should have paid. Certainly a lot of business transactions are handled verbally, but we use our purchase order system to check that the manufacturer comes through in the way we understood.

Inventory

The merchandise that Windward TV ordered on purchase order 7260 is delivered two weeks later. Enclosed in the shipment is a packing list (Exhibit 32). When the shipment is received, one of Windward TV's employees will verify the shipment with the enclosed packing list and sign it noting any discrepancies. The signed packing slip is then given to whoever will handle the recordkeeping.

Inventory is any item or material to be converted to sales. The flowers a lei maker uses are inventory as are the television sets that Windward TV sells. To understand the purpose of the inventory control system let us trace the movement of a television from the shipment just received. In this example:

EXHIBIT 29

THE MERCHANDISING PROCESS FOR A TYPICAL RETAIL STORE

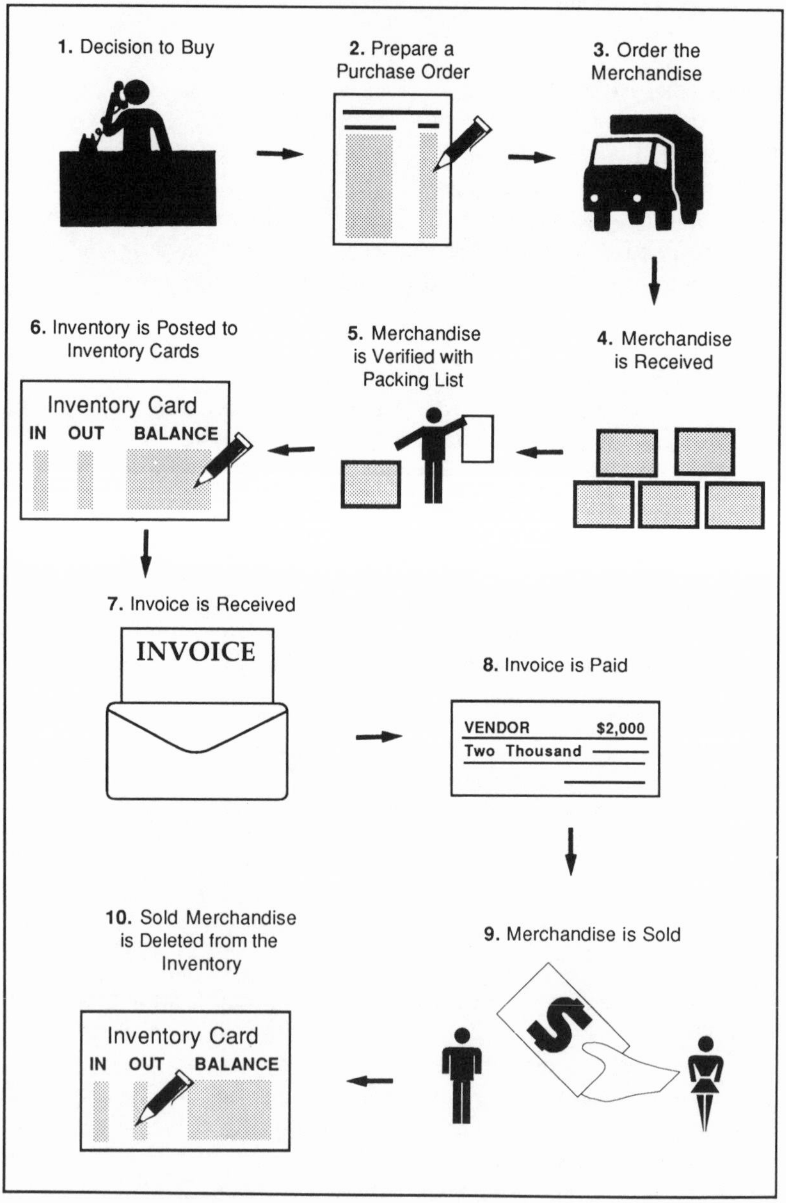

EXHIBIT 30

THE MERCHANDISING PROCESS OF A TYPICAL SERVICE BUSINESS

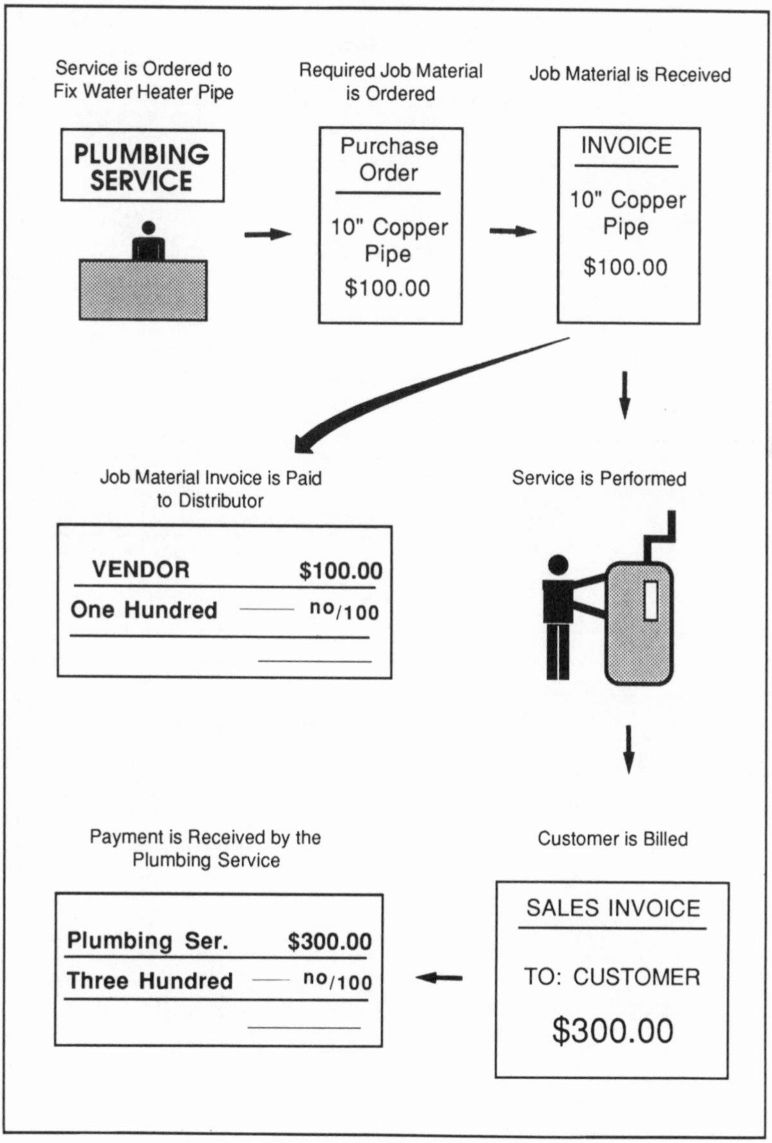

EXHIBIT 31

WINDWARD TV SHOP PURCHASE ORDER

Purchase Order

No.: 7260

WINDWARD TV SHOP
1234 Kaa Road
Kaneohe, HI 96744

Show this number on all correspondence, invoices, shipping order & packages.

Date: 4/15/87

To: Plantronics Electronic Corp.
1256 North Main St.
Van Nuys, CA 91250

Ship to: Windward TV Shop
1234 Kaa Rd.
Kaneohe, Hi 96744

Supplier information	Ship via	Freight charges	Terms
Supplier no. ____	☐ UPS	☐ Prepaid and add	☐ N/30
Date required 5/1/87	☐ Parcel post	☐ Collect	☐ ½% 10/N 30
Mark outside of carton:	☐ Air freight	☐ Prepaid and allowed	☐ 1% 10/N 30
	☒ Common carrier	☒ Prepaid	☐ 2% 10/N 30
Confirming phone order of ____ to ____	☐ Other	☐ Other Surface	☒ Other Net 60

Qty	Item no.	Description	Unit price	Total amount
10	PV1924	19" Color TV	250.00	2,500.00
10	PV13	13" Color TV	150.00	1,500.00
		Sub Total		4,000.00
		Less 10% Discount		(400.00)
			Total	3,600.00

Approved by Joe Gauahl

Title Manager

Special instructions Special 10% discount on opening order per Jerry Hoffman - Sales Manager

1. The television is received at the store;
2. The television is sold to a customer;
3. The customer returns the television as defective; and
4. The store sends the television back to the manufacturer.

Step 1: The television is received at the store.

The Plantronic packing list shows that the product was received at Windward TV on April 30 (Exhibit 32).

EXHIBIT 32
PACKING LIST

THE PLANTRONICS CORPORATION **Packing Slip**
1256 North Main St.
Van Nuys, LA 91250

Date: 4/15/87 Our order no: 99125
Your order no: 7260 Date:
Sold To: Windward TV Ship To: Same
1234 Kalia Rd.
Kailua, Hi 96744

Quantity ordered	Item number	Description	Quantity shipped	Number of cartons	Weight
10	PV1924	19 inch color TV	10	10	
10	PV1326	13 inch color TV	10	10	

Packed by: J.H. Balance to ship: 0

Step 2: The packing list is posted to inventory.

A card-filing system is one of several types of manual inventory control systems (there are computer systems too). This particular card system provides for a running log of products by model number. (There are different types of card systems for different types of businesses. A business forms company would be the best place to receive some assistance.) Each card represents one model from a manufacturer. Windward TV sells 35 different television models. Therefore, it has 35 cards in its inventory file to keep track of all its televisions. Exhibit 33 shows the entry to record the receipt of the ten televisions, model number PV1924.

Step 3: The television is sold to a customer.

A sales slip indicates the sale to Lee Yoshimoto on May 9, 1987 (Exhibit 34).

Step 4: The inventory card is updated.

Using the sales slip, the television is deleted from the inventory control card (Exhibit 35).

Step 5: The customer returns the television as defective.

If you have ever had to return something to a store, you probably had to fill out a return form. This merchandise return form is used to record the transaction of the incoming television (Exhibit 36).

EXHIBIT 33

INVENTORY CARD FOR MANUAL FILING SYSTEM

RECD. FROM	P.O. #	DATE RECEIVED	INVOICE #	QUANTITY	CUSTOMER'S NAME	WK. & DATE SOLD	RET. PRICE	BALANCE	
1 MANUF	7260	4/30/87	99125	10				10	21
2									20
3									19
4									18
5									17
6									16
7									15
8									14
9									13
10									12
11									11
12									10
13									9
14									8
15									7
16									6
17									5
18									4
19									3
20									2
21									1

MFG. Plantronics Corp. STYLE TYPE PV 1924

Step 6: The inventory card file is updated.

The inventory card file now shows the return of the television (Exhibit 37).

Step 7: The defective television is returned to the manufacturer.

Having first received authorization to return the defective television to the manufacturer, the dealer (Windward TV) then prepares an invoice and sends the defective unit back to the manufacturer (Exhibit 38).

Step 8: The inventory card is updated.

The defective television is removed from the inventory using the dealer invoice to the manufacturer (Exhibit 39).

How many times was the inventory card updated? How many different forms were used? Three months from the date Windward TV returned the television to the manufacturer could someone re-create what happened?

By looking at Exhibit 40 can you re-create what happened?

An inventory control system manages inventory, but the management of the payment of the manufacturer's invoice is called accounts payable.

Accounts Payable

"Accounts payable" is accounting terminology for bills that you owe. Windward TV had ordered the televisions on credit terms and now

EXHIBIT 34
SALES RECEIPT

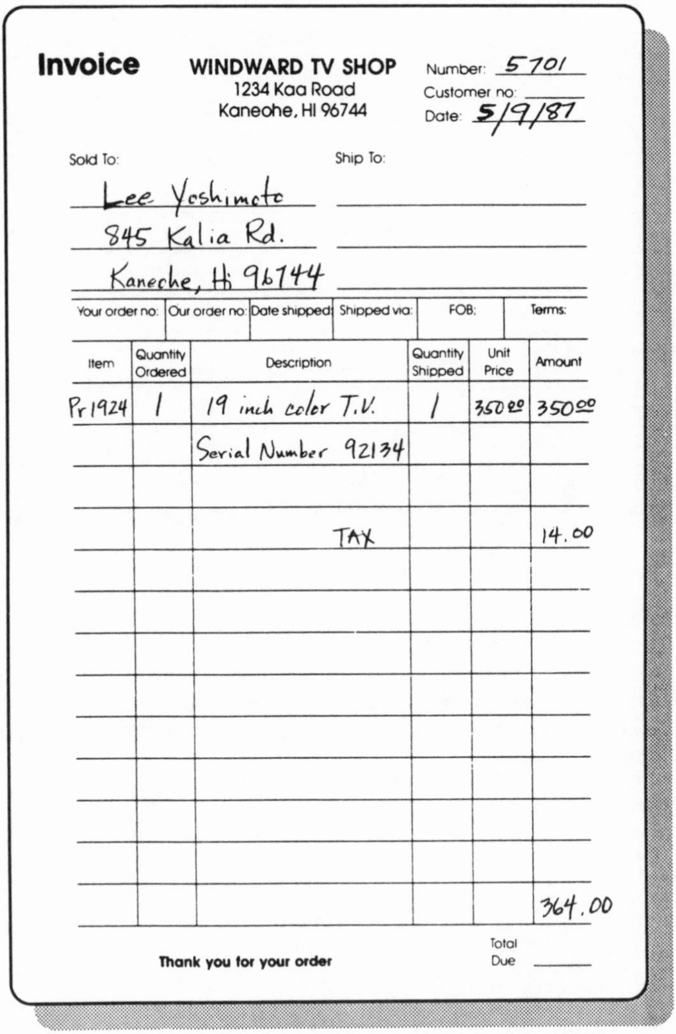

Invoice **WINDWARD TV SHOP**
1234 Kaa Road
Kaneohe, HI 96744

Number: 5701
Customer no:
Date: 5/19/87

Sold To: Ship To:

Lee Yoshimoto
845 Kalia Rd.
Kaneohe, Hi 96744

Your order no:	Our order no:	Date shipped:	Shipped via:	FOB:	Terms:

Item	Quantity Ordered	Description	Quantity Shipped	Unit Price	Amount
Pr1924	1	19 inch color T.V.	1	350.00	350.00
		Serial Number 92134			
		TAX			14.00
					364.00

Thank you for your order
Total Due

receives the invoice for payment in the mail (a manufacturer may send the invoice with the merchandise in the shipment in lieu of a packing slip).

By attaching the purchase order to the manufacturer invoice, Windward TV has a ready reference to see if the billing is correct. Exhibit 41 is the invoice they received with the shipment of televisions they ordered on purchase order 7260. Reviewing purchase order 7260 (see Exhibit 31) for this order, we see two problems. The businessowner will have to call or write Plantronics Corporation to rectify the discrepancies before payment can be made. Can you find the two problems?

EXHIBIT 35

INVENTORY CARD SHOWING SALE OF ONE TELEVISION

RECD. FROM	P.O. #	DATE RECEIVED	INVOICE #	QUANTITY	CUSTOMER'S NAME	WK. & DATE SOLD	RET. PRICE	BALANCE	
1 MANUF	7260	4/30/87	99125	10				10	21
2				1	Lee Yoshimoto	5/9		9	20
3									19
4									18
5									17
6									16
7									15
8									14
9									13
10									12
11									11
12									10
13									9
14									8
15									7
16									6
17									5
18									4
19									3
20									2
21									1

MFG. Plantronics Corp. STYLE TYPE PV 1924

Retailer: Once we verify the purchase order with the invoice and merchandise receipt, we write "OK to Pay" on the invoice and then staple the invoice with the purchase order and packing slip showing that someone in our store signed for the receipt of the goods. We then paper clip all the invoices from the same supplier together and verify each with the supplier's monthly statement.

A good accounts payable system will:

1. Verify that the invoice is valid to pay;
2. Flag any early payment discounts;
3. Show when the invoice should be paid; and
4. Be stored for ease of retrieval after payment.

Exhibit 42 shows the steps in the documentation of a single expense from the initial purchase order to how that expense is finally posted to the accounting ledger. These steps are:

1. Issue the Purchase Order—purchase orders can be issued for single expenses, such as advertising, just as they can be for merchandise.
2. Invoice is received and verified similar to merchandise purchases.
3. Cash Disbursements Journal is a listing by date of all cash disbursements. Just as your personal checking account ledger could be used for this purpose, a small business will often use its business checkbook ledger as its cash disbursements ledger.
4. Expenses Ledger—the purpose of the expense ledger is to summarize

EXHIBIT 36
MERCHANDISE REFUND FORM

WINDWARD TV SHOP
1234 Kaa Road
Kaneohe, HI 96744

Merchandise Refund

Sold To: Lee Yoshimoto
845 Kalea Rd.
Kaneohe, Hi 96744

Shipped To:

Reason for credit: Defective Tuner

Approved by: Bill Ching Date: 5/20/87

Your order no:	Order date:	Our order no:

Item	Quantity	Invoice no/description	Unit Price	Amount
PV1924	1	Serial No. 92134	350.00	350.00
		invoice 5701		
		tax		14.00

Customer Signature Lee Yoshimoto Total refund amount 364.00

similar expenses from the cash disbursements journal. For each expense category, such as advertising, phone expenses, or wages, you will have a separate sheet of paper. As a result, you will have a monthly summary of all the advertising expenses for the month on the advertising expense ledger. These ledgers may be separate pages in a folder or separate ledger cards.

EXHIBIT 37

INVENTORY CARD SHOWING RETURN OF ONE TELEVISION

	RECD. FROM	P.O. #	DATE RECEIVED	INVOICE #	QUANTITY	CUSTOMER'S NAME	WK. & DATE RET. SOLD	PRICE	BALANCE	
1	MANUF	7260	4/30/87	99125	10				10	21
2					1	Lee Yoshimoto	5/9		9	20
3	Yoshimoto		5/20/87	101	1	Defective return			10	19
4										18
5										17
6										16
7										15
8										14
9										13
10										12
11										11
12										10
13										9
14										8
15										7
16										6
17										5
18										4
19										3
20										2
21										1

MFG. Plantronics Corp. STYLE TYPE PV 1924

Daily Cash/Income Ledger

During the course of a business day, a business may have many sales and refund transactions. Some of these transactions will involve cash, checks, or charge cards. The accountability of these funds is the purpose of the daily cash report. Exhibit 43 is the daily cash report for Windward TV for March 5, 19--.

At the end of the day the cash is totaled, in this case $363. Checks and credit cards are added bringing the received income to $750. This figure is compared against the sales slips or the cash register tape. In our example, both figures agree. There is no overage or shortage. The bank deposit is then completed with the difference becoming the end cash for that day or the start cash for the following day.

Waikiki Tax Service, the free-lance situation, does not receive many cash or credit card sales, nor do they need to keep a cash register and start cash. Their primary sales payments are made by check, so their Daily Cash Receipt Report may look like Exhibit 44.

The Income Ledger

Each daily cash report is summarized on a monthly income ledger (Exhibits 45 and 46). These income ledgers are important business records, for they provide a monthly sales summary by day. Can you see

EXHIBIT 38

Defective-Return Invoice to the Manufacturer

WINDWARD TV SHOP
1234 Kaa Road
Kaneohe, HI 96744

Invoice

Number: 5702
Customer no:
Date: 5/30

Sold To:
Plantronics Corp
1256 N. Main St.
Van Nuys, CA. 91250

Ship To:

Your order no:	Our order no:	Date shipped:	Shipped via:	FOB:	Terms:

Item	Quantity Ordered	Description	Quantity Shipped	Unit Price	Amount
	1	PV1924 (SN92134)	1	175.00	175.00
		Defective Return			
		Freight collect			

Thank you for your order

Total Due 175.00

how each day's sales can be re-created by the sales slips? Can you see how a monthly income ledger can be re-created by using the daily cash receipt reports? This income accountability process is illustrated in Exhibit 47.

In addition to monitoring sales income and accounts payables, you will have to account for the money owed to you for trade credit you may extend —accounts receivables.

EXHIBIT 39

Updated Inventory Card

	RECD. FROM	P.O. #	DATE RECEIVED	INVOICE #	QUANTITY	CUSTOMER'S NAME	WK. & DATE RET. SOLD	PRICE	BALANCE	
1	MANUF	7260	4/30/87	99125	10				10	21
2					1	Lee Yoshimoto	5/9		9	20
3	Yoshimoto		5/20/87	101	1	Defective Return			10	19
4				5702	1	Return defective to Manuf.	5/30		9	18
5										17
6										16
7										15
8										14
9										13
10										12
11										11
12										10
13										9
14										8
15										7
16										6
17										5
18										4
19										3
20										2
21										1

MFG. Plantronics Corp. STYLE TYPE PV 1924

EXHIBIT 40

Inventory Card: Test Your Knowledge

	RECD. FROM	P.O. #	DATE RECEIVED	INVOICE #	QUANTITY	CUSTOMER'S NAME	WK. & DATE RET. SOLD	PRICE	BALANCE	
1	MANUF	2599	1/2/87		10				10	21
2				5311	2	Mark Buyers	1/20		8	20
3				00112	8	XYZ Distribution-Returned	2/1		0	19
4										18
5										17
6										16
7										15
8										14
9										13
10										12
11										11
12										10
13										9
14										8
15										7
16										6
17										5
18										4
19										3
20										2
21										1

MFG. XYZ Distributing STYLE TYPE Model 250

EXHIBIT 41

MANUFACTURER'S INVOICE

The Plantronics Corporation
1256 North Main St.
Van Nuys, CA 91250

To: Windward TV Shoppe
1234 Kaa St.
Kaneohe, HI 97609

Invoice Number 99125
Shipper: Northern Air
Invoice Date: 4/15/87
Customer P.O. 7260

Freight: prepaid
Terms: Net30

Model	Quantity	Price	Total
PV1924	10	$250.00	$2,500.00
PV1326	10	150.00	1,500.00
TOTAL			$4,000.00

Sales/Accounts Receivables

Windward TV does not have any accounts receivables because it's customers pay for the merchandise at the time of purchase. Waikiki Tax Service, the free-lance business, however, allows its clients credit terms. This granting of credit will create bills that are owed to Waikiki Tax Service. These are called accounts receivables.

One way to keep track of accounts receivables is to set up an accounts receivable ledger system similar to the inventory card system. Exhibit 48 shows the Western Services Group file. This card file shows Western Services Group billings and payments. In the exhibit we can see that Western Services Group was billed $350 on March 15 and $1,000 on April 2. They paid $500 on April 30 and have a current balance of $850.

Personnel Records

Good personnel files can minimize personnel problems by documenting your personnel management. Each employee should have a personnel file. This file should contain:

1. A statement signed by the employee that he has read and understood the employee manual, if the business has an employee manual (from chapter 13).

EXHIBIT 42

The Accounts Payable Process

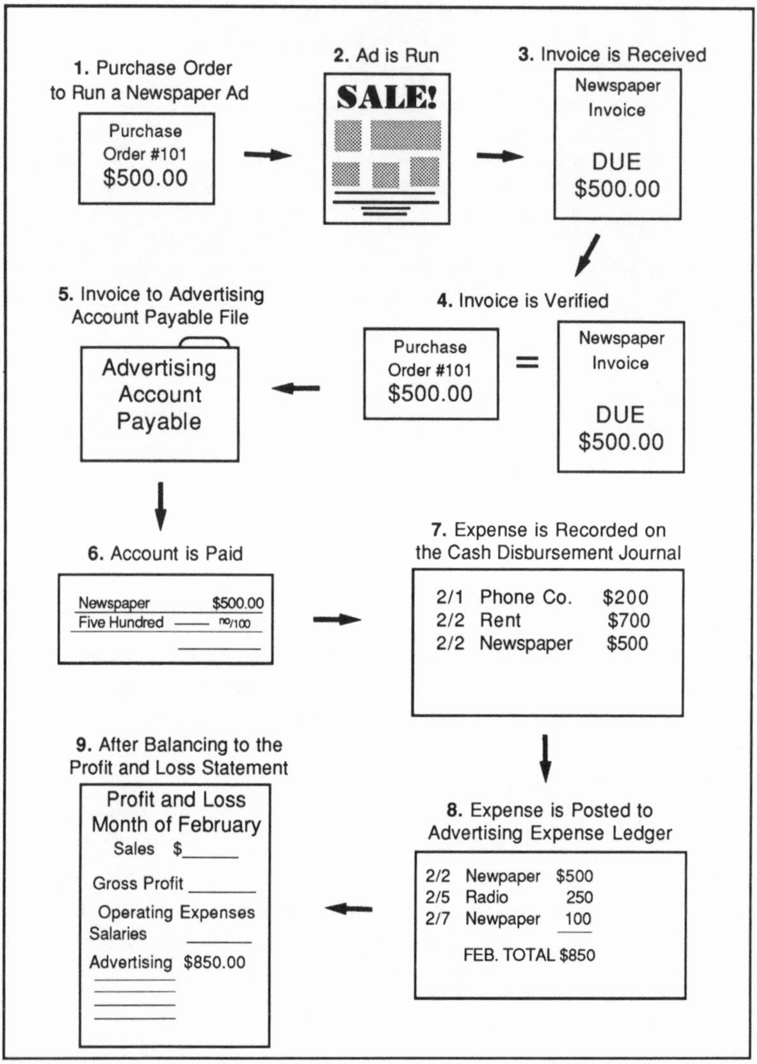
1. Purchase Order to Run a Newspaper Ad
Purchase Order #101 $500.00
2. Ad is Run
SALE!
3. Invoice is Received
Newspaper Invoice DUE $500.00
4. Invoice is Verified
Purchase Order #101 $500.00
=
Newspaper Invoice DUE $500.00
5. Invoice to Advertising Account Payable File
Advertising Account Payable
6. Account is Paid
Newspaper $500.00
Five Hundred no/100
7. Expense is Recorded on the Cash Disbursement Journal
2/1 Phone Co. $200
2/2 Rent $700
2/2 Newspaper $500
8. Expense is Posted to Advertising Expense Ledger
2/2 Newpaper $500
2/5 Radio 250
2/7 Newpaper 100
FEB. TOTAL $850
9. After Balancing to the Profit and Loss Statement
Profit and Loss
Month of February
Sales $
Gross Profit
Operating Expenses
Salaries
Advertising $850.00

EXHIBIT 43

DAILY CASH REPORT

Date 3/5/

Start Cash

$ 20	100	$ 10	50	$ 5	25	$ 1	30
$ .25	5.00	$ .10	2.00	$ .05	.50	$ .01	.50

Total Start Cash $ 213.00

End Cash

$ 20	240	$ 10	60	$ 5	25	$ 1	30
$ .25	5.00	$ .10	2.00	$ .05	.50	$ .01	.50

Total End Cash $ 363.00

Checks

Name	Amount
1. Bill Souza	$250.00

Total Checks $ 250.00

Credit Card Purchases

Name	Type of Card	Amount
1. Karen Fukunaga	MC	$350.00

Total Charges $ 350.00

Refunds

Name	Amount
1.	

Total Refunds $ 0

Balancing

Total sales (from sales invoices or cash register)			$ 750.00
Total ending cash		$ 363.00	
Total checks		$ 250.00	
Total charges		$ 350.00	
Refunds		$ 0.00	
Subtotal	$ 963.00		
Less start cash	$ 213.00		
Less refunds	$ 0.00		
Net cash received	$ 750.00		
Less net cash received			$ 750.00
Overage/shortage			$ 0.00
Bank deposit			
Cash		$ 200.00	
Checks		$ 250.00	
Charge		$ 350.00	
Total deposit			$ 800.00
End cash for register			
Total cash		$ 363.00	
Less cash deposit		$ 200.00	
End cash			$ 163.00

Prepared by Bill

EXHIBIT 44

WAIKIKI TAX SERVICE
DAILY CASH RECEIPT REPORT

Date 3/7/--

Checks Received

Name	Amount
1. Western Services Group	$150.00
2. Bill Martin	175.00
3. Windward TV Shoppe	250.25
TOTAL	$575.25

Bank deposit $575.25

Prepared by Cindy

2. His employment application (from chapter 13).
3. His employment test (from chapter 13).
4. His prior employment verification (from chapter 13).
5. Company status/payroll change report.
6. Copies of the federal and state employee's withholding allowance forms.
7. Copies of a medical application or exemption.
8. A copy of the employee's Form I-9 "Employment Eligibility Verification" (chapter 13).
9. Any disciplinary memos or letters of commendation.
10. Payroll time cards if not filed separately.

The Company Status/Payroll Change Report

The company status/payroll change report simply states a change in the employee's status such as a promotion or a pay change. There are preprinted forms available in office supply stores (Exhibit 49).

The Federal and State Employee's Withholding Allowance

The federal Employee's Withholding Allowance Certificate (Form W-4) and the state Employee's Withholding Exemption and Status Certificate (HW-4) are completed by the employee for the employer. These forms tell the employer how much to withhold in federal and state withholding taxes from the employee's paycheck (see Exhibits 50 and 51).

EXHIBIT 45

Monthly Income Ledger, Windward TV Shop

Monthly Receipt Record

Month Of: MARCH, 1987

Daily Receipts

Day	Total Sales
1	982.95
2	267.38
3	646.29
4	445.25
5	780.00
6	650.00
7	988.00
8	
9	
10	
11	
12	
13	
14	
15	
16	
17	
18	
19	
20	
21	
22	
23	
24	
25	
26	
27	
28	
29	
30	
31	
Total Month	
Total Year to Date	

Comments:

Prepared by:

Date:

Approved by:

Date:

EXHIBIT 46

Monthly Income Ledger, Waikiki Tax Service

Monthly Receipt Record

Month Of: MARCH, 1987

Daily Receipts

Day	Total Sales
1	858.00
2	676.00
3	329.76
4	430.56
5	650.00
6	322.40
7	546.26
8	
9	
10	
11	
12	
13	
14	
15	
16	
17	
18	
19	
20	
21	
22	
23	
24	
25	
26	
27	
28	
29	
30	
31	
Total Month	
Total Year to Date	

Comments:

Prepared by:

Date:

Approved by:

Date:

EXHIBIT 47

The Sales Accountability Process

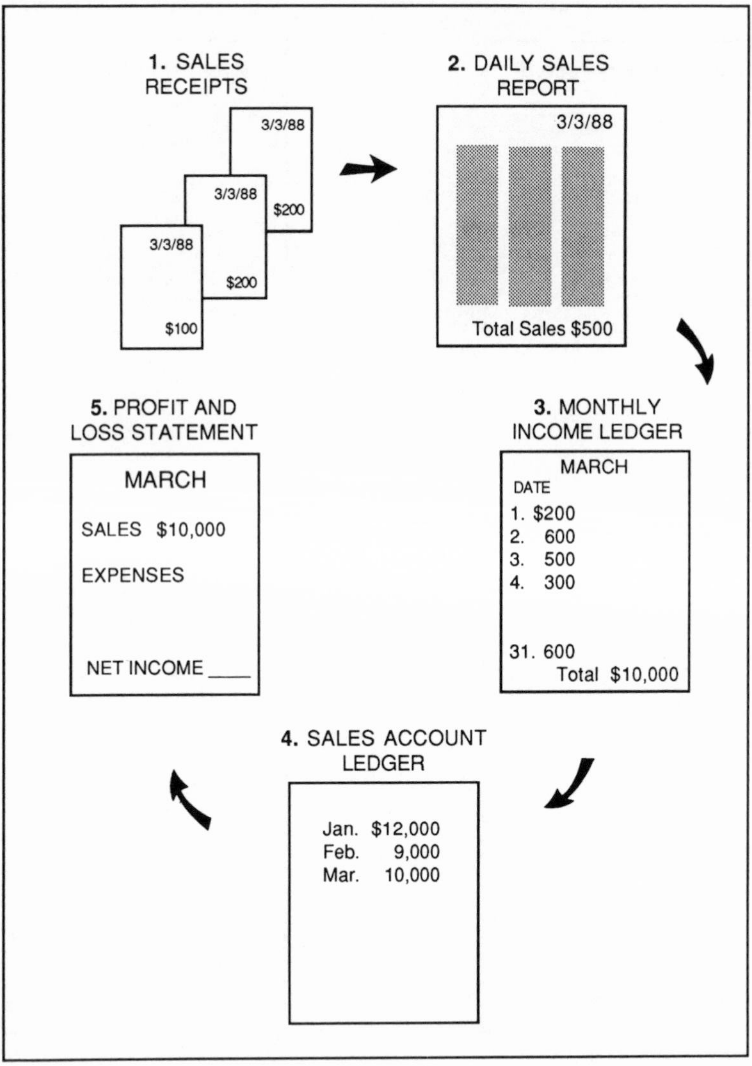

EXHIBIT 48

Accounts Receivable Ledger

NAME: Western Services Group

ADDRESS: 2828 Paa St.
Honolulu, HI 96819

DATE	INVOICE/ CHECK #	DESCRIPTION	CHARGES	PAYMENTS	BALANCE
3/15/87	6601	Prepared Payroll Taxes	350.00		350.00
4/2/87	6723	Prepared Tax Returns	1,000.00		1,350.00
4/30/87	1520	Payment		500.00	850.00

EXHIBIT 49

Status/Payroll Change Report

Employee Status Change

Date ____________________

Employee ____________________

Social Security No. ____________________

Status Change

CHANGE	FROM	TO	EFFECTIVE
Job Position			
Rate			
Hours			

Reason For Change ____________________

____

____

____

Authorized by ____________________ Date ____________

Medical Application or Exemption

Under Hawaii law the employer is required to provide a state-approved medical health program for any full-time employees. A copy of this application might be kept in the employee's file. If the employee claims exemption from this coverage, the employer must ask the employee to complete the state exemption HC-5 (Exhibit 52) and retain it on file. This form needs to be completed each year.

State of Hawaii Employment Status Report

Every time an employer hires or terminates an employee the employer is required to complete and submit to the State an "Employment Status Report" (see Exhibit 27, chapter 13).

EXHIBIT 50

FEDERAL EMPLOYEE'S WITHHOLDING ALLOWANCE CERTIFICATE (W-4)

Form **W-4** Department of the Treasury Internal Revenue Service

Employee's Withholding Allowance Certificate

▶ **For Privacy Act and Paperwork Reduction Act Notice, see reverse.**

OMB No. 1545-0010 **1991**

1 Type or print your first name and middle initial: Shirley A. | Last name: Jurich | 2 Your social security number: 576-06-2835

Home address (number and street or rural route): 98-118 Pua Lane

3 Marital status: ☐ Single ☒ Married ☐ Married, but withhold at higher Single rate.
Note: *If married, but legally separated, or spouse is a nonresident alien, check the Single box.*

City or town, state, and ZIP code: Honolulu, Hawaii 96817

4 Total number of allowances you are claiming (from line G above or from the Worksheets on back if they apply) . . . 4 | 2

5 Additional amount, if any, you want deducted from each pay . . . 5 | $

6 I claim exemption from withholding and I certify that I meet **ALL** of the following conditions for exemption:
- Last year I had a right to a refund of **ALL** Federal income tax withheld because I had **NO** tax liability; **AND**
- This year I expect a refund of **ALL** Federal income tax withheld because I expect to have **NO** tax liability; **AND**
- This year if my income exceeds $550 and includes nonwage income, another person cannot claim me as a dependent.

If you meet all of the above conditions, enter the year effective and "EXEMPT" here . . . ▶ 6 | 19

7 Are you a full-time student? (**Note:** *Full-time students are not automatically exempt.*) . . . 7 ☐ Yes ☒ No

Under penalties of perjury, I certify that I am entitled to the number of withholding allowances claimed on this certificate or entitled to claim exempt status.

Employee's signature ▶ Shirley A. Jurich **Date** ▶ 8-14, 19 91

8 Employer's name and address (**Employer:** Complete 8 and 10 **only if sending to IRS**) | 9 Office code (optional) | 10 Employer identification number

EXHIBIT 51

HAWAII EMPLOYEE'S WITHHOLDING EXEMPTION AND STATUS CERTIFICATE (HW-4)

FORM HW-4
(REV. 1989)

STATE OF HAWAII — DEPARTMENT OF TAXATION

EMPLOYEE'S WITHHOLDING EXEMPTION AND STATUS CERTIFICATE

Section A (to be completed by the employee)

1 Type or print your full name: Shirley Ann Jurich | 2 Your social security number: 576-06-2835

Home address (number and street or rural route): 98-118 Pua Lane

3 Marital Status: ☐ Single ☒ Married ☐ Married, but withhold at higher Single rate ☐ Certified Disabled Person (not subject to withholding)

City or town, state and ZIP code: Honolulu, Hawaii 96817

4 Total number of allowances you are claiming (from line H of the worksheet on page 2.) . . . 4 |

5 Additional amount, if any, you want deducted each pay period . . . 5 | $

I CERTIFY that I have correctly indicated my marital status and that the number of withholding exemptions claimed on this certificate does not exceed the number to which I am entitled.

(Date) 8-14 19 91 (Signed) Shirley A. Jurich

Section B (to be completed by the employer)

1 Employer's name | 2 Employer identification number

Employer's address

City or town, state and zip code

EMPLOYER: Keep this certificate with your records. If the employee is believed to have claimed an excess of exemptions according to the employee's situation or misstated employee's marital status, the Tax Assessor shall be advised.

Employment Verification Report

Every employer is required to hire only US citizens and aliens lawfully eligible to work in the United States. The I-9 form must be completed for every new hire (see Exhibit 28, chapter 13).

EXHIBIT 52

Hawaii Form HC-5

State of Hawaii
Department of Labor and Industrial Relations
DISABILITY COMPENSATION DIVISION
P. O. Box 3769, Honolulu, Hawaii 96813-3769

Form HC-5
(Rev. 1/83)

FOR CALENDAR YEAR 1983

EMPLOYEE NOTIFICATION TO EMPLOYER

Instructions to Employee: This form, to be completed in triplicate, is to be used for the following purposes as provided by the Hawaii Prepaid Health Care Law and Regulations: (A) If you work for two or more employers, you must notify each employer whether he is the principal employer (the employer responsible for providing health care coverage) by checking item 1, or the secondary employer by checking item 2. (B) If you are claiming exemption from health care coverage, indicate the reason in the appropriate block under item 3. (C) If you are changing your principal and/or secondary employer designation, or if you are terminating your exempt status, complete item 5.

NOTE: This form need not be filed if (1) you work for only one employer and your employer provides health care coverage, or (2) you work less than 20 hours per week for your employer.

To determine who would be the principal employer, Section 393-6, as amended, explains that (1) the principal employer shall be the employer who pays you the most wages; or (2) if one of the employers, who does not pay you the most wages, employs you for at least 35 hours a week, you shall determine which of the employers shall be your principal employer.

Employer Name	DOL Account Number
WAIKIKI TAX SERVICE	0000192620
Address	**Phone Number**
2828 PAA ST.	836-1400

In accordance with the provisions of the Hawaii Prepaid Health Care Law (Chapter 393, Hawaii Revised Statutes), this is to notify you that: (Check one block only):

☐ 1. Of the two or more concurrent employers that the undersigned works for (at least 20 or more hours a week), you have been selected as **principal** employer and are therefore required to provide health care coverage for the undersigned (Section 393-6).

☐ 2. Of the two or more concurrent employers that the undersigned works for (at least 20 or more hours a week), you have been selected as **secondary** employer and are therefore relieved of the responsibility to provide health care coverage for the undersigned until you are notified otherwise (Section 393-16).

3. I am exempt from health care coverage because I am (Section 393-17):

☐ a. covered by a Federally established health insurance or prepaid health care plan, such as Medicare, Medicaid or medical care benefits provided for military dependents and military retirees and their dependents.

☒ b. covered as a dependent under a qualified health care plan.

☐ c. a recipient of public assistance or covered by a State-legislated health care plan governing medical assistance.

☐ d. a follower of a religious group who depends for healing upon prayer or other spiritual means.

☐ e. other: specify ______________________

☐ 4. I waive coverage from my employer's health care plan; in lieu I have obtained a plan from ______________________ (name of health care plan contractor) which meets the Hawaii Prepaid Health Care Law (attach copy of plan and send to the DC Division).

☐ 5. The coverage exemption previously indicated in items 2, 3 or 4 is no longer applicable; you are therefore required to provide health care coverage for the undersigned (Section 393-18) effective ______________ (give date).

Employee Signature	Address	Date	Phone No.
Margaret Floyd	92-1299 KALEO PLACE	7/15/87	642-1111

Instructions to Employer: Enter your firm's Department of Labor (DOL) Account Number in the space provided. Provide coverage as required by 1 and 5 above. Send original copy of notice to the address listed at the top of this form; second copy for employer; third copy for employee.

EXHIBIT 53
Time Card

TIME CARD

WESTERN SERVICES GROUP

NAME________________________

PAY PERIOD________________

DATE	IN	OUT	HOURS	REMARKS
1 /16				
2 /17				
3 /18				
4 /19				
5 /20				
6 /21				
7 /22				
8 /23				
9 /24				
10/25				
11/26				
12/27				
13/28				
14/29				
15/30				
/31				

TOTAL HOURS WORKED________________

RATE OF PAY________________

OVERTIME________________

EMPLOYEE SIGNATURE__________________________

SUPERVISOR__________________________________

EXHIBIT 54

Payroll Records

Employee MILES KAMAKA

Social Security No. 565-53-9992

Marital Status S

Exemptions Claimed 1

Pay Period	Hours Reg.	OT	Rate	Gross Salary	FICA	Fed. With. Tax	State With. Tax	Other Deductions	Net Pay
2/1-2/15	67¼		4.00	269.00	19.23	13.00	7.00		229.67
2/16-2/28	63		4.00	252.00	18.02	11.00	6.45		216.53

Time Cards and Payroll Records

Each employee should maintain a time card (Exhibit 53) of days and times worked. These records should be signed by the employee. Payroll records (Exhibit 54) show actual dollars paid to and deductions made from each employee's pay.

If your systems are able to document accurately your business transactions and provide a way to check on its operation, you have a good system. Although we have seen 6 systems in this section, an average small business may have between 10 and 50 such systems. Your accountant, banker, and other business associates can be of great help in assessing your current systems. You can be sure that, if you do not work to develop and maintain an excellent system, a tax audit, a disagreement over a supplier invoice, a shortage in cash, or a misunderstanding with an employee will eventually make you more efficient.

Additional Reading

Doyle, Dennis M. 1977. *Efficient Accounting and Recordkeeping.* New York: John Wiley and Sons.

Dyer, Mary Lee. 1976. *Practical Bookkeeping for the Small Business.* Chicago: Contemporary Books, Inc.

Hayes, Rick Stephen, and C. Richard Baker. *Simplified Accounting for Non-Accountants.* New York: John Wiley and Sons, Inc.

PART IV

Financial Basics

15

Financial Statements: Let's See How Much You Have Made

The record-keeping systems discussed in chapter 14 document individual transactions. Financial statements summarize these transactions monthly, quarterly, or yearly. In chapter 3 we discovered that the operating expenses statement is nothing more than a numeric picture of the expenses of a business. We also discovered that without this picture we have no way to visualize fully all the different costs. This chapter will expand on that numeric picture by providing an overview of how the selling price and operating costs affect the profitability and cash flow of the business.

How to Set Your Selling Price

Artist: I had no idea what I should sell these items for. I just figured what it cost me to make them and doubled the price.

In many cases, someone starting a new business will determine their prices using a formula such as "doubling the cost." Although this method may be a satisfactory one for others to set their selling price, it may not be suitable for all businesses. A far more professional approach to setting your selling price is to look at what it is going to take to break even or to make the profit you want.

To illustrate, assume a business has the following costs for a month:

Operating costs	$6,000
Plus cost of goods sold	7,000
Total cost	$13,000

If sales were $11,000, then subtracting costs of $13,000 results in an operating loss of $2,000. In business terms:

Sales	$11,000
Less cost of goods	− 7,000
Gross profit	$4,000
Less operating expenses	− 6,000
Operating loss	− $2,000

We can see by this illustration that gross profit is sales less the cost of sales, and that the gross profit is the amount used to pay for the operating expenses and provide a profit.

Having suffered a $2,000 loss for the month, this business has three options to avoid future losses:

1. Cut some operating costs, and/or
2. Increase sales, and/or
3. Increase selling price.

If the business has done as much as possible with the first two categories, then increasing the selling price is the only alternative to avoiding future losses (in actuality, most businesses use a combination of all three options). In business terminology, the setting of the selling price is called the "percentage markup" or "gross margin."

Determining Your Gross Margin

The gross margin is the percentage difference between the selling price and the cost of the goods or service. This is best understood by using an example. Let us assume:

1. You are selling a sun visor for $1.00 each.
2. Your total cost of goods sold is $7,000 for the month.
3. Your operating cost for the month was $6,000.
4. Current month's sales were $11,000.

Given this information, the gross profit for the month was $4,000 and the gross margin was 36 percent.

Gross profit = Sales − Cost of goods sold

Sales	$11,000
Less cost of goods sold	− 7,000
Gross profit	$4,000

$$\text{Gross margin} = \frac{\text{Gross profit}}{\text{Total sales}} = \frac{\$4{,}000}{\$11{,}000} = 36 \text{ percent}$$

Simply stated, a gross margin of 36 percent says that for every $1.00 of sales, $.36 went to your gross profit and the balance ($.64 in this case) went to the cost of the goods sold. We now know that these visors cost $.64 each and that the business lost $2,040 this month:

Sales	$11,000
Units sold 11,000	
Less cost of sales (11,000 × $.64)	− 7,040
Gross profit	$3,960
Less operating expenses	− 6,000
Net loss	− $2,040

This method of determining your gross margin assumes an after-the-fact calculation where sales, cost of sales, and operating expenses are known. But what if you are attempting to determine your selling price for a new product you plan to sell and only know the gross margin you would like to make on each item?

Determining Your Selling Price for a Certain Gross Margin

In this case, we know that the visors cost us $.64 each and we would like a 36 percent gross margin markup. What is our selling price per unit?

Answer: Selling price = unit cost ÷ (1 − desired gross profit percentage),

or

$$\$.64 \div (1 - .36) = \$.64 \div .64 = \$1.00$$

The same procedure would be used to find the selling price of the visor at 40 percent gross margin.

Answer: $\$.64 \div (1 - .40) = \$.64 \div .60 = \$1.07$

At a 40 percent gross margin we would sell the visors for $1.07. Our dilemma is, we know that at 36 percent gross margin and a selling price of $1.00 per visor we are losing money, but will raising the gross margin to 40 percent help us break even?

The Break-even Point

If we plan to sell 11,000 visors next month with a cost of $.64 each, at what selling price would we break even (not incur a loss) with operating costs of $6,000? To answer this question we would total all the costs and divide by the number of units to be sold and arrive at a selling price of $1.19 per visor.

1. cost per visor × number of units to sell = cost of goods sold.
   $.64 × 11,000 = $7,040.
2. cost of goods sold + operating costs = total costs.
   $7,040 + $6,000 = $13,040.
3. total costs ÷ number of units to sell = break-even selling price
   $13,040 ÷ 11,000 = $1.19

What Sales Are Necessary at a Given Gross Margin?

For the sake of argument, let us say that the business cannot raise the selling price to $1.19. Because most businesses have to adjust their pricing with consideration to their competition and what the customer will pay, the art of pricing is far from an exact science. If it is felt that the best selling price of the visor is $1.00, then what sales must be generated at that selling price to break even?

Answer: Operating Expenses ÷ Gross Margin = Break-even Sales

or

$6,000 ÷ .36 = $16,667

Verification:

Sales	$16,667
Less cost of sales (64%)	− 10,667
Gross profit	$6,000
Less operating expenses	− 6,000
Net operating profit	0

If each unit this business was selling had a price of $1.00, then the business would have to sell 16,667 units per month to break even at $6,000 of operating expenses.

The Break-even Analysis

We can summarize our analysis of gross margins and break-even levels for the visor company.

Assuming (1) operating expenses of $6,000, and (2) unit cost of goods as $.64, two options open to this company are:

Option 1: At a selling price of $1.00 per unit (gross margin of 36 percent) the business needs to make sales of $16,667 to break even.

Option 2: If the business raises the unit selling price to $1.19 (gross margin of 46 percent), it must sell about 11,000 units (sales of $13,090) to break even.

Back to Margins

Each industry has a fairly consistent gross margin markup. For instance, the consumer electronics industry might see the following average markups for its retailers:

Cassette decks	20–35 percent
Stereo speakers	35–55 percent
Accessories	40–65 percent
Televisions	20–30 percent

Although a range of margins may be typical for a specific industry, individual product or service prices may vary with the product line, the demand for the product or service, and the business's marketing philosophy. Some other average industry gross margins for retail stores are:

Appliances	20 percent
Furniture	40–60 percent
Jewelry	100–300 percent

Car stereo retailer: We strive for 55 percent gross margins. We do not carry some lines because of the price competition with other retailers. These lines may be popular, but if too many retailers carry them and start cutting prices we cannot get the margin we need to cover our overhead. I've seen other retailers cut the price so that they only make 10 percent. That's OK on some clearance items, but on regular stock its murder for our type of business.

Here is a summary of the relationship between sales, cost of sales, operating expenses, and margins.

1. The larger the gross margin, the less you have to sell to cover operating costs.
2. Generally, the higher your selling price the fewer items you will sell based on price alone.
3. If the gross profit does not cover the operating expenses, then you will incur a loss.

Retailer: Our philosophy is to keep our prices up, but to offer a full line of choices and to advertise a lot. We may lose a certain percentage to discounters, but we don't feel that they offer the kind of products and services that we do. We may both end up with the same bottom-line profits, but we believe the heavy advertising pays extra dividends.

Determining Your Price for a Service Business

Although a service business, Waikiki Tax Service, the free-lance situation, operates under the same gross margin principles as the retailer, Windward TV. But because this business does not sell merchandise and has no direct cost of goods sold, how can it determine its gross margin or break-even point?

Engineer: I just started my own consulting business, but I don't know what to charge.

There are several ways to do this. Here is one way a professional who bills by the hour (such as an attorney or an accountant) might determine an hourly rate.

Let us assume that our accountant at Waikiki Tax Service would like to determine a daily and hourly rate. Let us further assume:

1. the professional wants a salary of $40,000;
2. 261 working days in a work year;
3. has total annual operating costs of $30,000;
4. projects a profit of 16 percent for the business; and
5. has 200 billable days.

Determine the Estimated Hourly Rate

1. Daily salary expectation:

$$\$40{,}000 \div 200 \text{ billable days} = \$200 \text{ per day.}$$

2. Daily overhead expectation:

$$\$30{,}000 \div 200 = \$150 \text{ per day.}$$

3. Total daily labor rate:

Daily salary rate	$200
Daily overhead rate	150
Total	$350

4. Daily profit:

$$\$350 \times 16 \text{ percent} = \$56 \text{ per day.}$$

5. Total daily rate:

Labor	$200
Overhead	150
Profit	56
Total	$406

6. Hourly rate:

$406 daily rate ÷ 8 hours per day = $51/hour.

To meet all it's income and profitability goals Waikiki Tax Service would need yearly sales of $81,200 ($406 × 200 days). If it eliminated the profit goal and just considered the salary and overhead, the break-even point would be $70,000 ($350 × 200 days).

Another way for a service business to estimate its break-even point is by totaling one year's operating expenses. For the business to break-even, it must have sales that equal these expenses.

Business seems simple enough—just get the required sales at the gross margin you need to cover operating expenses with a little left over for a profit. The problem in business, however, is that you have fixed monthly operating expenses but fluctuating monthly sales. Balancing the sales and expenses will affect whether a business will report a profit or a loss.

The Profit and Loss Statement

We have already reviewed a way to figure a profit or loss in our discussion of the gross margin for the visors.

Sales	$11,000
Less cost of goods	− 7,000
Gross profit	$4,000
Less operating expenses	− 6,000
Operating loss	− $2,000

This is a profit and loss statement. In chapter 3 we prepared an operating expenses statement for Windward TV (Exhibit 8). Look at that statement again. From this operating statement we will prepare a complete profit and loss statement (Exhibit 55). To expand this statement into a profit and loss statement, all we need to add is:

1. an estimate of sales for the month;
2. the estimated cost of sales;

EXHIBIT 55

WINDWARD TV SHOP
PROFIT AND LOSS STATEMENT
JANUARY, 19__

Sales		$15,200
Less cost of sales		(10,500)
GROSS PROFIT		$4,700
Operating expenses		
Rent	$1,125	
Salaries	2,580	
Office equipment	50	
Utilities	100	
Office supplies	50	
Vehicle	200	
Medical insurance	200	
Professional fees	300	
Freight	200	
Alarm	30	
Maintainence	50	
Advertising	300	
Payroll tax	260	
General Excise Tax	800	
Interest	100	
Phone	278	
Depreciation	200	
Miscellaneous	100	
Less total operating expenses		($6,923)
NET OPERATING PROFIT OR LOSS BEFORE INCOME TAXES		($2,223)

3. the resulting gross profit;
4. the depreciation expense;
5. the resulting net profit before income taxes.

Depreciation

Based on this statement Windward TV had a net loss of $2,223 for the month of January. The only new expense added to the original operating expenses is depreciation. Under tax rules, a business cannot charge totally in the month it is purchased the cost of major lease improvements or equipment that may be used over a number of years. As a result, the cost of that equipment must be prorated over its estimated useful life. For instance, if a piece of equipment is estimated to have a five-year life, under one type of depreciation schedule, one fifth of the cost of the equipment is applied to that year. The depreciation expense applies the cost of the asset to the period in which it is being used.

We already know what the businessowner needs to do to avert a similar loss in the next month:

1. increase the sales; and/or
2. reduce costs; and/or
3. increase the margin by increasing the selling price.

Assuming that the businessowner is able to negotiate lower costs from his supplier and now estimates cost of sales at $7,250 instead of $10,500, then his proforma (accounting terminology for projected) profit and loss statement for February would look like Exhibit 56.

Exhibit 57 illustrates how each sales dollar is spent based on the proforma profit and loss statement shown in Exhibit 56. Here we are able to see that of each sales dollar, salaries accounted for $.17 (or 17 percent); cost of sales took $.48; and operating profit before taxes was $.068. If you are interested in comparing your business with others in your industry, your banker and the Hawaii State Library, main branch, have several publications that provide just such industry averages.

One such publication is *Annual Statement Studies,* published by Robert Morris Associates. This annual publication lists national averages for different types of businesses. For instance, the 1986 report for retailers of radios, televisions, and record players shows that an average retailer in this industry with sales under $1 million has operating expenses of 31.7 percent of sales, a gross profit of 36.2 percent, and profits before taxes of 3.7 percent. These national averages are especially useful in assessing your operation and in projecting realistic new business estimates.

When you review these publications it is often a revelation to find that most profitable businesses earn between 3 and 8 percent of sales as operating profit before taxes. If you are a prospective businessowner, are your estimates for operating profits realistic? If you are currently in business, how does your percentage compare with the national averages for your industry and type of business? Your banker or the business section of the main library will be glad to help you.

> **Retailer:** When we look at our profit and loss statement, I am usually surprised at how low it is. Although we use a standard gross margin of 35 percent, it usually comes in lower because of the discounting we have done on slower moving stock.

With a little instruction from your accountant, you should be able to prepare your own profit and loss statement as soon as you desire. The

EXHIBIT 56

Windward TV Shop Proforma Profit and Loss Statement February 19__	
Sales	$15,200
Less cost of sales	($7,250)
Gross Profit	$7,950
Less total operating expenses (see Exhibit 55)	($6,923)
Net operating profit	$1,027

EXHIBIT 57

How Each Sales Dollar is Used

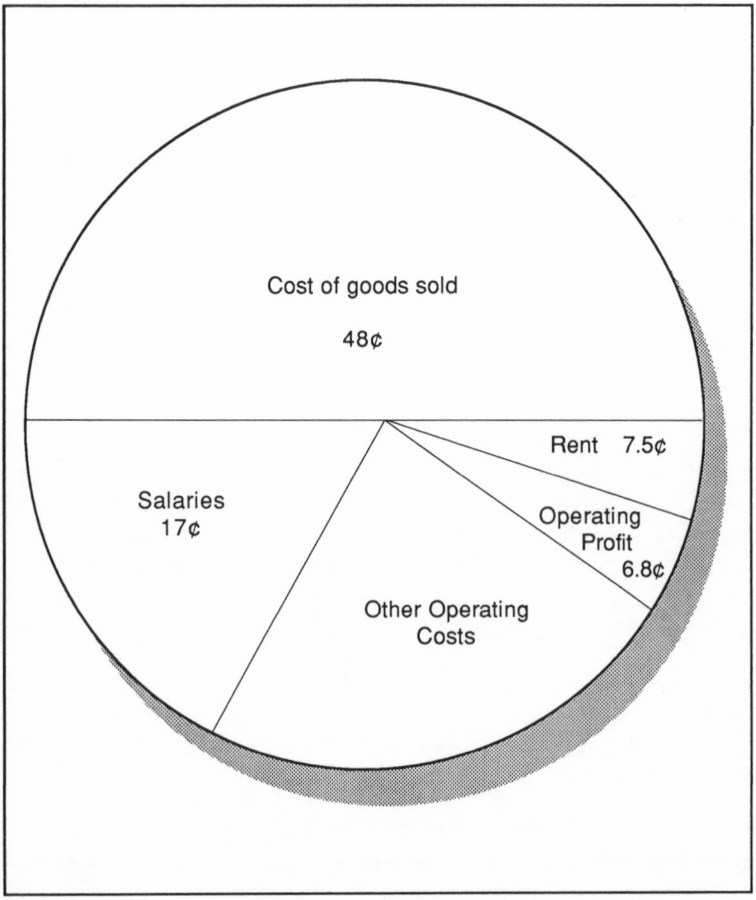

accountant can always review your work—and at a lower cost when it is prepared this way.

Controlling your profit or loss is only one part of the successful financial management of your business. The other is cash flow.

Cash Flow

Cash flow is what most of us are experts at. Cash flow is simply matching incoming cash with expenses. Take your paycheck and pay your bills. What do you pay now and what do you defer? Do you ever have more bills due than you have cash in your checking account? A great myth is that all businesses have enough money all the time to pay all their bills. Medium and small businesses are often cash poor. Consequently, the businessowner will be the decisionmaker on which bills get paid and which get delayed. For instance, here are some of the accounts payables from Windward TV:

	Past Due	Current	Due in 30 days
Monthly rent		$500	$500
Payroll		2,580	2,580
Suppliers			
Plantronics	$1,000	2,000	3,600
XYZ Distribution		1,000	3,000
Hawaii Isles	500	3,000	2,000
Telephone		278	278
Advertising			
KIII Radio	200	800	600
Newspaper		500	500
Accounting Service	200	200	200
Insurance		75	75
Bank loan		200	200
Equipment Lease		100	100
Total	$1,900	$11,233	$13,633

To pay all current bills the businessowner will need $1,900 plus $11,233 for a total of $13,133. What happens when you are a little short of cash in your personal life? If the business is short of cash, then some of these bills will have to be postponed. We will see in a minute why there is a shortage of funds, but to continue in this example let us assume:

1. The business has only $7,000 available to pay bills.
2. Plantronics is its major supplier but has a lax credit policy.
3. XYZ Distribution is a new supplier that Windward TV is hoping to impress.

4. The bank loan and equipment lease payments are important.
5. Salaries and rent must be paid on time.

Based on these assumptions, the businessowner decides to pay as follows:

Monthly rent	$500
Payroll	2,580
Suppliers	
Plantronics	1,000
XYZ Distribution	1,000
Hawaii Isles	500
Telephone	0
Advertising	
KIII Radio	200
Newspaper	500
Accounting service	200
Insurance	75
Bank loan	200
Equipment lease	100
Total	$6,855

If the businessowner pays in this manner, phone calls asking for payment may come from:

1. Hawaii Isle—now past due $3,000. This distributor may deny future orders except on a COD basis.
2. Telephone company—now past due $278.
3. Plantronics—if this distributor has a lax collection policy, orders might still be received, although the business is now past due $2,000.
4. KIII Radio—past due $1,000.

Retailer: All businesses and especially new businesses always seem to have more bills than money. Knowing how to conserve your cash starts by having a system of identifying all your payables and knowing how long you can stretch certain bills without hurting your operation. One of the first things we all learn is how to tell people you owe money that payment will be a little late. I can't tell you how many times I have been on credit hold with my suppliers.

Printshop owner: One of my bleakest memories happened in my first year in business. I needed $2,000 to make payroll and rent expenses, and I didn't know where the money was going to come from. I even contemplated suicide by driving up to the Pali. Fortunately, I didn't jump, but it was painful. That was over ten years ago.

A cash flow diagram for Windward TV is illustrated in Exhibit 58. Incoming money comes from sales, owner's equity, and loans. The outgo-

EXHIBIT 58

Cash Flow Diagram For Windward TV Shop

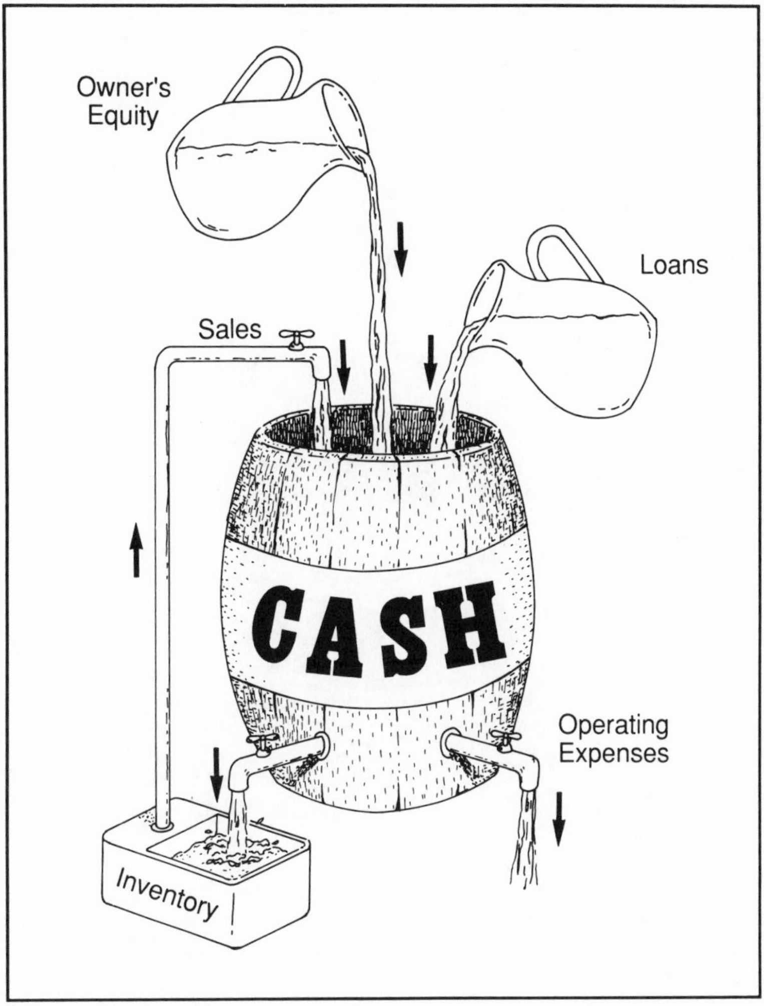

ing flow of money is to pay operating expenses and inventory purchases. Exhibit 59 shows the cash flow for Waikiki Tax Service. The major difference is that Waikiki Tax Service does not have inventory to purchase.

The primary ingredients for a positive cash flow are: (1) steady sales, (2) profitability, (3) controlled growth. When sales fluctuate, cash flow may be uneven. A good sales month may result in excess cash on hand, while a poor sales month may eventually result in a shortage of cash. But even if sales are satisfactory, higher or unexpected expenses can draw down cash reserves. The same thing happens in your personal life when your water heater breaks down unexpectedly.

EXHIBIT 59

Cash Flow Diagram For Waikiki Tax Service

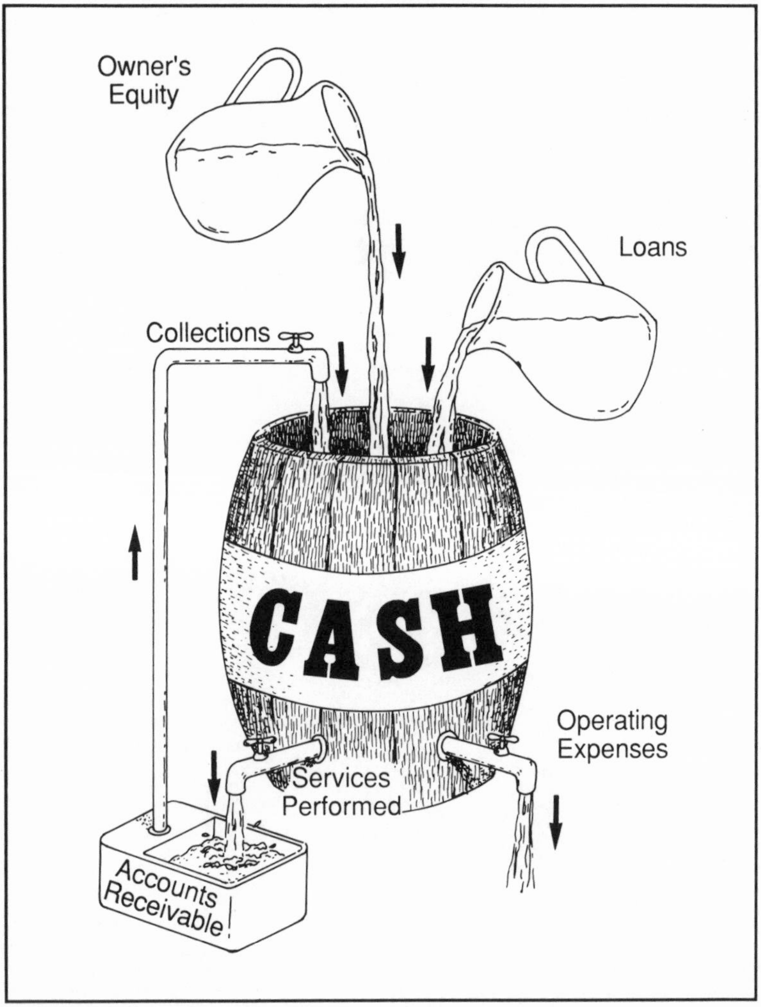

Although it is easy to see how an unprofitable business depletes cash reserves, a common anomaly is a profitable business that has a backorder of sales which fails because of poor cash flow. A fast-growing business is caught in a dilemma: the need to increase operating expenses and other costs to meet the surge in sales. This increase in operating costs increases the vulnerability of the company to a cash crunch should sales slow even temporarily.

The characteristics of a business with a good cash flow are steady sales with comfortable checking account balances and the ability to pay current bills.

EXHIBIT 60

WINDWARD TV SHOP
MONTHLY CASH FLOW BUDGET FORECAST
JANUARY TO MARCH 19__

	Jan	Feb	Mar
Cash Available			
Cash on hand	$2,000	$1,360	($1,780)
Cash Sales	$11,000	$8,000	$8,000
TOTAL	$13,000	$9,360	$6,220
Cash Requirements			
Inventory	$6,000	$5,500	$4,400
Operating expenses	5,640	5,640	4,450
TOTAL	$11,640	$11,140	$8,850
Excess cash after expenses	$1,360	($1,780)	($2,630)
Additional cash required	0	$1,780	$2,630

Where does the money come from to pay the bills? It comes from (1) sales, (2) prior profits (savings from prior profits), (3) owner's contributions and (4) loans. If sales and prior profits are not sufficient to provide cash for the payment of current obligations, then the businessowner has a limited number of options: (1) add owner's money; (2) get a loan; and/or (3) delay the payment of bills. As you can see, it is very much like your personal life. If your salary and savings cannot cover your monthly obligations, you will need other income or a loan.

Because every business faces this cash flow dilemma each month, it is especially important for a new business to establish its cash flow immediately, or to plan for outside funds to cover the shortages until it can develop a consistent cash flow.

Exhibit 60 shows a negative cash flow. (Exhibit A7 in appendix A is an example of a cash flow statement.) Let us assume Windward TV has $2,000 of cash and Net 30 terms from its suppliers. We can sympathize with the plight of Windward TV. It is experiencing a negative cash flow and has depleted cash reserves and cannot meet its current obligations. It has taken some corrective action by cutting some operating expenses—advertising, salaries, and equipment purchases—but other fixed costs, such as rent and loan payments, cannot be reduced. For the three months, Windward TV needs a total of $2,630. Its options are: (1) hope that April sales bring in a cash surplus; (2) put in more owner's equity; and/or (3) get a loan.

If Windward TV was able to obtain a $10,000 loan at $300 per month

EXHIBIT 61

WINDWARD TV SHOP
REVISED MONTHLY CASH FLOW BUDGET FORECAST
JANUARY TO MARCH 19__

	Months		
	Jan	Feb	Mar
Receipts			
Cash sales	$11,000	$8,000	$8,000
Loans	10,000		
Other			
Total receipts	$21,000	$8,000	$8,000
Disbursements			
Rent	$500	$500	$500
Salaries	2,580	2,580	2,200
Insurance	300	300	300
Advertising	200	200	
Taxes	1,060	1,060	800
Loan payment	150	450	450
Equipment purchase	200	200	
Equipment lease	100	100	100
Vehicle	200	200	150
Freight	200	200	100
Utilities	50	50	50
Phone	100	100	100
Maintenance			
Suppliers	6,000	5,500	4,400
Total disbursements	$11,640	$11,440	$9,150
Total cashflow	9,360	(3,440)	(1,150)
Beginning balance	2,000	11,360	7,920
Ending balance	11,360	7,920	6,770

repayment, how long could it remain in business while losing $500 per month? Other things being equal, for quite some time. Exhibit 61 shows the same cash flow statement after Windward TV was able to obtain a $10,000 bank loan in January. With the bank loan, Windward TV is able to cover easily all the current obligations and have cash to spare. This is true even though total operating expenses have increased (repayment of the bank loan) and the operation continues to be unprofitable.

Your accountant and banker can be your guides in reviewing your cash flow projections.

EXHIBIT 62

MR. AND MRS. BILL SPACE
STATEMENT OF NET WORTH
JANUARY 1, 19__

Assets	
Home	$150,000
Cash in bank	10,000
Stocks and bonds	5,00
Automobile	8,000
Household goods	3,000
TOTAL ASSETS	$176,000
Liabilities and Net Worth	
Mortgage on home	$100,000
Charge card bills	2,000
Bank loan	3,000
Automobile loan	5,000
TOTAL LIABILITIES	$110,000
Net worth	$66,000
TOTAL LIABILITIES AND NET WORTH	$176,000

The Balance Sheet

The balance sheet lists all your company's assets and liabilities. Instead of showing sales, margins, or operating expenses, the balance sheet shows all that the company owns and owes. Exhibit 62 shows an example of a statement of personal net worth. The difference between Mr. and Mrs. Space's assets and liabilities equals their net worth. Theoretically, if they sold all their assets and paid all their liabilities they would have $66,000 left before income taxes—their net worth. A business has a similar statement called a balance sheet. Exhibit 63 is the balance sheet for Windward TV.

A balance sheet balances. Total assets equal total liabilities and owner's equity. If Windward TV sold all the assets at the stated value and paid all the liabilities it would have $24,000 of owner's equity left. The balance sheet gives us another numeric picture different from the profit and loss or cash flow statement.

Financial statements are summaries. These summaries of information are used by managers and owners to plan and assess. Although there are many types of financial reports, the three most common are the profit and

EXHIBIT 63

Windward TV Shop Balance Sheet January 1, 19__	
Assets	
Cash	$8,000
Inventory	38,000
Prepaid deposit	500
Equipment	2,500
Total assets	$49,000
Total Liabilities and Owner's Equity	
Current bills	$20,000
Bank loan	5,000
Total liabilities	$25,000
Owner's equity	$24,000
Total liabilities and owner's equity	$49,000

loss statement, the cash flow statement, and the balance sheet. It is only through these financial statements that a businessowner can determine profits; if expenses are too high; if inventory is too great; or if enough cash is available to cover current bills.

Now that we have seen some of the reasons a business will need money, let us look at some of the methods available for raising money.

Additonal Reading

Kamoroff, Bernard. 1985. *Small Time Operator.* Laytonville, CA: Bell Springs Publishing.

Merrill, Lynch, Pierce, Fenner, and Smith, Inc. 1984. *How to Read a Financial Report.*

Small Business Administration. *A Pricing Checklist for Small Retailers.* Management Aid no. 4.013. Fort Worth, TX.

16

How to Raise Money

In chapter 3 we attempted to provide a rough estimate of what it might cost to start a new business by calculating the start-up costs and adding an estimated six months of operating costs. However, as we saw in chapter 15, every business needs not only start-up capital, but also periodic infusions of money to keep going.

A person with a sound business attitude assumes that any sales received in a new venture are the exception and not the rule. Those businesses that hope to make a major portion of their start-up cash from projected first-year sales are not operating with a sound business attitude.

> **Businessman:** I have started a number of businesses and offshoots of businesses over the years and I have always overestimated our sales, no matter how conservative I have been. Building a steady sales record just takes more time than most people want to believe.

Raising Start-up Capital

An old business adage states: "It takes money to make money." We have seen why this adage is true—start-up and operating costs can be extensive. The start-up costs in chapter 3 for Waikiki Tax Service and Windward TV Shop were:

Waikiki Tax Service		Windward TV Shop	
Item	Cost	Item	Cost
Rent	$ 0	Rent	$ 2,250
Salaries	0	Salaries	1,580
Office equipment	780	Equipment	5,926

Continued

Waikiki Tax Service *(cont.)*

Item	Cost
Office supplies	150
Vehicle	0
Renovation	0
Prof. subscript.	200
Legal fees	0
Accounting fees	0
Insurance	500
Med. insurance	0
Phone hookup	164
Miscellaneous	180
Total	$1,974

Windward TV *(cont.)*

Item	Cost
Office supplies	200
Vehicle	0
Renovation	8,000
Govt. fees	75
Legal fees	500
Accounting fees	500
Insurance	1,500
Med. insurance	100
Inventory	5,000
Miscellaneous	2,000
	$27,631

In chapter 3 we estimated the minimum monies needed for each business as the start-up costs plus six months of operating expenses. Using this arbitrary formula as a starting point, we estimated the minimum total capital needed for each operation as:

Waikiki Tax Service

Start-up cost	$1,974
6 months operating expenses (6 × $2,339)	14,034
Minimum total capital needed	$16,008

Windward TV Shop

Start-up cost	$27,631
6 months operating expenses	39,709
Minimum total capital needed	$67,340

We can now refine this estimate by preparing a cash flow statement for the first year (or more). For the sake of simplicity, let us assume that this cash flow statement estimates an amount close to $67,000. If you agree with these estimates then all you need do is take $67,000 out of your savings account to start Windward TV Shop. Unfortunately, most of us do not have $67,000 sitting in a bank.

Here are five sources of start-up capital:

1. Personal savings accounts
2. Bank loans
3. Rich individuals called "angels" or friends and family

4. Venture capital organizations
5. Government loans

Personal Sources of Start-up Capital

First, review your personal savings and other assets. You may not have all the required start-up capital, but you may have some. In any case, other investors or banks will want to see how much money you can provide in the initial capitalization. These investors will be comforted by the fact that you think highly enough of your venture to risk your personal assets. In addition, they will feel that, if you have a large personal stake in the business, you will be less likely to give up when the going gets tough.

Restaurant owner: Our company is a corporation. I used my own savings and got some other friends to invest.

Wholesaler: We started by using our personal savings and a small bank loan.

The most common methods of raising personal funds for business investment are from savings, selling stocks and bonds, cashing in a life insurance policy, selling other assets, or by taking a second mortgage on your home. Let us say you are trying to capitalize Windward TV and must raise $67,000. This is a lot of money, but, as you will see, it can be done with only $7,000 of your personal funds.

First, let us say you are able to take $5,000 from personal savings and another $2,000 from your credit card for a total of $7,000. Since you are short of the required goal, you have two options: (1) to borrow and/or (2) to give up part of the business by taking on partners. Borrowing money means incurring additional monthly overhead costs in the form of monthly payments and the loss of some profit. The danger in borrowing is the increased obligation to the business. On the other hand, people who give you loans are not interested in owning a part of your business.

Friends and Family

Let us say that you would like to retain as much of the ownership as possible and will first seek loans to meet your capitalization goal. The easiest loan may come from friends or family, since they already know you and there is no need to prove your character, as you would have to with a bank. Borrowing from friends and family, however, does create a risk of future strained family ties and friendships should the business fail or not perform well.

For the sake of this example, let us assume that you are able to persuade your parents to lend you $10,000 and your sister-in-law to lend an additional $5,000. You plan to repay these loans at 10 percent interest over a couple of years.

Equity Capital Financing

Another way to raise money without borrowing is to offer ownership or equity in the business in exchange for money. The advantage to equity capital financing is that there is no increased overhead or obligation to pay back the investment. Equity owners share the risk of a business in the hope of rewards from profits generated by the business. A disadvantage of equity financing is the possibility that you may not get along with your partner as the business develops and will be stuck with an unsuitable relationship.

Up to this point you have raised $22,000—$7,000 from personal assets and $15,000 from family loans—and still retain full equity ownership. Your next move is to offer a friend—someone you feel has a good business background—a part ownership. Equity can be exchanged for money and/or skills. Generally, the more money invested the more one should own. Your plan is to offer 20 percent of the business for $10,000 and part-time management skills while the partner keeps another job. Your friend accepts and you now have $32,000 and 80 percent of the business.

Angels

Your partner recommends that you visit a wealthy retired businessman in the hope that he will be an "angel" and lend you some additional money. After several discussions with this businessman, you decide his requirements for a loan are much too stringent. Instead, you decide to finance your inventory.

Inventory Finance Companies and Banks

You contact an inventory finance company and work out a $25,000 line of credit. Inventory finance companies are large, well-respected financial institutions that specialize in inventory financing. Although this line of credit can be used only to purchase inventory for resale, you feel inventory financing will be a major use of your funds.

Your next step is to visit a bank. You have $57,000 and need an additional $10,000. In chapter 6 we learned that a banker is not especially excited about a start-up business, preferring a business with a track record. The banker will worry also that more than half of the total capitalization for your business is in loans. A banker would prefer a smaller percentage of loans and more equity funds.

With $17,000 of equity funds and $50,000 of borrowed money, this business is starting out more "leveraged" (when debt exceeds equity). While there is no "right" leverage balance for a new venture (or an ongoing business), the lower the leverage amount, the more flexibility a business will have, since it will not have exhausted its borrowing capacity nor have a large fixed monthly loan repayment. Because your personal credit references have been good, however, and your loan proposal instills confidence, the banker approves your loan. You are set to start.

Would you start this business with less than $67,000? Remember, we arrived at this capital requirement by making a purely arbitrary estimate of the start-up cost plus six months of average monthly operating expenses. Any formula could have been used. Many people given the same situation would start with less than $67,000 and some would require more.

The level at which one may be considered undercapitalized depends on the individual's interpretation of risk. However, a major cause of business failure in the first year is undercapitalization. Although there are many undercapitalized businesses that succeed, they require the best of luck, skill, and stout-heartedness. Both your banker and your accountant can help you determine if you are undercapitalized.

> **Accountant:** Most businesses will take two to three years to break even. That means that the owners will have to carry the business for quite a while before it can return any profit.

Other Types of Financing

Venture Capital: Venture capital companies want to invest in businesses that will eventually go public, sell out, and make a profit. Minimum investments are normally $500,000 with the venture capital company assuming a major ownership interest. New ventures that hope to market products nationally and that understand a venture capital company hopes to make money on its investment by selling the company within a stated period are best suited for seeking venture capital. The Hawaii Department of Business, Economic Development and Tourism or The Chamber of Commerce of Hawaii can help businesses seeking venture capital companies.

Government Loans: Both the federal and state governments offer special low-interest government loans for small businesses. In chapter 6 we covered the Small Business Administration program. The State of Hawaii has a similar program through its Department of Business, Economic Development and Tourism, Financial Assistance Branch.

Office of Hawaiian Affairs: Direct loans for persons of Hawaiian ancestry who may not be able to get bank loans.

Buying an Existing Business

When you buy an existing business it has an established track record and customer base. Since it takes years to build both, by buying an existing business you are shortening the start-up period. Of course, if that business has established a poor reputation or does not have a good market, the track record may be a disadvantage or of little value.

Buying a business is a lot like buying a used car. The seller of a used car has a rough idea of its selling price and knows its idiosyncrasies and problems (some of which may be covered in a fresh coat of paint). The current businessowner is exactly like that used-car seller. You hope to buy that used car. How do you go about it? Generally, after some inspection and negotiation both buyer and seller agree on a price. A fair price for a used car is established when the seller and buyer both are happy with the terms of the sale. The same holds true for the sale of a business. A good selling price is an amount and terms that satisfy both seller and buyer.

To help both the seller and buyer quantify their decisionmaking, accountants use several methods to determine a business's worth. The point to remember is that much of the determination is subjective and, like the "blue book" used to rate used cars, is just a guide. One method to value an existing business is by assessing it's book value.

Book Value

The book value of a business is the net worth, as reported on the balance sheet. Remember, net worth is all the liabilities subtracted from the assets. For instance:

Windward TV Shop
Balance Sheet
December 31, 19__

Assets		
Cash		$ 5,000
Equipment		18,000
Inventory		30,000
Total assets		$53,000
Liabilities		
Accounts payables	$ 2,000	
Supplier accounts payables	10,000	
Bank loan	2,000	
Total liabilities	$14,000	
Owner's Equity	$39,000	
Total liabilities and net worth		$53,000

The owner's equity book value (the value on the accounting books) for Windward TV as of December 31 is $39,000. If Windward TV has good records of sales, profitability, and customers, the current Windward TV owner could argue justifiably that $39,000 is much too low a price for the business. Three times the book value might be suggested as a more appropriate price. That would bring the estimate of the value to $117,000 (3 × $39,000).

Because you feel that you could start a similar television shop with $67,000, the difference or $50,000 is the price for the "goodwill" established over the years for a proven track record and for a customer base. Is it worth it? Only the buyer and seller can determine that. A lot can be said, however, for an ongoing, successful business because most new businesses do fail.

Of course, the reason the business is being sold also could affect the selling price. Many good businesses can be bought relatively inexpensively because the owners decide to retire or try something else. Mainland owners, whether individuals or corporations, also may wish to divest themselves of their successful Hawaii operations from time to time. Many businesses up for sale, however, are in trouble. The reasons could be errors in the assessment of the market, zoning changes, or large incurred liabilities.

If you are interested in buying a business, you will need the assistance of a professional, such as a certified public accountant, preferably one who has experience with the type of business you are attempting to buy. Through good research you can ensure that you are buying what you intend and not a business with problems that have been "painted over."

This research is similar to that which you would do if you were starting a new business. For a clear view of the value of the business, review with your accountant the financial records of the business; do market research by talking to the business's suppliers and customers; check the competition; and review market trends and governmental plans for the area. In addition, you must consider exactly what you will be buying. Inventory? Accounts receivables? Lease? Accounts payables? Other liabilities? If a decision to purchase is reached, then an attorney's services will be needed to prepare the buy-sell contract and to review your specific liabilities.

Restaurant consultant: If someone else is selling a restaurant and you feel you can make money, you have to ask why they are selling it. Either they are doing something wrong or you may have an idea that you can do something better. Otherwise, if they were turning a 25 percent profit, I don't see how they would be selling. If the business is ill, you have to diagnose what the illness is.

Financing a Business Out of Its Profits

A new business cannot be financed out of operating profits for it has none, but an existing business can be financed in this way. Earlier in the chapter we saw how you might need $67,000 to start Windward TV from scratch. We also saw how buying Windward TV as an existing business might cost $117,000.

Let us assume that you agree with the $117,000 valuation but propose instead of cash-in-full an agreement that says you will pay $17,000 in cash and then pay off the additional $100,000 over five years at monthly installments of $1,666 per month. For the purchase you assume the existing inventory and payables (both verified and satisfactory to the business level). In addition, you request that the owner (1) advise and train you for three months and (2) sign a noncompetition clause.

If the owner agrees and you estimate the business can meet profitability projections with the additional $1,666 monthly payments, you have in essence received a long-term loan from the owner. In other words, you hope that a portion of the profit will pay off the business loan made by the previous owner. If the business is satisfactorily run within that five-year period, it could pay for itself. Of course, if it is not, the previous owner could re-acquire the business if not paid according to the purchase contract.

Buying a Franchise

If starting a business from scratch is risky and buying an ongoing, successful business is too expensive, a compromise would be to buy a franchise. A franchise is a blueprint of a particular business. The originator of a franchise has developed a successful business and is willing to let others share that plan for a fee and a percentage of sales.

Buying a franchise is like buying both an ongoing business and starting a new business at the same time. On the one hand you have the assurance of successful past experience, a ready made market, and an operating plan which includes training. On the other hand, you must take that information and transform it into a new business in your franchise area in Hawaii.

In addition to the plan and training, the franchiser (the person you buy the franchise from) will grant you a certain geographic exclusivity, say the State of Hawaii or the Kailua area. The advantages of a franchise are:

1. a prepared marketing program;
2. systematized operations;
3. training;
4. franchise assistance in solving some problems; and
5. in some cases, financial assistance.

The disadvantages are:

1. having to follow the franchise rules on marketing and advertising;
2. the inability to expand the operation except by adding more franchise outlets.

More than 1,300 available franchises are described in the *Franchise Opportunities Handbook* published by the United States Department of Commerce.

If you are looking at a franchise, you should consult an attorney familiar with franchises and have an accountant review the financial forecasts forwarded by the franchiser.

> **Consultant:** A franchise is a long-term business relationship between the franchiser and the franchisee. This business relationship is a partnership which is subject to many emotional problems.

One final caution on franchises: If you are planning to buy a franchise, make sure that it is registered with the State of Hawaii. Having the franchise registered in the state affords you more legal protection than you would have otherwise.

Raising Capital for an Ongoing Business

In chapter 15 we saw how a business has ongoing needs for new capital. For example, if a business is making a lot of sales, it may need more money to buy more products, expand warehouse facilities, or add employees. If, on the other hand, its sales are less than satisfactory, it will still need more capital to cover costs until sales improve.

One of the major roles of a businessowner is to continually raise capital for the business. It is a major error to assume that once you raise the capital necessary to open your business, the business will generate all its future cash needs through its operations. Even major corporations often have to renegotiate new lines of bank credit and raise capital through stock and bond issuance.

Although the sources of additional capital for an ongoing business are the same as for a new business, an existing business will eventually turn to the banks for most of its money raising efforts. After a year or two the business will have a track record. Although it may not yet be profitable, if it can show the banker a progression of steady sales growth and a successful market niche, the banker will be attentive to the future needs of the business. These financial needs will include inventory, working capital, and facility improvement loans.

> **Wholesaler:** A business needs to ask: when will we need more outside capital and where will we get it? If you don't have that next step figured out now when you don't need it, it may be too late when you do.

> **Retailer:** One of my biggest accomplishments was to secure a new bank loan package even though we had lost money the previous year. I had to use all my selling skills in getting the bank to see the merit of our proposal.

No one is born with the skills to convince people to invest or lend money to a business. A successful selling technique often depends on the enthusiasm of the individual businessowner. That enthusiasm and a confidence that says you know what you are doing are essential ingredients in all money requests (see chapter 6). The best way to get to know what you are doing is to do your homework about all aspects of the business.

After finally making your business work, the government is going to want their share. In the next chapter—taxes—you will see how a businessowner becomes a tax collector.

Additional Reading

Hayes, Rick Stephen. 1980. *Business Loans: A Guide to Money Sources and How to Approach Them Successfully.* New York: Van Norstand Reinhold Co., Inc.

"Money, Money, Everywhere but . . ." *Hawaii Business* 32 (3): 35–40.

"Selling a Business Can Be Fraught with Mistakes." *Pacific Business News* (September 9, 1985): 43.

17

Taxes: Your Job as a Tax Collector

Little did you realize when you started a business you would also become a tax collector. In addition to all the other work in operating your business, you must collect and pay taxes too. Some of these business taxes are:

1. The Hawaii State General Excise Tax (GET)
2. State of Hawaii Use Tax
3. The State of Hawaii Unemployment Insurance Tax
4. The Federal Unemployment Tax (FUTA)
5. Social Security (FICA)
6. Federal Withholding Tax (FWT)
7. State Withholding Tax (SWT)
8. Income Tax

Actually, you become a tax collector for only the general excise tax, the state and federal withholding taxes, and the FICA tax. The rest of the taxes you simply pay when due. New businessowners are often surprised at the various types of taxes that affect businesses and the different due dates for each tax. Since these two items are the most confusing, we will answer two questions for each tax: (1) how do you determine what you owe? and (2) when is it due?

Fortunately, acquiring a basic background on most of these taxes is not difficult. However, since this area is more complicated than can be fully covered here, businessowners should review their specific situations with an accountant and with the appropriate tax agency.

Hawaii General Excise Tax (GET)

The Hawaii General Excise Tax is a regressive state tax which is not dependent upon whether you make a profit, as with income tax. This tax is determined as a percentage of gross sales.

There are two rates of tax, 4 percent and ½ percent. The type of sale will determine the tax rate a business will use. All retail sales (sales to the end user) are in the 4 percent category. Sales made to other businesses *for resale* are taxed at the ½ percent rate. For example, a retail store with sales of $10,000 would be subject to $400 in general excise taxes at the 4 percent rate. A wholesale business, on the other hand, which uses the ½ percent rate, would be subject to a tax of $50 for the same $10,000 of sales (remember ½ percent equals .005). Because businesses pass this tax on by adding it to the invoice, the purchaser pays this tax and the business becomes a tax collector.

Once you know the rate that applies to your sales, you need to know when it is due. Like most other business taxes, the due date for your tax payment is determined by how much you owe.

You pay the tax:

1. Semiannually if your general excise tax liability does not exceed $1,000 for the calendar year. That means if your sales for the calendar year do not exceed $25,000 and you use a 4 percent general excise tax rate, you can pay the GET every six months.
2. Quarterly if your general excise tax liability does not exceed $2,000 for the calendar year ($50,000 in calendar year sales or roughly $4,166 of monthly average sales at 4 percent).
3. Monthly if your average monthly sales are more than $4,166 (at 4 percent).

Let us look at an example for both Windward TV, which had December sales of $15,753, and Waikiki Tax Service which received a quarterly income of $14,378. In this example, Windward TV projects annual sales of $100,000 for the year and files its GET monthly. Waikiki Tax Service estimates income for the year of $40,000 and files its GET quarterly. Exhibits 64 and 65 illustrate the GET paid by each business.

At the end of the year, the business is also required to complete a year end GET report (Exhibit 66). This form is due on the 20th day of the fourth month following the close of the fiscal year. For a business which uses a fiscal year of January to December, this report is due on April 20th.

The penalties for late payments of this tax and other taxes are severe. However, only a maximum penalty of 10 per cent of the tax due will be assessed for timely filed returns within 90 days of the prescribed filing date. This means if you file the GET form within the required time but do not pay all or any of the tax due at that time, the maximum penalty should be 10 percent of the tax due and not the 25 percent when you do not file at all.

Interest may also be charged on the portion of the tax due and if the state determines intentional disregard or fraud, additional penalties could be added. Questions about the GET should be directed to the Hawaii Department of Taxation.

EXHIBIT 64

WINDWARD TV SHOP DECEMBER GET

FORM G-45 (Rev. 1990) STATE OF HAWAII – DEPARTMENT OF TAXATION

GENERAL EXCISE/USE TAX RETURN

DO NOT WRITE IN THIS AREA **10**

NAME: Windward TV Shop

☒ **MONTH OF** December 19 91
(Do not combine your income for more than one month, if filing monthly.)

☐ **QUARTER OF** ________ 19 ___
(Do not combine your income for more than one quarter, if filing quarterly.)

G.E./USE ID. NO. 10288724

☐ **SEMIANNUAL PERIOD OF** ________ 19 ___
(Do not combine your income for more than one semiannual period, if filing semiannually.)

NOTE: SCHEDULE C (FORM G-45) MUST BE COMPLETED AND ATTACHED TO THIS FORM G-45.

SCHEDULE A - ACTIVITIES UNDER CHAPTER 237, HRS - GENERAL EXCISE TAX LAW

BUSINESS ACTIVITIES	BUS. ACT. CODE	a VALUES, GROSS PROCEEDS OR GROSS INCOME	b EXEMPTIONS / DEDUCTIONS (EXPLAIN ON REVERSE SIDE)	c TAXABLE INCOME	RATE	d TAXES	
WHOLESALING	1				.005		1
MANUFACTURING	2				.005		2
PRODUCING	3				.005		3
SUGAR PROCESSING	4				.005		4
PINEAPPLE CANNING	5				.005		5
SERVICES RENDERED FOR (OR TO) AN INTERMEDIARY	6				.005		6
INSURANCE COMMISSIONS	7				.0015		7
RETAILING	8	15,753 00		15,753 00	.04	630 12	8
SERVICES INCL. PROFESSIONAL	9				.04		9
CONTRACTING	10				.04		10
THEATER AMUSEMENT AND BROADCASTING	11				.04		11
INTEREST	12				.04		12
COMMISSIONS	13				.04		13
HOTEL RENTALS	14				.04		14
OTHER RENTALS	15				.04		15
ALL OTHERS	16				.04		16
SCHEDULE B - ACTIVITIES UNDER CHAPTER 238, HRS - USE TAX LAW							
IMPORTS FOR RESALE AT RETAIL	17				.005		17
IMPORTS FOR CONSUMPTION	18				.04		18

IF THERE IS NO TAX DUE, ENTER "NONE" ON LINE 19, SIGN THIS RETURN AND SUBMIT IT TO THE PROPER DISTRICT OFFICE.	19.	TOTAL TAXES DUE	630 12	19
FOR LATE FILING ONLY➔	20a.	PENALTY ➔		20a
	20b.	INTEREST ➔		20b
Make check payable to "HAWAII STATE TAX COLLECTOR" in U.S. dollars drawn on any U.S. bank. Write your general excise/use I.D. number on the check.	21.	TOTAL PAYMENT ➔ PAY IN U.S. DOLLARS	630 12	21
GRAND TOTAL EXEMPTIONS / DEDUCTIONS FROM BACK OF FORM	22.			

I declare, under the penalties set forth in sections 237-48 and 238-12, HRS, that this is a true and correct return, prepared in accordance with the provisions of the General Excise and Use Tax Laws and the rules issued thereunder.

IN CASE OF A CORPORATION OR PARTNERSHIP, THIS RETURN MUST BE SIGNED BY AN OFFICER OR PARTNER.

THIS SPACE FOR DATE RECEIVED STAMP

Debbie Miura (SIGNATURE) Partner (TITLE) 1/8/92 (DATE)

MAILING ADDRESS

OAHU DISTRICT OFFICE, P.O. BOX 1425, HONOLULU, HI 96806-1425
MAUI DISTRICT OFFICE, P.O. BOX 1427, WAILUKU, HI 96793-1427
HAWAII DISTRICT OFFICE, P.O. BOX 937, HILO, HI 96821-0937
KAUAI DISTRICT OFFICE, P.O. BOX 1687, LIHUE, HI 96766-5687

FORM G-45 **10**

Hawaii Use Tax

While the general excise tax is a tax on gross sales, the use tax is an import tax. It is a tax paid on any merchandise that is brought into the state from anywhere out of state. This tax may apply whether the merchandise is for resale or for internal business use (there are other implications and exceptions; contact the Hawaii Department of Taxation for more information). The rate of this use tax is ½ of 1 percent (.005) of the value of the goods for resale and 4 percent for items to be used in the business.

EXHIBIT 65
Waikiki Tax Service Quarterly GET

FORM G-45 (Rev. 1990) STATE OF HAWAII – DEPARTMENT OF TAXATION
GENERAL EXCISE/USE TAX RETURN

DO NOT WRITE IN THIS AREA **10**

NAME: Waikiki Tax Service

☐ **MONTH OF** ________ 19 __
(Do not combine your income for more than one month, if filing monthly.)

☒ **QUARTER OF** December 1991 **G.E./USE ID. NO.** 1 1 2 5 9 1 2 3
(Do not combine your income for more than one quarter, if filing quarterly.)

☐ **SEMIANNUAL PERIOD OF** ________ 19 __
(Do not combine your income for more than one semiannual period, if filing semiannually.)

NOTE: SCHEDULE C (FORM G-45) MUST BE COMPLETED AND ATTACHED TO THIS FORM G-45.

BUSINESS ACTIVITIES	BUS. ACT. CODE	a VALUES, GROSS PROCEEDS OR GROSS INCOME	b EXEMPTIONS / DEDUCTIONS (EXPLAIN ON REVERSE SIDE)	c TAXABLE INCOME	RATE	d TAXES	
SCHEDULE A - ACTIVITIES UNDER CHAPTER 237, HRS - GENERAL EXCISE TAX LAW							
WHOLESALING	1				.005		1
MANUFACTURING	2				.005		2
PRODUCING	3				.005		3
SUGAR PROCESSING	4				.005		4
PINEAPPLE CANNING	5				.005		5
SERVICES RENDERED FOR (OR TO) AN INTERMEDIARY	6				.005		6
INSURANCE COMMISSIONS	7				.0015		7
RETAILING	8				.04		8
SERVICES INCL. PROFESSIONAL	9	14,378 00		14,378 00	.04	575 12	9
CONTRACTING	10				.04		10
THEATER AMUSEMENT AND BROADCASTING	11				.04		11
INTEREST	12				.04		12
COMMISSIONS	13				.04		13
HOTEL RENTALS	14				.04		14
OTHER RENTALS	15				.04		15
ALL OTHERS	16				.04		16
SCHEDULE B - ACTIVITIES UNDER CHAPTER 238, HRS - USE TAX LAW							
IMPORTS FOR RESALE AT RETAIL	17				.005		17
IMPORTS FOR CONSUMPTION	18				.04		18

IF THERE IS NO TAX DUE, ENTER "NONE" ON LINE 19, SIGN THIS RETURN AND SUBMIT IT TO THE PROPER DISTRICT OFFICE.	19. TOTAL TAXES DUE	575 12	19
FOR LATE FILING ONLY▶	20a. PENALTY		20a
	20b. INTEREST		20b
Make check payable to "HAWAII STATE TAX COLLECTOR" in U.S. dollars drawn on any U.S. bank. Write your general excise/use I.D. number on the check.	21. TOTAL PAYMENT PAY IN U.S. DOLLARS	575 12	21
GRAND TOTAL EXEMPTIONS / DEDUCTIONS FROM BACK OF FORM	22.		

I declare, under the penalties set forth in sections 237-48 and 238-12, HRS, that this is a true and correct return, prepared in accordance with the provisions of the General Excise and Use Tax Laws and the rules issued thereunder.

THIS SPACE FOR DATE RECEIVED STAMP

IN CASE OF A CORPORATION OR PARTNERSHIP, THIS RETURN MUST BE SIGNED BY AN OFFICER OR PARTNER.

Jozie Akana (SIGNATURE) Owner (TITLE) 1/8/92 (DATE)

MAILING ADDRESS

OAHU DISTRICT OFFICE P.O. BOX 1425 HONOLULU, HI 96806-1425
MAUI DISTRICT OFFICE P.O. BOX 1427 WAILUKU, HI 96793-1427
HAWAII DISTRICT OFFICE P.O. BOX 937 HILO, HI 96821-0937
KAUAI DISTRICT OFFICE P.O. BOX 1687 LIHUE, HI 96766-5687

FORM G-45 **10**

Let us assume that Windward TV purchases some televisions for resale from a manufacturer in California. The total invoice for the order is $5,000. The use tax on that order is $25.00 ($5,000 × .005). But if Windward TV purchased $5,000 of new test equipment to be used in its repair section from a mainland supplier, the use tax would be $200 ($5,000 × .04).

This tax is payable:

1. Monthly for tax liabilities over $2,000 per month;
2. Quarterly for tax liabilities of more than $1,000 but less than $2,000 per quarter;
3. Semiannually for tax liabilities that do not exceed $1,000 in a calendar year.

EXHIBIT 66

WAIKIKI TAX SERVICE YEAR'S END GET REPORT

FORM G-49 (Rev. 1992)

STATE OF HAWAII — DEPARTMENT OF TAXATION
ANNUAL RETURN & RECONCILIATION
GENERAL EXCISE/USE TAX RETURN
FOR CALENDAR YEAR 1991
OR FISCAL YEAR ENDING 12 / 31 / 91 (MO. DAY YR.)

DO NOT WRITE IN THIS AREA **16**

NAME: WAIKIKI TAX SERVICE

G.E./USE ID. NO. 1 1 2 5 9 1 2 3

THIS ANNUAL RETURN MUST BE FILED ON OR BEFORE THE TWENTIETH DAY OF THE FOURTH MONTH FOLLOWING THE CLOSE OF THE CALENDAR OR FISCAL YEAR.

NOTE: SCHEDULE C (FORM G-49) MUST BE COMPLETED AND ATTACHED TO THIS FORM G-49.

• ATTACH CHECK OR MONEY ORDER HERE •

SCHEDULE A — ACTIVITIES UNDER CHAPTER 237, HRS — GENERAL EXCISE TAX LAW

BUSINESS ACTIVITIES	BUS. ACT. CODE	VALUES, GROSS PROCEEDS OR GROSS INCOME a	EXEMPTIONS/DEDUCTIONS (EXPLAIN ON REVERSE SIDE) b	TAXABLE INCOME c	RATE	TAXES d	
WHOLESALING	1				.005		1
MANUFACTURING	2				.005		2
PRODUCING	3				.005		3
SUGAR PROCESSING	4				.005		4
PINEAPPLE CANNING	5				.005		5
SERVICES RENDERED FOR (OR TO) AN INTERMEDIARY	6				.005		6
INSURANCE COMMISSIONS	7				.0015		7
RETAILING	8				.04		8
SERVICES INCL. PROFESSIONAL	9	47,250 00		47,250 00	.04	1,890 00	9
CONTRACTING	10				.04		10
THEATER AMUSEMENT AND BROADCASTING	11				.04		11
INTEREST	12				.04		12
COMMISSIONS	13				.04		13
HOTEL RENTALS	14				.04		14
OTHER RENTALS	15				.04		15
ALL OTHERS	16				.04		16
SCHEDULE B — ACTIVITIES UNDER CHAPTER 238, HRS — USE TAX LAW							
IMPORTS FOR RESALE AT RETAIL	17				.005		17
IMPORTS FOR CONSUMPTION	18				.04		18

TAX OFFICE COPY

NATURE OF BUSINESS

19.	TOTAL TAXES DUE (ADD LINES 1 — 18)	1,890 00	19
20a.	PENALTY $		
20b.	INTEREST $		20
21.	TOTAL AMOUNT (ADD LINES 19 AND 20)	1,890 00	21
22.	TOTAL TAXES PAID WITH YOUR MONTHLY, QUARTERLY, OR SEMIANNUAL RETURNS FOR THE PERIOD. EACH MONTHLY, QUARTERLY, OR SEMIANNUAL TAX PAYMENT SHOULD BE LISTED ON THE REVERSE SIDE OF THIS FORM. — 22. 1,820 00		
23.	ADDITIONAL ASSESSMENTS PAID FOR THE PERIOD, IF INCLUDED ON LINE 19. — 23.		
24.	PENALTIES $ INTEREST $ PAID DURING THE PERIOD. — 24.		
25.	TOTAL PAYMENTS MADE (LINES 22 TO 24 INCLUSIVE).	1,820 00	25
26.	CREDIT TO BE REFUNDED (LINE 25 MINUS LINE 21).		26
27.	TAXES DUE AND PAYABLE (LINE 21 MINUS LINE 25).	70 00	27
28.	**FOR LATE FILING ONLY ➡** 28a. PENALTY $ 28b. INTEREST $		28
29.	TOTAL AMOUNT DUE AND PAYABLE (ADD LINES 27 AND 28).	70 00	29
30.	PLEASE ENTER AMOUNT OF YOUR PAYMENT (Make check payable to "HAWAII STATE TAX COLLECTOR" in U.S. DOLLARS DRAWN ON ANY U.S. BANK. Write your general excise/use I.D. number on the check.	70 00	30
31.	GRAND TOTAL EXEMPTIONS/DEDUCTIONS FROM BACK OF FORM. — 31.		

DECLARATION: I declare, under the penalties set forth in sections 237-48 and 238-12, HRS, that this return (including any accompanying schedules or statements) has been examined by me and, to the best of my knowledge and belief, is a true, correct, and complete return, made in good faith for the tax period stated, pursuant to the General Excise and Use Tax Laws, and the rules issued thereunder. I also reaffirm the statements on my application (as amended).
IN THE CASE OF A CORPORATION OR PARTNERSHIP, THIS RETURN MUST BE SIGNED BY AN OFFICER, PARTNER, OR DULY AUTHORIZED AGENT.

SIGNATURE: Josie Akana TITLE: OWNER DATE: 1/8/92

— MAILING ADDRESSES —

OAHU DISTRICT OFFICE
P.O. BOX 1425
HONOLULU, HI 96806-1425

MAUI DISTRICT OFFICE
P.O. BOX 1427
WAILUKU, HI 96793-6427

HAWAII DISTRICT OFFICE
P.O. BOX 937
HILO, HI 96721-0937

KAUAI DISTRICT OFFICE
P.O. BOX 1687
LIHUE, HI 96766-5687

SCHEDULE C (FORM G-49) MUST BE FILED WITH THIS FORM G-49.
See the back of the Schedule C (Form G-49) for Instructions.

THIS SPACE FOR DATE RECEIVED STAMP

FORM G-49 **16**

The use tax is reported and paid with the general excise tax form. Since there are many exemptions and exceptions to both the general excise and use tax, questions about both these taxes should be directed to the Hawaii Department of Taxation.

Getting Federal and State Identification Numbers

Your GET number is issued by the state when you complete the GET application (chapter 5). If you plan to have employees, you must apply to both

EXHIBIT 67

Application for Employer Identification Number (Form SS-4)

Form **SS-4**
(Rev August 1989)
Department of the Treasury
Internal Revenue Service

Application for Employer Identification Number

(For use by employers and others. Please read the attached instructions before completing this form.) Please type or print clearly.

EIN

OMB No 1545-0003
Expires 7-31-91

1 Name of applicant (True legal name) (See instructions.)

2 Trade name of business, if different from name in line 1

3 Executor, trustee, "care of name"

4a Mailing address (street address) (room, apt., or suite no.)

5a Address of business. (See instructions.)

4b City, state, and ZIP code

5b City, state, and ZIP code

6 County and state where principal business is located

7 Name of principal officer, grantor, or general partner. (See instructions.) ▶

8a Type of entity (Check only one box.) (See instructions.)
☐ Individual SSN ____
☐ REMIC
☐ Personal service corp.
☐ State/local government
☐ National guard
☐ Other nonprofit organization (specify) ____
☐ Other (specify) ▶
☐ Estate
☐ Plan administrator SSN ____
☐ Other corporation (specify) ____
☐ Federal government/military
☐ Church or church controlled organization
If nonprofit organization enter GEN (if applicable) ____
☐ Trust
☐ Partnership
☐ Farmers' cooperative

8b If a corporation, give name of foreign country (if applicable) or state in the U.S. where incorporated ▶ | Foreign country | State

9 Reason for applying (Check only one box)
☐ Started new business
☐ Hired employees
☐ Created a pension plan (specify type) ▶
☐ Banking purpose (specify) ▶
☐ Changed type of organization (specify) ▶
☐ Purchased going business
☐ Created a trust (specify) ▶
☐ Other (specify) ▶

10 Date business started or acquired (Mo., day, year) (See instructions.)

11 Enter closing month of accounting year. (See instructions.)

12 First date wages or annuities were paid or will be paid (Mo., day, year). **Note:** *If applicant is a withholding agent, enter date income will first be paid to nonresident alien. (Mo., day, year)* ▶

13 Enter highest number of employees expected in the next 12 months. **Note:** *If the applicant does not expect to have any employees during the period, enter "0."* ▶ | Nonagricultural | Agricultural | Household

14 Does the applicant operate more than one place of business? ☐ Yes ☐ No
If "Yes," enter name of business. ▶

15 Principal activity or service (See instructions.) ▶

16 Is the principal business activity manufacturing? ☐ Yes ☐ No
If "Yes," principal product and raw material used ▶

17 To whom are most of the products or services sold? Please check the appropriate box. ☐ Business (wholesale)
☐ Public (retail) ☐ Other (specify) ▶ ☐ N/A

18a Has the applicant ever applied for an identification number for this or any other business? ☐ Yes ☐ No
Note: *If "Yes," please complete lines 18b and 18c.*

18b If you checked the "Yes" box in line 18a, give applicant's true name and trade name, if different than name shown on prior application.
True name ▶ Trade name ▶

18c Enter approximate date, city, and state where the application was filed and the previous employer identification number if known.
Approximate date when filed (Mo., day, year) | City and state where filed | Previous EIN

Under penalties of perjury, I declare that I have examined this application, and to the best of my knowledge and belief, it is true, correct, and complete

Telephone number (include area code)

Name and title (Please type or print clearly.) ▶

Signature ▶ Date ▶

Note: *Do not write below this line. For official use only.*

Please leave blank ▶	Geo	Ind	Class	Size	Reason for applying

For Paperwork Reduction Act Notice, see attached instructions. Form **SS-4** (Rev 8-89)

the federal and state governments for employer identification numbers before you can pay the next category of tax—federal and state payroll taxes.

The request for the federal employer identification number is made using Form SS-4 (Exhibit 67). This form must be sent to the Internal Revenue Service before you plan to file payroll tax payments.

To obtain your State of Hawaii employer number you submit the State of Hawaii Form UC-1, "Report To Determine Liability Under the Hawaii Employment Security Law" (Exhibit 68). This form is the application form for the state unemployment tax rate determination. However, the resulting Department of Labor (DOL) number is also the state identification number you will use to pay most of your state taxes.

Once you have both the employer federal identification number and the State of Hawaii DOL number you can submit payroll and other payroll-related taxes such as unemployment insurance.

EXHIBIT 68

REPORT TO DETERMINE LIABILITY UNDER THE HAWAII EMPLOYMENT SECURITY LAW (FORM UC-1)

FORM UC-1
Rev. 10/87

ORIGINAL COPY

REPORT TO DETERMINE LIABILITY UNDER THE HAWAII EMPLOYMENT SECURITY LAW

DEPARTMENT OF LABOR AND INDUSTRIAL RELATIONS
DIVISION OF UNEMPLOYMENT INSURANCE

☐ OAHU	☐ HAWAII	☐ MAUI	☐ KAUAI
830 Punchbowl St., Room 437 Honolulu, Hawaii 96813 Ph: 548-3024	180 Kinoole St. Hilo, Hawaii 96720 Ph: 961-7461	54 So. High St. Wailuku, Maui 96793 Ph: 244-4377	3016 Umi St. Lihue, Kauai 96766 Ph: 245-4485

DO NOT WRITE IN THIS SPACE
Registration
No. ______
Federal Identification
No. ______

Under Section 12-5-17 Administrative Rules relating to the Hawaii Employment Security Law, any individual or organization who employs one or more individuals in the State of Hawaii (or who acquires the ownership of a business or operation in which there have been employees), must file this report within twenty (20) days after services in employment are first performed. (TYPE OR PRINT LEGIBLY)

1. Employer's Name ______
   Trade Name or DBA ______ Business Telephone ______
2. Business Location ______ (Number and Street (Do not use post office box)) ______ City ______ State ______ Zip Code ______
3. Mailing Address if different from above [item 2]: ______ Number and Street or P. O. Box ______ City ______ State ______ Zip Code ______
4. Was business purchased or transferred? Yes ☐ No ☐ If "yes," was all or part of business purchased or transferred?
   All ☐ Part ☐ Give date of acquisition and name and address of predecessor.
   Date ______ Name ______ Trade Name ______ Address ______
   [A successor may assume the rate of the predecessor if [1] employer newly subject to law files Form UC-86 "Waiver of Employer's Experience Record" within sixty days after acquisition of the business, and [2] predecessor files all reports and pays all contributions due up to date of his termination within the same sixty day period. A successor filing a waiver after the 60 day period but on or before the next March 1st will be eligible for an experience rating determination for the following year if predecessor has filed all reports and paid all contributions due **(IT IS THE EMPLOYER'S RESPONSIBILITY TO OBTAIN FORM UC-86 FROM THE UNEMPLOYMENT INSURANCE DIVISION.)**]
5. Type of organization: Individual ☐ Partnership ☐ Corporation ☐ Other ☐ ______
6. Date business established ______ Date employment began in Hawaii ______ No. of employees on date employment began: ______
   To obtain an account number, this form must be submitted with Form UC-BP-5(A), "Report of New Hire(s)".
   If no employees, when do you anticipate hiring employees? ______
7. If individual owner, list name and home address of owner: if partnership, list names and home addresses of all partners; if corporation, list names and home addresses of all officers:

Name	Social Security No.	Home Address	Home Phone

8. Were you previously registered as an employer in Hawaii?
   Yes ☐ No ☐ If "yes," give date and trade name under which business was operated ______

Do Not Write In This Space

UC-1 prepared by ______
Follow-Up ______ Exempt ______
Liable ______ Fld. Rep. Code ______
New Acct. Cd. ______ TOB Cd. ______
Ac. Stat Dte. ______ TCC ______
MIFS ______ Pending ______
Approved by ______
Other Remarks ______

Hawaii Unemployment Insurance Tax

The state administers an Unemployment Insurance Fund which provides weekly reimbursements for qualified employees who have been released from employment for no fault of their own. This program is funded entirely by employers. While the GET was computed as a percentage of your *sales*, the Unemployment Insurance Tax is computed as a per-

EXHIBIT 69

RATE NOTICE AND EXPERIENCE RATING TABULATION FOR CALENDAR YEAR (FORM UC-DP-30)

FORM UC-DP-30 (REV. 12/85)
(EDP #2816)

STATE OF HAWAII
Department of Labor and Industrial Relations
Unemployment Insurance Division

RATE NOTICE & EXPERIENCE RATING TABULATION
FOR CALENDAR YEAR 1987

EMPLOYER ACCOUNT NUMBER	FEDERAL IDENTIFICATION NO.
0000197220	990238942

DATE MAILED:
DATE TABULATED:
LIABLE DATE:
ELIGIBILITY CODE:

ANNUAL TAXABLE PAYROLL			AVERAGE ANNUAL PAYROLL
1984	1985	1986	
0.00	0.00	0.00	0.00

RESERVE		CONTRIBUTIONS		1986 BENEFITS CHARGED		RESERVE 12/31/86
0.00	+	0.00	−	0.00	=	0.00

RESERVE 12/31/86		AVERAGE ANNUAL PAYROLL		RATIO
0.00	÷	0.00	=	0.00

BASIC EXPERIENCE RATE		SOLVENCY RATE		CONTRIBUTION RATE
3.60	+	0.00	=	3.60

IMPORTANT INFORMATION

This is your "Rate Notice and Experience Rating Tabulation" for calendar year 1987. The tabulation shows wage and contribution data reported by you on your quarterly contribution reports for years 1984, 1985, and 1986. Also included are benefits charged to your account for 1986.

If you are not in accord with the rate assigned to your account, the law provides you with a right to appeal. Please submit your request for review and redetermination in writing, setting forth your reasons, within 15 days from the date of mailing of this rate notice.

See reverse side for additional rate information and for explanation of this notice.

Windward TV Shop
234 Kaa St.
Kaneohe, HI 96744

centage of your total *employee payroll.* The percentage that each employer contributes to this fund is determined by the state and varies depending on the number of years in business, the claims submitted by that business, and the general usage of other businesses. The current range charged employers is from .2 to 5.4 percent.

After you submit your application UC-1 Form you will receive the "Rate Notice and Experience Rating Tabulation for Calendar Year" form UC-DP-30 (Exhibit 69). In this form the state will inform you of your unemployment "contribution" (tax) rate for the year. Most new businesses are charged a set introductory rate established by the state each year.

Although the employer pays the unemployment tax, the amount of tax is limited to a certain wage ceiling for each employee. For example, in 1995 that limit per employee for unemployment insurance was $25,000 (this limit changes annually). Consequently, the employer only has to pay a rated percentage up to the first $25,000 in wages per employee in 1995. Here is an example of how the eligible wages for this tax are calculated. Assume that you have two employees with salaries of $7,000 and $33,000. The total wages subject to the unemployment tax are shown on page 217. The table shows that in the third quarter, employee 2 has reached the contribution limit of $25,000 and the amount in excess of that limit in the fourth quarter, is not subject to the unemployment insurance tax.

The form that you use to pay your state unemployment tax is Form UC-B6. The state sends this form every quarter. Assuming that Windward TV had a quarterly payroll of $15,000 and a contribution rate of 3.6 percent, Exhibit 70 shows that the tax due for this quarter is $540. (Note: a temporary Employment and Training Assessment was added for the period of 1992–1996.)

	1st Quarter	2nd Quarter	3rd Quarter	4th Quarter	Total
Employee 1	$1,000	$ 2,000	$ 2,000	$ 2,000	$ 7,000
Employee 2	$5,000	$10,000	$ 8,900	$10,000	$33,900
Total wages	$6,000	$12,000	$10,900	$12,000	
Excess wages	0	0	0	$ 8,900	
Taxable wages	$6,000	$12,000	$10,900	$ 3,100	

EXHIBIT 70

Windward TV Shop Unemployment Contribution

FORM UC-B6 (REV. 1/92)
ICSD # 2614

STATE OF HAWAII
DEPARTMENT OF LABOR AND INDUSTRIAL RELATIONS
UNEMPLOYMENT INSURANCE DIVISION

QUARTERLY WAGE, CONTRIBUTION AND EMPLOYMENT AND TRAINING ASSESSMENT REPORT

DO NOT WRITE IN THIS SPACE

WINDWARD TV SHOP

FEDERAL I.D. NUMBER: 990023892

ACCOUNT NUMBER: 0000197220

FOR QUARTER ENDING: 033192

DELINQUENT AFTER:

DO NOT USE GRID MARKS FOR TYPEWRITTEN ENTRIES. SEE SAMPLE ON REVERSE

PLEASE PRINT OR TYPE IN BLACK INK

1) EMPLOYEE'S SSA#	2) EMPLOYEE'S NAME (LAST, FIRST)	3) TOTAL QTR WAGES PAID
576463569	ADRES, TED	4500.00
567429333	ARTEAGA, HILDA	4700.00
553072801	SMITH, WESLEEN	3300.00
576993300	KAMAKA, MILES	2500.00

MAIL OR DELIVER REPORTS AND REMITTANCES TO: **STATE TAX COLLECTOR**
P.O. Box 3223, Honolulu, Hawaii 96801
OR
830 Punchbowl Street
Honolulu, Hi. 96813

4) TOTAL WAGES ON THIS PAGE: 15000.00

CONTRIBUTION RATE: 3.6%

EMPLOYMENT & TNG ASSESSMENT RATE: 0.05 %

17) NUMBER OF COVERED WORKERS IN THE PAY PERIOD INCLUDING THE 12TH DAY OF EACH MONTH

1ST MONTH	2ND MONTH	3RD MONTH
4	4	4

5) TOTAL FROM OTHER PAGES		0 00
6) TOTAL WAGES PAID THIS QUARTER (sum of items 4 and 5)		15,000 00
7) LESS WAGES PAID THIS QUARTER to Each Employee in Excess of Year's First $		0 00
8) NET TAXABLE WAGES (subtract item 7 from item 6)		15,000 00
9) CONTRIBUTIONS DUE (multiply item 8 by >>>>	.036	540 00
10) E & T ASSESSMENT DUE (multiply item 8 by >>>>	.0005	7 50
11) AMOUNT DUE (SUM OF ITEM 9 AND 10)		547 50
12) OVERPAYMENT (enter amount from Form UC-306)		
13) ADJUSTED CONTRIBUTIONS DUE (subtract item 12 from item 11)		
14) PENALTY AND INTEREST		
15) TOTAL PAYMENT DUE (sum of items 13 and 14)		547 50
16) TOTAL REMITTANCE – PAY IN US DOLLARS ONLY MAKE CHECK PAYABLE TO HAWAII STATE TAX COLLECTOR PLEASE INDICATE YOUR U.I. ACCT NUMBER ON CHECK		547 50

I CERTIFY THAT THE INFORMATION ON THIS REPORT IS TRUE AND CORRECT

SIGNED BY: Debbie Miura

PRINT NAME: DEBBIE MIURA

TITLE: PARTNER

TELEPHONE NUMBER: 836-1400

DATE: 4/15/92

RETURN THIS COPY WITH PAYMENT

Print your characters like this ▶ 0 1 2 3 4 5 6 7 8 9 A B C D E F G H I J K L M N O P Q R S T U V W X Y Z

The UC-B6 form is due within 30 days of the end of the quarter. Penalties for nonpayment are (1) $10 or 10 percent of the tax whichever is greater and/or, (2) the assignment of the maximum rate. Questions on the completion of this form can be directed to the Hawaii Department of Labor and Industrial Relations, Unemployment Insurance Division.

Federal Unemployment Tax (FUTA)

In addition to the state unemployment tax, there is a Federal Unemployment Tax. The FUTA rate is 6.2 percent for the first $7,000 of wages (in 1991) for each employee (however, you do receive a credit if you paid the required amounts into a State's Unemployment Insurance Fund). This tax is paid quarterly using the federal tax deposit coupon Form 8109 (Exhibit 71). This federal deposit coupon will be used for many different tax payments. You will receive these coupons automatically when you apply for your federal identification number. Since this coupon is used to pay for several types of federal taxes, you must indicate on the coupon which type of tax you are paying. You accomplish this by checking the section "Type of Tax, Mark One" on the coupon. The type of tax you will mark on the coupon for the payment of FUTA is "940." Other types of taxes paid with this coupon are:

- 941 - Federal Withholding and Social Security (FICA)
- 943 - Agricultural Income and Social Security
- 720 - Federal Excise Tax
- CT-1 - Railroad Taxes
- 1120 - Corporation Income Tax
- 999-C - Farmer's Cooperative Income Tax
- 1042 - Withholding at the source

Fortunately, most businesses only use 940 and 941.

At the end of the year you will have to complete Form 940 or 940-EZ "Employer's Annual Federal Unemployment (FUTA) Tax Return" (Exhibit 72). This form is a summary of your year's FUTA liability. Questions concerning the FUTA can be directed to the Internal Revenue Service.

Employee's Withholding Tax (FWT and SWT)

Before you can withhold payroll taxes from the employee, your employee needs to inform you of the number of tax exemptions claimed. At the time of initial employment, each employee is required to complete a Federal Employee's Withholding Allowance Form, Form W-4 (see Exhibit 50, chapter 14). On this form the employee notifies the employer of the exemptions claimed for income tax withholding from each paycheck. This

EXHIBIT 71
Federal Tax Deposit Coupon

AMOUNT OF DEPOSIT (Do NOT type, please print.)

DOLLARS | CENTS

TAX YEAR MONTH →

EMPLOYER IDENTIFICATION NUMBER →

BANK NAME/ DATE STAMP

Name ______

Address ______

City ______

State ______ ZIP ______

Telephone number ( )

IRS USE ONLY

Darken only one TYPE OF TAX		and	Darken only one TAX PERIOD
941	Sch. A		1st Quarter
990C	1120		2nd Quarter
943	990-T		3rd Quarter
720	990PF		4th Quarter
CT-1	1042		
940			

35

FOR BANK USE IN MICR ENCODING

Federal Tax Deposit Coupon
Form 8109-B (Rev. 8-88)

EXHIBIT 72
Employer's Annual Federal Unemployment Tax Return (Form 940)

Form **940**

Department of the Treasury
Internal Revenue Service

Employer's Annual Federal Unemployment (FUTA) Tax Return

▶ **For Paperwork Reduction Act Notice, see separate instructions.**

OMB No. 1545-0028

1992

If incorrect, make any necessary change. ▶

Name (as distinguished from trade name) | Calendar year

Trade name, if any

Address and ZIP code | Employer identification number

T	
FF	
FD	
FP	
I	
T	

A Are you required to pay unemployment contributions to only one state? . . . . ☐ **Yes** ☐ **No**

B Did you pay all state unemployment contributions by February 1, 1993? (If a 0% experience rate is granted check "Yes.") . . . . ☐ **Yes** ☐ **No**

C Were all wages that were taxable for FUTA tax also taxable for your state's unemployment tax? . . . . ☐ **Yes** ☐ **No**

D Did you pay all wages in a state other than Michigan? . . . . ☐ **Yes** ☐ **No**

If you answered "No" to any of these questions, you must file Form 940. If you answered "Yes" to all the questions, you may file Form 940-EZ which is a simplified version of Form 940. You can get Form 940-EZ by calling 1-800-TAX-FORM (1-800-829-3676).

If you will not have to file returns in the future, check here, complete, and sign the return . . . . ▶ ☐

If this is an Amended Return, check here . . . . ▶ ☐

Part I **Computation of Taxable Wages**

1 Total payments (including exempt payments) during the calendar year for services of employees . **1**

2 Exempt payments. (Explain each exemption shown, attach additional sheets if necessary.) ▶ .... | Amount paid | **2**

3 Payments of more than $7,000 for services. Enter only amounts over the first $7,000 paid to each employee. Do not include payments from line 2. The $7,000 amount is the Federal wage base. Your state wage base may be different. **Do not use the state wage limitation** **3**

4 Total exempt payments (add lines 2 and 3) **4**

5 **Total taxable wages** (subtract line 4 from line 1) . . . . ▶ **5**

6 Additional tax resulting from credit reduction for unrepaid advances to the State of Michigan. Enter the wages included on line 5 for Michigan and multiply by .011. (See the separate Instructions for Form 940.) Enter the credit reduction amount here and in Part II, line 5: Michigan wages ______ × .011 = ... ▶ **6**

Be sure to complete both sides of this return and sign in the space provided on the back. Cat. No. 11234O Form **940** (1992)

EXHIBIT 73

INTERNAL REVENUE SERVICE CIRCULAR E

MARRIED Persons—**SEMIMONTHLY** Payroll Period
(For Wages Paid in 1995)

If the wages are–		And the number of withholding allowances claimed is—										
At least	But less than	0	1	2	3	4	5	6	7	8	9	10
		The amount of income tax to be withheld is—										
$0	$270	0	0	0	0	0	0	0	0	0	0	0
270	280	1	0	0	0	0	0	0	0	0	0	0
280	290	3	0	0	0	0	0	0	0	0	0	0
290	300	4	0	0	0	0	0	0	0	0	0	0
300	310	6	0	0	0	0	0	0	0	0	0	0
310	320	7	0	0	0	0	0	0	0	0	0	0
320	330	9	0	0	0	0	0	0	0	0	0	0
330	340	10	0	0	0	0	0	0	0	0	0	0
340	350	12	0	0	0	0	0	0	0	0	0	0
350	360	13	0	0	0	0	0	0	0	0	0	0
360	370	15	0	0	0	0	0	0	0	0	0	0
370	380	16	1	0	0	0	0	0	0	0	0	0
380	390	18	2	0	0	0	0	0	0	0	0	0
390	400	19	4	0	0	0	0	0	0	0	0	0
400	410	21	5	0	0	0	0	0	0	0	0	0
410	420	22	7	0	0	0	0	0	0	0	0	0
420	430	24	8	0	0	0	0	0	0	0	0	0
430	440	25	10	0	0	0	0	0	0	0	0	0
440	450	27	11	0	0	0	0	0	0	0	0	0
450	460	28	13	0	0	0	0	0	0	0	0	0
460	470	30	14	0	0	0	0	0	0	0	0	0
470	480	31	16	0	0	0	0	0	0	0	0	0
480	490	33	17	2	0	0	0	0	0	0	0	0
490	500	34	19	3	0	0	0	0	0	0	0	0
500	520	37	21	5	0	0	0	0	0	0	0	0
520	540	40	24	8	0	0	0	0	0	0	0	0
540	560	43	27	11	0	0	0	0	0	0	0	0
560	580	46	30	14	0	0	0	0	0	0	0	0
580	600	49	33	17	2	0	0	0	0	0	0	0
600	620	52	36	20	5	0	0	0	0	0	0	0
620	640	55	39	23	8	0	0	0	0	0	0	0
640	660	58	42	26	11	0	0	0	0	0	0	0
660	680	61	45	29	14	0	0	0	0	0	0	0
680	700	64	48	32	17	1	0	0	0	0	0	0
700	720	67	51	35	20	4	0	0	0	0	0	0
720	740	70	54	38	23	7	0	0	0	0	0	0
740	760	73	57	41	26	10	0	0	0	0	0	0
760	780	76	60	44	29	13	0	0	0	0	0	0
780	800	79	63	47	32	16	0	0	0	0	0	0
800	820	82	66	50	35	19	3	0	0	0	0	0
820	840	85	69	53	38	22	6	0	0	0	0	0
840	860	88	72	56	41	25	9	0	0	0	0	0
860	880	91	75	59	44	28	12	0	0	0	0	0
880	900	94	78	62	47	31	15	0	0	0	0	0
900	920	97	81	65	50	34	18	3	0	0	0	0
920	940	100	84	68	53	37	21	6	0	0	0	0
940	960	103	87	71	56	40	24	9	0	0	0	0
960	980	106	90	74	59	43	27	12	0	0	0	0
980	1,000	109	93	77	62	46	30	15	0	0	0	0
1,000	1,020	112	96	80	65	49	33	18	2	0	0	0
1,020	1,040	115	99	83	68	52	36	21	5	0	0	0
1,040	1,060	118	102	86	71	55	39	24	8	0	0	0
1,060	1,080	121	105	89	74	58	42	27	11	0	0	0
1,080	1,100	124	108	92	77	61	45	30	14	0	0	0
1,100	1,120	127	111	95	80	64	48	33	17	2	0	0
1,120	1,140	130	114	98	83	67	51	36	20	5	0	0
1,140	1,160	133	117	101	86	70	54	39	23	8	0	0
1,160	1,180	136	120	104	89	73	57	42	26	11	0	0
1,180	1,200	139	123	107	92	76	60	45	29	14	0	0
1,200	1,220	142	126	110	95	79	63	48	32	17	1	0
1,220	1,240	145	129	113	98	82	66	51	35	20	4	0
1,240	1,260	148	132	116	101	85	69	54	38	23	7	0
1,260	1,280	151	135	119	104	88	72	57	41	26	10	0
1,280	1,300	154	138	122	107	91	75	60	44	29	13	0
1,300	1,320	157	141	125	110	94	78	63	47	32	16	0
1,320	1,340	160	144	128	113	97	81	66	50	35	19	3
1,340	1,360	163	147	131	116	100	84	69	53	38	22	6
1,360	1,380	166	150	134	119	103	87	72	56	41	25	9
1,380	1,400	169	153	137	122	106	90	75	59	44	28	12
1,400	1,420	172	156	140	125	109	93	78	62	47	31	15

Page 44

W-4 is kept by the employer. The employee is also required to complete a similar form for the state. That form is the HW-4 (see Exhibit 51, chapter 14).

Based on the claimed exemptions, the employer will deduct the required tax using the appropriate tax tables or tax calculation provided by the federal and state governments. The federal tax tables used to deduct the required federal payroll taxes are provided in an Internal Revenue Service Circular E, *Employer's Tax Guide,* and a similar guide is provided by the State of Hawaii in their *Employer's Tax Guide* for state taxes. Exhibits 73 and 74 show the federal and state tax tables for a married person receiving a

EXHIBIT 74

HAWAII DEPARTMENT OF TAXATION, BOOKLET A, EMPLOYER'S TAX GUIDE

***Semimonthly* PAYROLL PERIOD** – continued
For Calendar Year 1991
***Married* PERSONS**

WAGES ARE		NUMBER OF WITHHOLDING EXEMPTIONS CLAIMED										
AT LEAST	BUT LESS THAN	0	1	2	3	4	5	6	7	8	9	10 or more
		AMOUNT OF INCOME TAX TO BE WITHHELD										
301	312	11.90	9.10	6.50	4.60	2.80	1.80	.90	.10			
312	323	12.70	9.80	7.20	5.00	3.30	2.00	1.20	.30			
323	334	13.50	10.50	7.90	5.40	3.70	2.20	1.40	.50			
334	345	14.30	11.10	8.50	5.90	4.10	2.50	1.60	.70			
345	356	15.10	11.90	9.20	6.60	4.60	2.90	1.80	.90	.10		
356	367	15.90	12.70	9.80	7.20	5.00	3.30	2.00	1.20	.30		
367	378	16.70	13.50	10.50	7.90	5.50	3.70	2.30	1.40	.50		
378	389	17.50	14.30	11.20	8.60	6.00	4.20	2.50	1.60	.70		
389	400	18.30	15.10	12.00	9.20	6.60	4.60	2.90	1.80	1.00	.10	
400	411	19.10	15.90	12.80	9.90	7.30	5.10	3.30	2.00	1.20	.30	
411	422	19.90	16.70	13.60	10.50	7.90	5.50	3.80	2.30	1.40	.50	
422	433	20.70	17.50	14.40	11.20	8.60	6.00	4.20	2.50	1.60	.80	
433	444	21.50	18.30	15.20	12.00	9.30	6.70	4.60	2.90	1.80	1.00	.10
444	455	22.20	19.10	16.00	12.80	9.90	7.30	5.10	3.30	2.10	1.20	.30
455	470	23.30	20.00	16.90	13.80	10.70	8.10	5.60	3.90	2.30	1.50	.60
470	485	24.50	21.10	18.00	14.90	11.70	9.00	6.40	4.50	2.70	1.80	.90
485	500	25.70	22.20	19.10	15.90	12.80	9.90	7.30	5.10	3.30	2.10	1.20
500	515	26.90	23.40	20.20	17.00	13.90	10.80	8.20	5.70	3.90	2.40	1.50
515	530	28.10	24.60	21.30	18.10	15.00	11.80	9.10	6.50	4.50	2.80	1.80
530	545	29.30	25.80	22.30	19.20	16.10	12.90	10.00	7.40	5.10	3.40	2.10
545	560	30.50	27.00	23.50	20.30	17.20	14.00	10.90	8.30	5.70	4.00	2.40
560	575	31.70	28.20	24.70	21.40	18.20	15.10	12.00	9.20	6.60	4.60	2.90
575	590	32.90	29.40	25.90	22.50	19.30	16.20	13.00	10.10	7.50	5.20	3.50
590	605	34.10	30.60	27.10	23.70	20.40	17.30	14.10	11.00	8.40	5.80	4.10
605	620	35.30	31.80	28.30	24.90	21.50	18.40	15.20	12.10	9.30	6.70	4.70
620	635	36.50	33.00	29.50	26.10	22.60	19.40	16.30	13.20	10.20	7.60	5.30
635	650	37.70	34.20	30.70	27.30	23.80	20.50	17.40	14.30	11.10	8.50	5.90
650	665	38.90	35.40	31.90	28.50	25.00	21.60	18.50	15.30	12.20	9.40	6.80
665	680	40.10	36.60	33.10	29.70	26.20	22.70	19.60	16.40	13.30	10.30	7.70
680	695	41.30	37.80	34.30	30.90	27.40	23.90	20.70	17.50	14.40	11.20	8.60
695	710	42.50	39.00	35.50	32.10	28.60	25.10	21.70	18.60	15.50	12.30	9.50
710	725	43.70	40.20	36.70	33.30	29.80	26.30	22.80	19.70	16.50	13.40	10.40
725	740	44.90	41.40	37.90	34.50	31.00	27.50	24.10	20.80	17.60	14.50	11.40
740	755	46.10	42.60	39.10	35.70	32.20	28.70	25.30	21.90	18.70	15.60	12.40
755	770	47.30	43.80	40.30	36.90	33.40	29.90	26.50	23.00	19.80	16.70	13.50
770	785	48.50	45.00	41.50	38.10	34.60	31.10	27.70	24.20	20.90	17.80	14.60
785	800	49.70	46.20	42.70	39.30	35.80	32.30	28.90	25.40	22.00	18.80	15.70
800	815	50.90	47.40	43.90	40.50	37.00	33.50	30.10	26.60	23.10	19.90	16.80
815	830	52.10	48.60	45.10	41.70	38.20	34.70	31.30	27.80	24.30	21.00	17.90
830	845	53.30	49.80	46.30	42.90	39.40	35.90	32.50	29.00	25.50	22.10	19.00
845	860	54.50	51.00	47.50	44.10	40.60	37.10	33.70	30.20	26.70	23.30	20.10
860	875	55.70	52.20	48.70	45.30	41.80	38.30	34.90	31.40	27.90	24.50	21.10
875	890	56.90	53.40	49.90	46.50	43.00	39.50	36.10	32.60	29.10	25.70	22.20
890	905	58.10	54.60	51.10	47.70	44.20	40.70	37.30	33.80	30.30	26.90	23.40
		8.00% OF EXCESS OVER $905 PLUS										
905 & OVER		58.70	55.20	51.70	48.30	44.80	41.30	37.90	34.40	30.90	27.50	24.00

37

paycheck twice a month. From these tables it is easy to calculate the amount of tax to be withheld based on the marital status, the times per month the employee is paid, the exemptions claimed, and the wages paid.

To illustrate, if your employee is paid twice a month, is married, claims one exemption, and had total wages of $900 for the first two weeks we would calculate the federal and state withholding tax as follows:

1. Using the federal tax circular turn to "semimonthly payroll period; married persons."
2. On that table (Exhibit 73) look for wages of $900.

3. Using our exhibit, that wage falls in the category of "wages are at least" $900 "but less than" $920.
4. Read across the columns of exemptions until you reach the column for one exemption. The figure in that column is $81. That is the amount you will deduct as federal withholding tax for this paycheck.

Using the State of Hawaii *Employer's Tax Guide* (Exhibit 74), you follow the same process to determine the State of Hawaii withholding tax. You should arrive at the figure of $54.60.

Every month you total separately all your federal and state withholding and determine if you need submit them for payment based on the amount you accumulate. Before you can determine if you should pay the federal tax weekly, monthly, or quarterly, you must calculate the social security liability.

Social Security (FICA)

The Social Security Tax (also known as FICA) is a percentage of the employee's gross salary. This percentage will vary in different years as prescribed by federal law. The current percentage for 1995 is 7.65% of gross payroll (6.2% for FICA and 1.45% for Medicare).

Consequently, for 1995, the employer will be required to deduct for FICA 7.65 percent of each employee's gross pay on each paycheck. Similar to unemployment insurance, there is a limit on wages subject to this deduction for each employee. This limit for FICA was $61,200 for wages in 1995 and $135,000 in wages for Medicare.

To calculate the FICA deduction for our sample payroll of $465, we would multiple that wage times 7.65 percent (.0765). Our payroll deductions would look like this:

Employee: Shirley Jurich
Pay period: 1/15/95–1/31/95

Total gross salary		$900.00
Less deductions		
FICA (6.2%)	55.80	
Medicare (1.45%)	13.05	
Federal Withholding Tax (FWT)	81.00	
State Withholding Tax (SWT)	54.60	
Total deductions		204.45
Net pay		$695.55

Congratulations, you have just done payroll.

Paying Federal Withholding Tax and FICA Taxes

As a federal tax collector you have withheld federal payroll taxes and FICA taxes from your employee's pay to deposit to the federal government. In addition, you have to pay a tax matching your employee's FICA contribution—the matching employer's FICA. That is to say, when you finally pay the FWT and the FICA tax to the federal government, you will pay:

Federal Withholding Tax + 2 times FICA and Medicare Tax.

When to pay this total tax depends on how much you owe. These are your alternatives (there are other exceptions that the Internal Revenue Service or your accountant can answer):

Amount of Tax Due	When Due
1. A business has reported $50,000 or less in payroll tax liability in the prior four quarters.	Pay by the 15th day of the following month.
2. Over $50,000 in payroll tax liability in the prior four quarters.	A firm will make deposits up to semi weekly.

Once you have computed the tax amount you owe, you pay this tax using the Federal Tax Deposit Coupon—checking in the block "941" (see Exhibit 71). Here is an example assuming that the payment is for the first month:

FWT collected for the month	$820
FICA collected for the month	$239
Medicare collected for the month	$56

Total taxes due:

$$\text{FWT} + 2 \times \text{FICA} + \text{Medicare}$$

$$\$820 + 2 \times \$295 = \$1{,}410$$

Exhibit 75 shows this payment on the federal tax deposit coupon. This coupon is normally paid to your bank which in turns pays the federal government. The government will also mail you Form 941, "Employer's Quarterly Federal Tax Return," which will request a summary of these payments (Exhibit 76).

EXHIBIT 75

FEDERAL DEPOSIT COUPON

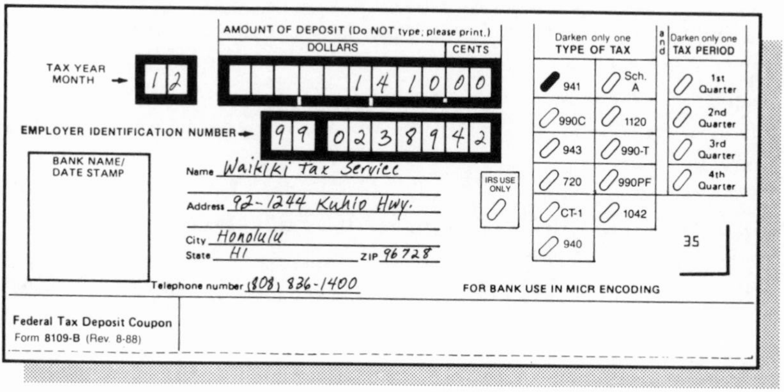

AMOUNT OF DEPOSIT (Do NOT type; please print.)

DOLLARS | CENTS

TAX YEAR MONTH → 12

1410 | 00

EMPLOYER IDENTIFICATION NUMBER → 99 0238942

BANK NAME/ DATE STAMP

Name Waikiki Tax Service

Address 92-1244 Kuhio Hwy.

City Honolulu

State HI ZIP 96728

Telephone number (808) 836-1400

IRS USE ONLY

Darken only one TYPE OF TAX: 941, Sch. A, 990C, 1120, 943, 990-T, 720, 990PF, CT-1, 1042, 940

Darken only one TAX PERIOD: 1st Quarter, 2nd Quarter, 3rd Quarter, 4th Quarter

35

FOR BANK USE IN MICR ENCODING

Federal Tax Deposit Coupon
Form 8109-B (Rev. 8-88)

The government frowns upon keeping money owed it. The penalties for late filing are expensive. A number of penalties and interest charges may be assessed for late or nonpayment of this tax. From the Internal Revenue Service, Notice 746 (Rev. 7-86), here is a sampling of the different penalties. First the disclaimer:

> Elimination of Penalties—Reasonable Cause. Except for certain cases of the Underpayment of Estimated Tax Penalty and for Fraud and Negligence penalties, the law provides that the penalties explained below can be removed if you have an acceptable reason. If you believe that you have a good reason but have not yet sent us an explanation, please send it to us.

Some of the penalty notices you can receive are:

> 01 Filing and Paying Late—A combined penalty has been added because your return was filed late and the tax was not paid when due. The penalty is 5 percent of the unpaid tax for each month (or part of a month) the return was late. It cannot be more than 25 percent of the tax paid late. If your return was more than 90 days late, the minimum penalty is the lesser of $100 or 100 percent of the balance of the tax due on the return.
>
> 09 Interest—Interest is figured from the due date of the return to the date of full payment or to the date of this notice.

There are 31 types of penalties and notices that are listed on the information bulletin.

Paying the Hawaii State Withholding Tax (SWT)

The formula for paying the SWT is simply to total the tax withheld and to pay it monthly. Returns may be filed quarterly if the withholding tax liability for the taxable year does not exceed $1,000. The state provides you a reporting form (HW-14) for this purpose. Exhibit 77 assumes that Windward TV files a monthly return.

EXHIBIT 76

EMPLOYER'S QUARTERLY FEDERAL TAX RETURN
(FORM 941)

Form **941** (Rev. January 1993) Department of the Treasury Internal Revenue Service

4141

Employer's Quarterly Federal Tax Return

▶ See separate instructions for information on completing this form.
Please type or print.

Enter state code for state in which deposits made . ▶ (see page 2 of instructions).

Name (as distinguished from trade name) — Date quarter ended
Trade name, if any — Employer identification number
Address (number and street) — City, state, and ZIP code

OMB No. 1545-0029
Expires 1-31-96

T
FF
FD
FP
I
T

If address is different from prior return, check here ▶ ☐

IRS Use

If you do not have to file returns in the future, check here . ▶ ☐ Date final wages paid . . . ▶

If you are a seasonal employer, see **Seasonal employers** on page 1 and check here ▶ ☐

1 Number of employees (except household) employed in the pay period that includes March 12th ▶

2 Total wages and tips subject to withholding, plus other compensation 2
3 Total income tax withheld from wages, tips, pensions, annuities, sick pay, gambling, etc. . 3
4 Adjustment of withheld income tax for preceding quarters of calendar year (see instructions) . . 4
5 Adjusted total of income tax withheld (line 3 as adjusted by line 4—see instructions) . . . 5
6a Taxable social security wages . . . . . $ × 12.4% (.124) = 6a
b Taxable social security tips . . . . . $ × 12.4% (.124) = 6b
7 Taxable Medicare wages and tips . . . $ × 2.9% (.029) = 7
8 Total social security and Medicare taxes (add lines 6a, 6b, and 7) 8
9 Adjustment of social security and Medicare taxes (see instructions for required explanation) . 9
10 Adjusted total of social security and Medicare taxes (line 8 as adjusted by line 9—see instructions) 10
11 Backup withholding (see instructions) 11
12 Adjustment of backup withholding tax for preceding quarters of calendar year 12
13 Adjusted total of backup withholding (line 11 as adjusted by line 12) 13
14 **Total taxes** (add lines 5, 10, and 13) 14
15 Advance earned income credit (EIC) payments made to employees, if any 15
16 Net taxes (subtract line 15 from line 14). **This should equal line 20, col. (d), below or line D of Schedule B** (plus line D of Schedule A if you treated backup withholding as a separate liability) 16
17 **Total deposits for quarter,** including overpayment applied from a prior quarter, from your records 17
18 **Balance due** (subtract line 17 from line 16). This should be less than $500. Pay to the Internal Revenue Service 18
19 **Overpayment,** if line 17 is more than line 16, enter excess here ▶ $ ________ and check if to be: ☐ Applied to next return **OR** ☐ Refunded.
20 **Monthly Summary of Federal Tax Liability. If line 16 is less than $500, you need not complete line 20.** If you are a monthly depositor, summarize your monthly tax liability below. If you are a semiweekly depositor or have accumulated a tax liability of $100,000 or more on any day, attach Schedule B (Form 941) and check here (see instructions) . . . . ▶ ☐

	(a) First month	(b) Second month	(c) Third month	(d) Total for quarter
Liability for month				

Sign Here Under penalties of perjury, I declare that I have examined this return, including accompanying schedules and statements, and to the best of my knowledge and belief, it is true, correct, and complete.
Signature ▶ Print Your Name and Title ▶ Date ▶

For Paperwork Reduction Act Notice, see page 1 of separate instructions. Cat. No. 17001Z Form **941** (Rev. 1-93)

☆ U.S. GOVERNMENT PRINTING OFFICE: 1993 339-478

The penalties for late and nonpayment of the SWT are similar to those of the federal government.

Business Income Tax

If you are fortunate enough to make a profit by year's end, you must pay a tax on that. The process is much too complicated to address here.

In chapter 4 we discussed the legal structure of businesses (sole proprietorship, partnership, and corporation). One of the major differences in

EXHIBIT 77

WINDWARD TV SHOP MONTHLY HAWAII WITHHOLDING TAX RETURN

Form HW-14
(Rev. 1992)

STATE OF HAWAII
DEPARTMENT OF TAXATION
WITHHOLDING TAX RETURN
CALENDAR YEAR 1992

DO NOT WRITE IN THIS AREA **30**

NAME:

HAWAII WITHHOLDING ID. NO. 1 0 2 8 8 7 2 4

☒ **MONTH OF** December **19** 92
(Do not combine your reporting for more than one month, if filing monthly.)

☐ **QUARTER OF** ______ **19** ___
(Do not combine your reporting for more than one quarter, if filing quarterly.)

♣ If your annual withholding tax liability is $100,000 or more, this return must be filed on or before the **10th** day of the month following the close of the filing period.
♣ If your annual withholding tax liability is less than $100,000, this return must be filed on or before the **15th** day of the month following the close of the filing period.

(NOTE: Enter "0" if no wages were paid or no tax withheld. Otherwise, complete this return and enclose applicable payment.)

• ATTACH CHECK OR MONEY ORDER HERE •

MAKE YOUR CHECK OR MONEY ORDER PAYABLE TO "HAWAII STATE TAX COLLECTOR" AND PAYABLE IN U.S. DOLLARS DRAWN ON ANY U.S. BANK.
WRITE YOUR HAWAII WITHHOLDING ID. NO. ON THE CHECK.

TOTAL WAGES PAID (include COLA)		8,150	00
TOTAL TAXES WITHHELD		352	21
FOR LATE FILING ONLY	PENALTY		
	INTEREST		
AMOUNT OF PAYMENT "PAY IN U.S. DOLLARS ONLY"		352	21

I declare under the penalties set forth in Chapter 235 HRS, that this is a true and correct return, prepared in accordance with the provisions of the Withholding Tax Laws and the rules issued thereunder.

Debbie Miura — SIGNATURE
1/8/93 — DATE
PARTNER — TITLE

THIS SPACE FOR DATE RECEIVED STAMP

MAILING ADDRESSES

OAHU DISTRICT OFFICE
P.O. BOX 3827
HONOLULU, HI 96812-3827

MAUI DISTRICT OFFICE
P.O. BOX 923
WAILUKU, HI 96793-0923

HAWAII DISTRICT OFFICE
P.O. BOX 1377
HILO, HI 96721-1377

KAUAI DISTRICT OFFICE
P.O. BOX 1686
LIHUE, HI 96766-5686

FORM HW-14 **30**

legal business structures is how each pays its taxes. Sole proprietorships and partnerships pay no business income taxes. Any income or loss is added to the personal tax return of the proprietor or the partners. Only corporations will be subject to business income taxes. Your accountant will help you.

This chapter has surveyed the taxes that affect you as a business owner. The two questions we reviewed about these business taxes were: (1) how do you calculate the tax you owe and (2) when do you pay it.

FICA	Percentage of employee's salary plus matching employer portion	When combined with FWT liability if tax is less than: $500 in any quarter pay by last day of following month from end of quarter; is more than $500 but less than $3,000 for any month pay by 15th day of following month; more than $3,000 due in any month pay that month.
SWT	State tax tables	By 15th day of following month for each month; if tax liability for entire year does not exceed $1,000 can file quarterly.
FUTA	.8% of employee's salary to $7,000	Quarterly
Income Tax	Based on a percentage of income	Corporate returns due March 30. Sole proprietorship and partnership returns due April 15.
Hawaii Unemployment Tax	Based on percentage of gross salary	Quarterly

Additional Reading

Bock, Russell S. *Taxes of Hawaii.* Honolulu: Crossroads Publishers. (Published annually).

Dyer, Mary Lee. 1976. *Practical Bookkeeping for the Small Business.* Chicago: Contemporary Books.

US Dept. of the Treasury. Internal Revenue Service. *Tax Guide for Small Business.* Publication 334.

Appendix A

A Sample Business Plan

The business plan is a roadmap for a business. It has two purposes: (1) to provide a comprehensive overview of the business for the businessowners and managers and (2) to act as a sales tool for securing initial or additional funds.

A business plan must be based on your realistic answers to tough questions. The three steps in writing a business plan are: (1) asking the right questions; (2) giving realistic answers; (3) writing a plan based on your answers. To illustrate, let us write a business plan for Windward TV Shop. Steps 1 and 2 are combined below. The answers to the questions apply to Windward TV Shop. To develop your own business plan answer the questions as they may apply to you.

Asking the Right Questions and Giving Realistic Answers

Company Background

1. *What is the name of the business?* Windward TV Shop.
2. *Does the business use any other names?* No.
3. *Is the business a sole proprietorship, a partnership, or a corporation?* A partnership.
4. *When will the business open?* On June 1 to take advantage of the Christmas season.
5. *Is this a new or existing business?* A new business.
6. *What industry is the business in?* Consumer electronics. We plan to sell televisions, video recorders, and hi-fi equipment.
7. *What does the business specialize in?* Retail sales and repair of consumer electronics.
8. *What does the business hope to achieve?* The business will fill a void by offering a full line of high-end video equipment and video accessory prod-

ucts that are not now available in the area. In addition, special distributor arrangements have been negotiated to offer a new type of custom-installed audio/video system.

9. *Where is the business principally located?* We are looking at a site in the Kalia Shopping Center.

Business Principals and Business Management

1. *Who are the principal owners of the business?* Joe Ganahl is the majority partner. Debbie Miura is the minority partner. It is a general partnership.

2. *What are their educational and business backgrounds?* Joe Ganahl graduated from the University of Hawaii in Business Administration. He was a sales representative for four years in the consumer electronics industry. Prior to that he worked as a salesperson in a stereo store.

Debbie Miura graduated from Leeward Community College in business. She is an accounting clerk and supervisor in a department store. She has been a video enthusiast for five years. She has known Joe Ganahl for six years.

3. *Have any of the principals owned a business before?* No, but Joe Ganahl was a manager in a stereo store for two years. In this capacity he acted as a sales person, helped order merchandise, and ran internal operations.

4. *What background in the business's industry does each principal have?* See above.

5. *Who will be the principal executives or managers?* Joe Ganahl will be the principal manager. Debbie Miura will work part-time.

6. *Are any of the owners going to be full-time managers?* Joe will be a full-time manager. Debbie will draw no salary from the business for the first two years, but she will be an advising partner and will establish and maintain the bookkeeping system.

7. *What are the educational and employment backgrounds of the executives and managers if they are not the owners?* Not applicable.

8. *Are there any other key employees?* Ted Adres will be the chief technician.

9. *How do you think the skills of the business owners will contribute to the success of the business?* Joe's industry background should complement Debbie's financial and record-keeping background.

10. *In which areas do the businessowners lack expertise?* Running a business; raising capital.

Your Market

1. *How big is the national market for your business?* In 1987, the consumer electronics industry reported retail sales of $35 billion. The fastest growing segment of the market was video products. Unit sales to retailers of such items as color televisions, videocassette recorders, and cameras set all time records in 1986. Color television sets continued as the industry's largest

dollar value product, with estimated sales of more than $8.5 billion, while the sales of videocassette recorders climbed to $7 billion in 1986, a 100 percent increase from the year before.

2. *How big is the Hawaii market?* Current data suggest that Hawaii has 0.3 percent of the national consumer electronics market. At that estimate, the Hawaii market should be $25,500,000 for color televisions and $21,000,000 for video recorders. The windward area of Oahu represents 11 percent of the Hawaii population, therefore the sales potential of this area for color televisions and video equipment is estimated at $5,000,000.

3. *Is the industry growing?* The consumer electronics industry has grown at a rate of 8 percent in the past two years, color televisions 6 percent, and video recorders 100 percent.

4. *What are the major trends in the industry?* Current data suggest that certain segments of the consumer electronics industry have experienced a decline in sales in the past couple of years. Sales of products such as telephones and personal computers experienced problems in growth, however, color televisions and video recorders showed sharp increases in growth.

5. *What is your geographic market?* Kailua and Kaneohe on the windward side of Oahu.

6. *What is your universe of customers?* The 1980 census showed that Kaneohe had a resident population of 35,553 with 9,698 households. Kailua had a resident population of 41,291 with 12,099 households. The median household income was about $28,500. Also, approximately 19,000 military personnel in 5,200 households live at the Kaneohe marine base. With this demographic distribution we estimate that 25 percent of the households will be shopping for our product line.

7. *Of this universe which ones are your target customers?* Our target customers are going to be the households in Kaneohe, at the Kaneohe marine base, and in Kailua.

8. *From whom are these customers receiving their products and services now?* Four specialty sales and service shops, two repair-only shops, and two department stores. In addition, the Kaneohe marine base has a base exchange which offers similar electronic equipment at discount prices. Research shows that customers also will be willing to drive to Honolulu to shop for this product. Television repair service is offered by six other specialty shops and by local manufacturer service centers.

9. *What are the strengths of the competition?* The base exchange offers good selection at good prices. Military customers prefer shopping there. The two department stores offer good selection and financing and they accept charge cards. They have good store visibility and advertising. Four of the specialty stores offer repair service, financing, and charge card purchases. Two of the specialty shops offer only repair service.

10. *What is the market share of each competitor?* Military customers—70 percent of this market to the military exchange, 20 percent to department stores, and 10 percent of the 5,200 housholds, or 520, to the six specialty

shops. That equals 130 households per shop. Civilian customers—50 percent to the department stores or to the Honolulu competition and 50 percent to the windward area specialty stores.

Your Sales Program

1. *How will your business be superior to that of your competitors?* (1) Location will be one key advantage. None of the specialty shops is located in a major shopping center. (2) Product line—we will have the largest selection of video camera equipment and accessories in the area. (3) Service—no other competitor will have the custom audio/video installation that we offer.

2. *How do you plan to capture the target customers?* (1) By advertising our custom audio/video installation service and our video expertise. (2) By offering product lines not available in the military exchange system. (3) By offering a full line of video accessories not available in this area. (4) By holding video seminars for the public.

3. *What percentage of the target customers do you hope to capture?* The first year we hope to capture 8 to 10 percent of the Windward specialty store business or $124,000.

4. *Who are your major suppliers?* XYZ Electronic Corp. and Plantronics Corp.

5. *What is your sales program?* The first six months, from June to January, we intend to advertise our name and service abilities using regional advertising and direct mail. Two of these promotions will feature give-away custom video installations for which the manufacturers are donating the equipment. During the summer we will concentrate on video equipment promotions, and during the fall on custom television installation. Throughout the year we will advertise special video accessories and hold video camera classes.

6. *What is your purchasing program?* We plan to purchase half of our products from local distributors and the other half from the mainland. We have negotiated special product arrangements with some mainland manufacturers. To finance these purchases we have arranged credit lines with the manufacturers and with an inventory finance company.

7. *What do you think your competition will do when you open?* They probably will expand their video lines or accessories.

8. *What problems do you anticipate in your sales program?* Although we hope to sell exclusive video accessories to those who already own video equipment and custom audio/video systems to the more affluent resident, we feel that half of our sales for the first two years will comprise standard color TVs and video recorders. Until we can establish our custom installation program, we must depend on low margin products for our sales. The problem is, we will face stiff competition on similar brand products from all competitors.

9. *What is your market niche?* Our market niche is offering video specialty products and custom audio/video installations.

Business Location

1. *Describe your business location?* We will be located in a shopping center in the Kaneohe area. The store will be 750 square feet with an option to expand another 500 square feet within two years. Our lease is for three years with an option for an additional five years if we take the additional 500 square feet.

2. *How is your location an advantage in selling your target market?* The area has high visibility with convenient parking. The shopping center is well designed and maintained. Center figures show that they average 5,000 customers per day. We will be located next to a major drug store which has a high traffic pattern.

3. *What special equipment do you need?* The store itself will only need standard shelving. But we will require special test equipment for our repair service. That equipment will cost $5,000.

4. *What renovations will you need?* As part of the lease the landlord will paint the walls, install the required electricity, and put in a carpet. We will add display shelving ourselves and order an outside sign.

Internal Operations

1. *Who will handle your record-keeping systems?* Debbie Miura will set up and maintain the record-keeping systems to include: purchase orders, accounts payable, checkbook, cash disbursement, general ledgers, payroll, inventory, and taxes. We will be using a CPA to oversee our systems and to file our annual income taxes and year-end financial reports.

2. *What are her qualifications?* Debbie Miura is an accountant for a department store. In addition, Joe Ganahl was a manager for a electronics store and will implement some of the same systems for the new store.

Financial Plan

1. *What are your estimated start-up costs?* We estimate about $27,000 in start-up costs and in addition hope to have six months of estimated monthly operating costs for a total of about $67,000.

2. *What are your estimated monthly operating costs for the first year?* We estimate average monthly operating costs of $6,700.

3. *What assumptions are you making when you arrived at these figures?* (1) That we will have first year (June to December) sales totaling $124,000; (2) that 60 percent of our sales will occur in the last quarter; (3) that cost of goods will average 35 percent gross margin.

4. *What are your profit and loss estimates for the first year?* On sales of $124,000 we anticipate a loss of about $28,000 the first year. This loss will be due to start-up expenses, paydown of start-up loans, and low sales for the first six months.

5. *When do you think the business will break even?* By the end of our second year we anticipate sales up to $260,000. Operating profit is anticipated at $6,000 for that year.

6. *What will your balance sheet look like after the first year?* It will be typical of a consumer electronics store with 40 percent of assets in inventory and 60 percent of liabilities in supplier accounts receivable.

7. *How do you plan to raise the start-up capital?* $17,000 in owners equity and $50,000 in borrowed funds.

8. *If you borrow funds, how do you plan to repay them?* Our loan repayment program calls for installment payments during the first year to the bank. If cash flow justifies it, we plan to pay off the loan from Joe Ganahl's sister-in-law after twelve months.

9. *How do you plan to raise additional money if you need it?* Debbie Miura is prepared to cash out a company pension plan with an estimated value of $5,000 should additional funds be needed.

You may add any other questions that apply to your specific business. The more questions you ask the more refined your business plan should become. In most cases, the questions of your banker, accountant, or investors will help you further refine your business plan.

Write the Business Plan

The foregoing questions and the answers you supplied will provide you and your managers with a basic business plan. If, however, you must present the plan to a banker when seeking a loan, its form should resemble that of the sample plan that follows. You can do this yourself or hire a professional such as an accountant.

BUSINESS PLAN
WINDWARD TV SHOP

Company Background

The Windward TV Shop is a Hawaii partnership. Formed on January 14, 1987, the partnership plans to open a retail television/video sales and service store on June 1, 1987, in the Kalia Shopping Center serving the Kaneohe and Kailua area.

As a new business Windward TV Shop will offer retail television equipment, a full line of video products, and technical assistance not now available in the Windward area. The goal of the business is to become the premiere video and television store in the windward area.

Business Principals

As a general partnership, Windward TV Shop has two partners: Joseph Ganahl and Debbie Miura (see Exhibit A1 for resumes). Mr. Ganahl, 31, is a graduate of the University of Hawaii with a degree in Business Administration. For the past four years he has been a sales representative in the consumer electronics industry for a major Hawaii distributor. In this capacity, Mr. Ganahl worked with retail establishments in television and video products. He helped develop sales programs and trained store personnel. Prior to his job as a sales representative, he worked as a sales person and salesmanager for a large television and video store in Honolulu for three years. In this role, Mr. Ganahl handled store sales and operation.

Miss Miura, 27, is a graduate of Leeward Community College. For the past six years she has been an accounting supervisor for a large department store. In this capacity she has been responsible for cash receipts, accounts payable, and some general ledger posting. Although she has no professional experience in the consumer electronics field, Miss Miura has been a video enthusiast for five years and is quite knowledgeable about video and television equipment.

While neither business principal has ever owned a business before, both have had prior management experience. In preparation for this business venture, both principals have completed the Chamber of Commerce's entrepreneurial training course on small business and have conducted some market and business operation research with similar businesses on the island of Maui.

The current plan calls for Mr. Ganahl to be the principal managing partner and for Miss Miura to retain her position with the department store while working part-time in the business. Miss Miura will draw no salary for the first two years.

Mr. Ganahl will handle store operation, sales, purchasing, and inventory control. Miss Miura will set up and maintain all record-keeping systems, bookkeeping, and financial records. Mr. Ted Adres will handle technical repair and custom installation. He has worked for the past three years as a technician and video installer for a small service center.

The Industry

In 1986, the consumer electronics industry reported retail sales of $35 billion and experienced a 6 percent growth rate. The fastest growing segment of the consumer electronics industry was the video market. Unit sales to retailers of such items as color televisions, video cassette recorders, and video cameras set all-time records. As product categories, color televisions grew 8 percent and video recorders 100 percent during the past year. Color television sets continued as the industry's largest dollar-value product with estimated sales of more than $8 billion, while sales of video equipment doubled to $7 billion in 1986.

Current data suggest that Hawaii has 0.3 percent of the national market. The Hawaii market is estimated to be $25,500,000 for color televisions and $21,000,000 for video recorders (this data is supported by the Hawaiian Electric Company report, *Major Appliance, Air Conditioning, and Television Sales Report,* which reported sales of 63,624 color television sets and 51,795 video recorders in 1986).

Nationally, just under 17 million color television sets were sold in 1986—an all-time record. With color sets already in use in more than 90 percent of TV homes, it is not surprising that only about 10 percent of these sales were made to first-time buyers. Replacements accounted for an estimated 40 percent of sales. The largest market segment, representing 50 percent of sales, went to consumers buying an additional set.

The shape of what many feel will be the video of tomorrow has already appeared on the market in the form of audio/video systems. These systems, which combine high resolution screens, high fidelity sound systems, and large screens are expected by some to change home entertainment systems.

Although certain parts of the consumer electronics industry have experienced a decline in sales in the past couple of years, color televisions and video recorders have experienced sharp growth. Current data suggest that this growth will continue for the next couple of years.

The Market

The 1980 census showed that Kaneohe had a resident population of 35,553 with 9,698 households. Kailua had a resident population of 41,291 with 12,099 households. The median household income was about $28,500. There are also approximately 19,000 military personnel in 5,200 households on the Kaneohe marine base. With this demographic distribution we estimate that 10 percent of the households will be shopping for video and television products.

We base this estimate on the following assumptions: (1) The military market will shop 70 percent in the military exchange, 20 percent in department and Honolulu stores, and 10 percent in windward area specialty stores. (2) Of the rest of the market 50 percent will buy from Honolulu shops and department stores and 50 percent from windward specialty stores.

The Competition

Four other specialty sales-and-service shops like the proposed business exist in the geographic area. In addition, there are two repair shops and two department stores offering similar products and service. Discussions with area residents, businesses, and business organizations indicate that the area customers are willing to drive into Honolulu to shop for this product and service. The Kaneohe Marine Corps Air Station exchange offers similar television and video products.

The strengths of the competition are:

1. Kaneohe base exchange: (a) good selection of equipment; (b) strong customer loyalty; (c) good prices.
2. Department stores and Honolulu stores: (a) high visibility (b) extensive advertising; (c) good selection of equipment; (d) customer financing.
3. Specialty stores: (a) specialized service; (b) customer financing.

Market Niche

Although there are similar specialty stores, Windward TV Shop will offer three types of service not offered by the competition:

1. A full line of high-end video accessories;
2. Custom video expertise; and
3. Custom audio/video system installation.

To capture a significant portion of the current market, Windward TV Shop will offer the lowest prices on standard television and video recorders. To offset these low margin sales Windward TV Shop will market exclusive video accessories and custom installation at higher margins.

The Sales Program

Immediate high visibility will be a key factor in the sales program. The partnership has already arrived at tentative negotiations for space in the Kalia Shopping Center in Kaneohe. Advertising will be localized to the Kaneohe, Kailua, and Kahuku areas. A direct mail campaign is planned with a regional newspaper for the first six months. Several manufacturers have committed special advertising funds and give-away equipment for these promotions.

Because Windward TV Shop is to open for retail business in June 1987, first year sales will represent only six months of the calendar year. Sales for this first six-month period are projected at $124,000 (Exhibit A2). The first twelve-month plan is to capture 10 percent of the current market or about $209,000 in sales (Exhibit A3). The second year goal is to reach sales of $260,000. The overall goal is to be able to capture 20 percent of the specialty market or $400,000 by the third year.

Financial Planning

The sales plan, which calls for high visibility and low prices, stipulates low initial margins. To compensate for low initial sales and low margins, Windward TV Shop is planning to raise six months of operating expenses as part of its initial capitalization.

Current market research shows that most of the competition sells products at between 20 to 30 percent gross margin. The current plan is to sell televisions and video recorders as "leader" items at 15 to 20 percent gross margin and accessories and custom services at 40 to 70 percent. Projected estimates call for half of the sales to come from low margin products and total gross margins to average 35 percent.

At estimated sales of $124,000 the first calendar year, we estimate Windward TV Shop will lose about $28,000 (see Exhibit A2). We project the business will make a profit starting the second year of about $6,000 on sales of $260,000 (Exhibit A2).

Estimated monthly operating expenses are anticipated to average $6,700 during the first year (Exhibit A4). At that level, break even should occur at $18,000 of monthly sales with projected gross margins of 35 percent. The balance sheet after the first year is shown in Exhibit A5.

To start the business we will need about $67,000. This includes $27,000 start-up costs (Exhibit A6) and $39,000 to cover six months of operating costs (Exhibit A6). This estimated capitalization should allow the business to meet anticipated cash flow requirements (Exhibit A7) without additional loans during the first year.

To raise the total capitalization amount the partners plan to invest $17,000 of equity funds and to secure or borrow $50,000 in credit lines or loans (Exhibit A8).

Location

Because high visibility is important, Windward TV Shop will be located in a 750 square-foot space at the Kalia Shopping Center in Kaneohe. The space is next to a major drug store. Shopping center personnel estimate that traffic is currently 5,000 customers per day. This lease is for three years with an option for an additional five years. The lease cost is $1.50 per square foot gross rent for the first three years and $2.00 per square foot for the option period. Planned renovations are outlined in Exhibit A9 and will cost about $8,000.

EXHIBIT A1

RESUMÉS OF THE BUSINESS PARTNERS

Joseph Ganahl
1931 Kaleo Pl.
Honolulu, HI 96821
Phone: 836-1400

Employment History

1978 to 1981	Video salesperson/Sales manager, The Sound Choice
1981 to present	Sales representative for video and TV lines. Since 1984 Assistant Sales Manager, American Distributors.

Education

Kaimuki High School, graduated 1976
University of Hawaii, graduated 1970; BBA Business

Family

Married with no children. Volunteer Director with the Special Olympics. Wife is a receptionist with one of the local television stations.

References

Don Akutagawa
President
American Distribution
13-235 Kalani Dr.
Honolulu, HI 96823
Phone: 521-0000

Michael Columbo
Engineer
1348 25th St.
Honolulu, HI 96823
Phone: 857-1567

Debbie Miura
19-231 Ahua St.
Aiea, HI 96871
Phone: 488-5400

Employment History

1979 to 1982	Accountant, Pacific Teletec
1982 to 1985	Accountant, Sears Department Stores
1985 to present	Assistance Accounting Manager, Sears

Education

Aiea High School, graduated 1977
Leeward Community College, graduated 1979, AS in accounting

Family

Single. Representative of the Aiea Neighborhood Board.

References

Michael Ching	Barbara Barkley
President	Supervisor
Pacific Teletec	Sears Department Stores
18-546 Leokane St.	Honolulu, HI 96817
Waipahu, HI 96891	Phone: 523-9865

EXHIBIT A2

WINDWARD TV SHOP
ESTIMATED PROFIT AND LOSS STATEMENTS
FOR 1987 AND 1988

	1987*	1988
Sales	$124,000	$260,000
Less cost of goods sold	85,000	170,000
Gross profit	$39,000	$90,000
Operating Expenses		
Rent	$9,000	$13,500
Salaries	19,640	29,160
Office equipment	1,276	600
Depreciation	1,400	2,400
Utilities	700	2,400
Vehicle	1,370	1,200
Medical insurance	1,600	1,800
Insurance	1,500	1,900
Office supplies	550	600
Professional fees	1,400	1,500
Freight	1,500	2,000
Alarm	410	360
Maintenance/improvements	8,350	600
Advertising	4,000	6,000
Payroll taxes	1,820	3,200
General excise tax	4,984	10,400
Interest	700	1,200
Phone	2,046	3,336
Miscellaneous	5,725	1,200
TOTAL	$67,971	$83,356
Net operating profit (loss)	($28,971)	$6,644

*1987 estimates for seven months May to December.

EXHIBIT A3

WINDWARD TV SHOP
ESTIMATED PROFIT AND LOSS STATEMENT
FIRST 12 MONTHS

	May	Jun	Jul	Aug	Sept
Sales	$0	8,000	10,000	15,000	18,000
Less cost of goods sold		6,400	8,000	12,000	11,700
Gross profit	0	1,600	2,000	3,000	6,300
Operating expenses					
Rent	1,125	1,125	1,125	1,125	1,125
Salaries	1,580	2,580	2,580	2,580	2,580
Office equipment	926	50	50	50	50
Utilities	0	100	100	100	100
Vehicle	0	170	200	200	200
Medical insurance	200	200	200	200	200
Insurance	1,500	0	0	0	0
Office supplies	200	50	50	50	50
Professional fees	1,000	300	300	300	300
Freight	0	200	100	200	200
Alarm	200	30	30	30	30
Maintenance/ improvements	8,000	50	50	50	50
Advertising	0	1,000	700	200	300
Payroll taxes	0	260	260	260	260
General excise taxes	0	320	400	600	732
Interest	0	100	100	100	100
Phone	0	278	278	278	278
Miscellaneous	5,025	100	100	100	100
TOTAL	$19,756	6,913	6,623	6,423	6,655
Net operating profit (loss)	$(19,756)	(5,313)	(4,623)	(3,423)	(355)

Oct	Nov	Dec	Jan	Feb	Mar	Apr	Total
18,000	25,000	30,000	15,000	20,000	25,000	25,000	$209,000
11,700	16,200	18,500	10,500	13,000	16,300	16,300	140,600
6,300	8,800	11,500	4,500	7,000	8,700	8,700	68,400
1,125	1,125	1,125	1,125	1,125	1,125	1,125	13,500
2,580	2,580	2,580	2,580	2,580	2,580	2,580	29,960
50	50	50	50	50	50	50	1,475
100	100	100	100	100	100	100	1,100
200	200	200	200	200	200	200	2,170
200	200	200	200	200	200	200	2,400
0	0	0	0	0	0	0	1,500
50	50	50	50	50	50	50	750
300	300	300	300	300	300	300	4,300
200	300	300	100	100	200	200	2,100
30	30	30	30	30	30	30	530
50	50	50	50	50	50	50	8,550
300	500	1,000	200	200	200	200	4,800
260	260	260	260	260	260	260	2,860
732	1,000	1,200	400	800	1,000	1,000	8,184
100	100	100	100	100	100	100	1,100
278	278	278	278	278	278	278	3,058
100	100	100	100	100	100	100	6,125
6,655	7,223	7,923	6,123	6,523	6,823	6,823	94,463
(355)	1,577	3,577	(1,623)	477	1,877	1,877	(26,063)

EXHIBIT A4

WINDWARD TV SHOP ESTIMATED MONTHLY OPERATING COSTS	Cost
Rent	$1,125
Salaries	$2,580
Office equipment (copy machine lease)	50
Utilities	100
Office supplies	50
Vehicle	200
Medical insurance	200
Professional fees	300
Freight	200
Alarm	30
Repairs and maintenance	50
Advertising	300
Payroll taxes	260
General excise tax	800
Interest (bank loan)	100
Phone	278
Miscellaneous	$100
TOTAL	$6,723

EXHIBIT A5

WINDWARD TV SHOP
ESTIMATED FIRST-YEAR BALANCE SHEET
DECEMBER 31, 19__

Assets		
Cash		$18,000
Equipment		18,000
Inventory		25,000
TOTAL ASSETS		$61,000
Liabilities		
Accounts payable	$ 2,000	
Supplier accounts payable	19,500	
Bank loan	4,700	
TOTAL LIABILITIES	$26,200	
Owner's equity	$34,800	
TOTAL LIABILITIES AND NET WORTH		$61,000

EXHIBIT A6

WINDWARD TV SHOP
ESTIMATED START-UP COSTS

	Cost
Rent (first month plus rental deposit)	$ 2,250
500 square feet at $2.25/sq ft = $1,125	
Rental deposit = $1,125	
Salaries	1,580
Owner = $800	
Part-time clerk = $320 ($5.00/hr)	
Part-time technician = $460 ($6.00/hr)	
Part-time salesman—not hired yet	
Office equipment	926
2 desks = $338	
2 chairs = $178	
File cabinet = $160	
Typewriter = $200	
Calculator = $50	
Improvements	8,000
Sign = $300	
Electrical = $1,500	
Office partition = $1,000	
Display shelves = $5,000	
Painting = $200 (painted by owner)	
Service equipment	5,000
Digital test equipment = $2,189	
Oscilloscope = $1,478	
Hand tools = $745	
Parts = $588	
Office supplies	200
Vehicle (will use own car)	0
Legal fees	500
Accounting fees	500
Insurance (one-year premiums)	1,500
Medical insurance (first month)	100
Government fees	75
Inventory	5,000
Display models (10 @ $250) = $2,500	
Back-up stock (10 @ $250) = $2,500	
Miscellaneous	2,000
TOTAL	$27,631

EXHIBIT A7

WINDWARD TV SHOP

ESTIMATED CASH FLOW FOR FIRST 12 MONTHS

	May	Jun	Jul	Aug	Sept
Sales receipts	0	8,000	10,000	15,000	18,000
Cash disbursements					
Cost of goods sold	0	0	9,400	8,000	12,000
Rent	1,125	1,125	1,125	1,125	1,125
Salaries	1,580	2,580	2,580	2,580	2,580
Office equipment	926	50	50	50	50
Utilities	0	100	100	100	100
Vehicle	0	170	200	200	200
Medical insurance	200	200	200	200	200
Insurance	1,500	0	0	0	0
Office supplies	200	50	50	50	50
Professional fees	1,000	300	300	300	300
Freight	0	200	100	200	200
Alarm	200	30	30	30	30
Maintenance/ improve.	8,000	50	50	50	50
Advertising	0	1,000	700	200	300
Payroll taxes	0	260	260	260	260
General excise tax	0	320	400	600	732
Interest	0	100	100	100	100
Phone	0	278	278	278	278
Miscellaneous	5,025	100	100	100	100
Loan repayment	0	900	900	900	900
Total cash disbursements	19,756	7,813	16,923	15,323	19,555
Net cash flow	(19,756)	187	(6,923)	(323)	(1,555)
Cash on hand	32,000				
Opening balance	32,000	12,244	12,431	5,508	5,185
+ net cash flow	(19,756)	187	(6,923)	(323)	(1,555)
TOTAL NEW CASH BALANCE	12,244	12,431	5,508	5,185	3,630

ASSUMPTIONS: (1) net 30-day terms; (2) $3,000 of display equipment purchased in June; (3) received $1,000 in equipment discount for December purchases—cooperative advertising; (4) repay $5,000 loan to Joe Ganahl's sister-in-law in April 1988.

Oct	Nov	Dec	Jan	Feb	Mar	Apr	Total
18,000	25,000	30,000	15,000	20,000	25,000	25,000	209,000
11,700	11,700	16,200	18,500	7,000	13,000	16,300	123,800
1,125	1,125	1,125	1,125	1,125	1,125	1,125	13,500
2,580	2,580	2,580	2,580	2,580	2,580	2,580	29,960
50	50	50	50	50	50	50	1,476
100	100	100	100	100	100	100	1,100
200	200	200	200	200	200	200	2,170
200	200	200	200	200	200	200	2,400
0	0	0	0	0	0	0	1,500
50	50	50	50	50	50	50	750
300	300	300	300	300	300	300	4,300
200	300	300	100	100	200	200	2,100
30	30	30	30	30	30	30	530
50	50	50	50	50	50	50	8,550
300	500	1,000	200	200	200	200	4,800
260	260	260	260	260	260	260	2,860
732	1,000	1,200	400	800	1,000	1,000	8,184
100	100	100	100	100	100	100	1,100
278	278	278	278	278	278	278	3,058
100	100	100	100	100	100	100	6,125
900	900	900	900	900	900	6,400	15,400
19,255	19,823	25,023	25,523	14,423	20,723	29,523	
(1,255)	5,177	4,977	(10,523)	5,577	4,277	(4,523)	
3,630	2,375	7,552	12,529	2,006	7,583	11,860	
(1,255)	5,177	4,977	(10,523)	5,577	4,277	(4,523)	
2,375	7,552	12,529	2,006	7,583	11,860	7,337	

EXHIBIT A8

Windward TV Shop Estimated Start-Up Capitalization	
Partners contribution	$17,000
Loans from relatives	15,000
Inventory loans	25,000
Bank loan	10,000
Total	$67,000

EXHIBIT A9

Windward TV Shop Estimated Site Renovation Costs	
Electrical	$1,500
Signs	300
Office partition	1,000
Display shelving	5,000
Paint	200
Total	$8,000

Appendix B
The Sample Loan Proposal

The loan proposal is derived from the business plan (appendix A). Presented together with the business plan to your bank or other loan sources, the loan proposal will:

1. Request a certain dollar amount;
2. Show why the loan is needed;
3. Show how the loan will be repaid.

To illustrate we will develop a bank loan request for a $10,000 one-year loan for Windward TV Shop using the business plan in appendix A. As with the business plan we must first answer some questions about the loan. Our answers will be for Windward TV Shop, but you will want to supply answers for your own business when you prepare your loan proposal.

Questions and Answers about a Loan

1. *What is the amount of money needed?* Windward TV Shop requests a bank loan of $10,000 for one year.

2. *What is the purpose of the loan?* The loan is needed for specialized test equipment and for store improvement (new display racks).

3. *Why do you need that exact amount?* Cost estimates:

Digital test equipment	$ 2,189
Oscilloscope	1,478
Hand tools	745
Parts	588
Display shelves	5,000
Total	$10,000

4. *What has been the recent sales performance of the business?* This will be a new business. We project first six-month sales of $124,000; first twelve-month sales of $209,000; and second year sales of $260,000.

5. *What has been the recent net profit or loss history of the business?* This is a new business with no history. We estimate that in the first calendar year from June to December the business will incur a loss of $28,000 from start-up expenses. Thereafter, projections call for a net profit of $6,000 in the second year.

6. *How is the loan to be repaid?* The request is for a 12-month loan to be repaid in 12 monthly installments. Income from sales will be used to make the monthly payments.

7. *What collateral will be used to secure the loan?* The bank will have first claim on all the assets of the business. In addition, Joe Ganahl will allow the bank a second mortgage on his real estate with an equity balance of $30,000.

8. *What other loans does the business have?* The business has two other loans and a credit line with an inventory finance company:

1. A loan from Mr. Sam Ganahl, father of Joe Ganahl. This two-year loan for $10,000 is payable in December 1989.
2. A loan of $5,000 from Mrs. Marjorie Helgeson, sister-in-law of Joe Ganahl. This one-year loan at 10 percent interest is due in April 1988. The partnership has an option to extend all or part of the repayment to April 1989.
3. A credit line of $23,000 has been established with an inventory finance company.

9. *Do any of these loans have a priority on the collateral pledged for this loan request?* No.

10. *How will this new loan affect the current debt ratio?* Of the estimated $67,000 in capitalization needed, the partners plan to invest $17,000 of equity and borrow the remaining $50,000—that equates to a debt-to-equity ratio of 2.94 to 1 (50,000/17,000). In other words, for every dollar of equity put into the business, $2.94 will be put in from a loan.

11. *How will the additional monthly obligation in overhead affect the cash flow of the business?* Cash flow projections for the 12 months of the loan show no difficulty in the repayment of the loan.

Write the Loan Proposal

The written loan proposal need not be long but should include all the information you gathered to answer the questions. As with the business plan you may write it yourself or seek professional assistance.

A Loan Proposal for Windward TV Shop

Loan Application

The Windward TV Shop is requesting a $10,000 one-year loan.

Purpose of the Loan

The loan will be used to purchase test equipment and to provide for improvements to the store site. The exact cost estimates are provided in Exhibit B1.

Repayment of the Loan

The loan will be repaid from sales generated from the business.

Other Loans

The business has two existing loans and an inventory finance credit line:

1. A two-year loan of $10,000 from Mr. Sam Ganahl, father of one of the partners, Joe Ganahl.
2. A $5,000 loan from Mrs. Marjorie Helgeson, sister-in-law of Joe Ganahl. This loan is a one year loan due in April 1988 but may be extended to April 1989.
3. Inventory finance credit lines have been established with an inventory finance company. The size of the line is $23,000.

All of these loans will hold a subordinate priority to the bank loan for a collateral position regarding the assets of the business.

Collateral

In addition to the assets of the business, Joe Ganahl will place his residence at 1931 Poki St. as collateral. The estimated equity position is $30,000 and is outlined in Exhibit B2. Miss Muira's net worth is shown in Exhibit B3.

The Debt to Equity Ratio

Of the estimated $67,000 of initial capitalization needed to start this business, the partners plan to put in $17,000 and borrow $50,000.

Company History

The company history and market plan are provided in the business plan attached. (You would submit your business plan, as developed in appendix A, with your loan proposal to the lending institutions.)

EXHIBIT B1

Cost Estimates for Bank Loan	
Digital test equipment	$ 2,189
Oscilloscope	1,478
Hand tools	745
Parts	588
Display shelving	5,000
Total loan request	$10,000

EXHIBIT B2

Mr. and Mrs. Joe Ganahl
Statement of Net Worth
May 1, 19__

Assets	
House	$130,000
Household goods	3,000
Cash	8,000
Auto	5,000
	$146,000
Liabilities and Net Worth	
House mortgage	$100,000
Car loan	3,000
Credit cards	1,000
Net worth	42,000
	$146,000

EXHIBIT B3

Miss Debbie Miura
Statement of Net Worth

Assets	
Cash	$15,000
Auto	8,000
Household goods	3,000
	$26,000
Liabilities and Net Worth	
Auto loan	$ 2,000
Credit cards	500
Net worth	23,500
	$26,000

Appendix C

A Sample Employee Manual

What follows is an actual employee manual used by a small business in Hawaii. Since all businesses vary, this sample is not recommended for use by any other business but is presented only to show how one company approached the preparation of an employee manual. For the purpose of this sample, the phrase "the Company" has been substituted for the actual company name.

Employee Manual

I. Welcome

To each employee:

This manual explains the policies of our Company and the benefits for which each employee is qualified. Please read and study this manual and retain it for future reference.

If you do not understand any of the material in this booklet, or if you have any questions, please ask your store manager.

The management wants each and every employee to know that it is the objective of our business to share the success of the operation with the employees through salaries, benefits, and improved job opportunities. Our success has come from the concerted efforts of all our employees. It is these efforts that will make us successful in the future. Although this manual is not to be construed as a guarantee of permanent employment, we sincerely hope that you will be part of our success story.

II. Policies

Hours of Operation: Business hours are from 8:00 AM to 4:30 PM, Monday through Friday. (Kapiolani: Weekdays 8:30 AM—5:00 PM and Weekends 9:00 AM—4:00 PM).

Dress Code: Normal business attire is required. Clean jeans in good repair are acceptable. Unacceptable attire includes T-shirts, tennis shoes, and rubber slippers. A name tag should be worn during business hours.

Customer Relations: At all times customers must be treated with courtesy and respect. Actions contrary to this policy will be considered cause for dismissal.

Discrimination: Work assignments, rates of pay, and promotions will be based on skill, ability, physical fitness, length of service, satisfactory attendance, satisfactory conduct, productivity, and quality of work.

Absence: If, for any reason, you cannot report for work on time, you are to notify the store manager as far in advance of your starting time as possible. State why you will be or are absent and how long you expect to be absent or tardy. Any employee being absent for two or more days who does not notify the office shall be terminated from employment with this Company. Notify the office at least twenty-four (24) hours in advance for any necessary absence (e.g., doctor appointments, dentist appointments, court appearances, etc.).

Pay Periods: Pay checks are distributed semimonthly on the 15th and the 30th, or 31st. If payday falls on a weekend, pay checks are issued on the last work day prior to that weekend. The pay period ends three work days before payday.

Termination: An employee will be subject to discharge if he/she cannot or will not perform satisfactory work (after proper instruction and a trial period), if his/her behavior adversely affects the work of others, or if his/her attendance record is unsatisfactory.

An employee receiving three or more EMPLOYEE WARNING SLIPS for violation of Company policies will be subject to termination with exception of the following, which will result in immediate termination of employment:

1. Pilfering (stealing)
2. Unauthorized possession of Company, employee, or customer property.
3. Willful abuse or deliberate damage to or destruction of Company or personal property.
4. Purchasing merchandise for personal use under the Company's name.
5. Deliberate falsification of : (a) purchase orders; (b) bills; (c) invoices; or (d) other business records.
6. Under the influence of narcotics or liquor on Company premises or during working hours.

III. Responsibilities

Store Manager: Responsibilities include: opening and closing the store; balancing the cash register at the end of the day; doing the bank deposit tally; supervising the equipment and personnel, ordering supplies; making sure time sheets and pay records are accurate and timely; preparing month-end billings for open (charge) accounts; sending in the monthly meter readings on the machines; making suggestions for changes in store lay-out and products; customer satisfaction calls; sending employees to canvass for business during slow periods; making sure employees wear name tags; ensuring that the minimum dress code is adhered to; production scheduling (deciding priorities and making sure that work is performed on a timely basis); evaluating employees on the quality of their work for periodic review for pay raises and benefits; keeping records in the invoice book; contacting delinquent accounts; and other duties as required.

Other Employees: Responsibilities include: carrying out the instructions of the store managers; operating the cash register, invoicing, and recording properly in the open account records; operating copy bindery equipment; displaying adequate math and verbal skills; servicing customers in a prompt and courteous manner and filling out the service request form properly (for customers who leave work instead of waiting for it); occasional pick-up and delivery of work; occasional sales calls (which include passing out of handbills); minor maintenance on copy and bindery equipment; and other duties as required.

IV. Employee Benefits

Probationary Period and Evaluations: All employees must pass a three-month probationary period, after which they are evaluated for possible pay raises and/or benefits. After the initial three-month evaluation, periodic raise and/or benefit evaluations will be given every six months.

Social Security: All employees are eligible to receive benefits under Social Security. The Company matches the employee's contribution.

Workers' Compensation: Workers' Compensation is a wage replacement program. This means that if you are unable to work because of a work-related sickness or injury and you meet the qualifying conditions of the law, you will be paid disability or sick leave benefits to partially replace the wages you lost. Workers' Compensation includes paying one hundred percent (100%) of the medical costs associated with the sickness or injury.

The Company provides Workers' Compensation benefits by purchasing insurance from a licensed insurance carrier. The cost of providing the benefits is financed entirely by the Company.

Any worker, whether hired on a part-time, intermittent, or full-time basis shall be provided Workers' Compensation.

TDI: TDI, or Temporary Disability Insurance, is a wage replacement program. This means that if you are unable to work because of an "off-the-job" sickness or injury and you meet the qualifying conditions of the law, you will be paid disability or sick leave benefits to partially replace the wages you lost. TDI does not include medical care.

The Company finances the entire cost of providing TDI benefits for any worker working twenty (20) hours or more per week, through a licensed insurance carrier.

Medical Benefits: Medical benefits may be chosen from plans by HMSA, Kaiser, or Island Care. The Company is required by law to pay one-half of the individual rate for the chosen plan, but, at the option of the Company, full individual or family coverage may be provided to the employee, possibly including dental coverage.

Vacation: After twelve (12) consecutive months of employment all part-time and full-time employees will receive the following vacation benefits:

Full-time Vacation Benefits:
- one (1) week after the first year;
- two (2) weeks after the second year.

Full-time Managers' Vacation Benefits:
- one (1) week after the first year;
- two (2) weeks after the second year;
- three (3) weeks after five years;
- four (4) weeks after 10 years.

Sick Leave and Personal Time: After the first year of employment, all employees will receive three (3) days of paid sick leave. Two (2) of these days may be used by employees in the event of an unforeseen circumstance, such as a child's illness, the need to appear in court, etc. After two (2) years of employment, all employees will receive five (5) days of paid sick leave. Two of these days may be used by the employee as personal time.

Sick leave must be used during the period it is earned. It can not be accumulated or carried forward from year to year.

If an employee must call in sick, the employee's manager or immediate supervisor should be informed as soon as possible so arrangements can be made to insure that the employee's time and work will be covered.

Hourly to Salary Status: After twelve (12) consecutive months of employment, all full-time employees will be paid on a salary basis instead of an hourly basis. The rate of pay may or may not change. This change is essentially for the employees benefit to provide them with continuity in the dollar amount they will receive with each pay check and pay period.

Retirement/Pension Plan: At the current time, the Company does not provide a retirement or pension plan. Employees who wish to do so may open an IRA (Individual Retirement Account) in which they can invest up to $2,000 per year.

V. This employee manual outlines company policies and is not a contractual agreement.

Appendix D

Hawaii Business Assistance Organizations

Nonprofit Organizations

The Small Business Center
The Chamber of Commerce of Hawaii
1132 Bishop St., Suite 200
Honolulu, HI 96813-2830

Provides information, referral, business consulting, and financial assistance. Also provides business training class under its Entrepreneurial Training Course.

Small Business Hawaii
6600 Kalanianaole Hwy., Suite 212
Honolulu, HI 96825

A private, independent corporation with statewide membership which provides educational seminars, bipartisan lobbying, counseling, and business forums.

Hawaii Business League
677 Ala Moana Blvd., Suite 815
Honolulu, HI 96813

An employer association which provides lobbying efforts, business consulting, and information on state laws.

Alu Like Business Development Center
1024 Mapunapuna St.
Honolulu, HI 96819

Assists native Hawaiians by offering assistance in business planning, loan packaging, business consulting, and classroom training in business start up.

Hawaii Employers Council
2682 Waiwai Lp.
Honolulu, HI 96819

Provides information on labor relations, collective bargaining procedures, workshops.

Economic Development Corporation of Honolulu
1001 Bishop St.
Pacific Tower, Suite 735
Honolulu, HI 96813
Promotes the business sector, referrals, research and development.

Hawaii Chamber of Commerce
75–5737 Kuakini Highway, #206
Kailua-Kona, HI 96740
Provides lobbying, loan counseling, business trends, and business information.

Maui Chamber of Commerce
26 N. Puunene Ave.
Kahului, Maui, HI 96732
Provides seminars, general island business information.

Kauai Chamber of Commerce
2970 Kele St.
Lihue, Kauai, HI 96766
Provides informational brochures, workshops, and business counseling.

Governmental Agencies and Government Supported Programs

Business Action Center
Hawaii Department of Business, Economic Development and Tourism
1130 N. Nimitz Highway, Suite A–254
Honolulu, HI 96817
Provides a "one-stop" business permit and license center for basic tax licenses, business and trade name registration, and employer related information and forms.

The International Business Center of Hawaii
201 Merchant St., Suite 1510
Honolulu, HI 96813
An agency of the State's Department of Business, Economic Development and Tourism. The Center provides Hawaii firms a single contact point for complete international trade services to help these firms compete globally.

Small Business Development Centers (SBDCN)

Hawaii—University of Hawaii at Hilo, Small Business Development Center Network
Kauai—Kauai Community College
Maui—Maui Community College
Oahu—130 Merchant St., Suite 1000

The UHH-SBDCN provides management and technical assistance to small and medium sized businesses through individual business consulting (free) and through seminars and workshops.

Honolulu Minority Business Development Center (HMBDC)

Grant Thornton
First Hawaiian Tower, 1132 Bishop St., Suite 1000
Honolulu, HI 96813

Provides business consulting to ethnic minorities in business planning, financial packaging, SBA 8A packaging, and government contracting assistance.

Pacific Business Center Program

University of Hawaii at Manoa
204 Maile Way
Honolulu, HI 96822

Provides consulting, counseling, and referral.

Small Business Information Center

Hawaii Department of Business, Economic Development and Tourism
737 Bishop St., Suite 1900
Honolulu, HI 96813

Provides information and referral service on permits, licensing, market data, business plan writing.

US Small Business Administration

Prince Kuhio Federal Bldg., Room 2213
Honolulu, HI 96850

Provides business guidance and counseling. Conducts workshops on general business. Provides financial assistance.

US International Trade Administration

Prince Kuhio Federal Building, Suite 4106
Honolulu, HI 96850

Provides counseling and information on exporting goods into foreign markets.

Appendix E

Check List for Starting a Business

Personal Assessment

1. If you have no previous business experience, how have you prepared for owning your own business?
   A. List at least one business course taken from the Chamber of Commerce, Small Business Administration, University of Hawaii, or a private organization:
   ____
   B. List at least one business book you have read:
   ____
   C. List one business owner you have talked to about starting a business: ______________________________
2. What management skills do you possess?
   A. List the previous job positions where you had to make sales, personnel, or policy decisions: ____________________
   ____
   B. List your experience with managing people in a business or organization: ______________________________
   C. List your experience at managing money: ____________________
   ____
   D. List your sales experience at selling a product or service: __________
   ____
3. What industry background do you have?
   A. How many years have you been in the industry (e.g., a Chinese restaurant is in the restaurant industry) of your proposed new business?
   none ______________
   at least one year ______________
   2 to 5 years ______________
   B. Name at least one trade publication in this industry:
   ____

4. What are your personal monthly cost-of-living expenses?

Rent or mortage	$ ______
Car	______
Food	______
Clothing	______
Current bills	______
Medical	______
Utilities	______
Taxes	______
Other	______
Total	$______

5. If the new business cannot pay for your salary for the first six months, how do you plan to meet your cost-of-living expenses?
   A. From savings ______
   B. From a loan ______
   C. From a second job ______
   D. From spouse wages ______

6. Can you and your family accept the following statement?
"I am going to start a new business that will require 10 to 12 hours per day, six to seven days a week for at least the first one or two years. As a result, I will have no spare time to do much else. I fully understand and accept this."

Market Analysis (chapter 2)

1. Describe your target market.
2. Describe your typical customer.
3. Determine a preliminary business location (chapter 8).
4. Determine your geographic boundaries.
5. Estimate the number of typical customers within the geographic boundaries.
6. Estimate the percentage of buying customers from the total possible number of customers.
7. Estimate the average sales per customer.
8. Estimate the average sales per month and per year.
9. Survey other similar businesses, potential customers, industry suppliers, and industry publications to revise your sales estimate.

Cost Estimates (chapter 3)

1. Prepare a start-up cost estimate.
2. Prepare an estimated monthly and yearly operating cost budget.
3. Determine the total money necessary to start the business.
4. Prepare cash flow projections for the first year (chapter 15).

Business Organization

1. Determine the need for any special government permits or licenses.

2. Determine the legal structure of the business and any business agreements between the owners (chapter 4).
3. Determine the accounting method and tax requirements (chapters 5 and 17).
4. Prepare a written business plan (appendix A).
5. Arrange for preliminary funding (chapters 6 and 16).
6. Register the business name (chapter 4).
7. Apply for any special government permits or licenses.
8. Apply for the Hawaii General Excise Tax license (chapter 5).
9. Complete the corporation and/or tax filings if necessary (chapters 4 and 17).
10. Obtain a business checking account.
11. Secure funding.
12. Implement the business plan.

Index

About the Author

Dennis Kondo was born and raised in Hawaii and graduated from the University of Hawaii with a degree in business management. After a number of years in major corporations, he has spent the last fifteen years involved in the formation and management of small businesses as a private entrepreneur, consultant, and instructor. As a consultant, he has worked on economic development and entrepreneurship projects for private industry, the State of Hawaii, the U.S. Government, and the United Nations. Mr. Kondo is also very much in demand as a lecturer with the University of Hawaii Small Business Management Program, the Chamber of Commerce, Kapiolani Community College, and the American Institute of Banking.